The Ultimate Guide to Tax Resolution

Sixth Edition

Helping Tax Professionals Help Their Clients™
A Tax Resolution Institute Publication

Peter Stephan
Matthew Cohen

First Edition, June 2006
Second Edition, July 2008
Third Edition, July 2009
Fourth Edition, November 2010
Fifth Edition, July 2013 (updated October 31, 2014)
Sixth Edition, November 25, 2014 (updated April 2016)

ISBN: 978-0-9829148-0-9

Library of Congress Control Number: 2010934247

Printed and bound in the United States

Published by the Tax Resolution Institute
21700 Oxnard Street, Suite 1160
Woodland Hills, CA 91367
www.taxresolutioninstitute.org

Cover Design: Matt Cohen

Table of Contents

When the tax agencies are breathing down your client's necks, don't throw up your hands and surrender. As the director of the Tax Resolution Institute, Peter Stephan has settled hundreds of complex and hard luck cases, sometimes for just one penny on the dollar. Learn how to counsel your clients who find themselves staring down the barrel of the IRS cannon. You will be amazed by the relief and resolution possibilities shared by Mr. Stephan.

About the Author:

Peter Y. Stephan's early research into IRS tax code led him to specialize in IRS practices and procedures; in particular the area of collection which led him to enter into practicing tax resolution. Peter built his firm by combining his unique blend of skills in the areas of accounting, taxation, and business consulting. In addition to practicing tax resolution, Mr. Stephan is frequently retained by fellow CPAs and Attorneys to perform forensic accounting and provide litigation support including expert witness services relating to various accounting, fraud and tax compliance matters. Peter is qualified by the ***State Bar of California***, ***California Board of Accountancy*** and the ***Internal Revenue Service*** to provide continuing professional education to Attorneys, Certified Public Accountants and Enrolled Agents in the area of tax resolution. In addition to authoring this textbook ***The Ultimate Guide to Tax Resolution***, Peter has created several tax resolution manuals providing fellow professionals with "one-of-a-kind" instruction allowing them to resolve all types of tax resolution issues. As a professional speaker, Mr. Stephan frequently appears at seminars, radio talk show programs relating to tax matters. In addition Peter has been quoted in newspaper and magazine articles. Mr. Stephan is a member of the ***California Society of Certified Public Accountants*** as well as the ***American Institute of Certified Public Accountants***.

About Tax Resolution Institute:

Tax Resolution Institute is comprised of experienced Certified Public Accountants and Tax Attorneys who are well versed in Taxation, Collection and Assessment Law, Business Management, Finance and Accounting. His senior associates have served well over 1000 businesses successfully through comprehensive understanding, along with subsequent design and implementation of appropriate solutions.

If you have any questions or comments, or require assistance with any tax resolution issue, please contact Peter Stephan and his team at **(877) 829-8370**. Or if you would prefer, you may e-mail us at:

info@taxresolutioninstitute.com

Be sure to include your telephone number as well as your email address so that we may respond to our questions in a timely manner. Additionally, if you need sample forms, we are happy to assist.

If you would like to order additional copies of this textbook, you may email us at the Tax Resolution Institute at **info@taxresolutioninstitute.com** or visit our website at:

www.taxresolutioninstitute.org

A Message about IRS Forms and Publications Herein

The IRS forms and publications included in this book are provided for the sole purpose of familiarizing the reader with materials relevant to the topics to which they are attached. If you plan on using any of the forms or publications shown in this book, please go to **http://www.taxresolutioninstitute.org/forms-library/** to locate the most recent version/s.

Chapter 1:

Introduction

Tax Resolution (also known as Tax Controversy) is the practice of resolving tax issues whether they relate to a person's business or personal matters the Federal, State, and local levels. The two main focuses of tax liability that will be covered in this textbook are income taxes and payroll taxes.

Solving Income Tax Issues

The majority of all income tax issues are best resolved using one of the following 5 methods:

- Preparing an Installment Agreement.
- Placement into Currently Not Collectible ("CNC") Status.
- Preparing a Partial Pay Installment Agreement ("PPIA").
- Preparing an Offer in Compromise ("OIC").
- Filing for Bankruptcy - (under the 3-year rule, 2-year rule or 240-day rule).

Other possible solutions include items such as subordination of a federal tax lien and providing Innocent Spouse relief. You will find in this manual that certain things such as obtaining transcripts to determine your client's income as well as which returns have yet to be filed (by obtaining both IRS wage & income transcripts and IRS tax return transcripts) are done for most if not all of the above mentioned items.

Solving Payroll Tax Issues

Unlike income taxes, payroll taxes are non-dischargeable in bankruptcy. There are four main aspects which comprise delinquent payroll taxes. They are:

- Trust fund portion ("Responsible Persons" are liable for this portion as a Civil Penalty)
- Non trust fund portion
- Interest (compounded daily)
- Penalties

Possible Payroll Tax Solutions:

- Preparing an Installment Agreement.
- Partial Pay Installment Agreement *(PPIA)*.
- Preparing an in-business Offer in Compromise ("OIC").
- Selling the business with complete knowledge of the IRS for liquidation value then submitting an Offer in Compromise on behalf of the Responsible Person/s.

Concerns about IRS Collection Policies[i]

By statute, the national taxpayer advocate is required to identify at least 20 of the most serious problems encountered by taxpayers each year. Seven of the most serious problems discussed in last year's report relate to IRS collection policies. Rather than intervening early and making personal contact with taxpayers, the IRS often waits until taxpayer's debts become so large that they warrant intervention of much more expensive IRS field collection personnel

The reports noted the following: The lack of early, meaningful interventions by the IRS on delinquent tax accounts contributes to the long-term financial problems for many taxpayers and costs the government billions of dollars in lost revenue. Taxpayers are harmed because many of them could pay off all or most of the original debt if contacted promptly, but are unable to pay off the debt by the time the IRS personally contacts them after interest and penalties have accrued. The government is harmed because the **IRS collects only about 15 cents on the dollar on tax debts that are two years old and virtually nothing on tax debts that are older than three years.**

Any debt-collection operation will acknowledge that as delinquent accounts receivable age, their collection potential declines. Yet it appears that as IRS collection cases age, IRS policies and procedures make it very difficult for taxpayers to obtain reasonable collection alternatives, with the result that the IRS often collects nothing.

The IRS uses automated processes, such as the Federal Payment Levy Program (FPLP), to impose levies against taxpayers who owe tax debts. However, about 84 percent of FPLP levies historically have been imposed against Social Security payments to the elderly or disabled, many of whom are fully dependent on these benefits to cover their basic living expenses. Despite the National Taxpayer Advocate's repeated urging, the IRS does not have screens in place to protect vulnerable, low income taxpayers from these automated levies.

Concerns about IRS Transparency

One former IRS Commissioner stated that transparency plays an important role in tax administration. “It goes without saying that the IRS needs to comply with the requirements of the law…but we believe FOIA represents a floor on transparency, not a ceiling. Transparency benefits taxpayers and the IRS. It benefits taxpayers because they are entitled to know what legal standards and procedures the IRS is applying, and it benefits the IRS because we can improve our procedures when we receive meaningful feedback from informed taxpayers and practitioners.”

The service is free, confidential, tailored to meet taxpayers’ needs, and available for businesses as well as individuals. There is at least one local taxpayer advocate in each state, the District of Columbia and Puerto Rico.

Taxpayers can contact the Taxpayer Advocate Service by calling a toll-free case intake line at 1-877-777-4778 or TTY/TTD 1-800-829-4059 to determine whether they are eligible for assistance. They can also call or write to their local taxpayer advocate, whose phone number and address are listed in the local telephone directory and in Publication 1546, The Taxpayer Advocate Service of the IRS - How to Get Help With Unresolved Tax Problems, which is available on the IRS web site at www.irs.gov.

Chapter 2:

Practicing Before the IRS

Circular 230 is the document that governs the practice of Attorneys, Certified Public Accountants and Enrolled Agents before the Internal Revenue Service. Below is a summary showing pertinent provisions from the document. Refer to Appendix A for the entire document.

Part A: Who may practice

Attorneys
Certified Public Accountants
Enrolled Agents
Enrolled Actuaries

Part B: Duties and restrictions relating to practice before the Internal Revenue Service

Fees, including contingent fees.
Retention & definition of client records.
Negotiation of taxpayer checks (**NO!)**
Types of opinions and requirements.

Part C: Sanctions

If you have to read this part, you should probably consult an attorney.

For those so inclined the entire Circular 230 document is included in the appendix for your "reading pleasure"

Circular 230 Overview

Conflicting Interests

A CPA may not represent a client before the IRS if the representation involves a conflict of interest. (Circular 230, §10.9(a))

Conflicts of interest occur where:

Representation of one client is adverse to the interests of another client;

There is significant risk that the representation of one client will be materially limited by the CPA's responsibilities to another client, a former client, a third party, or by the CPA's personal interests.

The practitioner may represent a client if:

The practitioner reasonably believes that the practitioner will be able to provide competent and diligent representation to each affected client;

The representation is not prohibited by law; and

Each affected client waives the conflict of interest and gives informed consent, confirmed in writing by each affected client, at the time the existence of the conflict of interest is known by the practitioner. The confirmation may be made within a reasonable period of time after the informed consent, but in no event later than 30 days.

(Circular 230,§10.29(b))

Conflicts of Interest can occur under the following circumstances:

Clients get divorced;

Owners of business entities have internal dispute; or

Practitioner prepares a business tax return for Corp, LLC or Trust and also prepares the individual tax returns for one of the owners.

Divorce and business entity disputes are two of the most common, conflict of interests faced by tax professionals

Circular 230 provides that "no…[tax professional]… shall represent conflicting interests in his practice before the IRS, except by express consent of all directly interested parties after full disclosure has been made.'' (§10.29)

The AICPA Code of Professional Conduct, §102-2, states that, " A conflict of interest may occur if a member performs a professional service… or has relationship … that could… be viewed… as impairing the member's objectivity. If the member believes that the professional service can be performed with objectivity, and the relationship is disclosed to and consent is obtained… the rule shall not operate to prohibit of the professional service.

It is not necessary that the professional had not intended to benefit from a conflict of interest. Merely the appearance of conflict may put the professional at risk

The AICPA has also created an *Ethics Decision Tree* for CPAs in business to help them make decisions in situations that may involve conflict of interest is a good chart to review. The chart can be found at their website www.aicpa.org

Furnishing Information and Records

CPAs are required to respond to proper and lawful requests for information by the IRS. Where the requested information or records are not in the possession of, or subject to the control of the CPA or the CPA's client, the CPA must notify the requesting IRS officer or employee. The CPA must do both of the following:

Provide any information the CPA has regarding who may have possession or control of the requested; and

Inquire of his or her client as to the location of the records and relay that information to the IRS.

The CPA is not required to make inquiries of any third person. The CPA also not required to verify any information regarding the identity of such persons provided by the client. (Circular230, §10.20(a)(2))

There is no requirement to contract information before relaying it to IRS.

Responsibility to Accuracy and Reliance on Others

Circular 230, §10.22 establishes the due diligence for CPAs. Generally, CPAs must exercise due diligence in:

Preparing tax returns or other documents relating to IRS matters;

Determining the correctness of representations made by the CPA to the Department of the Treasury; and

Determining the correctness of representations made by the CPA to clients with reference to any matter administered by IRS. (Circular 230, §10.22)

A CPA is presumed to have exercised due diligence when relying on work of another as long as the CPA used reasonable care in engaging, supervising, training, and evaluating such person. This presumption does not apply for purposed of tax shelter opinions. This applies in both of the contexts in which reliance may be issue:

The work of an employee or subordinate; and

The work of an outside specialist.

Fees (Generally)

A CPA may not charge an "unconscionable" fee for representing a client in a matter before the IRS. (Circular 230, §10) *There are no actual dollar limitations on the fees that CPAs can charge, but there are ethical limitations.

Circular 230 defines a "contingent fee" as any fee that is based, in whole or in part, on whether a position taken on a tax return or other filing will avoid challenge by the IRS, or whether the position is sustained (either by the IRS or through litigation). Contingent fee arrangements include any arrangement where the CPA will reimburse the client for all or a portion of the client's fee in the event that a position taken is challenged by the IRS or is not sustained. (Circular 230, §10.27(a))

A CPA may not charge a contingent fee for preparing an original tax return or for any advice rendered in connection with a position taken on an original tax return. (Circular 230, §10.27(b)(2)) A CPA may charge a contingent fee for preparation or advice in connection with an amended tax return or a claim for refund. (Circular 230, §10.27(b)(3)) The CPA may only charge a contingent fee if, at the time of entering into the fee agreement, the CPA reasonably anticipates that the amended tax return or refund claim will receive substantive review by the IRS.

Return of Client's Records

CPAs must return a client's records at the client's request, regardless of a fee dispute. (Circular 230, §10.28(a)). The CPA cannot hold the client's records hostage in an effort to get the client to pay the bill.

This requirement is limited to records that are necessary for a client to comply with his or her federal tax obligations. Additionally, a CPA can retain copies of the records, but must return the originals to the client. However, if an applicable state law allows the CPA to keep the client's records in situations where there is a fee dispute, the CPA only has to:

Return those records that must actually be attached to the client's *tax return;* and

Allow the client access to review and copy any records that are necessary to comply with his or her tax obligations.

"Records of the client" are defined to include written or electronic materials furnished by the client, materials prepared by a third party that are relevant to representation of the client, and any return, schedule, or other document prepared by the CPA in a prior representation that the client must have to comply with his or her current tax obligations. (Circular 230, §10.28(b))

Circular 230 specifically excludes items such as returns or other documents originally prepared by a CPA that the CPA is withholding because the client has not paid the fees for those documents.

Solicitation and Advertising

Circular 230, §10.30 places restrictions on public communication or advertising by CPAs, including:

Deceptive advertising;

Advertising that is in violation of federal or state law;

Misleading descriptions of professional designation; and

Fee information.

CPAs may not use, or participate in the use of, any form of public communication or private solicitation containing a false, fraudulent, misleading or coercive statement or claim.

A CPA is prohibited from making written or oral solicitations of potential clients in matters related to the IRS if those solicitations of employment would violate any federal or state statutes regarding the uninvited solicitation of prospective clients.

CPAs may disseminate the following fee information:

Fixed fees for specific routine services;

Hourly rates;

Range of fees for particular services; and

Fee charged for an initial consultation. (Circular 230, §10.30(b))

Once a CPA has published his or her rates the CPA is prevented from increasing those rates for at least 30 calendar days after the last date that the schedule of fees was published.

Retaining Records of Advertisements

When a CPA uses some form of advertisement or solicitation, he or she must keep a copy for at least 36 months from the date of the last transmission or use. (Circular 230, §10.30(c))

Negotiation of Taxpayer Checks

A CPA who prepares tax returns cannot endorse or otherwise negotiate any check issued to a client by the government with respect to a federal tax liability. (Circular 230, §10.31)

Preparer Penalties §6694

Beginning with the Tax Reform Act of 1976, the Code has imposed various penalties on income tax return preparers if:

There is an understatement on the return, and the understated return position did not have at least a specified threshold of authoritative support.

Since 1976, the specified threshold has progressively heightened, as have the associated penalties.

Historical Standards		
Standard	**Likelihood**	**Description**
Not frivolous	5%	Frivolous means patently improper on its face.
Reasonable basis	20-25%	Not merely arguable. Must be reasonably based on one or more authorities described in Treas. Regs. §1.6662-4(d)(3)(iii).
Realistic possibility of success	33%	Satisfied if a reasonable and well-informed person knowledgeable in the tax law concludes that the position has a one-in three of being sustained on its merits.
Substantial authority	40-45%	Satisfied if the weight of authorities supporting the position is substantial in relation to the weight of authorities in opposition.
More likely than not	>50%	Reasonable belief that the position is more likely than not sustainable on its merits.

The Small Business and Work Opportunity Act of 2007

On May 25, 2007, the ***Small Business and Work Opportunity Act of 2007*** brought major changes to IRC §6694:

It extends application of *income* tax preparers to *all tax return* preparers. It broadened the scope of IRC §6694 to include preparers of estate and gift returns, employment tax returns, excise tax returns, returns of exempt organizations and refund claims.

Raises the authoritative standard:

For undisclosed positions, the new standard is "more likely than not." It replaces the" realistic possibility" standard.

For disclosed positions, the new standard is "reasonable basis." This replaces the "not frivolous" standard.

Increases the monetary penalties.

Tier 1 penalty for understatement due to unreasonable positions is increased from $250 to the *greater of $1,000* or 50% of the income derived by the return preparer from the preparation of the return or claim.

Tier 2 penalty for willful, reckless, or intentional is increased from $1,000 to the greater of $5,000 or 50% of the income derived by the return preparer from the preparation of the return or claim.

Reasonable cause exception: No penalty applies if the understatement was due to reasonable cause and the preparer acted in good faith. (IRC §6694(a)(3))

To view the complete Circular 230 see Appendix A.

Power of Attorney[ii] see ***IRS Transcripts*** section

Tax Information Authorization[iii]

Form **8821** (Rev. October 2012) Department of the Treasury Internal Revenue Service

Tax Information Authorization

▶ **Information about Form 8821 and its instructions is at *www.irs.gov/form8821*.**
▶ **Do not sign this form unless all applicable lines have been completed.**
▶ **To request a copy or transcript of your tax return, use Form 4506, 4506-T, or 4506T-EZ.**

OMB No. 1545-1165
For IRS Use Only
Received by:
Name ____
Telephone ____
Function ____
Date

1 Taxpayer information. Taxpayer must sign and date this form on line 7.

Taxpayer name and address (type or print)	Taxpayer identification number(s)	
	Daytime telephone number	Plan number (if applicable)

2 Appointee. If you wish to name more than one appointee, attach a list to this form.

Name and address

CAF No. ____
PTIN ____
Telephone No. ____
Fax No. ____
Check if new: Address ☐ Telephone No. ☐ Fax No. ☐

3 Tax matters. The appointee is authorized to inspect and/or receive confidential tax information for the tax matters listed on this line. Do not use Form 8821 to request copies of tax returns.

(a) Type of Tax (Income, Employment, Payroll, Excise, Estate, Gift, Civil Penalty, etc.) (see instructions)	(b) Tax Form Number (1040, 941, 720, etc.)	(c) Year(s) or Period(s) (see the instructions for line 3)	(d) Specific Tax Matters (see instr.)

4 Specific use not recorded on Centralized Authorization File (CAF). If the tax information authorization is for a specific use not recorded on CAF, check this box. See the instructions. If you check this box, skip lines 5 and 6 . . . . ▶ ☐

5 Disclosure of tax information (you **must** check a box on line 5a or 5b unless the box on line 4 is checked):

a If you want copies of tax information, notices, and other written communications sent to the appointee on an ongoing basis, check this box . . . ▶ ☐

Note. Appointees will no longer receive forms, publications and other related materials with the notices.

b If you do not want any copies of notices or communications sent to your appointee, check this box . . . . ▶ ☐

6 Retention/revocation of tax information authorizations. This tax information authorization automatically revokes all prior authorizations for the same tax matters you listed on line 3 above unless you checked the box on line 4. If you do not want to revoke a prior tax information authorization, you **must** attach a copy of any authorizations you want to remain in effect **and** check this box . . . ▶ ☐

To revoke this tax information authorization, see the instructions.

7 Signature of taxpayer. If signed by a corporate officer, partner, guardian, executor, receiver, administrator, trustee, or party other than the taxpayer, I certify that I have the authority to execute this form with respect to the tax matters and tax periods shown on line 3 above.

▶ **IF NOT SIGNED AND DATED, THIS TAX INFORMATION AUTHORIZATION WILL BE RETURNED.**

▶ **DO NOT SIGN THIS FORM IF IT IS BLANK OR INCOMPLETE.**

Signature ____ Date ____

Print Name ____ Title (if applicable) ____

☐☐☐☐☐ PIN number for electronic signature

For Privacy Act and Paperwork Reduction Act Notice, see instructions. Cat. No. 11596P Form **8821** (Rev. 10-2012)

General Instructions

Section references are to the Internal Revenue Code unless otherwise noted.

Future developments. For the latest information about developments related to Form 8821 and its instructions, such as legislation enacted after they were published, go to *www.irs.gov/form8821*.

Purpose of Form

Form 8821 authorizes any individual, corporation, firm, organization, or partnership you designate to inspect and/or receive your confidential information for the type of tax and the years or periods you list on Form 8821. You may file your own tax information authorization without using Form 8821, but it must include all the information that is requested on Form 8821.

Form 8821 does not authorize your appointee to advocate your position with respect to federal tax laws; to execute waivers, consents, or closing agreements; or to otherwise represent you before the IRS. If you want to authorize an individual to represent you, use Form 2848, Power of Attorney and Declaration of Representative.

Use Form 4506, Request for Copy of Tax Return, to get a copy of your tax return.

Use Form 4506-T, Request for Transcript of Tax Return, to order: (a) transcript of tax account information and (b) Form W-2 and Form 1099 series information.

Use Form 4506T-EZ, Short Form Request for Individual Tax Return Transcript, to request a tax return transcript for the current and three prior tax years that includes most lines of the original return. The transcript will not show payments, penalty assessments, or adjustments made to the originally filed return.

Use Form 56, Notice Concerning Fiduciary Relationship, to notify the IRS of the existence of a fiduciary relationship. A fiduciary (trustee, executor, administrator, receiver, or guardian) stands in the position of a taxpayer and acts as the taxpayer. Therefore, a fiduciary does not act as an appointee and should not file Form 8821. If a fiduciary wishes to authorize an appointee to inspect and/or receive confidential tax information on behalf of the fiduciary, Form 8821 must be filed and signed by the fiduciary acting in the position of the taxpayer.

When To File

Form 8821 must be received by the IRS within 120 days of the date it was signed and dated by the taxpayer.

Where To File

Generally, mail or fax Form 8821 directly to the IRS. See the *Where To File Chart,* below. Exceptions are listed next.

If Form 8821 is for a specific tax matter, mail or fax it to the office handling that matter. For more information, see the instructions for line 4.

Where To File Chart

IF you live in . . .	THEN use this address . . .	Fax Number*
Alabama, Arkansas, Connecticut, Delaware, District of Columbia, Florida, Georgia, Illinois, Indiana, Kentucky, Louisiana, Maine, Maryland, Massachusetts, Michigan, Mississippi, New Hampshire, New Jersey, New York, North Carolina, Ohio, Pennsylvania, Rhode Island, South Carolina, Tennessee, Vermont, Virginia, or West Virginia	Internal Revenue Service Memphis Accounts Management Center PO Box 268, Stop 8423 Memphis, TN 38101-0268	855-214-7519
Alaska, Arizona, California, Colorado, Hawaii, Idaho, Iowa, Kansas, Minnesota, Missouri, Montana, Nebraska, Nevada, New Mexico, North Dakota, Oklahoma, Oregon, South Dakota, Texas, Utah, Washington, Wisconsin, or Wyoming	Internal Revenue Service 1973 N. Rulon White Blvd. MS 6737 Ogden, UT 84404	855-214-7522
All APO and FPO addresses, American Samoa, nonpermanent residents of Guam or the U.S. Virgin Islands**, Puerto Rico (or if excluding income under section 933), a foreign country, U.S. citizens and those filing Form 2555, 2555-EZ, or 4563.	Internal Revenue Service International CAF 2970 Market St. MS 3-E08.123 Philadelphia, PA 19104	855-772-3156

*These numbers may change without notice. For updates to these fax numbers, go to *www.irs.gov/form8821*.

**Permanent residents of Guam should use Department of Taxation, Government of Guam, P.O. Box 23607, GMF, GU 96921; permanent residents of the U.S. Virgin Islands should use: V.I. Bureau of Internal Revenue, 6115 Estate Smith Bay, Suite 225, St. Thomas, V.I. 00802.

Your appointee may be able to file Form 8821 electronically with the IRS from the IRS website. For more information, go to IRS.gov. Under the *for Tax Pros* tab, go to *Other Tools & Information* and click on *Use e-Services for Tax Pros*. If you complete Form 8821 for electronic signature authorization, do not file a Form 8821 with the IRS. Instead, give it to your appointee, who will retain the document.

Taxpayer Identification Number (TIN)

A TIN is used to confirm the identity of a taxpayer and identify the taxpayer's return and return information. It is important that you furnish your correct name, social security number (SSN), individual taxpayer identification number (ITIN), and/or employer identification number (EIN).

Partnership Items

A Tax Matter Partner is authorized to perform certain acts on behalf of an affected partnership. Rules governing the use of Form 8821 do not replace any provisions of law concerning the tax treatment of partnership items.

Appointee Address Change

If your appointee's address changes, a new Form 8821 is not required. The appointee can provide the IRS with the new information by sending written notification of the new address to the location where the Form 8821 was filed. Your appointee must sign and date the written notice.

Specific Instructions

Line 1. Taxpayer Information

Individual. Enter your name, TIN, and your street address in the space provided. Do not enter your appointee's address or post office box. If a return is a joint return, the appointee(s) identified will only be authorized for you. Your spouse, or former spouse, must submit a separate Form 8821 to designate an appointee.

Corporation, partnership, or association. Enter the name, EIN, and business address.

Employee plan or exempt organization. Enter the name, address, and EIN or SSN of the plan sponsor/plan name, exempt organization or bond issuer. Enter the three-digit plan number when applicable. If you are the plan's trustee and you are authorizing the IRS to disclose the tax information of the plan's trust, see the instructions relating to trust.

Trust. Enter the name, title, and address of the trustee, and the name and EIN of the trust.

Estate. Enter the name and address of the estate. If the estate does not have an identification number, enter the decedent's SSN or ITIN.

Line 2. Appointee

Enter your appointee's full name. Use the identical full name on all submissions and correspondence. Enter the nine-digit CAF number for each appointee. If an appointee has a CAF number for any previously filed Form 8821 or power of attorney (Form 2848), use that number. If a CAF number has not been assigned, enter "NONE," and the IRS will issue one directly to your appointee. The IRS does not assign CAF numbers to requests for employee plans and exempt organizations.

If you want to name more than one appointee, indicate so on this line and attach a list of appointees to Form 8821. If more than two appointees are listed and you request copies of notices and communications be sent to your new appointees (see line 5), copies of notices and communications will be sent only to the first two appointees.

Note. Because the IRS will send copies of notices and communications to no more than two persons, if you previously filed a Form 2848, Power of Attorney and Declaration of Representative, for the same tax matters and periods and you requested copies of notices and communications be sent to your representative(s) at that time, requesting your new appointee(s) receive copies of notices and communications may stop notices and communications from being sent to your authorized representative(s).

Check the appropriate box to indicate if either the address, telephone number, or fax number is new.

Line 3. Matters

Enter the type of tax, the tax form number, the years or periods, and the specific matter. Enter "Not applicable," in any of the columns that do not apply.

For example, you may list "Income, 1040" for calendar year "2010" and "Excise, 720" for "2010" (this covers all quarters in 2010). Multiple years or a series of inclusive periods, including quarterly periods, you may list 2008 through (thru or a hyphen) 2010. For example, "2008 thru 2010" or "2nd 2009-3rd 2010." For fiscal years, enter the ending year and month, using the YYYYMM format. Do not use a general reference such as "All years," "All periods," or "All taxes." Any tax information authorization with a general reference will be returned.

You may list the current year or period and any tax years or periods that have already ended as of the date you sign the tax information authorization. However, you may include on a tax information authorization only future tax periods that end no later than 3 years after the date the tax information authorization is received by the IRS. The 3 future periods are determined starting after December 31 of the year the tax information authorization is received by the IRS. You must enter the type of tax, the tax form number, and the future year(s) or period(s). Only tax forms directly related to the taxpayer may be listed on line 3. If the matter relates to estate tax, enter the date of the decedent's death instead of the year or period.

If you appoint someone only with respect to a penalty and interest due on that penalty, enter "civil penalty" in the description of matters column. If applicable, enter the tax year(s) for the penalty. Enter "NA" (not applicable) in the tax form number column. You do not have to enter the specific penalty.

Column (d). Enter any specific information you want the IRS to provide. Examples of column (d) information are: lien information, a balance due amount, a specific tax schedule, or a tax liability. Enter "not applicable" in column (d) if you are not limiting your appointee's authority to inspect and/or receive confidential tax information described in columns (a), (b), and (c).

For requests regarding Form 8802, Application for United States Residency Certification, enter "Form 8802" in column (d) and check the specific use box on line 4. Also, enter the appointee's information as instructed on Form 8802.

Note. If the taxpayer is subject to penalties related to an individual retirement account (IRA) (for example, a penalty for excess contributions) enter, "IRA civil penalty" on line 3, column a.

Note. If Form W-2 is listed on line 3, then the appointee may receive information regarding any civil penalties charged that relate to that Form W-2.

A Form 8821 that lists a particular tax return will also entitle the appointee to receive the taxpayer notices regarding any return-related civil penalties and a specific reference to penalties is not required. However, any civil penalty that is not return-related is not covered by the Form 8821 unless it references "civil penalties" or a specific penalty is stated.

Line 4. Specific Use Not Recorded on CAF

Generally, the IRS records all tax information authorizations on the CAF system. However, authorizations relating to a specific issue are not recorded.

Check the box on line 4 if Form 8821 is filed for any of the following reasons:

(a) requests to disclose information to loan companies or educational institutions,

(b) requests to disclose information to federal or state agency investigators for background checks,

(c) application for EIN, or

(d) claims filed on Form 843, Claim for Refund and Request for Abatement.

If you check the box on line 4, your appointee should mail or fax Form 8821 to the IRS office handling the matter. Otherwise, your appointee should bring a copy of Form 8821 to each appointment to inspect or receive information. A specific-use tax information authorization will not revoke any prior tax information authorizations.

Line 6. Retention/Revocation of Tax Information Authorizations

Check the box on this line and attach a copy of any tax information authorization you do not want to revoke. The filing of Form 8821 will not revoke any Form 2848 that is in effect.

If you want to revoke an existing tax information authorization and do not want to name a new appointee, send a copy of the previously executed tax information authorization to the IRS, using the *Where To File Chart*, earlier. The copy of the tax information authorization must have a current signature of the taxpayer and date under the original signature on line 7. Write "REVOKE" across the top of Form 8821.

If you do not have a copy of the tax information authorization you want to revoke, send a statement to the IRS. In the statement:

(a) indicate that the authority of the appointee is revoked,

(b) list the name and address of each recognized appointee whose authority is revoked,

(c) list the tax matters and tax periods, and

(d) sign and date the statement.

If you are completely revoking the authority of the appointee, state "remove all years/periods" instead of listing the specific tax matters, years, or periods.

To revoke a specific use tax information authorization, send the tax information authorization or statement of revocation to the IRS office handling your case, using the above instructions.

Line 7. Signature of Taxpayer

Individual. You must sign and date the authorization. If a joint return has been filed, your spouse must execute his or her own authorization on a separate Form 8821 to designate an appointee.

Corporation. Generally, Form 8821 can be signed by:

(a) an officer having authority under applicable state law to bind the corporation,

(b) any person designated by the board of directors or other governing body,

(c) any officer or employee on written request by any principal officer and attested to by the secretary or other officer, and

(d) any other person authorized to access information under section 6103(e)(1)(D), except for a person described in section 6103(a)(1)(D)(ii) (bona fide shareholders of record owning 1% or more of the outstanding stock of the corporation).

Partnership. Generally, Form 8821 can be signed by any person who was a member of the partnership during any part of the tax period covered by Form 8821. See *Partnership Items*, earlier. If the Form 8821 covers more than one tax year or tax period, the person must have been a member of the partnership for all or part of each tax year or period covered by Form 8821.

Employee plan. If the plan is listed as the taxpayer on line 1, a duly authorized individual having authority to bind the taxpayer must sign and that individual's exact title must be entered.

If the trust is the taxpayer, listed on line 1, a trustee having the authority to bind the trust must sign with the title of trustee entered. If the trust has not previously submitted a completed Form 56, Notice Concerning Fiduciary Relationship, identifying the current trustee, the trust must submit a Form 56 to identify the current trustee.

Estate. If there is more than one executor, only one executor having the authority to bind the estate is required to sign. See regulations section 601.503(d).

All others. See section 6103(e) if the taxpayer has died, is insolvent, is a dissolved corporation, or if a trustee, guardian, executor, receiver, or administrator is acting for the taxpayer.

Privacy Act and Paperwork Reduction Act Notice

We ask for the information on this form to carry out the Internal Revenue laws of the United States. Form 8821 authorizes the IRS to disclose your confidential tax information to the person you appoint. This form is provided for your convenience and its use is voluntary. The information is used by the IRS to determine what confidential tax information your appointee can inspect and/or receive. Section 6103(c) and its regulations require you to provide this information if you want to designate an appointee to inspect and/or receive your confidential tax information. Under section 6109, you must disclose your identification number. If you do not provide all the information requested on this form, we may not be able to honor the authorization. Providing false or fraudulent information may subject you to penalties.

We may disclose this information to the Department of Justice for civil or criminal litigation, and to cities, states, the District of Columbia, and U.S. commonwealths and possessions for use in administering their tax laws. We may also disclose this information to other countries under a tax treaty, to federal and state agencies to enforce federal nontax criminal laws, or to federal law enforcement and intelligence agencies to combat terrorism.

You are not required to provide the information requested on a form that is subject to the Paperwork Reduction Act unless the form displays a valid OMB control number. Books or records relating to a form or its instructions must be retained as long as their contents may become material in the administration of any Internal Revenue law.

The time needed to complete and file this form will vary depending on individual circumstances. The estimated average time is: **Recordkeeping**, 6 min.; **Learning about the law or the form**, 12 min.; **Preparing the form**, 24 min.; **Copying and sending the form to the IRS**, 20 min.

If you have comments concerning the accuracy of these time estimates or suggestions for making Form 8821 simpler, we would be happy to hear from you. You can write to Internal Revenue Service, Individual and Specialty Forms and Publications Branch, SE:W:CAR:MP:T:I, 1111 Constitution Ave. NW, IR-6526, Washington, DC 20224. **Do not** send Form 8821 to this address. Instead, see the *Where To File Chart,* earlier.

Chapter 3:

Sequence of Events

The handling of tax resolution matters is a rigorous activity that requires a systematic approach. The proper sequence of events for handling tax resolution matters is briefly described in the following annotated outline.

It is important to stress that careful and thorough documentation is vitally important throughout the process; as is the awareness that the resolution of tax issues often means that you will probably have to make adjustments to your strategies while you are moving through the process as new information emerges. Tax issues are complex, and clients frequently fail to retrieve material information.

Steps in the handling of tax resolution cases are as follows:

1. **Meet with the client.** This initial client meeting involves several important steps:

   - Define the extent of the issue(s) and obtain information in order to identify the years, periods, and tax form types in question. Keep in mind that the client is often unaware of the full scope of their issues. They may be unaware that they have unfiled returns or they may be basing the estimate of how much they owe on a span of time less than that which encompasses their entire problem.
   - Estimate fees and discuss them with the client.
   - Obtain a signed Power of Attorney from the client. IRS Form 2848, which is used for Federal taxes, can also often be used to pursue cases involving state agencies if the box indicating the appropriate type of tax is properly filled out with the appropriate state form numbers. The Power of Attorney is the call to action demonstrating that the client is committed to addressing the tax issue by hiring a professional.

2. **Prepare letter of engagement and retainer agreement** that spells out what you will be doing to resolve the client's issue. This letter should include:
   - Specific periods/forms identifying items that need to be addressed.
   - Scope of services you will be addressing.

     Although these documents can be sent to the client for signature, it is preferable to have them available at the time of the initial consultation so an agreement can be reached on the spot.
   - Obtain a retainer deposit check at the time your services are engaged, and make sure that the client understands that you will cease work on his or her case if at any time the retainer is exhausted, and will not commence work until the retainer has been replenished. **Obtaining a retainer check at the time of engagement is a must.** Consider having your clients pay by credit card (Visa, Master Card or American Express) to ease the process of collecting from your clients. The ability to process these types of cards are

relatively easy, and you will find that they not only help expedite collection in the tax resolution area, but also in your general accounting or law practice.

3. **Fax the Power of Attorney form** to East or West Coast Internal Revenue Service unit. The fax number for the West Coast IRS Unit, which is located in Ogden, Utah, is (801) 620-4249. The fax number of the East Coast IRS Unit, which is located in Memphis, Tennessee, is (901) 546-4115 or use e-Services online.
4. **Call the IRS or use e-services available to tax professionals online at www.irs.gov to order the client's transcripts**.
5. **Call the Revenue Officer** if one is assigned, and:
    - Introduce yourself. It's always good to develop a rapport with the Revenue Officer. You should also always ask for his or her name, badge number, and phone number and document this information.
    - Determine the status of case. Is the IRS planning to levy against the client tomorrow? Talk to the Revenue Officer about holding off for 30 to 120 days. Typically, the IRS will put a hold on any account that will be full paid in 60 days. Please note that this 60-day time period seems to be a "moving target".
    - Determine what other information may be needed from the client in order to proceed with and resolve the case.
6. **Call Automated Collections** ("ACS") if no one has been assigned to the client's case
7. **Obtain Tax Returns from client**. This step is important because if a filing or payment is delinquent. In some cases, you may find that the client has the necessary Tax Returns in his or her possession, while in other cases, it may be necessary for the client to go back to his or her accountant and have the returns prepared.
8. **Prepare tax returns if necessary**. In order to negotiate with the government, the client must be in compliance. This includes have all tax returns filed. If the client has unfiled delinquent returns which have not yet been prepared, you should prepare said returns as soon as possible. You should always be care to prepare complete and accurate returns. Often with delinquent returns a tax preparer will rush to prepare returns and cause their clients to acquire a much higher liability than should have been assessed.
9. **Send the client a Collection Information Statement** (i.e. form 433A or 433B) relating to them personally or if appropriate, their business. The questionnaire will not only be used to negotiate with the government but may be initially be used for your benefit in order to capture all relevant information including contact information (address, phone numbers, etc.), earnings information, living expense information or business information for both the taxpayer and spouse.
10. **Compare the following**:
    - Returns filed by you or the client with the Internal Revenue Service's records (via the transcripts that you requested in number 4).
    - Payments by the client to Internal Revenue Service records.

      You will also need to compare client filings and payment to payments made to other tax boards, which including state taxing agencies such as the California Franchise Tax Board, the California Employment Development Department, and the California State Board of Equalization. Keep in mind that although each of the above-mentioned agencies are in California, you must telephone each of these agencies separately as they each act alone.
11. **Calculate the penalties and interest.** You may do this by asking for the information when you contact the Revenue Officer or automated collections. You may also call separately to acquire this information. It is always good practice to cross-compare the numbers you obtain from the government with a "tax interest program" or other appropriate software program. This way you determine that the information you received is accurate. These programs can be downloaded from the Internet.
12. **Determine if:**
    - Assessments for all Federal and State taxing authorities are correct.

- There are still returns that need to be filed.
- The taxpayer has made all tax payments currently due (i.e. estimated tax payments, prior year tax payments, etc.)

13. **Review the Collection Information Statement** sent by the client. Note that the information supplied by the client in the collection information statement is most often incomplete and a good portion of it will most likely be inaccurate. It is important that the client supply the actual amounts they earn and spend and do not make "ballpark" estimates. When negotiating with the government, your goal is to minimize the amount the client will have to pay via a settlement or monthly payment. In order to do so, you must accurately show that your client monthly disposable income ("MDI"); which is calculated by taking the client's take home pay amount and subtracting their necessary and reasonable living expenses, is as low as possible and is an amount they can continually afford to pay over an extended period of time. If you provide an inaccurate Collection Information Statement which may include expenses that are not allowed, you are most likely going to obtain a result that is not as desirable as could have been accepted.
14. **Revise the Collection Information Statement as necessary.** See above.
15. **Contact the Government to Negotiate.** Be sure you are prepared when you contact the government. Whether you are billing hourly or charging a fixed fee, you should know that it takes a fair amount of time to get in touch with someone at the IRS. In addition, you may be transferred multiple times prior to reaching the person with whom you need to speak.

    For example, assume you are calling the IRS to negotiate an installment agreement and have a wage levy removed. Also assume that you have been on the phone for over an hour both waiting on hold and being transferred from ACS to the large dollar unit of collections. You finally reach the "right" person, make your case, supply the Collection Information Statement and come to an agreement. The Revenue Officer or representative then tells you that he or she will send the client instructions regarding the installment payment. All good, right? Not necessarily. They then ask you for the fax number to the taxpayer's payroll department so they can fax over a release to remove the wage garnishment. You then realize that you forgot to get a fax number for the client's payroll department. At this point you may have to call back after getting the number from your client. This may involve another 1+ hour phone call to the IRS to supply a fax number, or even worse, the representative you spoke with earlier did not take good notes and you may have to re-argue some or all of your case. In this particular instance, you can ask for a copy of the release to be sent to you and you can in turn forward it to your client's payroll tax department. The point is…BE PREAPERED!!!
16. **Contact the Client to discuss the results of your Negotiations.** As you practice more and more you will become better at estimating what the outcome of your client's case will be. That being said you never know when the IRS will throw you a curve ball. If you did your homework and everything is in order prior to contacting the IRS, you should be able to discuss with your client prior to making contact what you expect the outcome to be. Assuming you were right, it should be an easy conversation with your client after you are done negotiating with the IRS. On the other hand if the outcome is different, either the conversation will be quite pleasant when you share the news that you did better than expected. If the news is not good, make sure you explain why the outcome was worse than expected and be sure to refer to the information you were provided by the client. Often the less desirable outcomes stem from information you were not provided such as the taxpayer had defaulted on previous agreements or they have an S-Corp with unfiled returns.

    Make sure you are "paid up" when you are ready to negotiate with the IRS. Often you will receive final word when you least expect it. If your client has a balance owing to you, it may be hard to collect your final payment. Keep in mind that some clients go years without paying the IRS. Once you solve their case you may go to the bottom of the list.

Chapter 4:

Tax Handles™

"Tips for Tax Professionals who Handle Tax Collection and Resolution Matters"

Assessment v. Collection (Issue #1)

Most CPAs and enrolled agents are well versed in the area of assessment. That is to say they are experts in the preparation of income tax returns and from time to time the tax returns they prepared get audited. Therefore, by default most Attorneys', CPAs and enrolled agents become quite proficient at the audit process as well. From the Internal Revenue Service side, audits are handled by what are termed to be Revenue Agents.

On the other hand, most CPAs, enrolled agents, bankruptcy and tax attorneys are not well versed in the area of collections. These matters are handled by Revenue Officers. The collection encompasses various sub-categories. A few sub-categories can be classified as follows:

- Installment agreement(s).
- Subordination agreement(s).
- Offers in Compromise.
- Appeals
- Various types of bankruptcy - chapters 7, 11, and 13.

There are many additional areas that make up the tax resolution process. You may e-mail us at ***info@TaxResolutionInstitute.com*** if you have further questions regarding the foregoing.

First Contact with Revenue Officer (Issue #2)

The following list of procedures will guide your first contact with a revenue officer regarding any collection matter.

1. Always get the name (verifying that it is spelled correctly) and the ID number of any Revenue Officer with whom you speak.
2. Don't concern yourself with the fact that the Internal Revenue Service doesn't have the Power of Attorney you sent before you call. If you have faxed Form 2848 to either of the central Power of Attorney unit fax numbers on the east or west coast, it can take 2 to 3 days, or at times longer, for the forms to be processed. As such, it is unlikely that the Revenue Officer will receive it before you call. Note: you must appropriately choose the appropriate (West or East Power of Attorney) unit to fax your completed 2848. You should choose dependent on your client's state of residence and not the location of your practice. You should also consider using e-Services online. The ***Tax Resolution Institute*** will be glad to provide the appropriate fax numbers to you.
3. You may be asked to fax the Power of Attorney directly to the Revenue Officer while he or she is on the telephone with you. The officer will put you on hold, retrieve it, and subsequently begin speaking with you regarding your client's case.

4. After verifying the identification information of both you and your client, including your Centralized Authorization File (CAF) number (even though he or she may already have it), the Revenue Officer will give you most, if not all, of the information about any taxes owed by your client.

5. If your client owes payroll taxes as well as income taxes, be sure that the power of attorney is prepared with the business' Federal ID number, the type of form filed (*e.g., 941, 940 and/or 1040),* and the type of tax in question (e.g., employment and/or income). Be sure to list the applicable years or quarters in question individually. Do not list the years collectively, such as 2000-2005. Some revenue officers prefer that the years be spelled out (*e.g., 2003, 2004, 2005, 2006, 2007 or 3/31/07, 6/30/07, 9/30/07, 12/31/07*).

6. You can typically use the Internal Revenue Service's Power of Attorney Form 2848 for discussions with the State taxing agencies including without limitation the California Franchise Tax Board. These organizations will usually accept the Internal Revenue Service Power of Attorney in lieu of their own designated form to discuss your client's case with you. If you are using Form 2848 to obtain state tax information, be sure to list the applicable State form number in the appropriate section of the form.

The Importance of Engagement Letters (Issue #3)

At the Tax Resolution Institute we cannot stress enough, the importance of having an adequate engagement letter setting forth all issues regarding tax resolution matters.

The failure to provide a proper engagement letter may not only hinder your ability to collect your fees, it may also put you in a potentially dangerous position regarding exposure and liability. Without a properly prepared engagement letter, it is highly likely that you will not be able to collect the fees due you, and may jeopardize you coverage of liability insurance.

It is essential that you have an engagement letter that is as "bullet proof" as possible, especially if you are charging a percentage of the tax savings gained plus your premium hourly fee. This engagement letter will serve as the basis for collecting both your hourly and your contingency success fee. In the Tax Resolution arena, always make sure to get a retainer.

Dealing with the IRS (Issue #4)

The most important thing to remember when you are dealing with the IRS, is that you are dealing with a large bureaucratic organization that behaves like a bureaucratic organization!

The Internal Revenue Service is the world's largest (and most powerful) collection agency, and that in order to successfully deal with the IRS it is necessary to understand how they work. Some key concepts to remember are listed below:

- The IRS' strategy of tax collection is to scare tax payers into voluntarily paying their taxes.
- The mission of the IRS is to asses and collect Federal Taxes and thereby increase voluntary tax payer compliance based upon tax requirements.
- The basic and primary offices of the IRS are the district offices.
- The primary contact point of the IRS is the Regional Service Center.
- **Revenue Agents** assigned to the examination division are responsible for tax payer compliance and examination of tax returns.
- **Revenue officers** assigned to the collections division have the responsibility of monitoring delinquent tax returns, enforcing collection of taxes, penalties, and interest, and referring cases to the Criminal Investigations Division.
- **Special Agents** assigned to the **Criminal Investigations Division** are the *"police force"* of the IRS.
- The primary responsibility of the Examination Division (**Revenue Agents**) is to encourage voluntary taxpayer compliance by way of tax requirements. This is typically done by examining and auditing selected tax returns.

- The primary responsibility of the Collections Division is to collect taxes, penalties, and interest. Normally the Collection Division does not assess additional taxes; however, they may refer cases for audit.
- Revenue Officers have a great deal of power as well as discretion when dealing with taxpayers.

An ongoing problem for both the IRS and you (the taxpayer's representative) is the never-ending inconsistencies that arise when navigating the tax assessment and collection process.

You may e-mail us at ***info@TaxResolutionInstitute.com*** with any questions regarding the forgoing.

Chapter 5:

Installment Agreements

An **Installment Agreement** is a workable payment plan between a taxpayer and the IRS or State. The IRS and State encourages one to pay the tax debt they owe as well as to file all unfiled income tax returns as quickly as possible. When an individual or a business is unable to resolve a tax debt immediately, an **Installment Agreement** becomes an option that can be reasonable to the taxpayer while at the same time is acceptable to the IRS and State. Some Installment Agreements require the full payment of the tax liability which is set into monthly installments paid over time. Other **Installment Agreements** allow the taxpayer to partial pay their liability in monthly installments over time.

In order to be eligible for an **Installment Agreement** with the IRS or state, all unfiled tax returns must first be filed. Once all returns are filed and an accurate tax liability is determined, a qualified tax professional may begin negotiating an **Installment Agreement**. Keep in mind that it is the goal of the IRS and State is to collect as much tax due before the statute of limitations for collection expires. By law, the IRS has the authority to collect outstanding federal taxes for ten years from the date of assessment. State statutes vary.

If a taxpayer is able to prove that they cannot full-pay their liability, even over time they may enter into a payment plan that allows them to continue covering their monthly expenses and pay less than the amount owed in taxes by making monthly installments. This is what is referred to as a **Partial Pay Installment Agreement** ("**PPIA**"). The IRS charges a nominal fee to set-up an **Installment Agreement**. In addition, the taxpayer is required to stay in compliance. This means that they must, in addition to making the agreed upon monthly installments, continue to file future tax returns and pay all future tax liabilities in full. This must be done over the entire course of the **Installment Agreement** period otherwise the taxpayer will be in default and responsible for their full liability due immediately.

Streamlined Installment Agreements – Fresh Start Initiative

If the taxpayer is in compliance and able to pay his or her liability in full over a given period of time (up to 72 months), they may qualify for a "**Streamlined Installment Agreement**". In order to qualify the taxpayer must owe less than $50,000. If the taxpayer owes less than $25,000 then the qualifications become a little easier and the taxpayer may be able to have a Federal tax lien removed if one exists (note: The $25,000 and $50,000 thresholds are based upon the tax liability and do not include interest and penalties).

Without question, a negotiated payment plan in the form of an **Installment Agreement** is more favorable than a Wage Garnishment, Bank Levy, or Asset Seizure. If one cannot afford to pay their back taxes in full and at the present time, and they do not qualify for an **Offer in Compromise** or placement into **Currently Not Collectible** ("**CNC**") status, an **Installment Agreement** may be the best way to resolve their tax debt.

Installment Agreement Forms

The IRS states that the taxpayer should use Form 9465 to request a monthly installment plan if they cannot pay the full amount they owe. Generally, one has up to 72 months to pay. In certain circumstances, they can have longer to pay or their agreement may be approved for an amount that is less than the amount of tax you owe. However, before requesting an installment agreement, the IRS contends that the taxpayer should consider other less costly alternatives, such as getting a bank loan or using available credit on a credit card. We realize that neither of these alternatives are generally practical.

IRS Form 9465 Installment Agreement Request[iv]

Form **9465** (Rev. December 2013) Department of the Treasury Internal Revenue Service

Installment Agreement Request

► Information about Form 9465 and its separate instructions is at *www.irs.gov/form9465*.
► If you are filing this form with your tax return, attach it to the front of the return.
► See separate instructions.

OMB No. 1545-0074

Tip: If you owe $50,000 or less, you may be able to establish an installment agreement online, even if you have not yet received a bill for your taxes. Go to IRS.gov to apply to pay online. **Caution:** *Do not file this form if you are currently making payments on an installment agreement or can pay your balance in full within 120 days. Instead, call 1-800-829-1040. Do not file if your business is still operating and owes employment or unemployment taxes. Instead, call the telephone number on your most recent notice. If you are in bankruptcy or we have accepted your offer-in-compromise, see* **Bankruptcy or offer-in-compromise,** *in the instructions.*

Part I

This request is for Form(s) (for example, Form 1040 or Form 941) ► and for tax year(s) (for example, 2012 and 2013) ►

1a Your first name and initial | Last name | **Your social security number**

If a joint return, spouse's first name and initial | Last name | **Spouse's social security number**

Current address (number and street). If you have a P.O. box and no home delivery, enter your box number. | Apt. number

City, town or post office, state, and ZIP code. If a foreign address, also complete the spaces below (see instructions)

Foreign country name | Foreign province/state/county | Foreign postal code

1b If this address is new since you filed your last tax return, check here . . . . ► ☐

2 Name of your business (must be no longer operating) | Employer identification number (EIN)

3 Your home phone number | Best time for us to call

4 Your work phone number | Ext. | Best time for us to call

5 Name of your bank or other financial institution: | Address | City, state, and ZIP code

6 Your employer's name: | Address | City, state, and ZIP code

7 Enter the total amount you owe as shown on your tax return(s) (or notice(s)) 7

8 Enter the amount of any payment you are making with your tax return(s) (or notice(s)). See instructions 8

9 Subtract line 8 from line 7 and enter the result 9

10 Enter the amount you can pay each month. Make your payments as large as possible to limit interest and penalty charges. **The charges will continue until you pay in full. If no payment amount is listed on line 10, a payment will be determined for you by dividing the balance due by 72 months** . . 10

11 Divide the amount on line 9 by 72 and enter the result 11

- If the amount on line 10 is less than the amount on line 11 and you are unable to increase your payment to the amount on line 11, complete and attach Form 433-F, Collection Information Statement.
- If the amount on line 10 is equal to or greater than the amount on line 11 but the amount you owe is greater than $25,000 but not more than $50,000, you must complete either line 13 or 14, if you do not wish to complete Form 433-F.
- If the amount on line 9 is greater than $50,000, complete and attach Form 433-F, Collection Information Statement.

12 Enter the date you want to make your payment each month. **Do not** enter a date later than the 28th ►

13 If you want to make your payments by direct debit from your checking account, see the instructions and fill in lines 13a and 13b. This is the most convenient way to make your payments and it will ensure that they are made on time.

► a Routing number ☐☐☐☐☐☐☐☐☐

► b Account number ☐☐☐☐☐☐☐☐☐☐☐☐☐☐☐☐☐

I authorize the U.S. Treasury and its designated Financial Agent to initiate a monthly ACH debit (electronic withdrawal) entry to the financial institution account indicated for payments of my Federal taxes owed, and the financial institution to debit the entry to this account. This authorization is to remain in full force and effect until I notify the U.S. Treasury Financial Agent to terminate the authorization. To revoke payment, I must contact the U.S. Treasury Financial Agent at **1-800-829-1040** no later than 14 business days prior to the payment (settlement) date. I also authorize the financial institutions involved in the processing of the electronic payments of taxes to receive confidential information necessary to answer inquiries and resolve issues related to the payments.

14 If you want to make your payments by payroll deduction, check this box and attach a completed Form 2159, Payroll Deduction Agreement . . . . ☐

Your signature | Date | Spouse's signature. If a joint return, **both** must sign. | Date

For Privacy Act and Paperwork Reduction Act Notice, see instructions. Cat. No. 14842Y Form **9465** (Rev. 12-2013)

Form 9465 (Rev. 12-2013) Page 2

Part II **Additional information.** Complete this part only if you have defaulted on an installment agreement within the past 12 months and the amount you owe is greater than $25,000 but not more $50,000 and the amount on line 10 is equal to or greater than the amount on line 11. If you owe more than $50,000, complete and attach Form 433-F, Collection Information Statement.

15 In which county is your primary residence? ______

16a Marital status:
- ☐ Single. Skip question 16b and go to question 17.
- ☐ Married. Go to question 16b.

b Do you share household expenses with your spouse?
- ☐ Yes.
- ☐ No.

17 How many dependents will you be able to claim on this year's tax return? . . . . 17 ______

18 How many people in your household are 65 or older? . . . . 18 ______

19 How often are you paid?
- ☐ Once a week.
- ☐ Once every two weeks.
- ☐ Once a month.
- ☐ Twice a month.

20 What is your net income per pay period (take home pay)? . . . . 20 $ ______

21 How often is your spouse paid?
- ☐ Once a week.
- ☐ Once every two weeks.
- ☐ Once a month.
- ☐ Twice a month.

22 What is your spouse's net income per pay period (take home pay)? . . . . 22 $ ______

23 How many vehicles do you own? . . . . 23 ______

24 How many car payments do you have each month? . . . . 24 ______

25a Do you have health insurance?
- ☐ Yes. Go to question 25b.
- ☐ No. Skip question 25b and go to question 26a.

b Are your premiums deducted from your paycheck?
- ☐ Yes. Skip question 25c and go to question 26a.
- ☐ No. Go to question 25c.

c How much are your monthly premiums? . . . . 25c $ ______

26a Do you make court-ordered payments?
- ☐ Yes. Go to question 26b.
- ☐ No. Go to question 27.

b Are your court-ordered payments deducted from your paycheck?
- ☐ Yes. Go to question 27.
- ☐ No. Go to question 26c.

c How much are your court-ordered payments each month? . . . . 26c $ ______

27 Not including any court-ordered payments for child and dependent support, how much do you pay for child or dependent care each month? . . . . 27 $ ______

Form **9465** (Rev. 12-2013)

Case Study – CS1

Little information is needed to enter into a streamlined installment agreement. In order to illustrate how a non-streamlined installment agreement works we have will look at the "Doe" family. The Doe family is made up of John (Taxpayer), Jane (Spouse) and their two children Jimmy and Jeannie. John and Jane own a home with a mortgage. John and Jane both work. They own Jane's automobile and lease John's. John and Jane owe $247,000 stemming from unpaid taxes.

To summarize the Doe's situation, they are a:

- family of 4;
- living in Los Angeles;
- both husband and wife work;
- they own 1 vehicle and lease another;
- they own a single family home and
- owe $247,000 in unpaid taxes

First we will take a look at the Doe's income, expenses, assets and liabilities via a collection information statement. In this case we will assume that John and Jane are in automated collections and therefore will need to complete a 433-F. If a Revenue Officer had been assigned to their case, John and Jane would most likely need to submit a 433-A (referenced later in this manual).

The information found on form 433-F is used to calculate on a monthly basis the amount a taxpayer must pay toward their delinquent taxes. It is important to be thorough and accurate when completing this form.

At first appearance this seems like a simple form. The information you see here is similar to that you would find on a loan application. If you do not fill out a loan form correctly, you may be rejected which is disappointing but typically you can apply for another loan and being rejected is not going to change your day-to-day living circumstances. On the other hand, if you fill out this form incorrectly you could condemn yourself to a ten-year sentence of paying a much higher monthly installment payment than you can otherwise afford.

The top of the form is where you will enter your static information. Make sure you are accurate when entering your name and tax identification numbers. For instance, spell everything correctly and include your middle initials if they appear on your tax returns. The IRS will often cross reference this information with the information they have on file.

Below the top section, you will see a section asking for basic business information. This section pertains to taxpayers that are self-employed. Once again be sure to enter the requested business information accurately. If you are a wage earner, you should but "N/A" in the first box in this section and move onto the next section.

Be sure to enter the number of people in the household that are under and over the age of 65. The IRS will use this information to determine which National and Local standards apply to you. Typically to include someone in your expenses they must appear in your tax return as a taxpayer, spouse, or dependent.

The subsequent section, **Section 'A'** of the form asks for bank, investment and retirement account information. Be sure to include **ALL** applicable accounts. The IRS will most likely have at least a snapshot of this information and if something is excluded, it will bode poorly on the outcome of the installment agreement request. If there are too many accounts to fit on the form, include an addendum listing additional accounts placing the total of all accounts on the main form.

Section 'B' of the form covers Real property you own. As mentioned earlier, be complete and thorough. If the current value of the property is less than the balance owed, enter $0 in the equity box. Do not enter a negative amount. If you have two house payments (i.e. a 1st mortgage and a 2nd mortgage), be sure to include the applicable information.

Section 'C' of the form lists personal property you own or lease. The majority of information listed in this section pertains to vehicles. Note that if you are single, the IRS will almost always allow the ownership cost of only one vehicle. If you are marred, the IRS will typically allow for two vehicles. If a person or couple has more than one vehicle per person, the IRS will not allow the cost to own or lease the additional vehicles. In some cases, the IRS has disallowed the second vehicle because only one spouse was working.

We will now look at Page 1 of Form 433-F using the John and Jane Doe's information as described above…

Make sure the names match previous filed tax returns

Collection Information Statement

Name(s) and Address	Your Social Security Number or Individual Taxpayer Identification Number
John and Jane Doe 1234 Memory Lane Los Angeles, CA 90000	789-65-4321
	Your Spouse's Social Security Number or Individual Taxpayer Identification Number: 123-45-6789
☐ If address provided above is different than last return filed, please check here	Your Telephone Numbers — Home: (818) 555-1212 Work: Cell: / Spouse's Telephone Numbers — Home: Work: Cell:
County of Residence: Los Angeles	

Enter the number of people in the household who can be claimed on this year's tax return including you and your spouse. Under 65 4 65 and Over ____

If you or your spouse are self employed or have self employment income, provide the following information:

Name of Business	Business EIN	Type of Business	Number of Employees *(not counting owner)*

A. ACCOUNTS / LINES OF CREDIT Include checking, online, mobile (e.g., PayPal) and savings accounts, Certificates of Deposit, Trusts, Individual Retirement Accounts (IRAs), Keogh Plans, Simplified Employee Pensions, 401(k) Plans, Profit Sharing Plans, Mutual Funds, Stocks, Bonds and other investments. If applicable, include business accounts. *(Use additional sheets if necessary.)*

Name and Address of Institution	Account Number	Type of Account	Current Balance/Value	Check if Business Account
Wells Fargo	1234567	Checking	1,769	☐
ACME Credit Union	9999888777	Savings	814	☐
				☐
				☐
				☐
				☐
				☐

Put the most current balances from your statements here

B. REAL ESTATE Include ...ty, timeshares, vacant land and other real estate. *(Use additional sheets if necessary.)*

Place 2nd mortgage information here

Description/Location/County	Monthly Payment	Financing		Current Value	Balance Owed	Equity
1234 Memory Lane Los Angeles, CA 90000 Los Angeles ☒ Primary Residence ☐ Other	2,900	Year Purchased: 2008 Year Refinanced:	Purchase Price: 661,000 Refinance Amount:	435,000	517,000	0
☐ Primary Residence ☐ Other		Year Purchased Year Refinanced	Purchase Price Refinance Amount			

C. OTHER ASSETS Include cars, boats, recreational vehicles, whole life policies, etc. Include make, model and year of vehicles and name of Life Insurance company in Description. If applicable, include business assets such as tools, equipment, inventory, etc. *(Use additional sheets if necessary.)*

Description	Monthly Payment	Year Purchased	Final Payment *(mo/yr)*	Current Value	Balance Owed	Equity
Nissan Sentra	473	2002	8 / 17	1,438	0	1,438
Acura MDX (lease)	517	2014	7 / 17	0	12,408	0
			/			
			/			
			/			
			/			
			/			

NOTES *(For IRS Use Only)*

TURN PAGE TO CONTINUE

Form 433-F (Rev. 1-2013) Catalog 62053J Department of the Treasury **Internal Revenue Service** publish.no.irs.gov

Now we will cover Page 2 of Form 433F…

Section 'D' is where you put your credit card information. It is important to know that credit card payments are; for practical purposes, not considered an allowable expense. While the IRS contends that minimum credit card payments are allowable, they consider these payments as part of the Food, Clothing and Miscellaneous Items section below. In a minute when we cover that portion, you will see why credit card payments carry no practical bearing.

Section 'E' is where if you are self-employed, you will enter your business-related assets and liabilities. You will notice that this section is very similar to the bank account section and credit card sections we previously covered. As always be complete and accurate when entering information here. If your information does not fit on the form, include additional information in an addendum as necessary.

Section 'F' is a critical section. Here you will enter your employer, wage and income information. Even if you are not an employee earning a wage, you should still enter the static information for the company in which you work. You will see check boxes in this section asking for the frequency in which you receive pay. **PAY CLOSE ATTENTION TO THIS SECTION.** When you calculate your take-home income, be sure to do the math properly. When estimating what you will pay as a monthly installment payment, you take your income and subtract necessary and reasonable living expenses. If you calculate your income incorrectly, you lose substantial leverage in negotiation. If you get paid monthly, the math is easy. If you get paid semi-monthly, once again it is not hard to calculate. On the other hand, if you get paid weekly be sure to multiply the average net income of the checks you are including by 52 and divide by 12. If you get paid bi-weekly (every other week) you must multiply the average net income by 26 and divide by 12. When determining what numbers to include as gross pay and corresponding taxes withheld, you typically take the average of three-months pay over the given period. If you can show that you earned less over an expanded period of time, you may go back either 6 months, 1 year, or 2 years.

Section 'G' addresses other income. Here you will include income other than wages such as social security income and net business income if you are self-employed. If you are self-employed and earn net business income, the IRS may ask for additional substantiation which may include a Profit and Loss Statement to tie in the amount on the form.

Lastly is **Section 'H'**. This too is a critical section. The number included here, along with the income amounts and car and mortgage payments determine how much you will pay in monthly installments. In #1, Food, Clothing & Miscellaneous Items, #2 Transportation, and #4 Out of Pocket Health Care, you typically enter the IRS National and Local Standards (see *www.irs.gov* and enter "national and local standards for living') based upon the number of people in your household. In these three sections the IRS allows you to enter the standard and requires **no substantiation**. As mentioned earlier, minimum credit card payments are allowed under the Food, Clothing and Miscellaneous items section. Because the entire Standard is allowed with no substantiation, if credit card payments are included in this section they will have no practical bearing and in essence makes you no better off in terms of ability to pay. The other items you include on the form such as Housing and Utilities, Health Insurance and the items listed under section #5 "Other" should be the actual amounts you pay. Keep in mind that **all** income and expenses other than those that are allowed with no substantiation as listed above need to be substantiated. To prove the amount you take home in income you need to provide three-months check stubs. To substantiate non-standard expenses you need to provide three-months proof of expense and payment. Simply owing something does not make it an allowable expense. In addition you must provide three-months bank statements for all personal accounts listed on page one, and business accounts listed on page two.

Be sure to include the amount you paid for current tax payments as well as the amount you pay for delinquent payments of governmental agencies other than the IRS on this form. **You do not want to include a current IRS installment payment because the IRS will assume you are able to include this expense toward the proposed payment amount your are trying to negotiate**.

Once the form is complete you can calculate your net take-home pay and subtract out the necessary and reasonable living expenses to determine a proposed payment amount for the monthly installment agreement.

We will now look at page 2 of the form using John and Jane Doe's information…

Page 2 of 4

D. CREDIT CARDS *(Visa, MasterCard, American Express, Department Stores, etc.)*

Type	Credit Limit	Balance Owed	Minimum Monthly Payment
Wells Fargo Visa	500	468	61

E. BUSINESS INFORMATION Complete E1 for Accounts Receivable owed to you or your business. *(Use additional sheets if necessary.)* Complete E2 if you or your business accepts credit card payments.

E1. Accounts Receivable owed to you or your business

Name	Address	Amount Owed
	List total amount owed from additional sheets	
	Total amount of accounts receivable available to pay to IRS now	

E2. Name of individual or business on account

Credit Card *(Visa, Master Card, etc.)*	Issuing Bank Name and Address	Merchant Account Number

F. EMPLOYMENT INFORMATION If you have more than one employer, include the information on another sheet of paper. *(If attaching a copy of current pay stub, you do not need to complete this section.)*

Be sure to calculate your monthly income accurately

Your current Employer *(name and address)*	Spouse's current Employer *(name and address)*
ACME Inc 999 Industrial Way Los Angeles, CA 90000	Little Red School 4321 School Way Los Angeles, CA 90000
How often are you paid? *(Check one)* ☐ Weekly ☐ Biweekly ☐ Semi-monthly ☐ Monthly	How often are you paid? *(Check one)* ☐ Weekly ☐ Biweekly ☐ Semi-monthly ☒ Monthly
Gross per pay period 7,661	Gross per pay period 3,767
Taxes per pay period *(Fed)* 1,882 *(State)* 716 *(Local)*	Taxes per pay period *(Fed)* 681 *(State)* 216 *(Local)*
How long at current employer 4 yrs 1 mo	How long at current employer 11 yrs 3 mos

G. NON-WAGE HOUSEHOLD INCOME List monthly amounts. For Self-Employment and Rental Income, list the monthly amount received after expenses or taxes and attach a copy of your current year profit and loss statement.

Alimony Income		Net Rental Income		Interest/Dividends Income	
Child Support Income		Unemployment Income		Social Security Income	
Net Self Employment Income		Pension Income		Other:	

H. MONTHLY NECESSARY LIVING EXPENSES List monthly amounts. (For expenses paid other than monthly, see instructions.)

1. Food / Personal Care ***See instructions. If you do not spend more than the standard allowable amount for your family size, fill in the Total amount only.***

Food	821
Housekeeping Supplies	78
Clothing and Clothing Services	244
Personal Care Products & Services	70
Miscellaneous	300
Total	1,513

2. Transportation

Gas/Insurance/Licenses/Parking/ Maintenance etc.	590
Public Transportation	

3. Housing & Utilities

Rent	
Electric, Oil/Gas, Water/Trash	473
Telephone/Cell/Cable/Internet	90
Real Estate Taxes and Insurance *(if not included in B above)*	170
Maintenance and Repairs	
Total	733

4. Medical

Health Insurance	195
Out of Pocket Health Care Expenses	240

5. Other

Child / Dependent Care	
Estimated Tax Payments	
Term Life Insurance	270
Retirement *(Employer Required)*	
Retirement *(Voluntary)*	
Union Dues	
Delinquent State & Local Taxes *(minimum payment)*	
Student Loans *(minimum payment)*	
Court Ordered Child Support	
Court Ordered Alimony	
Other Court Ordered Payments	319
Other *(specify)*	
Other *(specify)*	
Other *(specify)*	

Do not include current IRS payments here

Under penalty of perjury, I declare to the best of my knowledge and belief this statement of assets, liabilities and other information is true, correct and complete

Your Signature	Spouse's Signature	Date

Form 433-F (Rev. 1-2013) Catalog 62... ...venue Service publish no irs ...

Transportation, Food/Personal Care and Out of Pocket Health Expenses are based upon IRS Standards

Now that we have looked at Form 433-F in detail, let's review the information we included in the form to see how much the Doe's will pay on a monthly basis…

Analysis

Installment Agreement - Family of Four (CS-1)

Item	Amount Allowed for IA		Notes
Income			
Gross Wages			
Taxpayer	7,661		Actual
Spouse	3,767		Actual
Total gross earnings:		11,428	
Taxes			
Taxpayer	(2,186)		Actual
Spouse	(1,026)		Actual
Total taxes withheld:		(3,212)	
Total net income:		**8,216**	
Personal Living Expenses			
Housing and Utilities			
Mortgage	3,200		Actual for IA
Utilities	433		Actual for IA
		3,633	OIC amount is based upon IRS local std.
Food/Clothing/Etc.	1,513		IRS national standard
		1,513	
Transportation			
Car payments	990		Actual
Maint./gas/insurance	590		IRS local standard
		1,580	
Medical			
Health insruance	195		Actual
Out-of-pocket health	240		IRS national standard
		435	
Other			
Childcare	319		
Life insurance	270		
		589	
Total living expeneses:		**7,750**	
Monthly Disposible Income:		**466**	

As you can see, the Doe's should offer $466 per month. In the pages prior you will find Form 9465. This is the form used to request an installment agreement. This form is used for submitting a streamlined installment agreement request and sometimes is requested by the IRS to be included with a Form 433. We have included the form for reference. As you will see it is simple to complete.

Tips and Traps - Installment Agreements

1. Be sure to complete Form 433-F or 433-A before you contact the IRS.

2. The information in Form 433-F is often supplied to the IRS over the phone. Be sure to fill on all boxes in sections that apply to your client. The IRS does not like blanks.

3. Create a separate sheet showing your income and expenses. Calculate your client's take-home income minus their living expenses prior to contacting the IRS. This will be the amount the IRS will expect you to pay on a monthly basis.

4. The installment agreement calculation may be negative. If the amount is less than zero, request to be placed into Currently Non Collectable status.

5. If your calculation is too low (i.e. substantially below zero) then the IRS may not consider your client's expenses to be real.

6. The IRS will compare your client's bank account deposits with the amount they claim as take-home income. Be sure that either these amounts match or that you can trace excess deposits as non-income (i.e. loans, transfers from savings, transfers from other accounts listed on the 433).

7. Provide three months billing statements, invoices, etc. to substantiate living expenses. Also include proof of payment either as copies of checks or bank statements showing the paid expenses. Simply owing the money is not enough to make an expense allowable.

8. If your client has more Monthly Disposable Income ("MDI") than they are able to pay to the IRS as an ongoing installment payment, they can increase their expenses to lower their MDI. For example they could:

    a. Trade in a car they own outright and lease or purchase another car. Note that leasing a car will add a new allowable expense without adding an additional asset.

    b. If they are self-employed they can make or increase estimated tax payments for the current tax year. This will lower their disposable income and increase the chance of staying in compliance moving forward.

    c. If your client is an employee they can increase their withholding tax if they typically owe taxes at the end of the year. Be careful not to have them over withhold as refunds will be kept by the IRS and applied to the back taxes owed.

    d. They can buy term life insurance. This is an allowable expense that carries no cash value.

9. Ask for 72 months to pay. If your client's MDI is too high, try taking their total liability and dividing it by 72. If the amount is less than their MDI, you may request that their full liability be paid over the 6-year period. This does not always work but it is worth a try.

Chapter 6:

Offers in Compromise

An Offer in Compromise (OIC) is an agreement between a taxpayer and the IRS that resolves the taxpayer's tax debt. The IRS has the authority to settle or "compromise" federal tax liabilities by accepting less than full payment under certain circumstances. A tax debt may be legally compromised under any of the following conditions:

Doubt as to Collectability - doubt exists that the taxpayer would ever be able to pay the full amount of tax owed.

Doubt as to Liability - doubt exists that the assessed tax is correct.

Effective Tax Administration - there is no doubt the assessed tax is correct, and there is no doubt that the full amount owed could be collected, but an extraordinary circumstance exists that allows the IRS to consider a taxpayer's OIC. To be eligible for a compromise on this basis, the taxpayer must demonstrate that collection of the tax would create an economic hardship or would be unfair and inequitable.

Taxpayers should be aware of false claims that their tax debts can be settled for "pennies on the dollar" through the Offer in Compromise Program. While this is true in some instances, it is imperative that they check the OIC requirements to verify if they qualify to submit an offer in compromise.

The ultimate goal of an Offer in Compromise is to settle, reduce and/or eliminate a tax liability that is in both the Government's and the taxpayer's best interest. The IRS will accept an offer-in-compromise to settle unpaid accounts for less than the amount owed when there is doubt that the liability can be collected in full and the amount you offer reasonably reflects collection potential. In addition to the forms necessary to file an Offer, we include a cover page that describes what forms and substantiation we have included in the package as well as a personal description of the taxpayer which provides the Offer Specialist a depiction that supports our case.

The IRS will also consider doubt as to liability and effective tax administration as acceptable platforms for abatement. The issue of "liability" is a complex legal issue (*e.g., whether a person is a "responsible person" to pay the payroll taxes*) requiring sophisticated and well-reasoned issues of fact and law.

To submit an offer-in-compromise you must complete Form 656. **The IRS will not accept an offer unless it is clear that you have complied with all current filing requirements.**

The IRS will not process an OIC for those working as employees unless all un-filed tax returns are filed, although it is not required that you make payment with the tax returns you file. This means that "employees" need to file all un-filed tax returns if you are considering eliminating your tax liability in an OIC. **The IRS cannot settle a tax liability for which there is no tax assessment**. Filed tax returns are important because they result in IRS tax assessments. Self-employed persons will be considered in compliance (for purposes of filing an OIC) if they file their quarterly tax returns "timely" (e.g. not late in making payment) for the current quarter and the preceding two quarters.

The Form 656 was redesigned in May of 2012 in order to assist taxpayer in the correct preparation of an OIC, as well as reduce the burden associated with the process. The 2012 revision is the culmination of a partnership effort involving the IRS, national Taxpayer Advocate, as well as a number of tax professional organizations.

National and Local Standards

Allowances for food, clothing, medications and other items, known as the National and Local Standards apply nationwide, with Local standards based on State and County of residence for Housing and Utilities, and Transportation. National Standards are also determined based on family size.

Filing Delinquent Tax Returns Eliminates the Risk of Imprisonment

Section 7230 of the Internal Revenue Code permits the IRS to charge you with the "willful failure to file a tax return." The statute subjects you to a risk of being guilty of a misdemeanor and a $25,000 penalty ($100,000 in case of a corporation,) and imprisonment for not more than one year. If the failure to file is "willful" the charge is a "felony" and the imprisonment is up to five years.

YOU ELIMINATE THE RISK OF IMPRISONMENT IF YOU VOLUNTARILY FILE YOUR TAX RETURNS and make payment of your tax liability.

Bankruptcy

The IRS will not process an OIC if you are currently in bankruptcy.

Internal Revenue Service Offer in Compromise Practice Problem Facts

Taxpayer "A" owes $50,000 in personal Federal income taxes (1040) and $200,000 in Federal payroll taxes from a business that went bankrupt 3 years ago.

Currently, Taxpayer "A" earns $3,500 per month from his automotive repair business. He makes an estimated tax payment of $2,500 per quarter ($833.33/mo). Taxpayer "A's" spouse earns $3,000 per month as a telemarketer. She receives a W-2 with the following withholdings, FIT – $450, FICA & Medicare – $229.50, SIT – $100, SDI – $24, Health Insurance – $250. Taxpayer "A" has a monthly mortgage payment of $2,600, real estate taxes of $450 and utilities of $250. Taxpayer "A" leases 1 automobile for $625 per month. Taxpayer "A" purchased automobile and has a monthly payment of $400 per month. There are 24 payments remaining. Taxpayer "A" has a term life insurance policy and pays $175 per month in premiums.

Look in the index of this book for reference and find print forms 433A (OIC) and 656 online at **http://www.taxresolutioninstitute.org/forms-library/.** With the information provided, prepare Form 433A OIC (OIC). In accordance with IRS National & Local Standards (also in this book and online) complete the form. You will see that this couple at least on the surface seems to qualify for an Offer. Keep in mind there are mitigating circumstances that will affect the outcome of an offer including the taxpayer's age as it relates to their ability to work (i.e. retired seniors have the advantage), the taxpayer's assets (keep in mind that the taxpayer's "Quick Sale Value of Assets" will bill included in the offer), and the taxpayer's ability to earn going forward (i.e. an out of work lawyer previously earning seven figures and currently seeking employment in the same field will most likely have trouble having an offer accepted).

Assuming the couple in this example have little to few assets and will most likely earn the same amount or less than they are currently earning, they fit the model to submit an Offer in Compromise. Once you have completed the 433A (OIC), complete Form 656. Notice that both forms have a checklist including items necessary to submit with the form/s. Always be sure to send a complete package when submitting documents to the taxing agencies.

Offer in Compromise Tax Practice and Procedures:

New OIC Requirement Poses a Hardship – New OIC 20% Partial Payment Requirement Could Backfire

The IRS, Tax Increase Prevention and Reconciliation Act of 2005 (TIPRA) amended Sec. 7122(c) (1) to require most taxpayers to make a 20% partial payment with an offer-in-compromise (OIC) application, effective July 16, 2006. The legislation was passed despite opposition from the AICPA, the American Bar Association's Section of Taxation and other stakeholders.

The change applies to lump-sum OICs. "Lump sum" is defined by Sec. 7122(c)(1)(A)(ii) as an offer to make payments in five or fewer installments. Any applicable OIC that does not include a partial payment may be returned to the taxpayer as un-processable; see Sec. 7122(d)(3)(C).

Under Sec. 7122(f), the IRS will consider any properly submitted OIC to be acceptable if it has not made a determination within 24 months of the submission date. However, a tax liability covered under the OIC that involves any judicial proceeding will suspend the 24-month period. Taxpayers must be current with their filings and any payments subsequent to the period covered by the OIC while they are waiting a resolution.

The $150 user fee imposed on OIC applicants beginning November 1, 2003, is still in effect; see Notice 2006-68.

Brief History of OIC Program

Since the 1860s, taxpayers have had the ability to compromise and settle deficiencies as a last resort. Historically, this has been good business for the government. In testimony before the House Small Business Committee on April 5, 2006 Nina Olsen, an IRS Taxpayer Advocate, said that, on average accepted OICs have resulted in the Service collecting 16 cents on every dollar owed. This is a statistically significant improved return compared to the 13 cents on the dollar which is what the IRS had typically collected on debts aged two or more years. According to Ms. Olsen, for cases in which OIC applications are rejected, the IRS collects an average of less than 80% of what it could have collected under an initial taxpayer offer, and in over 20% of the rejected cases, the Service recoups nothing at all.

Below is a chart showing the number of Offers submitted compared to the Offers accepted for 2007 through 2012:

Offers	2007	2008	2009	2010	2011	2012
Received by IRS	46,000	44,000	52,000	57,000	59,000	64,000
Accepted by IRS	12, 000	11,000	11,000	14,000	20,000	24,000
Percentage Accepted	26%	25%	21%	25%	33.9%	37.5%

Due to impediments introduced with the TIPRA, many practitioners and advocates have expressed concern that the new legislation will effectively kill the OIC program. How many taxpayers will be willing to incur the emotional and financial costs of providing a partial payment, believing their chances of having an offer accepted are slim? The most common means of financing an OIC payment are:

1. Cashing in an IRA and paying tax and penalties
2. Refinancing real estate with a loan
3. Obtaining funds from family or friends

Is it Possible to avoid the 20% down payment?

As a way to avoid the 20% initial payment, some commentators propose structuring an OIC to include more than five installments. Under this scenario, taxpayers would make monthly installments while awaiting IRS approval. However, as final approval may take several years, this approach may be impractical.

Conclusion

The Joint Committee on Taxation has estimated that revenue will increase by almost $2 billion from this provision. On the contrary, many practitioners predict that the 20% partial payment is a significant barrier that will encourage taxpayers not to apply for an OIC and will result in an overall decrease in revenue. We have found that typically if someone qualifies for an Offer and has the ability to pay for the Offer, they typically will not let the 20% down payment stand in their way.

New Law

The Tax Increase Prevention and Reconciliation Act of 2005 (TIPRA), section 509, made major changes to the IRS OIC program. These changes affect all offers received by the IRS on or after July 16, 2006. The postmark date on the offer is irrelevant. TIPRA section 509 amends IRC section 7122 by adding a new subsection (c) "Rules for Submission of Offers-in-Compromise."

A taxpayer filing a lump-sum offer must pay 20% of the offer amount with the application (IRC 7122(c) (1) (A)). A lump-sum offer means any offer of payments made in five or fewer installments.

A taxpayer filing a periodic-payment offer must pay the first proposed installment payment with the application and pay additional installments while the IRS is evaluating the offer (IRC section 7122(c) (1) (B)). A periodic-payment offer means any offer of payments made in six or more installments.

Taxpayers can avoid delays in processing their OIC applications by making all required payments in full and on time. Failure to pay the 20 percent on a lump-sum offer, or the first installment payment on a periodic-payment offer, will result in the IRS returning the offer to the taxpayer as non-processable (IRC section 7122(d) (3) (C) as amended by TIPRA).

The 20 percent payment for a lump-sum offer and the installment payments on a periodic payment offer are "payments on tax" and are not refundable deposits (IRC section 7809(b) and Treasury Regulation 301.7122-1(h)).

Taxpayers must specify in writing when submitting their offers how to apply the payments to the tax, penalty and interest due. Otherwise, the IRS will apply the payments in the best interest of the government (IRC section 7122(c) (2) (A)).

The OIC application fee reduces the assessed tax or other amounts due. A taxpayer may not specify how to apply the $150 application fee. Taxpayers failing to make installment payments on periodic-payment offers after providing the initial payment will cause the IRS to treat the offer as a withdrawal. The IRS will return the offer application to the taxpayer (IRC section 7122(c) (1) (B) (ii)).

A lump-sum offer accompanied by a payment that is below the required 20 percent threshold will be deemed processable. However, the taxpayer will be asked to pay the remaining balance in order to avoid having the offer returned. Failure to submit the remaining balance will cause the IRS to return the offer and retain the $150 application fee.

Taxpayers filing periodic-payment offers must submit the full amount of their first installment payment in order to meet the processability criteria. Otherwise, the IRS will deem the offer as non-processable and will return the application to the taxpayer along with the $150 fee.

Under the new law, taxpayers qualifying as low-income or filing an offer solely based on doubt as to liability qualify for a waiver of the new partial payment requirements. Taxpayers qualifying for the low-income exemption or filing a doubt-as-to- liability offer only are not liable for paying the application fee, or the payments imposed by TIPRA section 509.

A low-income taxpayer is an individual whose income falls at or below poverty levels based on guidelines established by the U.S. Department of Health and Human Services (HHS). Taxpayers claiming the low-income exception must complete and submit the Income Certification for Offer in Compromise Application Fee worksheet, along with their Form 656 application package.

The IRS will deem an OIC "accepted" that is not withdrawn, returned, or rejected within 24 months after IRS receipt. When calculating the 24-month timeframe, the IRS will disregard any time periods during which a liability included in the OIC is the subject of a dispute in any judicial proceeding (IRC section 7122(f) as amended by TIPRA).

Changes to the Offer Program ("Fresh Start" Initiative of 2012)

As of May 2012 the IRS eased up on the requirements necessary to qualify for an Offer as part of their "Fresh Start" initiative. In order to make it easier to qualify for an Offer the IRS reduced the minimum multiple of Monthly Disposable Income ("MDI") used to determine the MDI portion of the Offer to submit from 48 to 12 months and the maximum from 60 to 24 months which may equate to a tremendous reduction in the amount necessary to submit for an Offer. In addition the IRS broadened the spectrum for which items they now include as "Allowable Expenses" (refer to the chapter on National and Local Standards for amounts). Everyday expenditures such as credit card payments and student loan payments are now included as Allowable Expenses which was not the case previous to May of 2012. These changes dramatically lower the bar to determine who is qualified to submit an Offer but it remains to be seen if the IRS will dramatically increase the number of Offers accepted.

According to a report created by the Treasury Inspector General for Tax Administration ("TIGTA") that was released on March 30, 2012 "Increasing Requests for Offers in Compromise Have Created Inventory Backlogs and Delayed Responses to Taxpayers".

TIGTA prepared the audit of the Offer program because National Taxpayer Advocate reported the OIC Program as one of the most serious problems facing taxpayers from 2001 to 2009. TITGA set out to assess the effectiveness of the OIC Program to timely process requests, consistently apply OIC issuing an interim letter if contact is not made guidelines, accurately measure Program results, and effectively promote the Program.

Inventory of Total Unassigned Offers at Each COIC Site

Source: IRS AOIC Inventory Management Reports, as of October 2011

TITGA's Findings

"The combined impact of a weak economy and IRS efforts to promote the OIC Program has increased the number of requested offers by 28 percent between Fiscal Year 2007 and Fiscal Year 2011. However, the resources available to work the offers have decreased. TIGTA reviewed a statistically valid sample of offers and found the IRS did not process all offers timely. In 73 (74 percent) of 99 offers, the IRS failed to contact the taxpayer by the promised date. TIGTA estimates that 9,509 taxpayers who submitted offers between July 1 and December 31, 2010, may not have been contacted when promised. Additionally, as of October 25, 2011, there were 7,472 unassigned offers in holding queues awaiting assignment to OIC staff. TIGTA found that one processing site had more than four times as many unassigned offers from self-employed taxpayers compared with the other site, and 37 percent of the offers were more than six months old. TIGTA also determined that an incorrect date was used when offers were returned to the IRS because of IRS processing errors. TIGTA estimates that the wrong date may have been used for 712 taxpayers who submitted offers between July 1 and December 31, 2010. Finally, the IRS does not have formal Government that settles a tax liability for performance measures for streamlined offers."

What TITGA Recommended

"TIGTA recommended that the IRS revise OIC processing procedures, train employees, add a formal performance measure for the streamlined offers or apply the streamlined process to all offers.

In their response to the report, IRS officials agreed with the recommendations and plan to take appropriate corrective actions. The plans to keep taxpayers better informed by increasing the amount of time they tell taxpayers it will take until they are contacted as well as issuing an interim letter if contact is not made within the specified time. The IRS plans to initiate reassignment of offers between the sites as needed. In addition, the IRS plans to most aspects of the streamlined process to the remainder of the OIC cases. Also, the IRS agreed with the outcome measures in the report."

Analysis of Timeliness of Taxpayer Contact for Offers With a "Combo A" Letter Sent

Type of Sampled Case	Offers With a "Combo A" Letter Sent	Offers in Which Taxpayer Was Not Contacted by the Date Promised	Offers With an Interim Letter Sent	Number of Days Late Contacting the Taxpayer (Range)
Non-Streamlined Cases	39	24	5	10 – 195 days
Streamlined Cases	60	49	2	8 – 155 days
Total Cases	99	73	7	8 – 195 days

Source: TITGA's analysis of sampled offer cases received from July 1 through December 31, 2010

Sample Cover Letter

Via Certified Mail #________________________

Return Receipt Requested

Memphis Internal Revenue Service
Center COIC Unit
P O Box 30803, AMC
Memphis, Tenn. 38130-0803

-or-

Brookhaven Internal Revenue Service
Center COIC Unit
P.O. Box 9007
Holtsville, New York 11742-9007

RE: ________________________

SSN/EIN: ___________________

Offer in Compromise

Dear Offer in Compromise Reviewer:

I represent the above taxpayer(s). The taxpayer(s) would like to compromise his tax _______ liabilities for tax year(s) _________ to __________, totaling approximately $________. This offer is based solely upon the taxpayer's assets, which are nominal. A review of the enclosed 433-A Section 9, monthly income and expense, substantiates that this Offer in Compromise has no future income component

Enclosed please find the following documents:

1. *Power of Attorney, which should already be registered with the CAF Unit.*
2. *Original Form 656*
3. *Copy of the taxpayer's completed 433-A (and/or 433-B) with supporting documentation.*
4. *A deposit of $______, representing the required 20% payment (or first monthly payment).*

We would like the enclosed payments to be designated to the following tax periods __________.

If you have any questions or require additional information please do not hesitate to contact the undersigned

Implementing a Future Income Collateral Agreement In Lieu of Income Averaging

There is an important development you should be aware of if you are working on an Offer in Compromise or a Lien Release case. This is also pertinent if you are working on a Collection Due Process stemming from an Offer in Compromise or a Lien Release case.

The Internal Revenue Service has insisted upon utilizing income averaging in cases that involve a citizen that is (1) unemployed, (2) underemployed or (3) a self-employed person whose income has decreased due to conditions such as recession. When income averaging is implemented, it is often impossible for an individual to fund an Offer in Compromise.

Internal Revenue Manual section 5.8.5.6, Future Income (09-23-2008), paragraph (7) states:

"In some instances, a future income collateral agreement may be used in lieu of including the estimated value of future income in RCP [Reasonable Collection Potential]. When investigating an offer where current or past income does not provide an ability to accurately estimate future income, the use of a future income collateral agreement may provide a better means of calculating an acceptable offer amount."

The argument that a future income collateral agreement is a better solution than income averaging is also supported by the Tax Court case of **Sampson v. Commissioner**, T.C. Summ. Op. 2006-75, in which the Tax Court in a Collections Due Process judicial appeal held that the Internal Revenue Service abused its discretion in establishing future income without considering a collateral agreement.

An important development occurred in March of 2010 regarding this matter. The Internal Revenue Service issued **IR-20 10-29** that addressed said argument. The Internal Revenue Service specifically stated in a press release that under the current economic conditions, the agency should be using a future income collateral agreement and not projecting future income on the basis of income averaging.

In the same press release, the Internal Revenue Service also addressed the issue of releasing liens. The Internal Revenue Service stated that they "will accelerate lien relief" for individuals who are attempting to "refinance or sell" property but cannot "because of a tax lien". This situation arises in many cases, including Collections Due Process lien appeals.

Case Study – CS2

In order to illustrate how an Offer in Compromise works we will once again look at the "Doe" family. In this case the Doe family is once again made up of John (Taxpayer), Jane (Spouse) and their two children Jimmy and Jeannie. John and Jane own a home. John and Jane both are employees of the same company. They own Jane's automobile and lease John's. John and Jane owe $247,000 stemming from unpaid taxes. To summarize:

- Family of 4
- Living in Los Angeles
- Taxpayer and Spouse both work
- Owns 1 vehicle and leases another
- Owns a single family home
- Owes $247,000 from unpaid taxes

Form 433-A (OIC)

Again we will take a look at the Doe's income, expenses, assets and liabilities via the offer in compromise collection information statement (433A-OIC). This form is similar to the 433-F described in earlier pages in this manual. There are two significant differences. The first is that this form takes 7 pages to input information that was covered in two pages in the 433-F. It is very important to be thorough and accurate when completing this form. The second main difference is that unlike the 433-F where you can input actual expenses for items such as housing and utility payments and car payments, in this form you must include the amount you pay up to the IRS standard. If you pay more than the IRS standard for living expenses, the amount over the standard is disallowed for purposes of an offer.

You will see that the Doe's exhibit assets worth, for the purpose of an offer in compromise $4,438. This is significant because the IRS considers the quick sale value of your assets, not the top dollar amount possible to obtain if you were to sell your assets. You will also notice that the Doe's Monthly Disposable Income ("MDI") for purposes of the offer equals $1,000 per month. Below you will see how these numbers equate to an Offer in the amount of $15,471 which is significantly less than the $247,000 they currently owe.

Take a careful look at each section to see how it is completed. You will note that each section has an amount in the total box. If the Doe's do not have anything to enter in a particular section, the amount in the total box is shown as $0 and there is an 'N/A' in the first box of the section.

Each section has a total box where you add all of the elements in that section. It is important to calculate properly. You will notice that 'Box A' on page 4 and 'Box B' on Page 5 show the totals of boxes from their related sections. Do not forget to enter numbers in these boxes. They are used to calculate your offer on Page 7.

Be very careful when completing Page 6 of the form. Here you will enter your expenses as you did in the 433-F. The difference once again is that you must not exceed the IRS National and Local Standards. You will see that the actual Housing payment was higher than the IRS standard. In this case the standard was supplied.

On Page 7 of the offer you transfer numbers from the previous section totals to calculate the amount of your offer. You will see you have a 12-month option and a 24-month option. Yes, you read this correctly. The Offer in Compromise amount is double if you decide to pay in more than 5 months from the date of acceptance of the offer. It almost always makes sense to choose the 12-month option.

Finally, Page 8 is a checklist of items to include with the offer. Be sure that each item on the list is either not applicable or included with the offer. Do not forget to sign and date the form. Once this form is complete, you will move onto completing the actual offer application, Form 656. This is covered after the 433-A (OIC) sample form that follows.

Form **433-A (OIC)**
(Rev. January 2015)

Department of the Treasury — Internal Revenue Service

Collection Information Statement for Wage Earners and Self-Employed Individuals

Use this form if you are

- An individual who owes income tax on a Form 1040, U.S. Individual Income Tax Return
- An individual with a personal liability for Excise Tax
- An individual responsible for a Trust Fund Recovery Penalty
- An individual who is self-employed or has self-employment income. You are considered to be self-employed if you are in business for yourself, or carry on a trade or business.
- An individual who is personally responsible for a partnership liability (only if the partnership is submitting an offer)

Wage earners Complete Sections 1, 2, 3, 7, 8, 9 and the signature line in Section 10.
Self-employed individuals Complete Sections 4, 5, 6, in addition to Sections 1, 2 (if applicable), 3, 7, 8, 9 and the signature line in Section 10.
Note: Include attachments if additional space is needed to respond completely to any question.

Section 1 Personal and Household Information

Last Name	First Name	Date of Birth *(mm/dd/yyyy)*	Social Security Number
Doe	John	4/15/1965	123 - 45 - 6789

Marital status: ☐ Unmarried ☒ Married

Home Address *(Street, City, State, ZIP Code)*: 1234 Memory Lane, Los Angeles, CA 90000

Do you: ☒ Own your home ☐ Rent ☐ Other *(specify e.g., share rent, live with relative, etc.)*

County of Residence	Primary Phone	Mailing Address *(if different from above or Post Office Box number)*
Los Angeles	(213) 555 - 1212	

Secondary Phone	Fax Number
( ) -	( ) -

Provide information about your spouse.

Spouse's Last Name	Spouse's First Name	Date of Birth *(mm/dd/yyyy)*	Social Security Number
Doe	Jane	10/15/1970	789 - 65 - 1234

Provide information for all other persons in the household or claimed as a dependent.

Name	Age	Relationship	Claimed as a dependent on your Form 1040?	Contributes to household income?
Jimmy Doe	12	Son	☒ Yes ☐ No	☐ Yes ☒ No
Jenny Doe	7	Daughter	☒ Yes ☐ No	☐ Yes ☒ No
			☐ Yes ☐ No	☐ Yes ☐ No
			☐ Yes ☐ No	☐ Yes ☐ No

Section 2 Employment Information for Wage Earners

If you or your spouse have self-employment income (that is you file a Schedule C, E, F, etc.) instead of, or in addition to wage income, you must complete Business Information in Sections 4, 5, and 6.

Your Employer's Name: ACME Inc.

Employer's Address *(street, city, state, zip code)*: 9999 Industrial Way, Los Angeles, CA 90000

Do you have an interest in this business? ☐ Yes ☒ No

If yes, check the business interest that applies: ☐ Partner ☐ Officer ☐ Sole proprietor

Your Occupation: Consultant

How long with this employer: 4 (years) 1 (months)

Spouse's Employer's Name: Little Red School

Employer's Address *(street, city, state, zip code)*: 4321 School Way, Los Angeles, CA 90000

Does your spouse have an interest in this business? ☐ Yes ☒ No

If yes, check the business interest that applies: ☐ Partner ☐ Officer ☐ Sole proprietor

Spouse's Occupation:

How long with this employer: 11 (years) 3 (months)

Section 3 Personal Asset Information

Use the **most current** statement for each type of account, such as checking, savings, money market and online accounts, stored value cards *(such as, a payroll card from an employer)*, investment and retirement accounts *(IRAs, Keogh, 401(k) plans, stocks, bonds, mutual funds, certificates of deposit)*, life insurance policies that have a cash value, and safe deposit boxes. Asset value is subject to adjustment by IRS based on individual circumstances. Enter the total amount available for each of the following *(If additional space is needed include attachments)*.

Round to the nearest dollar. Do not enter a negative number. If any line item is a negative number, enter "0"

For offer purposes included the lowest average daily balance over the past three months

Cash and Investments (domestic and foreign)

☐ Cash ☒ Checking ☐ Savings ☐ Money Market/CD ☐ Online Account ☐ Stored Value Card

Bank Name	Account Number		
Wells Fargo Bank	1234567	(1a) $	1,769

☐ Checking ☒ Savings ☐ Money Market/CD ☐ Online Account ☐ Stored Value Card

Bank Name	Account Number		
ACME Credit Union	999888777666	(1b) $	814
	Total of bank accounts from attachment	(1c) $	
	Add lines (1a) through (1c) less ($1,000) =	**(1) $**	1,583

Note that this total is $1,000 less that sum of accounts. See note to the left of this total.

Investment Account: ☐ Stocks ☐ Bonds ☐ Other

Name of Financial Institution: N/A

Account Number:

Current Market Value $ ___ X .8 = $ ___ Less Loan Balance – $ ___ = (2a) $

Investment Account: ☐ Stocks ☐ Bonds ☐ Other

Name of Financial Institution:

Account Number:

Current Market Value $ ___ X .8 = $ ___ Less Loan Balance – $ ___ = (2b) $

Enter 'N/A' for sections that do not apply. Enter '0' in the totals for these sections.

Total of investment accounts from attachment. [current market value X.8 less loan balance(s)] (2c) $

Add lines (2a) through (2c) = (2) $ 0

Retirement Account: ☐ 401K ☐ IRA ☐ Other

Name of Financial Institution: N/A

Account Number:

Current Market Value $ ___ X .7 = $ ___ Less Loan Balance – $ ___ = (3a) $

Retirement Account: ☐ 401K ☐ IRA ☐ Other

Name of Financial Institution:

Account Number:

Current Market Value $ ___ X .7 = $ ___ Less Loan Balance – $ ___ = (3b) $

Total of investment accounts from attachment. [current market value X .7 less loan balance(s)] (3c) $

Add lines (3a) through (3c) = (3) $ 0

Cash Value of Life Insurance Policies

Name of Insurance Company: N/A

Policy Number:

Current Cash Value $ ___ Less Loan Balance – $ ___ = (4a) $

Total of life insurance policies from attachment $ ___ Less Loan Balance(s) – $ ___ = (4b) $

Add lines (4a) through (4b) = (4) $ 0

Section 3 ***(Continued)*** **Personal Asset Information**

Real Estate (Enter information about any house, condo, co-op, time share, etc. that you own or are buying)

Property Address *(Street Address, City, State, ZIP Code)* 1234 Memory Lane Los Angeles, CA 90000	Primary Residence [x] Yes [ ] No Date Purchased 04/15/2008	
County and Country Los Angeles, USA	Date of Final Payment 04/15/2038	
How title is held *(joint tenancy, etc.)* Joint Tenancy	Description of Property Single Family Residence	
Current Market Value $ 435,000 X .8 = $ 348,000	Less Loan Balance *(Mortgages, etc.)* – $ 517,000 (Total Value of Real Estate) =	(5a) $ 0
Property Address *(Street Address, City, State, ZIP Code)*	Primary Residence [ ] Yes [ ] No Date Purchased	
County and Country	Date of Final Payment	
How title is held *(joint tenancy, etc.)*	Description of Property	
Current Market Value $ X .8 = $	Less Loan Balance *(Mortgages, etc.)* – $ (Total Value of Real Estate) =	(5b) $
Total value of property(s) from attachment [current market value X .8 less any loan balance(s)]		(5c) $
	Add lines (5a) through (5c) =	**(5) $** 0

Vehicles ***(Enter information about any cars, boats, motorcycles, etc. that you own or lease)***

Vehicle Make & Model Nissan Sentra	Year 2012	Date Purchased 06/15/2002	Mileage 153,484	
[ ] Lease [ ] Loan — Name of Creditor N/A		Date of Final Payment N/A	Monthly Lease/Loan Amount $ N/A	
Current Market Value $ 15,938 X .8 = $ 12,750		Less Loan Balance *(Mortgages, etc.)* – $ 11,600	Total value of vehicle *(if the vehicle is leased, enter 0 as the total value)* =	(6a) $ 1,150
			Subtract $3,450 from line (6a). If line (6a) less line (6b) is a negative number, enter "0".	(6b) $ 0
Vehicle Make & Model Acura MDX	Year 2014	Date Purchased 06/15/2014	Mileage 13,781	
[x] Lease [ ] Loan — Name of Creditor Acura Dudes		Date of Final Payment 06/15/2018	Monthly Lease/Loan Amount $ 517	
Current Market Value $ N/A X .8 = $ N/A		Less Loan Balance *(Mortgages, etc.)* – $ N/A	Total value of vehicle *(if the vehicle is leased, enter 0 as the total value)* =	(6c) $ 0
			If you are filing a joint offer, subtract $3,450 from line (6c). If line (6c) less line (6d) is a negative number, enter "0".	(6d) $ 0
Total value of vehicles listed from attachment [current market value X .8 less any loan balance(s)]				(6e) $
			Total lines (6a) through (6e) =	**(6) $** 0

Section 3 *(Continued)* Personal Asset Information

Other valuable items *(artwork, collections, jewelry, items of value in safe deposit boxes, interest in a company or business that is not publicly traded, etc.)*

Description of asset: Furniture and Fixtures				
Current Market Value $ 2,879	X .8 = $ 2,303	Less Loan Balance – $ 0	=	(7a) $ 2,303
Description of asset: Personal Effects				
Current Market Value $ 350	X .8 = $ 280	Less Loan Balance – $ 0	=	(7b) $ 280
Total value of valuable items listed from attachment [current market value X .8 less any loan balance(s)]				(7c) $
Add lines (7a) through (7c) =				**(7) $** 2,583
Do not include amount on the lines with a letter beside the number. Round to the nearest whole dollar. Do not enter a negative number. If any line item is a negative, enter "0" on that line. **Add lines (1) through (7) and enter the amount in Box A =**				Box A Available Individual Equity in Assets $ 2,583

NOTE: If you or your spouse are self-employed, Sections 4, 5, and 6 must be completed before continuing with Sections 7 and 8.

Section 4 Self-Employed Information

If you or your spouse are self-employed (e.g., files Schedule(s) C, E, F, etc.), complete this section.

Is your business a sole proprietorship? ☐ Yes ☐ No		Address of Business *(If other than personal residence)*		
Name of Business N/A				
Business Telephone Number ( ) -	Employer Identification Number	Business Website		Trade Name or DBA
Description of Business	Total Number of Employees	Frequency of Tax Deposits	Average Gross Monthly Payroll $	

Do you or your spouse have any other business interests? Include any interest in an LLC, LLP, corporation, partnership, etc. ☐ Yes *(Percentage of ownership:*) Title: ☐ No	Business Address *(Street, City, State, ZIP code)*	
Business Name	Business Telephone Number ( ) -	Employer Identification Number

Type of business *(Select one)*

☐ Partnership ☐ LLC ☐ Corporation ☐ Other ______

Section 5 Business Asset Information *(for Self-Employed)*

List business assets such as bank accounts, tools, books, machinery, equipment, business vehicles and real property that is owned/leased/rented. If additional space is needed, attach a list of items.

Round to the nearest whole dollar. Do not enter a negative number. If any line item is a negative number, enter "0".

☐ Cash ☐ Checking ☐ Savings ☐ Money Market/CD ☐ Online Account ☐ Stored Value Card		
Bank Name N/A	Account Number	(8a) $
☐ Cash ☐ Checking ☐ Savings ☐ Money Market/CD ☐ Online Account ☐ Stored Value Card		
Bank Name	Account Number	(8b) $
Total value of bank accounts from attachment		(8c) $
Add lines (8a) through (8c) =		**(8) $** 0

Section 5 ***(Continued)*** **Business Asset Information** ***(for Self-Employed)***

Complete this page if you are self-employed. Otherwise enter 'N/A's and '0's

Description of asset: N/A		
Current Market Value $ ______ X .8 = $ ______	Less Loan Balance – $ ______ *(If leased or used in the production of income, enter 0 as the total value)* =	(9a) $
Description of asset:		
Current Market Value $ ______ X .8 = $ ______	Less Loan Balance – $ ______ *(If leased or used in the production of income, enter 0 as the total value)* =	(9b) $
Total value of assets listed from attachment [current market value X .8 less any loan balance(s)]		(9c) $
Add lines (9a) through (9c) =		**(9) $**
IRS allowed deduction for professional books and tools of trade –		(10) $ [4,540]
Enter the value of line (9) minus line (10). If less than zero enter zero. =		**(11) $**

Notes Receivable

Do you have notes receivable? ☐ Yes ☒ No

If yes, attach current listing which includes name and amount of note(s) receivable.

Accounts Receivable

Do you have accounts receivable, including e-payment, factoring companies, and any bartering or online auction accounts? ☐ Yes ☒ No

If yes, you may be asked to provide a list of the account(s) receivable.

Do not include amount on the lines with a letter beside the number. Round to the nearest whole dollar. Do not enter a negative number. If any line item is a negative, enter "0" on that line.
Add lines (8) and (11) and enter the amount in Box B = Box B Available Business Equity in Assets $ 0

Section 6 Business Income and Expense Information ***(for Self-Employed)***

Note: If you provide a current profit and loss (P&L) statement for the information below, enter the total gross monthly income on line 17 and your monthly expenses on line 29 below. Do not complete lines (12) - (16) and (18) - (28). You may use the amounts claimed for income and expenses on your most recent Schedule C; however, if the amount has changed significantly within the past year, a current P&L should be submitted to substantiate the claim.

Round to the nearest whole dollar. Do not enter a negative number. If any line item is a negative number, enter "0".

Business Income ***(You may average 6-12 months income/receipts to determine your Gross monthly income/receipts.)***	
Gross receipts	(12) $ 0
Gross rental income	(13) $
Interest income	(14) $
Dividends	(15) $
Other income	(16) $
Add lines (12) through (16) =	**(17) $**

Business Expenses ***(You may average 6-12 months expenses to determine your average expenses.)***	
Materials purchased *(e.g., items directly related to the production of a product or service)*	(18) $
Inventory purchased *(e.g., goods bought for resale)*	(19) $
Gross wages and salaries	(20) $
Rent	(21) $
Supplies *(items used to conduct business and used up within one year, e.g., books, office supplies, professional equipment, etc.)*	(22) $
Utilities/telephones	(23) $
Vehicle costs *(gas, oil, repairs, maintenance)*	(24) $
Business Insurance	(25) $
Current Business Taxes *(e.g., Real estate, excise, franchise, occupational, personal property, sales and employer's portion of employment taxes)*	(26) $
Other secured debts *(not credit cards)*	(27) $
Other business expenses *(include a list)*	(28) $
Add lines (18) through (28) =	**(29) $**

Round to the nearest whole dollar. Do not enter a negative number. If any line item is a negative, enter "0" on that line.
Subtract line (29) from line (17) and enter the amount in Box C = Box C Net Business Income $ 0

Section 7 Monthly Household Income and Expense Information

Enter your household's gross monthly income. The information below is for yourself, your spouse, and anyone else who contributes to your household's income. The entire household includes spouse, significant other, children, and others who contribute to the household. This is necessary for the IRS to accurately evaluate your offer.

Monthly Household Income

Round to the nearest whole dollar.

Primary taxpayer Wages $7,661 + Social Security $ + Pension(s) $ + Other Income *(e.g. unemployment)* $ Total primary taxpayer income =	(30) $ 7,661
Spouse Wages $3,767 + Social Security $ + Pension(s) $ + Other Income *(e.g. unemployment)* $ Total spouse income =	(31) $ 3,767
Additional sources of income used to support the household, e.g., non-liable spouse, or anyone else who may contribute to the household income, etc.	(32) $
Interest and dividends	(33) $
Distributions *(e.g., income from partnerships, sub-S Corporations, etc.)*	(34) $
Net rental income	(35) $
Net business income from Box C	(36) $
Child support received	(37) $
Alimony received	(38) $
Round to the nearest whole dollar. Do not enter a negative number. If any line item is a negative, enter "0" on that line. **Add lines (30) through (38) and enter the amount in Box D =**	Box D Total Household Income $ 11,428

Enter total income here from gross income numbers above. Taxes are taken out on next page

Monthly Household Expenses

Enter your average monthly expenses.

Note: Expenses may be adjusted based on IRS Collection Financial Standards. The standards may be found at www.irs.gov.

Round to the nearest whole dollar.

Food, clothing, and miscellaneous *(e.g., housekeeping supplies, personal care products, minimum payment on credit card). A reasonable estimate of these expenses may be used.*	(39) $ 1,513
Housing and utilities *(e.g., rent or mortgage payment and average monthly cost of property taxes, home insurance, maintenance, dues, fees and utilities including electricity, gas, other fuels, trash collection, water, cable television and Internet, telephone, and cell phone).*	(40) $ 3,133
Vehicle loan and/or lease payment(s)	(41) $ 990
Vehicle operating costs *(e.g., average monthly cost of maintenance, repairs, insurance, fuel, registrations, licenses, inspections, parking, tolls, etc.).* A reasonable estimate of these expenses may be used.	(42) $ 590
Public transportation costs *(e.g., average monthly cost of fares for mass transit such as bus, train, ferry, taxi, etc.). A reasonable estimate of these expenses may be used.*	(43) $
Health insurance premiums	(44) $ 195
Out-of-pocket health care costs *(e.g. average monthly cost of prescription drugs, medical services, and medical supplies like eyeglasses, hearing aids, etc.)*	(45) $ 240
Court-ordered payments *(e.g., monthly cost of any alimony, child support, etc.)*	(46) $ 319
Child/dependent care payments *(e.g., daycare, etc.)*	(47) $
Life insurance premiums	(48) $ 270
Current taxes *(e.g., monthly cost of federal, state, and local tax, personal property tax, etc.)*	(49) $ 3,178

Note that the actual housing expense is $500 greater than the IRS standard. For offer purposes the IRS standard of $3,133 is used, not the

Page 7 of 8

Section 7 Monthly Household Income and Expense Information ***(Continued)***

Other secured debts *(e.g., any loan where you pledged an asset as collateral not previously listed, government guaranteed Student Loan)*	(50) $
Delinquent State and Local Taxes	(51) $
Round to the nearest whole dollar. Do not enter a negative number. If any line item is a negative, enter "0" on that line. **Add lines (39) through (51) and enter the amount in Box E =**	Box E Total Household Expenses $ 10,428
Round to the nearest whole dollar. Do not enter a negative number. If any line item is a negative, enter "0" on that line. **Subtract Box E from Box D and enter the amount in Box F =**	Box F Remaining Monthly Income $ 1,000

Section 8 Calculate Your Minimum Offer Amount

The next steps calculate your minimum offer amount. The amount of time you take to pay your offer in full will affect your minimum offer amount. Paying over a shorter period of time will result in a smaller minimum offer amount.

Round to the nearest whole dollar.

Monthly Disposable income for offer purposes

If you will pay your offer in 5 months or less, multiply "Remaining Monthly Income" *(Box F)* by 12 to get "Future Remaining Income" *(Box G)*. Do not enter a number less than $0.

Enter the total from Box F		Box G Future Remaining Income
$ 1,000	X 12 =	$ 12,000

If you will pay your offer in more than 5 months, multiply "Remaining Monthly Income" (Box F) by 24 to get "Future Remaining Income" (Box H). Do not enter a number less than $0.

Enter the total from Box F		Box H Future Remaining Income
$ 1,000	X 24 =	$ 24,000

Determine your minimum offer amount by adding the total available assets from Box A and Box B (if applicable) to the amount in either Box G or Box H.

Enter the amount from Box A plus Box B (if applicable)		Enter the amount from either Box G or Box H		Offer Amount Your offer must be more than zero ($0). Do not leave blank. Use whole dollars only.
$ 2,583	+	$ 12,000	=	$ 14,583

If you cannot pay the Offer Amount shown above due to special circumstances, explain on the Form 656, Offer in Compromise, Section 3. You must offer an amount more than $0.

Offer amount based upon paying within 5 months of acceptance

Section 9 Other Information

Additional information IRS needs to consider settlement of your tax debt. If you or your business are currently in a bankruptcy proceeding, you are not eligible to apply for an offer.

Are you the beneficiary of a trust, estate, or life insurance policy?
☐ Yes ☒ No

Are you currently in bankruptcy?
☐ Yes ☒ No

Have you filed bankruptcy in the past 10 years?
☐ Yes ☒ No

Discharge/Dismissal Date *(mm/dd/yyyy)*

Location Filed

Are you or have you been party to a lawsuit?
☐ Yes ☒ No
If yes, date the lawsuit was resolved: *(mm/dd/yyyy)*

In the past 10 years, have you transferred any assets for less than their full value?
☐ Yes ☒ No
If yes, date the asset was transferred: *(mm/dd/yyyy)*

Have you lived outside the U.S. for 6 months or longer in the past 10 years?
☐ Yes ☒ No

Do you have any funds being held in trust by a third party?
☐ Yes ☒ No If yes, how much $ Where:

Section 10 Signatures

Under penalties of perjury, I declare that I have examined this offer, including accompanying documents, and to the best of my knowledge it is true, correct, and complete.

Signature of Taxpayer	Date *(mm/dd/yyyy)*
Signature of Taxpayer	Date *(mm/dd/yyyy)*

Remember to include all applicable attachments listed below.

- [X] Copies of the most recent pay stub, earnings statement, etc., from each employer
- [X] Copies of the most recent statement for each investment and retirement account
- [X] Copies of the most recent statement, etc., from all other sources of income such as pensions, Social Security, rental income, interest and dividends (including any received from a related partnership, corporation, LLC, LLP, etc.), court order for child support, alimony, and rent subsidies
- [X] Copies of bank statements for the three most recent months
- [X] Copies of the most recent statement from lender(s) on loans such as mortgages, second mortgages, vehicles, etc., showing monthly payments, loan payoffs, and balances
- [X] List of Notes Receivable, if applicable
- [X] Verification of State/Local Tax Liability, if applicable
- [X] Documentation to support any special circumstances described in the "Explanation of Circumstances" on Form 656, if applicable
- [X] Attach a Form 2848, *Power of Attorney*, if you would like your attorney, CPA, or enrolled agent to represent you and you do not have a current form on file with the IRS.

Be sure to use this checklist to verify you submit a complete offer

Form 656

The Offer in Compromise application Form 656 is much simpler to complete than the 433-A (OIC). This 4-page form consists of information easy to obtain. Page 1 of the form is where you enter your static information, the type of tax you owe, and the years or periods for which you owe. It is very important to know for exactly which years or periods you owe. If you accidentally exclude a year or quarter, the amount you owe for said year or quarter will be excluded from the offer if it is accepted. If the amount is significant, this could wipe out the benefit of entering into an offer. At the bottom of Page 1 you enter your reason for the offer. Most offers are submitted for Doubt as to Collectability. If you are considering an offer for other reasons, you should consult a professional.

Page 2 of the offer is where you explain why you are submitting the offer. It is advantageous to show extenuating circumstances as why you were unable to pay your tax. For example if you were sick or you are disabled, you should mention your condition here. Also if you are at retirement age and unable to work or have to cut down on work, that should be mentioned here as well. At the **Tax Resolution Institute** we always include a letter of explanation with the submission of an offer. We recommend you do the same.

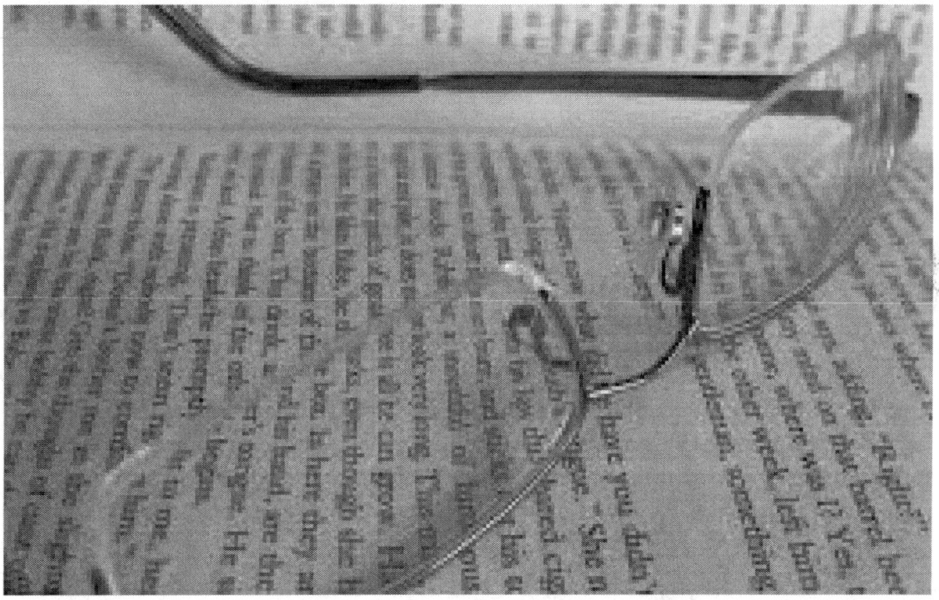

to

At the bottom of Page 2 is where you calculate your payments. You will transfer the offer amount from Page 7 of the 433-A (OIC). This amount is entered on Page 2 of the 656. You will then calculate 20% of the offer amount as a down payment. The down payment must be submitted in addition to the offer application fee of $186 with the offer. You will then break down the remaining 80% of the offer into 5 payments. These payments must be made within 5 months of acceptance of the offer.

Leave the top of Page 3 blank. In the next section on Page 3 you will explain where you are obtaining the funds to pay the offer. It is best if you are borrowing the funds from family and friends.

Page 4 of the offer is where you add your signature and date. Once the offer is complete you will mail it into the processing unit in your region. In order to determine to which processing unit you should send the offer, go to **www.irs.gov** and search for form 656 booklet. There you will find further instructions and applicable information including mailing addresses.

Form **656**
(Rev. January 2015)

Department of the Treasury — Internal Revenue Service

Offer in Compromise

Did you use the Pre-Qualifier tool located on our website at www.irs.gov prior to filling out this form?

☐ **Yes** ☐ **No**

Include the Application Fee and Payment *(personal check, cashier's check, or money order)* with your Form 656. You must also include the completed Form 433-A (OIC) and/or 433-B (OIC) and supporting documentation.

Section 1 — Your Information

Section 1A — Individual Information (Form 1040 Filers)

Your First Name, Middle Initial, Last Name	Social Security Number (SSN)	IRS Received Date
John Doe	123 - 45 - 6789	
If a Joint Offer, Spouse's First Name, Middle Initial, Last Name	Social Security Number (SSN)	
Jane Doe	789 - 65 - 1234	
Your Physical Home Address *(Street, City, State, ZIP Code)*		
1234 Memory Lane, Los Angeles, CA 90000		
Mailing Address *(If different from above or Post Office Box number)*		
Employer Identification Number *(For self-employed individuals only)*		
NA -		

Section 1B — Business Information (Form 1120, 1065, etc., filers)

If your business is a Corporation, Partnership, LLC, or LLP and you want to compromise those tax debts, you must complete this section. You must also include all required documentation including the Form 433-B (OIC), $186 application fee, and initial payment.

Business Name

N/A

Business Address *(Street, City, State, ZIP Code)*

Employer Identification Number *(EIN)*	Name and Title of Primary Contact	Telephone Number
-		( ) -

Type of liability is marked in this section

To: Commissioner of Internal Revenue Service

In the following agreement, the pronoun "we" may be assumed in place of "I" when there are joint liabilities and both parties are signing this agreement.

I submit this offer to compromise the tax liabilities plus any interest, penalties, additions to tax, and additional amounts required by law for the tax type and period(s) marked below:

Section 2 — Tax Periods

Section 2A — If Your Offer is for Individual Tax Debt Only
Complete this Section *only* if you completed Section 1A

☒ 1040 Income Tax-Year(s) 2008, 2009, 2010, 2011, 2012, 2013

☐ Trust Fund Recovery Penalty as a responsible person of *(enter corporation name)* ____________
for failure to pay withholding and Federal Insurance Contributions Act taxes (Social Security taxes), for period(s) ending ____________

☐ 941 Employer's Quarterly Federal Tax Return - Quarterly period(s) ____________

☐ 940 Employer's Annual Federal Unemployment (FUTA) Tax Return - Year(s) ____________

☐ Other Federal Tax(es) [specify type(s) and period(s)] ____________

Note: If you need more space, use attachment and title it "Attachment to Form 656 dated ____________." Make sure to sign and date the attachment.

Catalog Number 16728N www.irs.gov Form **656** (Rev. 1-2015)

Section 2 *(continued)* **Tax Periods**

Section 2B **If Your Offer is for Business Tax Debt**
Complete this Section *only* if you completed Section 1B

☐ 1120 Income Tax-Year(s) ____________

☐ 941 Employer's Quarterly Federal Tax Return - Quarterly period(s) ____________

☐ 940 Employer's Annual Federal Unemployment (FUTA) Tax Return - Year(s) ____________

☐ Other Federal Tax(es) [specify type(s) and period(s)] ____________

Note: If you need more space, use attachment and title it "Attachment to Form 656 dated ____________." Make sure to sign and date the attachment.

Reason for offer is marked here

Section 3 **Reason for Offer**

☒ **Doubt as to Collectibility** - I have insufficient assets and income to pay the full amount.

☐ **Exceptional Circumstances (Effective Tax Administration)** - I owe this amount and have sufficient assets to pay the full amount, but due to my exceptional circumstances, requiring full payment would cause an economic hardship or would be unfair and inequitable. I am submitting a written narrative explaining my circumstances.

Explanation of Circumstances *(Add additional pages, if needed)* – The IRS understands that there are unplanned events or special circumstances, such as serious illness, where paying the full amount or the minimum offer amount might impair your ability to provide for yourself and your family. If this is the case and you can provide documentation to prove your situation, then your offer may be accepted despite your financial profile. Describe your situation below and attach appropriate documents to this offer application.

I was a mortgage broker and hit hard times during the downturn. It took several years for us to get back on our feet but things seem to be turning around. While we do not have enough resources to full-pay our back taxes, We are requesting to compromise our prior liability to ensure that we can move forward and stay in current compliance.

Explanation of circumstances. Should also be included in a cover letter with offer package

Section 4 **Low-Income Certification** *(Individuals and Sole Proprietors Only)*

Do you qualify for Low-Income Certification? You qualify if your gross monthly household income is less than or equal to the amount shown in the chart below based on your family size and where you live. If you qualify, you are not required to submit any payments during the consideration of your offer. **Businesses other than sole proprietorships do not qualify for the low income waiver.**

☐ **Check here if you qualify for Low Income Certification based on the monthly income guidelines below.**

Size of family unit	48 contiguous states and D.C.	Hawaii	Alaska
1	$2,431	$2,796	$3,039
2	$3,277	$3,769	$4,096
3	$4,123	$4,742	$5,154
4	$4,969	$5,715	$6,213
5	$5,815	$6,688	$7,271
6	$6,660	$7,660	$8,329
7	$7,506	$8,633	$9,388
8	$8,352	$9,606	$10,446
For each additional person, add	$ 846	$ 973	$1,058

This section to be completed in extreme hardship cases

Page 3 of 6

Section 5 — Payment Terms

Check one of the payment options below to indicate how long it will take you to pay your offer in full. You must offer more than $0. The offer amount should be in whole dollars only.

Lump Sum Cash

[X] **Check here if you will pay your offer in 5 or fewer payments in 5 or fewer months from the date of acceptance:**
Enclose a check for 20% of the offer amount (waived if you are an individual or sole proprietorship and met the requirements for Low Income Certification) and fill in the amount(s) of your future payment(s).

Total Offer Amount	-	20% Initial Payment	=	Remaining Balance
$ 14,583	-	$ 2,917	=	$ 11,666

You may pay the remaining balance in one payment after acceptance of the offer or up to five payments, but cannot exceed 5 months.

Amount of payment $	2,917	payable within	1	Month after acceptance
Amount of payment $	2,917	payable within	2	Months after acceptance
Amount of payment $	2,917	payable within	3	Months after acceptance
Amount of payment $	2,917	payable within	4	Months after acceptance
Amount of payment $	2,915	payable within	5	Months after acceptance

Offer payment calculation. Note that you can pay balance of then offer at the end of the 5-month period

Periodic Payment

[ ] **Check here if you will pay your offer in full in 6 to 24 months.**

Enter the amount of your offer $ ____________

Note: The total amount must equal all of the proposed payments including the first and last payments.

Enclose a check for the first month's installment.

$ ________ is included with this offer then $ ________ will be sent in on the ________ day of each month for a total of ________ months with a final payment of $ ________ to be paid on the ________ day of the ________ month.

Note: The total months may not exceed a total of 24 months, including the first payment. Your first payment is considered to be month 1; therefore, the remainder of the payments must be made within 23 months for a total of 24.

You must continue to make these monthly payments while the IRS is considering the offer ***(waived if you are an individual or sole proprietorship and met the requirements for Low Income Certification).*** **Failure to make regular monthly payments will cause your offer to be returned with no appeal rights.**

IRS Use Only

[ ] Attached is an addendum dated (insert date) ____________ setting forth the amended offer amount and payment terms.

Section 6 — Designation of Down Payment and Deposit

If you want your payment to be applied to a specific tax year and a specific tax debt, please tell us the tax form ________ and tax year/quarter ________. If you do not designate a preference, we will apply any money you send to the government's best interest. If you wish to designate any payments not included with this offer, you must designate a preference for each payment at the time the payment is made. However, you cannot designate the $186 application fee or any payment after the IRS accepts the offer.

If you are paying **more than** the required payment when you submit your offer and want any part of that payment treated as a deposit, check the box below and insert the amount. Deposits will be refunded if the offer is rejected, returned, or withdrawn, unless you request it to be applied to your tax debt.

[ ] My payment of $ ________ includes the $186 application fee and $ ________ for my initial offer payment. I am requesting the additional payment of $ ________ be held as a deposit.

CAUTION: Do NOT designate the amounts sent in with your offer to cover the down payment and application fee as "deposits." Doing so will result in the return of your offer.

Catalog Number 16728N www.irs.gov Form **656** (Rev. 1-2015)

Section 7 Source of Funds, Making Your Payment, and Filing Requirements

Source of Funds

Tell us where you will obtain the funds to pay your offer. You may consider borrowing from friends and/or family, taking out a loan, or selling assets.

We will borrow funds from friends and/or family.

Making Your Payment

Include separate checks for the payment and application fee.
Make checks payable to the "United States Treasury" and attach to the front of your Form 656, Offer in Compromise. All payments must be in U.S. dollars. **Do not send cash.** Send a separate application fee with each offer; do not combine it with any other tax payments, as this may delay processing of your offer. Your offer will be returned to you if the application fee and the required payment is not included, or if your check is returned for insufficient funds.

Filing Requirements

☒ I certify that I have filed all required tax returns.

☐ I certify that I was not required to file a tax return for the following years:

Source of offer funds

Section 8 Offer Terms

By submitting this offer, I/we have read, understand and agree to the following terms and conditions:

Terms, Conditions, and Legal Agreement

a) I request that the IRS accept the offer amount listed in this offer application as payment of my outstanding tax debt (including interest, penalties, and any additional amounts required by law) as of the date listed on this form. I authorize the IRS to amend Section 2 on page 1 in the event I failed to list any of my assessed tax debt, or tax debt assessed before acceptance of my offer. I also authorize the IRS to amend Section 2 on page 1 by removing any tax years on which there is currently no outstanding liability. I understand that my offer will be accepted, by law, unless IRS notifies me otherwise, in writing, within 24 months of the date my offer was received by IRS. I also understand that if any tax debt that is included in the offer is in dispute in any judicial proceeding it/they will not be included in determining the expiration of the 24-month period.

IRS will keep my payments, fees, and some refunds.

b) I voluntarily submit the payments made on this offer and understand that they are not refundable even if I withdraw the offer or the IRS rejects or returns the offer. Unless I designate how to apply each required payment in Section 6 page 3, the IRS will apply my payment in the best interest of the government, choosing which tax years and tax debts to pay off. The IRS will also keep my application fee unless the offer is not accepted for processing.

c) The IRS will keep any refund, including interest, that I might be due for tax periods extending through the calendar year in which the IRS accepts my offer. I cannot designate that the refund be applied to estimated tax payments for the following year or the accepted offer amount. If I receive a refund after I submit this offer for any tax period extending through the calendar year in which the IRS accepts my offer, I will return the refund within 30 days of notification.

I understand that the amount I am offering may not include part or all of an expected or current tax refund, money already paid, funds attached by any collection action, or anticipated benefits from a capital or net operating loss.

d) The IRS will keep any monies it has collected prior to this offer. The IRS may levy my assets up to the time that the IRS official signs and acknowledges my offer as pending, which is accepted for processing and the IRS may keep any proceeds arising from such a levy. No levy will be issued on individual shared responsibility payments.

The IRS will keep any payments that I make related to this offer. I agree that any funds submitted with this offer will be treated as a payment unless I checked the box to treat an overpayment as a deposit. Only amounts that exceed the mandatory payments can be treated as a deposit. I also agree that any funds submitted with periodic payments made after the submission of this offer and prior to the acceptance, rejection, or return of this offer will be treated as payments, unless I identify an overpayment as a deposit on the check submitted with the corresponding periodic payment. A deposit will be refundable if the offer is rejected, returned, or withdrawn. I understand that the IRS will not pay interest on any deposit.

Pending status of an offer and right to appeal

e) Once an authorized IRS official signs this form, my offer is considered pending as of that signature date and it remains pending until the IRS accepts, rejects, returns, or I withdraw my offer. An offer is also considered pending for 30 days after any rejection of my offer by the IRS, and during the time that any rejection of my offer is being considered by the Appeals Office. An offer will be considered withdrawn when the IRS receives my written notification of withdrawal by personal delivery or certified mail or when I inform the IRS of my withdrawal by other means and the IRS acknowledges in writing my intent to withdraw the offer.

f) I waive the right to an Appeals hearing if I do not request a hearing in writing within 30 days of the date the IRS notifies me of the decision to reject the offer.

Section 8 ***(Continued)*** **Offer Terms**

I must comply with my future tax obligations and understand I remain liable for the full amount of my tax debt until all terms and conditions of this offer have been met.	g) I will comply with all provisions of the internal revenue laws, including requirements to timely file tax returns and timely pay taxes for the five year period beginning with the date of acceptance of this offer and ending through the fifth year, including any extensions to file and pay. I also agree to promptly pay any liabilities assessed after acceptance of this offer for tax years ending prior to acceptance of this offer that were not otherwise identified in Section 2 of this agreement. If this is an offer being submitted for joint tax debt, and one of us does not comply with future obligations, only the non-compliant taxpayer will be in default of this agreement. An accepted offer will not be defaulted solely due to the assessment of an individual shared responsibility payment.
	h) I agree that I will remain liable for the full amount of the tax liability, accrued penalties and interest, until I have met all of the terms and conditions of this offer. Penalty and interest will continue to accrue until all payment terms of the offer have been met. If I file for bankruptcy before the terms and conditions of the offer are met, I agree that the IRS may file a claim for the full amount of the tax liability, accrued penalties and interest, and that any claim the IRS files in the bankruptcy proceeding will be a tax claim.
	i) Once the IRS accepts my offer in writing, I have no right to challenge the tax debt(s) in court or by filing a refund claim or refund suit for any liability or period listed in Section 2, even if I default the terms of the accepted offer.
I understand what will happen if I fail to meet the terms of my offer (e.g., default).	j) If I fail to meet any of the terms of this offer, the IRS may levy or sue me to collect any amount ranging from the unpaid balance of the offer to the original amount of the tax debt (less payments made) plus penalties and interest that have accrued from the time the underlying tax liability arose. The IRS will continue to add interest, as Section 6601 of the Internal Revenue Code requires, on the amount the IRS determines is due after default.
I agree to waive time limits provided by law.	k) To have my offer considered, I agree to the extension of the time limit provided by law to assess my tax debt (statutory period of assessment). I agree that the date by which the IRS must assess my tax debt will now be the date by which my debt must currently be assessed plus the period of time my offer is pending plus one additional year if the IRS rejects, returns, or terminates my offer or I withdraw it. (Paragraph (e) of this section defines pending and withdrawal.) I understand that I have the right not to waive the statutory period of assessment or to limit the waiver to a certain length or certain periods or issues. I understand, however, that the IRS may not consider my offer if I refuse to waive the statutory period of assessment or if I provide only a limited waiver. I also understand that the statutory period for collecting my tax debt will be suspended during the time my offer is pending with the IRS, for 30 days after any rejection of my offer by the IRS, and during the time that any rejection of my offer is being considered by the Appeals Office.
I understand the IRS may file a Notice of Federal Tax Lien on my property.	l) The IRS may file a Notice of Federal Tax Lien during the offer investigation. The IRS may file a Notice of Federal Tax Lien to protect the Government's interest on offers that will be paid over time. This tax lien will be released when the payment terms of the accepted offer have been satisfied. The IRS will not file a Notice of Federal Tax Lien on any individual shared responsibility debt.
Correction Agreement	m) I/We authorize IRS, to correct any typographical or clerical errors or make minor modifications to my/our Form 656 that I/We signed in connection to this offer.
I authorize the IRS to contact relevant third parties in order to process my offer	n) By authorizing the IRS to contact third parties, I understand that I will not be notified of which third parties the IRS contacts as part of the offer application process, including tax periods that have not been assessed, as stated in section 7602 (c) of the Internal Revenue Code. In addition, I authorize the IRS to request a consumer report on me from a credit bureau.
I am submitting an offer as an individual for a joint liability	o) I understand if the liability sought to be compromised is the joint and individual liability of myself and my co-obligor(s) and I am submitting this offer to compromise my individual liability only, then if this offer is accepted, it does not release or discharge my co-obligor(s) from liability. The United States still reserves all rights of collection against the co-obligor(s).
Shared Responsibility Payment (SRP)	p) If your offer includes any shared responsibility payment (SRP) amount that you owe for not having minimum essential health coverage for you and, if applicable, your dependents per Internal Revenue Code Section 5000A – Individual shared responsibility payment, it is not subject to penalties or to lien and levy enforcement actions. However, interest will continue to accrue until you pay the total SRP balance due. We may apply your federal tax refunds to the SRP amount that you owe until it is paid in full.

Section 9 **Signatures**

Under penalties of perjury, I declare that I have examined this offer, including accompanying schedules and statements, and to the best of my knowledge and belief, it is true, correct and complete.

Signature of Taxpayer/Corporation Name	Phone Number	Date *(mm/dd/yyyy)*
Signature of Taxpayer/Authorized Corporate Officer	Phone Number	Date *(mm/dd/yyyy)*

Section 10	**Paid Preparer Use Only**	
Signature of Preparer	Phone Number	Date *(mm/dd/yyyy)*
Name of Paid Preparer	Preparer's CAF no. or PTIN	
Firm's Name (or yours if self-employed), Address, and ZIP Code		

Include a valid, signed Form 2848 or 8821 with this application, if one is not on file.

Section 11	**Third Party Designee**
Do you want to allow another person to discuss this offer with the IRS? ☐ Yes ☐ No	
If yes, provide designee's name	Telephone Number ( ) -

IRS Use Only. I accept the waiver of the statutory period of limitations on assessment for the Internal Revenue Service, as described in Section 8 (k).

Signature of Authorized Internal Revenue Service Official	Title	Date *(mm/dd/yyyy)*

Privacy Act Statement

We ask for the information on this form to carry out the internal revenue laws of the United States. Our authority to request this information is Section 7801 of the Internal Revenue Code.

Our purpose for requesting the information is to determine if it is in the best interests of the IRS to accept an offer. You are not required to make an offer; however, if you choose to do so, you must provide all of the taxpayer information requested. Failure to provide all of the information may prevent us from processing your request.

If you are a paid preparer and you prepared the Form 656 for the taxpayer submitting an offer, we request that you complete and sign Section 10 on Form 656, and provide identifying information. Providing this information is voluntary. This information will be used to administer and enforce the internal revenue laws of the United States and may be used to regulate practice before the Internal Revenue Service for those persons subject to Treasury Department Circular No. 230, Regulations Governing the Practice of Attorneys, Certified Public Accountants, Enrolled Agents, Enrolled Actuaries, and Appraisers before the Internal Revenue Service. Information on this form may be disclosed to the Department of Justice for civil and criminal litigation.

We may also disclose this information to cities, states and the District of Columbia for use in administering their tax laws and to combat terrorism. Providing false or fraudulent information on this form may subject you to criminal prosecution and penalties.

Enter your information in both sections

APPLICATION CHECKLIST

Review the entire application using the Application Checklist below. Include this checklist with your application.

Forms 433-A (OIC), 433-B (OIC), and 656

- ☐ Did you complete all fields and sign all forms?
- ☐ Did you make an offer amount that is equal to the offer amount calculated on the Form 433-A (OIC) or Form 433-B (OIC)? If not, did you describe the special circumstances that are leading you to offer less than the minimum in the "Explanation of Circumstances" Section 3 of Form 656, and did you provide supporting documentation of the special circumstances?
- ☐ Did you select a payment option on Form 656?
- ☐ If you want to allow the IRS to discuss your offer with another person, did you complete the "Third-Party Designee" section on the Form 656?
- ☐ If someone other than you completed the Form 656, did they sign it?
- ☐ Did you sign and attach the Form 433-A (OIC) if applicable?
- ☐ Did you sign and attach the Form 433-B (OIC) if applicable?
- ☐ Did you sign and attach the Form 656?
- ☐ If you are making an offer that includes business and individual tax debts, did you prepare a separate Form 656 package (including separate financial statements, supporting documentation, application fee, and initial payment)?

Supporting documentation and additional forms

- ☐ Did you include photocopies of all required supporting documentation?
- ☐ If you want a third party to represent you during the offer process, did you include a Form 2848 or Form 8821 unless one is already on file?

Payment

- ☐ Did you include a check or money order made payable to the "United States Treasury" for the initial payment? (Waived if you meet Low Income Certification guidelines—see Form 656.)
- ☐ Did you include a separate check or money order made payable to the "United States Treasury" for the $186 application fee? (Waived if you meet Low Income Certification guidelines—see Form 656.)

Mail your application package to the appropriate IRS facility

Mail the Form 656, 433-A (OIC) and/or 433-B (OIC), and related financial document(s) to the appropriate IRS processing office for your state. You may wish to send it by Certified Mail so you have a record of the date it was mailed.

If you reside in:	Mail your application to:
AK, AL, AR, AZ, CO, FL, GA, HI, ID, KY, LA, MS, MT, NC, NM, NV, OK, OR, SC, TN, TX, UT, WA, WI, WY	Memphis IRS Center COIC Unit P.O. Box 30803, AMC Memphis, TN 38130-0803 1-866-790-7117
CA, CT, DE, IA, IL, IN, KS, MA, MD, ME, MI, MN, MO, ND, NE, NH, NJ, NY, OH, PA, RI, SD, VT, VA, WV; DC, PR, or a foreign address	Brookhaven IRS Center COIC Unit P.O. Box 9007 Holtsville, NY 11742-9007 1-866-611-6191

Be sure to use this checklist to verify you submit a complete offer

Tips and Traps - Offers in Compromise

1. It can take up to two years for an Offer to be accepted or rejected. By IRS definition an Offer is deemed accepted if no answer is given within the 2-year period. The **Tax Resolution Institute** has yet to see an Offer be accepted based upon this rule.

2. A typical Offer takes 12-18 months to be accepted.

3. It can take up to 6 months for an Offer just to be deemed processable.

4. If an Offer is not processable, the taxpayer must correct the items that deem it non-processable and resubmit the Offer.

5. The chance of having an Offer accepted is much lower than the chance of entering into a manageable installment agreement.

6. There is a 10-year statute of limitation for the IRS to actively collect against a tax assessment. Submitting and Offer freezes the statute for the time the Offer is under consideration plus a time period following if the Offer is rejected or accepted and then the taxpayer defaults on the Offer.

7. If a taxpayer is near the end of their collection statute, it may make sense to forgo an Offer and request an installment agreement based upon hardship.

8. Acceptance of an Offer is based upon a taxpayer's ability to pay over the life of the statute of limitations on collection. Just because a taxpayer is unable to pay at the time an Offer is submitted, does not mean that their situation will not improve within the 10-year collection period. One example of this may be a realtor in a down market or a Lawyer that has been laid off by previously earned a significant salary.

9. A taxpayer must stay in compliance for 5 years after an Offer has been accepted. If they default on the Offer, the original liability, penalties and interest are placed back on the taxpayer's account and they will again be exposed to collection.

10. A taxpayer is often required to resubmit financial substantiation within the time period an Offer is being considered.

11. The IRS will often negotiate certain parts of an Offer in lieu of rejecting an Offer outright.

12. When an Offer is rejected, the IRS' reason is almost always that the taxpayer has the ability to full-pay their liability within the collection statute.

13. The amount to be paid for an Offer is formula based. That is 12 or 24 times one's monthly disposable income plus the quick-sale value of their assets. Some people, in planning for an Offer may try and sell, give away or transfer their assets in order to lower the Offer amount. If this is done solely with the intention of lowering one's Offer amount or done within a certain period of time prior to submission of the Offer, the asset in question may still be included in the Offer calculation by the IRS. For example, if a person refinances their home to pay off credit card debt, the IRS may include the cash taken out of the refinance as a dissipated asset for Offer purposes. Their contention is that Federal taxes should be paid prior to credit card companies.

14. When entering bank balances on Form 433-A (OIC) it is prudent to put the ending balance of the most current bank statement if the amount is relatively low. If not include the lowest average daily balance within the three-month period of the statements being submitted.

Request for Copy of Tax Return Form[v]

Form **4506**

(Rev. September 2013)

Department of the Treasury
Internal Revenue Service

Request for Copy of Tax Return

▶ **Request may be rejected if the form is incomplete or illegible.**

OMB No. 1545-0429

Tip. You may be able to get your tax return or return information from other sources. If you had your tax return completed by a paid preparer, they should be able to provide you a copy of the return. The IRS can provide a **Tax Return Transcript** for many returns free of charge. The transcript provides most of the line entries from the original tax return and usually contains the information that a third party (such as a mortgage company) requires. See **Form 4506-T, Request for Transcript of Tax Return,** or you can quickly request transcripts by using our automated self-help service tools. Please visit us at IRS.gov and click on "Order a Return or Account Transcript" or call 1-800-908-9946.

1a Name shown on tax return. If a joint return, enter the name shown first.

1b First social security number on tax return, individual taxpayer identification number, or employer identification number (see instructions)

2a If a joint return, enter spouse's name shown on tax return.

2b Second social security number or individual taxpayer identification number if joint tax return

3 Current name, address (including apt., room, or suite no.), city, state, and ZIP code (see instructions)

4 Previous address shown on the last return filed if different from line 3 (see instructions)

5 If the tax return is to be mailed to a third party (such as a mortgage company), enter the third party's name, address, and telephone number.

Caution. *If the tax return is being mailed to a third party, ensure that you have filled in lines 6 and 7 before signing. Sign and date the form once you have filled in these lines. Completing these steps helps to protect your privacy. Once the IRS discloses your tax return to the third party listed on line 5, the IRS has no control over what the third party does with the information. If you would like to limit the third party's authority to disclose your return information, you can specify this limitation in your written agreement with the third party.*

6 **Tax return requested.** Form 1040, 1120, 941, etc. and all attachments as originally submitted to the IRS, including Form(s) W-2, schedules, or amended returns. Copies of Forms 1040, 1040A, and 1040EZ are generally available for 7 years from filing before they are destroyed by law. Other returns may be available for a longer period of time. Enter only one return number. If you need more than one type of return, you must complete another Form 4506. ▶ ____________

Note. *If the copies must be certified for court or administrative proceedings, check here* . . . . . . ☐

7 **Year or period requested.** Enter the ending date of the year or period, using the mm/dd/yyyy format. If you are requesting more than eight years or periods, you must attach another Form 4506.

____________ ____________ ____________ ____________

____________ ____________ ____________ ____________

8 **Fee.** There is a $50 fee for each return requested. **Full payment must be included with your request or it will be rejected. Make your check or money order payable to "United States Treasury." Enter your SSN, ITIN, or EIN and "Form 4506 request" on your check or money order.**

a	Cost for each return	$ 50.00
b	Number of returns requested on line 7	
c	Total cost. Multiply line 8a by line 8b	$

9 If we cannot find the tax return, we will refund the fee. If the refund should go to the third party listed on line 5, check here . . . . . ☐

Caution. Do not sign this form unless all applicable lines have been completed.

Signature of taxpayer(s). I declare that I am either the taxpayer whose name is shown on line 1a or 2a, or a person authorized to obtain the tax return requested. If the request applies to a joint return, at least one spouse must sign. If signed by a corporate officer, partner, guardian, tax matters partner, executor, receiver, administrator, trustee, or party other than the taxpayer, I certify that I have the authority to execute Form 4506 on behalf of the taxpayer. **Note.** *For tax returns being sent to a third party, this form must be received within 120 days of the signature date.*

Phone number of taxpayer on line 1a or 2a

Sign Here

▶ **Signature** (see instructions) Date

▶ **Title** (if line 1a above is a corporation, partnership, estate, or trust)

▶ **Spouse's** signature Date

For Privacy Act and Paperwork Reduction Act Notice, see page 2. Cat. No. 41721E Form **4506** (Rev. 9-2013)

Section references are to the Internal Revenue Code unless otherwise noted.

Future Developments

For the latest information about Form 4506 and its instructions, go to *www.irs.gov/form4506*. Information about any recent developments affecting Form 4506, Form 4506T and Form 4506T-EZ will be posted on that page.

General Instructions

Caution. Do not sign this form unless all applicable lines have been completed.

Purpose of form. Use Form 4506 to request a copy of your tax return. You can also designate (on line 5) a third party to receive the tax return.

How long will it take? It may take up to 75 calendar days for us to process your request.

Tip. Use Form 4506-T, Request for Transcript of Tax Return, to request tax return transcripts, tax account information, W-2 information, 1099 information, verification of non-filing, and records of account.

Automated transcript request. You can quickly request transcripts by using our automated self-help service tools. Please visit us at IRS.gov and click on "Order a Return or Account Transcript" or call 1-800-908-9946.

Where to file. Attach payment and mail Form 4506 to the address below for the state you lived in, or the state your business was in, when that return was filed. There are two address charts: one for individual returns (Form 1040 series) and one for all other returns.

If you are requesting a return for more than one year and the chart below shows two different addresses, send your request to the address based on the address of your most recent return.

Chart for individual returns (Form 1040 series)

If you filed an individual return and lived in:	Mail to:
Alabama, Kentucky, Louisiana, Mississippi, Tennessee, Texas, a foreign country, American Samoa, Puerto Rico, Guam, the Commonwealth of the Northern Mariana Islands, the U.S. Virgin Islands, or A.P.O. or F.P.O. address	Internal Revenue Service RAIVS Team Stop 6716 AUSC Austin, TX 73301
Alaska, Arizona, Arkansas, California, Colorado, Hawaii, Idaho, Illinois, Indiana, Iowa, Kansas, Michigan, Minnesota, Montana, Nebraska, Nevada, New Mexico, North Dakota, Oklahoma, Oregon, South Dakota, Utah, Washington, Wisconsin, Wyoming	Internal Revenue Service RAIVS Team Stop 37106 Fresno, CA 93888
Connecticut, Delaware, District of Columbia, Florida, Georgia, Maine, Maryland, Massachusetts, Missouri, New Hampshire, New Jersey, New York, North Carolina, Ohio, Pennsylvania, Rhode Island, South Carolina, Vermont, Virginia, West Virginia	Internal Revenue Service RAIVS Team Stop 6705 P-6 Kansas City, MO 64999

Chart for all other returns

If you lived in or your business was in:	Mail to:
Alabama, Alaska, Arizona, Arkansas, California, Colorado, Florida, Hawaii, Idaho, Iowa, Kansas, Louisiana, Minnesota, Mississippi, Missouri, Montana, Nebraska, Nevada, New Mexico, North Dakota, Oklahoma, Oregon, South Dakota, Texas, Utah, Washington, Wyoming, a foreign country, or A.P.O. or F.P.O. address	Internal Revenue Service RAIVS Team P.O. Box 9941 Mail Stop 6734 Ogden, UT 84409
Connecticut, Delaware, District of Columbia, Georgia, Illinois, Indiana, Kentucky, Maine, Maryland, Massachusetts, Michigan, New Hampshire, New Jersey, New York, North Carolina, Ohio, Pennsylvania, Rhode Island, South Carolina, Tennessee, Vermont, Virginia, West Virginia, Wisconsin	Internal Revenue Service RAIVS Team P.O. Box 145500 Stop 2800 F Cincinnati, OH 45250

Specific Instructions

Line 1b. Enter your employer identification number (EIN) if you are requesting a copy of a business return. Otherwise, enter the first social security number (SSN) or your individual taxpayer identification number (ITIN) shown on the return. For example, if you are requesting Form 1040 that includes Schedule C (Form 1040), enter your SSN.

Line 3. Enter your current address. If you use a P.O. box, please include it on this line 3.

Line 4. Enter the address shown on the last return filed if different from the address entered on line 3.

Note. If the address on Lines 3 and 4 are different and you have not changed your address with the IRS, file Form 8822, Change of Address. For a business address, file Form 8822-B, Change of Address or Responsible Party — Business.

Signature and date. Form 4506 must be signed and dated by the taxpayer listed on line 1a or 2a. If you completed line 5 requesting the return be sent to a third party, the IRS must receive Form 4506 within 120 days of the date signed by the taxpayer or it will be rejected. Ensure that all applicable lines are completed before signing.

Individuals. Copies of jointly filed tax returns may be furnished to either spouse. Only one signature is required. Sign Form 4506 exactly as your name appeared on the original return. If you changed your name, also sign your current name.

Corporations. Generally, Form 4506 can be signed by: (1) an officer having legal authority to bind the corporation, (2) any person designated by the board of directors or other governing body, or (3) any officer or employee on written request by any principal officer and attested to by the secretary or other officer.

Partnerships. Generally, Form 4506 can be signed by any person who was a member of the partnership during any part of the tax period requested on line 7.

All others. See section 6103(e) if the taxpayer has died, is insolvent, is a dissolved corporation, or if a trustee, guardian, executor, receiver, or administrator is acting for the taxpayer.

Documentation. For entities other than individuals, you must attach the authorization document. For example, this could be the letter from the principal officer authorizing an employee of the corporation or the letters testamentary authorizing an individual to act for an estate.

Signature by a representative. A representative can sign Form 4506 for a taxpayer only if this authority has been specifically delegated to the representative on Form 2848, line 5. Form 2848 showing the delegation must be attached to Form 4506.

Privacy Act and Paperwork Reduction Act Notice. We ask for the information on this form to establish your right to gain access to the requested return(s) under the Internal Revenue Code. We need this information to properly identify the return(s) and respond to your request. If you request a copy of a tax return, sections 6103 and 6109 require you to provide this information, including your SSN or EIN, to process your request. If you do not provide this information, we may not be able to process your request. Providing false or fraudulent information may subject you to penalties.

Routine uses of this information include giving it to the Department of Justice for civil and criminal litigation, and cities, states, the District of Columbia, and U.S. commonwealths and possessions for use in administering their tax laws. We may also disclose this information to other countries under a tax treaty, to federal and state agencies to enforce federal nontax criminal laws, or to federal law enforcement and intelligence agencies to combat terrorism.

You are not required to provide the information requested on a form that is subject to the Paperwork Reduction Act unless the form displays a valid OMB control number. Books or records relating to a form or its instructions must be retained as long as their contents may become material in the administration of any Internal Revenue law. Generally, tax returns and return information are confidential, as required by section 6103.

The time needed to complete and file Form 4506 will vary depending on individual circumstances. The estimated average time is: **Learning about the law or the form,** 10 min.; **Preparing the form,** 16 min.; and **Copying, assembling, and sending the form to the IRS,** 20 min.

If you have comments concerning the accuracy of these time estimates or suggestions for making Form 4506 simpler, we would be happy to hear from you. You can write to:

Internal Revenue Service
Tax Forms and Publications Division
1111 Constitution Ave. NW, IR-6526
Washington, DC 20224.

Do not send the form to this address. Instead, see *Where to file* on this page.

Chapter 7:

IRS Transcripts

IRS Transcripts and Form 2848 (Power of Attorney)[vi]

There are three main types of tax transcripts you can obtain from the IRS. They are Account Transcripts, Wage and Income Transcripts and Tax Return Transcripts.

Account Transcripts include general activity relating to the taxpayers account including when and if a return was filed, what payments if any were made and how much is currently owed on the account. In addition other more specific items such as when a taxpayer was placed into Currently Non Collectable ("CNC") status or when an Offer in Compromise was accepted or rejected appears on the transcript. The Account Transcript offers valuable information pertaining to a taxpayer's fillings for the year in which the transcript was obtained. This transcript does not however include any information pertaining to the items that need to be included in the tax return itself.

The best place to find pertinent tax information that was reported directly to the IRS is the Wage and Income Transcript. If a taxpayer has unfiled returns and/or has prepared returns that do not correspond with the information that the IRS has on file, most information can be found in the Wage and Income transcript. Items such as wages and self-employment income (via form 1099) appear on a Wage and Income transcript. In addition reported Federal tax, Medicare and Social Security withholding will also appear on a Wage and Income transcript for employees. State tax withholding will not appear on a Federal transcript and must be obtained from the wage earner's W-2 or by contacting the State in which the tax was withheld. In addition interest income, dividend income and other investment income such as K-1 activity will appear on a Wage and Income transcript. If a taxpayer traded stocks, typically the proceeds from the sales of said stocks will appear on a Wage and Income transcript. However, the transactions showing the purchase of said stocks (the "basis") not only will not show up on the transcripts but will not be accounted for if the IRS prepares a Substitute for Return ("SFR") to determine the tax liability for an unfiled return. For this reason it is important for the tax preparer to obtain the basis information form the taxpayer for all stock transactions that occurred during the year of the delinquent return being prepared.

A Tax Return Transcript can be a valuable tool to determine what was included in a previously filed return. It is a hybrid of the Account Transcript and the Wage and Income Transcript. This Transcript is particularly valuable when altering or amending a return.

Below is a copy of the IRS Power of Attorney (Form 2848) used to obtain all three types of transcripts. In addition you will see form 4506T used to obtain transcripts as well.

Form **2848** (Rev. July 2014) Department of the Treasury Internal Revenue Service

Power of Attorney and Declaration of Representative

▶ Information about Form 2848 and its instructions is at *www.irs.gov/form2848*.

OMB No. 1545-0150

For IRS Use Only
Received by:
Name ____________
Telephone ____________
Function ____________
Date / /

Part I **Power of Attorney**

Caution: *A separate Form 2848 must be completed for each taxpayer. Form 2848 will not be honored for any purpose other than representation before the IRS.*

1 **Taxpayer information.** Taxpayer must sign and date this form on page 2, line 7.

Taxpayer name and address	Taxpayer identification number(s)	
	Daytime telephone number	Plan number (if applicable)

hereby appoints the following representative(s) as attorney(s)-in-fact:

2 **Representative(s)** must sign and date this form on page 2, Part II.

Name and address	CAF No. ____________ PTIN ____________ Telephone No. ____________ Fax No. ____________
Check if to be sent copies of notices and communications ☐	Check if new: Address ☐ Telephone No. ☐ Fax No. ☐
Name and address	CAF No. ____________ PTIN ____________ Telephone No. ____________ Fax No. ____________
Check if to be sent copies of notices and communications ☐	Check if new: Address ☐ Telephone No. ☐ Fax No. ☐
Name and address	CAF No. ____________ PTIN ____________ Telephone No. ____________ Fax No. ____________
(**Note.** IRS sends notices and communications to only two representatives.)	Check if new: Address ☐ Telephone No. ☐ Fax No. ☐
Name and address	CAF No. ____________ PTIN ____________ Telephone No. ____________ Fax No. ____________
(**Note.** IRS sends notices and communications to only two representatives.)	Check if new: Address ☐ Telephone No. ☐ Fax No. ☐

to represent the taxpayer before the Internal Revenue Service and perform the following acts:

3 **Acts authorized (you are required to complete this line 3).** With the exception of the acts described in line 5b, I authorize my representative(s) to receive and inspect my confidential tax information and to perform acts that I can perform with respect to the tax matters described below. For example, my representative(s) shall have the authority to sign any agreements, consents, or similar documents (see instructions for line 5a for authorizing a representative to sign a return).

Description of Matter (Income, Employment, Payroll, Excise, Estate, Gift, Whistleblower, Practitioner Discipline, PLR, FOIA, Civil Penalty, Sec. 5000A Shared Responsibility Payment, Sec. 4980H Shared Responsibility Payment, etc.) (see instructions)	Tax Form Number (1040, 941, 720, etc.) (if applicable)	Year(s) or Period(s) (if applicable) (see instructions)

4 **Specific use not recorded on Centralized Authorization File (CAF).** If the power of attorney is for a specific use not recorded on CAF, check this box. See the instructions for **Line 4. Specific Use Not Recorded on CAF** . . . . ▶ ☐

5a **Additional acts authorized.** In addition to the acts listed on line 3 above, I authorize my representative(s) to perform the following acts (see instructions for line 5a for more information):

☐ Authorize disclosure to third parties; ☐ Substitute or add representative(s); ☐ Sign a return; ____________

☐ Other acts authorized: ____________

Form 2848 (Rev. 7-2014) Page **2**

b Specific acts not authorized. My representative(s) is (are) not authorized to endorse or otherwise negotiate any check (including directing or accepting payment by any means, electronic or otherwise, into an account owned or controlled by the representative(s) or any firm or other entity with whom the representative(s) is (are) associated) issued by the government in respect of a federal tax liability.

List any specific deletions to the acts otherwise authorized in this power of attorney (see instructions for line 5b): ____________________

____

6 Retention/revocation of prior power(s) of attorney. The filing of this power of attorney automatically revokes all earlier power(s) of attorney on file with the Internal Revenue Service for the same matters and years or periods covered by this document. If you **do not** want to revoke a prior power of attorney, check here . . . . . ▶ ☐

YOU MUST ATTACH A COPY OF ANY POWER OF ATTORNEY YOU WANT TO REMAIN IN EFFECT.

7 Signature of taxpayer. If a tax matter concerns a year in which a joint return was filed, each spouse must file a separate power of attorney even if they are appointing the same representative(s). If signed by a corporate officer, partner, guardian, tax matters partner, executor, receiver, administrator, or trustee on behalf of the taxpayer, I certify that I have the authority to execute this form on behalf of the taxpayer.

▶ IF NOT COMPLETED, SIGNED, AND DATED, THE IRS WILL RETURN THIS POWER OF ATTORNEY TO THE TAXPAYER.

Signature	Date	Title (if applicable)
Print Name		Print name of taxpayer from line 1 if other than individual

Part II Declaration of Representative

Under penalties of perjury, by my signature below I declare that:

- I am not currently suspended or disbarred from practice before the Internal Revenue Service;
- I am subject to regulations contained in Circular 230 (31 CFR, Subtitle A, Part 10), as amended, governing practice before the Internal Revenue Service;
- I am authorized to represent the taxpayer identified in Part I for the matter(s) specified there; and
- I am one of the following:

a Attorney—a member in good standing of the bar of the highest court of the jurisdiction shown below.
b Certified Public Accountant—duly qualified to practice as a certified public accountant in the jurisdiction shown below.
c Enrolled Agent—enrolled as an agent by the Internal Revenue Service per the requirements of Circular 230.
d Officer—a bona fide officer of the taxpayer organization.
e Full-Time Employee—a full-time employee of the taxpayer.
f Family Member—a member of the taxpayer's immediate family (for example, spouse, parent, child, grandparent, grandchild, step-parent, step-child, brother, or sister).
g Enrolled Actuary—enrolled as an actuary by the Joint Board for the Enrollment of Actuaries under 29 U.S.C. 1242 (the authority to practice before the Internal Revenue Service is limited by section 10.3(d) of Circular 230).
h Unenrolled Return Preparer—Your authority to practice before the Internal Revenue Service is limited. You must have been eligible to sign the return under examination and have prepared and signed the return. **See Notice 2011-6 and *Special rules for registered tax return preparers and unenrolled return preparers* in the instructions (PTIN required for designation h).**
i Registered Tax Return Preparer—registered as a tax return preparer under the requirements of section 10.4 of Circular 230. Your authority to practice before the Internal Revenue Service is limited. You must have been eligible to sign the return under examination and have prepared and signed the return. **See Notice 2011-6 and *Special rules for registered tax return preparers and unenrolled return preparers* in the instructions (PTIN required for designation i).**
k Student Attorney or CPA—receives permission to represent taxpayers before the IRS by virtue of his/her status as a law, business, or accounting student working in an LITC or STCP. See instructions for Part II for additional information and requirements.
r Enrolled Retirement Plan Agent—enrolled as a retirement plan agent under the requirements of Circular 230 (the authority to practice before the Internal Revenue Service is limited by section 10.3(e)).

▶ IF THIS DECLARATION OF REPRESENTATIVE IS NOT COMPLETED, SIGNED, AND DATED, THE IRS WILL RETURN THE POWER OF ATTORNEY. REPRESENTATIVES MUST SIGN IN THE ORDER LISTED IN PART I, LINE 2. See the instructions for Part II.

Note. For designations d-f, enter your title, position, or relationship to the taxpayer in the "Licensing jurisdiction" column. See the instructions for Part II for more information.

Designation—Insert above letter **(a–r)**	Licensing jurisdiction (state) or other licensing authority (if applicable)	Bar, license, certification, registration, or enrollment number (if applicable). See instructions for Part II for more information.	Signature	Date

Form **2848** (Rev. 7-2014)

Request for Transcripts Form[vii]

Form **4506T-EZ**
(Rev. August 2014)
Department of the Treasury
Internal Revenue Service

Short Form Request for Individual Tax Return Transcript

▶ **Request may not be processed if the form is incomplete or illegible.**
▶ **For more information about Form 4506T-EZ, visit *www.irs.gov/form4506tez*.**

OMB No. 1545-2154

Tip. Use Form 4506T-EZ to order a 1040 series tax return transcript free of charge, or you can quickly request transcripts by using our automated self-help service tools. Please visit us at IRS.gov and click on "Get Transcript of Your Tax Records" under "Tools" or call 1-800-908-9946.

1a Name shown on tax return. If a joint return, enter the name shown first.

1b First social security number or individual taxpayer identification number on tax return

2a If a joint return, enter spouse's name shown on tax return.

2b Second social security number or individual taxpayer identification number if joint tax return

3 Current name, address (including apt., room, or suite no.), city, state, and ZIP code (see instructions)

4 Previous address shown on the last return filed if different from line 3 (see instructions)

5 If the transcript is to be mailed to a third party (such as a mortgage company), enter the third party's name, address, and telephone number. The IRS has no control over what the third party does with the tax information.

Third party name

Telephone number

Address (including apt., room, or suite no.), city, state, and ZIP code

Caution. If the tax transcript is being mailed to a third party, ensure that you have filled in line 6 before signing. Sign and date the form once you have filled in this line. Completing this step helps to protect your privacy. Once the IRS discloses your IRS transcript to the third party listed on line 5, the IRS has no control over what the third party does with the information. If you would like to limit the third party's authority to disclose your transcript information, you can specify this limitation in your written agreement with the third party.

6 **Year(s) requested.** Enter the year(s) of the return transcript you are requesting (for example, "2008"). Most requests will be processed within 10 business days.

Note. *If the IRS is unable to locate a return that matches the taxpayer identity information provided above, or if IRS records indicate that the return has not been filed, the IRS will notify you or the third party that it was unable to locate a return, or that a return was not filed, whichever is applicable.*

Caution. Do not sign this form unless all applicable lines have been completed.

Signature of taxpayer(s). I declare that I am the taxpayer whose name is shown on either line 1a or 2a. If the request applies to a joint return, **either** spouse must sign. **Note.** *For transcripts being sent to a third party, this form must be received within 120 days of the signature date.*

Phone number of taxpayer on line 1a or 2a

Sign Here

▶ **Signature** (see instructions) Date

▶ **Spouse's signature** Date

For Privacy Act and Paperwork Reduction Act Notice, see page 2. Cat. No. 54185S Form **4506T-EZ** (Rev. 08-2014)

Section references are to the Internal Revenue Code unless otherwise noted.

Future Developments

For the latest information about developments related to Form 4506T-EZ, such as legislation enacted after it was published, go to *www.irs.gov/form4506tez*.

Caution. Do not sign this form unless all applicable lines have been completed.

Purpose of form. Individuals can use Form 4506T-EZ to request a tax return transcript for the current and the prior three years that includes most lines of the original tax return. The tax return transcript will not show payments, penalty assessments, or adjustments made to the originally filed return. You can also designate (on line 5) a third party (such as a mortgage company) to receive a transcript. Form 4506T-EZ cannot be used by taxpayers who file Form 1040 based on a tax year beginning in one calendar year and ending in the following year (fiscal tax year). Taxpayers using a fiscal tax year must file Form 4506-T, Request for Transcript of Tax Return, to request a return transcript.

Use Form 4506-T to request tax return transcripts, tax account information, W-2 information, 1099 information, verification of non-filing, and record of account.

Automated transcript request. You can quickly request transcripts by using our automated self-help service tools. Please visit us at IRS.gov and click on "Get Transcript of Your Tax Records" under "Tools" or call 1-800-908-9946.

Where to file. Mail or fax Form 4506T-EZ to the address below for the state you lived in when the return was filed.

If you are requesting more than one transcript or other product and the chart below shows two different addresses, send your request to the address based on the address of your most recent return.

If you filed an individual return and lived in:	Mail or fax to the "Internal Revenue Service" at:
Alabama, Kentucky, Louisiana, Mississippi, Tennessee, Texas, a foreign country, American Samoa, Puerto Rico, Guam, the Commonwealth of the Northern Mariana Islands, the U.S. Virgin Islands, or A.P.O. or F.P.O. address	RAIVS Team Stop 6716 AUSC Austin, TX 73301 512-460-2272
Alaska, Arizona, Arkansas, California, Colorado, Hawaii, Idaho, Illinois, Indiana, Iowa, Kansas, Michigan, Minnesota, Montana, Nebraska, Nevada, New Mexico, North Dakota, Oklahoma, Oregon, South Dakota, Utah, Washington, Wisconsin, Wyoming	RAIVS Team Stop 37106 Fresno, CA 93888 559-456-7227
Connecticut, Delaware, District of Columbia, Florida, Georgia, Maine, Maryland, Massachusetts, Missouri, New Hampshire, New Jersey, New York, North Carolina, Ohio, Pennsylvania, Rhode Island, South Carolina, Vermont, Virginia, West Virginia	RAIVS Team Stop 6705 P-6 Kansas City, MO 64999 816-292-6102

Line 1b. Enter your employer identification number (EIN) if your request relates to a business return. Otherwise, enter the first social security number (SSN) or your individual taxpayer identification number (ITIN) shown on the return. For example, if you are requesting Form 1040 that includes Schedule C (Form 1040), enter your SSN.

Line 3. Enter your current address. If you use a P.O. box, include it on this line.

Line 4. Enter the address shown on the last return filed if different from the address entered on line 3.

Note. If the address on lines 3 and 4 are different and you have not changed your address with the IRS, file Form 8822, Change of Address.

Signature and date. Form 4506T-EZ must be signed and dated by the taxpayer listed on line 1a or 2a. If you completed line 5 requesting the information be sent to a third party, the IRS must receive Form 4506T-EZ within 120 days of the date signed by the taxpayer or it will be rejected. Ensure that all applicable lines are completed before signing.

Transcripts of jointly filed tax returns may be furnished to either spouse. Only one signature is required. Sign Form 4506T-EZ exactly as your name appeared on the original return. If you changed your name, also sign your current name.

Privacy Act and Paperwork Reduction Act Notice. We ask for the information on this form to establish your right to gain access to the requested tax information under the Internal Revenue Code. We need this information to properly identify the tax information and respond to your request. If you request a transcript, sections 6103 and 6109 require you to provide this information, including your SSN. If you do not provide this information, we may not be able to process your request. Providing false or fraudulent information may subject you to penalties.

Routine uses of this information include giving it to the Department of Justice for civil and criminal litigation, and cities, states, the District of Columbia, and U.S. commonwealths and possessions for use in administering their tax laws. We may also disclose this information to other countries under a tax treaty, to federal and state agencies to enforce federal nontax criminal laws, or to federal law enforcement and intelligence agencies to combat terrorism.

You are not required to provide the information requested on a form that is subject to the Paperwork Reduction Act unless the form displays a valid OMB control number. Books or records relating to a form or its instructions must be retained as long as their contents may become material in the administration of any Internal Revenue law. Generally, tax returns and return information are confidential, as required by section 6103.

The time needed to complete and file Form 4506T-EZ will vary depending on individual circumstances. The estimated average time is: **Learning about the law or the form,** 9 min.; **Preparing the form,** 18 min.; and **Copying, assembling, and sending the form to the IRS,** 20 min.

If you have comments concerning the accuracy of these time estimates or suggestions for making Form 4506T-EZ simpler, we would be happy to hear from you. You can write to:

Internal Revenue Service
Tax Forms and Publications Division
1111 Constitution Ave. NW, IR-6526
Washington, DC 20224

Do not send the form to this address. Instead, see *Where to file* on this page.

Sample IRS Account Transcript

In the pages following you will find a sample of an IRS Account transcript pertaining to an individual taxpayer's account. You will notice that in the transcript there is basic information including the name and taxpayer identification number of the taxpayer (which are redacted from this particluar transcript), the amount owed on account for the given tax year/period, whether a return has been filed and if so, when it was filed. In addtion to this basic information there is various other details that can be seen pertaining to a taxpayers account for a given tax year or period.

As you review the transcrit, be sure to read each line to see which type of events get recorded. In this case there are items that appear including levies, payments and submissions of an offer in compromise.

Internal Revenue Service e-services

DEPARTMENT OF THE TREASURY

This Product Contains Sensitive Taxpayer Data

Account Transcript

Request Date: 06-12-2009
Response Date: 05-12-2009
Tracking Number: 100045052838

FORM NUMBER: 1040A

TAX PERIOD: Dec 31, 2001

TAXPAYER IDENTIFICATION NUMBER: ████████

<<<<POWER OF ATTORNEY/TAX INFORMATION AUTHORIZATION (POA/TIA) ON FILE>>>>

--- ANY MINUS SIGN SHOWN BELOW SIGNIFIES A CREDIT AMOUNT ---

ACCOUNT BALANCE:	94,263.33	
ACCRUED INTEREST:	13,959.66	AS OF: Jun. 08, 2009
ACCRUED PENALTY:	0.00	AS OF: Jun. 08, 2009

ACCOUNT BALANCE PLUS ACCRUALS
(this is not a payoff amount): 58,225.21

** INFORMATION FROM THE RETURN OR AS ADJUSTED [16]

EXEMPTIONS:	04	FILING STATUS: Single
ADJUSTED GROSS INCOME:	80,102.00	
TAXABLE INCOME:	63,952.00	
TAX PER RETURN:	0.00	
SE TAXABLE INCOME TAXPAYER:	80,400.00	
SE TAX/\BLS INCOME SPOUSE:	0.00	
TOTAL SELF EMPLOYMENT TAX:	12,308.00	

RETURN DUE DATE OR RETURN RECEIVED DATE (WHICHEVER IS LATER)

PROCESSING DATE

TRANSACTIONS

CODE	EXPLANATION OF TRANSACTION	CYCLE	DATE	AMOUNT
150	Substitute tax return prepared by IRS		12-29-2003	$0.00

Code	Explanation	Cycle	Date	Amount
	49210-334-28288-3			
140	Inquiry for non-filing of tax return		03-17-2003	$0.00
570	Additional account action pending		12-29-2003	$0.00
420	Examination of tax return		12-23-2003	$0.00
170	Penalty for not pre-paying tax	20043508	09-13-2004	$936.00
160	Penalty for filing tax return after the due date	20043508	09-13-2004	$5,832.00
300	Additional tax assessed by examination	20043508	09-13-2004	$50,034.00
	49247-639-00298-4			
336	Interest charged for late payment	20043508	09-13-2004	$7,868.74
276	Penalty for late payment of tax	20043508	09-13-2004	$7,254.93
976	Duplicate return filed		08-13-2004	$0.00
	89221-228-31849-4			
977	Amended return filed		08-13-2004	$0.00
	49277-445-01093-5			
161	Reduced or removed penalty for filing tax return after the due date		09-13-2004	-$5,425.65
163	Penalty for filing tax return after the due date	20043508	09-13-2004	$5,425.65
171	Reduced or removed penalty for not pre-paying tax		09-13-2004	-$1,044.00
173	Penalty for not pre-paying tax	20043508	09-13-2004	$1,044.00
291	Prior tax abated		03-14-2005	-$24,114.00
	49254-445-00168-5			
277	Reduced or removed penalty for late payment of tax		03-14-2005	-$2,718.93
197	Reduced or removed interest charged for late payment		03-14-2005	-$2,771.19
530	Balance due account currently not collectable		04-28-2005	$0.00
960	Appointed representative		04-27-2005	$0.00
531	Account currently considered collectable		05-02-2005	$0.00
480	Offer in compromise received		06-21-2005	$0.00
971	Tax period blocked from automated levy program		07-11-2005	$0.00
481	Denied offer in compromise		08-18-2005	$0.00
582	Lien placed on assets due to balance owed		09-23-2005	$0.00
961	Removed appointed representative		12-08-2005	$0.00
480	Offer in compromise received		01-17-2006	$0.00
483	Removed offer in compromise		01-27-2006	$0.00
960	Appointed representative		03-02-2006	$0.00
971	Tax period blocked from automated levy program		05-08-2006	$0.00
480	Offer in compromise received		06-14-2006	$0.00
481	Denied offer in compromise		01-22-2007	$0.00
530	Balance due account currently not collectable		03-06-2007	$0.00

Sample IRS Wage and Income Transcript

Below is a partial sample of an IRS wage and income transcript. Notice how the 1099-B transactions show the proceeds from the sales of stocks but show no basis. The IRS includes the proceeds from these types of transactions in their Substitutes for Returns ("SFR"s). They exclude the basis amounts as they are not provided. Keep in mind that this will cause the income in the SFRs to be much high than the actual realized income of the taxpayer. This is one of many reasons why it is important to obtain wage and income transcripts and file actual returns to replace SFRs. Not doing so could cause the taxpayer to owe more than they should. In the case of a day trader this could amount to millions of dollars if not corrected.

Internal Revenue Service
United States Department of the Treasury

This Product Contains Sensitive Taxpayer Data

Wage and Income Transcript

Request Date: 03-07-2013
Response Date: 03-07-2013
Tracking Number: 100155526506

SSN Provided: [redacted]
Tax Period Requested: December, 2007

Form W-2 Wage and Tax Statement

Employer:
Employer Identification Number (EIN): [redacted]

Employee:
Employee's Social Security Number: [redacted]

Submission Type:	Original document
Wages, Tips and Other Compensation:	$114,915.00
Federal Income Tax Withheld:	$0.00
Social Security Wages:	$97,500.00
Social Security Tax Withheld:	$6,045.00
Medicare Wages and Tips:	$122,665.00
Medicare Tax Withheld:	$1,778.00
Social Security Tips:	$0.00
Allocated Tips:	$0.00
Advanced EIC Payment:	$0.00
Dependent Care Benefits:	$0.00
Deferred Compensation:	$7,750.00
Code "Q" Nontaxable Combat Pay:	$0.00
Code "W" Employer Contributions to a Health Savings Account:	$0.00
Code "Y" Deferrals under a section 409A nonqualified Deferred Compensation plan:	$0.00
Code "Z" Income under section 409A on a nonqualified Deferred Compensation plan:	$0.00
Code "R" Employer's Contribution to MSA:	$0.00
Code "S" Employer's Contribution to Simple Account:	$0.00
Code "T" Expenses Incurred for Qualified Adoptions:	$0.00
Code "V" Income from exercise of non-statutory stock options:	$0.00
Code "AA" Designated Roth Contributions under a Section 401(k) Plan:	$7,750.00
Code "BB" Designated Roth Contributions under a Section 403(b) Plan:	$0.00
Third Party Sick Pay Indicator:	Unanswered
Retirement Plan Indicator:	Yes
Statutory Employee:	Not Statutory Employee

Form 5498 Individual Retirement Arrangement Contribution Information

Trustee:

Trustee/Issuer's Federal Identification Number (FIN):

Participant:

Participant's Identification Number:

Submission Type:	Original document
Account Number (Optional):	
IRA Contributions:	0.00
Rollover Contributions:	0.00
Roth Conversion Amount:	0.00
Recharacterized Contributions:	0.00
Fair Market Value of Account:	$221.00
Life Insurance Cost Included in Box 1:	0.00
SEP Code:	Not Checked
IRA Code:	Checked
Simple Code:	Not Checked
Roth IRA Code:	Not Checked
RMD For Subsequent Year:	N/A
SEP Contributions:	0.00
SIMPLE Contributions:	0.00
Roth IRA Contributions:	0.00

Form 5498 Individual Retirement Arrangement Contribution Information

Trustee:

Trustee/Issuer's Federal Identification Number (FIN):

Participant:

Participant's Identification Number:

Submission Type:	Original document
Account Number (Optional):	
IRA Contributions:	0.00
Rollover Contributions:	$29.00
Roth Conversion Amount:	0.00
Recharacterized Contributions:	0.00
Fair Market Value of Account:	$36.00
Life Insurance Cost Included in Box 1:	0.00
SEP Code:	Not Checked
IRA Code:	Checked
Simple Code:	Not Checked
Roth IRA Code:	Not Checked

RMD For Subsequent Year:	N/A
SEP Contributions:	0.00
SIMPLE Contributions:	0.00
Roth IRA Contributions:	0.00

Form 5498 Individual Retirement Arrangement Contribution Information

Trustee:

Trustee/Issuer's Federal Identification Number (FIN):

Participant:

Participant's Identification Number:

Submission Type:	Original document
Account Number (Optional):	
IRA Contributions:	0.00
Rollover Contributions:	0.00
Roth Conversion Amount:	0.00
Recharacterized Contributions:	0.00
Fair Market Value of Account:	$117.00
Life Insurance Cost Included in Box 1:	0.00
SEP Code:	Not Checked
IRA Code:	Checked
Simple Code:	Not Checked
Roth IRA Code:	Not Checked
RMD For Subsequent Year:	N/A
SEP Contributions:	0.00
SIMPLE Contributions:	0.00
Roth IRA Contributions:	0.00

Form 1099-B Proceeds From Broker and Barter Exchange Transactions

Payer:

Payer's Federal Identification Number (FIN):

E TRADE CLEARING LLC

Recipient:

Recipient's Identification Number:

Submission Type:	Original document
Account Number:	
Date of Sale or Exchange:	07-25-2007
CUSIP Number:	73935A104

Gross Proceeds:	Gross proceeds minus commissions
Bartering:	0.00
Federal Income Tax Withheld:	0.00
Stocks and Bonds:	$24,599.00
Aggregate Profit or (Loss):	0.00
Realized Profit or (Loss):	0.00
Unrealized Profit or (Loss) 12/31 Prior Year:	0.00
Unrealized Profit or (Loss) 12/31 Current Year:	0.00
Description:	POWERSHARES QQQ TRUST
Second Notice Indicator:	No Second Notice
Number of Shares Exchanged:	0000000000000
Class/Classes of Stock Exchanged:	
Recipient Indicator:	Loss can be taken on tax return

Form 1099-B Proceeds From Broker and Barter Exchange Transactions

Payer:

Payer's Federal Identification Number (FIN):

E TRADE CLEARING LLC

Recipient:

Recipient's Identification Number:

Submission Type:	Original document
Account Number:	
Date of Sale or Exchange:	09-20-2007
CUSIP Number:	16941X105
Gross Proceeds:	Gross proceeds minus commissions
Bartering:	0.00
Federal Income Tax Withheld:	0.00
Stocks and Bonds:	$677.00
Aggregate Profit or (Loss):	0.00
Realized Profit or (Loss):	0.00
Unrealized Profit or (Loss) 12/31 Prior Year:	0.00
Unrealized Profit or (Loss) 12/31 Current Year:	0.00
Description:	CHINA SHENGHUO PHARMACEUTICAL
Second Notice Indicator:	No Second Notice
Number of Shares Exchanged:	0000000000000
Class/Classes of Stock Exchanged:	
Recipient Indicator:	Loss can be taken on tax return

Form 1099-B Proceeds From Broker and Barter Exchange Transactions

Payer:

Payer's Federal Identification Number (FIN): 320012683

E TRADE CLEARING LLC

PO BOX 1542

MERRIFIELD, VA 22116-9949

Recipient:

Code Definitions Required to Read IRS Account Transcripts

Most frequently seen Transaction Code numbers: in numerical sequence

150 = SFR filed or tax assessed

460 = Extension to file return

240 = Penalty - may indicate fraud or tax evasion conduct. Used with "reference" numbers.

290 = Additional tax assessed

300 = Additional tax assessed

320 = Fraud penalty

420 = Audit commenced (421 = ended)

480 = Offer-in-compromise submitted (481 = rejected, withdrawn)

520 = Prior bankruptcy, tax litigation or Due Process request filed (521 = ended)

582 = Tax lien filed (does not list which county)

608 = Statute of limitations expired

780 = Offer-in-compromise accepted (781 = defaulted)

971 = Could be one of many things:

971 + 031 = Discharged in BK

971 + 069 = Filed a request for due-process hearing

971 + 069 = Request for Due Process Hearing filed

976, 977 = "Amended tax return filed" (could be late original)

910, 914, 916, 918 = Criminal investigation

Chapter 8:

IRS Notices

With hundreds to choose from, an IRS notice can be difficult to navigate. Notices can range from showing how much unpaid tax is due, to showing how much of a refund is due to providing notice that a taxpayer's assets (most commonly their bank accounts) will be levied upon or their wages will be garnished. Some notices such as Notice of Unpaid Tax Due (CP501) or a Notice of Intent to Levy (CP504) are self-explanatory. To elaborate, the explanation provided within most notices explains clear detail as to why the notice was sent. Other notices are not as easy to decipher. If you or your client receives a notice that is "out of the box" refer to the chart below to determine why the notice was sent.

For example, it is not uncommon for a taxpayer to receive a notice of a tax lien being filed (2603C) after they have entered into an installment agreement and think the IRS is taking further active collection action against them. In the notice it states that the IRS has a right to and is exercising that right to protect their interest by filing a lien. Filing a lien does not typically affect a taxpayer on a day-to-day basis but many taxpayers mistake a lien for a levy and assume the funds in their bank accounts are again at risk of being frozen and remitted to the IRS. Once again, it is important to understand the process and read each notice, especially those that you do not see on a regular basis carefully.

Although most notices provide instructions, it is better to understand how the systems works before deciding to follow the instructions verbatim. For example, if your client receives a notice of tax due, it states that the balance must be paid in full within a prescribed period of time. If your client is unable to pay the liability in full, they will obviously be unable to fulfill the obligations set forth in the notice. In other cases your client may wish to prolong the payment period even if they can full-pay at the time the notice was received. Knowing the system will help you guide your client accordingly

It is important to know when a notice can be responded to via correspondence, when you should contact the IRS directly and when a notice can be ignored. These scenarios are covered in more detail throughout this book (*for examples see Installment Agreements, Offers in Compromise and Penalty Abatement*).

If you retain a new resolution client, it is important to request copies of all notices received to date. This will provide a clearer picture of what issues your client is facing. Often a client will claim to owe an amount of unpaid tax based upon a single year or a couple of years. They are usually basing their assessment upon collection activity such as a wage garnishment in which the notice of garnishment specifies a certain tax year or tax years owing. If your client provides ALL notices received to date rather than just the notice of garnishment, you will often find that the garnishment did not cover all years owing.

The IRS has redesigned their notices to be more clear and concise. In most cases the notice with describe an action that the taxpayer is expected to take. Below is a list of the most common IRS notices[viii] and a description of what they entail:

Notice Number	**Description**	**Topic**
CP01	We received the information that you provided and have verified your claim of identity theft. We have placed an identity theft indicator on your account.	Identity Theft
CP01A	This notice tells you about the Identity Protection Personal Identification Number (IP PIN) we sent you.	Identity Theft

Notice Number	Description	Topic
CP01H	You received a CP 01H notice because we were unable to process your tax return. The IRS has locked your account because the Social Security Administration informed us that the Social Security number (SSN) of the primary or secondary taxpayer on the return belongs to someone who was deceased prior to the current tax year (before January 1, 2010 for a 2010 tax return).	
CP01S	We received your Form 14039 or similar statement for your identity theft claim. We'll contact you when we finish processing your case or if we need additional information	
CP02H	You owe a balance due as a result of amending your tax return to show receipt of a grant received as a result of Hurricane Katrina, Rita or Wilma.	Balance Due
CP03C	You received a tax credit (called the First-Time Homebuyer Credit) for a house you purchased. You may need to file a form to report a change in ownership to the house you purchased.	
CP04	Our records show that you or your spouse served in a combat zone, a qualified contingency operation, or a hazardous duty station during the tax year specified on your notice. As a result, you may be eligible for tax deferment.	
CP05	We're reviewing your tax return.	
CP05A	We are examining your return and we need documentation.	
CP07	We received your tax return and are holding your refund until we complete a more thorough review of the benefits you claimed under a treaty and/or the deductions claimed on Schedule A.	
CP08	You may qualify for the Additional Child Tax Credit and be entitled to some additional money.	Additional Child Tax Credit
CP09	We've sent you this notice because our records indicate you may be eligible for the Earned Income Credit (EIC), but didn't claim it on your tax return.	

Notice Number	Description	Topic
CP10	We made a change(s) to your return because we believe there's a miscalculation. This change(s) affected the estimated tax payment you wanted applied to your taxes for next year.	Change To Your Estimated Tax Credit Amount
CP10A	We made a change(s) to your return because we believe there's a miscalculation involving your Earned Income Credit. This change(s) affected the estimated tax payment you wanted applied to your taxes for next year.	Change To Your Estimated Tax Credit Amount
CP11	We made changes to your return because we believe there's a miscalculation. You owe money on your taxes as a result of these changes.	Balance Due
CP11A	We made changes to your return because we believe there's a miscalculation involving your Earned Income Credit. You owe money on your taxes as a result of these changes.	Balance Due
CP11M	We made changes to your return involving the Making Work Pay and Government Retiree Credit. You owe money on your taxes as a result of these changes.	Balance Due
CP12	We made changes to correct a miscalculation on your return.	
CP12A	We made changes to correct the Earned Income Credit (EIC) claimed on your tax return.	
CP12E or CP12F	We made changes to correct a miscalculation on your return.	
CP12M	We made changes to the computation of the Making Work Pay and/or Government Retiree Credits on your return.	
CP12R	We made changes to the computation of the Rebate Recovery Credit on your return.	
CP13	We made changes to your return because we believe there's a miscalculation. You're not due a refund nor do you owe an additional amount because of our changes. Your account balance is zero.	

Notice Number	Description	Topic
CP13A	We made changes to your return because we found an error involving your Earned Income Credit. You're not due a refund nor do you owe an additional amount because of our changes. Your account balance is zero.	
CP13M	We made changes to your return involving the Making Work Pay credit or the Government Retiree Credit. You're not due a refund nor do you owe an additional amount because of our changes. Your account balance is zero.	
CP13R	We made changes to your return involving the Recovery Rebate Credit. You're not due a refund nor do you owe an additional amount because of our changes. Your account balance is zero.	
CP14	We sent you this notice because you owe money on unpaid taxes.	
LT14	You owe money on unpaid taxes.	
CP14I	You owe taxes and penalties because you didn't take out the minimum amount you had to from your traditional individual retirement arrangement (IRA). Or, you put into a tax-sheltered account more than you can legally.	
CP15B	We charged you a Trust Fund Recovery Penalty (TFRP) for not paying employment or excise taxes.	
CP16	We sent you this notice to tell you about changes we made to your return that affect your refund. We made these changes because we believe there was a miscalculation. Our records show you owe other tax debts and we applied all or part of your refund to them.	
CP18	We believe you incorrectly claimed one or more deductions or credits. As a result, your refund is less than you expected.	
CP19	We have increased the amount of tax you owe because we believe you incorrectly claimed one or more deductions or credits.	
CP20	We believe you incorrectly claimed one or more deductions or credits. As a result, your refund is less than you expected.	

Notice Number	Description	Topic
CP21A	We made the change(s) you requested to your tax return for the tax year specified on the notice. You owe money on your taxes as a result of the change(s).	Balance Due
CP21B	We made the change(s) you requested to your tax return for the tax year specified on the notice. You should receive your refund within 2-3 weeks of your notice.	Refund
CP21C	We made the change(s) you requested to your tax return for the tax year specified on the notice. You're not due a refund nor do you owe any additional amount. Your account balance for this tax form and tax year is zero.	Even Balance
CP21E	As a result of your recent audit, we made changes to your tax return for the tax year specified on the notice. You owe money on your taxes as a result of these changes.	Balance Due
CP21I	We made changes to your tax return for the tax year specified on the notice for Individual Retirement Arrangement (IRA) taxes. You owe money on your taxes as a result of these changes.	Balance Due
CP22A	We made the change(s) you requested to your tax return for the tax year specified on the notice. You owe money on your taxes as a result of the change(s).	Balance Due
CP22E	As a result of your recent audit, we made changes to your tax return for the tax year specified on the notice. You owe money on your taxes as a result of these changes.	Balance Due
CP22I	We made changes to your tax return for the tax year specified on the notice for Individual Retirement Arrangement (IRA) taxes. You owe money on your taxes as a result of these changes.	Balance Due
CP23	We made changes to your return because we found a difference between the amount of estimated tax payments on your tax return and the amount we posted to your account. You have a balance due because of these changes.	
CP24	We made changes to your return because we found a difference between the amount of estimated tax payments on your tax return and the amount we posted to your account. You have a potential overpayment credit because of these changes.	
CP24E	We made changes to your return because we found a difference between the amount of estimated tax payments on your tax return and the amount we posted to your account. You have a potential overpayment credit because of these changes.	

Notice Number	Description	Topic
CP25	We made changes to your return because we found a difference between the amount of estimated tax payments on your tax return and the amount we posted to your account. You're not due a refund nor do you owe an additional amount because of our changes. Your account balance is zero.	
LT26	You were previously asked information regarding the filing of your tax return for a specific tax period.	
CP27	We've sent you this notice because our records indicate you may be eligible for the Earned Income Credit (EIC), but didn't claim it on your tax return.	
CP30	We charged you a penalty for not pre-paying enough of your tax either by having taxes withheld from your income, or by making timely estimated tax payments.	
CP30A	We reduced or removed the penalty for underpayment of estimated tax reported on your tax return.	
CP31	Your refund check was returned to us, so you need to update your address.	Refund
CP32	We sent you a replacement refund check.	
CP32A	Call us to request your refund check.	
CP39	We used a refund from your spouse or former spouse to pay your past due tax debt. You may still owe money.	
CP42	The amount of your refund has changed because we used it to pay your spouse's past due tax debt.	
CP44	There is a delay processing your refund because you may owe other federal taxes.	
CP45	We were unable to apply your overpayment to your estimated tax as you requested.	Overpayment

Notice Number	Description	Topic
CP49	We sent you this notice to tell you we used all or part of your refund to pay a tax debt.	Overpayment
CP51A	We computed the tax on your Form 1040, 1040A or 1040EZ. You owe taxes.	
CP51B	We computed the tax on your Form 1040, 1040A or 1040EZ. You owe taxes.	
CP51C	We computed the tax on your Form 1040, 1040A or 1040EZ. You owe taxes.	
CP53	We can't provide your refund through direct deposit, so we're sending you a refund check by mail.	Direct Deposits
CP53A	We tried to direct deposit your refund, but the financial institution couldn't process it. We are researching your account, but it will take 8 to 10 weeks to reissue your refund.	
CP53B	We tried to direct deposit your refund, but the financial institution couldn't process it. We are researching your account, but it will take 8 to 10 weeks to complete our review and verify this refund.	
CP53C	We tried to direct deposit your refund, but the financial institution couldn't process it. When refund payments are questionable, we review related returns to ensure the return is valid. We are researching your account, but it will take 8 to 10 weeks to complete our review and verify this refund.	
CP54B	Your tax return shows a different name and/or ID number from the information we have for your account. Please provide more information to us in order to receive your refund.	
CP54E	Your tax return shows a different name and/or ID number from the information we have for your account. Please provide the requested information.	
CP54G	Your tax return shows a different name and/or ID number from the information we have for your account. Please provide the requested information.	

Notice Number	Description	Topic
CP54Q	Your tax return shows a different name and/or ID number from the information we have on file for you or from the information from the Social Security Administration (SSA).We previously sent you a notice asking you to provide us some updated information. We still haven't received a response from you.	
CP59	We sent you this notice because we have no record that you filed your prior personal tax return or returns.	
CP60	We removed a payment erroneously applied to your account.	
CP62	We applied a payment to your account.	
CP63	We are holding your refund because you have not filed one or more tax returns and we believe you will owe tax.	
CP71	You received this notice to remind you of the amount you owe in tax, penalty and interest.	
CP71A	You received this notice to remind you of the amount you owe in tax, penalty and interest.	
CP71C	You received this notice to remind you of the amount you owe in tax, penalty and interest.	
CP71D	You received this notice to remind you of the amount you owe in tax, penalty and interest.	
CP72	You may have claimed a frivolous position on your tax return. A frivolous return is identified when some information on the return has no basis in the law.	
CP74	You are recertified for EITC. You don't have to fill out Form 8862, Information To Claim Earned Income Credit After Disallowance, in the future. You'll receive your EIC refund within 6 weeks as long as you don't owe other tax or debts we're required to collect.	

Notice Number	Description	Topic
CP75	We're auditing your tax return and we need documentation to verify the Earned Income Credit (EIC) that you claimed. The Earned Income Credit and/or the Additional Child Tax Credit (ACTC) portion(s) of your refund is being held pending the results of the audit.	
CP75A	We're auditing your tax return and need documentation to verify the Earned Income Credit (EIC), dependent exemption(s) and filing status you claimed.	
CP75C	You were banned from claiming the Earned Income Credit (EIC) in a prior tax year due to your intentional disregard of the rules or a fraudulent claim. Since your ban is still in effect, we disallowed the EIC for your current tax year.	
CP75D	We're auditing your tax return and we need documentation to verify the income and withholding you reported on your tax return. This may affect your eligibility for the Earned Income Credit (EIC), dependent exemption(s) and other refundable credits that you claimed. We are holding your refund pending the results of the audit.	
CP76	We are allowing your Earned Income Credit as claimed on your tax return. You will receive any expected refund in 8 weeks provided you owe no other taxes or legal debts we are required to collect.	
CP80	We credited payments and/or other credits to your tax account for the tax period shown on your notice. However, we haven't received your tax return.	
CP080	We credited payments and/or other credits to your tax account for the form and tax period shown on your notice. However, we haven't received your tax return.	
CP81	We haven't received your tax return for a specific tax year. The statute of limitations to claim a refund of your credit or payment for that tax year is about to expire.	
CP081	We haven't received your tax return for a specific tax year. The statute of limitations to claim a refund of your credit or payment for that tax year is about to expire.	
CP88	We are holding your refund because you have not filed one or more tax returns and we believe you will owe tax.	
CP90C	We levied you for unpaid taxes. You have the right to a Collection Due Process hearing.	

Notice Number	Description	Topic
CP102	We made changes to your return because we believe there's a miscalculation. You owe money on your taxes as a result of these changes.	
CP103	We made changes to your railroad retirement tax return because we believe there was a miscalculation. As a result of these changes, you have a balance due.	
CP104	We made changes to your excise tax return because we believe there was a miscalculation. As a result of these changes, there is a balance due.	
CP108	You are receiving this notice because you made a payment of $XXXXX on XXXXX, and we can't determine the correct form or tax year to apply it to.	
CP112	We made changes to your return because we believe there's a miscalculation. As a result, you are due a refund.	
CP113	We made changes to your railroad retirement tax return because we believe there was a miscalculation. As a result of these changes, you have an overpayment on your account.	
CP114	We made changes to your excise tax return because we believe there was a miscalculation. As a result of these changes, there is an overpayment on your account.	
CP120	You need to send us documentation of your tax-exempt status.	Tax Exemptions
CP120A	Your organization's tax-exempt status has been revoked for failure to file a Form 990 series return for three consecutive years. In addition, you are no longer eligible to sponsor a tax-sheltered annuity plan (Internal Revenue Code section 403(b) retirement plan).	
CP123	We made changes to your excise tax return because we believe there was a miscalculation. As a result of these changes, you have a balance due of less than $1.	
CP124	We made changes to your excise tax return because we believe there was a miscalculation. As a result of these changes, there is a balance due of less than $1.	
CP130	Your tax return filing requirements may have changed: You may no longer need to pay the Alternative Minimum Tax.	Filing Requirements

Notice Number	Description	Topic
CP138	This notice tells you that all or part of the overpayment on a return you filed was applied to other federal taxes you owe.	
CP141C	You are receiving this notice because you did not respond to a previous request for missing or incomplete information on your return and your return is late.	
CP141I	You are receiving this notice because you did not respond to a previous request for missing or incomplete information on your return.	
CP141L	You are receiving this notice because you didn't file your return by the due date.	
CP142	We sent you this notice because you filed your information returns late.	
CP143	We accepted your explanation for filing your information return late. We will continue processing your returns.	
CP145	We were unable to credit the full amount you requested to the succeeding tax period.	
CP152	We have received your return.	Confirmation of Return Receipt
CP152A	We received your Form 8038-CP, Return for Credit Payments to Issuers of Qualified Bonds and provides an explanation for the reduced credit payment amount.	
CP153	We can't provide you with your refund through a direct deposit, so we're sending you a refund check/credit payment by mail.	Refund
CP156	We received your Form 990-T, Exempt Organization Business Income Tax Return and Form 8941, Credit for Small Employer Health Premiums.	
CP160	You received this notice to remind you of the amount you owe in tax, penalty and interest.	
CP161	You received this notice because of the money you owe from your tax return.	

Notice Number	Description	Topic
CP163	You received this notice to remind you of the amount you owe in tax, penalty and interest.	
CP166	We were unable to process your monthly payment because there were insufficient funds in your bank account.	Payment Process
CP169	You received this notice because we couldn't locate the return you said was previously filed.	
CP171	You received this notice to remind you of the amount you owe in tax, penalty and interest.	
CP178	Your tax return filing requirements may have changed: You may no longer owe excise tax.	Filing Requirements
CP180/CP181	We sent you this notice because your tax return is missing a schedule or form.	
CP182	We sent you this notice because your tax return is missing Form 3468.	
CP187	You received this notice to remind you of the amount you owe in tax, penalty and interest.	
CP188	We are holding your refund until we determine you owe no other taxes.	
CP210/CP220	We made change(s) for the tax year specified on the notice.	
CP211A	We approved your Form 8868, Application for Extension of Time To File an Exempt Organization Return.	
CP211B	We denied your request to extend the time to file your Exempt Organization Return because your Form 8868, Application for Extension of Time To File an Exempt Organization Return, wasn't signed or was signed by someone who wasn't authorized.	

Notice Number	Description	Topic
CP211C	We denied your request to extend the time to file your Exempt Organization Return because your Form 8868, Application for Extension of Time To File an Exempt Organization Return, wasn't received on time. A request for an extension of the time to file your Exempt Organization Return must be received on or before the due date of your return.	
CP211D	We denied your request to extend the time to file your Exempt Organization Return for an additional three months because your Form 8868, Application for Extension of Time To File an Exempt Organization Return, Part II, Line 7 didn't explain the need for additional time OR establish reasons that prevented you from filing by the extended due date.	
CP211E	We denied your request to extend the time to file your Exempt Organization Return because your Form 8868, Application for Extension of Time To File an Exempt Organization Return, didn't meet one or more of the requirements.	
CP231	Your refund or credit payment was returned to us and we need you to update your current address.	Address Update Needed
CP232A	We approved your request for an extension to file your Form 5330.	
CP232B	We denied your request to extend the time to file Form 5330 because your Form 5558, Application for Extension of Time To File Certain Employee Plan Returns, wasn't received on time. A request for an extension of the time to file Form 5330 must be received on or before the due date of your return.	
CP232C	We denied your request to extend the time to file Form 5330 because your Form 5558, Application for Extension of Time To File Certain Employee Plan Returns, wasn't signed or was signed by someone who wasn't authorized.	
CP232D	We denied your request to extend the time to file Form 5330 because your Form 5558, Application for Extension of Time To File Certain Employee Plan Returns, didn't state a reason why you need the extension.	
CP237	We sent you a replacement refund check.	
CP237A	Call us to request your refund check.	

Notice Number	Description	Topic
CP254	Your organization submitted a paper return for the tax period in question. Because our records show that you must file electronically, the paper return doesn't satisfy your filing obligation.	
CP255	We need information to complete the termination of your private foundation status.	
CP259	We've sent you this notice because our records indicate you didn't file the required business tax return identified in the notice.	
CP259A	We sent you this notice because our records indicate you did not file a required Form 990/990-EZ, Return of Organization Exempt From Income Tax.	
CP259B	We sent you this notice because our records indicate you didn't file a required Form 990-PF, Return of Private Foundation or Section 4947(a)(1) Nonexempt Charitable Trust Treated as a Private Foundation.	
CP259C	We sent you this notice because our records indicate you are presumed to be a private foundation and you didn't file a required Form 990-PF, Return of Private Foundation or Section 4947(a)(1) Nonexempt Charitable Trust Treated as a Private Foundation.	
CP259D	We sent you this notice because our records indicate you did not file a required Form 990-T, Exempt Organization Business Income Tax Return.	
CP259E	We sent you this notice because our records indicate you did not file a required Form 990-N, e-Postcard.	
CP259F	We're sending you this notice because our records indicate you did not file a required Form 5227, Split-Interest Trust information Return.	
CP259G	We sent you this notice because our records indicate you did not file a required Form 1120-POL, U.S. Income Tax Return for Certain Political Organizations.	
CP259H	We sent you this notice because our records indicate you are a tax-exempt political organization and you did not file a required Form 990/990-EZ, Return of Organization Exempt From Income Tax.	
CP261	CP261 is the approval notice for Form 2553, Election by a Small Business Corporation.	

Notice Number	Description	Topic
CP264	CP264 is the notice for denial of Form 2553, Election by a Small Business Corporation.	
CP267A	You received a CP267A Notice because you've overpaid the Branded Prescription Drug Fee.	
CP267B	You received a CP267B notice because you overpaid your Insurance Provider Fee under Section 9010 of ACA.	
CP268	We made changes to your return because we believe there is a miscalculation on your return. You have a potential overpayment credit because of this miscalculation.	
CP276A	We didn't receive a correctly completed tax liability schedule. We normally charge a Federal Tax Deposit (FTD) penalty when this happens. We decided not to do so this time.	FTD Penalty
CP276B	We didn't receive the correct amount of tax deposits. We normally charge a Federal Tax Deposit penalty when this happens. We decided not to do so this time.	FTD Penalty
CP279	CP279 is the notice of acceptance to the parent corporation of a Qualified Subchapter S Subsidiary (QSub) from Form 8869, Qualified Subchapter S Subsidiary Election.	
CP279A	CP279A is the notice of acceptance for a Qualified Subchapter S Subsidiary.	
CP282	You received this notice because you indicated on your Form 1065, U.S. Return of Partnership Income, or Form1065-B, U.S. Return of Income for Electing Large Partnerships, that you have foreign partners.	
CP283C	We charged you a penalty for filing a late or incomplete Form 8955-SSA, Annual Registration Statement Identifying Separated Participants with Deferred Vested Benefits.	
CP284	We approved your Form 1128, Application to Adopt, Change, or Retain a Tax Year.	
CP285	CP285 notifies BMF taxpayers the reason their Form 1128, Application To Adopt, Change, or Retain a Tax Year, was denied.	

Notice Number	Description	Topic
CP286	We send this notice when we approve Form 8716, Election To Have a Tax Year Other Than a Required Tax Year.	
CP288	We accepted your election to be treated as a Qualified Subchapter S Trust (QSST).	
CP290	We're approving your Electing Small Business Trust (ESBT) election.	
CP291	We're revoking your Electing Small Business Trust (ESBT) election.	
CP292	We're revoking your Qualified Subchapter S Trust (QSST) election.	
CP295	We charged you a penalty on your Form 5500.	
CP295A	We charged you a penalty on your Form 5500.	
CP297C	We levied you for unpaid taxes. You have the right to a Collection Due Process hearing.	
CP299	Your organization may be required to file an annual electronic notice (e-Postcard), Form 990-N.	
CP301	We sent you this notice to inform that you visited IRS online services website and went through Identity Verification process.	
CP501	You have a balance due (money you owe the IRS) on one of your tax accounts.	
CP503	We have not heard from you and you still have an unpaid balance on one of your tax accounts.	
CP504	You have an unpaid amount due on your account. If you do not pay the amount due immediately, the IRS will seize (levy) your state income tax refund and apply it to pay the amount you owe.	

Notice Number	Description	Topic
CP504B	You have an unpaid amount due on your account. If you do not pay the amount due immediately, the IRS will seize (levy) certain property or rights to property and apply it to pay the amount you owe.	
CP515I	This is a reminder notice that we still have no record that you filed your prior tax return or returns.	
CP515B	You received this reminder notice because our records indicate you didn't file a business tax return.	
CP516	This is a reminder notice that we still have no record that you filed your prior tax return or returns.	
CP518I	This is a final reminder notice that we still have no record that you filed your prior tax return(s).	
CP518B	This is a final reminder notice that our records still indicate you haven't filed a business tax return.	
CP521	This notice is to remind you that you have an installment agreement payment due. Please send your payment immediately.	
CP523	This notice informs you of our intent to terminate your installment agreement and seize (levy) your assets. You have defaulted on your agreement.	
CP547	We received your Form 2848, 8821, or 706, and we assigned you a Centralized Authorization File (CAF) number.	
CP563	We reviewed your Form W-7A, Application for Taxpayer Identification Number for Pending U.S. Adoptions, and we need additional information in order to process it.	
CP565	We gave you an Individual Taxpayer Identification Number (ITIN).	
CP566	We need more information to process your application for an Individual Taxpayer Identification Number (ITIN). You may have sent us an incomplete form. You may have sent us the wrong documents.	

Notice Number	Description	Topic
CP567	We rejected your application for an Individual Taxpayer Identification Number (ITIN). You may not be eligible for an ITIN. Your documents may be invalid. We may not have received a reply when we asked for more information.	
CP2000	The income and/or payment information we have on file doesn't match the information you reported on your tax return. This could affect your tax return; it may cause an increase or decrease in your tax, or may not change it at all.	
CP2005	We accepted the information you sent us. We're not going to change your tax return. We've closed our review of it.	
CP2006	We received your information. We'll look at it and let you know what we're going to do.	
CP2030	We are proposing changes in income, credits, and deductions reported on your U.S. Corporation Income Tax Return. We compared your information with items reported to us by banks, businesses and other payers.	
CP2057	You need to file an amended return. We've received information not reported on your tax return.	
CP2501	You need to contact us. We've received information not reported on your tax return.	
CP2531	Your Tax Return does not match the information we have on file.	
CP2566	We didn't receive your tax return. We have calculated your tax, penalty and interest based on wages and other income reported to us by employers, financial institutions and others.	
CP2566R	We previously sent you a CP63 notice informing you we are holding your refund until we receive one or more unfiled tax returns. Because we received no reply to our previous notice, we have calculated your tax, penalty and interest based on wages and other income reported to us by employers, financial institutions and others.	
CP3219A	We've received information that is different from what you reported on your tax return. This may result in an increase or decrease in your tax. The notice explains how the amount was calculated and how you can challenge it in U.S. Tax Court.	

Notice Number	Description	Topic
CP3219B	This Statutory Notice of Deficiency notifies you of the IRS's intent to assess a tax deficiency and informs you of your right to petition the United States Tax Court to dispute the proposed adjustments. .	
CP3219N	We didn't receive your tax return. We have calculated your tax, penalty and interest based on wages and other income reported to us by employers, financial institutions and others.	
-		
	Other Notices and Letters	
Notice or Letter Number	**Title**	-
CP 57	Notice of Insufficient Funds	
CP 90 / CP 297	Final Notice - Notice of Intent to Levy and Notice of Your Right to a Hearing	
CP 297A	Notice of Levy and Notice of Your Right to a Hearing	
CP 91 / CP 298	Final Notice Before Levy on Social Security Benefits	
Letter 0484C	Collection Information Statement Requested (Form 433F/433D); Inability to Pay/Transfer	
Letter 0549C	Balance Due on Account is Paid	
Letter 668D(LP 68)	We released the taxpayer's levy.	
Letter 0681C	Proposal to Pay Accepted	
Letter 0757C	Installment Privilege Terminated	
Letter 1058 (LT 11)	Final Notice prior to levy; your right to a hearing	
Letter 1615 (LT 18)	Mail us your overdue tax returns.	

Notice Number	Description	Topic
Letter 1731 (LP 64)	Please help us locate a taxpayer.	
Letter 1737 (LT 27)	Please complete and site Form 433F, Collection Information Statement.	
Letter 1961C	Installment Agreement for Direct Debit 433-G	
Letter 1962C	Installment Agreement Reply to Taxpayer	
Letter 2050 (LT 16)	Please call us about your overdue taxes or tax return.	
Letter 2257C	Balance Due Total to Taxpayer	
Letter 2271C	Installment Agreement for Direct Debit Revisions	
Letter 2272C	Installment Agreement Cannot be Considered	
Letter 2273C	Installment Agreement Accepted: Terms Explained	
Letter 2318C	Installment Agreement: Payroll Deduction (F2159) Incomplete	
Letter 2357C	Abatement of Penalties and Interest	
Letter 2603C	Installment Agreement Accepted - Notice of Federal Tax Lien Will be Filed	
Letter 2604C	Pre-assessed Installment Agreement	
Letter 2761C	Request for Combat Zone Service Dates	
Letter 2789C	Taxpayer Response to Reminder of Balance Due	
Letter 2800C	Incorrect Form W-4, Employee's Withholding Allowance Certificate	
Letter 2801C	Exempt Status May not be Allowed	

Notice Number	Description	Topic
Letter 2802C	Your withholding doesn't comply with IRS guidelines	
Letter 2840C	CC IAPND Installment Agreement Confirmation	
Letter 3030C	Balance Due Explained: Tax/Interest Not Paid	
Letter 3127C	Revision to Installment Agreement	
Letter 3217C	Installment Agreement Accepted: Terms Explained	
Letter 3228 (LT 39)	Reminder notice.	
Letter 4458C	We wrote to you because we didn't receive your monthly installment payment.	
Letter 4883C	We received your federal income tax return; however, we need more information from you to process it.	
Letter 5071C	We received your federal income tax return; however, we need more information from you to process it.	
Letter LP 47	Address Information Request	
Letter LP 59	Please contact us about the taxpayer levy.	

Chapter 9:

Restructuring & Reform Act

The Internal Revenue Service Restructuring and Reform Act of 1998 made some noteworthy tax law changes that will have ongoing effects. Among them are:

Change in capital gains holding period.

IRS restructuring.

IRS encouraged to accept offers in compromise and installment agreements.

IRS Restructuring

IRS Reorganization - In an effort to eliminate perceived abuses by the IRS, the Act contains the Taxpayers Bill of Rights which provides some of the most extensive taxpayer-protection provisions ever enacted. To see the most current version of this Bill of Rights, go to www.taxresolutioninstitute.org/forms-library and see Publication 1. Most notable were provisions which shifted the burden of proof from the taxpayer to the government in civil tax disputes and extend the attorney-client privilege to certain tax advisors other than attorneys.

The IRS eliminated or substantially modified the present geographic structure and replaced it with an organizational structure that features operating units serving particular groups of taxpayers with similar needs.

Congress had called for this restructuring because it believed that the IRS's current structure was one of the factors contributing to its inability to serve taxpayers properly. Restructuring the IRS into separate units that served particular groups of taxpayers with similar needs has enabled the IRS to serve them better. The IRS has identified four such groups, which are individual taxpayers, small businesses, large businesses and tax-exempt organizations.

<u>IRS Burden of Proof</u> - Under prior law, a rebuttable presumption always existed that the IRS's determination of tax liability was correct. This "presumption of correctness" in favor of the IRS placed the burden on the taxpayers to present evidence to support a finding contrary to the IRS's determination.

The Restructuring and Reform Act provided that, in any court proceeding, the IRS will have the burden of proof with respect to any factual issue if all of the following conditions are met:

The taxpayer introduces credible evidence with respect to the issue. Credible evidence means a quality of evidence which, after crucial analysis, the court would find sufficient upon which to base a decision on the issue if no contrary evidence were submitted.
The taxpayer has complied with the requirements to substantiate any item under the Internal Revenue Code and Treasury Regulations.
The taxpayer has maintained all records required under the Internal Revenue Code.
The taxpayer has cooperated with reasonable IRS requests for witnesses, information, documents, meetings, and interviews.
In the case of a partnership, corporation, or trust, the net worth of the entity is $7 million or less.

Expansion of Confidentiality Privilege - A common law privilege of confidentiality exists for communications between an attorney and client, or potential client, with respect to the legal advice the attorney gives the client. The privilege of confidentiality applies only where the attorney is advising the client, or potential client, on legal matters. It does not apply in situations where the attorney is acting in other capacities. For example, the attorney-client privilege will not automatically apply to communications and documents generated in the course of an attorney's preparation of a tax return. Attorney-client privilege is waived by any disclosure of the privileged information to a third party other than a third party who shares a common legal interest with the client or a third party necessary to the attorney-client consultation. Under pre-Act law, the attorney-client privilege was limited to communications between taxpayers and attorneys. No similar privilege existed for communications between taxpayers and other professionals, i.e., accountants and enrolled agents, practicing before the IRS.

The Act extended the application of the attorney-client privilege under the circumstances described below, to communicate between the taxpayer and any "federally authorized tax practitioner" (attorneys, certified public accountants, enrolled agents and enrolled actuaries) with respect to "tax advice," to the extent the communication would be considered a privileged communication if it were between a taxpayer and an attorney. The privilege may only be asserted in: (1) any non-criminal tax matter before IRS, and (2) any non-criminal tax proceeding in federal court brought by or against the United States.

The Restructuring and Reform Act provided that the privilege may be waived in the same manner as the attorney-client privilege. For example, if a taxpayer or federally authorized tax practitioner discloses to a third party the substance of a communication protected by the privilege, the privilege for that communication and any related communications is considered to be waived to the same extent and in the same manner as the privilege would be waived if the disclosure related to an attorney-client communication.

IRS Encouraged to Accept Offers-In-Compromise and Installment Agreements

The Restructuring and Reform Act encouraged the IRS to adopt a more liberal acceptance policy for taxpayer Offers-in-Compromise and installment agreements. The Restructuring and Reform Act generally prohibits the IRS from levying on a taxpayer's property or rights to property to collect tax while an offer-in-compromise is pending or while an installment agreement is pending or in effect. A procedure to allow taxpayers to appeal any rejected offer will be implemented, and notification of the appeal right must appear on the IRS form used by the taxpayers to apply for an offer-in-compromise.

The Restructuring and Reform Act stipulated that taxpayer's can under certain circumstances require the IRS to enter into an installment agreement for the payment of the taxpayer's deficiency.

Chapter 10:

IRS Contact Information

IRS Directory of Practitioners

SERVICE	TELEPHONE	HOURS OF OPERATION
Practitioner Priority Service	(866) 860-4259	M-F 8:00 a.m. - 8:00 p.m., local time
IRS Tax Help Line for Individuals	(800) 829-1040	M-F 8:00 a.m. - 8:00 p.m., local time
Business and Specialty Tax Line	(800) 829-4933	M-F 8:00 a.m. - 8:00 p.m., local time
e-Help (Practitioners Only)	(866) 255-0654	M-F 7:30 a.m. - 6:00 p.m., ET
e-Help (Practitioners Only)	(866) 255-0654	M-F 7:30 a.m. - 5:00 p.m., MT
Refund Hotline (Automated svc after hrs)	(800) 829-1954	M-F 8:00 a.m. - 8:00 p.m., local time
Forms and Publications	(800) 829-3676	M-F 8:00 a.m. - 8:00 p.m., local time
National Taxpayer Advocate's Help Line	(877) 777-4778	M-F 8:00 a.m. - 8:00 p.m., local time
Centralized Lien Payoff	(800) 913-6050	M-F 8:00 a.m. - 11:00 p.m., ET
Centralized Bankruptcy	(800) 913-9358	M-F 7:00 a.m. - 10:00 p.m., ET
Telephone Device for the Deaf (TDD)	(800) 829-4059	M-F 8:00 a.m. - 8:00 p.m., local time
Electronic Federal Tax Payment System	(800) 555-4477	24/7
Government Entities (TEGE) Help Line	(877) 829-5500	M-F 8:30 a.m. - 4:30 p.m., ET
Extension to File	(800) 829-4477	24/7
Forms 706 and 709 Help Line	(866) 699-4083	M-F 7:00 a.m. - 7:00 p.m., local time
Automated Collection System (Business)	(800) 829-3903	M-F 8:00 a.m. - 8:00 p.m., local time
Automated Collection System (Individual)	(800) 829-7650	M-F 8:00 a.m. - 8:00 p.m., local time
Criminal Investigation Informant Hotline	(800) 829-0433	M-F 8:00 a.m. - 8:00 p.m., local time
Employer Identification Number (EIN)	(800) 829-4933	M-F 8:00 a.m. - 8:00 p.m., local time
Excise Tax and Form 2290 Help Line	(866) 699-4096	M-F 8:00 a.m. - 6:00 p.m., ET
Information Return Reporting	(866) 455-7438	M-F 8:30 a.m. - 4:30 p.m., ET
Terrorist Act or Combat Zone Spcl Htlne	(866) 562-5227	M-F 8:00 a.m. - 8:00 p.m., local time

Last	**First**	**Agency**	**Title**	**Phone**	-	**Department**
Brooks	L'Tanya	IRS	Acting Area Director	(559) 454-6600		Acting Area Director
Donahue	Patricia	IRS	Area Counsel	(415) 227-5171		San Francisco
Nelson	James	IRS	Area Counsel	(213) 894-3027		Los Angeles
Patton	Collleen	IRS	Area Director	(720) 956-4533		Area Director
Petrillo	Linda	IRS	Area Director	(213) 576-3000		Area Director
Tarn	John	IRS	Area Director	(510) 637-3068		Area Director
Crawford	Joan	IRS	Area Director - Collection	(510) 637-2700		Area Director - Collection
Adams	Connie	IRS	Area Manager	(949) 389-4804		Laguna Niguel
Collins	Suzanne	IRS	Area Manager	(602) 207-8291		Area Manager
Curran	Dorry	IRS	Area Manager	(949) 389-4808		Los Angeles
Joan	Hirsch	IRS	Area Manager	(562) 400-1801		Area Manager
Peneau	Joyce	IRS	Area Manager	(510) 637-4360		Area Manager
Todaro	Tiffany	IRS	Area Manager	(510) 637-3079		Oakland
Fischer	Bernice	IRS	Area Manager - Western Area	(510) 637-3024		Western Area
Walshburn	Michael	IRS	Attorney	(213) 894-3027		
		IRS	Centralized Lien Function	(800) 913-6050		Centralized Lien Function
Shadrooz	Penina	IRS	Counsel	213) 894-3027		
Brantley	Charlie	IRS	Director	(732) 452-8101		Director
Coles	Glen	IRS	Director, Field Assistance	(559) 456-5066		Director, Field Assistance
Dial	Brenda	IRS	Director, Field Operations	(202) 283-2518		Director, Field Operations
Hunter	Charles	IRS	Director, Field Operations	(972) 308-1791		Director, Field Operations
Hwang	Maria	IRS	Director, Field Ops (West)	(510) 637-2570		Director, Field Operations (W)
Walker (acting)	Erwin	IRS	Director, Field Ops (West)	(818) 265-2313		Director, Field Operations (W)
De La Rocha	Lorena	IRS	Disclosure Officer	(213) 833-1203		Laguna Niguel/Los Angeles
Neal	Celeste	IRS	Disclosure Officer	(510) 637-2171		Oakland/Fresno
Bayer	Helen	IRS	Examination Technician	(818) 274-0747		Woodland Hills
Caruth	Michael	IRS	Examination Technician	(818) 274-0709		Woodland Hills
Garkanian	Rita	IRS	Examination Technician	(661) 753-5315		Santa Clarita
Grady	Richard	IRS	Examination Technician			Glendale
Fabin	Paulmikell	IRS	General Attorney	(213) 894-3027		
Renville	Gary	IRS	Governmental Liason	(916) 974-5585		Sacramento
Runow	Jill	IRS	Governmental Liason	(510) 637-3277		Fresno
Yau	David	IRS	Governmental Liason	(213) 576-4094		Los Angeles
John	Saltmarsh	IRS	Indian Tribal Gvts Area Mgr	(909) 388-8162		
Carter	Ms. R	IRS	Offer Specialist - OIC	(909) 388-8231		
Snyder	David	IRS	Offer Specialist - OIC	(818) 637-3933		

Last	**First**	**Agency**	**Title**	**Phone**	-	**Department**
Brenneman	Glenn	IRS	Offer Specialist Grp Mgr -OIC			
Tuler	Jeff	IRS	Offer Specialist Terri Mgr -OIC	(714) 347-9254		
Meyer	Ted	IRS	Program Manager	(818) 543-2300		Glendale
Simmons	Christopher	IRS	Program Manager	(818) 274-0833		Woodland Hills
Antell	Theresa	IRS	Program Manager	(510) 637-2707		Oakland
Larkin	Janice	IRS	Program Manager	(213) 576-3059		Program Manager
Checchi	Charles	IRS	Program Manager - Area 9	(415) 227-5075		San Francisco
Streeter	Annette	IRS	Program Manager - Area 9	(951) 276-6441		Laguna Niguel
Walker	Erwin	IRS	Program Manager - Terr 12	(818) 265-2313		
Topping	Jacquelyn	IRS	Program Manager - Terr 13	(602) 636-9412		
Acuna	Diego	IRS	Revenue Agent			Woodland Hills
Adafre	Marie	IRS	Revenue Agent	(818) 274-0716		Woodland Hills
Akopyan	Mariam	IRS	Revenue Agent	(818) 756-4558		Glendale
Alzate	Vicente	IRS	Revenue Agent	(818) 543-2317		Glendale
Arrieta	Crystal	IRS	Revenue Agent	(818) 274-0744		Woodland Hills
Batres	Xiomara	IRS	Revenue Agent	(818) 543-2294		Glendale
Bell	Zlpporah	IRS	Revenue Agent	(818) 274-0822		Woodland Hills
Bergeron	John	IRS	Revenue Agent	(818) 274-0732		Woodland Hills
Bohanon	Rosemary	IRS	Revenue Agent	(661) 753-5307		Santa Clarita
Capplello	Christopher	IRS	Revenue Agent	(818) 756-4558		Glendale
Cervantes	Walter	IRS	Revenue Agent	(818) 274-0735		Woodland Hills
Chan	Cheuk-MIng	IRS	Revenue Agent	(818) 274-0777		Woodland Hills
Chan	Maggie	IRS	Revenue Agent	(818) 543-2297		Glendale
Chong	Young	IRS	Revenue Agent	(818) 274-0743		Woodland Hills
Chow	Frances	IRS	Revenue Agent	(818) 543-2299		Glendale
Cortes	Carlos	IRS	Revenue Agent			
Cuenca	Luis	IRS	Revenue Agent	(818) 274-0772		Woodland Hills
Daei	Shahrouz	IRS	Revenue Agent	(818) 543-2243		Glendale
Denuna	Max	IRS	Revenue Agent	(818) 543-2309		Glendale
Galstian	Men	IRS	Revenue Agent	(818) 756-4549		Glendale
Gharibian	Karineh	IRS	Revenue Agent	(818) 543-2244		Glendale
Griffin	Sonya	IRS	Revenue Agent	(818) 756-4558		Glendale
Grigoryan	Sona	IRS	Revenue Agent	(818) 274-0758		Woodland Hills
Halfen	William	IRS	Revenue Agent	(661) 753-5317		Santa Clarita
HartMelanfeM		IRS	Revenue Agent	(818) 543-2501		Glendale
Heermans	Wanna	IRS	Revenue Agent	(818) 543-2513		Glendale
Holsombach	Carrie	IRS	Revenue Agent	(760) 866-6115		
Holt	Mercedes	IRS	Revenue Agent	(310) 543-2257		Glendale
Hu	Simln	IRS	Revenue Agent	(818) 543-2304		Glendale "
Huynh	Phuong	IRS	Revenue Agent	(661) 753-5319		Santa Clarita

Last	First	Agenc y	Title	Phone	-	Department
Iturbe	Marcia	IRS	Revenue Agent	(818) 274-0757		Woodland Hills
Jackson	Lupe	IRS	Revenue Agent	(818) 543-2245		Glendale
Johnson	Byron	IRS	Revenue Agent	(661) 753-5321		Santa Clarita
JouryAvfvaE		IRS	Revenue Agent	(818) 274-0761		Woodland Hills
Kabadaian	Sebouh	IRS	Revenue Agent	(818) 274-0830		Woodland Hills
Karaoglanian	Lilit	IRS	Revenue Agent	(818) 543-2302		Glendale
Karimi	Nahid	IRS	Revenue Agent	(661) 753-5346		Santa Clarita
Kawano	Sandra	IRS	Revenue Agent	(818) 543-2323		Glendale
Kim	Alicia	IRS	Revenue Agent	(818) 543-2238		Glendale
Kim	Michael	IRS	Revenue Agent	(818) 543-2306		Glendale
Landyshev	Michael	IRS	Revenue Agent			Woodland Hills
Lea	Jonathan	IRS	Revenue Agent	(818) 274-0773		Woodland Hills
Lee	Deborah	IRS	Revenue Agent	(818) 543-2314		Glendale
Lee	Dong	IRS	Revenue Agent	(818) 543-2364		Glendale
Leyva	Janette	IRS	Revenue Agent	(661) 753-5325		Santa Clarita
Magadamyan	Anet	IRS	Revenue Agent	(818) 543-2292		Glendale
MinAlexS		IRS	Revenue Agent			Glendale
Moon	Holly	IRS	Revenue Agent	(818) 543-2229		Glendate
Nwabueze	Joy	IRS	Revenue Agent	(661) 753-5336		Santa Clarita
Oaks	Erin	IRS	Revenue Agent	(661) 753-5340		Santa Clarita
Oh	Jennifer	IRS	Revenue Agent	(618) 274-805		Woodland Hills
Ortiz	Rafael	IRS	Revenue Agent	(818) 543-2315		Glendale
Osunsanmi	Kola	IRS	Revenue Agent	(661) 753-5339		Santa Clarita
Park	Byong	IRS	Revenue Agent	(818) 543-2296		Glendale
Peterson	Jennifer	IRS	Revenue Agent	(818) 756-4558		Glendale
Pham	Lan	IRS	Revenue Agent	(818) 543-2366		Glendale
Qazi	Zuhair	IRS	Revenue Agent	(818) 543-2288		Glendale
Reed	Eric	IRS	Revenue Agent	(661) 753-5338		Santa Clarita
Reinaga	Kristy	IRS	Revenue Agent	(818) 756-4549		Woodland Hills
Retana	Danny	IRS	Revenue Agent	(816) 543-2295		Glendale Woodland Hills
Rodriguez	Maria	IRS	Revenue Agent	(818) 274-0762		Woodland Hlits
Rubtsov	Ivan	IRS	Revenue Agent	(818) 756-4556		Glendale
Ruiz	Cindy	IRS	Revenue Agent	(661) 753-5341		Santa Clarita
Sahimi	Katherine	IRS	Revenue Agent	(818) 543-2307		Glendale
Santos	A	IRS	Revenue Agent	(818) 756-4554		Santa Clarita
Schwartz	Sherry	IRS	Revenue Agent	(818) 274-0723		Woodland Hiils
Shirvanian	Monfque	IRS	Revenue Agent	(818) 543-2312		Glendale
Shushetovsky	Danny	IRS	Revenue Agent	(818) 543-2293		Glendale
Singh	Tejinder	IRS	Revenue Agent	(818) 274-0721		Woodland Hills
Sivakumar	Pamawathy	IRS	Revenue Agent	(818) 274-0766		Woodland Hiils
Sohn	Grace	IRS	Revenue Agent	(818) 543-2508		Glendale
Ta	Quan	IRS	Revenue Agent	(818) 543-2319		Glendale
Tom	Kim	IRS	Revenue Agent	(818) 543-2298		Glendale
Trim	Kyle	IRS	Revenue Agent	(818) 543-2329		Glendale

Last	First	Agency	Title	Phone	-	Department
Tuazon	Melissa	IRS	Revenue Agent	(818) 543-2509		Glendale
Tuszynski	Nida	IRS	Revenue Agent	(818) 543-2318		Glendale
Ukagba	Thomas	IRS	Revenue Agent	(818) 274-0768		Woodland Hills
Vasquez-Mora	Magaiis	IRS	Revenue Agent	(661) 753-5324		Santa Clarita
Wallace	Kelvit	IRS	Revenue Agent	(818) 274-0756		Woodland Hills
Witter	Garth	IRS	Revenue Agent	(818) 274-0749		Woodland Hills
Wong	Sophia	IRS	Revenue Agent	(818) 274-0725		Woodland Hills
WungLesha		IRS	Revenue Agent	(818) 274-0712		Woodland Hills
Wyatt	Jordan	IRS	Revenue Agent	(661) 753-5349		Santa Clarita
Yaron	Ely	IRS	Revenue Agent	(818) 543-2242		Glendale
Zakaryan	Ani	IRS	Revenue Agent	(818) 543-2308		Glendale
Bates	Paul	IRS	Revenue Agent - Supervisor	(818) 274-0829		Woodland Hills
Lee	Chong	IRS	Revenue Agent - Supervisor	(661) 753-5326		Santa Clarita
Lopez	Gabriela	IRS	Revenue Agent - Supervisor	(818) 543-2224		Glendale
Muriiio	Alicia	IRS	Revenue Agent - Supervisor	(818) 274-0764		Woodland Hills
Ng	Carol	IRS	Revenue Agent - Supervisor	(818) 274-0741		Woodland Hills
Rakusin	Barry	IRS	Revenue Agent - Supervisor	(818) 543-2520		Glendale
Ryan	James	IRS	Revenue Agent - Supervisor	(818) 543-2470		Glendale
Sim	Tiffany	IRS	Revenue Agent - Supervisor	(626) 312-5092		Glendale
Andrews	John	IRS	Revenue Officer	(681) 753-5306		Santa Clarita
Arceo	Crystal	IRS	Revenue Officer	(818) 543-2402		Glendale
Austin	Steven	IRS	Revenue Officer	(818) 543-2485		Glendale
Barner		IRS	Revenue Officer	(909) 388-8223		
Bautista	Alex	IRS	Revenue Officer	(305) 445-4553		Camarillo
Bautista	Alex	IRS	Revenue Officer	(805) 445-4553		Camarillo
Breed	Ms. M	IRS	Revenue Officer	(619) 615-9445		San Diego
Bridgewater	Karen	IRS	Revenue Officer	(818) 756-4513		Santa Clarita
Calhoun	Albert	IRS	Revenue Officer	(818) 543-2487		Glendale
Capistrano	Ivan-Rey	IRS	Revenue Officer	(661) 753-5309		Santa Clarita
Carrillo	Lionel	IRS	Revenue Officer	(818) 543-2473		Glendale
Carter		IRS	Revenue Officer	(909)388-8231		
Charles	Sarah	IRS	Revenue Officer	(661) 753-5312		Santa Clarita
Chen	Christina	IRS	Revenue Officer	(714) 347-9366		Glendale
Contreras	Victor	IRS	Revenue Officer	(813) 543-2488		Glendale
Coombs	Marie	IRS	Revenue Officer	(305) 982-5165		
Davis	Patricia	IRS	Revenue officer	(360) 905-1177		
De Legarret	Jess	IRS	Revenue Officer	(818) 543-2499		Glendale
Descieux	Ms. S	IRS	Revenue Officer	(213) 833-1247		Los Angeles
Elliff	James	IRS	Revenue Officer	(318) 543-2493		Glendale

Last	First	Agenc y	Title	Phone	-	Department
Floras	Gilbert	IRS	Revenue Officer	(818) 543-2497		Glendale
Fox	Kenneth R.	IRS	Revenue Officer	(616) 487-4878		
Garcia	Alex	IRS	Revenue Officer	(210) 841-2425		Texas
Gonzales	Arturo	IRS	Revenue Officer	(818) 543-2502		Glendale
Greschner	Mr. J.	IRS	Revenue Officer	(914) 684-7166		New York
Hannosh	Loteta	IRS	Revenue Officer	(818) 543-2404		Glendale
Hanson	Ted	IRS	Revenue Officer	(818) 543-2504		Glendale
Harada	Yukio	IRS	Revenue Officer	(818) 543-2505		Glendale
Hernandez	Leticia	IRS	Revenue Officer	(818) 543-2475		Glendale
Hicks	Pier	IRS	Revenue Officer	(818) 543-2405		Glendale
Hill	Patricia	IRS	Revenue Officer	979-268-1504		
Hubbard		IRS	Revenue Officer	(949) 389-4237		
Huerta	Ms. B	IRS	Revenue Officer	(310) 414-3682		El Segundo
Jones	Latanuza	IRS	Revenue Officer	(661) 753-5322		Santa Clarita
Kalman	Robert	IRS	Revenue Officer			
Knight	Ms F.	IRS	Revenue Officer	(702) 868-5358		Las Vegas
Krause	Katherine	IRS	Revenue Officer	(203) 340-7743		Norwalk
Laohapanich	Mr.	IRS	Revenue Officer	(213) 576-3448		
Lewis	Romney	IRS	Revenue Officer	(818) 265-2335		Glendale
Lewis	David	IRS	Revenue Officer	(818) 543-2406		Glendale
Lin	TK	IRS	Revenue Officer	(818) 543-2407		Glendale
Lomax	Mr. C	IRS	Revenue Officer	(718) 760-6029		New York
Lopez	Roman	IRS	Revenue Officer	(818) 543-2527		Glendale
M'beguere	Monica	IRS	Revenue Officer	(818) 543-2408		Glendale
McBride	Kenneth	IRS	Revenue Officer	(661) 753-5333		Santa Clarita
Mejia	Mr. E	IRS	Revenue Officer	(213) 833-1120		Los Angeles
Mia	Mohammad	IRS	Revenue Officer	(661) 753-5329		Santa Clarita
Mohammad	Mia	IRS	Revenue Officer	(661) 753-5329		
Mohluddin	Fatema	IRS	Revenue Officer	(661) 753-5330		Santa Clarita
Murray	Erin	IRS	Revenue Officer	(818) 543-2489		Glendale
Parayno	Anna	IRS	Revenue Officer	(818) 543-2409		Glendale
Perin	Loifta	IRS	Revenue Officer	(818) 543-2478		Glendale
Pfelffer	Peter	IRS	Revenue Officer	(818) 543-2479		Glendale
Puig		IRS	Revenue Officer	(626) 312 - 5038		
Quach		IRS	Revenue Officer	(818) 543-2409		
Reed	Jennifer	IRS	Revenue Officer	(818) 543-2520		Glendale
Rennie	Georgia	IRS	Revenue Officer	(541) 342-8726		Oregon
Riddick-Parham	Eleanor	IRS	Revenue Officer	(562) 491-7713		Long Beach/SD
Ritchie	Noeline	IRS	Revenue Officer	(269) 323-4928		Michigan
Salvatore	Gary	IRS	Revenue Officer	(661) 753-5342		Santa Clarita
Scott	Nathan	IRS	Revenue Officer	(714) 347-9375		Santa Clarita
Shaw	Susan	IRS	Revenue Officer	(850) 475-7338		Florida
Sosa	Ms. E	IRS	Revenue Officer	(626) 927-1247		El Monte
Stallings	Kevin	IRS	Revenue Officer	(818) 543-2493		Glendale
Stayer	Laura	IRS	Revenue Officer	(618) 543-2410		Glendale

Last	First	Agency	Title	Phone	-	Department
Stevens	Farrell	IRS	Revenue Officer	(818) 543-2506		Glendale
Stiff	James	IRS	Revenue Officer	(818) 543-2498		Glendale
Strickle	Mr. R	IRS	Revenue Officer	(619) 615-9534		San Diego
Tchuldjian	Una	IRS	Revenue Officer	(818) 543-2411		Glendale
Wagner Tartagiino	Linda	IRS	Revenue Officer	(818) 543-2483		Glendale
Warner	J	IRS	Revenue Officer	(618) 543-2494		Glendale
Warr	Frank	IRS	Revenue Officer	(626) 927 -1240		
Webb	Jason	IRS	Revenue Officer	(281)721-3332		Texas
Wells	Leon	IRS	Revenue Officer	(818) 543-2528		Glendale
Wilkerson	David	IRS	Revenue Officer	(818) 543-2352		Glendale
Winker	Lisa	IRS	Revenue Officer	(818) 543-2495		Glendale
Witt	Jon	IRS	Revenue Officer	(502) 572-2223		Kentucky
Chavez	Thomas	IRS	Revenue Officer - Group Mgr	(626) 927-1440		
Chavez	Thomas	IRS	Revenue Officer - Group Mgr	(626) 927-1440		
Stayer	Laura	IRS	Revenue Officer - Group Mgr	(818) 543-2410		
Beeman	Donna	IRS	Revenue Officer - Supervisor	(818) 543-2480		Glendale
Borbon	Rhonda	IRS	Revenue Officer - Supervisor	(818) 543-2320		Glendale
Dipla	Brittanny	IRS	Revenue Officer - Supervisor	(805) 479-2552		Glendale
Ejimofdr	John	IRS	Revenue Officer - Supervisor	(818) 543-2490		Glendale
Jaymeson	Edward	IRS	Revenue Officer - Supervisor	(661) 753-5320		Santa Clarita
Olivas	Ms.	IRS	Revenue Officer - Supervisor			
Rodriguez	Sandra	IRS	Revenue Officer - Supervisor	(818) 543-2400		Glendale
Wingate	Terry	IRS	Revenue Offier	(805) 352- 0340		
Midgley	Elizabeth	IRS	Secretaiy (Office Automation)	(818) 543-2521		Glendale
Padilla	Zaira	IRS	Secretaiy (Office Automation)	(818) 274-0722		Woodland Hills
Minassian	Eileen	IRS	Secretary (OA)	(818) 543-2301		Glendale
Aguilar Garcia	Monica	IRS	Secretary (Office Automation)	(818) 543-2351		Glendale
Comett	Marjorie	IRS	Secretary (Office Automation)	(818) 543-2401		Glendale Woodiand Hills
Delmatoff	Marilyn	IRS	Secretary (Office Automation)	(818) 543-2491		Glendale
Kim	Sarah	IRS	Secretary (Office Automation)	(818) 543-2471		Glendale
Lam	Miu	IRS	Secretary (Office Automation)	(818) 543-2371		Glendale

Last	First	Agency	Title	Phone	-	Department
Nord	Helen	IRS	Secretary (Office Automation)	(661) 753-5334		Santa Clarita
Rhein	Erica	IRS	Secretary (Office Automation)	(818) 274-0737		
Scott	Karen	IRS	Secretary (Office Automation)	(818) 274-0750		Woodland Hills
Antal	Vivienne	IRS	SL Specialist	(415) 522-6384		Oakland
Breece	Dan	IRS	SL Specialist	(714) 347-9244		Santa Ana
Cacioppo	Lori	IRS	SL Specialist	(949) 389-4609		Laguna Niguel
Cervantes	Alejandro	IRS	SL Specialist	(213) 833-1258		Los Angeles
Footit	Christine	IRS	SL Specialist	(702) 868-5330		Las Vegas
Henrie-Brown	Jennifer	IRS	SL Specialist	(510) 637-2199		Oakland
Jaramillo	Maria	IRS	SL Specialist	(213) 833-1226		Los Angeles
Kelly-Brenner	Gerry	IRS	SL Specialist	(510) 637-3036		Oakland
Kershner	Keith	IRS	SL Specialist	(213) 435-8755		El Monte
Kinsey	James	IRS	SL Specialist	(408) 817-6842		San Jose
Lauridsen	Gina	IRS	SL Specialist	(619) 615-7768		San Diego
LeBlanc	Nancy	IRS	SL Specialist	(714) 347-9255		Santa Ana
Olsen	Kathy	IRS	SL Specialist	(702) 868-5307		Las Vegas
Ortiz	Cathy	IRS	SL Specialist	(213) 833-1227		Los Angeles
Sanchez	Christella	IRS	SL Specialist	(916) 974-5281		Sacramento
Sanders	Sharon	IRS	SL Specialist	(213) 833-1224		Los Angeles
Smith	Amy	IRS	SL Specialist	(909) 388-8234		San Bernardino
Vollmer	Traci	IRS	SL Specialist	(559) 443-7587		Fresno
Williams	Katie	IRS	SL Specialist	(619) 615-7771		San Diego
Zine	Marc	IRS	SL Specialist	(916) 974-5281		
Demarco	Leslie	IRS	Special Agent in Charge	(213) 576-3205		Los Angles
O'Briant	Scott	IRS	Special Agent in Charge, Los	(510) 637-2688		Oakland Field Office
Afmuete	Clarita	IRS	Supervisory Tax Specialist	(818) 274-0705		Woodland Hills
Bergsrud	Denise	IRS	Supervisory Tax Specialist	(818) 543-2350		Glendale
CapizzoLisaA		IRS	Supervisory Tax Specialist	(661) 753-5310		Santa Clarita
Heitmann	Karl	IRS	Supervisory Tax Specialist	(818) 274-0752		Woodland Hills
Phillips	Marsha	IRS	Supervisory Tax Specialist	(510) 637-2636		Supervisory Tax Specialist
Kwan	Bak	IRS	Tax Compliance Officer	(818) 543 - 2333		Glendale
Carrillo	Vivian	IRS	Tax Examining Technician	(818) 543-2496		Glendale
Griffin	Ethel	IRS	Tax Examining Technician	(818) 543-2503		Glendale
Hubbs	Michael	IRS	Tax Examining Technician	(818) 543-2412		
Lautsbaugh	Theresa	IRS	Tax Examining	(818) 543-2476		Glendale

Last	First	Agency	Title	Phone	-	Department
			Technician			
Mejia	Gilberto	IRS	Tax Examining Technician	(213) 576-4080		Glendale
Alessi	Mtehefe	IRS	Tax Specialist	(661) 753-5302		Santa Clarita
Anderson	Sandra	IRS	Tax Specialist	(818) 543-2332		Glendale
Arriola	Aldo	IRS	Tax Specialist			Woodland Hills
Becker	Alan	IRS	Tax Specialist	(818) 274-0748		Woodland Hills
Benson	Shauna	IRS	Tax Specialist	(818) 274-0734		Woodland Hilts
Britten	Fen	IRS	Tax Specialist	(818) 265-2309		Glendale
Chang	Raymond	IRS	Tax Specialist	(661) 753-5311		Santa Clarita
Chiou	Sheuerong	IRS	Tax Specialist	(818) 274-0707		Woodland Hills
Cross	Ronald	IRS	Tax Specialist	(661) 753-5313		Santa Clarita
Duarte	Heidi	IRS	Tax Specialist	(818) 274-0713		Woodland Hills
Garcia	Edras	IRS	Tax Specialist	(661) 353-5314		Santa Clarita
Gibbs	Shirley	IRS	Tax Specialist	(818) 756-4539		Woodland Hills
Hassricfc	Royal	IRS	Tax Specialist	(818) 543-2344		Glendale
Holbert	Sharon	IRS	Tax Specialist	(818) 274-0745		Woodland Hills
Howard-Rubinstein	Mia	IRS	Tax Specialist	(818) 274-0778		Woodland Hills
Kasparian	Hovannes	IRS	Tax Specialist	(818) 543-2346		Glendale
Kwan	Bak	IRS	Tax Specialist	(618) 543-2333		Glendale
Macis	Eric	IRS	Tax Specialist	(661) 753-5327		Santa Clarita
Mora	Alexander	IRS	Tax Specialist	(661) 753-5331		Santa Clarita
Morrow	Emily	IRS	Tax Specialist	(818) 274-0711		Woodland Hills
Mouradian	Ani	IRS	Tax Specialist	(818) 756-4539		Woodland Hills
Munro	Marie	IRS	Tax Specialist	(661) 753-5332		Santa Clarita
O Dena	Neil	IRS	Tax Specialist	(818) 543-2334		Glendale
Sanchez	Cleofas	IRS	Tax Specialist	(818) 274-0753		Woodland Hills
Sherman	Diana	IRS	Tax Specialist			Woodland Hills
Uvernois	Robert	IRS	Tax Specialist	(818) 274-0710		Woodland Hills
Vu	Heidi	IRS	Tax Specialist	(818) 274-0803		Woodland Hills
Vu-Nguyen	Cynthia	IRS	Tax Specialist	(818) 274-0751		Woodland Hills
Walsh	John	IRS	Tax Specialist	(818) 543-2348		Glendale
Wilson	Leticia	IRS	Tax Specialist	(661) 753-5348		Santa Clarita
Allevato	Anthony	IRS	Territory Manager	(949) 389-4391		Laguna Niguel
Alvarado	Leo	IRS	Territory Manager	(310) 535-7429		El Segundo
Bass	Leah	IRS	Territory Manager	(916) 974-5482		Sacramento
Bennett	Alonzo	IRS	Territory Manager	(408) 817-6705		San Jose
Branson	Nancy	IRS	Territory Manager	(415) 522-6165		San Francisco
Chezbaum	Rick	IRS	Territory Manager	(805) 352-0331		Fresno
Cox	Kathleen (acting)	IRS	Territory Manager	(510) 637-2707		Oakland
Cuomo	Donna	IRS	Territory Manager	(213) 576-3875		Los Angeles
Dunn	Shelly	IRS	Territory Manager	(510) 637-3163		Oakland
Edwards	Phil	IRS	Territory Manager	(909) 388-8239		San Diego
Fleming	Sandra	IRS	Territory Manager	(213) 576-3057		Los Angeles

Last	First	Agency	Title	Phone	-	Department
Focht	Don	IRS	Territory Manager	(415) 522-6083		San Francisco
Frank	Deirda	IRS	Territory Manager	(562) 491-7789		Long Beach/SD
Jaramillo	Mark	IRS	Territory Manager	(909) 388-8294		San Bernardino
Jones	Tamara	IRS	Territory Manager	(408) 817-6903		San Jose
Jones	Tamara	IRS	Territory Manager	(408) 817-6903		San Francisco
Kelly	Tim	IRS	Territory Manager	(707) 535-3850		San Franciso
Kuhns	Barbara	IRS	Territory Manager	(949) 389-4595		Southern CA/Alaska
LaCour	DeGina	IRS	Territory Manager	(213) 576-3847		PSP
Lee	Stella	IRS	Territory Manager	(408) 817-6554		Oakland/San Jose
McDaniel	Ethelyn	IRS	Territory Manager	(949) 389-4107		Laguna Niguel
Meyer	Ted	IRS	Territory Manager	(818) 265-2363		Glendale
Miller	Dorothy	IRS	Territory Manager	(916) 974-5371		Fresno
Mitchell	Tonya	IRS	Territory Manager	(626) 312-5068		El Monte
Parker	Sheryl	IRS	Territory Manager	(510) 637-4614		Oakland
Russell	Dorothy	IRS	Territory Manager	(714) 347-9511		Santa Ana
Schoonmaker	Neil	IRS	Territory Manager	(559) 443-7698		Fresno
Shabazz	Tony	IRS	Territory Manager	(408) 817-6275		San Jose
Stewart	Connie	IRS	Territory Manager	(213) 576-3439		Los Angeles
Thompson	Jim	IRS	Territory Manager	(805) 445-4437		Camarillo
Thomson	Diane	IRS	Territory Manager	(714) 347-9209		Santa Ana
Tracht	Mark	IRS	Territory Manager	(213) 576-3688		Central Coast
Turner	Steve (acting)	IRS	Territory Manager	(310) 535-4611		El Segundo
Veasiy	John	IRS	Territory Manager	(714) 347-9330		Santa Ana
Wreyford	Claudia	IRS	Territory Manager	(916) 974-5589		Oakland/Sacramento
Swarts	Howard	IRS	Territory Manager	(916) 974-5178		

Chapter 11:

Trust Fund Recovery

(Formerly the 100% Penalty)

Facing possible retributions such as civil liability for unpaid employment taxes, including penalties and interest, and possible criminal liability, employer delinquencies in the payment of employment taxes remain one of the most serious collection problems of the IRS.

Under the Internal Revenue Code certain persons, other than taxpayers, may be designated as agents or responsible persons for the collection of taxes due to the United States. The most common example of this type of provision is the requirement that employers collect and withhold income and social security (or more properly, Federal Insurance Contributions Act [FICA]) taxes, which are by far the most commonly collected from persons other than the taxpayers.

A corporation or partnership unable to obtain outside financing or having insufficient funds to pay all its obligations may attempt to continue in business by failing to pay employment taxes. Because the IRS does not immediately detect delinquencies or take enforced collection action, employers thus are tempted to treat the government as an ordinary creditor. In effect, they borrow from the government the amount of employment taxes required to be paid over.

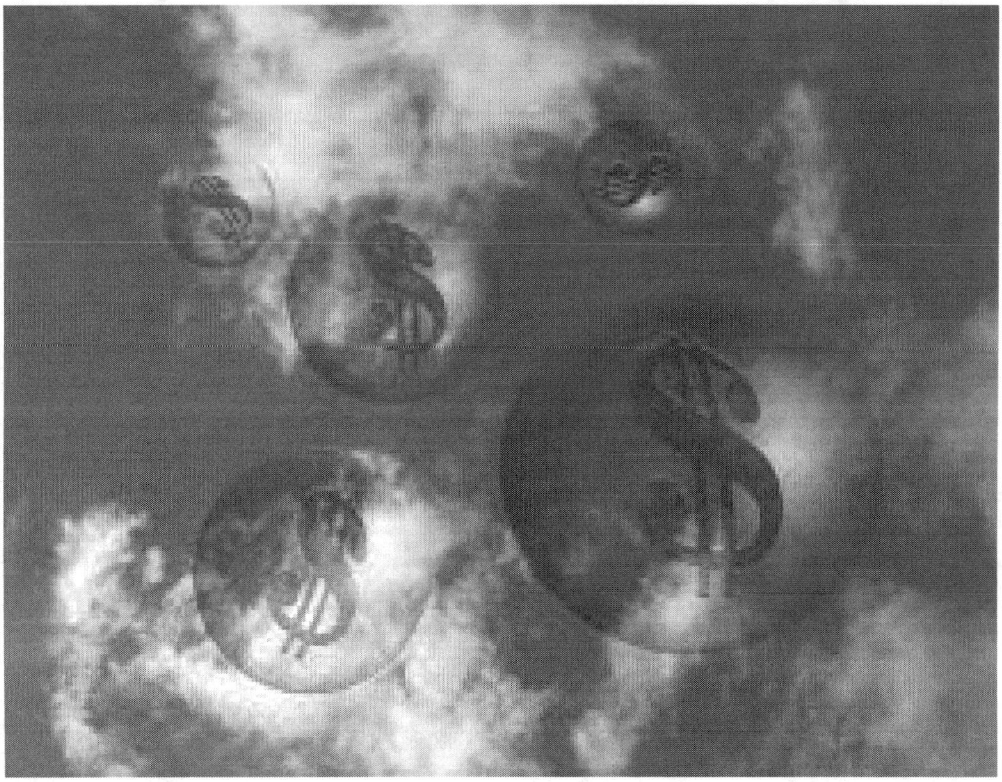

In most cases, persons responsible for deciding how the funds of the employer's business will be spent do not intend to defraud the government. They decide to prefer creditors other than the government in hope that the business will "turn the corner" so that sufficient funds will then be available to pay all creditors, including the government. To compensate the government for part of the taxes due it upon the failure of a business, Section 6672 of the Internal Revenue Code (which is included at the end of this chapter) imposes a penalty equal to the tax required to have been paid over (hence the former term "100% Penalty") on any person who (1) was required "to collect, truthfully account for and pay over" employment taxes; and (2) willfully failed to do so.

Under the so-called "Trust Fund Recovery Penalty" or TFRP provision, the IRS may assess and collect a penalty in the amount equal to the unpaid corporate **trust fund** taxes from any person who was required, but failed, "to collect, truthfully account for, and pay over the tax."

In order to assert the trust fund recovery penalty assessment, the IRS must establish two elements. First, the person subject to penalty must be "responsible" for seeing that the corporation's withheld trust fund taxes were paid to the government. Generally, a finding of responsibility will attach to persons charged with "control over the corporation's business affairs (and) who participate in decisions concerning payment of creditors, or those who have "the final word as to what bills should or should not be paid, and when." Second, the IRS must prove that the person "willfully" failed to pay over the taxes.

In this context, willfulness means a voluntary, conscious, and intentional choice to pay other creditors instead of the government at the time the wages were paid and the withholding taxes were due for deposit. Mere negligence is insufficient to establish willfulness under this provision. A reckless disregard of the risk that the tax may not be paid over to the government may, however, constitute willfulness.

The following points should be noted regarding the trust fund recovery penalty under IRC section 6672;

1. The trust fund recovery penalty does not make the government whole in the event of the failure to pay over employment taxes. The penalty only returns to the government the amount of the taxes collected and not paid over—that is, the trust fund portion of employment taxes and not the portion of the taxes imposed on the employer.

2. The term penalty is somewhat misleading. The amount of the liability imposed by Section 6672 is equal to the amount of the delinquent trust fund taxes and is not in addition to those taxes. Consequently, the "penalty" is actually a collection device designed for the purpose of collecting the taxes the employer should have paid over.

3. There is a distinction between the amount of the liability and the existence of liability for the penalty. The amount of the liability is affected by the lack of payment of trust fund taxes by the corporation. However, liability for the penalty is a direct and primary obligation of the responsible person for failure to withhold and pay over the trust fund tax. This liability is separate and distinct from the liability of the employer under this wage withholding provisions.

4. The trust fund recovery penalty is not necessary in the case where a business is conducted as a proprietorship. The individual owners are personally and directly liable for employment taxes. Accordingly, Section 6672 applies where a corporation or partnership is the "employer" and a "person" subject to the trust fund recovery penalty includes "an officer, or employee of a partnership, who …is under a duty to perform the act in respect of which the violation occurs." The statute states "any person" having the duty to collect and pay over may be liable for the penalty and, accordingly, the penalty may be, and frequently is, asserted against more than one person."

5. No negligence or fraud penalty may by assessed against a person in the event that the trust fund recovery penalty is assessed.

6. In addition to collecting and paying over income taxes from employees, an Employer is required to report and pay his own portion of FICA taxes, as well as federal unemployment tax, or FUTA taxes. These amounts are referred to as the employer's portions of employment taxes.

7. In the event that an employer fails to collect and pay over, he may be required, on notice, to create a special bank account in trust for the withheld taxes. If the employer fails to comply with these trust provisions, he may be prosecuted under Section 725 for committing a misdemeanor punishable by a fine of not more than $ 5,000 or imprisonment for not more than one year, or both.

8. Civil penalties and interest may be imposed if the employer fails to file returns or to pay over the entire correct amount of employment taxes.

9. In aggravated cases of nonpayment, criminal prosecution may be instituted. A felony prosecution might also be brought under one of the criminal statutes described in Section 7204 for fraudulent withholding statements or willful failure to supply such statements to employees, Section 7207 for fraudulent written statements given to the Service, or on Section 7203 for willful failure to supply information.

10. In the event that the employer has no assets, then no taxes, penalties, or interest can be collected from the employer. Nevertheless, employees are entitled to credit for the amount of income and FICA taxes withheld whether or not the employer pays over the withheld taxes to the government.

The IRS' practice is to assert 100% penalties against all executive officers. However, a person may be an officer (or a director) of a corporation without having real or effective control over financial affairs. This may be true even when an officer has authority to sign checks. Accordingly, the officer's scope of authority in dealing with the payment of taxes should be described. If the person has no authority over tax matters, an employment agreement, resolution, or other official documents should say so.

Joint-and-Several Liability and Contribution

A taxpayer who is jointly and severally liable for the payment of an unpaid tax along with other responsible persons cannot avoid collection on the basis that the government should first collect, or attempt to collect, the tax from the other persons. The obligation to collect and pay over is the individual and primary obligation of the responsible person. For this reason, some courts have also found that the IRS need not have first attempted to recover the tax from a corporation, although this may not be true if it can be established the corporation was solvent and had assets available at the time the Service should have collected the liability as joint and several. The amount of liability will not be apportioned or divided between or among alleged responsible persons.

Statute of Limitations

Except in cases of a failure to file a return, filing false returns, or willful attempted evasion, the statutory period of assessment is three years after a return is filed. This general rule applies to the assessment of the trust fund recovery penalty of Section 6672 against a responsible person. Tax returns for employment taxes are filed quarterly. Since the 100 percent penalty is a device for collection of the trust fund portion of these taxes, the penalty should be subject to the same period of limitations as the tax itself—that is, the three-year period following the filing of the employment tax return. The statute of limitations of assessment can remain open more than three years after the date of the failure to act. If the return is filed after the due date, the limitations period is measured from the actual filing date, and if no return is filed, the limitations period remains open indefinitely. Once the tax is assessed, the Service may collect the tax by a levy or proceeding in court within ten years after the assessment. The assessment that is collectible within the ten-year period is the assessment under Section 6672, not the assessment against the employer. An action against a responsible person has nevertheless been held timely when brought within ten years of the date of the assessment against the employer.

Corporate officers or other persons who might be considered responsible for paying over trust fund taxes should instruct the IRS to apply payments to the trust fund portions of employment taxes accrued during their period of responsibility before making any other application of the payment. The elimination of any delinquency in trust fund taxes eliminates the trust fund recovery penalty as well. Specific designation of a payment is necessary because the IRS's procedure is to consider that any payment on a corporate account represents a payment of the employer portions of the liability (including assessed penalty and interest) unless there is some specific designation to the contrary. Only the balance of the payment, if any is applied to the trust fund portion of the liability. The IRS will not recognize any right of designation where enforced collection of the delinquency is made.

The IRS determines whether to pursue the Trust Fund Recovery Penalty:

After the initial contact of trust fund taxpayer

As soon as possible but no later than 120 calendar days after assignment of the balance due accounts in the Collection Field.

Note: Although this decision must be made within six month period, there's no requirement that the entire investigation be completed within a specific time period. However, when the Revenue Officer makes the decision to assert, the investigation will proceed as expeditiously as possible. If the business is no longer operating, the Trust Fund Recovery Penalty will generally be completed within 120 days of the determination date.

In the event that certain facts surface during the IRS investigation, which may indicate that transfers of corporate stock and/or capital assets have occurred, the IRS will, in addition to pursuing the Trust Fund Recovery Penalty, consider recovery of the unpaid corporate liability by recommending:

Transferee assessment

Suit to establish a transferee liability

Suit to set aside a fraudulent transfer

Examination referral

TFRP Interviews and Investigations (4180 Interview)

1. During the initial contact with the taxpayer the Revenue Officer will attempt to conduct interviews with all potentially responsible persons. The revenue officer should take the following actions during the interview:
    a. Provide Publication 1, Your Rights as a Taxpayer, and document the history that the publication was delivered;
    b. Explain the Trust Fund Recovery Penalty;
    c. Advise all potentially responsible persons, to the extent possible, that they may be held personally liable for the Trust Fund Recovery Penalty;
    d. Provide Notice 784, Could You Be Personally Liable for Certain Unpaid Federal Taxes?
    e. Advise the person(s) being interviewed of the proper actions to take to avoid such liability;
    f. Begin asking questions and gathering information and documents, such as bank statements and cancelled checks, in support of assertion of the penalty;
    g. Attempt to secure at least one Form 4180, Report of Interview with Individual Relative to Trust Fund Recovery Penalty or Personal Liability for Excise Tax, from a potentially responsible person;
    h. Secure additional Forms 4180 from all potentially responsible personas to the extent possible;
    i. The Revenue Officer will not give or mail the form to the potentially responsible person(s) or representative for completion by that person. **It will be completed in person or over the phone;**
    j. The Revenue Officer will always request the presence of the potentially responsible person when conducting an interview with a representative having a Power of Attorney;
    k. A summons may be necessary to require the potentially responsible person's presence at the interview;
    l. A statement can be updated at a later date with the changes, initiated by the Revenue Officer and the person interviewed.

Third Party Interviews and Third Party Contact Considerations

It may be necessary to contact a third party for the purpose of gathering information concerning other officers or employees.

The Revenue Officer will secure and include in the file documentation of sources of income and assets and all necessary supporting documents in order for the initiating revenue officer to make a recommendation for assertion or non-assertion of the Trust Fund Revenue Penalty, including non-assertion due to collectability.

Evidence That May Support Recommendations

In the majority of cases, the largest portion of evidence that is secured to support recommendations of Trust Fund Recovery Penalty is either corporate records or bank records.

Note: Determination of the amount of documentation required to support the recommendation to assert the penalty is done so on a case by case basis. There must be sufficient documentation in the file to support each recommendation for assertion. Bank records and copies of the applicable tax returns will be secured on almost every case. If they are not secured, the case file must be documented with the reason(s) why they were not secured and why they are not necessary to support the recommendation.

Corporate records that can be reviewed include:

Articles of Incorporation

Minute Books

Forms 941 and 1120 or 1065

Payroll records

Any other records that may be relevant to determining the roles and responsibilities of individuals involved with the corporation

1. The corporate records should be reviewed to determine:

    Duties (and changes to duties) of officers, directors, etc.

    Appointments and resignations of officers, directors, etc.

    Responsibilities of individuals to file and pay tax returns

    Issuance of stock to officers

    Assets transferred to officers

    Loans made to officers

    Unreported payroll and other taxes

    Diversion of funds

    Borrowing of funds not used to pay taxes

2. Bank records that can be reviewed include:

    Cancelled checks and bank statements

    Signature cards and correspondence to the bank relative to changes affecting the signature cards

    Loan applications and records of loans

    Any other records that may be relevant to determining which individuals were involved in the financial affairs of the business

2. The bank records should be reviewed to determine:

    Authority of persons to sign checks and deposit funds

    Authority of persons to obligate the corporation by borrowing

    Diversion of funds to officers, members, etc.

    Deposits and withdrawals of alleged loans to corporation by officers, members, directors, etc.

    Excessive salaries, expenses, etc.

    Payment of other obligations

    Deposit records for monies received for sale of assets

    Deposit records of payments for stock in the corporation

    Any other relevant records

Calculating the TFRP

If a taxpayer submits a partial payment of a liability when there are assessments for more than one taxable period, and the taxpayer did not provide specific written instructions as to the application of the partial payment, the payment will be applied in a manner serving the best interests of the government. The payment will be applied to satisfy the liability for successive periods in descending order of priority until the payment is absorbed. If the amount applied to a period is less than the liability for the period, the amount will be applied to tax, penalty, and interest, in that order, until the amount is absorbed. When considering the best interest of the government and period of priority, in addition to statute and lien priority issues, consideration will be given to first applying payments to the non-trust funds.

Note: If returns were calculated under IRC 6020(b) and the liability is being included as part of the TFRP assessment, said returns must be submitted for processing and must be included as pre-assessed modules if the assessment has not yet posted.

Determining the TFRP balance applies:

On cases where the Letter 1153(DO) is issued on or after June 19, 2000
For all payments received on or after January 1, 2003 for cases where the Letter 1153(DO) was issued before June 19, 2000

All undesignated payments on a tax period are applied following the guidelines below:

SEQUENCE OF PAYMENT APPLICATION

Non-trust fund portion of tax (employer's share of FICA, or the non-trust fund reported on Form 720)

Trust fund portion of tax (withholding and employee's share of FICA, or the trust fund "collected" excise tax under IRC 6672 on communications or air transportation).

Assessed lien fees and collection costs

Assessed penalty

Assessed interest

Accrued penalty to date of payment

Accrued interest to date of payment

Special Payment Application Rules

Proceeds from an offset or a levy on a contract are applied to the liability incurred during the period of the contract even though the application may not serve the best interests of the government.

Payments by Responsible Party on Behalf of the Employer

When efforts to collect the tax, penalty, and interest from the employer have been unsuccessful, it may be suggested to the responsible persons that they have two options:

Pay the withheld tax liability on behalf of the corporation.

Have the Trust Fund Recovery Penalty.

1. If a responsible person chooses to pay on behalf of the corporation then:

    Payment will be made by cash, cashier's check, certified check, or other acceptable payment form.

    The responsible person may provide the funds to the corporation and pay with a corporate check.

    If the payment is not made with a corporate check, the responsible person(s) will provide a signed statement certifying that payment is being made on behalf of the corporation for the application to the trust fund liability.

    The statement will read as follows: "I/We {Name(s)}, hereby tender payment of $(Amount) and specifically request that such funds be applied to the trust fund tax liability of {Business Name}, {Business E.I.N} for the period(s) ending {List each period}."

    This statement protects the government's position in cases where a responsible person later files a claim for refund of the TFRP, claiming that their personal tax payment was misapplied or applied against their wishes to the corporate liability.

Retain the signed statement along with a copy of Form 4183 as part of both the balance due and any TFRP case files.

Note: if statement accompanying unsolicited payments are to be accepted as adequate they must clearly indicate the intent to designate payments, along the lines of the statement in (d) above.

The TFRP investigation will continue while awaiting designated payments from a responsible person.

Form 4183 Penalty Assessment Recommendation

The Revenue Officer will review all of the documentation in the case file as well as all Forms 4180 in order to make a determination regarding responsibility and willfulness for each potentially responsible party.

A collectability determination must be completed for each potentially responsible person determined to be both responsible and willful.

Manager's Review of Trust Fund Recommendations

1. The group manager must complete a thorough review of the Trust Fund Recovery Penalty recommendation to determine the adequacy of the TFRP recommendation prior to the revenue officer issuing the assessment.
2. The manager's review of the recommendation must address the same issues that the revenue officer addressed. When the answer to any of the questions is "no", the manager should consider whether to return the recommendation to the revenue officer for corrective action and/or further development. Managers must ensure all required documents are in the case file and a collectability determination has been made on each potential responsible officer.

Notification of Proposed Assessment

Once Form 4183 is approved by the group manager, the Revenue Officer should prepare Form 3177, Notice of Action on the Master File, to request input of the TC 130 to freeze any potential refunds for all individuals determined to be responsible for the TFRP. The form may be prepared using the ATFR program. Form 3177 should then be submitted to the CP 44 Unit in Accounting Control/Services for input of the TC 130.

Letter 1153 and Form 2751 are then prepared, and along with Publication 1, they are delivered to the taxpayer. A copy of page 4 of Form 4183 showing the penalty computation may also be included with the documents delivered to the taxpayer so they are aware of how payments were applied to the account.

Letter 1153

Notifies the responsible party of the proposed assessment

Contains a description of the available appeal rights

Affords the responsible party the opportunity to agree to or to appeal the assessment

Should be modified if the responsible person has filed a bankruptcy proceeding and the automatic stay is still in effect, to delete any references to: the Service "collecting" the TFRP, any actions the taxpayer should take to delay collection activity by the Service, and any collections the Service may take in Jeopardy circumstances

Form 2751

Provides a report of the corporate liability

Provides a breakdown of the proposed TFRP assessment for each quarter for which the TFRP assessment is proposed

Allows the responsible party to agree to the proposed assessment

Waives the 60 day restriction on notice and demand if signed by the taxpayer

May be signed by the responsible party at any time during the TFRP investigation or after the Service has issued Letter 1153(DO)

Payroll Tax Withholding and the IRS

It is tempting to "borrow" the payroll taxes withheld from your employees-in order to take advantage of the time between payday and the day you're supposed to pay those amounts over to the Internal Revenue Service.

Section 6672 of the tax code makes you liable' "in addition to other penalties provided by law... to a penalty equal to the total amount of the tax" not accounted for and paid over. There is a civil penalty that may, at the government's discretion be assessed. It may also be augmented by criminal prosecution. The Tax code (section 7202) makes it a felony to willfully fail "to accounts for; and pay over" taxes withheld from employees.

You are deemed to have withheld the taxes (withholding tax, as well as your employees' share of Social Security and Medicare taxes) by paying your employees their wages net the deductions. The withheld amounts constitute a fund you hold in trust for the government. This "trust fund" is not the same as a debt such as accounts payable.

A debt is what you owe your creditors for goods or services, or for a loan you received. Even your personal income tax is your debt to the government. The taxes you withhold from your employees' compensation are treated as the government's money that you hold in trust as agent or trustee. IRS regulations stipulate that once you have withheld the tax, your employees are entitled to credit for it, regardless of when (or if) you pay it over to the government.

You will be held personally liable for the withheld taxes, if: (a) you are responsible for its collection and payment. Whether as the owner of the business or a person authorized to handle its funds; and (b) your failure to collect the tax and pay it over are "willful." You have the burden of proving the absence of at least one of elements.

You do not have to be the owner of the business. The courts have made it clear that you can be held liable for the tax if you are in a position to exercise significant control even if you don't have the final word over the disbursement of funds. Whether you are called the chief financial officer or the bookkeeper, if you authorized to determine which creditors are to be paid, and to issue checks, you can be held responsible even if some payments are subject to a superior's approval.

The easier question has to do with the "willfulness," since the courts have provided an answer that is very simple: Failure to pay withholding taxes is willful within the meaning of irc section 6672 if you pay other creditors when you don't have sufficient funds to pay the taxes you know to be due. Even an employee to whom you owe wages is regarded as just another creditor.

If your company is teetering at the edge, you are generally better advised to close it down than to use the government's money as working capital.

Section 6672[ix]

Failure to collect and pay over tax, or attempt to evade or defeat tax

(a) General rule

Any person required to collect, truthfully account for, and pay over any tax imposed by this title who willfully fails to collect such tax, or truthfully account for and pay over such tax, or willfully attempts in any manner to evade or defeat any such tax or the payment thereof, shall, in addition to other penalties provided by law, be liable to a penalty equal to the total amount of the tax evaded, or not collected, or not accounted for and paid over. No penalty shall be imposed under section 6653 or part II of subchapter A of chapter 68 for any offense to which this section is applicable.

(b) Preliminary notice requirement

(1) In general

No penalty shall be imposed under subsection (a) unless the Secretary notifies the taxpayer in writing by mail to an address as determined under section 6212(b) or in person that the taxpayer shall be subject to an assessment of such penalty.

(2) Timing of notice

The mailing of the notice described in paragraph (1) (or, in the case of such a notice delivered in person, such delivery) shall precede any notice and demand of any penalty under subsection (a) by at least 60 days.

(3) Statute of limitations

If a notice described in paragraph (1) with respect to any penalty is mailed or delivered in person before the expiration of the period provided by section 6501 for the assessment of such penalty (determined without regard to this paragraph), the period provided by such section for the assessment of such penalty shall not expire before the later of –

(A) the date 90 days after the date on which such notice was mailed or delivered in person, or

(B) if there is a timely protest of the proposed assessment, the date 30 days after the Secretary makes a final administrative determination with respect to such protest.

(4) Exception for jeopardy

This subsection shall not apply if the Secretary finds that the collection of the penalty is in jeopardy.

(c) Extension of period of collection where bond is filed

(1) In general

If, within 30 days after the day on which notice and demand of any penalty under subsection (a) is made against any person, such person -

(A) pays an amount which is not less than the minimum amount required to commence a proceeding in court with respect to his liability for such penalty,

(B) files a claim for refund of the amount so paid, and

(C) furnishes a bond which meets the requirements of paragraph (3), no levy or proceeding in court for the collection of the remainder of such penalty shall be made, begun, or prosecuted until a final resolution of a proceeding begun as provided in paragraph (2). Notwithstanding the provisions of section 7421(a), the beginning of such proceeding or levy during the time such prohibition is in force may be enjoined by a proceeding in the proper court. Nothing in this paragraph shall be construed to prohibit any counterclaim for the remainder of such penalty in a proceeding begun as provided in paragraph (2).

(2) Suit must be brought to determine liability for penalty If,

within 30 days after the day on which his claim for refund with respect to any penalty under subsection (a) is denied, the person described in paragraph (1) fails to begin a proceeding in the appropriate United States district court (or in the Court of Claims) (FOOTNOTE 1) for the determination of his liability for such penalty, paragraph (1) shall cease to apply with respect to such penalty, effective on the day following the close of the 30-day period referred to in this paragraph.(FOOTNOTE 1) See References in Text note below.

(3) Bond

The bond referred to in paragraph (1) shall be in such form and with such sureties as the Secretary may by regulations prescribe and shall be in an amount equal to 1 1/2 times the amount of excess of the penalty assessed over the payment described in paragraph (1).

(4) Suspension of running of period of limitations on collection

The running of the period of limitations provided in section 6502 on the collection by levy or by a proceeding in court in respect of any penalty described in paragraph (1) shall be suspended for the period during which the Secretary is prohibited from collecting by levy or a proceeding in court.

(5) Jeopardy collection

If the Secretary makes a finding that the collection of the penalty is in jeopardy, nothing in this subsection shall prevent the immediate collection of such penalty.

(d) Right of contribution where more than 1 person liable for penalty

If more than 1 person is liable for the penalty under subsection (a) with respect to any tax, each person who paid such penalty shall be entitled to recover from other persons who are liable for such penalty an amount equal to the excess of the amount paid by such person over such person's proportionate share of the penalty. Any claim for such a recovery may be made only in a proceeding which is separate from, and is not joined or consolidated with -

(1) an action for collection of such penalty brought by the United States, or

(2) a proceeding in which the United States files a counterclaim or third-party complaint for the collection of such penalty.

(e) Exception for voluntary board members of tax-exempt organizations

No penalty shall be imposed by subsection (a) on any unpaid, volunteer member of any board of trustees or directors of an organization exempt from tax under subtitle A if such member -

(1) is solely serving in an honorary capacity,

(2) does not participate in the day-to-day or financial operations of the organization, and

(3) does not have actual knowledge of the failure on which such penalty is imposed.

The preceding sentence shall not apply if it results in no person being liable for the penalty imposed by subsection (a).

Chapter 12:

Collection Information

Tips and Traps - Nine Things You Should Know About Penalties

If you don't file your return and pay your tax by the due date you may have to pay a penalty. Here are nine things the IRS wants you to know about the two different penalties you may face if you do not pay or file on time.

1. If you do not file by the deadline, you might face a failure-to-file penalty.
2. If you do not pay by the due date, you could face a failure-to-pay penalty.
3. The failure-to-file penalty is generally more than the failure-to-pay penalty. So if you cannot pay all the taxes you owe, you should still file your tax return and explore other payment options in the meantime.
4. The penalty for filing late is usually 5% of the unpaid taxes for each month or part of month that return is late. This penalty will not exceed 25% of your unpaid taxes.
5. If you file your return more than 600 days after the due date or extended due date, the minimum penalty is the smaller of $135 or 100% of the unpaid tax.
6. You will have to pay a failure-to-pay penalty of ½ of 1% of your unpaid taxes for each month or part of a month after due date that the taxes are not paid. This penalty can be as much a 25% of your unpaid taxes.
7. If you filed an extension and you paid at least 90% of your actual tax liability by the due date, you will not face with a failure-to-pay penalty if the remaining balance is paid by the extended due date.
8. If both the failure-to-file penalty and the failure-to-pay penalty apply in any month, the 5% failure-to-file penalty is reduced by the failure-to-pay penalty. However, if you file return more than 60 days after the due date or extended due date, the minimum penalty is the smaller of $135 or 100% of the unpaid tax.

9. You will not have the pay a failure-to-file or failure-to-pay penalty if you can show that you failed to file or pay on time because of reasonable cause and not because of willful neglect.

Partial Pay Installment Agreements

When it is not possible for taxpayers to full pay delinquent tax liabilities they may be allowed to pay their liabilities over a prescribed period of time. If full payment cannot be achieved by the Collection Statute Expiration Date (CSED), and taxpayers have some ability to pay, the Service can grant Partial Payment Installment Agreements (PPIAs). The American Jobs Creation Act of 2004 amended IRC § 6159 to provide this authority.

IRC 6159 requires Partial Payment Installment Agreements (PPIA) be reviewed every two years. Centralized Case Processing (CCP) performs the two year financial review on all PPIAs.

Centralized Case Processing (CCP) monitors installment agreements to ensure taxpayers:

Make installment payments when due.

Pay required federal tax deposits.

File federal tax returns when due.

Pay additional liabilities when due.

IRC 6159 does not allow for an installment agreement to be defaulted for non-payment of estimated tax.

If taxpayers remain in compliance with filing, paying and depositing requirements, the IRS takes no further case action or makes any further contact with the taxpayer until the agreement is completed.

If the taxpayer does not complete any one of the items in (1) above, the IRS follows the procedures below:

The IRS contacts the taxpayer and requests the payment, deposit or return, whichever is appropriate.

If the taxpayer complies within the reasonable time frame given, the IRS does not begin default and termination procedures. They continue to monitor the installment agreement as before.

If the taxpayer does not comply with the deadline given the installment agreement will be considered in default and the IRS will resume collection activity.

Collection Information Statements

One of the most important things to remember when negotiating with the IRS on behalf of a taxpayer that is unable to pay their liability in full, is that the IRS collects based not upon what a taxpayer owes but rather based upon their ability to pay.

As someone who practices tax resolution, you will often be approached by people with tax liabilities, claiming that they are unable to pay their tax debt in full. In order to determine as far as the IRS is concerned, how much a taxpayer is able to afford, the IRS uses formulas similar to those used to determine how much a person can afford to make a mortgage payment. The big difference is that banks and other lenders use a multiple of earnings while the IRS takes a taxpayers "take home" income and subtracts out their necessary and reasonable living expenses. The IRS expects that all remaining funds will be paid to them in monthly installments. These payments are applied to the outstanding tax liability.

If you give the IRS information that does not fit their model, they will include funds as income that the taxpayer did not consider or disallow expenses that they taxpayer is making on the basis that they are either unnecessary or unreasonable. The result in either case is that the IRS will demand a larger monthly installment payment that the taxpayer is unable to make without altering their lifestyle or that the IRS will reject an Offer based upon their assertion that the taxpayer has the ability to pay more than they claimed was possible. For this reason it is imperative that a person practicing tax resolution know exactly what is and what is not considered an allowable expense. In addition the practitioner must know how much for each allowable expense is considered reasonable.

To make this determination for purposes of an Offer in Compromise the answer is simple. The IRS publishes at least two times a year, National and Local Standards for living expenses. Upon review of these published standards, you will see that some seem reasonable while others seem low. Especially when looking at large metropolitan areas such as Los Angeles and New York where the cost of living is much higher than other parts of the country.

For purposes of an Installment Agreement; at least at this time, the IRS typically will allow a taxpayer to claim actual living expenses as opposed to their published standards. That being said the living expenses must still be reasonable (i.e. the IRS will typically not allow someone be making mortgage payments on their mansion or car payments on their Rolls Royce).

In order to determine how much a taxpayer nets in monthly income, as well as how much they spend monthly on living expenses, the IRS requires that a delinquent taxpayer submit a Collection Information Statement (433A, 433B or 433F). In this form a taxpayer lists their income, expenses, assets and liabilities. Upon first glance of the forms they seem simple to complete. The problem is that when you ask a delinquent taxpayer to complete one of the above mentioned forms, you will find that they never complete the form completely correct.

One of the most common errors occurs when a taxpayer attempts to enter income information. If they are an employee earning w-2 wages, they will either enter biweekly paycheck information as bimonthly which fails to include two paychecks or they will enter the withholding information incorrectly which can greatly affect the amount they earn as it appears on the form. If they taxpayer is self-employed they typically never enter the correct monthly net business income but rather guess at the amount. In order to determine how much a self-employed person nets in monthly business income, they must supply a Profit and Loss statement for their business. The net monthly business income is determined by subtracting the business expenses from the gross income and dividing the net income by the number of months spanning the Profit and Loss statement.

Another common mistake taxpayers make when completing Collection Information Statements is to guess at their living expenses such as food, clothing, car maintenance, gas, car insurance and out of pocket medical expenses. It is difficult for someone to track all of these expenses which is not really an issue because unless a taxpayer can prove they have a very valid reason for spending more, the IRS will only allow the published amount for these items as listed in their National and Local Standards.

The biggest mistake one can make and is usually the case when a taxpayer takes a stab at completing a Collection Information Statement is to not complete the form in its entirety. Every section must be completed and done so accurately. The IRS does not like guesses. If a section does not apply to the taxpayer submitting the form, "N/A" should be placed in the appropriate boxes and "$0" should be entered in the "Total" for said section. Keep in mind that the IRS will typically ask for substantiation for all items that either exceed the amount or are not included in their National and Local Standards for living expenses. Substantiation includes both proof of the expense (i.e. invoices and statements) as well as proof that the expense was paid (i.e. a copy of cancelled check, credit card statements or bank statements). For example, if someone has a $3,500 mortgage payment that has not been paid in 6 months due to negotiation for a loan modification, the mortgage expense will be disallowed.

In the pages following, you will find the Collection Information Statement forms. Notice that the 433A and 433F ask for virtually the same information. The difference is that the 433F, typically used by automated collections is a short version (2 pages). The 433A typically requested by a Revenue Officer asked for similar information in more detail (6 pages). The 433B is used for business entities and is basically asked for static information in addition to the information one would find in the Company's Profit and Loss statement as well as their Balance Sheet. Note that all of the forms below come with instructions. Always be sure to read the instructions carefully and include all supporting information requested in the instructions.

Collection Information Statement (long form 433-A[x])

Form **433-A**
(Rev. December 2012)
Department of the Treasury
Internal Revenue Service

Collection Information Statement for Wage Earners and Self-Employed Individuals

Wage Earners Complete Sections 1, 2, 3, 4, and 5 including the signature line on page 4. *Answer all questions or write N/A if the question is not applicable.*

Self-Employed Individuals Complete Sections 1, 3, 4, 5, 6 and 7 and the signature line on page 4. *Answer all questions or write N/A if the question is not applicable.*

For Additional Information, refer to Publication 1854, "How To Prepare a Collection Information Statement."

Include attachments if additional space is needed to respond completely to any question.

Name on Internal Revenue Service (IRS) Account	Social Security Number *SSN* on IRS Account	Employer Identification Number *EIN*

Section 1: Personal Information

1a Full Name of Taxpayer and Spouse *(if applicable)*	1c Home Phone ( )	1d Cell Phone ( )
1b Address *(Street, City, State, ZIP code) (County of Residence)*	1e Business Phone ( )	1f Business Cell Phone ( )
	2b Name, Age, and Relationship of dependent(s)	
2a Marital Status: ☐ Married ☐ Unmarried *(Single, Divorced, Widowed)*		

	Social Security No. *(SSN)*	Date of Birth *(mmddyyyy)*	Driver's License Number and State
3a Taxpayer			
3b Spouse			

Section 2: Employment Information for Wage Earners

If you or your spouse have self-employment income instead of, or in addition to wage income, complete Business Information in Sections 6 and 7.

Taxpayer		Spouse	
4a Taxpayer's Employer Name		5a Spouse's Employer Name	
4b Address *(Street, City, State, and ZIP code)*		5b Address *(Street, City, State, and ZIP code)*	
4c Work Telephone Number ( )	4d Does employer allow contact at work ☐ Yes ☐ No	5c Work Telephone Number ( )	5d Does employer allow contact at work ☐ Yes ☐ No
4e How long with this employer *(years)* *(months)*	4f Occupation	5e How long with this employer *(years)* *(months)*	5f Occupation
4g Number of withholding allowances claimed on Form W-4	4h Pay Period: ☐ Weekly ☐ Bi-weekly ☐ Monthly ☐ Other	5g Number of withholding allowances claimed on Form W-4	5h Pay Period: ☐ Weekly ☐ Bi-weekly ☐ Monthly ☐ Other

Section 3: Other Financial Information *(Attach copies of applicable documentation)*

6 **Are you a party to a lawsuit** *(If yes, answer the following)* ☐ Yes ☐ No

☐ Plaintiff ☐ Defendant	Location of Filing	Represented by	Docket/Case No.
Amount of Suit $	Possible Completion Date *(mmddyyyy)*	Subject of Suit	

7 **Have you ever filed bankruptcy** *(If yes, answer the following)* ☐ Yes ☐ No

Date Filed *(mmddyyyy)*	Date Dismissed *(mmddyyyy)*	Date Discharged *(mmddyyyy)*	Petition No.	Location Filed

8 **In the past 10 years, have you lived outside of the U.S for 6 months or longer** *(If yes, answer the following)* ☐ Yes ☐ No

Dates lived abroad: from *(mmddyyyy)*	To *(mmddyyyy)*

9a **Are you the beneficiary of a trust, estate, or life insurance policy** *(If yes, answer the following)* ☐ Yes ☐ No

Place where recorded:		EIN:
Name of the trust, estate, or policy	Anticipated amount to be received $	When will the amount be received

9b **Are you a trustee, fiduciary, or contributor of a trust** ☐ Yes ☐ No

Name of the trust:	EIN:

10 **Do you have a safe deposit box (business or personal)** *(If yes, answer the following)* ☐ Yes ☐ No

Location *(Name, address and box number(s))*	Contents	Value $

11 **In the past 10 years, have you transferred any assets for less than their full value** *(If yes, answer the following)* ☐ Yes ☐ No

List Asset(s)	Value at Time of Transfer $	Date Transferred *(mmddyyyy)*	To Whom or Where was it Transferred

www.irs.gov Cat. No. 20312N Form **433-A** (Rev.12-2012)

Form 433-A (Rev. 12-2012) Page 2

Section 4: Personal Asset Information for All Individuals

12 **CASH ON HAND** Include cash that is not in a bank **Total Cash on Hand** $

PERSONAL BANK ACCOUNTS Include all checking, online and mobile *(e.g., PayPal)* accounts, money market accounts, savings accounts, and stored value cards *(e.g., payroll cards, government benefit cards, etc.)*.

	Type of Account	Full Name & Address *(Street, City, State, ZIP code)* of Bank, Savings & Loan, Credit Union, or Financial Institution	Account Number	**Account Balance** As of ______ *mmddyyyy*
13a				$
13b				$
13c				$

13d **Total Cash** *(Add lines 13a through 13c, and amounts from any attachments)* $

INVESTMENTS Include stocks, bonds, mutual funds, stock options, certificates of deposit, and retirement assets such as IRAs, Keogh, and 401(k) plans. Include all corporations, partnerships, limited liability companies, or other business entities in which you are an officer, director, owner, member, or otherwise have a financial interest.

	Type of Investment or Financial Interest	Full Name & Address *(Street, City, State, ZIP code)* of Company	Current Value	Loan Balance *(if applicable)* As of ______ *mmddyyyy*	**Equity** Value minus Loan
14a		Phone	$	$	$
14b		Phone	$	$	$
14c		Phone	$	$	$

14d **Total Equity** *(Add lines 14a through 14c and amounts from any attachments)* $

	AVAILABLE CREDIT Include all lines of credit and bank issued credit cards. Full Name & Address *(Street, City, State, ZIP code)* of Credit Institution	Credit Limit	Amount Owed As of ______ *mmddyyyy*	**Available Credit** As of ______ *mmddyyyy*
15a	Acct. No	$	$	$
15b	Acct. No	$	$	$

15c **Total Available Credit** *(Add lines 15a, 15b and amounts from any attachments)* $

16a **LIFE INSURANCE** Do you own or have any interest in any life insurance policies with cash value *(Term Life insurance does not have a cash value)*

☐ **Yes** ☐ **No** If yes, complete blocks 16b through 16f for each policy.

16b	Name and Address of Insurance Company(ies):			
16c	Policy Number(s)			
16d	Owner of Policy			
16e	Current Cash Value	$	$	$
16f	Outstanding Loan Balance	$	$	$

16g **Total Available Cash** *(Subtract amounts on line 16f from line 16e and include amounts from any attachments)* $

Form **433-A** (Rev. 12-2012)

Form 433-A (Rev. 12-2012) Page **3**

REAL PROPERTY Include all real property owned or being purchased

	Purchase Date *(mmddyyyy)*	Current Fair Market Value (FMV)	Current Loan Balance	Amount of Monthly Payment	Date of Final Payment *(mmddyyyy)*	**Equity** FMV Minus Loan
17a Property Description		$	$	$		$
Location *(Street, City, State, ZIP code)* and County	Lender/Contract Holder Name, Address *(Street, City, State, ZIP code)*, and Phone Phone					
17b Property Description		$	$	$		$
Location *(Street, City, State, ZIP code)* and County	Lender/Contract Holder Name, Address *(Street, City, State, ZIP code)*, and Phone Phone					

17c Total Equity *(Add lines 17a, 17b and amounts from any attachments)* $

PERSONAL VEHICLES LEASED AND PURCHASED Include boats, RVs, motorcycles, all-terrain and off-road vehicles, trailers, etc.

Description (Year, Mileage, Make/Model, Tag Number, Vehicle Identification Number)		Purchase/ Lease Date *(mmddyyyy)*	Current Fair Market Value (FMV)	Current Loan Balance	Amount of Monthly Payment	Date of Final Payment *(mmddyyyy)*	**Equity** FMV Minus Loan
18a Year	Make/Model		$	$	$		$
Mileage	License/Tag Number	Lender/Lessor Name, Address *(Street, City, State, ZIP code)*, and Phone Phone					
Vehicle Identification Number							
18b Year	Make/Model		$	$	$		$
Mileage	License/Tag Number	Lender/Lessor Name, Address *(Street, City, State, ZIP code)*, and Phone Phone					
Vehicle Identification Number							

18c Total Equity *(Add lines 18a, 18b and amounts from any attachments)* $

PERSONAL ASSETS Include all furniture, personal effects, artwork, jewelry, collections *(coins, guns, etc.)*, antiques or other assets. Include intangible assets such as licenses, domain names, patents, copyrights, mining claims, etc.

	Purchase/ Lease Date *(mmddyyyy)*	Current Fair Market Value (FMV)	Current Loan Balance	Amount of Monthly Payment	Date of Final Payment *(mmddyyyy)*	**Equity** FMV Minus Loan
19a Property Description		$	$	$		$
Location *(Street, City, State, ZIP code)* and County	Lender/Lessor Name, Address *(Street, City, State, ZIP code)*, and Phone Phone					
19b Property Description		$	$	$		$
Location *(Street, City, State, ZIP code)* and County	Lender/Lessor Name, Address *(Street, City, State, ZIP code)*, and Phone Phone					

19c Total Equity *(Add lines 19a, 19b and amounts from any attachments)* $

Form **433-A** (Rev. 12-2012)

Form 433-A (Rev. 12-2012) Page **4**

If you are self-employed, sections 6 and 7 must be completed before continuing.

Section 5: Monthly Income and Expenses

Monthly Income/Expense Statement *(For additional information, refer to Publication 1854.)*

Total Income		Total Living Expenses		IRS USE ONLY
Source	Gross Monthly	Expense Items [6]	Actual Monthly	Allowable Expenses
20 Wages (Taxpayer) [1]	$	35 Food, Clothing and Misc. [7]	$	
21 Wages (Spouse) [1]	$	36 Housing and Utilities [8]	$	
22 Interest - Dividends	$	37 Vehicle Ownership Costs [9]	$	
23 Net Business Income [2]	$	38 Vehicle Operating Costs [10]	$	
24 Net Rental Income [3]	$	39 Public Transportation [11]	$	
25 Distributions (K-1, IRA, etc.) [4]	$	40 Health Insurance	$	
26 Pension (Taxpayer)	$	41 Out of Pocket Health Care Costs [12]	$	
27 Pension (Spouse)	$	42 Court Ordered Payments	$	
28 Social Security (Taxpayer)	$	43 Child/Dependent Care	$	
29 Social Security (Spouse)	$	44 Life Insurance	$	
30 Child Support	$	45 Current year taxes (Income/FICA) [13]	$	
31 Alimony	$	46 Secured Debts (Attach list)	$	
Other Income (Specify below) [5]		47 Delinquent State or Local Taxes	$	
32	$	48 Other Expenses (Attach list)	$	
33	$	49 Total Living Expenses (add lines 35-48)	$	
34 Total Income (add lines 20-33)	$	50 Net difference (Line 34 minus 49)	$	

1 **Wages, salaries, pensions, and social security:** Enter gross monthly wages and/or salaries. Do not deduct tax withholding or allotments taken out of pay, such as insurance payments, credit union deductions, car payments, etc. To calculate the gross monthly wages and/or salaries:

If paid weekly - multiply weekly gross wages by 4.3. Example: $425.89 x 4.3 = $1,831.33

If paid biweekly (every 2 weeks) - multiply biweekly gross wages by 2.17. Example: $972.45 x 2.17 = $2,110.22

If paid semimonthly (twice each month) - multiply semimonthly gross wages by 2. Example: $856.23 x 2 = $1,712.46

2 **Net Income from Business:** Enter monthly net business income. This is the amount earned after ordinary and necessary monthly business expenses are paid. **This figure is the amount from page 6, line 89.** If the net business income is a loss, enter "0". Do not enter a negative number. If this amount is more or less than previous years, attach an explanation.

3 **Net Rental Income:** Enter monthly net rental income. This is the amount earned after ordinary and necessary monthly rental expenses are paid. Do not include deductions for depreciation or depletion. If the net rental income is a loss, enter "0." Do not enter a negative number.

4 **Distributions:** Enter the total distributions from partnerships and subchapter S corporations reported on Schedule K-1, and from limited liability companies reported on Form 1040, Schedule C, D or E. Enter total distributions from IRAs if not included under pension income.

5 **Other Income:** Include agricultural subsidies, unemployment compensation, gambling income, oil credits, rent subsidies, etc.

6 **Expenses not generally allowed:** We generally do not allow tuition for private schools, public or private college expenses, charitable contributions, voluntary retirement contributions or payments on unsecured debts. However, we may allow the expenses if proven that they are necessary for the health and welfare of the individual or family or the production of income. See Publication 1854 for exceptions.

7 **Food, Clothing and Miscellaneous:** Total of food, clothing, housekeeping supplies, and personal care products for one month. The miscellaneous allowance is for expenses incurred that are not included in any other allowable living expense items. Examples are credit card payments, bank fees and charges, reading material, and school supplies.

8 **Housing and Utilities:** For principal residence: Total of rent or mortgage payment. Add the average monthly expenses for the following: property taxes, homeowner's or renter's insurance, maintenance, dues, fees, and utilities. Utilities include gas, electricity, water, fuel, oil, other fuels, trash collection, telephone, cell phone, cable television and internet services.

9 **Vehicle Ownership Costs:** Total of monthly lease or purchase/loan payments.

10 **Vehicle Operating Costs:** Total of maintenance, repairs, insurance, fuel, registrations, licenses, inspections, parking, and tolls for one month.

11 **Public Transportation:** Total of monthly fares for mass transit *(e.g., bus, train, ferry, taxi, etc.)*

12 **Out of Pocket Health Care Costs:** Monthly total of medical services, prescription drugs and medical supplies *(e.g., eyeglasses, hearing aids, etc.)*

13 **Current Year Taxes:** Include state and Federal taxes withheld from salary or wages, or paid as estimated taxes.

Certification: *Under penalties of perjury, I declare that to the best of my knowledge and belief this statement of assets, liabilities, and other information is true, correct, and complete.*

Taxpayer's Signature	Spouse's signature	Date

After we review the completed Form 433-A, you may be asked to provide verification for the assets, encumbrances, income and expenses reported. Documentation may include previously filed income tax returns, pay statements, self-employment records, bank and investment statements, loan statements, bills or statements for recurring expenses, etc.

IRS USE ONLY *(Notes)*

Form **433-A** (Rev. 12-2012)

Sections 6 and 7 must be completed only if you are SELF-EMPLOYED.

Section 6: Business Information

51 Is the business a sole proprietorship *(filing Schedule C)* ☐ **Yes**, Continue with Sections 6 and 7. ☐ **No**, Complete Form 433-B.
All other business entities, including limited liability companies, partnerships or corporations, must complete Form 433-B.

52 Business Name & Address *(if different than 1b)*

53 Employer Identification Number	54 Type of Business	55 Is the business a Federal Contractor ☐ Yes ☐ No

56 Business Website (web address)	57 Total Number of Employees	58 Average Gross Monthly Payroll

59 Frequency of Tax Deposits	60 Does the business engage in e-Commerce *(Internet sales)* If yes, complete *lines 61a and 61b* ☐ Yes ☐ No

PAYMENT PROCESSOR *(e.g., PayPal, Authorize.net, Google Checkout, etc.)* Name & Address *(Street, City, State, ZIP code)*	Payment Processor Account Number
61a	
61b	

CREDIT CARDS ACCEPTED BY THE BUSINESS

Credit Card	Merchant Account Number	Issuing Bank Name & Address *(Street, City, State, ZIP code)*
62a		
62b		
62c		

63 **BUSINESS CASH ON HAND** Include cash that is not in a bank. **Total Cash on Hand** $

BUSINESS BANK ACCOUNTS Include checking accounts, online and mobile *(e.g., PayPal)* accounts, money market accounts, savings accounts, and stored value cards *(e.g., payroll cards, government benefit cards, etc.).* Report Personal Accounts in Section 4.

Type of Account	Full name & Address *(Street, City, State, ZIP code)* of Bank, Savings & Loan, Credit Union or Financial Institution.	Account Number	**Account Balance** As of ______ *mmddyyyy*
64a			$
64b			$
64c **Total Cash in Banks** *(Add lines 64a, 64b and amounts from any attachments)*			$

ACCOUNTS/NOTES RECEIVABLE Include e-payment accounts receivable and factoring companies, and any bartering or online auction accounts. *(List all contracts separately, including contracts awarded, but not started.)* **Include Federal, state and local government grants and contracts.**

Accounts/Notes Receivable & Address *(Street, City, State, ZIP code)*	Status *(e.g., age, factored, other)*	Date Due *(mmddyyyy)*	Invoice Number or Government Grant or Contract Number	**Amount Due**
65a				$
65b				$
65c				$
65d				$
65e				$
65f **Total Outstanding Balance** *(Add lines 65a through 65e and amounts from any attachments)*				$

Form 433-A (Rev. 12-2012) Page **6**

BUSINESS ASSETS Include all tools, books, machinery, equipment, inventory or other assets used in trade or business. Include a list and show the value of all intangible assets such as licenses, patents, domain names, copyrights, trademarks, mining claims, etc.

	Purchase/ Lease Date *(mmddyyyy)*	Current Fair Market Value (FMV)	Current Loan Balance	Amount of Monthly Payment	Date of Final Payment *(mmddyyyy)*	**Equity** FMV Minus Loan
66a Property Description		$	$	$		$
Location *(Street, City, State, ZIP code)* and Country		Lender/Lessor/Landlord Name, Address *(Street, City, State, ZIP code)*, and Phone Phone				
66b Property Description		$	$	$		$
Location *(Street, City, State, ZIP code)* and Country		Lender/Lessor/Landlord Name, Address *(Street, City, State, ZIP code)*, and Phone Phone				
66c Total Equity *(Add lines 66a, 66b and amounts from any attachments)*						$

Section 7 should be completed only if you are SELF-EMPLOYED

Section 7: Sole Proprietorship Information *(lines 67 through 87 should reconcile with business Profit and Loss Statement)*

Accounting Method Used: ☐ Cash ☐ Accrual

Use the prior 3, 6, 9 or 12 month period to determine your typical business income and expenses.

Income and Expenses during the period *(mmddyyyy)* *to (mmddyyyy)*

Provide a breakdown below of your average monthly income and expenses, based on the period of time used above.

Total Monthly Business Income		**Total Monthly Business Expenses** (Use attachments as needed)	
Source	Gross Monthly	Expense Items	Actual Monthly
67 Gross Receipts	$	77 Materials Purchased [1]	$
68 Gross Rental Income	$	78 Inventory Purchased [2]	$
69 Interest	$	79 Gross Wages & Salaries	$
70 Dividends	$	80 Rent	$
71 Cash Receipts not included in lines 67-70	$	81 Supplies [3]	$
Other Income (Specify below)		82 Utilities/Telephone [4]	$
72	$	83 Vehicle Gasoline/Oil	$
73	$	84 Repairs & Maintenance	$
74	$	85 Insurance	$
75	$	86 Current Taxes [5]	$
76 **Total Income** (Add lines 67 through 75)	$	87 Other Expenses, including installment payments (Specify)	$
		88 **Total Expenses (Add lines 77 through 87)**	$
		89 **Net Business Income (Line 76 minus 88)** [6]	$

Enter the monthly net income amount from line 89 on line 23, section 5. If line 89 is a loss, enter "0" on line 23, section 5. Self-employed taxpayers must return to page 4 to sign the certification.

1 **Materials Purchased:** Materials are items directly related to the production of a product or service.

2 **Inventory Purchased:** Goods bought for resale.

3 **Supplies:** Supplies are items used in the business that are consumed or used up within one year. This could be the cost of books, office supplies, professional equipment, etc.

4 **Utilities/Telephone:** Utilities include gas, electricity, water, oil, other fuels, trash collection, telephone, cell phone and business internet.

5 **Current Taxes:** Real estate, excise, franchise, occupational, personal property, sales and employer's portion of employment taxes.

6 **Net Business Income:** Net profit from Form 1040, Schedule C may be used if duplicated deductions are eliminated (e.g., expenses for business use of home already included in housing and utility expenses on page 4). Deductions for depreciation and depletion on Schedule C are not cash expenses and must be added back to the net income figure. In addition, interest cannot be deducted if it is already included in any other installment payments allowed.

IRS USE ONLY *(Notes)*

Collection Information Statement (form for businesses 433-B)[xi]

Form **433-B**
(Rev. December 2012)
Department of the Treasury
Internal Revenue Service

Collection Information Statement for Businesses

Note: *Complete all entry spaces with the current data available or "N/A" (not applicable). Failure to complete all entry spaces may result in rejection of your request or significant delay in account resolution.* **Include attachments if additional space is needed to respond completely to any question.**

Section 1: Business Information

1a Business Name
1b Business Street Address
Mailing Address
City State ZIP
1c County
1d Business Telephone ( )
1e Type of Business
1f Business Website (web address)

2a Employer Identification No. (EIN)
2b Type of entity *(Check appropriate box below)*
☐ Partnership ☐ Corporation ☐ Other
☐ Limited Liability Company (LLC) classified as a corporation
☐ Other LLC - Include number of members
2c Date Incorporated/Established *mmddyyyy*

3a Number of Employees
3b Monthly Gross Payroll
3c Frequency of Tax Deposits
3d Is the business enrolled in Electronic Federal Tax Payment System (EFTPS) ☐ **Yes** ☐ **No**

4 Does the business engage in e-Commerce *(Internet sales)* If yes, complete 5a and 5b. ☐ **Yes** ☐ **No**

PAYMENT PROCESSOR *(e.g., PayPal, Authorize.net, Google Checkout, etc.)* Name and Address *(Street, City, State, ZIP code)*	Payment Processor Account Number
5a	
5b	

CREDIT CARDS ACCEPTED BY THE BUSINESS

Type of Credit Card *(e.g., Visa, Mastercard, etc.)*	Merchant Account Number	Issuing Bank Name and Address *(Street, City, State, ZIP code)*
6a		Phone
6b		Phone
6c		Phone

Section 2: Business Personnel and Contacts

PARTNERS, OFFICERS, LLC MEMBERS, MAJOR SHAREHOLDERS, ETC.

7a Full Name
Title
Home Address
City State ZIP
Responsible for Depositing Payroll Taxes ☐ **Yes** ☐ **No**
Social Security Number
Home Telephone ( )
Work/Cell Phone ( )
Ownership Percentage & Shares or Interest
Annual Salary/Draw

7b Full Name
Title
Home Address
City State ZIP
Responsible for Depositing Payroll Taxes ☐ **Yes** ☐ **No**
Social Security Number
Home Telephone ( )
Work/Cell Phone ( )
Ownership Percentage & Shares or Interest
Annual Salary/Draw

7c Full Name
Title
Home Address
City State ZIP
Responsible for Depositing Payroll Taxes ☐ **Yes** ☐ **No**
Social Security Number
Home Telephone ( )
Work/Cell Phone ( )
Ownership Percentage & Shares or Interest
Annual Salary/Draw

7d Full Name
Title
Home Address
City State ZIP
Responsible for Depositing Payroll Taxes ☐ **Yes** ☐ **No**
Social Security Number
Home Telephone ( )
Work/Cell Phone ( )
Ownership Percentage & Shares or Interest
Annual Salary/Draw

www.irs.gov Cat. No. 16649P Form **433-B** (Rev. 12-2012)

Form 433-B (Rev. 12-2012) Page 2

Section 3: Other Financial Information *(Attach copies of all applicable documents)*

8 **Does the business use a Payroll Service Provider or Reporting Agent** *(If yes, answer the following)* ☐ Yes ☐ No

Name and Address *(Street, City, State, ZIP code)*	Effective dates *(mmddyyyy)*

9 **Is the business a party to a lawsuit** *(If yes, answer the following)* ☐ Yes ☐ No

☐ Plaintiff ☐ Defendant	Location of Filing	Represented by	Docket/Case No.
Amount of Suit $	Possible Completion Date *(mmddyyyy)*	Subject of Suit	

10 **Has the business ever filed bankruptcy** *(If yes, answer the following)* ☐ Yes ☐ No

Date Filed *(mmddyyyy)*	Date Dismissed *(mmddyyyy)*	Date Discharged *(mmddyyyy)*	Petition No.	District of Filing

11 **Do any related parties** *(e.g., officers, partners, employees)* **have outstanding amounts owed to the business** *(If yes, answer the following)* ☐ Yes ☐ No

Name and Address *(Street, City, State, ZIP code)*	Date of Loan	Current Balance As of ______ *mmddyyyy*	Payment Date	Payment Amount
		$		$

12 **Have any assets been transferred, in the last 10 years, from this business for less than full value** *(If yes, answer the following)* ☐ Yes ☐ No

List Asset	Value at Time of Transfer	Date Transferred *(mmddyyyy)*	To Whom or Where Transferred
	$		

13 **Does this business have other business affiliations** ***(e.g., subsidiary or parent companies)*** *(If yes, answer the following)* ☐ Yes ☐ No

Related Business Name and Address *(Street, City, State, ZIP code)*	Related Business EIN:

14 **Any increase/decrease in income anticipated** *(If yes, answer the following)* ☐ Yes ☐ No

Explain *(Use attachment if needed)*	How much will it increase/decrease	When will it increase/decrease
	$	

15 **Is the business a Federal Government Contractor** *(Include Federal Government contracts in #18, Accounts/Notes Receivable)* ☐ Yes ☐ No

Section 4: Business Asset and Liability Information

16a **CASH ON HAND** *Include cash that is not in the bank* **Total Cash on Hand** $

16b **Is there a safe on the business premises** ☐ Yes ☐ No Contents

BUSINESS BANK ACOUNTS Include online and mobile accounts *(e.g., PayPal)*, money market accounts, savings accounts, checking accounts and stored value cards *(e.g., payroll cards, government benefit cards, etc.)*
List safe deposit boxes including location, box number and value of contents. Attach list of contents.

	Type of Account	Full Name and Address *(Street, City, State, ZIP code)* of Bank, Savings & Loan, Credit Union or Financial Institution	Account Number	Account Balance As of ______ *mmddyyyy*
17a				$
17b				$
17c				$

17d **Total Cash in Banks** *(Add lines 17a through 17c and amounts from any attachments)* $

Form **433-B** (Rev. 12-2012)

Form 433-B (Rev. 12-2012) Page **3**

ACCOUNTS/NOTES RECEIVABLE Include e-payment accounts receivable and factoring companies, and any bartering or online auction accounts. *(List all contracts separately including contracts awarded, but not started).* ***Include Federal, state and local government grants and contracts.***

Name & Address *(Street, City, State, ZIP code)*	Status *(e.g., age, factored, other)*	Date Due *(mmddyyy)*	Invoice Number or Government Grant or Contract Number	**Amount Due**
18a Contact Name Phone				$
18b Contact Name Phone				$
18c Contact Name Phone				$
18d Contact Name Phone				$
18e Contact Name Phone				$
18f Outstanding Balance *(Add lines 18a through 18e and amounts from any attachments)*				$

INVESTMENTS List all investment assets below. Include stocks, bonds, mutual funds, stock options, certificates of deposit and commodities *(e.g., gold, silver, copper, etc.).*

Name of Company & Address *(Street, City, State, ZIP code)*	Used as collateral on loan	Current Value	Loan Balance	**Equity** Value Minus Loan
19a Phone	☐ **Yes** ☐ **No**	$	$	$
19b Phone	☐ **Yes** ☐ **No**	$	$	$
19c Total Investments *(Add lines 19a, 19b, and amounts from any attachments)*				$

AVAILABLE CREDIT Include all lines of credit and credit cards.

Full Name & Address *(Street, City, State, ZIP code)*	Credit Limit	Amount Owed As of ________ *mmddyyyy*	**Available Credit** As of ________ *mmddyyyy*
20a Account No.	$	$	$
20b Account No.	$	$	$
20c Total Credit Available *(Add lines 20a, 20b, and amounts from any attachments)*			$

Form **433-B** (Rev. 12-2012)

Form 433-B (Rev. 12-2012) Page **4**

REAL PROPERTY Include all real property and land contracts the business owns/leases/rents.

	Purchase/ Lease Date *(mmddyyyy)*	Current Fair Market Value (FMV)	Current Loan Balance	Amount of Monthly Payment	Date of Final Payment *(mmddyyyy)*	**Equity** FMV Minus Loan
21a Property Description		$	$	$		$
Location *(Street, City, State, ZIP code)* and County	Lender/Lessor/Landlord Name, Address, *(Street, City, State, ZIP code)* and Phone Phone					
21b Property Description		$	$	$		$
Location *(Street, City, State, ZIP code)* and County	Lender/Lessor/Landlord Name, Address, *(Street, City, State, ZIP code)* and Phone Phone					
21c Property Description		$	$	$		$
Location *(Street, City, State, ZIP code)* and County	Lender/Lessor/Landlord Name, Address, *(Street, City, State, ZIP code)* and Phone Phone					
21d Property Description		$	$	$		$
Location *(Street, City, State, ZIP code)* and County	Lender/Lessor/Landlord Name, Address, *(Street, City, State, ZIP code)* and Phone Phone					
21e Total Equity *(Add lines 21a through 21d and amounts from any attachments)*						$

VEHICLES, LEASED AND PURCHASED Include boats, RVs, motorcycles, all-terrain and off-road vehicles, trailers, mobile homes, etc.

		Purchase/ Lease Date *(mmddyyyy)*	Current Fair Market Value (FMV)	Current Loan Balance	Amount of Monthly Payment	Date of Final Payment *(mmddyyyy)*	**Equity** FMV Minus Loan
22a Year	Make/Model		$	$	$		$
Mileage	License/Tag Number	Lender/Lessor Name, Address, *(Street, City, State, ZIP code)* and Phone Phone					
Vehicle Identification Number (VIN)							
22b Year	Make/Model		$	$	$		$
Mileage	License/Tag Number	Lender/Lessor Name, Address, *(Street, City, State, ZIP code)* and Phone Phone					
Vehicle Identification Number (VIN)							
22c Year	Make/Model		$	$	$		$
Mileage	License/Tag Number	Lender/Lessor Name, Address, *(Street, City, State, ZIP code)* and Phone Phone					
Vehicle Identification Number (VIN)							
22d Year	Make/Model		$	$	$		$
Mileage	License/Tag Number	Lender/Lessor Name, Address, *(Street, City, State, ZIP code)* and Phone Phone					
Vehicle Identification Number (VIN)							
22e Total Equity *(Add lines 22a through 22d and amounts from any attachments)*							$

Form **433-B** (Rev. 12-2012)

Form 433-B (Rev. 12-2012) Page 5

BUSINESS EQUIPMENT AND INTANGIBLE ASSETS Include all machinery, equipment, merchandise inventory, and other assets in 23a through 23d. List intangible assets in 23e through 23g *(licenses, patents, logos, domain names, trademarks, copyrights, software, mining claims, goodwill and trade secrets.)*

	Purchase/ Lease Date *(mmddyyyy)*	Current Fair Market Value (FMV)	Current Loan Balance	Amount of Monthly Payment	Date of Final Payment *(mmddyyyy)*	**Equity** FMV Minus Loan
23a Asset Description		$	$	$		$
Location of asset *(Street, City, State, ZIP code)* and County	Lender/Lessor Name, Address, *(Street, City, State, ZIP code)* and Phone Phone					
23b Asset Description		$	$	$		$
Location of asset *(Street, City, State, ZIP code)* and County	Lender/Lessor Name, Address, *(Street, City, State, ZIP code)* and Phone Phone					
23c Asset Description		$	$	$		$
Location of asset *(Street, City, State, ZIP code)* and County	Lender/Lessor Name, Address, *(Street, City, State, ZIP code)* and Phone Phone					
23d Asset Description		$	$	$		$
Location of asset *(Street, City, State, ZIP code)* and County	Lender/Lessor Name, Address, *(Street, City, State, ZIP code)* and Phone Phone					
23e Intangible Asset Description						$
23f Intangible Asset Description						$
23g Intangible Asset Description						$
23h Total Equity *(Add lines 23a through 23g and amounts from any attachments)*						$

BUSINESS LIABILITIES Include notes and judgements not listed previously on this form.

Business Liabilities	Secured/ Unsecured	Date Pledged *(mmddyyyy)*	Balance Owed	Date of Final Payment *(mmddyyyy)*	Payment Amount
24a Description:	☐ Secured ☐ Unsecured		$		$
Name Street Address City/State/ZIP code Phone					
24b Description:	☐ Secured ☐ Unsecured		$		$
Name Street Address City/State/ZIP code Phone					
24c Total Payments *(Add lines 24a and 24b and amounts from any attachments)*					$

Form **433-B** (Rev. 12-2012)

Form 433-B (Rev. 12-2012) Page **6**

Section 5: Monthly Income/Expenses Statement for Business

Accounting Method Used: ☐ Cash ☐ Accrual

Use the prior 3, 6, 9 or 12 month period to determine your typical business income and expenses.

Income and Expenses during the period *(mmddyyyy)* *to (mmddyyyy)*

Provide a breakdown below of your average monthly income and expenses, based on the period of time used above.

Total Monthly Business Income		Total Monthly Business Expenses	
Income Source	Gross Monthly	Expense items	Actual Monthly
25 Gross Receipts from Sales/Services	$	36 Materials Purchased [1]	$
26 Gross Rental Income	$	37 Inventory Purchased [2]	$
27 Interest Income	$	38 Gross Wages & Salaries	$
28 Dividends	$	39 Rent	$
29 Cash Receipts (Not included in lines 25-28)	$	40 Supplies [3]	$
Other Income (Specify below)		41 Utilities/Telephone [4]	$
30	$	42 Vehicle Gasoline/Oil	$
31	$	43 Repairs & Maintenance	$
32	$	44 Insurance	$
33	$	45 Current Taxes [5]	$
34	$	46 Other Expenses (Specify)	$
35 **Total Income** (Add lines 25 through 34)	$	47 IRS Use Only-Allowable Installment Payments	$
		48 **Total Expenses** (Add lines 36 through 47)	$
		49 **Net Income** (Line 35 minus Line 48)	$

1 **Materials Purchased:** Materials are items directly related to the production of a product or service.

2 **Inventory Purchased:** Goods bought for resale.

3 **Supplies:** Supplies are items used to conduct business and are consumed or used up within one year. This could be the cost of books, office supplies, professional equipment, etc.

4 **Utilities/Telephone:** Utilities include gas, electricity, water, oil, other fuels, trash collection, telephone, cell phone and business internet.

5 **Current Taxes:** Real estate, state, and local income tax, excise, franchise, occupational, personal property, sales and the employer's portion of employment taxes.

Certification: *Under penalties of perjury, I declare that to the best of my knowledge and belief this statement of assets, liabilities, and other information is true, correct, and complete.*

Signature	Title	Date

Print Name of Officer, Partner or LLC Member

After we review the completed Form 433-B, you may be asked to provide verification for the assets, encumbrances, income and expenses reported. Documentation may include previously filed income tax returns, profit and loss statements, bank and investment statements, loan statements, financing statements, bills or statements for recurring expenses, etc.

IRS USE ONLY *(Notes)*

Collection Information Statement (short form 433-F)[xii]

Collection Information Statement

Name(s) and Address	Your Social Security Number or Individual Taxpayer Identification Number	
	Your Spouse's Social Security Number or Individual Taxpayer Identification Number	
☐ If address provided above is different than last return filed, please check here	Your Telephone Numbers Home: ______ Work: ______ Cell: ______	Spouse's Telephone Numbers Home: ______ Work: ______ Cell: ______
County of Residence		

Enter the number of people in the household who can be claimed on this year's tax return including you and your spouse. Under 65 ____ 65 and Over ____

If you or your spouse are self employed or have self employment income, provide the following information:

Name of Business	Business EIN	Type of Business	Number of Employees *(not counting owner)*

A. ACCOUNTS / LINES OF CREDIT Include checking, online, mobile (e.g., PayPal) and savings accounts, Certificates of Deposit, Trusts, Individual Retirement Accounts (IRAs), Keogh Plans, Simplified Employee Pensions, 401(k) Plans, Profit Sharing Plans, Mutual Funds, Stocks, Bonds and other investments. If applicable, include business accounts. *(Use additional sheets if necessary.)*

Name and Address of Institution	Account Number	Type of Account	Current Balance/Value	Check if Business Account
				☐
				☐
				☐
				☐
				☐
				☐
				☐

B. REAL ESTATE Include home, vacation property, timeshares, vacant land and other real estate. *(Use additional sheets if necessary.)*

Description/Location/County	Monthly Payment(s)	Financing		Current Value	Balance Owed	Equity
		Year Purchased	Purchase Price			
☐ Primary Residence ☐ Other		Year Refinanced	Refinance Amount			
		Year Purchased	Purchase Price			
☐ Primary Residence ☐ Other		Year Refinanced	Refinance Amount			

C. OTHER ASSETS Include cars, boats, recreational vehicles, whole life policies, etc. Include make, model and year of vehicles and name of Life Insurance company in Description. If applicable, include business assets such as tools, equipment, inventory, etc. *(Use additional sheets if necessary.)*

Description	Monthly Payment	Year Purchased	Final Payment *(mo/yr)*	Current Value	Balance Owed	Equity
			/			
			/			
			/			
			/			
			/			
			/			
			/			

NOTES *(For IRS Use Only)*

TURN PAGE TO CONTINUE

D. CREDIT CARDS *(Visa, MasterCard, American Express, Department Stores, etc.)*

Type	Credit Limit	Balance Owed	Minimum Monthly Payment

E. BUSINESS INFORMATION Complete E1 for Accounts Receivable owed to you or your business. *(Use additional sheets if necessary.)* Complete E2 if you or your business accepts credit card payments.

E1. Accounts Receivable owed to you or your business

Name	Address	Amount Owed
	List total amount owed from additional sheets	
	Total amount of accounts receivable available to pay to IRS now	

E2. Name of individual or business on account

Credit Card *(Visa, Master Card, etc.)*	Issuing Bank Name and Address	Merchant Account Number

F. EMPLOYMENT INFORMATION If you have more than one employer, include the information on another sheet of paper. *(If attaching a copy of current pay stub, you do not need to complete this section.)*

Your current Employer *(name and address)*	Spouse's current Employer *(name and address)*
How often are you paid? *(Check one)* ☐ Weekly ☐ Biweekly ☐ Semi-monthly ☐ Monthly	How often are you paid? *(Check one)* ☐ Weekly ☐ Biweekly ☐ Semi-monthly ☐ Monthly
Gross per pay period ____	Gross per pay period ____
Taxes per pay period *(Fed)* ____ *(State)* ____ *(Local)* ____	Taxes per pay period *(Fed)* ____ *(State)* ____ *(Local)* ____
How long at current employer ____	How long at current employer ____

G. NON-WAGE HOUSEHOLD INCOME List monthly amounts. For Self-Employment and Rental Income, list the monthly amount received after expenses or taxes and attach a copy of your current year profit and loss statement.

Alimony Income		Net Rental Income		Interest/Dividends Income	
Child Support Income		Unemployment Income		Social Security Income	
Net Self Employment Income		Pension Income		Other:	

H. MONTHLY NECESSARY LIVING EXPENSES List monthly amounts. (For expenses paid other than monthly, see instructions.)

1. Food / Personal Care ***See instructions. If you do not spend more than the standard allowable amount for your family size, fill in the Total amount only.***

Food	
Housekeeping Supplies	
Clothing and Clothing Services	
Personal Care Products & Services	
Miscellaneous	
Total	

2. Transportation

Gas/Insurance/Licenses/Parking/ Maintenance etc.	
Public Transportation	

3. Housing & Utilities

Rent	
Electric, Oil/Gas, Water/Trash	
Telephone/Cell/Cable/Internet	
Real Estate Taxes and Insurance *(if not included in B above)*	
Maintenance and Repairs	
Total	

4. Medical

Health Insurance	
Out of Pocket Health Care Expenses	

5. Other

Child / Dependent Care	
Estimated Tax Payments	
Term Life Insurance	
Retirement *(Employer Required)*	
Retirement *(Voluntary)*	
Union Dues	
Delinquent State & Local Taxes *(minimum payment)*	
Student Loans *(minimum payment)*	
Court Ordered Child Support	
Court Ordered Alimony	
Other Court Ordered Payments	
Other *(specify)*	
Other *(specify)*	
Other *(specify)*	

Under penalty of perjury, I declare to the best of my knowledge and belief this statement of assets, liabilities and other information is true, correct and complete.

Your Signature	Spouse's Signature	Date

IRS National and Local Standards

Allowable Living Expense Housing and Utilities Standards – effective 03/28/2016

Please note that the standards change. For updated IRS standards visit http://www.taxresolutioninstitute.org/forms-library/

Housing and Utilities – Local Standard

State Name	County	Housing and Utilities for a Family of 1	Housing and Utilities for a Family of 2	Housing and Utilities for a Family of 3	Housing and Utilities for a Family of 4	Housing and Utilities for a Family of 5 or more
Alabama	Autauga County	1,184	1,390	1,465	1,633	1,660
Alabama	Baldwin County	1,324	1,555	1,639	1,827	1,857
Alabama	Barbour County	978	1,148	1,210	1,349	1,371
Alabama	Bibb County	1,054	1,237	1,304	1,454	1,477
Alabama	Blount County	1,102	1,294	1,364	1,521	1,545
Alabama	Bullock County	1,091	1,281	1,350	1,505	1,530
Alabama	Butler County	998	1,172	1,235	1,377	1,399
Alabama	Calhoun County	1,079	1,267	1,335	1,489	1,513
Alabama	Chambers County	949	1,114	1,174	1,309	1,330
Alabama	Cherokee County	1,108	1,301	1,371	1,529	1,553
Alabama	Chilton County	1,065	1,251	1,318	1,470	1,493
Alabama	Choctaw County	961	1,128	1,189	1,326	1,347
Alabama	Clarke County	1,037	1,218	1,283	1,431	1,454
Alabama	Clay County	1,028	1,207	1,272	1,418	1,441
Alabama	Cleburne County	1,025	1,204	1,269	1,415	1,438
Alabama	Coffee County	1,201	1,411	1,487	1,658	1,685
Alabama	Colbert County	1,074	1,261	1,329	1,482	1,506
Alabama	Conecuh County	888	1,043	1,099	1,225	1,245
Alabama	Coosa County	966	1,134	1,195	1,332	1,354
Alabama	Covington	1,000	1,175	1,238	1,380	1,403
Alabama	Crenshaw County	996	1,170	1,233	1,375	1,397
Alabama	Cullman County	1,046	1,228	1,294	1,443	1,466
Alabama	Dale County	1,033	1,213	1,278	1,425	1,448
Alabama	Dallas County	1,053	1,237	1,303	1,453	1,476
Alabama	DeKalb County	1,011	1,187	1,251	1,395	1,417
Alabama	Elmore County	1,189	1,396	1,471	1,640	1,667
Alabama	Escambia County	993	1,166	1,229	1,370	1,392
Alabama	Etowah County	1,110	1,304	1,374	1,532	1,557
Alabama	Fayette County	979	1,150	1,212	1,351	1,373
Alabama	Franklin County	989	1,162	1,224	1,365	1,387
Alabama	Geneva County	952	1,118	1,178	1,313	1,335
Alabama	Greene County	968	1,137	1,198	1,336	1,357
Alabama	Hale County	1,041	1,222	1,288	1,436	1,459
Alabama	Henry County	1,047	1,230	1,296	1,445	1,468
Alabama	Houston County	1,087	1,276	1,345	1,500	1,524
Alabama	Jackson County	996	1,170	1,233	1,375	1,397
Alabama	Jefferson County	1,272	1,494	1,574	1,755	1,783
Alabama	Lamar County	925	1,087	1,145	1,277	1,297
Alabama	Lauderdale County	1,055	1,239	1,306	1,456	1,480
Alabama	Lawrence County	1,050	1,233	1,299	1,448	1,472
Alabama	Lee County	1,216	1,428	1,505	1,678	1,705
Alabama	Limestone County	1,166	1,369	1,443	1,609	1,635
Alabama	Lowndes County	982	1,153	1,215	1,355	1,377
Alabama	Macon County	1,025	1,203	1,268	1,414	1,437

State Name	County	Housing and Utilities for a Family of 1	Housing and Utilities for a Family of 2	Housing and Utilities for a Family of 3	Housing and Utilities for a Family of 4	Housing and Utilities for a Family of 5 or more
Alabama	Madison County	1,231	1,445	1,523	1,698	1,726
Alabama	Marengo County	1,064	1,250	1,317	1,468	1,492
Alabama	Marion County	931	1,093	1,152	1,284	1,305
Alabama	Marshall County	1,065	1,251	1,318	1,470	1,493
Alabama	Mobile County	1,198	1,407	1,483	1,654	1,680
Alabama	Monroe County	952	1,118	1,178	1,313	1,335
Alabama	Montgomery County	1,157	1,359	1,432	1,597	1,622
Alabama	Morgan County	1,092	1,282	1,351	1,506	1,531
Alabama	Perry County	1,075	1,262	1,330	1,483	1,507
Alabama	Pickens County	1,003	1,178	1,241	1,384	1,406
Alabama	Pike County	1,076	1,264	1,332	1,485	1,509
Alabama	Randolph County	938	1,102	1,161	1,295	1,315
Alabama	Russell County	1,098	1,290	1,359	1,515	1,540
Alabama	Shelby County	1,422	1,670	1,760	1,962	1,994
Alabama	St. Clair County	1,179	1,385	1,459	1,627	1,653
Alabama	Sumter County	975	1,145	1,207	1,346	1,368
Alabama	Talladega County	1,042	1,224	1,290	1,438	1,462
Alabama	Tallapoosa County	1,063	1,249	1,316	1,467	1,491
Alabama	Tuscaloosa County	1,231	1,446	1,524	1,699	1,727
Alabama	Walker County	1,012	1,188	1,252	1,396	1,419
Alabama	Washington	1,035	1,216	1,281	1,428	1,451
Alabama	Wilcox County	1,003	1,178	1,241	1,384	1,406
Alabama	Winston County	961	1,128	1,189	1,326	1,347
Alaska	Aleutians East Borough	1,050	1,234	1,300	1,450	1,473
Alaska	Aleutians West Census Area	1,791	2,103	2,216	2,471	2,511
Alaska	Anchorage Municipality	1,866	2,191	2,309	2,575	2,616
Alaska	Bethel Census Area	1,479	1,737	1,830	2,040	2,073
Alaska	Bristol Bay Borough	1,690	1,984	2,091	2,331	2,369
Alaska	Denali Borough	1,425	1,674	1,764	1,967	1,999
Alaska	Dillingham Census Area	1,532	1,799	1,896	2,114	2,148
Alaska	Fairbanks North Star Borough	1,788	2,100	2,213	2,467	2,507
Alaska	Haines Borough	1,411	1,657	1,746	1,947	1,978
Alaska	Hoonah-Angoon Census Area	1,492	1,752	1,846	2,058	2,092
Alaska	Juneau City and Borough	1,975	2,319	2,444	2,725	2,769
Alaska	Kenai Peninsula Borough	1,440	1,691	1,782	1,987	2,019
Alaska	Ketchikan Gateway Borough	1,721	2,021	2,130	2,375	2,413
Alaska	Kodiak Island Borough	1,932	2,269	2,391	2,666	2,709
Alaska	Lake and	1,527	1,794	1,890	2,107	2,141
	Peninsula Borough					
Alaska	Matanuska- Susitna Borough	1,613	1,894	1,996	2,226	2,261
Alaska	Nome Census Area	1,401	1,646	1,734	1,933	1,965
Alaska	North Slope Borough	1,130	1,327	1,398	1,559	1,584
Alaska	Northwest Arctic Borough	1,381	1,622	1,709	1,906	1,936
Alaska	Petersburg Census Area	1,425	1,673	1,763	1,966	1,997

State Name	County	Housing and Utilities for a Family of 1	Housing and Utilities for a Family of 2	Housing and Utilities for a Family of 3	Housing and Utilities for a Family of 4	Housing and Utilities for a Family of 5 or more
Alaska	Prince of Wales- Hyder Census Area	1,315	1,544	1,627	1,814	1,843
Alaska	Sitka City and Borough	1,789	2,101	2,214	2,469	2,508
Alaska	Skagway Municipality	1,944	2,283	2,406	2,683	2,726
Alaska	Southeast Fairbanks Census Area	1,392	1,635	1,723	1,921	1,952
Alaska	Valdez-Cordova Census Area	1,627	1,910	2,013	2,244	2,281
Alaska	Wade Hampton Census Area	736	865	911	1,016	1,032
Alaska	Wrangell City and Borough	1,403	1,647	1,736	1,936	1,967
Alaska	Yakutat City and Borough	1,266	1,487	1,567	1,747	1,775
Alaska	Yukon-Koyukuk Census Area	1,140	1,339	1,411	1,573	1,599
Arizona	Apache County	971	1,141	1,202	1,340	1,362
Arizona	Cochise County	1,214	1,426	1,503	1,676	1,703
Arizona	Coconino County	1,467	1,723	1,816	2,025	2,058
Arizona	Gila County	1,161	1,364	1,437	1,602	1,628
Arizona	Graham County	1,125	1,321	1,392	1,552	1,577
Arizona	Greenlee County	890	1,046	1,102	1,229	1,249
Arizona	La Paz County	1,079	1,267	1,335	1,489	1,513
Arizona	Maricopa County	1,424	1,672	1,762	1,965	1,996
Arizona	Mohave County	1,128	1,325	1,396	1,557	1,582
Arizona	Navajo County	1,136	1,334	1,406	1,568	1,593
Arizona	Pima County	1,336	1,570	1,654	1,844	1,874
Arizona	Pinal County	1,286	1,511	1,592	1,775	1,804
Arizona	Santa Cruz County	1,149	1,349	1,422	1,586	1,611
Arizona	Yavapai County	1,283	1,507	1,588	1,771	1,799
Arizona	Yuma County	1,176	1,381	1,455	1,622	1,649
Arkansas	Arkansas County	942	1,107	1,166	1,300	1,321
Arkansas	Ashley County	924	1,086	1,144	1,276	1,296
Arkansas	Baxter County	990	1,163	1,225	1,366	1,388
Arkansas	Benton County	1,202	1,412	1,488	1,659	1,686
Arkansas	Boone County	952	1,118	1,178	1,313	1,335
Arkansas	Bradley County	922	1,083	1,141	1,272	1,293
Arkansas	Calhoun County	966	1,134	1,195	1,332	1,354
Arkansas	Carroll County	995	1,168	1,231	1,373	1,395
Arkansas	Chicot County	964	1,132	1,193	1,330	1,352
Arkansas	Clark County	991	1,164	1,227	1,368	1,390
Arkansas	Clay County	835	980	1,033	1,152	1,170
Arkansas	Cleburne County	972	1,142	1,203	1,341	1,363
Arkansas	Cleveland County	988	1,161	1,223	1,364	1,386
Arkansas	Columbia County	982	1,153	1,215	1,355	1,377
Arkansas	Conway County	945	1,110	1,170	1,305	1,326
Arkansas	Craighead County	1,058	1,242	1,309	1,460	1,483
Arkansas	Crawford County	1,007	1,182	1,246	1,389	1,412
Arkansas	Crittenden County	1,083	1,272	1,340	1,494	1,518
Arkansas	Cross County	1,000	1,175	1,238	1,380	1,403
Arkansas	Dallas County	916	1,076	1,134	1,264	1,285
Arkansas	Desha County	963	1,131	1,192	1,329	1,351

State Name	County	Housing and Utilities for a Family of 1	Housing and Utilities for a Family of 2	Housing and Utilities for a Family of 3	Housing and Utilities for a Family of 4	Housing and Utilities for a Family of 5 or more
Arkansas	Drew County	987	1,160	1,222	1,363	1,385
Arkansas	Faulkner County	1,153	1,354	1,427	1,591	1,617
Arkansas	Franklin County	936	1,100	1,159	1,292	1,313
Arkansas	Fulton County	928	1,090	1,149	1,281	1,302
Arkansas	Garland County	1,054	1,238	1,305	1,455	1,479
Arkansas	Grant County	1,042	1,224	1,290	1,438	1,462
Arkansas	Greene County	1,015	1,192	1,256	1,400	1,423
Arkansas	Hempstead County	987	1,160	1,222	1,363	1,385
Arkansas	Hot Spring County	961	1,128	1,189	1,326	1,347
Arkansas	Howard County	939	1,103	1,162	1,296	1,317
Arkansas	Independence County	956	1,123	1,183	1,319	1,340
Arkansas	Izard County	869	1,020	1,075	1,199	1,218
Arkansas	Jackson County	792	930	980	1,093	1,110
Arkansas	Jefferson County	982	1,153	1,215	1,355	1,377
Arkansas	Johnson County	873	1,025	1,080	1,204	1,224
Arkansas	Lafayette County	879	1,033	1,088	1,213	1,233
Arkansas	Lawrence County	823	966	1,018	1,135	1,153
Arkansas	Lee County	903	1,060	1,117	1,245	1,266
Arkansas	Lincoln County	860	1,010	1,064	1,186	1,206
Arkansas	Little River County	935	1,098	1,157	1,290	1,311
Arkansas	Logan County	857	1,007	1,061	1,183	1,202
Arkansas	Lonoke County	1,099	1,291	1,360	1,516	1,541
Arkansas	Madison County	987	1,159	1,221	1,361	1,383
Arkansas	Marion County	880	1,033	1,089	1,214	1,234
Arkansas	Miller County	1,036	1,217	1,282	1,429	1,453
Arkansas	Mississippi County	956	1,123	1,183	1,319	1,340
Arkansas	Monroe County	869	1,021	1,076	1,200	1,219
Arkansas	Montgomery County	907	1,065	1,122	1,251	1,271
Arkansas	Nevada County	886	1,041	1,097	1,223	1,243
Arkansas	Newton County	925	1,087	1,145	1,277	1,297
Arkansas	Ouachita County	911	1,070	1,127	1,257	1,277
Arkansas	Perry County	946	1,111	1,171	1,306	1,327
Arkansas	Phillips County	977	1,147	1,209	1,348	1,370
Arkansas	Pike County	901	1,058	1,115	1,243	1,263
Arkansas	Poinsett County	946	1,111	1,171	1,306	1,327
Arkansas	Polk County	925	1,087	1,145	1,277	1,297
Arkansas	Pope County	994	1,167	1,230	1,371	1,394
Arkansas	Prairie County	893	1,049	1,105	1,232	1,252
Arkansas	Pulaski County	1,214	1,425	1,502	1,675	1,702
Arkansas	Randolph County	861	1,011	1,065	1,187	1,207
Arkansas	Saline County	1,161	1,364	1,437	1,602	1,628
Arkansas	Scott County	865	1,016	1,071	1,194	1,213
Arkansas	Searcy County	893	1,049	1,105	1,232	1,252
Arkansas	Sebastian County	1,019	1,197	1,261	1,406	1,429
Arkansas	Sevier County	873	1,025	1,080	1,204	1,224
Arkansas	Sharp County	829	974	1,026	1,144	1,162

State Name	County	Housing and Utilities for a Family of 1	Housing and Utilities for a Family of 2	Housing and Utilities for a Family of 3	Housing and Utilities for a Family of 4	Housing and Utilities for a Family of 5 or more
Arkansas	St. Francis County	920	1,081	1,139	1,270	1,290
Arkansas	Stone County	934	1,097	1,156	1,289	1,310
Arkansas	Union County	935	1,098	1,157	1,290	1,311
Arkansas	Van Buren County	915	1,074	1,132	1,262	1,283
Arkansas	Washington County	1,204	1,414	1,490	1,661	1,688
Arkansas	White County	1,017	1,195	1,259	1,404	1,426
Arkansas	Woodruff County	803	943	994	1,108	1,126
Arkansas	Yell County	945	1,109	1,169	1,303	1,324
California	Alameda County	2,418	2,839	2,992	3,336	3,390
California	Alpine County	2,100	2,466	2,599	2,898	2,945
California	Amador County	1,718	2,018	2,126	2,370	2,409
California	Butte County	1,479	1,738	1,831	2,042	2,075
California	Calaveras County	1,690	1,985	2,092	2,333	2,370
California	Colusa County	1,484	1,743	1,837	2,048	2,081
California	Contra Costa County	2,359	2,771	2,920	3,256	3,308
California	Del Norte County	1,362	1,600	1,686	1,880	1,910
California	El Dorado County	2,084	2,447	2,579	2,876	2,922
California	Fresno County	1,516	1,780	1,876	2,092	2,126
California	Glenn County	1,416	1,663	1,752	1,953	1,985
California	Humboldt County	1,556	1,828	1,926	2,147	2,182
California	Imperial County	1,407	1,652	1,741	1,941	1,973
California	Inyo County	1,628	1,912	2,015	2,247	2,283
California	Kern County	1,441	1,692	1,783	1,988	2,020
California	Kings County	1,450	1,703	1,794	2,000	2,033
California	Lake County	1,473	1,730	1,823	2,033	2,065
California	Lassen County	1,509	1,772	1,867	2,082	2,115
California	Los Angeles County	2,146	2,521	2,656	2,961	3,009
California	Madera County	1,482	1,740	1,834	2,045	2,078
California	Marin County	3,050	3,582	3,775	4,209	4,277
California	Mariposa County	1,572	1,847	1,946	2,170	2,205
California	Mendocino County	1,717	2,017	2,125	2,369	2,408
California	Merced County	1,458	1,713	1,805	2,013	2,045
California	Modoc County	1,134	1,332	1,404	1,565	1,591
California	Mono County	1,862	2,186	2,304	2,569	2,610
California	Monterey County	2,018	2,371	2,498	2,785	2,830
California	Napa County	2,243	2,634	2,776	3,095	3,145
California	Nevada County	1,921	2,257	2,378	2,651	2,694
California	Orange County	2,366	2,779	2,928	3,265	3,317
California	Placer County	2,066	2,427	2,557	2,851	2,897
California	Plumas County	1,556	1,828	1,926	2,147	2,182
California	Riverside County	1,799	2,112	2,226	2,482	2,522
California	Sacramento County	1,715	2,014	2,122	2,366	2,404
California	San Benito County	2,236	2,626	2,767	3,085	3,135
California	San Bernardino County	1,681	1,974	2,080	2,319	2,357
California	San Diego County	2,199	2,582	2,721	3,034	3,083
California	San Francisco County	2,918	3,427	3,611	4,026	4,091
California	San Joaquin County	1,789	2,101	2,214	2,469	2,508

State Name	County	Housing and Utilities for a Family of 1	Housing and Utilities for a Family of 2	Housing and Utilities for a Family of 3	Housing and Utilities for a Family of 4	Housing and Utilities for a Family of 5 or more
California	San Luis Obispo County	2,014	2,366	2,493	2,780	2,825
California	San Mateo County	2,871	3,372	3,553	3,962	4,026
California	Santa Barbara County	2,116	2,485	2,619	2,920	2,967
California	Santa Clara County	2,742	3,220	3,393	3,783	3,844
California	Santa Cruz County	2,443	2,870	3,024	3,372	3,426
California	Shasta County	1,462	1,717	1,809	2,017	2,050
California	Sierra County	1,332	1,564	1,648	1,838	1,867
California	Siskiyou County	1,335	1,568	1,652	1,842	1,872
California	Solano County	1,942	2,280	2,403	2,679	2,723
California	Sonoma County	2,111	2,480	2,613	2,913	2,961
California	Stanislaus County	1,614	1,896	1,998	2,228	2,264
California	Sutter County	1,529	1,796	1,892	2,110	2,144
California	Tehama County	1,325	1,556	1,640	1,829	1,858
California	Trinity County	1,467	1,722	1,815	2,024	2,056
California	Tulare County	1,366	1,605	1,691	1,885	1,916
California	Tuolumne County	1,547	1,816	1,914	2,134	2,169
California	Ventura County	2,242	2,633	2,775	3,094	3,144
California	Yolo County	1,904	2,236	2,356	2,627	2,669
California	Yuba County	1,486	1,745	1,839	2,050	2,084
Colorado	Adams County	1,502	1,764	1,859	2,073	2,106
Colorado	Alamosa County	1,079	1,267	1,335	1,489	1,513
Colorado	Arapahoe County	1,583	1,859	1,959	2,184	2,220
Colorado	Archuleta County	1,392	1,635	1,723	1,921	1,952
Colorado	Baca County	934	1,097	1,156	1,289	1,310
Colorado	Bent County	983	1,155	1,217	1,357	1,379
Colorado	Boulder County	1,765	2,073	2,184	2,435	2,474
Colorado	Broomfield County	1,709	2,007	2,115	2,358	2,396
Colorado	Chaffee County	1,418	1,665	1,755	1,957	1,988
Colorado	Cheyenne	1,158	1,360	1,433	1,598	1,624
	County					
Colorado	Clear Creek County	1,500	1,761	1,856	2,069	2,103
Colorado	Conejos County	1,029	1,208	1,273	1,419	1,442
Colorado	Costilla County	988	1,161	1,223	1,364	1,386
Colorado	Crowley County	1,043	1,225	1,291	1,439	1,463
Colorado	Custer County	1,406	1,651	1,740	1,940	1,971
Colorado	Delta County	1,260	1,480	1,560	1,739	1,767
Colorado	Denver County	1,541	1,810	1,907	2,126	2,161
Colorado	Dolores County	1,138	1,337	1,409	1,571	1,596
Colorado	Douglas County	1,959	2,300	2,424	2,703	2,746
Colorado	Eagle County	2,063	2,423	2,553	2,847	2,893
Colorado	El Paso County	1,485	1,744	1,838	2,049	2,082
Colorado	Elbert County	1,922	2,258	2,379	2,653	2,695
Colorado	Fremont County	1,196	1,405	1,480	1,650	1,677
Colorado	Garfield County	1,735	2,038	2,147	2,394	2,433
Colorado	Gilpin County	1,513	1,777	1,872	2,087	2,121
Colorado	Grand County	1,484	1,743	1,837	2,048	2,081

State Name	County	Housing and Utilities for a Family of 1	Housing and Utilities for a Family of 2	Housing and Utilities for a Family of 3	Housing and Utilities for a Family of 4	Housing and Utilities for a Family of 5 or more
Colorado	Gunnison County	1,547	1,817	1,915	2,135	2,170
Colorado	Hinsdale County	1,462	1,717	1,809	2,017	2,050
Colorado	Huerfano County	1,084	1,274	1,342	1,496	1,520
Colorado	Jackson County	1,026	1,205	1,270	1,416	1,439
Colorado	Jefferson County	1,630	1,914	2,017	2,249	2,285
Colorado	Kiowa County	963	1,131	1,192	1,329	1,351
Colorado	Kit Carson County	1,140	1,339	1,411	1,573	1,599
Colorado	La Plata County	1,565	1,838	1,937	2,160	2,195
Colorado	Lake County	1,262	1,482	1,562	1,742	1,770
Colorado	Larimer County	1,514	1,778	1,874	2,090	2,123
Colorado	Las Animas County	1,239	1,456	1,534	1,710	1,738
Colorado	Lincoln County	1,221	1,434	1,511	1,685	1,712
Colorado	Logan County	1,128	1,325	1,396	1,557	1,582
Colorado	Mesa County	1,361	1,599	1,685	1,879	1,909
Colorado	Mineral County	1,364	1,602	1,688	1,882	1,913
Colorado	Moffat County	1,342	1,576	1,661	1,852	1,882
Colorado	Montezuma County	1,180	1,386	1,461	1,629	1,655
Colorado	Montrose County	1,333	1,566	1,650	1,840	1,869
Colorado	Morgan County	1,248	1,466	1,545	1,723	1,750
Colorado	Otero County	1,017	1,195	1,259	1,404	1,426
Colorado	Ouray County	1,807	2,122	2,236	2,493	2,533
Colorado	Park County	1,499	1,760	1,855	2,068	2,102
Colorado	Phillips County	1,141	1,340	1,412	1,574	1,600
Colorado	Pitkin County	1,944	2,283	2,406	2,683	2,726
Colorado	Prowers County	1,017	1,195	1,259	1,404	1,426
Colorado	Pueblo County	1,197	1,406	1,482	1,652	1,679
Colorado	Rio Blanco County	1,274	1,497	1,577	1,758	1,787
Colorado	Rio Grande County	1,092	1,282	1,351	1,506	1,531
Colorado	Routt County	1,760	2,067	2,178	2,428	2,468
Colorado	Saguache County	1,084	1,274	1,342	1,496	1,520
Colorado	San Juan County	1,227	1,441	1,518	1,693	1,720
Colorado	San Miguel County	1,864	2,189	2,307	2,572	2,614
Colorado	Sedgwick County	1,006	1,182	1,245	1,388	1,411
Colorado	Summit County	1,907	2,240	2,360	2,631	2,674
Colorado	Teller County	1,452	1,705	1,797	2,004	2,036
Colorado	Washington County	1,103	1,295	1,365	1,522	1,547
Colorado	Weld County	1,454	1,708	1,800	2,007	2,039
Colorado	Yuma County	1,193	1,402	1,477	1,647	1,673
Connecticut	Fairfield County	2,481	2,914	3,071	3,424	3,479
Connecticut	Hartford County	1,799	2,113	2,227	2,483	2,523
Connecticut	Litchfield County	1,801	2,115	2,229	2,485	2,525
Connecticut	Middlesex County	1,930	2,266	2,388	2,663	2,706
Connecticut	New Haven County	1,884	2,213	2,332	2,600	2,642
Connecticut	New London County	1,775	2,085	2,197	2,450	2,489
Connecticut	Tolland County	1,827	2,146	2,261	2,521	2,562
Connecticut	Windham County	1,618	1,901	2,003	2,233	2,269
Delaware	Kent County	1,451	1,704	1,796	2,003	2,035

State Name	County	Housing and Utilities for a Family of 1	Housing and Utilities for a Family of 2	Housing and Utilities for a Family of 3	Housing and Utilities for a Family of 4	Housing and Utilities for a Family of 5 or more
Delaware	New Castle County	1,564	1,837	1,936	2,159	2,193
Delaware	Sussex County	1,382	1,624	1,711	1,908	1,939
District of Columbia	District of Columbia	2,127	2,498	2,632	2,935	2,982
Florida	Alachua County	1,388	1,630	1,718	1,916	1,946
Florida	Baker County	1,160	1,363	1,436	1,601	1,627
Florida	Bay County	1,349	1,585	1,670	1,862	1,892
Florida	Bradford County	1,093	1,284	1,353	1,509	1,533
Florida	Brevard County	1,306	1,534	1,616	1,802	1,831
Florida	Broward County	1,711	2,010	2,118	2,362	2,400
Florida	Calhoun County	1,012	1,188	1,252	1,396	1,419
Florida	Charlotte County	1,290	1,515	1,596	1,780	1,808
Florida	Citrus County	1,071	1,258	1,326	1,478	1,502
Florida	Clay County	1,378	1,619	1,706	1,902	1,933
Florida	Collier County	1,658	1,947	2,052	2,288	2,325
Florida	Columbia County	1,086	1,275	1,344	1,499	1,523
Florida	DeSoto County	1,097	1,289	1,358	1,514	1,539
Florida	Dixie County	999	1,173	1,236	1,378	1,400
Florida	Duval County	1,372	1,611	1,698	1,893	1,924
Florida	Escambia County	1,227	1,442	1,519	1,694	1,721
Florida	Flagler County	1,311	1,539	1,622	1,809	1,838
Florida	Franklin County	1,219	1,432	1,509	1,683	1,710
Florida	Gadsden County	1,138	1,336	1,408	1,570	1,595
Florida	Gilchrist County	1,091	1,281	1,350	1,505	1,530
Florida	Glades County	1,004	1,179	1,242	1,385	1,407
Florida	Gulf County	1,270	1,492	1,572	1,753	1,781
Florida	Hamilton County	917	1,077	1,135	1,266	1,286
Florida	Hardee County	1,013	1,190	1,254	1,398	1,421
Florida	Hendry County	1,079	1,267	1,335	1,489	1,513
Florida	Hernando County	1,159	1,362	1,435	1,600	1,626
Florida	Highlands County	1,073	1,260	1,328	1,481	1,505
Florida	Hillsborough County	1,462	1,717	1,809	2,017	2,050
Florida	Holmes County	995	1,168	1,231	1,373	1,395
Florida	Indian River County	1,327	1,558	1,642	1,831	1,860
Florida	Jackson County	1,029	1,209	1,274	1,421	1,443
Florida	Jefferson County	1,131	1,329	1,400	1,561	1,586
Florida	Lafayette County	1,166	1,369	1,443	1,609	1,635
Florida	Lake County	1,297	1,523	1,605	1,790	1,818
Florida	Lee County	1,432	1,682	1,772	1,976	2,008
Florida	Leon County	1,416	1,663	1,752	1,953	1,985
Florida	Levy County	1,069	1,256	1,323	1,475	1,499
Florida	Liberty County	984	1,156	1,218	1,358	1,380
Florida	Madison County	983	1,154	1,216	1,356	1,378
Florida	Manatee County	1,471	1,727	1,820	2,029	2,062
Florida	Marion County	1,126	1,323	1,394	1,554	1,579
Florida	Martin County	1,574	1,849	1,948	2,172	2,207

State Name	County	Housing and Utilities for a Family of 1	Housing and Utilities for a Family of 2	Housing and Utilities for a Family of 3	Housing and Utilities for a Family of 4	Housing and Utilities for a Family of 5 or more
Florida	Miami-Dade County	1,660	1,949	2,054	2,290	2,327
Florida	Monroe County	2,064	2,424	2,554	2,848	2,894
Florida	Nassau County	1,420	1,668	1,758	1,960	1,992
Florida	Okaloosa County	1,455	1,709	1,801	2,008	2,041
Florida	Okeechobee County	1,087	1,276	1,345	1,500	1,524
Florida	Orange County	1,482	1,740	1,834	2,045	2,078
Florida	Osceola County	1,405	1,650	1,739	1,939	1,970
Florida	Palm Beach County	1,639	1,925	2,028	2,261	2,298
Florida	Pasco County	1,321	1,552	1,635	1,823	1,852
Florida	Pinellas County	1,417	1,665	1,754	1,956	1,987
Florida	Polk County	1,214	1,425	1,502	1,675	1,702
Florida	Putnam County	1,005	1,181	1,244	1,387	1,409
Florida	Santa Rosa County	1,381	1,622	1,709	1,906	1,936
Florida	Sarasota County	1,420	1,667	1,757	1,959	1,991
Florida	Seminole County	1,492	1,753	1,847	2,059	2,093
Florida	St. Johns County	1,700	1,997	2,104	2,346	2,384
Florida	St. Lucie County	1,349	1,585	1,670	1,862	1,892
Florida	Sumter County	1,180	1,386	1,460	1,628	1,654
Florida	Suwannee County	1,027	1,206	1,271	1,417	1,440
Florida	Taylor County	990	1,163	1,225	1,366	1,388
Florida	Union County	1,080	1,269	1,337	1,491	1,515
Florida	Volusia County	1,255	1,474	1,553	1,732	1,760
Florida	Wakulla County	1,208	1,419	1,495	1,667	1,694
Florida	Walton County	1,334	1,567	1,651	1,841	1,871
Florida	Washington County	1,004	1,180	1,243	1,386	1,408
Georgia	Appling County	974	1,144	1,206	1,345	1,366
Georgia	Atkinson County	932	1,094	1,153	1,286	1,306
Georgia	Bacon County	891	1,047	1,103	1,230	1,250
Georgia	Baker County	1,055	1,239	1,306	1,456	1,480
Georgia	Baldwin County	1,179	1,385	1,459	1,627	1,653
Georgia	Banks County	1,219	1,432	1,509	1,683	1,710
Georgia	Barrow County	1,234	1,449	1,527	1,703	1,730
Georgia	Bartow County	1,200	1,409	1,485	1,656	1,683
Georgia	Ben Hill County	950	1,116	1,176	1,311	1,332
Georgia	Berrien County	986	1,158	1,220	1,360	1,382
Georgia	Bibb County	1,213	1,424	1,501	1,674	1,701
Georgia	Bleckley County	1,054	1,237	1,304	1,454	1,477
Georgia	Brantley County	996	1,170	1,233	1,375	1,397
Georgia	Brooks County	1,058	1,243	1,310	1,461	1,484
Georgia	Bryan County	1,465	1,721	1,813	2,021	2,054
Georgia	Bulloch County	1,194	1,403	1,478	1,648	1,675
Georgia	Burke County	981	1,152	1,214	1,354	1,375
Georgia	Butts County	1,217	1,429	1,506	1,679	1,706
Georgia	Calhoun County	978	1,149	1,211	1,350	1,372
Georgia	Camden County	1,428	1,677	1,767	1,970	2,002
Georgia	Candler County	1,055	1,239	1,306	1,456	1,480
Georgia	Carroll County	1,179	1,385	1,459	1,627	1,653

State Name	County	Housing and Utilities for a Family of 1	Housing and Utilities for a Family of 2	Housing and Utilities for a Family of 3	Housing and Utilities for a Family of 4	Housing and Utilities for a Family of 5 or more
Georgia	Catoosa County	1,159	1,361	1,434	1,599	1,625
Georgia	Charlton County	1,030	1,210	1,275	1,422	1,445
Georgia	Chatham County	1,397	1,641	1,729	1,928	1,959
Georgia	Chattahoochee County	994	1,167	1,230	1,371	1,394
Georgia	Chattooga County	977	1,147	1,209	1,348	1,370
Georgia	Cherokee County	1,500	1,761	1,856	2,069	2,103
Georgia	Clarke County	1,258	1,478	1,557	1,736	1,764
Georgia	Clay County	1,100	1,292	1,361	1,518	1,542
Georgia	Clayton County	1,215	1,427	1,504	1,677	1,704
Georgia	Clinch County	1,112	1,306	1,376	1,534	1,559
Georgia	Cobb County	1,546	1,815	1,913	2,133	2,167
Georgia	Coffee County	1,007	1,182	1,246	1,389	1,412
Georgia	Colquitt County	995	1,168	1,231	1,373	1,395
Georgia	Columbia County	1,358	1,595	1,681	1,874	1,905
Georgia	Cook County	1,048	1,231	1,297	1,446	1,470
Georgia	Coweta County	1,384	1,626	1,713	1,910	1,941
Georgia	Crawford County	1,132	1,330	1,401	1,562	1,587
Georgia	Crisp County	988	1,161	1,223	1,364	1,386
Georgia	Dade County	1,097	1,289	1,358	1,514	1,539
Georgia	Dawson County	1,492	1,753	1,847	2,059	2,093
Georgia	Decatur County	1,094	1,285	1,354	1,510	1,534
Georgia	DeKalb County	1,479	1,737	1,830	2,040	2,073
Georgia	Dodge County	1,013	1,190	1,254	1,398	1,421
Georgia	Dooly County	947	1,112	1,172	1,307	1,328
Georgia	Dougherty County	1,151	1,351	1,424	1,588	1,613
Georgia	Douglas County	1,352	1,588	1,673	1,865	1,896
Georgia	Early County	1,058	1,243	1,310	1,461	1,484
Georgia	Echols County	1,014	1,191	1,255	1,399	1,422
Georgia	Effingham County	1,336	1,569	1,653	1,843	1,873
Georgia	Elbert County	1,024	1,202	1,267	1,413	1,436
Georgia	Emanuel County	983	1,155	1,217	1,357	1,379
Georgia	Evans County	1,098	1,290	1,359	1,515	1,540
Georgia	Fannin County	1,172	1,376	1,450	1,617	1,643
Georgia	Fayette County	1,708	2,006	2,114	2,357	2,395
Georgia	Floyd County	1,172	1,377	1,451	1,618	1,644
Georgia	Forsyth County	1,726	2,027	2,136	2,382	2,420
Georgia	Franklin County	1,154	1,355	1,428	1,592	1,618
Georgia	Fulton County	1,753	2,059	2,170	2,420	2,459
Georgia	Gilmer County	1,183	1,389	1,464	1,632	1,659
Georgia	Glascock County	987	1,159	1,221	1,361	1,383
Georgia	Glynn County	1,311	1,540	1,623	1,810	1,839
Georgia	Gordon County	1,094	1,285	1,354	1,510	1,534
Georgia	Grady County	1,112	1,306	1,376	1,534	1,559
Georgia	Greene County	1,346	1,581	1,666	1,858	1,888
Georgia	Gwinnett County	1,511	1,775	1,870	2,085	2,119
Georgia	Habersham County	1,138	1,337	1,409	1,571	1,596

State Name	County	Housing and Utilities for a Family of 1	Housing and Utilities for a Family of 2	Housing and Utilities for a Family of 3	Housing and Utilities for a Family of 4	Housing and Utilities for a Family of 5 or more
Georgia	Hall County	1,334	1,567	1,651	1,841	1,871
Georgia	Hancock County	995	1,168	1,231	1,373	1,395
Georgia	Haralson County	1,137	1,335	1,407	1,569	1,594
Georgia	Harris County	1,453	1,706	1,798	2,005	2,037
Georgia	Hart County	1,124	1,320	1,391	1,551	1,576
Georgia	Heard County	1,087	1,276	1,345	1,500	1,524
Georgia	Henry County	1,403	1,648	1,737	1,937	1,968
Georgia	Houston County	1,218	1,430	1,507	1,680	1,707
Georgia	Irwin County	1,061	1,246	1,313	1,464	1,488
Georgia	Jackson County	1,382	1,624	1,711	1,908	1,939
Georgia	Jasper County	1,169	1,373	1,447	1,613	1,639
Georgia	Jeff Davis County	970	1,139	1,200	1,338	1,360
Georgia	Jefferson County	1,010	1,186	1,250	1,394	1,416
Georgia	Jenkins County	978	1,149	1,211	1,350	1,372
Georgia	Johnson County	995	1,169	1,232	1,374	1,396
Georgia	Jones County	1,239	1,455	1,533	1,709	1,737
Georgia	Lamar County	1,227	1,441	1,518	1,693	1,720
Georgia	Lanier County	1,076	1,264	1,332	1,485	1,509
Georgia	Laurens County	1,133	1,330	1,402	1,563	1,588
Georgia	Lee County	1,319	1,550	1,633	1,821	1,850
Georgia	Liberty County	1,216	1,428	1,505	1,678	1,705
Georgia	Lincoln County	1,135	1,333	1,405	1,567	1,592
Georgia	Long County	1,132	1,330	1,401	1,562	1,587
Georgia	Lowndes County	1,164	1,367	1,440	1,606	1,632
Georgia	Lumpkin County	1,262	1,482	1,562	1,742	1,770
Georgia	Macon County	1,001	1,176	1,239	1,381	1,404
Georgia	Madison County	1,131	1,329	1,400	1,561	1,586
Georgia	Marion County	1,087	1,276	1,345	1,500	1,524
Georgia	McDuffie County	1,122	1,317	1,388	1,548	1,573
Georgia	McIntosh County	1,214	1,426	1,503	1,676	1,703
Georgia	Meriwether County	1,099	1,291	1,360	1,516	1,541
Georgia	Miller County	1,073	1,260	1,328	1,481	1,505
Georgia	Mitchell County	1,018	1,196	1,260	1,405	1,428
Georgia	Monroe County	1,239	1,455	1,533	1,709	1,737
Georgia	Montgomery County	1,054	1,237	1,304	1,454	1,477
Georgia	Morgan County	1,294	1,520	1,602	1,786	1,815
Georgia	Murray County	999	1,173	1,236	1,378	1,400
Georgia	Muscogee County	1,219	1,432	1,509	1,683	1,710
Georgia	Newton County	1,255	1,474	1,553	1,732	1,760
Georgia	Oconee County	1,584	1,860	1,960	2,185	2,221
Georgia	Oglethorpe County	1,172	1,377	1,451	1,618	1,644
Georgia	Paulding County	1,305	1,533	1,615	1,801	1,830
Georgia	Peach County	1,154	1,355	1,428	1,592	1,618
Georgia	Pickens County	1,281	1,504	1,585	1,767	1,796
Georgia	Pierce County	1,038	1,219	1,285	1,433	1,456
Georgia	Pike County	1,370	1,609	1,695	1,890	1,920
Georgia	Polk County	1,194	1,403	1,478	1,648	1,675

State Name	County	Housing and Utilities for a Family of 1	Housing and Utilities for a Family of 2	Housing and Utilities for a Family of 3	Housing and Utilities for a Family of 4	Housing and Utilities for a Family of 5 or more
Georgia	Pulaski County	1,122	1,317	1,388	1,548	1,573
Georgia	Putnam County	1,173	1,378	1,452	1,619	1,645
Georgia	Quitman County	953	1,120	1,180	1,316	1,337
Georgia	Rabun County	1,266	1,487	1,567	1,747	1,775
Georgia	Randolph County	937	1,101	1,160	1,293	1,314
Georgia	Richmond County	1,127	1,324	1,395	1,555	1,581
Georgia	Rockdale County	1,336	1,569	1,653	1,843	1,873
Georgia	Schley County	1,162	1,365	1,438	1,603	1,629
Georgia	Screven County	1,028	1,207	1,272	1,418	1,441
Georgia	Seminole County	1,002	1,177	1,240	1,383	1,405
Georgia	Spalding County	1,216	1,428	1,505	1,678	1,705
Georgia	Stephens County	1,130	1,327	1,398	1,559	1,584
Georgia	Stewart County	834	979	1,032	1,151	1,169
Georgia	Sumter County	1,049	1,232	1,298	1,447	1,471
Georgia	Talbot County	1,039	1,220	1,286	1,434	1,457
Georgia	Taliaferro County	1,020	1,198	1,262	1,407	1,430
Georgia	Tattnall County	1,017	1,195	1,259	1,404	1,426
Georgia	Taylor County	962	1,129	1,190	1,327	1,348
Georgia	Telfair County	877	1,030	1,085	1,210	1,229
Georgia	Terrell County	945	1,110	1,170	1,305	1,326
Georgia	Thomas County	1,147	1,348	1,420	1,583	1,609
Georgia	Tift County	1,114	1,309	1,379	1,538	1,562
Georgia	Toombs County	1,006	1,182	1,245	1,388	1,411
Georgia	Towns County	1,150	1,350	1,423	1,587	1,612
Georgia	Treutlen County	888	1,043	1,099	1,225	1,245
Georgia	Troup County	1,181	1,387	1,462	1,630	1,656
Georgia	Turner County	1,050	1,233	1,299	1,448	1,472
Georgia	Twiggs County	1,012	1,189	1,253	1,397	1,420
Georgia	Union County	1,257	1,477	1,556	1,735	1,763
Georgia	Upson County	1,020	1,198	1,262	1,407	1,430
Georgia	Walker County	1,042	1,223	1,289	1,437	1,460
Georgia	Walton County	1,353	1,589	1,674	1,867	1,897
Georgia	Ware County	1,049	1,232	1,298	1,447	1,471
Georgia	Warren County	968	1,137	1,198	1,336	1,357
Georgia	Washington County	1,100	1,293	1,362	1,519	1,543
Georgia	Wayne County	1,071	1,257	1,325	1,477	1,501
Georgia	Webster County	975	1,145	1,207	1,346	1,368
Georgia	Wheeler County	994	1,167	1,230	1,371	1,394
Georgia	White County	1,234	1,449	1,527	1,703	1,730
Georgia	Whitfield County	1,104	1,296	1,366	1,523	1,548
Georgia	Wilcox County	978	1,149	1,211	1,350	1,372
Georgia	Wilkes County	1,138	1,337	1,409	1,571	1,596
Georgia	Wilkinson County	1,008	1,183	1,247	1,390	1,413
Georgia	Worth County	1,061	1,246	1,313	1,464	1,488
Hawaii	Hawaii County	1,624	1,907	2,010	2,241	2,277
Hawaii	Honolulu County	2,224	2,613	2,753	3,070	3,119

State Name	County	Housing and Utilities for a Family of 1	Housing and Utilities for a Family of 2	Housing and Utilities for a Family of 3	Housing and Utilities for a Family of 4	Housing and Utilities for a Family of 5 or more
Hawaii	Kalawao County	2,022	2,375	2,503	2,791	2,836
Hawaii	Kauai County	2,071	2,432	2,563	2,858	2,904
Hawaii	Maui County	2,164	2,541	2,678	2,986	3,034
Idaho	Ada County	1,347	1,582	1,667	1,859	1,889
Idaho	Adams County	1,142	1,341	1,413	1,575	1,601
Idaho	Bannock County	1,135	1,333	1,405	1,567	1,592
Idaho	Bear Lake County	1,029	1,209	1,274	1,421	1,443
Idaho	Benewah County	1,058	1,243	1,310	1,461	1,484
Idaho	Bingham County	1,154	1,355	1,428	1,592	1,618
Idaho	Blaine County	1,648	1,935	2,039	2,273	2,310
Idaho	Boise County	1,225	1,439	1,516	1,690	1,718
Idaho	Bonner County	1,287	1,512	1,593	1,776	1,805
Idaho	Bonneville County	1,202	1,412	1,488	1,659	1,686
Idaho	Boundary County	1,197	1,405	1,481	1,651	1,678
Idaho	Butte County	1,015	1,192	1,256	1,400	1,423
Idaho	Camas County	1,226	1,440	1,517	1,691	1,719
Idaho	Canyon County	1,135	1,333	1,405	1,567	1,592
Idaho	Caribou County	1,061	1,246	1,313	1,464	1,488
Idaho	Cassia County	1,044	1,226	1,292	1,441	1,464
Idaho	Clark County	1,042	1,223	1,289	1,437	1,460
Idaho	Clearwater County	1,160	1,363	1,436	1,601	1,627
Idaho	Custer County	1,113	1,308	1,378	1,536	1,561
Idaho	Elmore County	1,206	1,416	1,492	1,664	1,690
Idaho	Franklin County	1,183	1,389	1,464	1,632	1,659
Idaho	Fremont County	1,099	1,291	1,360	1,516	1,541
Idaho	Gem County	1,175	1,380	1,454	1,621	1,647
Idaho	Gooding County	1,077	1,265	1,333	1,486	1,510
Idaho	Idaho County	1,034	1,215	1,280	1,427	1,450
Idaho	Jefferson County	1,210	1,421	1,497	1,669	1,696
Idaho	Jerome County	1,115	1,310	1,380	1,539	1,564
Idaho	Kootenai County	1,301	1,528	1,610	1,795	1,824
Idaho	Latah County	1,269	1,490	1,570	1,751	1,779
Idaho	Lemhi County	1,055	1,239	1,306	1,456	1,480
Idaho	Lewis County	1,004	1,179	1,242	1,385	1,407
Idaho	Lincoln County	1,100	1,293	1,362	1,519	1,543
Idaho	Madison County	1,340	1,573	1,658	1,849	1,879
Idaho	Minidoka County	975	1,145	1,207	1,346	1,368
Idaho	Nez Perce County	1,209	1,420	1,496	1,668	1,695
Idaho	Oneida County	1,159	1,361	1,434	1,599	1,625
Idaho	Owyhee County	1,127	1,324	1,395	1,555	1,581
Idaho	Payette County	1,196	1,405	1,480	1,650	1,677
Idaho	Power County	1,103	1,295	1,365	1,522	1,547
Idaho	Shoshone County	1,019	1,197	1,261	1,406	1,429
Idaho	Teton County	1,537	1,805	1,902	2,121	2,155
Idaho	Twin Falls County	1,141	1,340	1,412	1,574	1,600
Idaho	Valley County	1,283	1,507	1,588	1,771	1,799
Idaho	Washington County	1,053	1,237	1,303	1,453	1,476

State Name	County	Housing and Utilities for a Family of 1	Housing and Utilities for a Family of 2	Housing and Utilities for a Family of 3	Housing and Utilities for a Family of 4	Housing and Utilities for a Family of 5 or more
Illinois	Adams County	1,047	1,230	1,296	1,445	1,468
Illinois	Alexander County	962	1,130	1,191	1,328	1,349
Illinois	Bond County	1,147	1,347	1,419	1,582	1,608
Illinois	Boone County	1,436	1,686	1,777	1,981	2,013
Illinois	Brown County	988	1,161	1,223	1,364	1,386
Illinois	Bureau County	1,129	1,326	1,397	1,558	1,583
Illinois	Calhoun County	1,160	1,363	1,436	1,601	1,627
Illinois	Carroll County	1,105	1,297	1,367	1,524	1,549
Illinois	Cass County	1,008	1,183	1,247	1,390	1,413
Illinois	Champaign County	1,301	1,528	1,610	1,795	1,824
Illinois	Christian County	989	1,162	1,224	1,365	1,387
Illinois	Clark County	1,066	1,252	1,319	1,471	1,494
Illinois	Clay County	901	1,058	1,115	1,243	1,263
Illinois	Clinton County	1,265	1,485	1,565	1,745	1,773
Illinois	Coles County	1,037	1,218	1,283	1,431	1,454
Illinois	Cook County	1,766	2,075	2,186	2,437	2,477
Illinois	Crawford County	937	1,101	1,160	1,293	1,314
Illinois	Cumberland County	1,014	1,191	1,255	1,399	1,422
Illinois	De Witt County	1,097	1,289	1,358	1,514	1,539
Illinois	DeKalb County	1,576	1,851	1,951	2,175	2,210
Illinois	Douglas County	1,096	1,287	1,356	1,512	1,536
Illinois	DuPage County	1,930	2,267	2,389	2,664	2,707
Illinois	Edgar County	1,012	1,189	1,253	1,397	1,420
Illinois	Edwards County	869	1,020	1,075	1,199	1,218
Illinois	Effingham County	1,060	1,245	1,312	1,463	1,486
Illinois	Fayette County	956	1,123	1,183	1,319	1,340
Illinois	Ford County	1,062	1,247	1,314	1,465	1,489
Illinois	Franklin County	901	1,058	1,115	1,243	1,263
Illinois	Fulton County	1,013	1,190	1,254	1,398	1,421
Illinois	Gallatin County	895	1,051	1,108	1,235	1,255
Illinois	Greene County	939	1,103	1,162	1,296	1,317
Illinois	Grundy County	1,555	1,827	1,925	2,146	2,181
Illinois	Hamilton County	984	1,156	1,218	1,358	1,380
Illinois	Hancock County	972	1,142	1,203	1,341	1,363
Illinois	Hardin County	880	1,033	1,089	1,214	1,234
Illinois	Henderson	963	1,131	1,192	1,329	1,351
	County					
Illinois	Henry County	1,116	1,311	1,381	1,540	1,565
Illinois	Iroquois County	1,109	1,302	1,372	1,530	1,554
Illinois	Jackson County	1,121	1,316	1,387	1,547	1,571
Illinois	Jasper County	970	1,139	1,200	1,338	1,360
Illinois	Jefferson County	1,051	1,235	1,301	1,451	1,474
Illinois	Jersey County	1,201	1,410	1,486	1,657	1,684
Illinois	Jo Daviess County	1,201	1,411	1,487	1,658	1,685
Illinois	Johnson County	1,050	1,234	1,300	1,450	1,473
Illinois	Kane County	1,777	2,087	2,199	2,452	2,491

State Name	County	Housing and Utilities for a Family of 1	Housing and Utilities for a Family of 2	Housing and Utilities for a Family of 3	Housing and Utilities for a Family of 4	Housing and Utilities for a Family of 5 or more
Illinois	Kankakee County	1,357	1,593	1,679	1,872	1,902
Illinois	Kendall County	1,854	2,177	2,294	2,558	2,599
Illinois	Knox County	985	1,157	1,219	1,359	1,381
Illinois	La Salle County	1,252	1,471	1,550	1,728	1,756
Illinois	Lake County	1,992	2,339	2,465	2,748	2,793
Illinois	Lawrence County	874	1,027	1,082	1,206	1,226
Illinois	Lee County	1,140	1,339	1,411	1,573	1,599
Illinois	Livingston County	1,176	1,382	1,456	1,623	1,650
Illinois	Logan County	1,027	1,206	1,271	1,417	1,440
Illinois	Macon County	1,071	1,258	1,326	1,478	1,502
Illinois	Macoupin County	1,084	1,274	1,342	1,496	1,520
Illinois	Madison County	1,230	1,444	1,522	1,697	1,724
Illinois	Marion County	949	1,114	1,174	1,309	1,330
Illinois	Marshall County	1,133	1,330	1,402	1,563	1,588
Illinois	Mason County	1,006	1,182	1,245	1,388	1,411
Illinois	Massac County	1,063	1,248	1,315	1,466	1,490
Illinois	McDonough County	1,023	1,201	1,266	1,412	1,434
Illinois	McHenry County	1,808	2,124	2,238	2,495	2,536
Illinois	McLean County	1,376	1,616	1,703	1,899	1,929
Illinois	Menard County	1,185	1,392	1,467	1,636	1,662
Illinois	Mercer County	1,100	1,293	1,362	1,519	1,543
Illinois	Monroe County	1,538	1,807	1,904	2,123	2,157
Illinois	Montgomery County	1,004	1,180	1,243	1,386	1,408
Illinois	Morgan County	1,083	1,272	1,340	1,494	1,518
Illinois	Moultrie County	1,052	1,236	1,302	1,452	1,475
Illinois	Ogle County	1,331	1,563	1,647	1,836	1,866
Illinois	Peoria County	1,190	1,398	1,473	1,642	1,669
Illinois	Perry County	998	1,172	1,235	1,377	1,399
Illinois	Piatt County	1,214	1,426	1,503	1,676	1,703
Illinois	Pike County	903	1,061	1,118	1,247	1,267
Illinois	Pope County	978	1,149	1,211	1,350	1,372
Illinois	Pulaski County	961	1,128	1,189	1,326	1,347
Illinois	Putnam County	1,198	1,407	1,483	1,654	1,680
Illinois	Randolph County	1,032	1,212	1,277	1,424	1,447
Illinois	Richland County	1,013	1,190	1,254	1,398	1,421
Illinois	Rock Island County	1,143	1,343	1,415	1,578	1,603
Illinois	Saline County	950	1,116	1,176	1,311	1,332
Illinois	Sangamon County	1,193	1,402	1,477	1,647	1,673
Illinois	Schuyler County	962	1,129	1,190	1,327	1,348
Illinois	Scott County	985	1,157	1,219	1,359	1,381
Illinois	Shelby County	998	1,172	1,235	1,377	1,399
Illinois	St. Clair County	1,324	1,554	1,638	1,826	1,856
Illinois	Stark County	1,033	1,213	1,278	1,425	1,448
Illinois	Stephenson County	1,112	1,306	1,376	1,534	1,559
Illinois	Tazewell County	1,182	1,388	1,463	1,631	1,658
Illinois	Union County	1,061	1,246	1,313	1,464	1,488
Illinois	Vermilion County	996	1,170	1,233	1,375	1,397

State Name	County	Housing and Utilities for a Family of 1	Housing and Utilities for a Family of 2	Housing and Utilities for a Family of 3	Housing and Utilities for a Family of 4	Housing and Utilities for a Family of 5 or more
Illinois	Wabash County	1,014	1,191	1,255	1,399	1,422
Illinois	Warren County	974	1,144	1,205	1,344	1,365
Illinois	Washington County	1,202	1,412	1,488	1,659	1,686
Illinois	Wayne County	942	1,107	1,166	1,300	1,321
Illinois	White County	935	1,098	1,157	1,290	1,311
Illinois	Whiteside County	1,071	1,258	1,326	1,478	1,502
Illinois	Will County	1,804	2,119	2,233	2,490	2,530
Illinois	Williamson County	1,048	1,231	1,297	1,446	1,470
Illinois	Winnebago County	1,237	1,453	1,531	1,707	1,735
Illinois	Woodford County	1,378	1,618	1,705	1,901	1,932
Indiana	Adams County	987	1,159	1,221	1,361	1,383
Indiana	Allen County	1,053	1,237	1,303	1,453	1,476
Indiana	Bartholomew County	1,155	1,356	1,429	1,593	1,619
Indiana	Benton County	985	1,157	1,219	1,359	1,381
Indiana	Blackford County	878	1,032	1,087	1,212	1,232
Indiana	Boone County	1,450	1,703	1,794	2,000	2,033
Indiana	Brown County	1,225	1,439	1,516	1,690	1,718
Indiana	Carroll County	1,075	1,262	1,330	1,483	1,507
Indiana	Cass County	936	1,100	1,159	1,292	1,313
Indiana	Clark County	1,146	1,346	1,418	1,581	1,607
Indiana	Clay County	1,010	1,186	1,250	1,394	1,416
Indiana	Clinton County	1,083	1,272	1,340	1,494	1,518
Indiana	Crawford County	921	1,082	1,140	1,271	1,292
Indiana	Daviess County	993	1,166	1,229	1,370	1,392
Indiana	Dearborn County	1,271	1,493	1,573	1,754	1,782
Indiana	Decatur County	1,045	1,227	1,293	1,442	1,465
Indiana	DeKalb County	1,036	1,217	1,282	1,429	1,453
Indiana	Delaware County	971	1,141	1,202	1,340	1,362
Indiana	Dubois County	1,098	1,290	1,359	1,515	1,540
Indiana	Elkhart County	1,067	1,254	1,321	1,473	1,497
Indiana	Fayette County	970	1,139	1,200	1,338	1,360
Indiana	Floyd County	1,222	1,435	1,512	1,686	1,713
Indiana	Fountain County	992	1,165	1,228	1,369	1,391
Indiana	Franklin County	1,183	1,389	1,464	1,632	1,659
Indiana	Fulton County	1,004	1,179	1,242	1,385	1,407
Indiana	Gibson County	1,017	1,195	1,259	1,404	1,426
Indiana	Grant County	912	1,071	1,129	1,259	1,279
Indiana	Greene County	993	1,166	1,229	1,370	1,392
Indiana	Hamilton County	1,524	1,790	1,886	2,103	2,137
Indiana	Hancock County	1,300	1,527	1,609	1,794	1,823
Indiana	Harrison County	1,084	1,273	1,341	1,495	1,519
Indiana	Hendricks County	1,315	1,545	1,628	1,815	1,845
Indiana	Henry County	1,011	1,187	1,251	1,395	1,417
Indiana	Howard County	1,025	1,203	1,268	1,414	1,437
Indiana	Huntington County	1,016	1,194	1,258	1,403	1,425
Indiana	Jackson County	1,028	1,207	1,272	1,418	1,441

State Name	County	Housing and Utilities for a Family of 1	Housing and Utilities for a Family of 2	Housing and Utilities for a Family of 3	Housing and Utilities for a Family of 4	Housing and Utilities for a Family of 5 or more
Indiana	Jasper County	1,148	1,349	1,421	1,584	1,610
Indiana	Jay County	909	1,068	1,125	1,254	1,275
Indiana	Jefferson County	1,028	1,207	1,272	1,418	1,441
Indiana	Jennings County	1,020	1,198	1,262	1,407	1,430
Indiana	Johnson County	1,240	1,457	1,535	1,712	1,739
Indiana	Knox County	936	1,100	1,159	1,292	1,313
Indiana	Kosciusko County	1,096	1,287	1,356	1,512	1,536
Indiana	LaGrange County	1,128	1,325	1,396	1,557	1,582
Indiana	Lake County	1,222	1,435	1,512	1,686	1,713
Indiana	LaPorte County	1,105	1,297	1,367	1,524	1,549
Indiana	Lawrence County	1,040	1,221	1,287	1,435	1,458
Indiana	Madison County	1,036	1,217	1,282	1,429	1,453
Indiana	Marion County	1,138	1,336	1,408	1,570	1,595
Indiana	Marshall County	1,088	1,277	1,346	1,501	1,525
Indiana	Martin County	1,011	1,187	1,251	1,395	1,417
Indiana	Miami County	966	1,134	1,195	1,332	1,354
Indiana	Monroe County	1,177	1,383	1,457	1,625	1,651
Indiana	Montgomery County	1,021	1,199	1,263	1,408	1,431
Indiana	Morgan County	1,186	1,393	1,468	1,637	1,663
Indiana	Newton County	1,064	1,250	1,317	1,468	1,492
Indiana	Noble County	1,055	1,239	1,306	1,456	1,480
Indiana	Ohio County	1,176	1,381	1,455	1,622	1,649
Indiana	Orange County	940	1,104	1,163	1,297	1,318
Indiana	Owen County	1,058	1,243	1,310	1,461	1,484
Indiana	Parke County	948	1,113	1,173	1,308	1,329
Indiana	Perry County	982	1,153	1,215	1,355	1,377
Indiana	Pike County	1,011	1,187	1,251	1,395	1,417
Indiana	Porter County	1,311	1,539	1,622	1,809	1,838
Indiana	Posey County	1,138	1,336	1,408	1,570	1,595
Indiana	Pulaski County	989	1,162	1,224	1,365	1,387
Indiana	Putnam County	1,178	1,384	1,458	1,626	1,652
Indiana	Randolph County	926	1,088	1,146	1,278	1,298
Indiana	Ripley County	1,139	1,338	1,410	1,572	1,598
Indiana	Rush County	1,020	1,198	1,262	1,407	1,430
Indiana	Scott County	1,057	1,241	1,308	1,458	1,482
Indiana	Shelby County	1,155	1,356	1,429	1,593	1,619
Indiana	Spencer County	1,035	1,216	1,281	1,428	1,451
Indiana	St. Joseph County	1,056	1,240	1,307	1,457	1,481
Indiana	Starke County	986	1,158	1,220	1,360	1,382
Indiana	Steuben County	1,079	1,268	1,336	1,490	1,514
Indiana	Sullivan County	966	1,134	1,195	1,332	1,354
Indiana	Switzerland County	1,071	1,258	1,326	1,478	1,502
Indiana	Tippecanoe County	1,147	1,348	1,420	1,583	1,609
Indiana	Tipton County	1,096	1,288	1,357	1,513	1,537
Indiana	Union County	1,097	1,289	1,358	1,514	1,539
Indiana	Vanderburgh County	1,073	1,260	1,328	1,481	1,505
Indiana	Vermillion County	946	1,111	1,171	1,306	1,327

State Name	County	Housing and Utilities for a Family of 1	Housing and Utilities for a Family of 2	Housing and Utilities for a Family of 3	Housing and Utilities for a Family of 4	Housing and Utilities for a Family of 5 or more
Indiana	Vigo County	990	1,163	1,225	1,366	1,388
Indiana	Wabash County	960	1,127	1,188	1,325	1,346
Indiana	Warren County	1,056	1,240	1,307	1,457	1,481
Indiana	Warrick County	1,224	1,438	1,515	1,689	1,716
Indiana	Washington County	1,012	1,189	1,253	1,397	1,420
Indiana	Wayne County	994	1,167	1,230	1,371	1,394
Indiana	Wells County	1,011	1,187	1,251	1,395	1,417
Indiana	White County	1,003	1,178	1,241	1,384	1,406
Indiana	Whitley County	1,118	1,313	1,384	1,543	1,568
Iowa	Adair County	1,041	1,222	1,288	1,436	1,459
Iowa	Adams County	1,018	1,196	1,260	1,405	1,428
Iowa	Allamakee County	1,073	1,260	1,328	1,481	1,505
Iowa	Appanoose County	977	1,147	1,209	1,348	1,370
Iowa	Audubon County	896	1,052	1,109	1,237	1,256
Iowa	Benton County	1,222	1,435	1,512	1,686	1,713
Iowa	Black Hawk County	1,100	1,292	1,361	1,518	1,542
Iowa	Boone County	1,196	1,405	1,480	1,650	1,677
Iowa	Bremer County	1,183	1,389	1,464	1,632	1,659
Iowa	Buchanan County	1,130	1,328	1,399	1,560	1,585
Iowa	Buena Vista County	1,003	1,178	1,241	1,384	1,406
Iowa	Butler County	1,015	1,192	1,256	1,400	1,423
Iowa	Calhoun County	905	1,063	1,120	1,249	1,269
Iowa	Carroll County	1,071	1,257	1,325	1,477	1,501
Iowa	Cass County	931	1,093	1,152	1,284	1,305
Iowa	Cedar County	1,163	1,366	1,439	1,604	1,630
Iowa	Cerro Gordo County	1,060	1,245	1,312	1,463	1,486
Iowa	Cherokee County	939	1,103	1,162	1,296	1,317
Iowa	Chickasaw County	1,014	1,191	1,255	1,399	1,422
Iowa	Clarke County	1,103	1,295	1,365	1,522	1,547
Iowa	Clay County	1,009	1,185	1,249	1,393	1,415
Iowa	Clayton County	1,092	1,282	1,351	1,506	1,531
Iowa	Clinton County	1,117	1,312	1,383	1,542	1,567
Iowa	Crawford County	999	1,174	1,237	1,379	1,402
Iowa	Dallas County	1,471	1,727	1,820	2,029	2,062
Iowa	Davis County	1,098	1,290	1,359	1,515	1,540
Iowa	Decatur County	1,005	1,181	1,244	1,387	1,409
Iowa	Delaware County	1,125	1,321	1,392	1,552	1,577
Iowa	Des Moines County	1,050	1,234	1,300	1,450	1,473
Iowa	Dickinson County	1,204	1,414	1,490	1,661	1,688
Iowa	Dubuque County	1,197	1,406	1,482	1,652	1,679
Iowa	Emmet County	1,004	1,180	1,243	1,386	1,408
Iowa	Fayette County	1,002	1,177	1,240	1,383	1,405
Iowa	Floyd County	971	1,141	1,202	1,340	1,362
Iowa	Franklin County	1,004	1,180	1,243	1,386	1,408
Iowa	Fremont County	1,011	1,187	1,251	1,395	1,417
Iowa	Greene County	1,004	1,179	1,242	1,385	1,407

State Name	County	Housing and Utilities for a Family of 1	Housing and Utilities for a Family of 2	Housing and Utilities for a Family of 3	Housing and Utilities for a Family of 4	Housing and Utilities for a Family of 5 or more
Iowa	Grundy County	1,120	1,315	1,386	1,545	1,570
Iowa	Guthrie County	1,101	1,293	1,363	1,520	1,544
Iowa	Hamilton County	1,049	1,232	1,298	1,447	1,471
Iowa	Hancock County	1,001	1,176	1,239	1,381	1,404
Iowa	Hardin County	1,025	1,204	1,269	1,415	1,438
Iowa	Harrison County	1,151	1,352	1,425	1,589	1,615
Iowa	Henry County	1,080	1,269	1,337	1,491	1,515
Iowa	Howard County	1,006	1,182	1,245	1,388	1,411
Iowa	Humboldt County	986	1,158	1,220	1,360	1,382
Iowa	Ida County	844	992	1,045	1,165	1,184
Iowa	Iowa County	1,201	1,411	1,487	1,658	1,685
Iowa	Jackson County	1,082	1,271	1,339	1,493	1,517
Iowa	Jasper County	1,161	1,364	1,437	1,602	1,628
Iowa	Jefferson County	1,036	1,217	1,282	1,429	1,453
Iowa	Johnson County	1,414	1,661	1,750	1,951	1,983
Iowa	Jones County	1,143	1,343	1,415	1,578	1,603
Iowa	Keokuk County	1,026	1,205	1,270	1,416	1,439
Iowa	Kossuth County	973	1,143	1,204	1,342	1,364
Iowa	Lee County	1,006	1,182	1,245	1,388	1,411
Iowa	Linn County	1,266	1,487	1,567	1,747	1,775
Iowa	Louisa County	1,068	1,255	1,322	1,474	1,498
Iowa	Lucas County	1,011	1,187	1,251	1,395	1,417
Iowa	Lyon County	1,055	1,239	1,306	1,456	1,480
Iowa	Madison County	1,373	1,612	1,699	1,894	1,925
Iowa	Mahaska County	1,058	1,243	1,310	1,461	1,484
Iowa	Marion County	1,156	1,358	1,431	1,596	1,621
Iowa	Marshall County	1,089	1,279	1,348	1,503	1,527
Iowa	Mills County	1,363	1,601	1,687	1,881	1,911
Iowa	Mitchell County	1,036	1,217	1,282	1,429	1,453
Iowa	Monona County	934	1,097	1,156	1,289	1,310
Iowa	Monroe County	1,149	1,349	1,422	1,586	1,611
Iowa	Montgomery County	999	1,174	1,237	1,379	1,402
Iowa	Muscatine County	1,186	1,393	1,468	1,637	1,663
Iowa	O'Brien County	1,071	1,257	1,325	1,477	1,501
Iowa	Osceola County	951	1,117	1,177	1,312	1,334
Iowa	Page County	1,002	1,177	1,240	1,383	1,405
Iowa	Palo Alto County	945	1,110	1,170	1,305	1,326
Iowa	Plymouth County	1,110	1,304	1,374	1,532	1,557
Iowa	Pocahontas County	905	1,063	1,120	1,249	1,269
Iowa	Polk County	1,324	1,555	1,639	1,827	1,857
Iowa	Pottawattamie County	1,190	1,398	1,473	1,642	1,669
Iowa	Poweshiek County	1,159	1,362	1,435	1,600	1,626
Iowa	Ringgold County	1,055	1,239	1,306	1,456	1,480
Iowa	Sac County	923	1,084	1,142	1,273	1,294
Iowa	Scott County	1,224	1,438	1,515	1,689	1,716
Iowa	Shelby County	1,082	1,271	1,339	1,493	1,517
Iowa	Sioux County	1,136	1,334	1,406	1,568	1,593

State Name	County	Housing and Utilities for a Family of 1	Housing and Utilities for a Family of 2	Housing and Utilities for a Family of 3	Housing and Utilities for a Family of 4	Housing and Utilities for a Family of 5 or more
Iowa	Story County	1,302	1,529	1,611	1,796	1,825
Iowa	Tama County	1,081	1,270	1,338	1,492	1,516
Iowa	Taylor County	928	1,090	1,149	1,281	1,302
Iowa	Union County	1,025	1,204	1,269	1,415	1,438
Iowa	Van Buren County	985	1,157	1,219	1,359	1,381
Iowa	Wapello County	963	1,131	1,192	1,329	1,351
Iowa	Warren County	1,327	1,558	1,642	1,831	1,860
Iowa	Washington County	1,201	1,410	1,486	1,657	1,684
Iowa	Wayne County	966	1,134	1,195	1,332	1,354
Iowa	Webster County	979	1,150	1,212	1,351	1,373
Iowa	Winnebago County	1,015	1,192	1,256	1,400	1,423
Iowa	Winneshiek	1,220	1,433	1,510	1,684	1,711
	County					
Iowa	Woodbury County	1,058	1,242	1,309	1,460	1,483
Iowa	Worth County	987	1,160	1,222	1,363	1,385
Iowa	Wright County	957	1,125	1,185	1,321	1,343
Kansas	Allen County	966	1,134	1,195	1,332	1,354
Kansas	Anderson County	1,136	1,334	1,406	1,568	1,593
Kansas	Atchison County	1,075	1,263	1,331	1,484	1,508
Kansas	Barber County	975	1,145	1,207	1,346	1,368
Kansas	Barton County	1,018	1,196	1,260	1,405	1,428
Kansas	Bourbon County	986	1,158	1,220	1,360	1,382
Kansas	Brown County	972	1,142	1,203	1,341	1,363
Kansas	Butler County	1,302	1,530	1,612	1,797	1,826
Kansas	Chase County	1,105	1,297	1,367	1,524	1,549
Kansas	Chautauqua County	956	1,123	1,183	1,319	1,340
Kansas	Cherokee County	987	1,159	1,221	1,361	1,383
Kansas	Cheyenne County	1,000	1,175	1,238	1,380	1,403
Kansas	Clark County	980	1,151	1,213	1,352	1,374
Kansas	Clay County	1,047	1,230	1,296	1,445	1,468
Kansas	Cloud County	920	1,080	1,138	1,269	1,289
Kansas	Coffey County	1,122	1,318	1,389	1,549	1,574
Kansas	Comanche County	1,033	1,213	1,278	1,425	1,448
Kansas	Cowley County	1,070	1,256	1,324	1,476	1,500
Kansas	Crawford County	1,042	1,223	1,289	1,437	1,460
Kansas	Decatur County	867	1,018	1,073	1,196	1,216
Kansas	Dickinson County	1,119	1,314	1,385	1,544	1,569
Kansas	Doniphan County	1,109	1,303	1,373	1,531	1,556
Kansas	Douglas County	1,399	1,644	1,732	1,931	1,962
Kansas	Edwards County	865	1,015	1,070	1,193	1,212
Kansas	Elk County	869	1,020	1,075	1,199	1,218
Kansas	Ellis County	1,209	1,420	1,496	1,668	1,695
Kansas	Ellsworth County	953	1,119	1,179	1,315	1,336
Kansas	Finney County	1,219	1,432	1,509	1,683	1,710
Kansas	Ford County	1,134	1,331	1,403	1,564	1,590
Kansas	Franklin County	1,210	1,421	1,497	1,669	1,696

State Name	County	Housing and Utilities for a Family of 1	Housing and Utilities for a Family of 2	Housing and Utilities for a Family of 3	Housing and Utilities for a Family of 4	Housing and Utilities for a Family of 5 or more
Kansas	Geary County	1,300	1,527	1,609	1,794	1,823
Kansas	Gove County	1,026	1,205	1,270	1,416	1,439
Kansas	Graham County	914	1,073	1,131	1,261	1,281
Kansas	Grant County	1,089	1,279	1,348	1,503	1,527
Kansas	Gray County	1,184	1,390	1,465	1,633	1,660
Kansas	Greeley County	911	1,070	1,128	1,258	1,278
Kansas	Greenwood County	974	1,144	1,206	1,345	1,366
Kansas	Hamilton County	1,086	1,275	1,344	1,499	1,523
Kansas	Harper County	1,000	1,175	1,238	1,380	1,403
Kansas	Harvey County	1,136	1,334	1,406	1,568	1,593
Kansas	Haskell County	1,057	1,241	1,308	1,458	1,482
Kansas	Hodgeman County	963	1,131	1,192	1,329	1,351
Kansas	Jackson County	1,252	1,470	1,549	1,727	1,755
Kansas	Jefferson County	1,253	1,472	1,551	1,729	1,757
Kansas	Jewell County	877	1,030	1,085	1,210	1,229
Kansas	Johnson County	1,597	1,875	1,976	2,203	2,239
Kansas	Kearny County	1,078	1,266	1,334	1,487	1,511
Kansas	Kingman County	1,138	1,337	1,409	1,571	1,596
Kansas	Kiowa County	1,096	1,288	1,357	1,513	1,537
Kansas	Labette County	1,021	1,200	1,264	1,409	1,432
Kansas	Lane County	915	1,075	1,133	1,263	1,284
Kansas	Leavenworth County	1,425	1,673	1,763	1,966	1,997
Kansas	Lincoln County	975	1,145	1,207	1,346	1,368
Kansas	Linn County	1,121	1,316	1,387	1,547	1,571
Kansas	Logan County	1,050	1,234	1,300	1,450	1,473
Kansas	Lyon County	1,075	1,263	1,331	1,484	1,508
Kansas	Marion County	1,035	1,216	1,281	1,428	1,451
Kansas	Marshall County	1,020	1,198	1,262	1,407	1,430
Kansas	McPherson County	1,154	1,355	1,428	1,592	1,618
Kansas	Meade County	1,060	1,245	1,312	1,463	1,486
Kansas	Miami County	1,489	1,749	1,843	2,055	2,088
Kansas	Mitchell County	997	1,171	1,234	1,376	1,398
Kansas	Montgomery County	970	1,140	1,201	1,339	1,361
Kansas	Morris County	1,084	1,273	1,341	1,495	1,519
Kansas	Morton County	1,071	1,258	1,326	1,478	1,502
Kansas	Nemaha County	1,128	1,325	1,396	1,557	1,582
Kansas	Neosho County	987	1,160	1,222	1,363	1,385
Kansas	Ness County	971	1,141	1,202	1,340	1,362
Kansas	Norton County	911	1,070	1,127	1,257	1,277
Kansas	Osage County	1,135	1,333	1,405	1,567	1,592
Kansas	Osborne County	943	1,107	1,167	1,301	1,322
Kansas	Ottawa County	1,100	1,292	1,361	1,518	1,542
Kansas	Pawnee County	979	1,150	1,212	1,351	1,373
Kansas	Phillips County	933	1,096	1,155	1,288	1,309
Kansas	Pottawatomie County	1,283	1,507	1,588	1,771	1,799
Kansas	Pratt County	1,079	1,267	1,335	1,489	1,513
Kansas	Rawlins County	1,052	1,236	1,302	1,452	1,475

State Name	County	Housing and Utilities for a Family of 1	Housing and Utilities for a Family of 2	Housing and Utilities for a Family of 3	Housing and Utilities for a Family of 4	Housing and Utilities for a Family of 5 or more
Kansas	Reno County	1,070	1,256	1,324	1,476	1,500
Kansas	Republic County	996	1,170	1,233	1,375	1,397
Kansas	Rice County	1,019	1,197	1,261	1,406	1,429
Kansas	Riley County	1,368	1,607	1,693	1,888	1,918
Kansas	Rooks County	960	1,127	1,188	1,325	1,346
Kansas	Rush County	887	1,042	1,098	1,224	1,244
Kansas	Russell County	971	1,141	1,202	1,340	1,362
Kansas	Saline County	1,172	1,377	1,451	1,618	1,644
Kansas	Scott County	1,240	1,457	1,535	1,712	1,739
Kansas	Sedgwick County	1,224	1,438	1,515	1,689	1,716
Kansas	Seward County	1,094	1,285	1,354	1,510	1,534
Kansas	Shawnee County	1,192	1,400	1,475	1,645	1,671
Kansas	Sheridan County	1,055	1,239	1,306	1,456	1,480
Kansas	Sherman County	995	1,168	1,231	1,373	1,395
Kansas	Smith County	1,054	1,238	1,305	1,455	1,479
Kansas	Stafford County	903	1,060	1,117	1,245	1,266
Kansas	Stanton County	966	1,134	1,195	1,332	1,354
Kansas	Stevens County	1,099	1,291	1,360	1,516	1,541
Kansas	Sumner County	1,125	1,321	1,392	1,552	1,577
Kansas	Thomas County	1,120	1,315	1,386	1,545	1,570
Kansas	Trego County	1,016	1,193	1,257	1,402	1,424
Kansas	Wabaunsee County	1,089	1,279	1,348	1,503	1,527
Kansas	Wallace County	949	1,115	1,175	1,310	1,331
Kansas	Washington County	910	1,069	1,126	1,255	1,276
Kansas	Wichita County	1,093	1,284	1,353	1,509	1,533
Kansas	Wilson County	915	1,074	1,132	1,262	1,283
Kansas	Woodson County	914	1,073	1,131	1,261	1,281
Kansas	Wyandotte County	1,199	1,408	1,484	1,655	1,681
Kentucky	Adair County	873	1,026	1,081	1,205	1,225
Kentucky	Allen County	1,008	1,184	1,248	1,392	1,414
Kentucky	Anderson County	1,172	1,377	1,451	1,618	1,644
Kentucky	Ballard County	989	1,162	1,224	1,365	1,387
Kentucky	Barren County	1,012	1,189	1,253	1,397	1,420
Kentucky	Bath County	942	1,107	1,166	1,300	1,321
Kentucky	Bell County	879	1,033	1,088	1,213	1,233
Kentucky	Boone County	1,358	1,595	1,681	1,874	1,905
Kentucky	Bourbon County	1,125	1,321	1,392	1,552	1,577
Kentucky	Boyd County	1,021	1,200	1,264	1,409	1,432
Kentucky	Boyle County	1,077	1,265	1,333	1,486	1,510
Kentucky	Bracken County	1,101	1,293	1,363	1,520	1,544
Kentucky	Breathitt County	983	1,154	1,216	1,356	1,378
Kentucky	Breckinridge County	928	1,090	1,149	1,281	1,302
Kentucky	Bullitt County	1,191	1,399	1,474	1,644	1,670
Kentucky	Butler County	922	1,083	1,141	1,272	1,293
Kentucky	Caldwell County	966	1,134	1,195	1,332	1,354
Kentucky	Calloway County	1,050	1,233	1,299	1,448	1,472

State Name	County	Housing and Utilities for a Family of 1	Housing and Utilities for a Family of 2	Housing and Utilities for a Family of 3	Housing and Utilities for a Family of 4	Housing and Utilities for a Family of 5 or more
Kentucky	Campbell County	1,232	1,447	1,525	1,700	1,728
Kentucky	Carlisle County	950	1,116	1,176	1,311	1,332
Kentucky	Carroll County	1,024	1,202	1,267	1,413	1,436
Kentucky	Carter County	967	1,136	1,197	1,335	1,356
Kentucky	Casey County	935	1,098	1,157	1,290	1,311
Kentucky	Christian County	1,100	1,292	1,361	1,518	1,542
Kentucky	Clark County	1,181	1,387	1,462	1,630	1,656
Kentucky	Clay County	859	1,009	1,063	1,185	1,204
Kentucky	Clinton County	842	989	1,042	1,162	1,181
Kentucky	Crittenden County	949	1,114	1,174	1,309	1,330
Kentucky	Cumberland County	837	983	1,036	1,155	1,174
Kentucky	Daviess County	1,055	1,239	1,306	1,456	1,480
Kentucky	Edmonson County	1,017	1,195	1,259	1,404	1,426
Kentucky	Elliott County	998	1,172	1,235	1,377	1,399
Kentucky	Estill County	983	1,154	1,216	1,356	1,378
Kentucky	Fayette County	1,275	1,498	1,578	1,759	1,788
Kentucky	Fleming County	927	1,089	1,147	1,279	1,300
Kentucky	Floyd County	995	1,169	1,232	1,374	1,396
Kentucky	Franklin County	1,180	1,386	1,461	1,629	1,655
Kentucky	Fulton County	955	1,122	1,182	1,318	1,339
Kentucky	Gallatin County	1,148	1,349	1,421	1,584	1,610
Kentucky	Garrard County	1,135	1,333	1,405	1,567	1,592
Kentucky	Grant County	1,243	1,460	1,538	1,715	1,743
Kentucky	Graves County	963	1,131	1,192	1,329	1,351
Kentucky	Grayson County	946	1,111	1,171	1,306	1,327
Kentucky	Green County	895	1,051	1,108	1,235	1,255
Kentucky	Greenup County	1,063	1,249	1,316	1,467	1,491
Kentucky	Hancock County	1,000	1,175	1,238	1,380	1,403
Kentucky	Hardin County	1,151	1,351	1,424	1,588	1,613
Kentucky	Harlan County	861	1,011	1,065	1,187	1,207
Kentucky	Harrison County	1,079	1,268	1,336	1,490	1,514
Kentucky	Hart County	937	1,101	1,160	1,293	1,314
Kentucky	Henderson County	1,056	1,240	1,307	1,457	1,481
Kentucky	Henry County	1,111	1,305	1,375	1,533	1,558
Kentucky	Hickman County	888	1,043	1,099	1,225	1,245
Kentucky	Hopkins County	967	1,136	1,197	1,335	1,356
Kentucky	Jackson County	880	1,033	1,089	1,214	1,234
Kentucky	Jefferson County	1,228	1,442	1,520	1,695	1,722
Kentucky	Jessamine County	1,284	1,508	1,589	1,772	1,800
Kentucky	Johnson County	965	1,133	1,194	1,331	1,353
Kentucky	Kenton County	1,269	1,491	1,571	1,752	1,780
Kentucky	Knott County	953	1,120	1,180	1,316	1,337
Kentucky	Knox County	953	1,119	1,179	1,315	1,336
Kentucky	Larue County	1,033	1,214	1,279	1,426	1,449
Kentucky	Laurel County	991	1,163	1,226	1,367	1,389
Kentucky	Lawrence County	965	1,133	1,194	1,331	1,353
Kentucky	Lee County	875	1,028	1,083	1,208	1,227

State Name	County	Housing and Utilities for a Family of 1	Housing and Utilities for a Family of 2	Housing and Utilities for a Family of 3	Housing and Utilities for a Family of 4	Housing and Utilities for a Family of 5 or more
Kentucky	Leslie County	892	1,048	1,104	1,231	1,251
Kentucky	Letcher County	850	998	1,052	1,173	1,192
Kentucky	Lewis County	905	1,063	1,120	1,249	1,269
Kentucky	Lincoln County	957	1,124	1,184	1,320	1,341
Kentucky	Livingston County	959	1,126	1,187	1,324	1,345
Kentucky	Logan County	1,020	1,198	1,262	1,407	1,430
Kentucky	Lyon County	1,150	1,350	1,423	1,587	1,612
Kentucky	Madison County	1,183	1,389	1,464	1,632	1,659
Kentucky	Magoffin County	970	1,140	1,201	1,339	1,361
Kentucky	Marion County	1,024	1,202	1,267	1,413	1,436
Kentucky	Marshall County	1,024	1,202	1,267	1,413	1,436
Kentucky	Martin County	1,062	1,247	1,314	1,465	1,489
Kentucky	Mason County	1,031	1,211	1,276	1,423	1,446
Kentucky	McCracken County	1,073	1,260	1,328	1,481	1,505
Kentucky	McCreary County	826	970	1,022	1,140	1,158
Kentucky	McLean County	965	1,133	1,194	1,331	1,353
Kentucky	Meade County	1,134	1,331	1,403	1,564	1,590
Kentucky	Menifee County	856	1,005	1,059	1,181	1,200
Kentucky	Mercer County	1,130	1,327	1,398	1,559	1,584
Kentucky	Metcalfe County	875	1,028	1,083	1,208	1,227
Kentucky	Monroe County	888	1,043	1,099	1,225	1,245
Kentucky	Montgomery County	1,025	1,204	1,269	1,415	1,438
Kentucky	Morgan County	903	1,061	1,118	1,247	1,267
Kentucky	Muhlenberg County	939	1,103	1,162	1,296	1,317
Kentucky	Nelson County	1,100	1,292	1,361	1,518	1,542
Kentucky	Nicholas County	968	1,137	1,198	1,336	1,357
Kentucky	Ohio County	898	1,055	1,112	1,240	1,260
Kentucky	Oldham County	1,590	1,868	1,968	2,194	2,230
Kentucky	Owen County	1,033	1,213	1,278	1,425	1,448
Kentucky	Owsley County	926	1,088	1,146	1,278	1,298
Kentucky	Pendleton County	1,108	1,301	1,371	1,529	1,553
Kentucky	Perry County	997	1,171	1,234	1,376	1,398
Kentucky	Pike County	990	1,163	1,225	1,366	1,388
Kentucky	Powell County	993	1,166	1,229	1,370	1,392
Kentucky	Pulaski County	997	1,171	1,234	1,376	1,398
Kentucky	Robertson County	1,021	1,199	1,263	1,408	1,431
Kentucky	Rockcastle County	928	1,090	1,149	1,281	1,302
Kentucky	Rowan County	1,019	1,197	1,261	1,406	1,429
Kentucky	Russell County	928	1,089	1,148	1,280	1,301
Kentucky	Scott County	1,236	1,452	1,530	1,706	1,733
Kentucky	Shelby County	1,318	1,548	1,631	1,819	1,848
Kentucky	Simpson County	1,058	1,243	1,310	1,461	1,484
Kentucky	Spencer County	1,326	1,557	1,641	1,830	1,859
Kentucky	Taylor County	947	1,112	1,172	1,307	1,328
Kentucky	Todd County	1,012	1,188	1,252	1,396	1,419
Kentucky	Trigg County	1,059	1,244	1,311	1,462	1,485

State Name	County	Housing and Utilities for a Family of 1	Housing and Utilities for a Family of 2	Housing and Utilities for a Family of 3	Housing and Utilities for a Family of 4	Housing and Utilities for a Family of 5 or more
Kentucky	Trimble County	1,144	1,344	1,416	1,579	1,604
Kentucky	Union County	953	1,119	1,179	1,315	1,336
Kentucky	Warren County	1,155	1,357	1,430	1,594	1,620
Kentucky	Washington County	1,028	1,207	1,272	1,418	1,441
Kentucky	Wayne County	865	1,015	1,070	1,193	1,212
Kentucky	Webster County	943	1,107	1,167	1,301	1,322
Kentucky	Whitley County	966	1,134	1,195	1,332	1,354
Kentucky	Wolfe County	884	1,038	1,094	1,220	1,240
Kentucky	Woodford County	1,277	1,500	1,581	1,763	1,791
Louisiana	Acadia Parish	959	1,126	1,187	1,324	1,345
Louisiana	Allen Parish	971	1,141	1,202	1,340	1,362
Louisiana	Ascension Parish	1,289	1,514	1,595	1,778	1,807
Louisiana	Assumption Parish	1,026	1,205	1,270	1,416	1,439
Louisiana	Avoyelles Parish	931	1,093	1,152	1,284	1,305
Louisiana	Beauregard Parish	1,058	1,243	1,310	1,461	1,484
Louisiana	Bienville Parish	937	1,101	1,160	1,293	1,314
Louisiana	Bossier Parish	1,210	1,422	1,498	1,670	1,697
Louisiana	Caddo Parish	1,155	1,357	1,430	1,594	1,620
Louisiana	Calcasieu Parish	1,101	1,293	1,363	1,520	1,544
Louisiana	Caldwell Parish	937	1,101	1,160	1,293	1,314
Louisiana	Cameron Parish	1,070	1,256	1,324	1,476	1,500
Louisiana	Catahoula Parish	852	1,001	1,055	1,176	1,195
Louisiana	Claiborne Parish	960	1,127	1,188	1,325	1,346
Louisiana	Concordia Parish	924	1,086	1,144	1,276	1,296
Louisiana	De Soto Parish	1,024	1,202	1,267	1,413	1,436
Louisiana	East Baton Rouge Parish	1,276	1,498	1,579	1,761	1,789
Louisiana	East Carroll Parish	836	982	1,035	1,154	1,173
Louisiana	East Feliciana Parish	1,058	1,242	1,309	1,460	1,483
Louisiana	Evangeline Parish	920	1,080	1,138	1,269	1,289
Louisiana	Franklin Parish	919	1,079	1,137	1,268	1,288
Louisiana	Grant Parish	956	1,123	1,183	1,319	1,340
Louisiana	Iberia Parish	1,079	1,267	1,335	1,489	1,513
Louisiana	Iberville Parish	1,108	1,301	1,371	1,529	1,553
Louisiana	Jackson Parish	941	1,105	1,164	1,298	1,319
Louisiana	Jefferson Davis Parish	1,057	1,241	1,308	1,458	1,482
Louisiana	Jefferson Parish	1,367	1,606	1,692	1,887	1,917
Louisiana	La Salle Parish	941	1,105	1,164	1,298	1,319
Louisiana	Lafayette Parish	1,246	1,463	1,542	1,719	1,747
Louisiana	Lafourche Parish	1,147	1,347	1,419	1,582	1,608
Louisiana	Lincoln Parish	1,135	1,333	1,405	1,567	1,592
Louisiana	Livingston Parish	1,227	1,441	1,518	1,693	1,720
Louisiana	Madison Parish	839	985	1,038	1,157	1,176
Louisiana	Morehouse Parish	950	1,116	1,176	1,311	1,332
Louisiana	Natchitoches Parish	1,058	1,242	1,309	1,460	1,483
Louisiana	Orleans Parish	1,526	1,792	1,888	2,105	2,139
Louisiana	Ouachita Parish	1,098	1,290	1,359	1,515	1,540
Louisiana	Plaquemines Parish	1,389	1,631	1,719	1,917	1,948

State Name	County	Housing and Utilities for a Family of 1	Housing and Utilities for a Family of 2	Housing and Utilities for a Family of 3	Housing and Utilities for a Family of 4	Housing and Utilities for a Family of 5 or more
Louisiana	Pointe Coupee Parish	1,163	1,366	1,439	1,604	1,630
Louisiana	Rapides Parish	1,125	1,321	1,392	1,552	1,577
Louisiana	Red River Parish	886	1,040	1,096	1,222	1,242
Louisiana	Richland Parish	930	1,092	1,151	1,283	1,304
Louisiana	Sabine Parish	988	1,161	1,223	1,364	1,386
Louisiana	St. Bernard Parish	1,133	1,330	1,402	1,563	1,588
Louisiana	St. Charles Parish	1,406	1,651	1,740	1,940	1,971
Louisiana	St. Helena Parish	1,043	1,225	1,291	1,439	1,463
Louisiana	St. James Parish	1,108	1,301	1,371	1,529	1,553
Louisiana	St. John the Baptist Parish	1,294	1,519	1,601	1,785	1,814
Louisiana	St. Landry Parish	961	1,128	1,189	1,326	1,347
Louisiana	St. Martin Parish	1,016	1,194	1,258	1,403	1,425
Louisiana	St. Mary Parish	1,101	1,293	1,363	1,520	1,544
Louisiana	St. Tammany Parish	1,457	1,711	1,803	2,010	2,043
Louisiana	Tangipahoa Parish	1,160	1,363	1,436	1,601	1,627
Louisiana	Tensas Parish	915	1,074	1,132	1,262	1,283
Louisiana	Terrebonne Parish	1,180	1,386	1,460	1,628	1,654
Louisiana	Union Parish	986	1,158	1,220	1,360	1,382
Louisiana	Vermilion Parish	1,030	1,210	1,275	1,422	1,445
Louisiana	Vernon Parish	978	1,149	1,211	1,350	1,372
Louisiana	Washington Parish	935	1,098	1,157	1,290	1,311
Louisiana	Webster Parish	1,069	1,256	1,323	1,475	1,499
Louisiana	West Baton Rouge Parish	1,203	1,413	1,489	1,660	1,687
Louisiana	West Carroll Parish	865	1,015	1,070	1,193	1,212
Louisiana	West Feliciana Parish	1,342	1,576	1,661	1,852	1,882
Louisiana	Winn Parish	865	1,016	1,071	1,194	1,213
Maine	Androscoggin County	1,326	1,557	1,641	1,830	1,859
Maine	Aroostook County	1,009	1,185	1,249	1,393	1,415
Maine	Cumberland County	1,597	1,876	1,977	2,204	2,240
Maine	Franklin County	1,082	1,271	1,339	1,493	1,517
Maine	Hancock County	1,251	1,469	1,548	1,726	1,754
Maine	Kennebec	1,212	1,424	1,500	1,673	1,700
	County					
Maine	Knox County	1,333	1,566	1,650	1,840	1,869
Maine	Lincoln County	1,223	1,436	1,513	1,687	1,714
Maine	Oxford County	1,126	1,322	1,393	1,553	1,578
Maine	Penobscot County	1,206	1,416	1,492	1,664	1,690
Maine	Piscataquis County	994	1,167	1,230	1,371	1,394
Maine	Sagadahoc County	1,374	1,613	1,700	1,896	1,926
Maine	Somerset County	1,063	1,248	1,315	1,466	1,490
Maine	Waldo County	1,194	1,403	1,478	1,648	1,675
Maine	Washington County	1,059	1,244	1,311	1,462	1,485
Maine	York County	1,501	1,763	1,858	2,072	2,105
Maryland	Allegany County	1,128	1,325	1,396	1,557	1,582
Maryland	Anne Arundel County	1,944	2,283	2,406	2,683	2,726
Maryland	Baltimore city	1,385	1,627	1,714	1,911	1,942

State Name	County	Housing and Utilities for a Family of 1	Housing and Utilities for a Family of 2	Housing and Utilities for a Family of 3	Housing and Utilities for a Family of 4	Housing and Utilities for a Family of 5 or more
Maryland	Baltimore County	1,666	1,957	2,062	2,299	2,336
Maryland	Calvert County	1,994	2,342	2,468	2,752	2,796
Maryland	Caroline County	1,570	1,844	1,943	2,166	2,201
Maryland	Carroll County	1,928	2,264	2,386	2,660	2,703
Maryland	Cecil County	1,671	1,963	2,068	2,306	2,343
Maryland	Charles County	1,997	2,346	2,472	2,756	2,801
Maryland	Dorchester County	1,436	1,686	1,777	1,981	2,013
Maryland	Frederick County	1,899	2,230	2,350	2,620	2,663
Maryland	Garrett County	1,187	1,394	1,469	1,638	1,664
Maryland	Harford County	1,780	2,091	2,203	2,456	2,496
Maryland	Howard County	2,301	2,703	2,848	3,176	3,227
Maryland	Kent County	1,460	1,715	1,807	2,015	2,047
Maryland	Montgomery County	2,272	2,669	2,812	3,135	3,186
Maryland	Prince George's County	1,941	2,279	2,402	2,678	2,721
Maryland	Queen Anne's County	2,000	2,349	2,475	2,760	2,804
Maryland	Somerset County	1,282	1,506	1,587	1,770	1,798
Maryland	St. Mary's County	1,850	2,173	2,290	2,553	2,595
Maryland	Talbot County	1,681	1,974	2,080	2,319	2,357
Maryland	Washington County	1,513	1,777	1,872	2,087	2,121
Maryland	Wicomico County	1,411	1,657	1,746	1,947	1,978
Maryland	Worcester County	1,505	1,768	1,863	2,077	2,111
Massachusetts	Barnstable County	1,758	2,065	2,176	2,426	2,465
Massachusetts	Berkshire County	1,392	1,635	1,723	1,921	1,952
Massachusetts	Bristol County	1,768	2,076	2,188	2,440	2,479
Massachusetts	Dukes County	2,132	2,503	2,638	2,941	2,989
Massachusetts	Essex County	2,035	2,391	2,519	2,809	2,854
Massachusetts	Franklin County	1,488	1,747	1,841	2,053	2,086
Massachusetts	Hampden County	1,503	1,765	1,860	2,074	2,107
Massachusetts	Hampshire County	1,623	1,907	2,009	2,240	2,276
Massachusetts	Middlesex County	2,198	2,581	2,720	3,033	3,082
Massachusetts	Nantucket County	2,742	3,220	3,393	3,783	3,844
Massachusetts	Norfolk County	2,182	2,562	2,700	3,011	3,059
Massachusetts	Plymouth County	1,999	2,348	2,474	2,759	2,803
Massachusetts	Suffolk County	2,056	2,415	2,545	2,838	2,883
Massachusetts	Worcester County	1,791	2,103	2,216	2,471	2,511
Michigan	Alcona County	973	1,143	1,204	1,342	1,364
Michigan	Alger County	1,074	1,261	1,329	1,482	1,506
Michigan	Allegan County	1,214	1,425	1,502	1,675	1,702
Michigan	Alpena County	1,010	1,186	1,250	1,394	1,416
Michigan	Antrim County	1,162	1,365	1,438	1,603	1,629
Michigan	Arenac County	1,036	1,217	1,282	1,429	1,453
Michigan	Baraga County	1,014	1,191	1,255	1,399	1,422
Michigan	Barry County	1,241	1,458	1,536	1,713	1,740
Michigan	Bay County	1,123	1,319	1,390	1,550	1,575
Michigan	Benzie County	1,203	1,413	1,489	1,660	1,687
Michigan	Berrien County	1,151	1,351	1,424	1,588	1,613
Michigan	Branch County	1,037	1,219	1,284	1,432	1,455

State Name	County	Housing and Utilities for a Family of 1	Housing and Utilities for a Family of 2	Housing and Utilities for a Family of 3	Housing and Utilities for a Family of 4	Housing and Utilities for a Family of 5 or more
Michigan	Calhoun County	1,138	1,337	1,409	1,571	1,596
Michigan	Cass County	1,151	1,351	1,424	1,588	1,613
Michigan	Charlevoix County	1,236	1,452	1,530	1,706	1,733
Michigan	Cheboygan County	1,020	1,198	1,262	1,407	1,430
Michigan	Chippewa County	1,069	1,256	1,323	1,475	1,499
Michigan	Clare County	965	1,133	1,194	1,331	1,353
Michigan	Clinton County	1,389	1,631	1,719	1,917	1,948
Michigan	Crawford County	1,020	1,198	1,262	1,407	1,430
Michigan	Delta County	1,048	1,231	1,297	1,446	1,470
Michigan	Dickinson County	1,061	1,246	1,313	1,464	1,488
Michigan	Eaton County	1,305	1,533	1,615	1,801	1,830
Michigan	Emmet County	1,258	1,478	1,557	1,736	1,764
Michigan	Genesee County	1,189	1,396	1,471	1,640	1,667
Michigan	Gladwin County	1,050	1,234	1,300	1,450	1,473
Michigan	Gogebic County	899	1,056	1,113	1,241	1,261
Michigan	Grand Traverse County	1,235	1,450	1,528	1,704	1,731
Michigan	Gratiot County	1,067	1,253	1,320	1,472	1,496
Michigan	Hillsdale County	1,103	1,295	1,365	1,522	1,547
Michigan	Houghton County	1,002	1,177	1,240	1,383	1,405
Michigan	Huron County	1,037	1,218	1,283	1,431	1,454
Michigan	Ingham County	1,264	1,484	1,564	1,744	1,772
Michigan	Ionia County	1,175	1,380	1,454	1,621	1,647
Michigan	Iosco County	955	1,122	1,182	1,318	1,339
Michigan	Iron County	1,012	1,189	1,253	1,397	1,420
Michigan	Isabella County	1,151	1,351	1,424	1,588	1,613
Michigan	Jackson County	1,182	1,388	1,463	1,631	1,658
Michigan	Kalamazoo County	1,256	1,475	1,554	1,733	1,761
Michigan	Kalkaska County	1,015	1,192	1,256	1,400	1,423
Michigan	Kent County	1,258	1,478	1,557	1,736	1,764
Michigan	Keweenaw County	1,056	1,240	1,307	1,457	1,481
Michigan	Lake County	934	1,097	1,156	1,289	1,310
Michigan	Lapeer County	1,281	1,505	1,586	1,768	1,797
Michigan	Leelanau County	1,391	1,634	1,722	1,920	1,951
Michigan	Lenawee County	1,201	1,411	1,487	1,658	1,685
Michigan	Livingston County	1,513	1,777	1,873	2,088	2,122
Michigan	Luce County	995	1,169	1,232	1,374	1,396
Michigan	Mackinac County	1,064	1,250	1,317	1,468	1,492
Michigan	Macomb County	1,326	1,557	1,641	1,830	1,859
Michigan	Manistee County	1,045	1,227	1,293	1,442	1,465
Michigan	Marquette County	1,106	1,299	1,369	1,526	1,551
Michigan	Mason County	1,116	1,311	1,381	1,540	1,565
Michigan	Mecosta County	1,101	1,293	1,363	1,520	1,544
Michigan	Menominee County	993	1,166	1,229	1,370	1,392
Michigan	Midland County	1,208	1,419	1,495	1,667	1,694
Michigan	Missaukee County	1,022	1,200	1,265	1,410	1,433
Michigan	Monroe County	1,310	1,538	1,621	1,807	1,837

State Name	County	Housing and Utilities for a Family of 1	Housing and Utilities for a Family of 2	Housing and Utilities for a Family of 3	Housing and Utilities for a Family of 4	Housing and Utilities for a Family of 5 or more
Michigan	Montcalm County	1,079	1,267	1,335	1,489	1,513
Michigan	Montmorency County	966	1,135	1,196	1,334	1,355
Michigan	Muskegon County	1,095	1,286	1,355	1,511	1,535
Michigan	Newaygo County	1,114	1,309	1,379	1,538	1,562
Michigan	Oakland County	1,550	1,820	1,918	2,139	2,173
Michigan	Oceana County	1,092	1,282	1,351	1,506	1,531
Michigan	Ogemaw County	991	1,164	1,227	1,368	1,390
Michigan	Ontonagon County	937	1,101	1,160	1,293	1,314
Michigan	Osceola County	1,042	1,223	1,289	1,437	1,460
Michigan	Oscoda County	960	1,127	1,188	1,325	1,346
Michigan	Otsego County	1,096	1,287	1,356	1,512	1,536
Michigan	Ottawa County	1,268	1,489	1,569	1,749	1,778
Michigan	Presque Isle County	983	1,154	1,216	1,356	1,378
Michigan	Roscommon County	977	1,147	1,209	1,348	1,370
Michigan	Saginaw County	1,130	1,327	1,398	1,559	1,584
Michigan	Sanilac County	1,067	1,253	1,320	1,472	1,496
Michigan	Schoolcraft County	1,023	1,201	1,266	1,412	1,434
Michigan	Shiawassee County	1,163	1,366	1,439	1,604	1,630
Michigan	St. Clair County	1,247	1,464	1,543	1,720	1,748
Michigan	St. Joseph County	1,061	1,246	1,313	1,464	1,488
Michigan	Tuscola County	1,101	1,293	1,363	1,520	1,544
Michigan	Van Buren	1,190	1,398	1,473	1,642	1,669
	County					
Michigan	Washtenaw County	1,623	1,907	2,009	2,240	2,276
Michigan	Wayne County	1,262	1,482	1,562	1,742	1,770
Michigan	Wexford County	1,063	1,249	1,316	1,467	1,491
Minnesota	Aitkin County	1,178	1,384	1,458	1,626	1,652
Minnesota	Anoka County	1,508	1,771	1,866	2,081	2,114
Minnesota	Becker County	1,277	1,500	1,581	1,763	1,791
Minnesota	Beltrami County	1,215	1,427	1,504	1,677	1,704
Minnesota	Benton County	1,344	1,578	1,663	1,854	1,884
Minnesota	Big Stone County	1,018	1,196	1,260	1,405	1,428
Minnesota	Blue Earth County	1,297	1,523	1,605	1,790	1,818
Minnesota	Brown County	1,130	1,328	1,399	1,560	1,585
Minnesota	Carlton County	1,287	1,512	1,593	1,776	1,805
Minnesota	Carver County	1,799	2,113	2,227	2,483	2,523
Minnesota	Cass County	1,199	1,408	1,484	1,655	1,681
Minnesota	Chippewa County	1,122	1,318	1,389	1,549	1,574
Minnesota	Chisago County	1,550	1,820	1,918	2,139	2,173
Minnesota	Clay County	1,295	1,521	1,603	1,787	1,816
Minnesota	Clearwater County	1,142	1,341	1,413	1,575	1,601
Minnesota	Cook County	1,467	1,723	1,816	2,025	2,058
Minnesota	Cottonwood County	999	1,174	1,237	1,379	1,402
Minnesota	Crow Wing County	1,235	1,450	1,528	1,704	1,731
Minnesota	Dakota County	1,596	1,874	1,975	2,202	2,238
Minnesota	Dodge County	1,395	1,638	1,726	1,924	1,956
Minnesota	Douglas County	1,308	1,536	1,619	1,805	1,834

State Name	County	Housing and Utilities for a Family of 1	Housing and Utilities for a Family of 2	Housing and Utilities for a Family of 3	Housing and Utilities for a Family of 4	Housing and Utilities for a Family of 5 or more
Minnesota	Faribault County	956	1,123	1,183	1,319	1,340
Minnesota	Fillmore County	1,252	1,470	1,549	1,727	1,755
Minnesota	Freeborn County	1,043	1,225	1,291	1,439	1,463
Minnesota	Goodhue County	1,435	1,685	1,776	1,980	2,012
Minnesota	Grant County	1,079	1,267	1,335	1,489	1,513
Minnesota	Hennepin County	1,635	1,921	2,024	2,257	2,293
Minnesota	Houston County	1,233	1,448	1,526	1,701	1,729
Minnesota	Hubbard County	1,260	1,480	1,560	1,739	1,767
Minnesota	Isanti County	1,436	1,686	1,777	1,981	2,013
Minnesota	Itasca County	1,181	1,387	1,462	1,630	1,656
Minnesota	Jackson County	1,042	1,224	1,290	1,438	1,462
Minnesota	Kanabec County	1,263	1,483	1,563	1,743	1,771
Minnesota	Kandiyohi County	1,260	1,479	1,559	1,738	1,766
Minnesota	Kittson County	1,021	1,199	1,263	1,408	1,431
Minnesota	Koochiching County	1,079	1,267	1,335	1,489	1,513
Minnesota	Lac qui Parle County	1,004	1,179	1,242	1,385	1,407
Minnesota	Lake County	1,184	1,390	1,465	1,633	1,660
Minnesota	Lake of the Woods County	1,068	1,255	1,322	1,474	1,498
Minnesota	Le Sueur County	1,385	1,627	1,714	1,911	1,942
Minnesota	Lincoln County	1,078	1,266	1,334	1,487	1,511
Minnesota	Lyon County	1,179	1,385	1,459	1,627	1,653
Minnesota	Mahnomen County	1,087	1,276	1,345	1,500	1,524
Minnesota	Marshall County	1,062	1,247	1,314	1,465	1,489
Minnesota	Martin County	1,073	1,260	1,328	1,481	1,505
Minnesota	McLeod County	1,301	1,528	1,610	1,795	1,824
Minnesota	Meeker County	1,315	1,544	1,627	1,814	1,843
Minnesota	Mille Lacs County	1,281	1,505	1,586	1,768	1,797
Minnesota	Morrison County	1,269	1,490	1,570	1,751	1,779
Minnesota	Mower County	1,122	1,317	1,388	1,548	1,573
Minnesota	Murray County	1,075	1,262	1,330	1,483	1,507
Minnesota	Nicollet County	1,325	1,556	1,640	1,829	1,858
Minnesota	Nobles County	1,101	1,293	1,363	1,520	1,544
Minnesota	Norman County	1,025	1,203	1,268	1,414	1,437
Minnesota	Olmsted County	1,395	1,638	1,726	1,924	1,956
Minnesota	Otter Tail County	1,199	1,408	1,484	1,655	1,681
Minnesota	Pennington County	1,087	1,276	1,345	1,500	1,524
Minnesota	Pine County	1,250	1,468	1,547	1,725	1,753
Minnesota	Pipestone County	1,020	1,198	1,262	1,407	1,430
Minnesota	Polk County	1,218	1,430	1,507	1,680	1,707
Minnesota	Pope County	1,215	1,427	1,504	1,677	1,704
Minnesota	Ramsey County	1,496	1,758	1,852	2,065	2,098
Minnesota	Red Lake County	1,088	1,278	1,347	1,502	1,526
Minnesota	Redwood County	1,054	1,237	1,304	1,454	1,477
Minnesota	Renville County	1,107	1,300	1,370	1,528	1,552
Minnesota	Rice County	1,461	1,716	1,808	2,016	2,048
Minnesota	Rock County	1,130	1,328	1,399	1,560	1,585

State Name	County	Housing and Utilities for a Family of 1	Housing and Utilities for a Family of 2	Housing and Utilities for a Family of 3	Housing and Utilities for a Family of 4	Housing and Utilities for a Family of 5 or more
Minnesota	Roseau County	1,193	1,402	1,477	1,647	1,673
Minnesota	Scott County	1,740	2,043	2,153	2,401	2,439
Minnesota	Sherburne County	1,531	1,798	1,895	2,113	2,147
Minnesota	Sibley County	1,278	1,501	1,582	1,764	1,792
Minnesota	St. Louis County	1,187	1,394	1,469	1,638	1,664
Minnesota	Stearns County	1,322	1,553	1,636	1,824	1,854
Minnesota	Steele County	1,321	1,552	1,635	1,823	1,852
Minnesota	Stevens County	1,175	1,380	1,454	1,621	1,647
Minnesota	Swift County	1,041	1,222	1,288	1,436	1,459
Minnesota	Todd County	1,151	1,352	1,425	1,589	1,615
Minnesota	Traverse County	1,055	1,239	1,306	1,456	1,480
Minnesota	Wabasha County	1,289	1,514	1,595	1,778	1,807
Minnesota	Wadena County	1,089	1,279	1,348	1,503	1,527
Minnesota	Waseca County	1,223	1,436	1,513	1,687	1,714
Minnesota	Washington County	1,648	1,936	2,040	2,275	2,311
Minnesota	Watonwan County	1,026	1,205	1,270	1,416	1,439
Minnesota	Wilkin County	1,149	1,349	1,422	1,586	1,611
Minnesota	Winona County	1,238	1,454	1,532	1,708	1,736
Minnesota	Wright County	1,541	1,810	1,907	2,126	2,161
Minnesota	Yellow Medicine	1,018	1,196	1,260	1,405	1,428
	County					
Mississippi	Adams County	963	1,131	1,192	1,329	1,351
Mississippi	Alcorn County	985	1,157	1,219	1,359	1,381
Mississippi	Amite County	925	1,087	1,145	1,277	1,297
Mississippi	Attala County	862	1,013	1,067	1,190	1,209
Mississippi	Benton County	1,012	1,188	1,252	1,396	1,419
Mississippi	Bolivar County	1,018	1,196	1,260	1,405	1,428
Mississippi	Calhoun County	844	991	1,044	1,164	1,183
Mississippi	Carroll County	946	1,111	1,171	1,306	1,327
Mississippi	Chickasaw County	896	1,052	1,109	1,237	1,256
Mississippi	Choctaw County	869	1,020	1,075	1,199	1,218
Mississippi	Claiborne County	895	1,051	1,108	1,235	1,255
Mississippi	Clarke County	889	1,044	1,100	1,227	1,246
Mississippi	Clay County	970	1,140	1,201	1,339	1,361
Mississippi	Coahoma County	940	1,104	1,163	1,297	1,318
Mississippi	Copiah County	983	1,154	1,216	1,356	1,378
Mississippi	Covington County	945	1,109	1,169	1,303	1,324
Mississippi	DeSoto County	1,264	1,484	1,564	1,744	1,772
Mississippi	Forrest County	1,129	1,326	1,397	1,558	1,583
Mississippi	Franklin County	946	1,111	1,171	1,306	1,327
Mississippi	George County	1,113	1,308	1,378	1,536	1,561
Mississippi	Greene County	1,037	1,218	1,283	1,431	1,454
Mississippi	Grenada County	951	1,117	1,177	1,312	1,334
Mississippi	Hancock County	1,188	1,395	1,470	1,639	1,666
Mississippi	Harrison County	1,230	1,444	1,522	1,697	1,724
Mississippi	Hinds County	1,117	1,312	1,382	1,541	1,566
Mississippi	Holmes County	906	1,064	1,121	1,250	1,270

State Name	County	Housing and Utilities for a Family of 1	Housing and Utilities for a Family of 2	Housing and Utilities for a Family of 3	Housing and Utilities for a Family of 4	Housing and Utilities for a Family of 5 or more
Mississippi	Humphreys County	886	1,041	1,097	1,223	1,243
Mississippi	Issaquena County	1,021	1,200	1,264	1,409	1,432
Mississippi	Itawamba County	948	1,113	1,173	1,308	1,329
Mississippi	Jackson County	1,259	1,479	1,558	1,737	1,765
Mississippi	Jasper County	948	1,113	1,173	1,308	1,329
Mississippi	Jefferson County	909	1,068	1,125	1,254	1,275
Mississippi	Jefferson Davis County	957	1,124	1,184	1,320	1,341
Mississippi	Jones County	1,022	1,200	1,265	1,410	1,433
Mississippi	Kemper County	834	979	1,032	1,151	1,169
Mississippi	Lafayette County	1,240	1,457	1,535	1,712	1,739
Mississippi	Lamar County	1,294	1,520	1,602	1,786	1,815
Mississippi	Lauderdale County	1,075	1,262	1,330	1,483	1,507
Mississippi	Lawrence County	971	1,141	1,202	1,340	1,362
Mississippi	Leake County	974	1,144	1,205	1,344	1,365
Mississippi	Lee County	1,110	1,304	1,374	1,532	1,557
Mississippi	Leflore County	1,008	1,183	1,247	1,390	1,413
Mississippi	Lincoln County	1,040	1,221	1,287	1,435	1,458
Mississippi	Lowndes County	1,069	1,256	1,323	1,475	1,499
Mississippi	Madison County	1,486	1,745	1,839	2,050	2,084
Mississippi	Marion County	975	1,145	1,207	1,346	1,368
Mississippi	Marshall County	1,122	1,318	1,389	1,549	1,574
Mississippi	Monroe County	968	1,137	1,198	1,336	1,357
Mississippi	Montgomery County	960	1,127	1,188	1,325	1,346
Mississippi	Neshoba County	941	1,106	1,165	1,299	1,320
Mississippi	Newton County	951	1,117	1,177	1,312	1,334
Mississippi	Noxubee County	901	1,058	1,115	1,243	1,263
Mississippi	Oktibbeha County	1,180	1,386	1,460	1,628	1,654
Mississippi	Panola County	995	1,168	1,231	1,373	1,395
Mississippi	Pearl River County	1,127	1,324	1,395	1,555	1,581
Mississippi	Perry County	967	1,136	1,197	1,335	1,356
Mississippi	Pike County	982	1,153	1,215	1,355	1,377
Mississippi	Pontotoc County	982	1,153	1,215	1,355	1,377
Mississippi	Prentiss County	938	1,102	1,161	1,295	1,315
Mississippi	Quitman County	781	917	966	1,077	1,094
Mississippi	Rankin County	1,227	1,442	1,519	1,694	1,721
Mississippi	Scott County	966	1,135	1,196	1,334	1,355
Mississippi	Sharkey County	1,058	1,242	1,309	1,460	1,483
Mississippi	Simpson County	968	1,137	1,198	1,336	1,357
Mississippi	Smith County	1,046	1,228	1,294	1,443	1,466
Mississippi	Stone County	1,146	1,346	1,418	1,581	1,607
Mississippi	Sunflower County	933	1,096	1,155	1,288	1,309
Mississippi	Tallahatchie County	870	1,022	1,077	1,201	1,220
Mississippi	Tate County	1,220	1,433	1,510	1,684	1,711
Mississippi	Tippah County	872	1,024	1,079	1,203	1,223
Mississippi	Tishomingo County	882	1,035	1,091	1,216	1,236
Mississippi	Tunica County	932	1,095	1,154	1,287	1,307

State Name	County	Housing and Utilities for a Family of 1	Housing and Utilities for a Family of 2	Housing and Utilities for a Family of 3	Housing and Utilities for a Family of 4	Housing and Utilities for a Family of 5 or more
Mississippi	Union County	987	1,160	1,222	1,363	1,385
Mississippi	Walthall County	1,064	1,250	1,317	1,468	1,492
Mississippi	Warren County	1,148	1,349	1,421	1,584	1,610
Mississippi	Washington County	1,030	1,210	1,275	1,422	1,445
Mississippi	Wayne County	949	1,114	1,174	1,309	1,330
Mississippi	Webster County	987	1,160	1,222	1,363	1,385
Mississippi	Wilkinson County	907	1,065	1,122	1,251	1,271
Mississippi	Winston County	966	1,134	1,195	1,332	1,354
Mississippi	Yalobusha County	949	1,115	1,175	1,310	1,331
Mississippi	Yazoo County	991	1,163	1,226	1,367	1,389
Missouri	Adair County	991	1,163	1,226	1,367	1,389
Missouri	Andrew County	1,176	1,382	1,456	1,623	1,650
Missouri	Atchison County	974	1,144	1,206	1,345	1,366
Missouri	Audrain County	1,037	1,218	1,283	1,431	1,454
Missouri	Barry County	978	1,149	1,211	1,350	1,372
Missouri	Barton County	985	1,157	1,219	1,359	1,381
Missouri	Bates County	1,097	1,289	1,358	1,514	1,539
Missouri	Benton County	1,003	1,178	1,241	1,384	1,406
Missouri	Bollinger County	961	1,128	1,189	1,326	1,347
Missouri	Boone County	1,269	1,491	1,571	1,752	1,780
Missouri	Buchanan County	1,100	1,292	1,361	1,518	1,542
Missouri	Butler County	974	1,144	1,206	1,345	1,366
Missouri	Caldwell County	1,120	1,315	1,386	1,545	1,570
Missouri	Callaway County	1,088	1,278	1,347	1,502	1,526
Missouri	Camden County	1,102	1,294	1,364	1,521	1,545
Missouri	Cape Girardeau County	1,110	1,304	1,374	1,532	1,557
Missouri	Carroll County	1,004	1,179	1,242	1,385	1,407
Missouri	Carter County	1,075	1,262	1,330	1,483	1,507
Missouri	Cass County	1,345	1,580	1,665	1,856	1,886
Missouri	Cedar County	937	1,101	1,160	1,293	1,314
Missouri	Chariton County	949	1,114	1,174	1,309	1,330
Missouri	Christian County	1,176	1,382	1,456	1,623	1,650
Missouri	Clark County	949	1,115	1,175	1,310	1,331
Missouri	Clay County	1,366	1,604	1,690	1,884	1,915
Missouri	Clinton County	1,233	1,448	1,526	1,701	1,729
Missouri	Cole County	1,173	1,378	1,452	1,619	1,645
Missouri	Cooper County	1,048	1,231	1,297	1,446	1,470
Missouri	Crawford County	1,011	1,187	1,251	1,395	1,417
Missouri	Dade County	938	1,102	1,161	1,295	1,315
Missouri	Dallas County	953	1,119	1,179	1,315	1,336
Missouri	Daviess County	1,048	1,231	1,297	1,446	1,470
Missouri	DeKalb County	1,147	1,347	1,419	1,582	1,608
Missouri	Dent County	959	1,126	1,187	1,324	1,345
Missouri	Douglas County	881	1,034	1,090	1,215	1,235
Missouri	Dunklin County	906	1,064	1,121	1,250	1,270
Missouri	Franklin County	1,203	1,413	1,489	1,660	1,687
Missouri	Gasconade County	1,057	1,241	1,308	1,458	1,482

State Name	County	Housing and Utilities for a Family of 1	Housing and Utilities for a Family of 2	Housing and Utilities for a Family of 3	Housing and Utilities for a Family of 4	Housing and Utilities for a Family of 5 or more
Missouri	Gentry County	1,015	1,192	1,256	1,400	1,423
Missouri	Greene County	1,077	1,265	1,333	1,486	1,510
Missouri	Grundy County	953	1,120	1,180	1,316	1,337
Missouri	Harrison County	966	1,134	1,195	1,332	1,354
Missouri	Henry County	1,010	1,186	1,250	1,394	1,416
Missouri	Hickory County	931	1,093	1,152	1,284	1,305
Missouri	Holt County	1,000	1,175	1,238	1,380	1,403
Missouri	Howard County	992	1,165	1,228	1,369	1,391
Missouri	Howell County	963	1,131	1,192	1,329	1,351
Missouri	Iron County	930	1,092	1,151	1,283	1,304
Missouri	Jackson County	1,286	1,511	1,592	1,775	1,804
Missouri	Jasper County	1,033	1,214	1,279	1,426	1,449
Missouri	Jefferson County	1,262	1,482	1,562	1,742	1,770
Missouri	Johnson County	1,200	1,409	1,485	1,656	1,683
Missouri	Knox County	911	1,070	1,127	1,257	1,277
Missouri	Laclede County	988	1,161	1,223	1,364	1,386
Missouri	Lafayette County	1,147	1,347	1,419	1,582	1,608
Missouri	Lawrence County	1,021	1,200	1,264	1,409	1,432
Missouri	Lewis County	923	1,084	1,142	1,273	1,294
Missouri	Lincoln County	1,234	1,449	1,527	1,703	1,730
Missouri	Linn County	947	1,112	1,172	1,307	1,328
Missouri	Livingston County	999	1,173	1,236	1,378	1,400
Missouri	Macon County	966	1,134	1,195	1,332	1,354
Missouri	Madison County	949	1,114	1,174	1,309	1,330
Missouri	Maries County	999	1,174	1,237	1,379	1,402
Missouri	Marion County	1,027	1,206	1,271	1,417	1,440
Missouri	McDonald County	970	1,139	1,200	1,338	1,360
Missouri	Mercer County	878	1,032	1,087	1,212	1,232
Missouri	Miller County	975	1,145	1,207	1,346	1,368
Missouri	Mississippi County	840	986	1,039	1,158	1,177
Missouri	Moniteau County	1,057	1,241	1,308	1,458	1,482
Missouri	Monroe County	975	1,145	1,207	1,346	1,368
Missouri	Montgomery County	1,046	1,229	1,295	1,444	1,467
Missouri	Morgan County	972	1,142	1,203	1,341	1,363
Missouri	New Madrid County	914	1,073	1,131	1,261	1,281
Missouri	Newton County	1,028	1,207	1,272	1,418	1,441
Missouri	Nodaway County	1,064	1,250	1,317	1,468	1,492
Missouri	Oregon County	894	1,050	1,106	1,233	1,253
Missouri	Osage County	1,041	1,222	1,288	1,436	1,459
Missouri	Ozark County	944	1,108	1,168	1,302	1,323
Missouri	Pemiscot County	943	1,107	1,167	1,301	1,322
Missouri	Perry County	1,096	1,287	1,356	1,512	1,536
Missouri	Pettis County	1,016	1,194	1,258	1,403	1,425
Missouri	Phelps County	1,118	1,313	1,384	1,543	1,568
Missouri	Pike County	1,033	1,214	1,279	1,426	1,449

State Name	County	Housing and Utilities for a Family of 1	Housing and Utilities for a Family of 2	Housing and Utilities for a Family of 3	Housing and Utilities for a Family of 4	Housing and Utilities for a Family of 5 or more
Missouri	Platte County	1,534	1,802	1,899	2,117	2,152
Missouri	Polk County	1,019	1,197	1,261	1,406	1,429
Missouri	Pulaski County	1,159	1,361	1,434	1,599	1,625
Missouri	Putnam County	1,025	1,204	1,269	1,415	1,438
Missouri	Ralls County	1,016	1,193	1,257	1,402	1,424
Missouri	Randolph County	983	1,154	1,216	1,356	1,378
Missouri	Ray County	1,172	1,377	1,451	1,618	1,644
Missouri	Reynolds County	980	1,151	1,213	1,352	1,374
Missouri	Ripley County	865	1,015	1,070	1,193	1,212
Missouri	Saline County	987	1,159	1,221	1,361	1,383
Missouri	Schuyler County	890	1,046	1,102	1,229	1,249
Missouri	Scotland County	986	1,158	1,220	1,360	1,382
Missouri	Scott County	966	1,134	1,195	1,332	1,354
Missouri	Shannon County	911	1,070	1,128	1,258	1,278
Missouri	Shelby County	948	1,113	1,173	1,308	1,329
Missouri	St. Charles County	1,461	1,716	1,808	2,016	2,048
Missouri	St. Clair County	932	1,095	1,154	1,287	1,307
Missouri	St. Francois County	1,012	1,188	1,252	1,396	1,419
Missouri	St. Louis city	1,193	1,402	1,477	1,647	1,673
Missouri	St. Louis County	1,403	1,647	1,736	1,936	1,967
Missouri	Ste. Genevieve County	1,126	1,322	1,393	1,553	1,578
Missouri	Stoddard County	958	1,126	1,186	1,322	1,344
Missouri	Stone County	1,071	1,257	1,325	1,477	1,501
Missouri	Sullivan County	947	1,112	1,172	1,307	1,328
Missouri	Taney County	1,089	1,279	1,348	1,503	1,527
Missouri	Texas County	953	1,120	1,180	1,316	1,337
Missouri	Vernon County	1,007	1,182	1,246	1,389	1,412
Missouri	Warren County	1,244	1,461	1,540	1,717	1,745
Missouri	Washington County	920	1,081	1,139	1,270	1,290
Missouri	Wayne County	845	993	1,046	1,166	1,185
Missouri	Webster County	999	1,174	1,237	1,379	1,402
Missouri	Worth County	870	1,022	1,077	1,201	1,220
Missouri	Wright County	920	1,081	1,139	1,270	1,290
Montana	Beaverhead County	1,141	1,340	1,412	1,574	1,600
Montana	Big Horn County	920	1,081	1,139	1,270	1,290
Montana	Blaine County	1,076	1,264	1,332	1,485	1,509
Montana	Broadwater County	1,244	1,461	1,539	1,716	1,744
Montana	Carbon County	1,225	1,439	1,516	1,690	1,718
Montana	Carter County	1,370	1,610	1,696	1,891	1,922
Montana	Cascade County	1,207	1,418	1,494	1,666	1,693
Montana	Chouteau County	1,105	1,298	1,368	1,525	1,550
Montana	Custer County	1,063	1,248	1,315	1,466	1,490
Montana	Daniels County	1,096	1,287	1,356	1,512	1,536
Montana	Dawson County	1,131	1,329	1,400	1,561	1,586
Montana	Deer Lodge County	974	1,144	1,206	1,345	1,366
Montana	Fallon County	984	1,156	1,218	1,358	1,380
Montana	Fergus County	1,073	1,260	1,328	1,481	1,505

State Name	County	Housing and Utilities for a Family of 1	Housing and Utilities for a Family of 2	Housing and Utilities for a Family of 3	Housing and Utilities for a Family of 4	Housing and Utilities for a Family of 5 or more
Montana	Flathead County	1,363	1,601	1,687	1,881	1,911
Montana	Gallatin County	1,514	1,778	1,874	2,090	2,123
Montana	Garfield County	1,006	1,182	1,245	1,388	1,411
Montana	Glacier County	1,016	1,194	1,258	1,403	1,425
Montana	Golden Valley County	1,169	1,373	1,447	1,613	1,639
Montana	Granite County	1,218	1,430	1,507	1,680	1,707
Montana	Hill County	1,127	1,324	1,395	1,555	1,581
Montana	Jefferson County	1,421	1,669	1,759	1,961	1,993
Montana	Judith Basin County	1,060	1,245	1,312	1,463	1,486
Montana	Lake County	1,273	1,495	1,575	1,756	1,784
Montana	Lewis and Clark County	1,350	1,586	1,671	1,863	1,893
Montana	Liberty County	870	1,022	1,077	1,201	1,220
Montana	Lincoln County	1,099	1,291	1,360	1,516	1,541
Montana	Madison County	1,385	1,627	1,714	1,911	1,942
Montana	McCone County	1,180	1,386	1,460	1,628	1,654
Montana	Meagher County	1,014	1,191	1,255	1,399	1,422
Montana	Mineral County	1,193	1,401	1,476	1,646	1,672
Montana	Missoula County	1,445	1,697	1,788	1,994	2,026
Montana	Musselshell County	1,130	1,327	1,398	1,559	1,584
Montana	Park County	1,286	1,511	1,592	1,775	1,804
Montana	Petroleum County	1,154	1,355	1,428	1,592	1,618
Montana	Phillips County	1,021	1,199	1,263	1,408	1,431
Montana	Pondera County	1,132	1,330	1,401	1,562	1,587
Montana	Powder River County	1,167	1,370	1,444	1,610	1,636
Montana	Powell County	1,016	1,194	1,258	1,403	1,425
Montana	Prairie County	943	1,107	1,167	1,301	1,322
Montana	Ravalli County	1,320	1,551	1,634	1,822	1,851
Montana	Richland County	1,144	1,344	1,416	1,579	1,604
Montana	Roosevelt County	951	1,117	1,177	1,312	1,334
Montana	Rosebud County	1,117	1,312	1,383	1,542	1,567
Montana	Sanders County	1,145	1,345	1,417	1,580	1,605
Montana	Sheridan County	1,159	1,362	1,435	1,600	1,626
Montana	Silver Bow County	1,022	1,200	1,265	1,410	1,433
Montana	Stillwater County	1,324	1,554	1,638	1,826	1,856
Montana	Sweet Grass County	1,262	1,482	1,562	1,742	1,770
Montana	Teton County	1,138	1,337	1,409	1,571	1,596
Montana	Toole County	1,016	1,194	1,258	1,403	1,425
Montana	Treasure County	1,030	1,210	1,275	1,422	1,445
Montana	Valley County	1,053	1,237	1,303	1,453	1,476
Montana	Wheatland County	962	1,130	1,191	1,328	1,349
Montana	Wibaux County	1,050	1,234	1,300	1,450	1,473
Montana	Yellowstone County	1,319	1,549	1,632	1,820	1,849
Nebraska	Adams County	1,113	1,308	1,378	1,536	1,561
Nebraska	Antelope County	961	1,128	1,189	1,326	1,347
Nebraska	Arthur County	1,096	1,287	1,356	1,512	1,536
Nebraska	Banner County	1,297	1,523	1,605	1,790	1,818

State Name	County	Housing and Utilities for a Family of 1	Housing and Utilities for a Family of 2	Housing and Utilities for a Family of 3	Housing and Utilities for a Family of 4	Housing and Utilities for a Family of 5 or more
Nebraska	Blaine County	1,134	1,332	1,404	1,565	1,591
Nebraska	Boone County	1,092	1,282	1,351	1,506	1,531
Nebraska	Box Butte County	1,073	1,260	1,328	1,481	1,505
Nebraska	Boyd County	1,049	1,232	1,298	1,447	1,471
Nebraska	Brown County	987	1,159	1,221	1,361	1,383
Nebraska	Buffalo County	1,286	1,510	1,591	1,774	1,803
Nebraska	Burt County	1,137	1,335	1,407	1,569	1,594
Nebraska	Butler County	1,124	1,320	1,391	1,551	1,576
Nebraska	Cass County	1,370	1,610	1,696	1,891	1,922
Nebraska	Cedar County	1,092	1,283	1,352	1,507	1,532
Nebraska	Chase County	987	1,159	1,221	1,361	1,383
Nebraska	Cherry County	1,144	1,344	1,416	1,579	1,604
Nebraska	Cheyenne County	1,138	1,337	1,409	1,571	1,596
Nebraska	Clay County	1,055	1,239	1,306	1,456	1,480
Nebraska	Colfax County	1,059	1,244	1,311	1,462	1,485
Nebraska	Cuming County	981	1,152	1,214	1,354	1,375
Nebraska	Custer County	1,034	1,215	1,280	1,427	1,450
Nebraska	Dakota County	1,144	1,344	1,416	1,579	1,604
Nebraska	Dawes County	1,084	1,274	1,342	1,496	1,520
Nebraska	Dawson County	1,061	1,246	1,313	1,464	1,488
Nebraska	Deuel County	954	1,121	1,181	1,317	1,338
Nebraska	Dixon County	1,063	1,249	1,316	1,467	1,491
Nebraska	Dodge County	1,130	1,327	1,398	1,559	1,584
Nebraska	Douglas County	1,355	1,591	1,677	1,870	1,900
Nebraska	Dundy County	907	1,066	1,123	1,252	1,272
Nebraska	Fillmore County	980	1,151	1,213	1,352	1,374
Nebraska	Franklin County	928	1,090	1,149	1,281	1,302
Nebraska	Frontier County	1,024	1,202	1,267	1,413	1,436
Nebraska	Furnas County	946	1,111	1,171	1,306	1,327
Nebraska	Gage County	1,122	1,318	1,389	1,549	1,574
Nebraska	Garden County	934	1,097	1,156	1,289	1,310
Nebraska	Garfield County	873	1,026	1,081	1,205	1,225
Nebraska	Gosper County	1,018	1,196	1,260	1,405	1,428
Nebraska	Grant County	911	1,070	1,127	1,257	1,277
Nebraska	Greeley County	1,006	1,182	1,245	1,388	1,411
Nebraska	Hall County	1,162	1,365	1,438	1,603	1,629
Nebraska	Hamilton County	1,134	1,331	1,403	1,564	1,590
Nebraska	Harlan County	957	1,125	1,185	1,321	1,343
Nebraska	Hayes County	1,142	1,341	1,413	1,575	1,601
Nebraska	Hitchcock County	854	1,003	1,057	1,179	1,198
Nebraska	Holt County	1,037	1,219	1,284	1,432	1,455
Nebraska	Hooker County	1,027	1,206	1,271	1,417	1,440
Nebraska	Howard County	1,250	1,468	1,547	1,725	1,753
Nebraska	Jefferson County	938	1,102	1,161	1,295	1,315
Nebraska	Johnson County	992	1,165	1,228	1,369	1,391
Nebraska	Kearney County	1,058	1,242	1,309	1,460	1,483
Nebraska	Keith County	1,027	1,206	1,271	1,417	1,440

State Name	County	Housing and Utilities for a Family of 1	Housing and Utilities for a Family of 2	Housing and Utilities for a Family of 3	Housing and Utilities for a Family of 4	Housing and Utilities for a Family of 5 or more
Nebraska	Keya Paha County	1,134	1,332	1,404	1,565	1,591
Nebraska	Kimball County	1,027	1,206	1,271	1,417	1,440
Nebraska	Knox County	1,003	1,178	1,241	1,384	1,406
Nebraska	Lancaster County	1,297	1,523	1,605	1,790	1,818
Nebraska	Lincoln County	1,227	1,441	1,518	1,693	1,720
Nebraska	Logan County	1,192	1,400	1,475	1,645	1,671
Nebraska	Loup County	1,250	1,468	1,547	1,725	1,753
Nebraska	Madison County	1,132	1,330	1,401	1,562	1,587
Nebraska	McPherson County	1,360	1,597	1,683	1,877	1,907
Nebraska	Merrick County	1,007	1,182	1,246	1,389	1,412
Nebraska	Morrill County	1,008	1,183	1,247	1,390	1,413
Nebraska	Nance County	972	1,142	1,203	1,341	1,363
Nebraska	Nemaha County	1,040	1,221	1,287	1,435	1,458
Nebraska	Nuckolls County	918	1,078	1,136	1,267	1,287
Nebraska	Otoe County	1,200	1,409	1,485	1,656	1,683
Nebraska	Pawnee County	1,014	1,191	1,255	1,399	1,422
Nebraska	Perkins County	1,017	1,195	1,259	1,404	1,426
Nebraska	Phelps County	1,061	1,246	1,313	1,464	1,488
Nebraska	Pierce County	1,096	1,287	1,356	1,512	1,536
Nebraska	Platte County	1,113	1,308	1,378	1,536	1,561
Nebraska	Polk County	1,026	1,205	1,270	1,416	1,439
Nebraska	Red Willow County	996	1,170	1,233	1,375	1,397
Nebraska	Richardson County	856	1,005	1,059	1,181	1,200
Nebraska	Rock County	890	1,046	1,102	1,229	1,249
Nebraska	Saline County	1,129	1,326	1,397	1,558	1,583
Nebraska	Sarpy County	1,437	1,687	1,778	1,982	2,014
Nebraska	Saunders County	1,355	1,591	1,677	1,870	1,900
Nebraska	Scotts Bluff County	1,138	1,336	1,408	1,570	1,595
Nebraska	Seward County	1,277	1,500	1,581	1,763	1,791
Nebraska	Sheridan County	899	1,056	1,113	1,241	1,261
Nebraska	Sherman County	1,021	1,199	1,263	1,408	1,431
Nebraska	Sioux County	1,025	1,204	1,269	1,415	1,438
Nebraska	Stanton County	1,066	1,252	1,319	1,471	1,494
Nebraska	Thayer County	966	1,135	1,196	1,334	1,355
Nebraska	Thomas County	1,155	1,356	1,429	1,593	1,619
Nebraska	Thurston County	1,009	1,185	1,249	1,393	1,415
Nebraska	Valley County	945	1,109	1,169	1,303	1,324
Nebraska	Washington County	1,469	1,725	1,818	2,027	2,060
Nebraska	Wayne County	1,015	1,192	1,256	1,400	1,423
Nebraska	Webster County	966	1,135	1,196	1,334	1,355
Nebraska	Wheeler County	1,065	1,251	1,318	1,470	1,493
Nebraska	York County	1,079	1,267	1,335	1,489	1,513
Nevada	Carson City	1,471	1,727	1,820	2,029	2,062
Nevada	Churchill County	1,212	1,424	1,500	1,673	1,700
Nevada	Clark County	1,557	1,829	1,927	2,149	2,183
Nevada	Douglas County	1,643	1,930	2,034	2,268	2,305

State Name	County	Housing and Utilities for a Family of 1	Housing and Utilities for a Family of 2	Housing and Utilities for a Family of 3	Housing and Utilities for a Family of 4	Housing and Utilities for a Family of 5 or more
Nevada	Elko County	1,437	1,688	1,779	1,984	2,016
Nevada	Esmeralda County	998	1,172	1,235	1,377	1,399
Nevada	Eureka County	1,171	1,375	1,449	1,616	1,642
Nevada	Humboldt County	1,226	1,440	1,517	1,691	1,719
Nevada	Lander County	1,237	1,453	1,531	1,707	1,735
Nevada	Lincoln County	1,112	1,306	1,376	1,534	1,559
Nevada	Lyon County	1,283	1,507	1,588	1,771	1,799
Nevada	Mineral County	1,032	1,212	1,277	1,424	1,447
Nevada	Nye County	1,205	1,415	1,491	1,662	1,689
Nevada	Pershing County	1,217	1,429	1,506	1,679	1,706
Nevada	Storey County	1,418	1,665	1,755	1,957	1,988
Nevada	Washoe County	1,601	1,880	1,981	2,209	2,244
Nevada	White Pine County	1,117	1,312	1,383	1,542	1,567
New Hampshire	Belknap County	1,611	1,892	1,994	2,223	2,259
New Hampshire	Carroll County	1,431	1,681	1,771	1,975	2,007
New Hampshire	Cheshire County	1,568	1,841	1,940	2,163	2,198
New Hampshire	Coos County	1,209	1,420	1,496	1,668	1,695
New Hampshire	Grafton County	1,501	1,763	1,858	2,072	2,105
New Hampshire	Hillsborough County	1,885	2,214	2,333	2,601	2,643
New Hampshire	Merrimack County	1,766	2,075	2,186	2,437	2,477
New Hampshire	Rockingham County	1,995	2,343	2,469	2,753	2,797
New Hampshire	Strafford County	1,773	2,082	2,194	2,446	2,486
New Hampshire	Sullivan County	1,495	1,756	1,850	2,063	2,096
New Jersey	Atlantic County	1,807	2,123	2,237	2,494	2,535
New Jersey	Bergen County	2,650	3,113	3,280	3,657	3,716
New Jersey	Burlington County	1,936	2,274	2,396	2,672	2,715
New Jersey	Camden County	1,813	2,130	2,244	2,502	2,542
New Jersey	Cape May County	1,789	2,101	2,214	2,469	2,508
New Jersey	Cumberland County	1,555	1,827	1,925	2,146	2,181
New Jersey	Essex County	2,520	2,960	3,119	3,478	3,534
New Jersey	Gloucester County	1,887	2,216	2,335	2,604	2,646
New Jersey	Hudson County	2,426	2,850	3,003	3,348	3,402
New Jersey	Hunterdon County	2,434	2,858	3,012	3,358	3,413
New Jersey	Mercer County	2,107	2,475	2,608	2,908	2,955
New Jersey	Middlesex County	2,210	2,596	2,735	3,050	3,099
New Jersey	Monmouth County	2,385	2,801	2,952	3,291	3,345
New Jersey	Morris County	2,548	2,993	3,154	3,517	3,573
New Jersey	Ocean County	1,898	2,229	2,349	2,619	2,661
New Jersey	Passaic County	2,390	2,807	2,958	3,298	3,351
New Jersey	Salem County	1,675	1,967	2,073	2,311	2,349
New Jersey	Somerset County	2,455	2,883	3,038	3,387	3,442
New Jersey	Sussex County	2,107	2,475	2,608	2,908	2,955
New Jersey	Union County	2,422	2,845	2,998	3,343	3,397
New Jersey	Warren County	2,036	2,391	2,520	2,810	2,855
New Mexico	Bernalillo County	1,347	1,582	1,667	1,859	1,889
New Mexico	Catron County	1,055	1,239	1,306	1,456	1,480

State Name	County	Housing and Utilities for a Family of 1	Housing and Utilities for a Family of 2	Housing and Utilities for a Family of 3	Housing and Utilities for a Family of 4	Housing and Utilities for a Family of 5 or more
New Mexico	Chaves County	1,010	1,186	1,250	1,394	1,416
New Mexico	Cibola County	1,016	1,193	1,257	1,402	1,424
New Mexico	Colfax County	1,075	1,262	1,330	1,483	1,507
New Mexico	Curry County	1,092	1,283	1,352	1,507	1,532
New Mexico	DeBaca County	1,009	1,185	1,249	1,393	1,415
New Mexico	Dona Ana County	1,171	1,375	1,449	1,616	1,642
New Mexico	Eddy County	1,054	1,238	1,305	1,455	1,479
New Mexico	Grant County	1,023	1,201	1,266	1,412	1,434
New Mexico	Guadalupe County	1,024	1,202	1,267	1,413	1,436
New Mexico	Harding County	995	1,169	1,232	1,374	1,396
New Mexico	Hidalgo County	930	1,092	1,151	1,283	1,304
New Mexico	Lea County	1,066	1,252	1,319	1,471	1,494
New Mexico	Lincoln County	1,197	1,406	1,482	1,652	1,679
New Mexico	Los Alamos County	1,774	2,083	2,195	2,447	2,487
New Mexico	Luna County	956	1,123	1,183	1,319	1,340
New Mexico	McKinley County	1,035	1,216	1,281	1,428	1,451
New Mexico	Mora County	1,063	1,249	1,316	1,467	1,491
New Mexico	Otero County	1,037	1,218	1,283	1,431	1,454
New Mexico	Quay County	913	1,072	1,130	1,260	1,280
New Mexico	Rio Arriba County	1,161	1,364	1,437	1,602	1,628
New Mexico	Roosevelt County	1,072	1,259	1,327	1,480	1,503
New Mexico	San Juan County	1,224	1,438	1,515	1,689	1,716
New Mexico	San Miguel County	1,147	1,347	1,419	1,582	1,608
New Mexico	Sandoval County	1,353	1,590	1,675	1,868	1,898
New Mexico	Santa Fe County	1,534	1,801	1,898	2,116	2,150
New Mexico	Sierra County	904	1,062	1,119	1,248	1,268
New Mexico	Socorro County	1,047	1,230	1,296	1,445	1,468
New Mexico	Taos County	1,279	1,502	1,583	1,765	1,794
New Mexico	Torrance County	996	1,170	1,233	1,375	1,397
New Mexico	Union County	1,007	1,182	1,246	1,389	1,412
New Mexico	Valencia County	1,143	1,343	1,415	1,578	1,603
New York	Albany County	1,597	1,875	1,976	2,203	2,239
New York	Allegany County	1,040	1,221	1,287	1,435	1,458
New York	Bronx County	2,190	2,572	2,710	3,022	3,070
New York	Broome County	1,181	1,387	1,462	1,630	1,656
New York	Cattaraugus County	1,112	1,306	1,376	1,534	1,559
New York	Cayuga County	1,202	1,412	1,488	1,659	1,686
New York	Chautauqua County	1,038	1,219	1,285	1,433	1,456
New York	Chemung County	1,128	1,325	1,396	1,557	1,582
New York	Chenango County	1,137	1,335	1,407	1,569	1,594
New York	Clinton County	1,277	1,499	1,580	1,762	1,790
New York	Columbia County	1,627	1,910	2,013	2,244	2,281
New York	Cortland County	1,229	1,443	1,521	1,696	1,723
New York	Delaware County	1,154	1,355	1,428	1,592	1,618
New York	Dutchess County	2,085	2,448	2,580	2,877	2,923
New York	Erie County	1,261	1,481	1,561	1,741	1,769

State Name	County	Housing and Utilities for a Family of 1	Housing and Utilities for a Family of 2	Housing and Utilities for a Family of 3	Housing and Utilities for a Family of 4	Housing and Utilities for a Family of 5 or more
New York	Essex County	1,256	1,476	1,555	1,734	1,762
New York	Franklin County	1,139	1,338	1,410	1,572	1,598
New York	Fulton County	1,188	1,395	1,470	1,639	1,666
New York	Genesee County	1,209	1,420	1,496	1,668	1,695
New York	Greene County	1,474	1,731	1,824	2,034	2,067
New York	Hamilton County	1,191	1,399	1,474	1,644	1,670
New York	Herkimer County	1,135	1,333	1,405	1,567	1,592
New York	Jefferson County	1,248	1,466	1,545	1,723	1,750
New York	Kings County	2,365	2,778	2,927	3,264	3,316
New York	Lewis County	1,107	1,300	1,370	1,528	1,552
New York	Livingston County	1,269	1,490	1,570	1,751	1,779
New York	Madison County	1,252	1,470	1,549	1,727	1,755
New York	Monroe County	1,343	1,577	1,662	1,853	1,883
New York	Montgomery County	1,238	1,454	1,532	1,708	1,736
New York	Nassau County	2,779	3,264	3,439	3,834	3,896
New York	New York County	3,669	4,309	4,541	5,063	5,145
New York	Niagara County	1,220	1,433	1,510	1,684	1,711
New York	Oneida County	1,232	1,447	1,525	1,700	1,728
New York	Onondaga County	1,341	1,575	1,660	1,851	1,881
New York	Ontario County	1,326	1,557	1,641	1,830	1,859
New York	Orange County	2,119	2,489	2,623	2,925	2,972
New York	Orleans County	1,226	1,440	1,517	1,691	1,719
New York	Oswego County	1,212	1,424	1,500	1,673	1,700
New York	Otsego County	1,252	1,471	1,550	1,728	1,756
New York	Putnam County	2,461	2,891	3,046	3,396	3,451
New York	Queens County	2,236	2,626	2,767	3,085	3,135
New York	Rensselaer County	1,534	1,801	1,898	2,116	2,150
New York	Richmond County	2,207	2,593	2,732	3,046	3,095
New York	Rockland County	2,651	3,114	3,281	3,658	3,717
New York	Saratoga County	1,622	1,905	2,007	2,238	2,274
New York	Schenectady County	1,496	1,758	1,852	2,065	2,098
New York	Schoharie County	1,332	1,565	1,649	1,839	1,868
New York	Schuyler County	1,143	1,342	1,414	1,577	1,602
New York	Seneca County	1,150	1,350	1,423	1,587	1,612
New York	St. Lawrence County	1,114	1,309	1,379	1,538	1,562
New York	Steuben County	1,116	1,311	1,381	1,540	1,565
New York	Suffolk County	2,494	2,930	3,087	3,442	3,498
New York	Sullivan County	1,550	1,820	1,918	2,139	2,173
New York	Tioga County	1,209	1,420	1,496	1,668	1,695
New York	Tompkins County	1,420	1,667	1,757	1,959	1,991
New York	Ulster County	1,779	2,090	2,202	2,455	2,495
New York	Warren County	1,411	1,657	1,746	1,947	1,978
New York	Washington County	1,328	1,559	1,643	1,832	1,862
New York	Wayne County	1,239	1,455	1,533	1,709	1,737
New York	Westchester County	2,928	3,439	3,624	4,041	4,106
New York	Wyoming County	1,148	1,349	1,421	1,584	1,610
New York	Yates County	1,151	1,351	1,424	1,588	1,613

State Name	County	Housing and Utilities for a Family of 1	Housing and Utilities for a Family of 2	Housing and Utilities for a Family of 3	Housing and Utilities for a Family of 4	Housing and Utilities for a Family of 5 or more
North Carolina	Alamance County	1,193	1,401	1,476	1,646	1,672
North Carolina	Alexander County	1,008	1,184	1,248	1,392	1,414
North Carolina	Alleghany County	1,145	1,345	1,417	1,580	1,605
North Carolina	Anson County	957	1,124	1,184	1,320	1,341
North Carolina	Ashe County	1,079	1,268	1,336	1,490	1,514
North Carolina	Avery County	1,072	1,259	1,327	1,480	1,503
North Carolina	Beaufort County	1,196	1,405	1,480	1,650	1,677
North Carolina	Bertie County	1,053	1,237	1,303	1,453	1,476
North Carolina	Bladen County	1,033	1,213	1,278	1,425	1,448
North	Brunswick	1,293	1,518	1,600	1,784	1,813
Carolina	County					
North Carolina	Buncombe County	1,270	1,492	1,572	1,753	1,781
North Carolina	Burke County	1,042	1,223	1,289	1,437	1,460
North Carolina	Cabarrus County	1,329	1,561	1,645	1,834	1,864
North Carolina	Caldwell County	997	1,171	1,234	1,376	1,398
North Carolina	Camden County	1,624	1,907	2,010	2,241	2,277
North Carolina	Carteret County	1,283	1,507	1,588	1,771	1,799
North Carolina	Caswell County	1,033	1,213	1,278	1,425	1,448
North Carolina	Catawba County	1,119	1,314	1,385	1,544	1,569
North Carolina	Chatham County	1,434	1,684	1,775	1,979	2,011
North Carolina	Cherokee County	1,007	1,182	1,246	1,389	1,412
North Carolina	Chowan County	1,291	1,517	1,598	1,782	1,811
North Carolina	Clay County	1,055	1,239	1,306	1,456	1,480
North Carolina	Cleveland County	1,055	1,239	1,306	1,456	1,480
North Carolina	Columbus County	1,058	1,242	1,309	1,460	1,483
North Carolina	Craven County	1,271	1,493	1,573	1,754	1,782
North	Cumberland	1,210	1,421	1,497	1,669	1,696
Carolina	County					
North Carolina	Currituck County	1,523	1,789	1,885	2,102	2,136
North Carolina	Dare County	1,593	1,870	1,971	2,198	2,233
North Carolina	Davidson County	1,126	1,323	1,394	1,554	1,579
North Carolina	Davie County	1,210	1,421	1,497	1,669	1,696
North Carolina	Duplin County	1,073	1,260	1,328	1,481	1,505
North Carolina	Durham County	1,386	1,628	1,715	1,912	1,943
North Carolina	Edgecombe County	1,043	1,225	1,291	1,439	1,463
North Carolina	Forsyth County	1,212	1,424	1,500	1,673	1,700
North Carolina	Franklin County	1,191	1,399	1,474	1,644	1,670
North Carolina	Gaston County	1,180	1,386	1,460	1,628	1,654
North Carolina	Gates County	1,277	1,500	1,581	1,763	1,791
North Carolina	Graham County	920	1,080	1,138	1,269	1,289
North Carolina	Granville County	1,213	1,424	1,501	1,674	1,701
North Carolina	Greene County	1,091	1,281	1,350	1,505	1,530
North Carolina	Guilford County	1,277	1,499	1,580	1,762	1,790
North	Halifax County	1,092	1,282	1,351	1,506	1,531
Carolina						
North Carolina	Harnett County	1,221	1,434	1,511	1,685	1,712

State Name	County	Housing and Utilities for a Family of 1	Housing and Utilities for a Family of 2	Housing and Utilities for a Family of 3	Housing and Utilities for a Family of 4	Housing and Utilities for a Family of 5 or more
North Carolina	Haywood County	1,185	1,391	1,466	1,635	1,661
North Carolina	Henderson County	1,199	1,408	1,484	1,655	1,681
North Carolina	Hertford County	1,049	1,232	1,298	1,447	1,471
North Carolina	Hoke County	1,186	1,393	1,468	1,637	1,663
North Carolina	Hyde County	936	1,100	1,159	1,292	1,313
North Carolina	Iredell County	1,281	1,505	1,586	1,768	1,797
North Carolina	Jackson County	1,153	1,354	1,427	1,591	1,617
North Carolina	Johnston County	1,242	1,459	1,537	1,714	1,741
North Carolina	Jones County	1,105	1,298	1,368	1,525	1,550
North Carolina	Lee County	1,148	1,349	1,421	1,584	1,610
North Carolina	Lenoir County	1,088	1,278	1,347	1,502	1,526
North Carolina	Lincoln County	1,201	1,410	1,486	1,657	1,684
North Carolina	Macon County	1,102	1,294	1,364	1,521	1,545
North Carolina	Madison County	1,180	1,386	1,460	1,628	1,654
North Carolina	Martin County	1,093	1,284	1,353	1,509	1,533
North Carolina	McDowell County	988	1,161	1,223	1,364	1,386
North Carolina	Mecklenburg County	1,406	1,651	1,740	1,940	1,971
North Carolina	Mitchell County	1,016	1,193	1,257	1,402	1,424
North Carolina	Montgomery County	1,050	1,233	1,299	1,448	1,472
North Carolina	Moore County	1,270	1,492	1,572	1,753	1,781
North Carolina	Nash County	1,193	1,401	1,476	1,646	1,672
North Carolina	New Hanover County	1,445	1,697	1,788	1,994	2,026
North Carolina	Northampton County	1,037	1,219	1,284	1,432	1,455
North Carolina	Onslow County	1,245	1,462	1,541	1,718	1,746
North Carolina	Orange County	1,663	1,953	2,058	2,295	2,332
North Carolina	Pamlico County	1,227	1,441	1,518	1,693	1,720
North Carolina	Pasquotank County	1,386	1,628	1,715	1,912	1,943
North Carolina	Pender County	1,253	1,472	1,551	1,729	1,757
North Carolina	Perquimans County	1,327	1,558	1,642	1,831	1,860
North Carolina	Person County	1,124	1,320	1,391	1,551	1,576
North Carolina	Pitt County	1,244	1,461	1,539	1,716	1,744
North Carolina	Polk County	1,171	1,375	1,449	1,616	1,642
North Carolina	Randolph County	1,088	1,278	1,347	1,502	1,526
North Carolina	Richmond County	991	1,164	1,227	1,368	1,390
North Carolina	Robeson County	1,043	1,225	1,291	1,439	1,463
North Carolina	Rockingham County	1,059	1,244	1,311	1,462	1,485
North Carolina	Rowan County	1,105	1,298	1,368	1,525	1,550
North Carolina	Rutherford County	1,001	1,176	1,239	1,381	1,404
North Carolina	Sampson County	1,070	1,256	1,324	1,476	1,500
North Carolina	Scotland County	1,021	1,199	1,263	1,408	1,431
North Carolina	Stanly County	1,179	1,385	1,459	1,627	1,653
North Carolina	Stokes County	1,076	1,264	1,332	1,485	1,509
North Carolina	Surry County	1,063	1,248	1,315	1,466	1,490
North Carolina	Swain County	1,090	1,280	1,349	1,504	1,528
North Carolina	Transylvania County	1,122	1,317	1,388	1,548	1,573

State Name	County	Housing and Utilities for a Family of 1	Housing and Utilities for a Family of 2	Housing and Utilities for a Family of 3	Housing and Utilities for a Family of 4	Housing and Utilities for a Family of 5 or more
North Carolina	Tyrrell County	1,077	1,265	1,333	1,486	1,510
North Carolina	Union County	1,421	1,669	1,759	1,961	1,993
North Carolina	Vance County	1,076	1,264	1,332	1,485	1,509
North Carolina	Wake County	1,496	1,757	1,851	2,064	2,097
North Carolina	Warren County	1,093	1,284	1,353	1,509	1,533
North Carolina	Washington County	1,020	1,198	1,262	1,407	1,430
North Carolina	Watauga County	1,287	1,512	1,593	1,776	1,805
North Carolina	Wayne County	1,117	1,312	1,382	1,541	1,566
North Carolina	Wilkes County	1,050	1,233	1,299	1,448	1,472
North Carolina	Wilson County	1,198	1,407	1,483	1,654	1,680
North Carolina	Yadkin County	1,029	1,209	1,274	1,421	1,443
North Carolina	Yancey County	1,085	1,275	1,343	1,497	1,522
North Dakota	Adams County	1,021	1,200	1,264	1,409	1,432
North Dakota	Barnes County	1,079	1,268	1,336	1,490	1,514
North Dakota	Benson County	928	1,089	1,148	1,280	1,301
North Dakota	Billings County	1,051	1,235	1,301	1,451	1,474
North Dakota	Bottineau County	1,071	1,257	1,325	1,477	1,501
North Dakota	Bowman County	996	1,170	1,233	1,375	1,397
North Dakota	Burke County	1,094	1,285	1,354	1,510	1,534
North Dakota	Burleigh County	1,334	1,567	1,651	1,841	1,871
North Dakota	Cass County	1,364	1,602	1,688	1,882	1,913
North Dakota	Cavalier County	961	1,128	1,189	1,326	1,347
North Dakota	Dickey County	1,046	1,229	1,295	1,444	1,467
North Dakota	Divide County	1,128	1,325	1,396	1,557	1,582
North Dakota	Dunn County	922	1,083	1,141	1,272	1,293
North Dakota	Eddy County	858	1,008	1,062	1,184	1,203
North Dakota	Emmons County	910	1,069	1,126	1,255	1,276
North Dakota	Foster County	1,021	1,200	1,264	1,409	1,432
North Dakota	Golden Valley County	848	996	1,050	1,171	1,190
North Dakota	Grand Forks County	1,286	1,510	1,591	1,774	1,803
North Dakota	Grant County	1,041	1,222	1,288	1,436	1,459
North Dakota	Griggs County	993	1,166	1,229	1,370	1,392
North Dakota	Hettinger County	913	1,072	1,130	1,260	1,280
North Dakota	Kidder County	1,037	1,219	1,284	1,432	1,455
North Dakota	LaMoure County	1,039	1,220	1,286	1,434	1,457
North Dakota	Logan County	1,019	1,197	1,261	1,406	1,429
North Dakota	McHenry County	1,096	1,288	1,357	1,513	1,537
North Dakota	McIntosh County	875	1,028	1,083	1,208	1,227
North Dakota	McKenzie County	1,025	1,203	1,268	1,414	1,437
North Dakota	McLean County	1,119	1,314	1,385	1,544	1,569
North Dakota	Mercer County	1,104	1,296	1,366	1,523	1,548
North Dakota	Morton County	1,271	1,493	1,573	1,754	1,782
North Dakota	Mountrail County	999	1,173	1,236	1,378	1,400
North Dakota	Nelson County	1,018	1,196	1,260	1,405	1,428
North Dakota	Oliver County	1,042	1,224	1,290	1,438	1,462

State Name	County	Housing and Utilities for a Family of 1	Housing and Utilities for a Family of 2	Housing and Utilities for a Family of 3	Housing and Utilities for a Family of 4	Housing and Utilities for a Family of 5 or more
North Dakota	Pembina County	978	1,149	1,211	1,350	1,372
North Dakota	Pierce County	1,008	1,184	1,248	1,392	1,414
North Dakota	Ramsey County	1,013	1,190	1,254	1,398	1,421
North Dakota	Ransom County	1,117	1,312	1,382	1,541	1,566
North Dakota	Renville County	1,075	1,262	1,330	1,483	1,507
North Dakota	Richland County	1,100	1,292	1,361	1,518	1,542
North Dakota	Rolette County	934	1,097	1,156	1,289	1,310
North Dakota	Sargent County	1,022	1,200	1,265	1,410	1,433
North Dakota	Sheridan County	955	1,122	1,182	1,318	1,339
North Dakota	Sioux County	985	1,157	1,219	1,359	1,381
North Dakota	Slope County	948	1,113	1,173	1,308	1,329
North Dakota	Stark County	1,262	1,482	1,562	1,742	1,770
North Dakota	Steele County	954	1,121	1,181	1,317	1,338
North Dakota	Stutsman County	1,079	1,267	1,335	1,489	1,513
North Dakota	Towner County	928	1,089	1,148	1,280	1,301
North Dakota	Traill County	1,149	1,349	1,422	1,586	1,611
North Dakota	Walsh County	987	1,159	1,221	1,361	1,383
North Dakota	Ward County	1,259	1,479	1,558	1,737	1,765
North Dakota	Wells County	928	1,090	1,149	1,281	1,302
North Dakota	Williams County	1,119	1,314	1,385	1,544	1,569
Ohio	Adams County	1,002	1,177	1,240	1,383	1,405
Ohio	Allen County	1,102	1,294	1,364	1,521	1,545
Ohio	Ashland County	1,117	1,312	1,383	1,542	1,567
Ohio	Ashtabula	1,096	1,288	1,357	1,513	1,537
	County					
Ohio	Athens County	1,134	1,331	1,403	1,564	1,590
Ohio	Auglaize County	1,168	1,371	1,445	1,611	1,637
Ohio	Belmont County	1,011	1,187	1,251	1,395	1,417
Ohio	Brown County	1,131	1,329	1,400	1,561	1,586
Ohio	Butler County	1,370	1,610	1,696	1,891	1,922
Ohio	Carroll County	1,125	1,321	1,392	1,552	1,577
Ohio	Champaign County	1,164	1,368	1,441	1,607	1,633
Ohio	Clark County	1,116	1,311	1,381	1,540	1,565
Ohio	Clermont County	1,373	1,612	1,699	1,894	1,925
Ohio	Clinton County	1,182	1,388	1,463	1,631	1,658
Ohio	Columbiana County	1,053	1,237	1,303	1,453	1,476
Ohio	Coshocton County	1,004	1,179	1,242	1,385	1,407
Ohio	Crawford County	1,004	1,180	1,243	1,386	1,408
Ohio	Cuyahoga County	1,308	1,536	1,619	1,805	1,834
Ohio	Darke County	1,100	1,293	1,362	1,519	1,543
Ohio	Defiance County	1,117	1,312	1,382	1,541	1,566
Ohio	Delaware County	1,815	2,131	2,246	2,504	2,545
Ohio	Erie County	1,197	1,406	1,482	1,652	1,679
Ohio	Fairfield County	1,401	1,646	1,734	1,933	1,965
Ohio	Fayette County	1,083	1,272	1,340	1,494	1,518
Ohio	Franklin County	1,387	1,629	1,717	1,914	1,945
Ohio	Fulton County	1,197	1,405	1,481	1,651	1,678

State Name	County	Housing and Utilities for a Family of 1	Housing and Utilities for a Family of 2	Housing and Utilities for a Family of 3	Housing and Utilities for a Family of 4	Housing and Utilities for a Family of 5 or more
Ohio	Gallia County	1,125	1,321	1,392	1,552	1,577
Ohio	Geauga County	1,571	1,845	1,944	2,168	2,203
Ohio	Greene County	1,380	1,621	1,708	1,904	1,935
Ohio	Guernsey County	1,022	1,200	1,265	1,410	1,433
Ohio	Hamilton County	1,355	1,591	1,677	1,870	1,900
Ohio	Hancock County	1,193	1,401	1,476	1,646	1,672
Ohio	Hardin County	1,033	1,213	1,278	1,425	1,448
Ohio	Harrison County	948	1,113	1,173	1,308	1,329
Ohio	Henry County	1,147	1,348	1,420	1,583	1,609
Ohio	Highland County	1,071	1,257	1,325	1,477	1,501
Ohio	Hocking County	1,125	1,321	1,392	1,552	1,577
Ohio	Holmes County	1,107	1,300	1,370	1,528	1,552
Ohio	Huron County	1,147	1,347	1,419	1,582	1,608
Ohio	Jackson County	1,063	1,249	1,316	1,467	1,491
Ohio	Jefferson County	982	1,153	1,215	1,355	1,377
Ohio	Knox County	1,200	1,409	1,485	1,656	1,683
Ohio	Lake County	1,329	1,561	1,645	1,834	1,864
Ohio	Lawrence County	1,050	1,234	1,300	1,450	1,473
Ohio	Licking County	1,333	1,566	1,650	1,840	1,869
Ohio	Logan County	1,126	1,322	1,393	1,553	1,578
Ohio	Lorain County	1,294	1,519	1,601	1,785	1,814
Ohio	Lucas County	1,201	1,410	1,486	1,657	1,684
Ohio	Madison County	1,282	1,506	1,587	1,770	1,798
Ohio	Mahoning County	1,099	1,291	1,360	1,516	1,541
Ohio	Marion County	1,077	1,265	1,333	1,486	1,510
Ohio	Medina County	1,437	1,687	1,778	1,982	2,014
Ohio	Meigs County	1,004	1,179	1,242	1,385	1,407
Ohio	Mercer County	1,142	1,341	1,413	1,575	1,601
Ohio	Miami County	1,197	1,406	1,482	1,652	1,679
Ohio	Monroe County	927	1,089	1,147	1,279	1,300
Ohio	Montgomery County	1,216	1,428	1,505	1,678	1,705
Ohio	Morgan County	1,062	1,247	1,314	1,465	1,489
Ohio	Morrow County	1,201	1,411	1,487	1,658	1,685
Ohio	Muskingum County	1,074	1,261	1,329	1,482	1,506
Ohio	Noble County	911	1,070	1,127	1,257	1,277
Ohio	Ottawa County	1,218	1,431	1,508	1,681	1,709
Ohio	Paulding County	1,042	1,224	1,290	1,438	1,462
Ohio	Perry County	1,036	1,217	1,282	1,429	1,453
Ohio	Pickaway County	1,311	1,540	1,623	1,810	1,839
Ohio	Pike County	1,084	1,274	1,342	1,496	1,520
Ohio	Portage County	1,313	1,542	1,625	1,812	1,841
Ohio	Preble County	1,155	1,357	1,430	1,594	1,620
Ohio	Putnam County	1,126	1,323	1,394	1,554	1,579
Ohio	Richland County	1,084	1,273	1,341	1,495	1,519
Ohio	Ross County	1,134	1,331	1,403	1,564	1,590
Ohio	Sandusky County	1,122	1,317	1,388	1,548	1,573

State Name	County	Housing and Utilities for a Family of 1	Housing and Utilities for a Family of 2	Housing and Utilities for a Family of 3	Housing and Utilities for a Family of 4	Housing and Utilities for a Family of 5 or more
Ohio	Scioto County	1,045	1,227	1,293	1,442	1,465
Ohio	Seneca County	1,034	1,215	1,280	1,427	1,450
Ohio	Shelby County	1,159	1,362	1,435	1,600	1,626
Ohio	Stark County	1,157	1,359	1,432	1,597	1,622
Ohio	Summit County	1,262	1,482	1,562	1,742	1,770
Ohio	Trumbull County	1,081	1,270	1,338	1,492	1,516
Ohio	Tuscarawas County	1,072	1,259	1,327	1,480	1,503
Ohio	Union County	1,518	1,783	1,879	2,095	2,129
Ohio	Van Wert County	1,016	1,194	1,258	1,403	1,425
Ohio	Vinton County	1,025	1,203	1,268	1,414	1,437
Ohio	Warren County	1,537	1,805	1,902	2,121	2,155
Ohio	Washington County	1,063	1,248	1,315	1,466	1,490
Ohio	Wayne County	1,167	1,370	1,444	1,610	1,636
Ohio	Williams County	1,046	1,228	1,294	1,443	1,466
Ohio	Wood County	1,323	1,554	1,637	1,825	1,855
Ohio	Wyandot County	1,050	1,234	1,300	1,450	1,473
Oklahoma	Adair County	923	1,084	1,142	1,273	1,294
Oklahoma	Alfalfa County	890	1,046	1,102	1,229	1,249
Oklahoma	Atoka County	978	1,149	1,211	1,350	1,372
Oklahoma	Beaver County	1,117	1,312	1,383	1,542	1,567
Oklahoma	Beckham County	1,146	1,346	1,418	1,581	1,607
Oklahoma	Blaine County	1,016	1,193	1,257	1,402	1,424
Oklahoma	Bryan County	1,042	1,223	1,289	1,437	1,460
Oklahoma	Caddo County	931	1,093	1,152	1,284	1,305
Oklahoma	Canadian County	1,299	1,526	1,608	1,793	1,822
Oklahoma	Carter County	1,098	1,290	1,359	1,515	1,540
Oklahoma	Cherokee County	1,056	1,240	1,307	1,457	1,481
Oklahoma	Choctaw County	903	1,061	1,118	1,247	1,267
Oklahoma	Cimarron County	866	1,017	1,072	1,195	1,215
Oklahoma	Cleveland County	1,281	1,504	1,585	1,767	1,796
Oklahoma	Coal County	897	1,053	1,110	1,238	1,258
Oklahoma	Comanche County	1,126	1,323	1,394	1,554	1,579
Oklahoma	Cotton County	988	1,161	1,223	1,364	1,386
Oklahoma	Craig County	943	1,107	1,167	1,301	1,322
Oklahoma	Creek County	1,104	1,296	1,366	1,523	1,548
Oklahoma	Custer County	1,122	1,317	1,388	1,548	1,573
Oklahoma	Delaware County	1,041	1,222	1,288	1,436	1,459
Oklahoma	Dewey County	939	1,103	1,162	1,296	1,317
Oklahoma	Ellis County	918	1,078	1,136	1,267	1,287
Oklahoma	Garfield County	1,025	1,203	1,268	1,414	1,437
Oklahoma	Garvin County	1,016	1,193	1,257	1,402	1,424
Oklahoma	Grady County	1,156	1,358	1,431	1,596	1,621
Oklahoma	Grant County	904	1,062	1,119	1,248	1,268
Oklahoma	Greer County	892	1,048	1,104	1,231	1,251
Oklahoma	Harmon County	788	925	975	1,087	1,105
Oklahoma	Harper County	932	1,094	1,153	1,286	1,306
Oklahoma	Haskell County	927	1,089	1,147	1,279	1,300

State Name	County	Housing and Utilities for a Family of 1	Housing and Utilities for a Family of 2	Housing and Utilities for a Family of 3	Housing and Utilities for a Family of 4	Housing and Utilities for a Family of 5 or more
Oklahoma	Hughes County	923	1,084	1,142	1,273	1,294
Oklahoma	Jackson County	1,029	1,209	1,274	1,421	1,443
Oklahoma	Jefferson County	904	1,062	1,119	1,248	1,268
Oklahoma	Johnston County	928	1,089	1,148	1,280	1,301
Oklahoma	Kay County	999	1,173	1,236	1,378	1,400
Oklahoma	Kingfisher County	1,109	1,303	1,373	1,531	1,556
Oklahoma	Kiowa County	930	1,092	1,151	1,283	1,304
Oklahoma	Latimer County	901	1,058	1,115	1,243	1,263
Oklahoma	Le Flore County	942	1,107	1,166	1,300	1,321
Oklahoma	Lincoln County	1,032	1,212	1,277	1,424	1,447
Oklahoma	Logan County	1,255	1,474	1,553	1,732	1,760
Oklahoma	Love County	1,022	1,200	1,265	1,410	1,433
Oklahoma	Major County	928	1,090	1,149	1,281	1,302
Oklahoma	Marshall County	937	1,101	1,160	1,293	1,314
Oklahoma	Mayes County	1,017	1,195	1,259	1,404	1,426
Oklahoma	McClain County	1,288	1,513	1,594	1,777	1,806
Oklahoma	McCurtain County	925	1,087	1,145	1,277	1,297
Oklahoma	McIntosh County	979	1,150	1,212	1,351	1,373
Oklahoma	Murray County	1,018	1,196	1,260	1,405	1,428
Oklahoma	Muskogee County	1,025	1,203	1,268	1,414	1,437
Oklahoma	Noble County	1,029	1,209	1,274	1,421	1,443
Oklahoma	Nowata County	939	1,103	1,162	1,296	1,317
Oklahoma	Okfuskee County	910	1,069	1,126	1,255	1,276
Oklahoma	Oklahoma County	1,236	1,452	1,530	1,706	1,733
Oklahoma	Okmulgee County	1,002	1,177	1,240	1,383	1,405
Oklahoma	Osage County	1,129	1,326	1,397	1,558	1,583
Oklahoma	Ottawa County	949	1,114	1,174	1,309	1,330
Oklahoma	Pawnee County	1,076	1,264	1,332	1,485	1,509
Oklahoma	Payne County	1,199	1,408	1,484	1,655	1,681
Oklahoma	Pittsburg County	979	1,150	1,212	1,351	1,373
Oklahoma	Pontotoc County	1,046	1,229	1,295	1,444	1,467
Oklahoma	Pottawatomie County	1,042	1,224	1,290	1,438	1,462
Oklahoma	Pushmataha County	919	1,079	1,137	1,268	1,288
Oklahoma	Roger Mills County	1,038	1,219	1,285	1,433	1,456
Oklahoma	Rogers County	1,233	1,448	1,526	1,701	1,729
Oklahoma	Seminole County	941	1,105	1,164	1,298	1,319
Oklahoma	Sequoyah County	920	1,080	1,138	1,269	1,289
Oklahoma	Stephens County	1,036	1,217	1,282	1,429	1,453
Oklahoma	Texas County	1,048	1,231	1,297	1,446	1,470
Oklahoma	Tillman County	897	1,053	1,110	1,238	1,258
Oklahoma	Tulsa County	1,239	1,456	1,534	1,710	1,738
Oklahoma	Wagoner County	1,232	1,447	1,525	1,700	1,728
Oklahoma	Washington County	1,066	1,252	1,319	1,471	1,494
Oklahoma	Washita County	911	1,070	1,128	1,258	1,278
Oklahoma	Woods County	955	1,122	1,182	1,318	1,339
Oklahoma	Woodward County	1,005	1,181	1,244	1,387	1,409

State Name	County	Housing and Utilities for a Family of 1	Housing and Utilities for a Family of 2	Housing and Utilities for a Family of 3	Housing and Utilities for a Family of 4	Housing and Utilities for a Family of 5 or more
Oregon	Baker County	1,151	1,351	1,424	1,588	1,613
Oregon	Benton County	1,567	1,840	1,939	2,162	2,197
Oregon	Clackamas County	1,776	2,086	2,198	2,451	2,490
Oregon	Clatsop County	1,487	1,746	1,840	2,052	2,085
Oregon	Columbia County	1,450	1,703	1,794	2,000	2,033
Oregon	Coos County	1,241	1,458	1,536	1,713	1,740
Oregon	Crook County	1,221	1,434	1,511	1,685	1,712
Oregon	Curry County	1,344	1,578	1,663	1,854	1,884
Oregon	Deschutes County	1,508	1,771	1,866	2,081	2,114
Oregon	Douglas County	1,261	1,481	1,561	1,741	1,769
Oregon	Gilliam County	1,081	1,270	1,338	1,492	1,516
Oregon	Grant County	1,073	1,260	1,328	1,481	1,505
Oregon	Harney County	1,043	1,225	1,291	1,439	1,463
Oregon	Hood River County	1,648	1,935	2,039	2,273	2,310
Oregon	Jackson County	1,456	1,710	1,802	2,009	2,042
Oregon	Jefferson County	1,230	1,444	1,522	1,697	1,724
Oregon	Josephine County	1,342	1,576	1,661	1,852	1,882
Oregon	Klamath County	1,214	1,425	1,502	1,675	1,702
Oregon	Lake County	1,117	1,312	1,382	1,541	1,566
Oregon	Lane County	1,435	1,685	1,776	1,980	2,012
Oregon	Lincoln County	1,362	1,600	1,686	1,880	1,910
Oregon	Linn County	1,326	1,557	1,641	1,830	1,859
Oregon	Malheur County	1,161	1,364	1,437	1,602	1,628
Oregon	Marion County	1,425	1,673	1,763	1,966	1,997
Oregon	Morrow County	1,129	1,326	1,397	1,558	1,583
Oregon	Multnomah County	1,670	1,962	2,067	2,305	2,342
Oregon	Polk County	1,478	1,736	1,829	2,039	2,072
Oregon	Sherman County	1,085	1,275	1,343	1,497	1,522
Oregon	Tillamook County	1,287	1,512	1,593	1,776	1,805
Oregon	Umatilla County	1,211	1,423	1,499	1,671	1,698
Oregon	Union County	1,161	1,364	1,437	1,602	1,628
Oregon	Wallowa County	1,234	1,449	1,527	1,703	1,730
Oregon	Wasco County	1,328	1,560	1,644	1,833	1,863
Oregon	Washington County	1,746	2,051	2,161	2,410	2,448
Oregon	Wheeler County	1,134	1,331	1,403	1,564	1,590
Oregon	Yamhill County	1,514	1,778	1,874	2,090	2,123
Pennsylvania	Adams County	1,485	1,744	1,838	2,049	2,082
Pennsylvania	Allegheny County	1,291	1,517	1,598	1,782	1,811
Pennsylvania	Armstrong County	1,063	1,248	1,315	1,466	1,490
Pennsylvania	Beaver County	1,196	1,405	1,480	1,650	1,677
Pennsylvania	Bedford County	1,077	1,265	1,333	1,486	1,510
Pennsylvania	Berks County	1,453	1,706	1,798	2,005	2,037
Pennsylvania	Blair County	1,071	1,258	1,326	1,478	1,502
Pennsylvania	Bradford County	1,143	1,343	1,415	1,578	1,603
Pennsylvania	Bucks County	1,931	2,268	2,390	2,665	2,708
Pennsylvania	Butler County	1,391	1,633	1,721	1,919	1,950
Pennsylvania	Cambria County	1,041	1,222	1,288	1,436	1,459

State Name	County	Housing and Utilities for a Family of 1	Housing and Utilities for a Family of 2	Housing and Utilities for a Family of 3	Housing and Utilities for a Family of 4	Housing and Utilities for a Family of 5 or more
Pennsylvania	Cameron County	995	1,168	1,231	1,373	1,395
Pennsylvania	Carbon County	1,319	1,550	1,633	1,821	1,850
Pennsylvania	Centre County	1,411	1,657	1,746	1,947	1,978
Pennsylvania	Chester County	2,027	2,381	2,509	2,798	2,843
Pennsylvania	Clarion County	1,036	1,217	1,282	1,429	1,453
Pennsylvania	Clearfield County	1,051	1,235	1,301	1,451	1,474
Pennsylvania	Clinton County	1,134	1,331	1,403	1,564	1,590
Pennsylvania	Columbia County	1,190	1,398	1,473	1,642	1,669
Pennsylvania	Crawford County	1,084	1,273	1,341	1,495	1,519
Pennsylvania	Cumberland County	1,433	1,684	1,774	1,978	2,010
Pennsylvania	Dauphin County	1,365	1,603	1,689	1,883	1,914
Pennsylvania	Delaware County	1,745	2,050	2,160	2,408	2,447
Pennsylvania	Elk County	1,006	1,182	1,245	1,388	1,411
Pennsylvania	Erie County	1,147	1,348	1,420	1,583	1,609
Pennsylvania	Fayette County	1,031	1,211	1,276	1,423	1,446
Pennsylvania	Forest County	923	1,084	1,142	1,273	1,294
Pennsylvania	Franklin County	1,332	1,564	1,648	1,838	1,867
Pennsylvania	Fulton County	1,211	1,423	1,499	1,671	1,698
Pennsylvania	Greene County	1,040	1,221	1,287	1,435	1,458
Pennsylvania	Huntingdon County	1,087	1,276	1,345	1,500	1,524
Pennsylvania	Indiana County	1,127	1,324	1,395	1,555	1,581
Pennsylvania	Jefferson County	985	1,157	1,219	1,359	1,381
Pennsylvania	Juniata County	1,175	1,380	1,454	1,621	1,647
Pennsylvania	Lackawanna County	1,300	1,527	1,609	1,794	1,823
Pennsylvania	Lancaster	1,428	1,677	1,767	1,970	2,002
	County					
Pennsylvania	Lawrence County	1,105	1,297	1,367	1,524	1,549
Pennsylvania	Lebanon County	1,342	1,576	1,661	1,852	1,882
Pennsylvania	Lehigh County	1,529	1,796	1,892	2,110	2,144
Pennsylvania	Luzerne County	1,218	1,431	1,508	1,681	1,709
Pennsylvania	Lycoming County	1,203	1,413	1,489	1,660	1,687
Pennsylvania	McKean County	964	1,132	1,193	1,330	1,352
Pennsylvania	Mercer County	1,086	1,275	1,344	1,499	1,523
Pennsylvania	Mifflin County	1,056	1,240	1,307	1,457	1,481
Pennsylvania	Monroe County	1,638	1,924	2,027	2,260	2,297
Pennsylvania	Montgomery County	1,900	2,231	2,351	2,621	2,664
Pennsylvania	Montour County	1,246	1,463	1,542	1,719	1,747
Pennsylvania	Northampton County	1,594	1,872	1,973	2,200	2,235
Pennsylvania	Northumberland County	1,107	1,300	1,370	1,528	1,552
Pennsylvania	Perry County	1,312	1,541	1,624	1,811	1,840
Pennsylvania	Philadelphia County	1,240	1,457	1,535	1,712	1,739
Pennsylvania	Pike County	1,485	1,744	1,838	2,049	2,082
Pennsylvania	Potter County	1,091	1,281	1,350	1,505	1,530
Pennsylvania	Schuylkill County	1,146	1,346	1,418	1,581	1,607
Pennsylvania	Snyder County	1,188	1,395	1,470	1,639	1,666
Pennsylvania	Somerset County	1,084	1,274	1,342	1,496	1,520

State Name	County	Housing and Utilities for a Family of 1	Housing and Utilities for a Family of 2	Housing and Utilities for a Family of 3	Housing and Utilities for a Family of 4	Housing and Utilities for a Family of 5 or more
Pennsylvania	Sullivan County	1,149	1,349	1,422	1,586	1,611
Pennsylvania	Susquehanna County	1,209	1,420	1,496	1,668	1,695
Pennsylvania	Tioga County	1,153	1,354	1,427	1,591	1,617
Pennsylvania	Union County	1,273	1,495	1,575	1,756	1,784
Pennsylvania	Venango County	974	1,144	1,206	1,345	1,366
Pennsylvania	Warren County	1,016	1,194	1,258	1,403	1,425
Pennsylvania	Washington County	1,256	1,475	1,554	1,733	1,761
Pennsylvania	Wayne County	1,361	1,599	1,685	1,879	1,909
Pennsylvania	Westmoreland County	1,214	1,426	1,503	1,676	1,703
Pennsylvania	Wyoming County	1,251	1,469	1,548	1,726	1,754
Pennsylvania	York County	1,465	1,721	1,813	2,021	2,054
Puerto Rico	Adjuntas Municipio	865	1,016	1,071	1,194	1,213
Puerto Rico	Aguada Municipio	911	1,070	1,128	1,258	1,278
Puerto Rico	Aguadilla Municipio	1,052	1,236	1,302	1,452	1,475
Puerto Rico	Aguas Buenas Municipio	1,045	1,227	1,293	1,442	1,465
Puerto Rico	Aibonito Municipio	1,012	1,188	1,252	1,396	1,419
Puerto Rico	Añasco Municipio	855	1,004	1,058	1,180	1,199
Puerto Rico	Arecibo Municipio	1,004	1,179	1,242	1,385	1,407
Puerto Rico	Arroyo Municipio	811	953	1,004	1,119	1,138
Puerto Rico	Barceloneta	911	1,070	1,128	1,258	1,278
	Municipio					
Puerto Rico	Barranquitas Municipio	924	1,086	1,144	1,276	1,296
Puerto Rico	Bayamón Municipio	1,199	1,408	1,484	1,655	1,681
Puerto Rico	Cabo Rojo Municipio	948	1,113	1,173	1,308	1,329
Puerto Rico	Caguas Municipio	1,129	1,326	1,397	1,558	1,583
Puerto Rico	Camuy Municipio	929	1,091	1,150	1,282	1,303
Puerto Rico	Canóvanas Municipio	1,039	1,220	1,286	1,434	1,457
Puerto Rico	Carolina Municipio	1,203	1,413	1,489	1,660	1,687
Puerto Rico	Cataño Municipio	1,375	1,615	1,702	1,898	1,928
Puerto Rico	Cayey Municipio	1,078	1,266	1,334	1,487	1,511
Puerto Rico	Ceiba Municipio	928	1,089	1,148	1,280	1,301
Puerto Rico	Ciales Municipio	878	1,032	1,087	1,212	1,232
Puerto Rico	Cidra Municipio	1,096	1,287	1,356	1,512	1,536
Puerto Rico	Coamo Municipio	882	1,036	1,092	1,218	1,237
Puerto Rico	Comerío Municipio	982	1,153	1,215	1,355	1,377
Puerto Rico	Corozal Municipio	939	1,103	1,162	1,296	1,317
Puerto Rico	Culebra Municipio	1,128	1,325	1,396	1,557	1,582
Puerto Rico	Dorado Municipio	1,286	1,510	1,591	1,774	1,803
Puerto Rico	Fajardo Municipio	1,000	1,175	1,238	1,380	1,403
Puerto Rico	Florida Municipio	948	1,113	1,173	1,308	1,329
Puerto Rico	Guánica Municipio	888	1,043	1,099	1,225	1,245
Puerto Rico	Guayama Municipio	973	1,143	1,204	1,342	1,364
Puerto Rico	Guayanilla Municipio	966	1,134	1,195	1,332	1,354
Puerto Rico	Guaynabo Municipio	1,761	2,068	2,179	2,430	2,469
Puerto Rico	Gurabo Municipio	1,183	1,389	1,464	1,632	1,659
Puerto Rico	Hatillo Municipio	973	1,143	1,204	1,342	1,364
Puerto Rico	Hormigueros Municipio	928	1,089	1,148	1,280	1,301

State Name	County	Housing and Utilities for a Family of 1	Housing and Utilities for a Family of 2	Housing and Utilities for a Family of 3	Housing and Utilities for a Family of 4	Housing and Utilities for a Family of 5 or more
Puerto Rico	Humacao Municipio	1,016	1,194	1,258	1,403	1,425
Puerto Rico	Isabela Municipio	888	1,043	1,099	1,225	1,245
Puerto Rico	Jayuya Municipio	851	999	1,053	1,174	1,193
Puerto Rico	Juana Díaz Municipio	880	1,033	1,089	1,214	1,234
Puerto Rico	Juncos Municipio	1,054	1,238	1,305	1,455	1,479
Puerto Rico	Lajas Municipio	886	1,040	1,096	1,222	1,242
Puerto Rico	Lares Municipio	881	1,034	1,090	1,215	1,235
Puerto Rico	Las Marías Municipio	823	966	1,018	1,135	1,153
Puerto Rico	Las Piedras Municipio	980	1,151	1,213	1,352	1,374
Puerto Rico	Loíza Municipio	1,006	1,182	1,245	1,388	1,411
Puerto Rico	Luquillo Municipio	1,004	1,180	1,243	1,386	1,408
Puerto Rico	Manatí Municipio	1,000	1,175	1,238	1,380	1,403
Puerto Rico	Maricao Municipio	770	904	953	1,063	1,080
Puerto Rico	Maunabo Municipio	898	1,055	1,112	1,240	1,260
Puerto Rico	Mayagüez Municipio	1,069	1,256	1,323	1,475	1,499
Puerto Rico	Moca Municipio	942	1,107	1,166	1,300	1,321
Puerto Rico	Morovis Municipio	884	1,038	1,094	1,220	1,240
Puerto Rico	Naguabo Municipio	953	1,119	1,179	1,315	1,336
Puerto Rico	Naranjito Municipio	953	1,119	1,179	1,315	1,336
Puerto Rico	Orocovis Municipio	898	1,055	1,112	1,240	1,260
Puerto Rico	Patillas Municipio	897	1,053	1,110	1,238	1,258
Puerto Rico	Peñuelas Municipio	811	953	1,004	1,119	1,138
Puerto Rico	Ponce Municipio	1,004	1,179	1,242	1,385	1,407
Puerto Rico	Quebradillas Municipio	953	1,119	1,179	1,315	1,336
Puerto Rico	Rincón Municipio	971	1,141	1,202	1,340	1,362
Puerto Rico	Río Grande Municipio	1,046	1,229	1,295	1,444	1,467
Puerto Rico	Sabana Grande Municipio	890	1,045	1,101	1,228	1,247
Puerto Rico	Salinas Municipio	864	1,014	1,069	1,192	1,211
Puerto Rico	San Germán Municipio	884	1,038	1,094	1,220	1,240
Puerto Rico	San Juan Municipio	1,386	1,628	1,715	1,912	1,943
Puerto Rico	San Lorenzo Municipio	971	1,141	1,202	1,340	1,362
Puerto Rico	San Sebastián Municipio	903	1,060	1,117	1,245	1,266
Puerto Rico	Santa Isabel Municipio	920	1,081	1,139	1,270	1,290
Puerto Rico	Toa Alta Municipio	1,258	1,478	1,557	1,736	1,764
Puerto Rico	Toa Baja Municipio	1,154	1,355	1,428	1,592	1,618
Puerto Rico	Trujillo Alto Municipio	1,286	1,510	1,591	1,774	1,803
Puerto Rico	Utuado Municipio	861	1,011	1,065	1,187	1,207
Puerto Rico	Vega Alta Municipio	986	1,158	1,220	1,360	1,382
Puerto Rico	Vega Baja Municipio	1,081	1,270	1,338	1,492	1,516
Puerto Rico	Vieques Municipio	967	1,136	1,197	1,335	1,356
Puerto Rico	Villalba Municipio	924	1,086	1,144	1,276	1,296
Puerto Rico	Yabucoa Municipio	993	1,166	1,229	1,370	1,392
Puerto Rico	Yauco Municipio	948	1,113	1,173	1,308	1,329
Rhode Island	Bristol County	1,980	2,326	2,451	2,733	2,777
Rhode Island	Kent County	1,724	2,025	2,134	2,379	2,418
Rhode Island	Newport County	1,921	2,256	2,377	2,650	2,693

State Name	County	Housing and Utilities for a Family of 1	Housing and Utilities for a Family of 2	Housing and Utilities for a Family of 3	Housing and Utilities for a Family of 4	Housing and Utilities for a Family of 5 or more
Rhode Island	Providence County	1,685	1,979	2,085	2,325	2,362
Rhode Island	Washington County	1,866	2,191	2,309	2,575	2,616
South Carolina	Abbeville County	1,057	1,241	1,308	1,458	1,482
South Carolina	Aiken County	1,138	1,337	1,409	1,571	1,596
South Carolina	Allendale County	984	1,156	1,218	1,358	1,380
South Carolina	Anderson County	1,128	1,325	1,396	1,557	1,582
South Carolina	Bamberg County	952	1,118	1,178	1,313	1,335
South Carolina	Barnwell County	995	1,168	1,231	1,373	1,395
South Carolina	Beaufort County	1,604	1,884	1,985	2,213	2,249
South Carolina	Berkeley County	1,277	1,499	1,580	1,762	1,790
South Carolina	Calhoun County	1,038	1,219	1,285	1,433	1,456
South Carolina	Charleston County	1,594	1,872	1,973	2,200	2,235
South	Cherokee County	983	1,155	1,217	1,357	1,379
Carolina						
South Carolina	Chester County	983	1,154	1,216	1,356	1,378
South Carolina	Chesterfield County	954	1,121	1,181	1,317	1,338
South Carolina	Clarendon County	999	1,174	1,237	1,379	1,402
South Carolina	Colleton County	1,080	1,269	1,337	1,491	1,515
South Carolina	Darlington County	1,041	1,222	1,288	1,436	1,459
South Carolina	Dillon County	942	1,107	1,166	1,300	1,321
South Carolina	Dorchester County	1,377	1,617	1,704	1,900	1,931
South Carolina	Edgefield County	1,088	1,278	1,347	1,502	1,526
South Carolina	Fairfield County	1,075	1,263	1,331	1,484	1,508
South Carolina	Florence County	1,115	1,310	1,380	1,539	1,564
South Carolina	Georgetown County	1,281	1,505	1,586	1,768	1,797
South Carolina	Greenville County	1,221	1,434	1,511	1,685	1,712
South Carolina	Greenwood County	1,040	1,221	1,287	1,435	1,458
South Carolina	Hampton County	973	1,143	1,204	1,342	1,364
South Carolina	Horry County	1,229	1,443	1,521	1,696	1,723
South	Jasper County	1,046	1,229	1,295	1,444	1,467
Carolina						
South Carolina	Kershaw County	1,113	1,307	1,377	1,535	1,560
South Carolina	Lancaster County	1,139	1,338	1,410	1,572	1,598
South Carolina	Laurens County	975	1,145	1,207	1,346	1,368
South Carolina	Lee County	950	1,116	1,176	1,311	1,332
South Carolina	Lexington County	1,188	1,395	1,470	1,639	1,666
South Carolina	Marion County	974	1,144	1,206	1,345	1,366
South Carolina	Marlboro County	903	1,061	1,118	1,247	1,267
South Carolina	McCormick County	1,022	1,200	1,265	1,410	1,433
South Carolina	Newberry County	1,100	1,292	1,361	1,518	1,542
South Carolina	Oconee County	1,130	1,327	1,398	1,559	1,584
South Carolina	Orangeburg County	1,051	1,235	1,301	1,451	1,474
South Carolina	Pickens County	1,096	1,288	1,357	1,513	1,537
South Carolina	Richland County	1,262	1,482	1,562	1,742	1,770
South Carolina	Saluda County	1,060	1,245	1,312	1,463	1,486
South Carolina	Spartanburg County	1,122	1,317	1,388	1,548	1,573
South	Sumter County	1,082	1,271	1,339	1,493	1,517

State Name	County	Housing and Utilities for a Family of 1	Housing and Utilities for a Family of 2	Housing and Utilities for a Family of 3	Housing and Utilities for a Family of 4	Housing and Utilities for a Family of 5 or more
Carolina						
South Carolina	Union County	940	1,104	1,163	1,297	1,318
South Carolina	Williamsburg County	970	1,139	1,200	1,338	1,360
South Carolina	York County	1,257	1,477	1,556	1,735	1,763
South Dakota	Aurora County	945	1,110	1,170	1,305	1,326
South Dakota	Beadle County	1,024	1,202	1,267	1,413	1,436
South Dakota	Bennett County	1,003	1,178	1,241	1,384	1,406
South Dakota	Bon Homme County	918	1,078	1,136	1,267	1,287
South Dakota	Brookings County	1,218	1,431	1,508	1,681	1,709
South Dakota	Brown County	1,139	1,338	1,410	1,572	1,598
South Dakota	Brule County	1,162	1,365	1,438	1,603	1,629
South Dakota	Buffalo County	879	1,033	1,088	1,213	1,233
South Dakota	Butte County	1,109	1,303	1,373	1,531	1,556
South Dakota	Campbell County	1,072	1,259	1,327	1,480	1,503
South Dakota	Charles Mix County	966	1,134	1,195	1,332	1,354
South Dakota	Clark County	912	1,071	1,129	1,259	1,279
South Dakota	Clay County	1,211	1,423	1,499	1,671	1,698
South Dakota	Codington County	1,151	1,351	1,424	1,588	1,613
South Dakota	Corson County	883	1,037	1,093	1,219	1,238
South Dakota	Custer County	1,210	1,421	1,497	1,669	1,696
South Dakota	Davison County	1,087	1,276	1,345	1,500	1,524
South Dakota	Day County	1,003	1,178	1,241	1,384	1,406
South Dakota	Deuel County	1,070	1,256	1,324	1,476	1,500
South Dakota	Dewey County	873	1,025	1,080	1,204	1,224
South Dakota	Douglas County	924	1,085	1,143	1,274	1,295
South Dakota	Edmunds County	1,131	1,329	1,400	1,561	1,586
South Dakota	Fall River County	1,159	1,361	1,434	1,599	1,625
South Dakota	Faulk County	1,059	1,244	1,311	1,462	1,485
South Dakota	Grant County	1,126	1,322	1,393	1,553	1,578
South Dakota	Gregory County	964	1,132	1,193	1,330	1,352
South Dakota	Haakon County	973	1,143	1,204	1,342	1,364
South Dakota	Hamlin County	1,120	1,315	1,386	1,545	1,570
South Dakota	Hand County	1,097	1,289	1,358	1,514	1,539
South Dakota	Hanson County	1,165	1,368	1,442	1,608	1,634
South Dakota	Harding County	1,257	1,477	1,556	1,735	1,763
South Dakota	Hughes County	1,298	1,524	1,606	1,791	1,820
South Dakota	Hutchinson County	1,005	1,181	1,244	1,387	1,409
South Dakota	Hyde County	1,050	1,233	1,299	1,448	1,472
South Dakota	Jackson County	1,076	1,264	1,332	1,485	1,509
South Dakota	Jerauld County	952	1,118	1,178	1,313	1,335
South Dakota	Jones County	939	1,103	1,162	1,296	1,317
South Dakota	Kingsbury County	1,007	1,182	1,246	1,389	1,412
South Dakota	Lake County	1,178	1,384	1,458	1,626	1,652
South Dakota	Lawrence County	1,281	1,505	1,586	1,768	1,797
South Dakota	Lincoln County	1,407	1,652	1,741	1,941	1,973
South Dakota	Lyman County	1,036	1,217	1,282	1,429	1,453

State Name	County	Housing and Utilities for a Family of 1	Housing and Utilities for a Family of 2	Housing and Utilities for a Family of 3	Housing and Utilities for a Family of 4	Housing and Utilities for a Family of 5 or more
South Dakota	Marshall County	1,108	1,301	1,371	1,529	1,553
South Dakota	McCook County	1,099	1,291	1,360	1,516	1,541
South Dakota	McPherson County	1,004	1,179	1,242	1,385	1,407
South Dakota	Meade County	1,330	1,562	1,646	1,835	1,865
South Dakota	Mellette County	1,008	1,183	1,247	1,390	1,413
South Dakota	Miner County	978	1,149	1,211	1,350	1,372
South Dakota	Minnehaha County	1,227	1,441	1,518	1,693	1,720
South Dakota	Moody County	1,150	1,350	1,423	1,587	1,612
South Dakota	Pennington County	1,282	1,506	1,587	1,770	1,798
South Dakota	Perkins County	930	1,092	1,151	1,283	1,304
South Dakota	Potter County	992	1,165	1,228	1,369	1,391
South Dakota	Roberts County	1,079	1,268	1,336	1,490	1,514
South Dakota	Sanborn County	957	1,124	1,184	1,320	1,341
South Dakota	Shannon County	752	884	931	1,038	1,055
South Dakota	Spink County	969	1,138	1,199	1,337	1,358
South Dakota	Stanley County	1,210	1,422	1,498	1,670	1,697
South Dakota	Sully County	1,179	1,385	1,459	1,627	1,653
South Dakota	Todd County	765	899	947	1,056	1,073
South Dakota	Tripp County	1,058	1,242	1,309	1,460	1,483
South Dakota	Turner County	1,129	1,326	1,397	1,558	1,583
South Dakota	Union County	1,288	1,513	1,594	1,777	1,806
South Dakota	Walworth	1,006	1,182	1,245	1,388	1,411
	County					
South Dakota	Yankton County	1,131	1,329	1,400	1,561	1,586
South Dakota	Ziebach County	865	1,015	1,070	1,193	1,212
Tennessee	Anderson County	1,149	1,349	1,422	1,586	1,611
Tennessee	Bedford County	1,092	1,282	1,351	1,506	1,531
Tennessee	Benton County	930	1,092	1,151	1,283	1,304
Tennessee	Bledsoe County	1,021	1,200	1,264	1,409	1,432
Tennessee	Blount County	1,188	1,395	1,470	1,639	1,666
Tennessee	Bradley County	1,103	1,295	1,365	1,522	1,547
Tennessee	Campbell County	985	1,157	1,219	1,359	1,381
Tennessee	Cannon County	1,071	1,258	1,326	1,478	1,502
Tennessee	Carroll County	930	1,092	1,151	1,283	1,304
Tennessee	Carter County	970	1,139	1,200	1,338	1,360
Tennessee	Cheatham County	1,219	1,432	1,509	1,683	1,710
Tennessee	Chester County	1,058	1,242	1,309	1,460	1,483
Tennessee	Claiborne County	932	1,094	1,153	1,286	1,306
Tennessee	Clay County	882	1,035	1,091	1,216	1,236
Tennessee	Cocke County	974	1,144	1,205	1,344	1,365
Tennessee	Coffee County	1,101	1,293	1,363	1,520	1,544
Tennessee	Crockett County	972	1,142	1,203	1,341	1,363
Tennessee	Cumberland County	999	1,174	1,237	1,379	1,402
Tennessee	Davidson County	1,339	1,572	1,657	1,848	1,877
Tennessee	Decatur County	915	1,074	1,132	1,262	1,283
Tennessee	DeKalb County	987	1,159	1,221	1,361	1,383
Tennessee	Dickson County	1,155	1,357	1,430	1,594	1,620

State Name	County	Housing and Utilities for a Family of 1	Housing and Utilities for a Family of 2	Housing and Utilities for a Family of 3	Housing and Utilities for a Family of 4	Housing and Utilities for a Family of 5 or more
Tennessee	Dyer County	1,084	1,274	1,342	1,496	1,520
Tennessee	Fayette County	1,297	1,523	1,605	1,790	1,818
Tennessee	Fentress County	941	1,105	1,164	1,298	1,319
Tennessee	Franklin County	1,002	1,177	1,240	1,383	1,405
Tennessee	Gibson County	1,025	1,203	1,268	1,414	1,437
Tennessee	Giles County	1,088	1,278	1,347	1,502	1,526
Tennessee	Grainger County	944	1,108	1,168	1,302	1,323
Tennessee	Greene County	967	1,136	1,197	1,335	1,356
Tennessee	Grundy County	890	1,046	1,102	1,229	1,249
Tennessee	Hamblen County	1,038	1,219	1,285	1,433	1,456
Tennessee	Hamilton County	1,231	1,445	1,523	1,698	1,726
Tennessee	Hancock County	835	981	1,034	1,153	1,172
Tennessee	Hardeman County	962	1,129	1,190	1,327	1,348
Tennessee	Hardin County	1,005	1,181	1,244	1,387	1,409
Tennessee	Hawkins County	995	1,168	1,231	1,373	1,395
Tennessee	Haywood County	1,015	1,192	1,256	1,400	1,423
Tennessee	Henderson County	990	1,163	1,225	1,366	1,388
Tennessee	Henry County	940	1,104	1,163	1,297	1,318
Tennessee	Hickman County	1,011	1,187	1,251	1,395	1,417
Tennessee	Houston County	927	1,089	1,147	1,279	1,300
Tennessee	Humphreys County	1,033	1,213	1,278	1,425	1,448
Tennessee	Jackson County	1,026	1,205	1,270	1,416	1,439
Tennessee	Jefferson County	1,029	1,208	1,273	1,419	1,442
Tennessee	Johnson County	972	1,142	1,203	1,341	1,363
Tennessee	Knox County	1,235	1,451	1,529	1,705	1,732
Tennessee	Lake County	945	1,109	1,169	1,303	1,324
Tennessee	Lauderdale County	991	1,164	1,227	1,368	1,390
Tennessee	Lawrence County	1,009	1,185	1,249	1,393	1,415
Tennessee	Lewis County	988	1,161	1,223	1,364	1,386
Tennessee	Lincoln County	1,063	1,248	1,315	1,466	1,490
Tennessee	Loudon County	1,172	1,376	1,450	1,617	1,643
Tennessee	Macon County	985	1,157	1,219	1,359	1,381
Tennessee	Madison County	1,158	1,360	1,433	1,598	1,624
Tennessee	Marion County	1,071	1,258	1,326	1,478	1,502
Tennessee	Marshall County	1,056	1,240	1,307	1,457	1,481
Tennessee	Maury County	1,164	1,368	1,441	1,607	1,633
Tennessee	McMinn County	1,050	1,233	1,299	1,448	1,472
Tennessee	McNairy County	970	1,140	1,201	1,339	1,361
Tennessee	Meigs County	1,033	1,213	1,278	1,425	1,448
Tennessee	Monroe County	1,002	1,177	1,240	1,383	1,405
Tennessee	Montgomery County	1,195	1,404	1,479	1,649	1,676
Tennessee	Moore County	992	1,165	1,228	1,369	1,391
Tennessee	Morgan County	1,037	1,219	1,284	1,432	1,455
Tennessee	Obion County	977	1,147	1,209	1,348	1,370
Tennessee	Overton County	913	1,072	1,130	1,260	1,280
Tennessee	Perry County	912	1,071	1,129	1,259	1,279

State Name	County	Housing and Utilities for a Family of 1	Housing and Utilities for a Family of 2	Housing and Utilities for a Family of 3	Housing and Utilities for a Family of 4	Housing and Utilities for a Family of 5 or more
Tennessee	Pickett County	1,025	1,204	1,269	1,415	1,438
Tennessee	Polk County	996	1,170	1,233	1,375	1,397
Tennessee	Putnam County	1,096	1,288	1,357	1,513	1,537
Tennessee	Rhea County	995	1,169	1,232	1,374	1,396
Tennessee	Roane County	1,118	1,313	1,384	1,543	1,568
Tennessee	Robertson County	1,238	1,454	1,532	1,708	1,736
Tennessee	Rutherford County	1,269	1,490	1,570	1,751	1,779
Tennessee	Scott County	856	1,006	1,060	1,182	1,201
Tennessee	Sequatchie County	1,037	1,219	1,284	1,432	1,455
Tennessee	Sevier County	1,169	1,373	1,447	1,613	1,639
Tennessee	Shelby County	1,354	1,591	1,676	1,869	1,899
Tennessee	Smith County	1,086	1,275	1,344	1,499	1,523
Tennessee	Stewart County	1,059	1,244	1,311	1,462	1,485
Tennessee	Sullivan County	1,062	1,247	1,314	1,465	1,489
Tennessee	Sumner County	1,334	1,567	1,651	1,841	1,871
Tennessee	Tipton County	1,247	1,464	1,543	1,720	1,748
Tennessee	Trousdale County	1,051	1,235	1,301	1,451	1,474
Tennessee	Unicoi County	928	1,090	1,149	1,281	1,302
Tennessee	Union County	941	1,106	1,165	1,299	1,320
Tennessee	Van Buren County	887	1,042	1,098	1,224	1,244
Tennessee	Warren County	960	1,127	1,188	1,325	1,346
Tennessee	Washington County	1,118	1,313	1,384	1,543	1,568
Tennessee	Wayne County	872	1,024	1,079	1,203	1,223
Tennessee	Weakley County	988	1,161	1,223	1,364	1,386
Tennessee	White County	937	1,101	1,160	1,293	1,314
Tennessee	Williamson County	1,827	2,146	2,261	2,521	2,562
Tennessee	Wilson County	1,395	1,638	1,726	1,924	1,956
Texas	Anderson County	1,074	1,261	1,329	1,482	1,506
Texas	Andrews County	1,155	1,356	1,429	1,593	1,619
Texas	Angelina County	1,075	1,262	1,330	1,483	1,507
Texas	Aransas County	1,294	1,520	1,602	1,786	1,815
Texas	Archer County	1,164	1,367	1,440	1,606	1,632
Texas	Armstrong County	1,076	1,264	1,332	1,485	1,509
Texas	Atascosa County	1,142	1,341	1,413	1,575	1,601
Texas	Austin County	1,470	1,726	1,819	2,028	2,061
Texas	Bailey County	1,009	1,185	1,249	1,393	1,415
Texas	Bandera County	1,250	1,468	1,547	1,725	1,753
Texas	Bastrop County	1,289	1,514	1,595	1,778	1,807
Texas	Baylor County	1,134	1,332	1,404	1,565	1,591
Texas	Bee County	1,046	1,229	1,295	1,444	1,467
Texas	Bell County	1,262	1,482	1,562	1,742	1,770
Texas	Bexar County	1,307	1,535	1,617	1,803	1,832
Texas	Blanco County	1,227	1,441	1,518	1,693	1,720
Texas	Borden County	1,206	1,417	1,493	1,665	1,692
Texas	Bosque County	1,039	1,220	1,286	1,434	1,457
Texas	Bowie County	1,136	1,334	1,406	1,568	1,593

State Name	County	Housing and Utilities for a Family of 1	Housing and Utilities for a Family of 2	Housing and Utilities for a Family of 3	Housing and Utilities for a Family of 4	Housing and Utilities for a Family of 5 or more
Texas	Brazoria County	1,574	1,849	1,948	2,172	2,207
Texas	Brazos County	1,386	1,628	1,715	1,912	1,943
Texas	Brewster County	1,189	1,396	1,471	1,640	1,667
Texas	Briscoe County	903	1,060	1,117	1,245	1,266
Texas	Brooks County	984	1,156	1,218	1,358	1,380
Texas	Brown County	1,098	1,290	1,359	1,515	1,540
Texas	Burleson County	1,088	1,277	1,346	1,501	1,525
Texas	Burnet County	1,279	1,502	1,583	1,765	1,794
Texas	Caldwell County	1,231	1,446	1,524	1,699	1,727
Texas	Calhoun County	1,215	1,427	1,504	1,677	1,704
Texas	Callahan County	1,011	1,187	1,251	1,395	1,417
Texas	Cameron County	1,103	1,295	1,365	1,522	1,547
Texas	Camp County	1,118	1,313	1,384	1,543	1,568
Texas	Carson County	1,158	1,360	1,433	1,598	1,624
Texas	Cass County	956	1,123	1,183	1,319	1,340
Texas	Castro County	943	1,107	1,167	1,301	1,322
Texas	Chambers County	1,483	1,741	1,835	2,046	2,079
Texas	Cherokee County	1,079	1,268	1,336	1,490	1,514
Texas	Childress County	911	1,070	1,127	1,257	1,277
Texas	Clay County	1,125	1,321	1,392	1,552	1,577
Texas	Cochran County	802	942	993	1,107	1,125
Texas	Coke County	1,093	1,284	1,353	1,509	1,533
Texas	Coleman County	927	1,089	1,147	1,279	1,300
Texas	Collin County	1,765	2,074	2,185	2,436	2,476
Texas	Collingsworth County	1,052	1,236	1,302	1,452	1,475
Texas	Colorado County	1,264	1,484	1,564	1,744	1,772
Texas	Comal County	1,540	1,809	1,906	2,125	2,159
Texas	Comanche County	1,004	1,179	1,242	1,385	1,407
Texas	Concho County	936	1,100	1,159	1,292	1,313
Texas	Cooke County	1,230	1,444	1,522	1,697	1,724
Texas	Coryell County	1,132	1,330	1,401	1,562	1,587
Texas	Cottle County	835	980	1,033	1,152	1,170
Texas	Crane County	903	1,061	1,118	1,247	1,267
Texas	Crockett County	1,027	1,206	1,271	1,417	1,440
Texas	Crosby County	940	1,104	1,163	1,297	1,318
Texas	Culberson County	934	1,097	1,156	1,289	1,310
Texas	Dallam County	1,105	1,297	1,367	1,524	1,549
Texas	Dallas County	1,421	1,669	1,759	1,961	1,993
Texas	Dawson County	992	1,165	1,228	1,369	1,391
Texas	Deaf Smith County	1,103	1,295	1,365	1,522	1,547
Texas	Delta County	1,061	1,246	1,313	1,464	1,488
Texas	Denton County	1,676	1,968	2,074	2,313	2,350
Texas	DeWitt County	1,049	1,232	1,298	1,447	1,471
Texas	Dickens County	983	1,155	1,217	1,357	1,379
Texas	Dimmit County	984	1,156	1,218	1,358	1,380
Texas	Donley County	990	1,163	1,225	1,366	1,388

State Name	County	Housing and Utilities for a Family of 1	Housing and Utilities for a Family of 2	Housing and Utilities for a Family of 3	Housing and Utilities for a Family of 4	Housing and Utilities for a Family of 5 or more
Texas	Duval County	1,076	1,264	1,332	1,485	1,509
Texas	Eastland County	948	1,113	1,173	1,308	1,329
Texas	Ector County	1,175	1,380	1,454	1,621	1,647
Texas	Edwards County	1,068	1,255	1,322	1,474	1,498
Texas	El Paso County	1,150	1,350	1,423	1,587	1,612
Texas	Ellis County	1,412	1,658	1,747	1,948	1,979
Texas	Erath County	1,206	1,416	1,492	1,664	1,690
Texas	Falls County	1,014	1,191	1,255	1,399	1,422
Texas	Fannin County	1,168	1,372	1,446	1,612	1,638
Texas	Fayette County	1,087	1,276	1,345	1,500	1,524
Texas	Fisher County	906	1,064	1,121	1,250	1,270
Texas	Floyd County	985	1,157	1,219	1,359	1,381
Texas	Foard County	919	1,079	1,137	1,268	1,288
Texas	Fort Bend County	1,734	2,037	2,146	2,393	2,431
Texas	Franklin County	1,129	1,326	1,397	1,558	1,583
Texas	Freestone County	1,102	1,294	1,364	1,521	1,545
Texas	Frio County	1,074	1,261	1,329	1,482	1,506
Texas	Gaines County	957	1,124	1,184	1,320	1,341
Texas	Galveston County	1,581	1,857	1,957	2,182	2,217
Texas	Garza County	962	1,129	1,190	1,327	1,348
Texas	Gillespie County	1,426	1,675	1,765	1,968	2,000
Texas	Glasscock County	1,155	1,357	1,430	1,594	1,620
Texas	Goliad County	1,085	1,275	1,343	1,497	1,522
Texas	Gonzales County	1,017	1,195	1,259	1,404	1,426
Texas	Gray County	1,088	1,278	1,347	1,502	1,526
Texas	Grayson County	1,216	1,428	1,505	1,678	1,705
Texas	Gregg County	1,218	1,430	1,507	1,680	1,707
Texas	Grimes County	1,114	1,309	1,379	1,538	1,562
Texas	Guadalupe County	1,388	1,630	1,718	1,916	1,946
Texas	Hale County	1,006	1,182	1,245	1,388	1,411
Texas	Hall County	981	1,152	1,214	1,354	1,375
Texas	Hamilton County	1,123	1,319	1,390	1,550	1,575
Texas	Hansford County	1,022	1,200	1,265	1,410	1,433
Texas	Hardeman County	925	1,087	1,145	1,277	1,297
Texas	Hardin County	1,222	1,435	1,512	1,686	1,713
Texas	Harris County	1,457	1,711	1,803	2,010	2,043
Texas	Harrison County	1,179	1,385	1,459	1,627	1,653
Texas	Hartley County	1,220	1,433	1,510	1,684	1,711
Texas	Haskell County	951	1,117	1,177	1,312	1,334
Texas	Hays County	1,515	1,779	1,875	2,091	2,124
Texas	Hemphill County	1,173	1,378	1,452	1,619	1,645
Texas	Henderson County	1,134	1,331	1,403	1,564	1,590
Texas	Hidalgo County	1,112	1,306	1,376	1,534	1,559
Texas	Hill County	1,185	1,391	1,466	1,635	1,661
Texas	Hockley County	1,075	1,263	1,331	1,484	1,508
Texas	Hood County	1,352	1,588	1,673	1,865	1,896
Texas	Hopkins County	1,108	1,301	1,371	1,529	1,553

State Name	County	Housing and Utilities for a Family of 1	Housing and Utilities for a Family of 2	Housing and Utilities for a Family of 3	Housing and Utilities for a Family of 4	Housing and Utilities for a Family of 5 or more
Texas	Houston County	1,008	1,184	1,248	1,392	1,414
Texas	Howard County	1,037	1,219	1,284	1,432	1,455
Texas	Hudspeth County	928	1,089	1,148	1,280	1,301
Texas	Hunt County	1,206	1,416	1,492	1,664	1,690
Texas	Hutchinson County	961	1,128	1,189	1,326	1,347
Texas	Irion County	1,271	1,493	1,573	1,754	1,782
Texas	Jack County	1,134	1,331	1,403	1,564	1,590
Texas	Jackson County	1,083	1,272	1,340	1,494	1,518
Texas	Jasper County	1,051	1,235	1,301	1,451	1,474
Texas	Jeff Davis County	1,022	1,200	1,265	1,410	1,433
Texas	Jefferson County	1,221	1,434	1,511	1,685	1,712
Texas	Jim Hogg County	1,020	1,198	1,262	1,407	1,430
Texas	Jim Wells County	1,142	1,341	1,413	1,575	1,601
Texas	Johnson County	1,273	1,495	1,575	1,756	1,784
Texas	Jones County	1,037	1,218	1,283	1,431	1,454
Texas	Karnes County	1,008	1,183	1,247	1,390	1,413
Texas	Kaufman County	1,433	1,684	1,774	1,978	2,010
Texas	Kendall County	1,830	2,149	2,265	2,525	2,566
Texas	Kenedy County	1,048	1,231	1,297	1,446	1,470
Texas	Kent County	877	1,030	1,085	1,210	1,229
Texas	Kerr County	1,276	1,498	1,579	1,761	1,789
Texas	Kimble County	1,057	1,241	1,308	1,458	1,482
Texas	King County	1,094	1,285	1,354	1,510	1,534
Texas	Kinney County	995	1,169	1,232	1,374	1,396
Texas	Kleberg County	1,140	1,339	1,411	1,573	1,599
Texas	Knox County	894	1,050	1,106	1,233	1,253
Texas	La Salle County	1,073	1,260	1,328	1,481	1,505
Texas	Lamar County	1,033	1,214	1,279	1,426	1,449
Texas	Lamb County	977	1,147	1,209	1,348	1,370
Texas	Lampasas County	1,303	1,531	1,613	1,798	1,828
Texas	Lavaca County	1,025	1,203	1,268	1,414	1,437
Texas	Lee County	1,273	1,496	1,576	1,757	1,786
Texas	Leon County	1,120	1,315	1,386	1,545	1,570
Texas	Liberty County	1,193	1,402	1,477	1,647	1,673
Texas	Limestone County	1,037	1,218	1,283	1,431	1,454
Texas	Lipscomb County	1,028	1,207	1,272	1,418	1,441
Texas	Live Oak County	1,075	1,263	1,331	1,484	1,508
Texas	Llano County	1,214	1,425	1,502	1,675	1,702
Texas	Loving County	1,467	1,722	1,815	2,024	2,056
Texas	Lubbock County	1,214	1,426	1,503	1,676	1,703
Texas	Lynn County	1,066	1,252	1,319	1,471	1,494
Texas	Madison County	1,194	1,403	1,478	1,648	1,675
Texas	Marion County	1,072	1,259	1,327	1,480	1,503
Texas	Martin County	1,025	1,204	1,269	1,415	1,438
Texas	Mason County	1,154	1,355	1,428	1,592	1,618
Texas	Matagorda County	1,170	1,374	1,448	1,615	1,641

State Name	County	Housing and Utilities for a Family of 1	Housing and Utilities for a Family of 2	Housing and Utilities for a Family of 3	Housing and Utilities for a Family of 4	Housing and Utilities for a Family of 5 or more
Texas	Maverick County	1,079	1,267	1,335	1,489	1,513
Texas	McCulloch County	1,067	1,254	1,321	1,473	1,497
Texas	McLennan County	1,244	1,461	1,540	1,717	1,745
Texas	McMullen County	914	1,073	1,131	1,261	1,281
Texas	Medina County	1,217	1,429	1,506	1,679	1,706
Texas	Menard County	844	992	1,045	1,165	1,184
Texas	Midland County	1,379	1,620	1,707	1,903	1,934
Texas	Milam County	1,105	1,298	1,368	1,525	1,550
Texas	Mills County	1,108	1,301	1,371	1,529	1,553
Texas	Mitchell County	939	1,103	1,162	1,296	1,317
Texas	Montague County	1,079	1,268	1,336	1,490	1,514
Texas	Montgomery County	1,544	1,814	1,911	2,131	2,165
Texas	Moore County	1,081	1,270	1,338	1,492	1,516
Texas	Morris County	970	1,140	1,201	1,339	1,361
Texas	Motley County	905	1,063	1,120	1,249	1,269
Texas	Nacogdoches County	1,161	1,364	1,437	1,602	1,628
Texas	Navarro County	1,131	1,329	1,400	1,561	1,586
Texas	Newton County	1,054	1,237	1,304	1,454	1,477
Texas	Nolan County	1,004	1,179	1,242	1,385	1,407
Texas	Nueces County	1,341	1,575	1,660	1,851	1,881
Texas	Ochiltree County	999	1,174	1,237	1,379	1,402
Texas	Oldham County	1,147	1,348	1,420	1,583	1,609
Texas	Orange County	1,194	1,403	1,478	1,648	1,675
Texas	Palo Pinto County	1,189	1,396	1,471	1,640	1,667
Texas	Panola County	1,113	1,308	1,378	1,536	1,561
Texas	Parker County	1,477	1,735	1,828	2,038	2,071
Texas	Parmer County	1,149	1,349	1,422	1,586	1,611
Texas	Pecos County	1,078	1,266	1,334	1,487	1,511
Texas	Polk County	1,122	1,318	1,389	1,549	1,574
Texas	Potter County	1,060	1,245	1,312	1,463	1,486
Texas	Presidio County	941	1,105	1,164	1,298	1,319
Texas	Rains County	1,204	1,414	1,490	1,661	1,688
Texas	Randall County	1,332	1,564	1,648	1,838	1,867
Texas	Reagan County	1,060	1,245	1,312	1,463	1,486
Texas	Real County	919	1,079	1,137	1,268	1,288
Texas	Red River County	1,002	1,177	1,240	1,383	1,405
Texas	Reeves County	960	1,127	1,188	1,325	1,346
Texas	Refugio County	1,058	1,242	1,309	1,460	1,483
Texas	Roberts County	1,160	1,363	1,436	1,601	1,627
Texas	Robertson County	1,050	1,233	1,299	1,448	1,472
Texas	Rockwall County	1,637	1,923	2,026	2,259	2,295
Texas	Runnels County	975	1,145	1,207	1,346	1,368
Texas	Rusk County	1,065	1,251	1,318	1,470	1,493
Texas	Sabine County	1,027	1,206	1,271	1,417	1,440
Texas	San Augustine County	974	1,144	1,206	1,345	1,366
Texas	San Jacinto County	1,201	1,410	1,486	1,657	1,684
Texas	San Patricio County	1,268	1,489	1,569	1,749	1,778

State Name	County	Housing and Utilities for a Family of 1	Housing and Utilities for a Family of 2	Housing and Utilities for a Family of 3	Housing and Utilities for a Family of 4	Housing and Utilities for a Family of 5 or more
Texas	San Saba County	1,012	1,189	1,253	1,397	1,420
Texas	Schleicher County	984	1,156	1,218	1,358	1,380
Texas	Scurry County	1,075	1,262	1,330	1,483	1,507
Texas	Shackelford County	1,164	1,367	1,440	1,606	1,632
Texas	Shelby County	991	1,163	1,226	1,367	1,389
Texas	Sherman County	1,091	1,281	1,350	1,505	1,530
Texas	Smith County	1,255	1,474	1,553	1,732	1,760
Texas	Somervell County	1,333	1,566	1,650	1,840	1,869
Texas	Starr County	1,015	1,192	1,256	1,400	1,423
Texas	Stephens County	999	1,173	1,236	1,378	1,400
Texas	Sterling County	999	1,174	1,237	1,379	1,402
Texas	Stonewall County	861	1,011	1,065	1,187	1,207
Texas	Sutton County	1,214	1,425	1,502	1,675	1,702
Texas	Swisher County	993	1,166	1,229	1,370	1,392
Texas	Tarrant County	1,444	1,696	1,787	1,993	2,025
Texas	Taylor County	1,140	1,339	1,411	1,573	1,599
Texas	Terrell County	842	989	1,042	1,162	1,181
Texas	Terry County	1,046	1,228	1,294	1,443	1,466
Texas	Throckmorton County	959	1,126	1,187	1,324	1,345
Texas	Titus County	1,073	1,260	1,328	1,481	1,505
Texas	Tom Green County	1,142	1,341	1,413	1,575	1,601
Texas	Travis County	1,664	1,954	2,059	2,296	2,333
Texas	Trinity County	1,042	1,224	1,290	1,438	1,462
Texas	Tyler County	990	1,163	1,225	1,366	1,388
Texas	Upshur County	1,057	1,241	1,308	1,458	1,482
Texas	Upton County	974	1,144	1,205	1,344	1,365
Texas	Uvalde County	1,029	1,208	1,273	1,419	1,442
Texas	Val Verde County	1,151	1,351	1,424	1,588	1,613
Texas	Van Zandt County	1,112	1,306	1,376	1,534	1,559
Texas	Victoria County	1,233	1,448	1,526	1,701	1,729
Texas	Walker County	1,222	1,435	1,512	1,686	1,713
Texas	Waller County	1,406	1,651	1,740	1,940	1,971
Texas	Ward County	979	1,150	1,212	1,351	1,373
Texas	Washington County	1,218	1,431	1,508	1,681	1,709
Texas	Webb County	1,295	1,521	1,603	1,787	1,816
Texas	Wharton County	1,206	1,416	1,492	1,664	1,690
Texas	Wheeler County	1,057	1,241	1,308	1,458	1,482
Texas	Wichita County	1,148	1,349	1,421	1,584	1,610
Texas	Wilbarger County	992	1,165	1,228	1,369	1,391
Texas	Willacy County	983	1,155	1,217	1,357	1,379
Texas	Williamson County	1,564	1,837	1,936	2,159	2,193
Texas	Wilson County	1,409	1,655	1,744	1,945	1,976
Texas	Winkler County	972	1,142	1,203	1,341	1,363
Texas	Wise County	1,319	1,550	1,633	1,821	1,850
Texas	Wood County	1,134	1,331	1,403	1,564	1,590
Texas	Yoakum County	1,061	1,246	1,313	1,464	1,488

State Name	County	Housing and Utilities for a Family of 1	Housing and Utilities for a Family of 2	Housing and Utilities for a Family of 3	Housing and Utilities for a Family of 4	Housing and Utilities for a Family of 5 or more
Texas	Young County	1,110	1,304	1,374	1,532	1,557
Texas	Zapata County	966	1,134	1,195	1,332	1,354
Texas	Zavala County	915	1,074	1,132	1,262	1,283
Utah	Beaver County	1,124	1,320	1,391	1,551	1,576
Utah	Box Elder County	1,252	1,471	1,550	1,728	1,756
Utah	Cache County	1,283	1,507	1,588	1,771	1,799
Utah	Carbon County	1,100	1,292	1,361	1,518	1,542
Utah	Daggett County	1,158	1,360	1,433	1,598	1,624
Utah	Davis County	1,467	1,723	1,816	2,025	2,058
Utah	Duchesne County	1,218	1,430	1,507	1,680	1,707
Utah	Emery County	1,046	1,229	1,295	1,444	1,467
Utah	Garfield County	1,079	1,268	1,336	1,490	1,514
Utah	Grand County	1,171	1,375	1,449	1,616	1,642
Utah	Iron County	1,232	1,447	1,525	1,700	1,728
Utah	Juab County	1,186	1,393	1,468	1,637	1,663
Utah	Kane County	1,108	1,301	1,371	1,529	1,553
Utah	Millard County	1,077	1,265	1,333	1,486	1,510
Utah	Morgan County	1,715	2,014	2,122	2,366	2,404
Utah	Piute County	923	1,084	1,142	1,273	1,294
Utah	Rich County	1,240	1,457	1,535	1,712	1,739
Utah	Salt Lake County	1,496	1,757	1,851	2,064	2,097
Utah	San Juan County	1,063	1,248	1,315	1,466	1,490
Utah	Sanpete County	1,193	1,401	1,476	1,646	1,672
Utah	Sevier County	1,075	1,262	1,330	1,483	1,507
Utah	Summit County	2,041	2,397	2,526	2,816	2,862
Utah	Tooele County	1,345	1,580	1,665	1,856	1,886
Utah	Uintah County	1,304	1,532	1,614	1,800	1,829
Utah	Utah County	1,462	1,717	1,809	2,017	2,050
Utah	Wasatch County	1,706	2,003	2,111	2,354	2,392
Utah	Washington County	1,408	1,654	1,743	1,943	1,975
Utah	Wayne County	1,164	1,368	1,441	1,607	1,633
Utah	Weber County	1,300	1,527	1,609	1,794	1,823
Vermont	Addison County	1,500	1,762	1,857	2,071	2,104
Vermont	Bennington County	1,415	1,662	1,751	1,952	1,984
Vermont	Caledonia County	1,290	1,515	1,596	1,780	1,808
Vermont	Chittenden County	1,688	1,982	2,089	2,329	2,367
Vermont	Essex County	1,121	1,316	1,387	1,547	1,571
Vermont	Franklin County	1,422	1,670	1,760	1,962	1,994
Vermont	Grand Isle County	1,605	1,885	1,986	2,214	2,250
Vermont	Lamoille County	1,467	1,722	1,815	2,024	2,056
Vermont	Orange County	1,364	1,602	1,688	1,882	1,913
Vermont	Orleans County	1,216	1,428	1,505	1,678	1,705
Vermont	Rutland County	1,370	1,609	1,695	1,890	1,920
Vermont	Washington County	1,503	1,765	1,860	2,074	2,107
Vermont	Windham County	1,424	1,672	1,762	1,965	1,996
Vermont	Windsor County	1,492	1,752	1,846	2,058	2,092
Virginia	Accomack County	1,164	1,367	1,440	1,606	1,632

State Name	County	Housing and Utilities for a Family of 1	Housing and Utilities for a Family of 2	Housing and Utilities for a Family of 3	Housing and Utilities for a Family of 4	Housing and Utilities for a Family of 5 or more
Virginia	Albemarle County	1,635	1,920	2,023	2,256	2,292
Virginia	Alexandria city	2,315	2,719	2,865	3,194	3,246
Virginia	Alleghany County	1,007	1,182	1,246	1,389	1,412
Virginia	Amelia County	1,264	1,484	1,564	1,744	1,772
Virginia	Amherst County	1,109	1,302	1,372	1,530	1,554
Virginia	Appomattox County	1,108	1,301	1,371	1,529	1,553
Virginia	Arlington County	2,456	2,884	3,039	3,388	3,443
Virginia	Augusta County	1,252	1,471	1,550	1,728	1,756
Virginia	Bath County	979	1,150	1,212	1,351	1,373
Virginia	Bedford city	1,272	1,494	1,574	1,755	1,783
Virginia	Bedford County	1,272	1,494	1,574	1,755	1,783
Virginia	Bland County	948	1,113	1,173	1,308	1,329
Virginia	Botetourt County	1,391	1,634	1,722	1,920	1,951
Virginia	Bristol city	1,008	1,184	1,248	1,392	1,414
Virginia	Brunswick County	1,079	1,267	1,335	1,489	1,513
Virginia	Buchanan County	936	1,099	1,158	1,291	1,312
Virginia	Buckingham County	1,112	1,306	1,376	1,534	1,559
Virginia	Buena Vista city	1,187	1,394	1,469	1,638	1,664
Virginia	Campbell	1,140	1,339	1,411	1,573	1,599
	County					
Virginia	Caroline County	1,446	1,699	1,790	1,996	2,028
Virginia	Carroll County	948	1,113	1,173	1,308	1,329
Virginia	Charles City County	1,193	1,401	1,476	1,646	1,672
Virginia	Charlotte County	1,099	1,291	1,360	1,516	1,541
Virginia	Charlottesville city	1,563	1,836	1,935	2,158	2,192
Virginia	Chesapeake city	1,702	2,000	2,107	2,349	2,387
Virginia	Chesterfield County	1,539	1,808	1,905	2,124	2,158
Virginia	Clarke County	1,785	2,096	2,209	2,463	2,503
Virginia	Colonial Heights city	1,292	1,517	1,599	1,783	1,812
Virginia	Covington city	920	1,081	1,139	1,270	1,290
Virginia	Craig County	1,260	1,479	1,559	1,738	1,766
Virginia	Culpeper County	1,648	1,935	2,039	2,273	2,310
Virginia	Cumberland County	1,162	1,365	1,438	1,603	1,629
Virginia	Danville city	990	1,163	1,225	1,366	1,388
Virginia	Dickenson County	960	1,127	1,188	1,325	1,346
Virginia	Dinwiddie County	1,303	1,531	1,613	1,798	1,828
Virginia	Emporia city	1,230	1,444	1,522	1,697	1,724
Virginia	Essex County	1,157	1,359	1,432	1,597	1,622
Virginia	Fairfax city	2,193	2,576	2,714	3,026	3,075
Virginia	Fairfax County	2,313	2,717	2,863	3,192	3,244
Virginia	Falls Church city	2,657	3,120	3,288	3,666	3,725
Virginia	Fauquier County	2,037	2,392	2,521	2,811	2,856
Virginia	Floyd County	1,073	1,260	1,328	1,481	1,505
Virginia	Fluvanna County	1,442	1,694	1,785	1,990	2,022
Virginia	Franklin city	1,336	1,570	1,654	1,844	1,874
Virginia	Franklin County	1,173	1,378	1,452	1,619	1,645

State Name	County	Housing and Utilities for a Family of 1	Housing and Utilities for a Family of 2	Housing and Utilities for a Family of 3	Housing and Utilities for a Family of 4	Housing and Utilities for a Family of 5 or more
Virginia	Frederick County	1,536	1,804	1,901	2,120	2,154
Virginia	Fredericksburg city	1,751	2,056	2,167	2,416	2,455
Virginia	Galax city	917	1,077	1,135	1,266	1,286
Virginia	Giles County	1,038	1,219	1,285	1,433	1,456
Virginia	Gloucester County	1,422	1,670	1,760	1,962	1,994
Virginia	Goochland County	1,715	2,015	2,123	2,367	2,405
Virginia	Grayson County	951	1,117	1,177	1,312	1,334
Virginia	Greene County	1,495	1,756	1,850	2,063	2,096
Virginia	Greensville County	1,014	1,191	1,255	1,399	1,422
Virginia	Halifax County	1,042	1,224	1,290	1,438	1,462
Virginia	Hampton city	1,439	1,690	1,781	1,986	2,018
Virginia	Hanover County	1,626	1,909	2,012	2,243	2,280
Virginia	Harrisonburg city	1,240	1,457	1,535	1,712	1,739
Virginia	Henrico County	1,502	1,764	1,859	2,073	2,106
Virginia	Henry County	956	1,123	1,183	1,319	1,340
Virginia	Highland County	1,119	1,314	1,385	1,544	1,569
Virginia	Hopewell city	1,138	1,337	1,409	1,571	1,596
Virginia	Isle of Wight	1,661	1,951	2,056	2,292	2,329
	County					
Virginia	James City County	1,691	1,986	2,093	2,334	2,371
Virginia	King and Queen County	1,214	1,426	1,503	1,676	1,703
Virginia	King George County	1,845	2,168	2,284	2,547	2,588
Virginia	King William County	1,433	1,683	1,773	1,977	2,009
Virginia	Lancaster County	1,327	1,558	1,642	1,831	1,860
Virginia	Lee County	909	1,068	1,125	1,254	1,275
Virginia	Lexington city	1,360	1,597	1,683	1,877	1,907
Virginia	Loudoun County	2,458	2,887	3,042	3,392	3,447
Virginia	Louisa County	1,408	1,654	1,743	1,943	1,975
Virginia	Lunenburg County	1,012	1,189	1,253	1,397	1,420
Virginia	Lynchburg city	1,208	1,419	1,495	1,667	1,694
Virginia	Madison County	1,330	1,562	1,646	1,835	1,865
Virginia	Manassas city	1,777	2,087	2,199	2,452	2,491
Virginia	Manassas Park city	1,938	2,277	2,399	2,675	2,718
Virginia	Martinsville city	1,006	1,182	1,245	1,388	1,411
Virginia	Mathews County	1,332	1,564	1,648	1,838	1,867
Virginia	Mecklenburg County	1,084	1,273	1,341	1,495	1,519
Virginia	Middlesex County	1,512	1,776	1,871	2,086	2,120
Virginia	Montgomery County	1,391	1,633	1,721	1,919	1,950
Virginia	Nelson County	1,227	1,442	1,519	1,694	1,721
Virginia	New Kent County	1,561	1,833	1,932	2,154	2,189
Virginia	Newport News city	1,416	1,664	1,753	1,955	1,986
Virginia	Norfolk city	1,526	1,793	1,889	2,106	2,140
Virginia	Northampton County	1,236	1,452	1,530	1,706	1,733
Virginia	Northumberland County	1,389	1,631	1,719	1,917	1,948
Virginia	Norton city	891	1,047	1,103	1,230	1,250
Virginia	Nottoway County	1,118	1,313	1,384	1,543	1,568
Virginia	Orange County	1,421	1,669	1,759	1,961	1,993

State Name	County	Housing and Utilities for a Family of 1	Housing and Utilities for a Family of 2	Housing and Utilities for a Family of 3	Housing and Utilities for a Family of 4	Housing and Utilities for a Family of 5 or more
Virginia	Page County	1,195	1,404	1,479	1,649	1,676
Virginia	Patrick County	970	1,139	1,200	1,338	1,360
Virginia	Petersburg city	1,135	1,333	1,405	1,567	1,592
Virginia	Pittsylvania County	1,048	1,231	1,297	1,446	1,470
Virginia	Poquoson city	1,803	2,117	2,231	2,488	2,528
Virginia	Portsmouth city	1,471	1,728	1,821	2,030	2,063
Virginia	Powhatan County	1,557	1,829	1,927	2,149	2,183
Virginia	Prince Edward County	1,250	1,468	1,547	1,725	1,753
Virginia	Prince George County	1,392	1,635	1,723	1,921	1,952
Virginia	Prince William County	2,074	2,436	2,567	2,862	2,908
Virginia	Pulaski County	1,113	1,307	1,377	1,535	1,560
Virginia	Radford city	1,140	1,339	1,411	1,573	1,599
Virginia	Rappahannock County	1,780	2,091	2,203	2,456	2,496
Virginia	Richmond city	1,442	1,694	1,785	1,990	2,022
Virginia	Richmond County	1,182	1,388	1,463	1,631	1,658
Virginia	Roanoke city	1,153	1,354	1,427	1,591	1,617
Virginia	Roanoke County	1,349	1,585	1,670	1,862	1,892
Virginia	Rockbridge County	1,280	1,503	1,584	1,766	1,795
Virginia	Rockingham County	1,295	1,521	1,603	1,787	1,816
Virginia	Russell County	938	1,102	1,161	1,295	1,315
Virginia	Salem city	1,265	1,486	1,566	1,746	1,774
Virginia	Scott County	949	1,114	1,174	1,309	1,330
Virginia	Shenandoah County	1,353	1,590	1,675	1,868	1,898
Virginia	Smyth County	932	1,094	1,153	1,286	1,306
Virginia	Southampton County	1,340	1,573	1,658	1,849	1,879
Virginia	Spotsylvania County	1,662	1,952	2,057	2,294	2,331
Virginia	Stafford County	1,980	2,325	2,450	2,732	2,776
Virginia	Staunton city	1,182	1,388	1,463	1,631	1,658
Virginia	Suffolk city	1,723	2,023	2,132	2,377	2,416
Virginia	Surry County	1,211	1,423	1,499	1,671	1,698
Virginia	Sussex County	1,176	1,382	1,456	1,623	1,650
Virginia	Tazewell County	1,001	1,176	1,239	1,381	1,404
Virginia	Virginia Beach	1,711	2,009	2,117	2,360	2,399
	city					
Virginia	Warren County	1,471	1,728	1,821	2,030	2,063
Virginia	Washington County	1,100	1,292	1,361	1,518	1,542
Virginia	Waynesboro city	1,210	1,421	1,497	1,669	1,696
Virginia	Westmoreland County	1,280	1,503	1,584	1,766	1,795
Virginia	Williamsburg city	1,420	1,667	1,757	1,959	1,991
Virginia	Winchester city	1,509	1,772	1,867	2,082	2,115
Virginia	Wise County	968	1,137	1,198	1,336	1,357
Virginia	Wythe County	1,005	1,181	1,244	1,387	1,409
Virginia	York County	1,749	2,054	2,164	2,413	2,452
Washington	Adams County	1,213	1,424	1,501	1,674	1,701
Washington	Asotin County	1,231	1,445	1,523	1,698	1,726
Washington	Benton County	1,353	1,589	1,674	1,867	1,897

State Name	County	Housing and Utilities for a Family of 1	Housing and Utilities for a Family of 2	Housing and Utilities for a Family of 3	Housing and Utilities for a Family of 4	Housing and Utilities for a Family of 5 or more
Washington	Chelan County	1,358	1,595	1,681	1,874	1,905
Washington	Clallam County	1,366	1,604	1,690	1,884	1,915
Washington	Clark County	1,603	1,883	1,984	2,212	2,248
Washington	Columbia County	1,145	1,345	1,417	1,580	1,605
Washington	Cowlitz County	1,361	1,598	1,684	1,878	1,908
Washington	Douglas County	1,347	1,582	1,667	1,859	1,889
Washington	Ferry County	1,137	1,335	1,407	1,569	1,594
Washington	Franklin County	1,294	1,520	1,602	1,786	1,815
Washington	Garfield County	1,080	1,269	1,337	1,491	1,515
Washington	Grant County	1,206	1,416	1,492	1,664	1,690
Washington	Grays Harbor County	1,229	1,443	1,521	1,696	1,723
Washington	Island County	1,651	1,939	2,043	2,278	2,315
Washington	Jefferson County	1,439	1,690	1,781	1,986	2,018
Washington	King County	2,070	2,431	2,562	2,857	2,903
Washington	Kitsap County	1,665	1,956	2,061	2,298	2,335
Washington	Kittitas County	1,485	1,744	1,838	2,049	2,082
Washington	Klickitat County	1,357	1,594	1,680	1,873	1,903
Washington	Lewis County	1,294	1,520	1,602	1,786	1,815
Washington	Lincoln County	1,184	1,390	1,465	1,633	1,660
Washington	Mason County	1,336	1,570	1,654	1,844	1,874
Washington	Okanogan County	1,128	1,325	1,396	1,557	1,582
Washington	Pacific County	1,140	1,339	1,411	1,573	1,599
Washington	Pend Oreille County	1,100	1,293	1,362	1,519	1,543
Washington	Pierce County	1,704	2,001	2,109	2,352	2,389
Washington	San Juan County	1,744	2,049	2,159	2,407	2,446
Washington	Skagit County	1,607	1,888	1,989	2,218	2,254
Washington	Skamania County	1,461	1,716	1,808	2,016	2,048
Washington	Snohomish County	1,869	2,195	2,313	2,579	2,621
Washington	Spokane County	1,347	1,582	1,667	1,859	1,889
Washington	Stevens County	1,232	1,447	1,525	1,700	1,728
Washington	Thurston County	1,648	1,935	2,039	2,273	2,310
Washington	Wahkiakum County	1,291	1,517	1,598	1,782	1,811
Washington	Walla Walla County	1,365	1,603	1,689	1,883	1,914
Washington	Whatcom County	1,571	1,845	1,944	2,168	2,203
Washington	Whitman County	1,333	1,566	1,650	1,840	1,869
Washington	Yakima County	1,275	1,498	1,578	1,759	1,788
West Virginia	Barbour County	911	1,070	1,127	1,257	1,277
West Virginia	Berkeley County	1,316	1,546	1,629	1,816	1,846
West Virginia	Boone County	1,016	1,193	1,257	1,402	1,424
West Virginia	Braxton County	890	1,045	1,101	1,228	1,247
West Virginia	Brooke County	959	1,126	1,187	1,324	1,345
West Virginia	Cabell County	1,024	1,202	1,267	1,413	1,436
West Virginia	Calhoun County	747	878	925	1,031	1,048
West Virginia	Clay County	1,002	1,177	1,240	1,383	1,405
West Virginia	Doddridge County	886	1,041	1,097	1,223	1,243
West Virginia	Fayette County	883	1,037	1,093	1,219	1,238
West Virginia	Gilmer County	773	908	957	1,067	1,084

State Name	County	Housing and Utilities for a Family of 1	Housing and Utilities for a Family of 2	Housing and Utilities for a Family of 3	Housing and Utilities for a Family of 4	Housing and Utilities for a Family of 5 or more
West Virginia	Grant County	981	1,152	1,214	1,354	1,375
West Virginia	Greenbrier County	936	1,099	1,158	1,291	1,312
West Virginia	Hampshire County	1,023	1,201	1,266	1,412	1,434
West Virginia	Hancock County	956	1,123	1,183	1,319	1,340
West Virginia	Hardy County	983	1,155	1,217	1,357	1,379
West Virginia	Harrison County	980	1,151	1,213	1,352	1,374
West Virginia	Jackson County	960	1,127	1,188	1,325	1,346
West Virginia	Jefferson County	1,541	1,810	1,907	2,126	2,161
West Virginia	Kanawha County	1,026	1,205	1,270	1,416	1,439
West Virginia	Lewis County	879	1,033	1,088	1,213	1,233
West Virginia	Lincoln County	886	1,040	1,096	1,222	1,242
West Virginia	Logan County	974	1,144	1,206	1,345	1,366
West Virginia	Marion County	998	1,172	1,235	1,377	1,399
West Virginia	Marshall County	924	1,086	1,144	1,276	1,296
West Virginia	Mason County	863	1,014	1,068	1,191	1,210
West Virginia	McDowell County	793	932	982	1,095	1,113
West Virginia	Mercer County	943	1,107	1,167	1,301	1,322
West Virginia	Mineral County	1,037	1,218	1,283	1,431	1,454
West Virginia	Mingo County	954	1,121	1,181	1,317	1,338
West Virginia	Monongalia County	1,188	1,395	1,470	1,639	1,666
West Virginia	Monroe County	945	1,110	1,170	1,305	1,326
West Virginia	Morgan County	1,194	1,403	1,478	1,648	1,675
West Virginia	Nicholas County	921	1,082	1,140	1,271	1,292
West Virginia	Ohio County	987	1,159	1,221	1,361	1,383
West Virginia	Pendleton County	912	1,071	1,129	1,259	1,279
West Virginia	Pleasants County	1,033	1,213	1,278	1,425	1,448
West Virginia	Pocahontas County	905	1,063	1,120	1,249	1,269
West Virginia	Preston County	986	1,158	1,220	1,360	1,382
West Virginia	Putnam County	1,166	1,369	1,443	1,609	1,635
West Virginia	Raleigh County	991	1,163	1,226	1,367	1,389
West Virginia	Randolph County	905	1,063	1,120	1,249	1,269
West Virginia	Ritchie County	824	968	1,020	1,137	1,156
West Virginia	Roane County	935	1,098	1,157	1,290	1,311
West Virginia	Summers County	867	1,018	1,073	1,196	1,216
West Virginia	Taylor County	997	1,171	1,234	1,376	1,398
West Virginia	Tucker County	947	1,112	1,172	1,307	1,328
West Virginia	Tyler County	861	1,012	1,066	1,189	1,208
West Virginia	Upshur County	946	1,111	1,171	1,306	1,327
West Virginia	Wayne County	949	1,115	1,175	1,310	1,331
West Virginia	Webster County	770	904	953	1,063	1,080
West Virginia	Wetzel County	894	1,051	1,107	1,234	1,254
West Virginia	Wirt County	831	976	1,028	1,146	1,165
West Virginia	Wood County	978	1,148	1,210	1,349	1,371
West Virginia	Wyoming County	840	986	1,039	1,158	1,177
Wisconsin	Adams County	1,194	1,403	1,478	1,648	1,675
Wisconsin	Ashland County	1,120	1,315	1,386	1,545	1,570

State Name	County	Housing and Utilities for a Family of 1	Housing and Utilities for a Family of 2	Housing and Utilities for a Family of 3	Housing and Utilities for a Family of 4	Housing and Utilities for a Family of 5 or more
Wisconsin	Barron County	1,185	1,392	1,467	1,636	1,662
Wisconsin	Bayfield County	1,172	1,377	1,451	1,618	1,644
Wisconsin	Brown County	1,323	1,554	1,637	1,825	1,855
Wisconsin	Buffalo County	1,245	1,462	1,541	1,718	1,746
Wisconsin	Burnett County	1,168	1,372	1,446	1,612	1,638
Wisconsin	Calumet County	1,370	1,610	1,696	1,891	1,922
Wisconsin	Chippewa County	1,224	1,438	1,515	1,689	1,716
Wisconsin	Clark County	1,125	1,321	1,392	1,552	1,577
Wisconsin	Columbia County	1,430	1,680	1,770	1,974	2,005
Wisconsin	Crawford County	1,124	1,320	1,391	1,551	1,576
Wisconsin	Dane County	1,636	1,922	2,025	2,258	2,294
Wisconsin	Dodge County	1,336	1,570	1,654	1,844	1,874
Wisconsin	Door County	1,282	1,506	1,587	1,770	1,798
Wisconsin	Douglas County	1,186	1,393	1,468	1,637	1,663
Wisconsin	Dunn County	1,312	1,541	1,624	1,811	1,840
Wisconsin	Eau Claire County	1,269	1,491	1,571	1,752	1,780
Wisconsin	Florence County	1,235	1,451	1,529	1,705	1,732
Wisconsin	Fond du Lac County	1,307	1,535	1,617	1,803	1,832
Wisconsin	Forest County	1,034	1,215	1,280	1,427	1,450
Wisconsin	Grant County	1,185	1,392	1,467	1,636	1,662
Wisconsin	Green County	1,387	1,629	1,717	1,914	1,945
Wisconsin	Green Lake County	1,173	1,378	1,452	1,619	1,645
Wisconsin	Iowa County	1,411	1,657	1,746	1,947	1,978
Wisconsin	Iron County	1,050	1,233	1,299	1,448	1,472
Wisconsin	Jackson County	1,169	1,373	1,447	1,613	1,639
Wisconsin	Jefferson County	1,419	1,666	1,756	1,958	1,990
Wisconsin	Juneau County	1,175	1,380	1,454	1,621	1,647
Wisconsin	Kenosha County	1,482	1,740	1,834	2,045	2,078
Wisconsin	Kewaunee County	1,240	1,457	1,535	1,712	1,739
Wisconsin	La Crosse County	1,342	1,576	1,661	1,852	1,882
Wisconsin	Lafayette County	1,264	1,484	1,564	1,744	1,772
Wisconsin	Langlade County	1,034	1,215	1,280	1,427	1,450
Wisconsin	Lincoln County	1,155	1,357	1,430	1,594	1,620
Wisconsin	Manitowoc County	1,169	1,373	1,447	1,613	1,639
Wisconsin	Marathon County	1,267	1,488	1,568	1,748	1,777
Wisconsin	Marinette County	1,064	1,250	1,317	1,468	1,492
Wisconsin	Marquette County	1,176	1,382	1,456	1,623	1,650
Wisconsin	Menominee County	1,032	1,212	1,277	1,424	1,447
Wisconsin	Milwaukee County	1,420	1,667	1,757	1,959	1,991
Wisconsin	Monroe County	1,218	1,431	1,508	1,681	1,709
Wisconsin	Oconto County	1,260	1,479	1,559	1,738	1,766
Wisconsin	Oneida County	1,176	1,381	1,455	1,622	1,649
Wisconsin	Outagamie County	1,353	1,590	1,675	1,868	1,898
Wisconsin	Ozaukee County	1,664	1,955	2,060	2,297	2,334
Wisconsin	Pepin County	1,218	1,430	1,507	1,680	1,707
Wisconsin	Pierce County	1,577	1,852	1,952	2,176	2,212
Wisconsin	Polk County	1,345	1,579	1,664	1,855	1,885

State Name	County	Housing and Utilities for a Family of 1	Housing and Utilities for a Family of 2	Housing and Utilities for a Family of 3	Housing and Utilities for a Family of 4	Housing and Utilities for a Family of 5 or more
Wisconsin	Portage County	1,225	1,439	1,516	1,690	1,718
Wisconsin	Price County	1,121	1,316	1,387	1,547	1,571
Wisconsin	Racine County	1,417	1,665	1,754	1,956	1,987
Wisconsin	Richland County	1,179	1,385	1,459	1,627	1,653
Wisconsin	Rock County	1,257	1,477	1,556	1,735	1,763
Wisconsin	Rusk County	1,091	1,281	1,350	1,505	1,530
Wisconsin	Sauk County	1,345	1,579	1,664	1,855	1,885
Wisconsin	Sawyer County	1,168	1,371	1,445	1,611	1,637
Wisconsin	Shawano County	1,201	1,410	1,486	1,657	1,684
Wisconsin	Sheboygan County	1,279	1,502	1,583	1,765	1,794
Wisconsin	St. Croix County	1,554	1,825	1,923	2,144	2,179
Wisconsin	Taylor County	1,187	1,394	1,469	1,638	1,664
Wisconsin	Trempealeau County	1,235	1,450	1,528	1,704	1,731
Wisconsin	Vernon County	1,215	1,427	1,504	1,677	1,704
Wisconsin	Vilas County	1,228	1,442	1,520	1,695	1,722
Wisconsin	Walworth County	1,504	1,766	1,861	2,075	2,109
Wisconsin	Washburn County	1,154	1,355	1,428	1,592	1,618
Wisconsin	Washington County	1,559	1,832	1,930	2,152	2,187
Wisconsin	Waukesha County	1,702	1,999	2,106	2,348	2,386
Wisconsin	Waupaca County	1,214	1,425	1,502	1,675	1,702
Wisconsin	Waushara County	1,204	1,414	1,490	1,661	1,688
Wisconsin	Winnebago County	1,267	1,488	1,568	1,748	1,777
Wisconsin	Wood County	1,122	1,317	1,388	1,548	1,573
Wyoming	Albany County	1,380	1,621	1,708	1,904	1,935
Wyoming	Big Horn County	1,108	1,301	1,371	1,529	1,553
Wyoming	Campbell County	1,472	1,729	1,822	2,032	2,064
Wyoming	Carbon County	1,180	1,386	1,461	1,629	1,655
Wyoming	Converse County	1,329	1,561	1,645	1,834	1,864
Wyoming	Crook County	1,306	1,534	1,616	1,802	1,831
Wyoming	Fremont County	1,266	1,487	1,567	1,747	1,775
Wyoming	Goshen County	1,107	1,300	1,370	1,528	1,552
Wyoming	Hot Springs County	1,155	1,356	1,429	1,593	1,619
Wyoming	Johnson County	1,330	1,562	1,646	1,835	1,865
Wyoming	Laramie County	1,373	1,612	1,699	1,894	1,925
Wyoming	Lincoln County	1,353	1,590	1,675	1,868	1,898
Wyoming	Natrona County	1,295	1,521	1,603	1,787	1,816
Wyoming	Niobrara County	1,087	1,276	1,345	1,500	1,524
Wyoming	Park County	1,263	1,483	1,563	1,743	1,771
Wyoming	Platte County	1,085	1,275	1,343	1,497	1,522
Wyoming	Sheridan County	1,356	1,592	1,678	1,871	1,901
Wyoming	Sublette County	1,656	1,945	2,050	2,286	2,323
Wyoming	Sweetwater County	1,428	1,677	1,767	1,970	2,002
Wyoming	Teton County	2,061	2,421	2,551	2,844	2,890
Wyoming	Uinta County	1,275	1,498	1,578	1,759	1,788
Wyoming	Washakie County	1,201	1,411	1,487	1,658	1,685
Wyoming	Weston County	1,290	1,516	1,597	1,781	1,809

National Standards: Food, Clothing and Other Items

Expense	One Person	Two Persons	Three Persons	Four Persons
Food	$307	$583	$668	$815
Housekeeping supplies	$30	$60	$60	$71
Apparel & services	$80	$148	$193	$227
Personal care products & services	$34	$61	$62	$74
Miscellaneous	$119	$231	$266	$322
Total	**$570**	**$1,083**	**$1,249**	**$1,509**

More than four persons	Additional Persons Amount
For each additional person, add to four-person total allowance:	**$341**

Please note that the standards change. For updated IRS standards visit http://www.taxresolutioninstitute.org/forms-library/

Local Standards: Transportation

Public Transportation		
National	$173	

Ownership Costs		
	One Car	**Two Cars**
National	$471	$942

Operating Costs		
	One Car	**Two Cars**
Northeast Region	$251	$502
Boston	$250	$500
New York	$308	$616
Philadelphia	$270	$540
Midwest Region	$191	$382
Chicago	$236	$472
Cleveland	$204	$408
Detroit	$266	$532
Minneapolis-St. Paul	$196	$392
South Region	$220	$440
Atlanta	$231	$462
Baltimore	$225	$450
Dallas-Ft. Worth	$250	$500
Houston	$281	$562
Miami	$312	$624
Washington, D.C.	$250	$500
West Region	$213	$426
Los Angeles	$266	$532
Phoenix	$262	$524
San Diego	$271	$542
San Francisco	$276	$552
Seattle	$173	$346

National Standards: Out-of-Pocket Health Care

	Out of Pocket Costs
Under 65	$54
65 and Older	$130

Please note that the standards change. For updated IRS standards visit http://www.taxresolutioninstitute.org/forms-library/

IRS Collection Procedures

The Power of the IRS to Collect Taxes:

The IRS has the power to collect taxes by levying on taxpayer's property stemming from the filing of the Federal Tax Lien. When a person owes taxes, the IRS is able to file a lien on all of said person's assets once they meet necessary statutory requirements. The lien attaches to all rights, title and interest of the taxpayer wherever it may be situated. [IRC § 6321] Once the IRS has a lien on a taxpayer's assets, it may enforce said lien by administratively levying his or her assets.

Lien Rights

Let's take the following example: *a person buys a car and finances the purchase through a bank. The purchase price for the car is $20,000. The purchaser pays a down payment of $2,000 and signs a note with a bank giving it a lien on the car. The bank then lends the buyer $18,000 to complete the purchase. If the buyer defaults on the note, the bank may repossess the car.*

In the case of the IRS it gains a lien on all of a taxpayer's assets and therefore it has the right to seize most of those assets to satisfy unpaid taxes.

Creation of Lien:

The liability of a taxpayer for Internal Revenue taxes is personal in nature and, except for the taxes imposed under Subtitle E of the Code relating to distilled spirits, wines, and beer, does not directly attach to his or her property. In this respect the liability is analogous to a simple debt, and without anything more could be enforced only by a court action. To protect the revenue Congress has provided an administrative means by which collection of assessment may be affected. Congress also has statutorily provided for a lien which attaches to a taxpayer's property. The lien is often referred to as the "statutory" or the "general" lien. The following requirements for establishing the lien are contained in the code.

An assessment must have been made;

A notice and demand for payment must have been made (the first IRS notice meets this requirement); and

The taxpayer must have neglected or refused to pay. [IRC § 6321]

Meeting Statutory Requirements:

It is surprisingly easy for the IRS to meet the statutory requirements. An assessment occurs when the IRS encodes the return information to its system of records and an assessment officer signs a certificate of assessment. A machine now automatically imposes a signature on assessment documents when return information is posted to the IRS computer system. The notice and demand requirement is met by sending the taxpayer a notice requesting payment.

Correspondence with Compliance Center:

It is typically ineffective to write to a Compliance Center. It can take Compliance Centers more than six weeks to process correspondence. For example, if your client receives a Notice 504 even though he paid the tax upon receipt of the Notice 503, a letter to the IRS will not stop assignment to Automated Collection System ("ACS"). The IRS may not process your letter for six weeks, yet the computer continues to automatically refer the matter to ACS on a set cycle. You must speak with someone at the IRS and request that the computer process be stopped while the IRS searches for the lost payment. Even if the Compliance Center has processed your correspondence, the response can be useless. You might receive a postcard acknowledging that correspondence was received but failing to include pertinent basic information including identifying the client in question. If you have written more than one letter, there is no way of determining which matter or to whom the postcard received refers.

Small Dollar Payment Plans:

A taxpayer may be able to secure a 72-month payment plan for 1040 liabilities of less than $50,000. The IRS Restructuring and Reform Act of 1998 required the IRS to grant a payment plan to individual taxpayers who owe less than $25,000 but the amount has been increased to $50,000. If the taxpayer desires this type of plan, he or she should respond to the IRS upon receiving the first notice by writing to the Compliance Center requesting 72 months to pay the tax liability. A request for a payment arrangement on small dollar accounts could also be made by transmitting the new IRS Form 9465. On many occasions the IRS has granted the taxpayer a payment plan but failed to confirm the plan. If subsequent notices cease to be sent from the Compliance Center, the taxpayer should assume that the Service has granted a plan. If the Compliance Center continues to issue subsequent notices, the taxpayer should assume that his or her plan has been improperly processed by the Service and contact their support Staff or a Revenue Officer.

Quality of Compliance Centers:

Compliance Centers operate at varying degrees of efficiency. At the time this book was written, the Philadelphia Compliance Center was acknowledged to be one of the worst in the country. Fresno, Austin, Holtsville and Atlanta were in close competition to be the runner-ups for worst. Ogden was rated one of the best Compliance Centers. Inefficient Compliance Centers can create large unnecessary problems for your clients. At one time, the Philadelphia Compliance Center lost the federal tax deposit records of approximately 10,000 businesses and dealt with their error by proceeding to bill the companies.

Telephone Collection Efforts:

If an account cannot be collected by a Returns Processing Center using notices and/or levies upon the taxpayer's wages or bank account, the matter will then be transferred to a Customer Service Center for telephone collection efforts. Each Customer Service Center, including the Return Processing Center, has a computerized telephone collection system.

Payment Options Comparison Chart					
	Total of All Liabilities	**Time Frame for Full Payment**	**Other Basic Requirements**	**Financial Information**	**Verification of Financial Information**
Streamlined IA	Below $25,000	Within 60 months	Must stay current with all future taxes	Limited	No
Full-pay IA (< 60 mos.)	No Limits	Up to 60 months	Leverage equity in assets, must stay current with all future taxes, conditional expense may be allowed	Complete	Yes
Full-pay IA (60 mos.)	No Limits	61 months and up, prior to expiration of collection statute	Leverage equity in assets, must stay current with all future taxes, Transition period for conditional expenses may be allowed for up to 12 mos.	Complete	Yes
Partial Pay IA	No Limits	Payment made until collection statute expires	Leverage equity in assets, must stay current with all future taxes, no conditional expenses allowed, no transition period	Complete	Yes
Deferred Payment Offer in Compromise	No Limit	Payment made until statute date or until offer amount received	Net realizable equity must be accounted for in amount offered, No conditional expenses allowed, must stay current with all future taxes	Complete	Yes
Fresh Start Installment Agreement <$25,000	Below $25,000	72 months	Must qualify to make payments based upon income	None	No
Fresh Start Installment Agreement between $25,000 and $50,000	Between $25,000 and $50,000	72 months	Must qualify to make payments based upon income	Very Little	No

Chapter 13:

Engagement Agreements

Hourly Fee Agreement Sample

(please verify that any engagement agreement you use including this sample does not violate any of your local State laws):

Date

Client Name
Address
City, State, Zip

CLIENT AGREEMENT

This is intended to be a legally binding agreement under the laws of ***State in which company conducts business****.*
Please read it carefully before signing.

RETAINER AGREEMENT FOR TAX REPRESENTATION SERVICES

This Agreement is for tax representation services between NAME ("Client", "you", "your") and the Tax Resolution Institute Inc ("we", "our", "us"). The purpose of this document is to reduce this agreement to writing so that we will understand our obligations to each other.

MATTER IN WHICH REPRESENTATION WILL BE PROVIDED

At your request our engagement is limited to the: (1) Preparation of Power of Attorney for federal income taxes due; (2) Assessment of administrative procedures and administrative remedies available; (3) Meeting with Revenue Officers by telephone or in person; (4) Negotiation of a Federal Installment Agreement, as applicable.

SCOPE OF REPRESENTATION

Our responsibility will be to undertake the above matters, to represent the Client and to do everything necessary to properly handle this matter.

CLIENT TO BE KEPT INFORMED

We will keep the Client fully informed of the status of this matter and will provide copies of all relevant correspondence concerning this matter. We will meet (either in person or over the telephone) at any mutually agreeable time to discuss the status of this matter. The Client is urged to communicate any and all concerns or questions which the Client has in connection with this representation and we will endeavor to promptly respond.

NO PREDICTION OF RESULTS

ALTHOUGH WE WILL USE OUR BEST EFFORTS AS CERTIFIED PUBLIC ACCOUNTANTS FOR THE CLIENT TO REPRESENT THE CLIENT IN ACHIEVING THE MOST FAVORABLE POSSIBLE RESULT UNDER THE LAWS OF THE UNITED STATES, WE MAKE NO REPRESENTATION OR PREDICTION THAT ANY GIVEN RESULT WILL OCCUR AS A RESULT OF SUCH EFFORTS.

COOPERATION OF THE CLIENT

The Client agrees that he/she will (A) promptly respond to any oral or written request by us to provide information and (B) diligently assist us in obtaining any information from any third party. The Client understands that failure to diligently assist us in representing the Client could lead to a less favorable result in this matter and to additional representation fees which would not otherwise be incurred if the Client were to diligently cooperate and assist us.

FEES

The above-described services shall be provided by our firm in consideration of our normal hourly rate in the amount of $400 per hour. The Client agrees to remit a retainer in the amount of $4,000 for the services set forth above. In addition, the Client agrees to maintain a minimum retainer balance of $1,000. If at any time the retainer balance should fall below the $1,000 minimum, the Client agrees to make payment necessary to replenish retainer account within (3) days of notice. If the Client fails to replenish the retainer account as stated above, all work will cease until payments are made current. Please note that work performed before the IRS and other taxing agencies is document and time sensitive. For this reason it is imperative that the Client stays current with regards to payments and responds upon receipt of requests for information and documents. Because our firm has limited resources, we can only accept a finite number of cases. By agreeing to represent you, we are limiting our ability to represent other clients who may also be in need of our services. All fees paid to us by Client in the form of retainer payment or otherwise are non-refundable. We strongly recommend that Client supports our efforts to complete all work in a professional and timely manner including without limitation, supplying documents requested by the IRS, Client's local state taxing agency, and us; completing and returning forms; and making payments as set forth above. Should the Client fail to complete Client's responsibilities in a professional and timely manner as set forth above, we may at our discretion, cease all work in assisting Client to resolve Client's outstanding matters deeming all payments made by client fully earned and non-refundable. Please note that we bill in tenths (.1) of an hour and our minimum charge for any service (phone call, e-mail, etc.) is two-tenths (.2) of an hour.

OUT-OF-POCKET COSTS

The fees set forth in Paragraph 5 above do not include any out-of-pocket costs advanced by us on behalf of the Client, such as messenger fees, express mail, parking, and the like. These out-of-pocket costs will be advanced by us, will be invoiced to the Client by us, and will be due and payable in the same manner as the professional fees which are invoiced to the Client.

TERMINATION OF AGREEMENT

The Client may terminate this agreement at any time for any reason whatsoever, but such termination shall not affect the obligation to pay for any services already rendered or costs already advanced up to the date and time of the termination. We may terminate this Agreement at any time if the Client fails to pay fees when due under the terms of this agreement or fails to cooperate in any other way, or for other legal or just cause. Upon termination of this Agreement for failure to pay fees, we will return to the Client any of the Client's original documents. Upon termination of this Agreement following the payment of all costs and fees, the Tax Resolution Institute Inc will return all documents to which the client is entitled.

We maintain the right to terminate representation for your failure to cooperate and/or your failure to make payment of any fees and/or costs as provided for under the terms of this agreement. Failure to respond within 48 hours of request will result to no responsibility.

Invoices will be mailed monthly (or sooner) and are due when received. If we have not received payment within 7 days of our invoice, all work will be suspended until your account is brought current. Accounts past due more than 30 days will be charged interest and administrative costs at 1.5% per month.

In the event that any provisions or partial provision of this Agreement shall be held to be void, voidable, or unenforceable, the remaining portions hereof shall nevertheless remain in full force and effect.

Each party, by affixing his signature below, does further represent that, prior to entering into this agreement; he consulted with an attorney at law of his own choice, who explained the provisions of this agreement to his personal satisfaction.

This contract, consisting of Paragraphs 1 through 10, is our entire agreement. Any prior or contemporaneous agreements, understandings and representations are merged and superseded by these written terms. Any modification or waiver shall be in writing. Client has been advised that time is of the essence with respect to this matter.

Please sign, date and return this Agreement along with Forms 2848 Power of Attorney. Please return signed form along with a retainer check in the amount of $4,000 to the address listed above promptly so that we may begin working on your case.

Sincerely,

Your Name, Name of Firm

Acknowledged

By: ____***Client Name***____

Because delinquent taxpayers typically do not know the full extent of their tax issues and therefore additional work beyond the scope of work discussed in an initial consultation with the taxpayer often becomes necessary, it is usually preferable to enter into an agreement based upon collecting hourly fees as opposed to a fixed fee agreement. Sometimes clients are more comfortable entering into a fixed fee agreement knowing what they will pay in advance. This type of agreement can too be implemented but if you enter into a fixed fee agreement you must ensure that you specifically describe the work that is to be completed and make it clear that any additional work that becomes necessary to complete will be done so either under a separate agreement, and/or for an additional cost which can either be an additional fixed fee or done so on an hourly basis based upon your regular published fees. Below you will see a sample of a fixed fee agreement.

Fixed Fee Agreement Sample

(please verify that any engagement agreement you use including this sample does not violate any of your local State laws):

Date

VIA Email: ***email***

Name
Street
City, State, Zip

Dear ***Taxpayer***,

This document is being furnished to ***Name*** ('you", "your") in order to ensure that you have a full understanding of terms of our engagement. For this reason ***Your Company*** insists that you read this letter carefully.

Your Company will provide to you our services a follows:

Please note that the items listed below represent the general services necessary to complete the majority of tax resolution cases. It is possible that additional services be required to resolve unforeseen matters that may arise in a client's case. Should subsequent matters not listed below arise with your tax case, you agree to pay, in addition to the amount set forth in this agreement, for additional work necessary to resolve your matter(s). ***Your Company*** will contact you to discuss said matters as well as any applicable fees associated with additional work to be completed by ***Your Company***.

Based upon the information you have provided us, the services or a subset of the services described below are deemed appropriate to resolve your case. In the event that the information you provided us is incomplete, inaccurate or the circumstances of your case change, you authorize ***Your Company*** to employ additional services necessary to achieve the optimal resolution to your case.

Obtaining Transcripts: If necessary, *Your Company* **with your consent will contact the Internal Revenue Service ("IRS") and when appropriate the State in which you pay tax in order to acquire, examine, decipher and evaluate all applicable tax transcripts relating to your Individual and/or Business tax matters for the periods** *beginning year* **through** *ending year*.

Preparation of Tax Returns: *Your Company* **will prepare your Federal and when applicable State type of tax returns for the periods beginning year through ending year. Your Company will prepare your returns based upon the above-mentioned transcripts and information you provide us via documents and tax organizers.**

Protection Against Collection Activity: Assuming that there is no active collection activity, *Your Company* **will make a best effort attempt to keep the taxing agencies involved with your case from levying your bank account, garnishing your wages, garnishing your income (3rd Party Levy), or seizing your assets for the entire tenure of your engagement with us. If bank levies and/or wage garnishments are already in place, we will make a best effort attempt to have them removed and/or reduced.**

Installment Agreement: Assuming you are in "Current Compliance", *Your Company* **will negotiate with the IRS and when applicable the State in which you owe back taxes, a monthly installment plan in which you make payments based upon your ability to pay (which may be nothing if you qualify for Currently Non Collectible ["CNC"] status).**

Installment Agreement (FOR OFFERS ONLY): Assuming you do not qualify for an Offer in Compromise or you choose not to proceed with an Offer in Compromise and you are in "Current Compliance", *Your Company* **will negotiate with the IRS and when applicable the State in which you owe back taxes, a monthly installment plan in which you make payments based upon your ability to pay (which may be nothing if you qualify for Currently Non Collectible ["CNC"] status).**

Abatement of Penalties: If the facts of your case warrant so, *Your Company* **will negotiate to remove penalties when applicable.**

Preparation of an Offer in Compromise: If *Your Company* **determines you qualify as an Offer in Compromise candidate, we will prepare and submit an "Offer in Compromise" to the IRS on your behalf for your current tax liability. If the offer is rejected and you consent to proceed with the services of** *Your Company* **as they relate to the appeal of your offer, you will pay** *Your Company* **additional fees to warrant the time necessary to file and argue the appeal.**

YOUR COMPANY WILL AT ALL TIMES MAKE A BEST EFFORT ATTEMPT WITHIN THE CONFINES OF THE LAW TO OBTAIN THE BEST RESULT POSSIBLE TO YOU, HOWEVER, AT NO TIME DOES ***YOUR COMPANY*** MAKE ANY PREDICTION OR REPRESENTATION THAT ANY GIVEN RESULT WILL OCCUR AS A RESULT OF OUR EFFORTS.

Client Responsibilities

Current compliance: you agree to make and maintain payments and continue to file returns as required by any agreements, settlements, and/or compromises that are made with the Taxing Agencies involved in your case, or as is required by law.

Client representation: You agree that ***Your Company's*** representation of you is conditioned upon you continuing to remain current on all future tax liabilities as they become due. Failure to stay current with any and all tax liabilities will be cause for termination of this agreement, as it would greatly affect our ability to adequately represent you.

Taxing agency correspondence: Working with the taxing agencies is both time and document sensitive. You agree to respond within five (5) working days with all items requested by ***Your Company***, and the taxing agencies involved with your case.

Agreement execution: You agree and acknowledge that ***Your Company*** has advised you of your obligation to fully and accurately disclose the nature, source and extent of your income, expenses, assets and liabilities. Providing inaccurate information may jeopardize the outcome of your case.

Time is of the essence: ***Your Company*** must respond to tax notices quickly to in order to avoid additional complications to your case. Every notice you receive must be forwarded to us right away.

Time estimates: When requested by you ***Your Company*** will provide estimates of the time it should take to resolve your tax matters. In some instances, the period of time it takes for cases to be completed becomes extended due to factors that are out of our control including without limitation taxing agency delays.

Corresponding with IRS and if applicable the State in which you owe tax: For the tenure of our representation of you, you must not talk to, meet in person, or have any other correspondence with any taxing agency relating to your case without our consent.

Fees for services provided: Our work is typically completed on a retainer basis. ***Your Company*** will estimate a fee for the services to be rendered at the time of our engagement. We typically require anywhere from Fifty percent (50%) to one hundred percent (100%) of the estimated amount be paid prior to the commencement of services. The estimate of our fee is not binding as some cases become more complicated and time consuming than anticipated when the estimate was made. Fees are based on the value of the services rendered considering the expertise required in addition to expended time.

Out of pocket costs: The fees set forth below do not include any out-of-pocket costs advanced by us on behalf of the Client, including without limitation messenger fees, express mail, parking, and travel. The above-mentioned out-of-pocket costs may be advanced by us at our discretion and will be invoiced by us to the Client. The reimbursements of these costs by the Client to us are due and payable upon request.

Non-refundable retainer payments: ***Your Company*** strongly recommends that you contribute to and support our efforts as requested by us. Failure to do so may result in our withdrawal from a matter and all retainer payments and other payments collected by us will be deemed fully earned and non–refundable.

If you fail to meet the responsibilities listed above *Your Company* **reserves the right to terminate this agreement or apply additional fees to compensate for additional work necessary to obtain a resolution to your case.**

Headings: Headings used in this agreement are for convenience of reference only and shall not constitute a part of this agreement for any other purpose or affect the construction of this agreement.

Fees

The cost for these services will be $______, assuming that the information you provided us thus far is complete and accurate, that you do not add additional work and that you are at all times cooperative and timely regarding our request for information. ***Your Company*** will require an initial payment in the amount of $________ prior to commencing work. The remaining balance of $_________ shall be due and payable as follows: Three (3) post-dated check(s), or the ACH Automatic Debit Authorization in the amount of $___________ each, dated 30 days apart from one another, starting 30 days after initial payment is made.

Your Company *reserves the right to increase the fees stipulated herein if we have not been retained within 7 days from the date of this Agreement. All work completed by us that exists outside the scope of work set forth above or is necessary to complete due to the lack of cooperation by you will be completed at hour standard hourly rates which range from* **hourly rates** *per hour. All retainer payments as well as other payments for services paid to* **Your Company** *are earned when paid; no refunds will be furnished. All invoices are due upon receipt. Failure to pay either retainer requests or to submit payment as per the agreed upon payment schedule stated above, shall cause our firm to immediately stop providing services without further notice.*

I acknowledge that ***Your Company*** has or will advise me that the dischargeability of this liability in Bankruptcy may or may not be possible.

By signing and dating below you understand and agree to the terms of this agreement. Please mail or scan and send this signed and dated agreement, along with the Powers of Attorney, your retainer deposit in the amount of $ and the 3 post-dated checks(s) or the ACH Automatic Debit Authorization.

Please do not hesitate to call us if we can assist you with any other matters or if you have any questions regarding this agreement.

Sincerely,

____

Tax Resolution Specialist
Your Company

____

READ, UNDERSTOOD, AGREED TO,
AND COPY RECEIVED BY CLIENT

Client Name

____

Date

Chapter 14:

Penalties and Interest

Introduction

When clients make initial contact with a tax resolution provider regarding their tax concerns, one of the first questions they ask is "can you remove the penalties and interest that has been assessed toward my delinquent taxes?" To be perfectly clear, you will most likely not be successful in removing interest. Interest generated from delinquent taxes will not be abated with the exception of a few extraordinary circumstances. In order to abate interest the taxpayer must prove that he or she was caused an unwarranted delay that was directly caused by the actions of an IRS employee; and, the delay itself caused the interest to be charged. The IRS and State taxing agencies have a steadfast policy that interest will be charged on delinquent taxes. There are other ways such as Offers in Compromise and Partial Pay Installment Agreement to remove or reduce the necessity to pay interest but simply asking for the interest to be removed will be unsuccessful. That being said, if you are able to abate penalties and/or have tax liabilities reduced, you can in turn reduce the interest that has accrued on said penalties and tax.

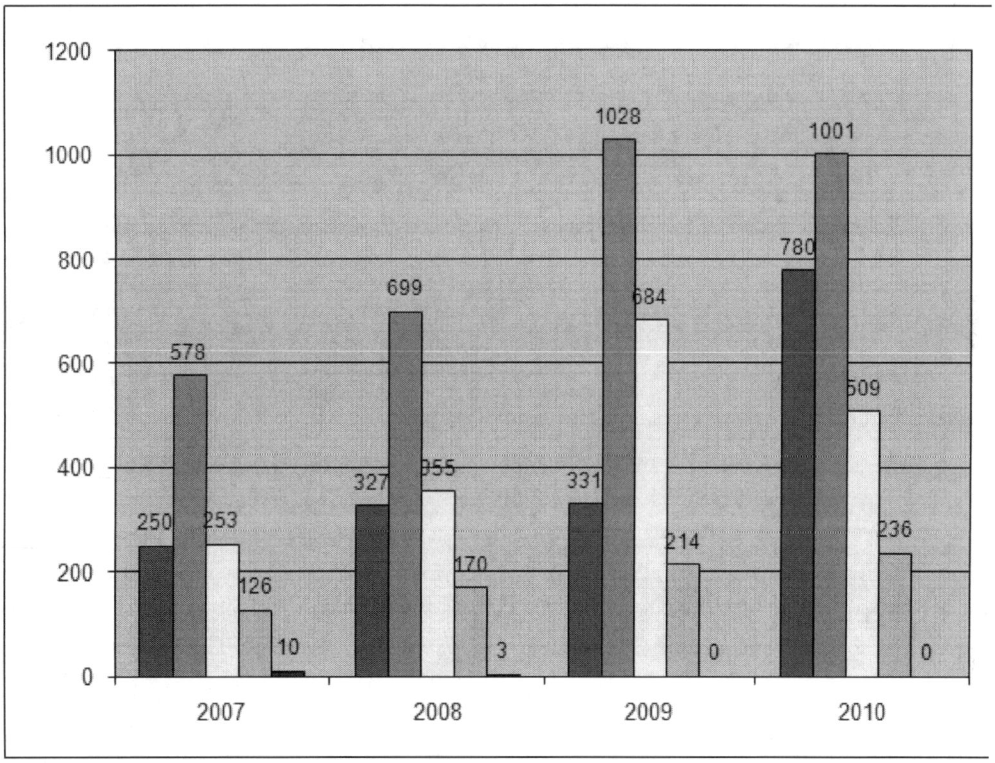

Having penalties waived (removed) on the other hand is a different story. There are several steps you can take to have penalties waived. Assuming you have the ability to have penalties waived, the question remains as to whether or not it makes economic sense to complete the work necessary to remove said penalties. For example, if a taxpayer owes $500,000 in back taxes, and the possibility exists to have a $10,000 penalty waived, should said taxpayer pay a professional to have the penalty removed? If the taxpayer has the ability to full-pay their liability within the statute of limitations, the answer would most likely be "yes". However, if the taxpayer is earning minimum wage and has no assets to speak of, he or she would be spending their limited funds more wisely to address the $500,000 liability as opposed to reducing it to a $490,000 liability and still having to address the same concerns.

There are certain things you must know if you wish to have penalties abated. First and foremost, the IRS will typically not abate a penalty unless it has already been paid. Beyond the necessary to prepay a penalty and related interest on a liability, it can be advantageous for a taxpayer to do so because it will stop the additional interest that continues to accrue if the penalty is ultimately not removed.

As a general rule of thumb, you may request an abatement of penalty if you show cause. A taxpayer who voluntarily steps forward and corrects a deficiency in a previously filed return is often successful in requesting penalty abatement. A taxpayer will most likely not be successful in requesting an abatement of a penalty that was assessed as a result of an audit.

The most common way to request that a penalty be abated is write a letter to the IRS office that issued the initial notice. The chances of having the abatement granted increase if the letter is in response to the first notice received and not sent once collection activity has commenced.

Correspondence to the IRS requesting the abatement should be clear and concise, including both a detail of the cause of the penalty assessment, as well as providing supporting documentation showing why the penalty should be removed.

What kinds of interest and penalties will I be charged for filing and paying taxes late?

Answer:

Interest is compounded daily and charged on any unpaid tax from the due date of the return (without regard to any extension of time to file) until the date of payment.

- The interest rate is the federal short-term rate plus 3 percent.
- That rate is determined every three months.

In addition, if you didn't pay your tax on time, you'll generally have to pay a late payment penalty.

- The late payment penalty is one-half of one percent of the tax (0.5%) owed for each month, or part of a month, that the tax remains unpaid after the due date, not exceeding 25 percent.
- The one-half of one percent rate increases to one percent if the tax remains unpaid after several bills have been sent to you and the IRS issues a notice of intent to levy.
- If you filed a timely return and are paying your tax via an installment agreement, the penalty is one-quarter of one percent for each month, or part of a month, that the installment agreement is in effect.

If you did not file on time and owe tax, you may owe an additional penalty for failure to file unless you can show reasonable cause.

- The combined penalty is 5 percent (4.5% late filing, 0.5% late payment) for each month, or part of a month, that your return was late, up to 25%.
- The late filing penalty applies to the net amount due, which is the tax shown on your return and any additional tax found to be due, as reduced by any credits for withholding and estimated tax payments.
- After five months, if you still have not paid, the 0.5% failure-to-pay penalty continues to run, up to 25%, until the tax is paid.
- The total penalty for failure to file and pay can be 47.5% (22.5% late filing, 25% late payment) of the tax owed.

If your return was over 60 days late, however, the minimum failure-to-file penalty is the smaller of $135 ($100 for returns required to be filed before January 1, 2009) or 100% of the tax required to be shown on the return

Determining Income Tax Interest[xiii]

20.2.6.1 (06-18-2010)
Method and Rates Used

The methods and rates for computing interest are:

Prior to February 1, 1980, simple annual interest was computed on a Year, Year, Month, Month, Day, Day (YYMMDD) basis.

Beginning February 1, 1980, the method changed to calculate total days times the daily factor.

On January 1, 1983, the method changed to daily compounding of interest (i.e., interest computed on interest).

20.2.6.2 (10-15-2011)
Compound Interest

The Service is required to compound interest on a daily basis per IRC 6622(a). This results in a daily recalculation of the principal amount **plus** accrued interest.

- Principal amount (P)
- Daily interest rate (R)
- Number of days (T)
- Interest (I)

2. The principal amount on which interest is compounded includes tax, penalties (at the point they become subject to interest per IRM 20.2.5.3, *Interest on Penalties and Additions to Tax*), additions to tax and all accrued interest.

3. The formula to compute interest is as follows:
    - Interest (I) equals principal (P) times the daily interest rate (R) or I = P x R.
    - New principal (New P) equals interest plus principal or New P= I + P and continues over the number of days (T) until the principal/new principal amounts are paid.

20.2.6.4 (10-15-2011) Interest Computation Tools

1. IDRS Command Code (CC) COMPA is used for non-complex interest computations. C C INTST is used if the module is not restricted (-I Freeze Code is one indicator of module restriction). In addition to these command codes, the IRS supports the use of a Commercial Off The Shelf (COTS) software program called InterestNet, commonly referred to as the Automated Computational Tool (DMI/ACT), which can be used for most interest computations, and is recommended for more complex interest computations. This software program is available to all employees, particularly those involved with the calculation of restricted interest. IRM 20.2.8.6, *Reasons for Restriction*, lists some of the reasons interest may need to be restricted on a tax module.
2. See IRM 2.3.39, *Command Code FTPIN*, for an explanation of CC FTPIN. See IRM 2.3.40, *Command Code PICRD*, for an explanation of CC PICRD. See IRM 2.3.29, *IDRS Terminal Input, Command Codes INTST, ICOMP, and COMPA*, for definers and examples using CC COMPA.

    Occasionally, CC INTST does not match the Master File (i.e., CFOL) interest and/or penalty computation. Therefore, before CC INTST results are used, compare total penalty and interest with CFOL command codes BMFOLT or IMFOLT (as appropriate) with total penalty and interest on INTST, computed to the interest date reflected on IMFOLT or BMFOLT. If unable to reconcile computational differences between CFOL and CC INTST, a manual computation must be made to determine which one is correct. If there is a systemic interest problem, send the results to the appropriate person per local procedures (consult your manager or lead), so that either programming can be corrected or an advisory can be issued. If there are no local referral procedures, then send to the Office of Servicewide Interest analyst responsible for programming problems. For contact information see http://sbseservicewide.web.irs.gov/interest/contacts/213.aspx.

    Caution:

    C C INTST does not update or cause an accurate interest computation on a tax module to be performed when interest is restricted. If the tax module is restricted, a manual interest computation **must** be done. Whenever possible, use a non-restricting TC 340. See IRM 20.2.8.11, *Non-Restricting TC 340.*

20.2.6.5 (10-15-2011) Computer Generated Interest Computations

1. Master File calculates interest by sorting all money amount transactions in effective date order and computing interest on balances from transaction to transaction (running module balance).
    A. When all transactions are sorted and a liability is established, interest is computed on that liability to the date of the next transaction.
    B. That transaction amount is added to the unpaid liability plus interest, and interest on this new balance is computed to the next transaction date and so on, through all transactions posted, to the current posting (23C) date.
    C. Master File compares the total interest accrued to the net amount of all posted interest transactions in the module and assesses or abates the difference with TC 19X or 33X as appropriate.
    D. No additional penalty or interest accrues on amounts paid within 21 calendar days of notice and demand (10 business days if the amount in the notice is $100,000 or more). See IRM 20.2.5.4, *Notice and Demand and Debit Interest.*

Penalty for Paying Income Taxes After They Were Due

Whether or not you can afford to pay your tax liability, you are better off filing your tax returns timely. If you fail to file your Federal income tax return in a timely manner, you will be charged an additional 5% of the overall liability per month for the first 5 months after the taxes are due. This equates to paying an additional 25% above the original tax liability plus other less significant penalties and interest on both the tax and penalties.

For this reason, a taxpayer would be foolish not to file an extension of time to file (Form 4868) giving them an extra 6 months or 180 days to prepare and file their tax return. The 4868 is a 1-page form requiring relatively little information.

Keep in mind that filing a 4868 does not extend the time necessary to pay the tax owed. That being said, it is still worth saving 25% of the overall tax liability in penalties. In order to avoid a late-payment penalty when filing an extension, a taxpayer must pay at least 90% of the amount they by the due date of the return which is typically April 15th

Example 1: if a taxpayer owes $11,000, they would be required to pay $9,900:

$11,000 x 0.90 = $9,900

If said taxpayer did not pay at least $9,900 when they filed their extension, the IRS would assess a late-payment penalty. The penalty is ½% of the amount you owe per month. This penalty continues to accrue until it reaches the prescribed maximum amount equaling 25%... Using the example above, the late-payment penalty would be:

Example 1a: $11,000 x 0.005 = $55 charged per month (this amount would continue to accrue until it reached $2,750 which is 25% of $11,000)

To sum up, the sooner a taxpayer is able to satisfy an outstanding balance, the less they will pay in penalties. If a taxpayer files their return on time and enters into a voluntary installment agreement, the IRS will reduce their late-payment penalty by ¼% per month.

Example 1c: $11,000 x 0.0025 = $27.50 (in this case the $55 penalty would be reduced to $27.50 which is ½ of the original)

In this same example, if the taxpayer does not file an extension, the late-filing payment fee would be 4.5% of the unpaid tax per month up to five months.

Example 1d: $11,000 x 0.045 = $495 per month

In addition to accruing penalties for failure to pay timely, any additional tax owed after the due date of the return will also accrue interest. Interest assessed for taxes is compounded daily and will continue to accrue as long as the tax is owed.

The interest rate for unpaid taxes is determined by adding 3% to the federal short-term rate. As of the second quarter of 2008, the interest rate on unpaid individual income taxes is 6%.

Example 1e: monthly interest amount would be $660,

$11,000 x .06 = $660

and the penalty would be $55 which combined would be

$660 + $55 = **$715 (penalty and interest)**

So the taxpayer would continue to accrue $715 for each month that they failed to pay the original $11,000 they owed in taxes to the IRS. Keep in mind that this example is simple in that it fails to account for interim payments that may have been made as well as interest accruing on penalties and interest accruing on interest.

Payroll Tax Interest and Penalties

If a business has employees, it is the business's responsibility to collect and submit via tax deposits to the IRS and local taxing agencies, the employee's income tax withholding as well as the employee's payroll taxes as well as the employer's matching share of payroll taxes. Unless an employee is exempt, an employer must withhold and submit, usually via electronic deposits, the items described above within a given time frame. If an employer fails to remit income tax withholding as well as payroll tax withholding and the employer's matching share, they will face severe consequences.

In addition to the employee's Federal income tax withholding IRS payroll taxes are made up of two parts: Social Security tax and Medicare tax. An employer is required to match the amount paid of each of these taxes. If the payroll tax liability is under $2,500, the employer may make tax deposits quarterly when they prepare and file their payroll tax returns (Form 941s). If the liability is over $2,500, the deposits must be made sooner (i.e. semi-monthly or monthly).

While most employers are required to make Federal payroll tax deposits semi-monthly or monthly, if they reported taxes greater than $50,000 for the look-back period, they are a semiweekly schedule depositor, and generally must deposit your employment taxes based on the following schedule[xiv]:

1. The employment taxes on payments made to their employees on Wednesday, Thursday, and/or Friday, must be deposited by the following Wednesday.

2. The employment taxes on payments made to their employees on Saturday, Sunday, Monday, and/or Tuesday, must be deposited by the following Friday.

If any of the 3 weekdays after the end of a semiweekly period is a legal holiday, you will have an additional day for each day that is a legal holiday to make the required deposit. Regardless of whether an employer is a monthly schedule depositor or a semiweekly schedule depositor, if they accumulate taxes of $100,000 or more on any day during a deposit period, they must deposit the tax by the next business day. If this happens, they become a semiweekly depositor for at least the remainder of the calendar year and for the following calendar year.

Since 2012, the IRS determines the late filing penalty based upon the number of days that has passed since the payroll taxes were due. For example, if an employer makes their Federal tax deposit within five days of being due, the IRS will assess a 2% penalty of the total amount. If they deposit is made within 6-15 days of the due date, the penalty increases to 5%. If the tax is more than 15 days late, the penalty increases to 10%. Note that if you outsource your payroll tax duties to a payroll service provider, the IRS holds you responsible for tax errors that the third party makes.

It is important to remember that payroll tax penalties and interest are not only assessed to the business but also to those considered by the IRS to be "Responsible" for determining that the funds withheld to pay the government were earmarked for other items (see *Trust Fund* and *Civil Penalty*).

100% Penalty (Trust Fund Recovery Penalty)

As mentioned above, section 6672 of the Internal Revenue Code allows the IRS to charge any "responsible party" who refuses or fails to collect and pay mandated federal taxes a 100% personal liability "Civil" penalty. The responsible person/s may be a corporate officer or someone who controls the employer's finances or has an authorized signature on the payroll account and will be jointly and severally liable if more than one person is found "Responsible"

The withholding process occurs as follows:

1. Employee's income taxes, Social Security taxes, and Medicare taxes are withheld from the employee's pay.

2. They amounts that were withheld are then paid (usually via electronica tax deposits).

3. The amounts withheld and the deposits that were made are reported via payroll tax returns.

4. At the end of the year, forms W-2 are prepared for each employee and submitted to the Social Security Administration ("SSA") along with a summary of all of the W-2's called Form W-3.

5. The SSA then forwards the reported withholding data to the IRS.

If an employer fails to satisfy the requirements set forth above, the employee may face issues that arise from the employer's actions or lack thereof.

Statute of Limitations

There is no statute of limitations to assess penalties and interest on a return that has not been prepared. There is also no statute of limitations for penalties and interest stemming from the failure to file and report payroll taxes (Social Security, Medicare, Unemployment, withheld income taxes). In addition, there also is no statute of limitations on assessment of tax, penalties and interest when a false tax return is filed.

IRS Civil Penalties

	Description	Code Section	Penalty	Defense
1	**Failure to Timely File Returns**	6651(a)(1)	5% of tax shown on return (reduced by credits claimed on taxes timely paid) for each month sot to exceed 25%. Minimum penalty of lesser of $100 or 100% of any unpaid tax for Income tax returns over 60 days late. If failure to pay penalty applies/ failure to file penalty reduced by 0.5%, i.e., aggregate penalties cannot exceed 5% per month for first 5 months. 25% ceilings of each penalty are independently applied.	Reasonable Cause and Not Willful Neglect
	a. Intentional Failure to Timely File Returns	6651(f)	15% of tax shown on return (reduced by taxes timely paid) for each month not to exceed 75%.	Gross Negligence, Honest Belief, Reliance on Tax Advisor
2	**Failure to Pay Tax on Return**	6651(a)(2)	0.5% of tax due per month not to exceed 25%. 1% of tax after notice of intent to levy. 0.25% during installment agreement, after 1999. Does not apply to Estimated Tax or when Civil Fraud Penalty applies.	Reasonable Cause and Not Willful Neglect
	a. Failure to Pay Tax on subsequent Assessment	6651(a)(3) & (h)	0.5% of tax due per month not to exceed 25% (0.25% during installment agreement). 1% of tax after notice of intent to levy. Does not apply to Estimated Tax or When Civil Fraud Penalty applies.	Reasonable Cause and Not Willful Neglect
3	**Failure to File Forms 1099, DIV or PATR relating to payments of less than $10**	6652(a)	$1 per return with $1,000 annual maximum	Reasonable Cause and Not Willful Neglect
4	**Failure to Report Tips**	6652(b)	50% of employee's share of F.I.C.A. tax on unreported amount.	Reasonable Cause and Not Willful Neglect
5	**Failure to File EO Return**	6652(c)(1)	$10 per day with maximum of lesser of $5,000 or 5% annual gross receipts.	Reasonable Cause

	Description	Code Section	Penalty	Defense
	a. Disclosure under I.R.C. §6033 (a)(2) [reportable transaction]	6653(c)(3)	$100 per each day failure to disclose continues, not to exceed $50,000.	Reasonable Cause
6	**Failure to File Plan Registration**	6652(d)	$1 per day for each with $5,000 annual maximum.	Reasonable Cause
7	**Failure to File Plan Returns**	6652(e)	$25 per day with $15,000 maximum.	Reasonable Cause
8	**Failure to File Returns re Foreign Persona investing in U.S. Real Property**	6652(f)	Lesser of $25 per day or 5% of property fair market value.	Reasonable cause and Not Willful Neglect
9	**Failure to File Timely Report for Merger, Consolidation or Termination of Plan or Name and Address of Administrator**	6652(d)(2)	$1 per day with $1,000 maximum.	Reasonable Cause
10	**Failure to File Return Regarding Corporate Changes in Control and Recapitalizations**	6652(1)(k)	$500 each day with $100,000 maximum.	Reasonable Cause, de minimus, exceptions
11	**Failure to Pay Estimated Tax by Individuals**	6654	Penalty computed on amount and duration of underpayment at prevailing rate set in S6621 (not compounded daily). Subject to exceptions plus special rules for farmers and fishermen. Does not apply if tax for current year after credit for withheld taxes is less than $1,000 if taxpayer had no tax liability in prior year, or qualifies under applicable safe harbor.	waiver of penalty— where imposition would be against equity and good conscience where prior year's overpayment credited against current year estimated tax is offset by IRS, aged or disabled taxpayer.
12	**Failure to Pay Estimated Tax by Corporation**	6655	Penalty computed on amount and duration of underpayment at prevailing rate set in S6621 (not compounded daily). Subject to statutory exceptions.	Exceptions
13	**Failure to Deposit**	6656(b)	2% if failure 1 to 5 days, 5% if failure 6 to 15 days, 10% if failure more than. 15 days, 15% if failure 10 days after first delinquency notice or day of jeopardy assessment.	Reasonable Cause and Not Willful Neglect
14	**Dishonored Check**	6657	2% of amount of the check, if check is less than $750, penalty is lesser of $15 or amount of the check.	Good Faith and Reasonable Cause to believe check would be paid.
15	**Accuracy-Related/ Negligence**	6662(a),(c)	20% of underpayment solely due to negligence. No penalty stacking rule.	Disclosure of non-frivolous position (returns due pre 1/1/94), Reasonable Cause, Good Faith

	Description	Code Section	Penalty	Defense
16	**Accuracy-Related/ Substantial understatement**	6662(a), (d)	20% of underpayment due to substantial understatement. No penalty stacking rule.	Reasonable Cause, Good Faith, Substantial. Authority or Disclosure (non-tax shelter), more likely than not (tax shelter)
	a. Individuals	6662(d)(1)(A)	understatement exceeds greater of 10% of required tax or $5,000.	
	b. Corporations	6662 (d)(1)(B)	Understatement exceeds greater of 10% of required tax (or, if greater, $10,000) or $10,000,000.	
17	**Accuracy - Related/Substantial Valuation Overstatement**	6662(a), (e) and (h)	For valuation overstatements in excess of $5,000 ["C" corporations $10,000], 20% for valuations 200% or more of correct amount, 40% if 400% or more of correct amount. No penalty stacking rule.	Reasonable Cause and Good Faith (Qualified Appraiser - charitable contributions)
18	**Accuracy - Related/Substantial Misstatements Under IRC §481**	6662(a), (e)	For misstatements regarding 482 price adjustments - [before 1/1/94] : 20% for 200% or more (50% or less) of correct amount, or $10,000,000 adjustment, 40% for 400% or more (25% or less) of correct amount, or $40,000,000 adjustment, [after 13/31/93]: lesser of $5,000,000 or 10% receipts (40% on $20,000,000 or 20% receipts). No penalty stacking rule.	Reasonable Cause and Good Faith
19	**Accuracy-Related/Substantial Overstatement Pension Liabilities**	6663(a), (f)	For pension liability in excess of $1,000 overstatement, 20% for liabilities 200% or more of correct amount, 40% if 400% or more of correct amount. No penalty stacking rule.	Reasonable Cause and Good Faith
20	**Accuracy - Related/Substantial Estate or Gift Tax Valuation understatement**	6663(a), (g)	For estate or gift tax liability in excess of $5,000 understatement, 20% for 50% or less of correct amount, 40% if 25% or less of correct amount. No penalty stacking rule.	Reasonable Cause and. Good Faith
21	**Accuracy-Related Listed or Reportable Transactions**	6662A	20% of underpayment if disclosed; 30% of underpayment if not disclosed. Transaction amount at highest income tax rate.	Reasonable cause and Good Faith, Adequate Disclosure, Substantial Authority, and Reasonable Belief (non-reliance on disqualified tax advisor or disqualified opinion).
	a. Accuracy-Related Transactions lacking economic substance	6662(b)(6) & (i)	20% of underpayment if disclosed, 40% of underpayment if not disclosed.	No Reasonable Cause exception
	b. Accuracy - Related Transactions involving	6662(b)(7)	40% of underpayment.	Reasonable Case and Good Faith

	Description	Code Section	Penalty	Defense
	undisclosed foreign asset			
22	**Civil Fraud**	6663	75% of underpayment solely due to fraud (tax on highest income tax rate).	Reasonable Cause and Good Faith, Gross Negligence, Honest Belief, Reliance on Tax Advisor, Son-Fraud by Spouse (Joint Return)
23	**Trust Fund Recovery Penalty (100% Penalty)**	6672 6682	Trust fund payroll taxes (withheld income and F.I.C.A. taxes).	Not Responsible and Not willful
24	**False W-4 Claims for withholding**	6692	$500 per statement. No penalty if no decrease In amount withheld or if tax liability does not exceed allowable credits and estimated tax payments.	Reasonable Cause
25	**Failure to File Actuarial Report (Schedule B of Form 5500)**	6694(a)	$1,000 per document.	Reasonable Cause
26	**Failure to File Form 5498 (IRA)**	6693	$50 per document.	Reasonable Cause
27	**Return Preparer - Nonwillful all tax returns**	6694 (a)	May 25. 2007 - Greater of $1,000 or 50% of preparer's income per return. Does not apply when penalty under §6701 is assessed. Pre-May 25, 2007 - $250 per return. Does not apply when penalty under §6701 is assessed.	Substantial Authority, Reasonable Belief & Disclosure Reasonable Case and Good Faith, Realistic Possibility of Being Sustained, Disclosure
28	**Return Preparer—Willful or Reckless Conduct Income Tax Returns**	6694 (b) 6694 (b)	May 25, 2007 - Greater of $5,000 or 50% of preparer's income per return. Does not apply when penalty under §6701 is assessed. Pre-Mav 25, 2007 - $1,000 reduced by penalty paid under §6694(a) per return. Doss not apply when penalty under §6701 is assessed.	Gross Negligence, Taxpayer's liability Not Understated Gross Negligence, Taxpayer's liability Not Understated
29	**Return Preparer - Failure to Provide Copy to Taxpayer**	6695 (a)	$50 per failure, not to exceed $25,000.	Reasonable Cause and Not Willful Neglect
30	**Return Preparer—Failure to Sign Return**	6695 (b)	$50 per failure, not to exceed $25,000.	Reasonable Cause and Not Willful Neglect
31	**Return Preparer—Failure to Provide TIN on Return**	6695 (c)	$50 per failure, not to exceed $25,000.	Reasonable Cause and Not Willful Neglect
32	**Return Preparer—Failure to Retain Copy or List of Taxpayers**	6695 (d)	$50 per failure, not to exceed $25,000.	Reasonable Cause and Not Willful Neglect
33	**Return Preparer—Failure to File Correct Information Returns**	6695 (e)	$50 per failure, not to exceed $25,000.	Reasonable Cause and Not Willful Neglect
34	**Return Preparer—Negotiation of Taxpayer Check**	6695 (f)	$500 per check.	Honest Belief.

	Description	Code Section	Penalty	Defense
35	**Failure to File Partnership Return or to Show Required Information on Form 1065**	6698	$195 per partner per month not to exceed 13 months per each partner (less for prior years).	Reasonable Cause
36	**Promoting Abusive Tax Shelters--Furnishing False Statements Representing Tax Benefits for Valuation Overstatement Exceeding 300* of Correct Valuation**	6700	Lesser of $1,000 per activity or 100% of gross income derived from activity (in addition to other penalties, except when penalty under §6701 1b assessed). 50% of gross income if statement false.	Honest Belief. With respect to Valuation Overstatement only, Reasonable Basis for Valuation and Good Faith.
37	**Aiding and Abetting in Understatement of Liability**	6701	$1,000 ($10,000 if corporation) per person per tax period. Applies in addition to any other penalties except when penalties under §6694 and §6700 are assessed.	Non Participant
38	**Frivolous Return and specified frivolous submissions**	6702	$5000 ($500 prior to 12/20/06). Applies in addition to any other penalties.	Non Frivolous
39	**Failure to Keep Trust and Annuity Plan Records**	6704	$50 with $50,000 annual maximum.	Reasonable Cause and Non Willful Neglect
40	**Failure to Furnish Tax Shelter information** Before October 23, 2005			
	a. General rule	6707 (a) (2)	Failure to Register—greater of $500 or 1% of total investment (with maximum of $10,000 pre-1986 Act).	Reasonable Cause
	b. Confidential Arrangements	6707 (a) (3)	Failure to register confidential arrangements - greater of 50% of fees to promoter (75% if intentional) or $10,000.	Reasonable Cause or non-participant in shelter
	c. Failure to Furnish Shelter ID Number	6707 (b) (1) & (2)	Failure to furnish shelter ID number -$100 for each failure. Failure to Include ID Number in Return--$250 for each failure.	Reasonable Cause
	Begin October 23, 3004 a. General rule	6707 (b) (1)	Failure to file return under 36111(a) re-reportable transaction - $50,000.	IRS Rescission to promote compliance
	b. Listed transaction	6707 (b) (2)	Greater of $200,000 or 50% gross income derived from transaction [75% if intentional].	None
41	**Failure to Include Reportable Transaction Information with Return**	6707A	**Reportable Transaction.** Natural Persona $10,000. Other Taxpayers $50,000. **Listed Transactions.** Natural Persons $100,000. Other Taxpayers $200,000.	IRS Rescission to promote compliance

	Description	Code Section	Penalty	Defense
42	**Failure to Maintain Tax Shelter List**	6708	$50 each person with $100,000 annual maximum. Applies in addition to any other penalties.	Reasonable Cause and Not Willful Neglect
43	**Begin October 22, 2004 - Failure to Maintain Reportable Transaction List**	6708	$10,000 per day after 20th day following IRS request for list.	Reasonable Cause
44	**Disclosure or use of information by Return Preparer**	6713	$250 each disclosure or use with $10,000 annual maximum.	Exceptions under Code, Order of Court, preparation of State and local tax returns
45	**Failure to File Information Returns; Failure to include Full and Correct Information (Forma 1099, Schedules K, etc.)**	6721	$50 per payee document with $250,000 annual maximum. Reductions: $15 per return (maximum $75,000) if correction within 30 days, $30 per return (maximum $150,000) if correction after 30 days prior to August 1.	Reasonable Cause and Not willful Neglect, de minimus exceptions, small business
	a. Intentional Failure to rile information Returns	6721 (c)	Greater of $100 or 10% of aggregate amount required to be reported fox. certain payors (e.g., cash payment exceeding $10,000) or 5% of aggregate amount required to be reported for certain filers (e.g., brokers, exchanges .of partnership interests, dispositions of donated property).	Gross Negligence, Honest Belief
	b. Intentional Failure to File form 8300	6721 (c) (2) (C)	Greater of $25,000 or cash received but not to exceed $100,000.	Gross negligence, Honest Belief
46	**Failure to Furnish Correct and Timely information Return**	6722	$50 per payee document with $100,000 annual maximum.	Reasonable Cause and Not Willful Neglect
	a. Intentional Failure to include Correct Information	6722 (c)	Greater of $100 or 10% of aggregate amount required to be reported for certain payers (e.g., cash receipt exceeding $10,000) or 5% of aggregate amount required to be reported for other certain filers (e.g., brokers, exchanges of partnership interests, dispositions of donated property).	Gross Negligence, Honest Belief
47	**Failure to include Required information in Information Return**	6723	$500 per return with $100,000 annual maximum.	Reasonable Cause and Not Willful Neglect
48	**Failure to Tile Foreign-Business Entity Returns (corporation and partnership):**			

	Description	Code Section	Penalty	Defense
	a. Form 8938 statement of Specified Foreign Financial Assets -individuals holding interest in foreign financial asset(account, stock or financial instrument from non-U.S. person, interest in foreign entity) exceeding $50,000	6038D (d)	Failure to file form (tax years beginning after 3/18/10) $10,000 with additional $10,000 added for each month failure continues beginning 90 days after taxpayer notified of delinquency, maximum - $50,000 per return.	Reasonable Cause and No Willful Neglect
	b. Form 3520, Annual Return to Report Transactions with Foreign Trusts and Receipt of Certain Foreign Gifts. Transactions involving foreign trusts, including creation of a foreign trust by U.S. parson to foreign trust and receipt of distributions from foreign trust. Report receipt of gifts from foreign sources greater than annual sun of100000	6677 (a) - reportable event 6039F (c) - foreign gifts	Failure to file return, or filing an incomplete return or reportable, event -greater of $10,000 or 35% of gross reportable amount; additional $10,000 each month failure continues beginning 90 days after taxpayer notified of delinquency. Return reporting gifts -penalty 5% of aggregate gifts per month, with maximum penalty of 25%.	Reasonable cause and No Willful Neglect
	c. Form 3520-A, Information Return of Foreign Trust with a U.S. Owner. Ownership interests in foreign trust, by U.S. person with various interests and powers *over* those trusts	6677 (b)	Greater of $10,000 or 5% of gross value of trust assets owned by U.S. person; additional $10,000 each month failure continues beginning 90 days after taxpayer notified of delinquency.	Reasonable cause and No Willful Neglect
	d. Form 5471, Information Return of U.S. Person with Respect to Certain Foreign Corporations . U.S. person, officers, directors or shareholders of foreign corporations (10% rule)	6038 (b) (1) [base penalty] 6038 (b) (2) [notification penalty]	Failure to file return $10,000, with additional $10,000. added for each month failure continues beginning 90 days after taxpayer notified of delinquency, maximum $50,000 per return.	Reasonable Cause
	e. Form 5472, Information Return of 25% Foreign-Owned U.S. Corporation or a Foreign Corporation Engaged in a U.S. Trade or Business. Transactions between 25% foreign-owned domestic corporation engaged in a trade or business in the U.S. and related party	6038 (d) (1)][base penalty] 6038 (d) (2) [notification penalty]	Failure to file return or keep records regarding reportable transactions -$10,000; additional $10,000 each month failure continues beginning 90 days after taxpayer notified of delinquency.	Reasonable Cause
	f. Form 926, Return of a U.S. Transferor of Property to a Foreign Corporation. Transfers of property to foreign corporations and other information.	6038B (c)	Failure to furnish Information - 10% of value of property transferred, with maximum $100,000 per return; no limit if failure to report transfer intentional.	Reasonable Cause and No Willful Neglect

	Description	Code Section	Penalty	Defense
	g. Form 8865, Return of U.S. Person with Respect to Certain Foreign Partnerships. U.S. persons with interests in foreign partnerships report interests in transactions of foreign partnerships, transfers of property to foreign partnerships, and acquisitions, dispositions and changes in foreign partnership interests	6038 (b) (1) [base penalty] 6038 (b) (2) [notification penalty] 6038B (c) [transfer penalty]	Failure to file return - $10,000; additional $10,000 for each month failure continues beginning 90 days after taxpayer notified of delinquency, maximum - $50,000 per return; 10% of value of non-reported property transferred in excess of $100,000, with maximum $100,000 per return; no limit if failure to report transfer intentional.	Reasonable Cause
	h. Form 8B58, Information Return of U.S. Persons with Respect to Foreign Disregarded Entities. U.S. persons direct owners of foreign disregarded entity ("FDE"). U.S. persons Category 4 or 5 filers of Form 5471 if controlled foreign corporations owner of FDE. U.S. persons Category 1 or 2 filers of Form 8865 if foreign controlled, partnership owner of FDE	8858 Instructions	None but could give rise to Form 5471 and Form 8865 penalties.	Reasonable Cause
49	**Failure to File Form TD F 90-22.1, Report of Foreign Bank and Financial Accounts (FBAR). Direct or indirect interest in, or signature authority (or other similar authority) of financial accounts in excess of $10,000 at any time during year.**	31 U.S.C. 5321 (a) (5)	October 22, 2004 - Negligent failure to file - Not greater than $10,000 per each account. Pre-October 22, 2004 Willful failure to file - Greater of $25,000 or balance in account but not to exceed $100,000. October 22, 2004 - Greater of $100,000 or 504 of highest amount in each account.	Reasonable Cause and Amount Reported None as of October 22, 2004
50	**Interest Suspension**	6604 (g)	IRS falls to notify individual of additional tax liability before 18 months following latex of date return filed or due date [36 months for written notice of adjustment after November 25, 2007].	Inapplicable for gross misstatement, Reportable Avoidance Transactions after 10/31/04 & fraud

Penalty Reference Chart[xv]

Penalty Name	IRC Section	R&TC Section	Penalty Reason	Computation
Limited Liability Company (LLC) Fee Estimate Penalty	None	17942(d)(2)	Underpayment of estimated fee.	10% of the underpayment.
			Exceptions - Safe harbor-100% of prior year.	
Tax on Joint Return Exceeds Tax on Separate Returns	6013(b)(5)	1853 0	Tax on a joint return exceeds tax shown on separate returns, due to negligence or intentional disregard of rules, or fraud. In lieu of penalties provided by Section 19164(a) and (b). 20% of total amount of excess if attributable to negligence/intentional disregard of rules.	75% of excess if attributable to fraud.
			Exceptions - None.	
Information Return From Owner of Real Property	6045	1864 2	Owners and transferors failing to file information return relating to interest in real property by the due date.	Penalty under 19183 applies. If information return not filed within 60 days of due date, the deduction of certain property-related expenses are disallowed.
			Exceptions - Reasonable cause and not willful neglect.	
Withholdin g Penalties	3403, 1461	18668(a)	Any person required to withhold tax, but fails to do so.	The greater of: • The actual amount withheld or • Payee's total tax liability (before application of any payments and credits), not to exceed the required 7% withholding amount.
			Exceptions - Reasonable cause.	
Withholdin g Penalties – Real Estate	3403, 1461	18668(d)	Any person required to withhold tax from the sale of real property when properly notified, but fails to do so.	The greater of: • $500 or • 10% of the amount required to be withheld.
				Exceptions - Reasonable cause.

Penalty Name	IRC Section	R&TC Section	Penalty Reason	Computation
Withholding Penalties – Real Estate Escrow Person		18668(e)(1)	Any real estate escrow person failing to provide written notification of withholding requirement to a transferee/buyer of a California real property interest.	The greater of: • $500 or • 10% of the amount required to be withheld.
			Exceptions - Reasonable cause.	
Withholding Penalties – Real Estate False Certificate		18668(e)(5)	Any transferor of California real property who knowingly files a false exemption certificate (Form 593-C, *Real Estate Withholding Certificate*) to avoid withholding.	The greater of: • $1,000 or • 20% of the amount required to be withheld.
			Exceptions - Reasonable cause.	
Withholding Penalties	None	18669	Successor on a sale, transfer, or disposition of a business for failing to pay required amounts or failing to withhold or to pay withheld amounts.	10% of amount not paid or personal liability for amounts not withheld or withheld amounts not paid.
			Exceptions - None.	
Electronic Funds Transfer (EFT) Penalty	6302	19011(c)	Any person required to remit payment by EFT, but who makes payment by other means.	10% of the amount paid by non-EFT.
			Exceptions - Reasonable cause and not willful neglect.	
Electronic Payment Requirements for Individuals	None	19011.5	Failure by individuals, whose tax liability is greater than $80,000 or who make an estimated tax or extension payment that exceeds $20,000, to remit their tax payments electronically.	1% of the amount paid.
			Exceptions - Reasonable cause and not willful neglect.	
Failure to File a Return/Late Filing Penalty	6651	1913 1	Any taxpayer who is required to file a return, but fails to do so by the due date.	5% of the tax due, after allowing for timely payments, for every month that the return is late, up to a maximum of 25%. For fraud, substitute 15% and 75% for 5% and 25%, respectively. For individuals and fiduciaries, minimum penalty is the lesser of: • $135 or • 100% of the tax required to be shown on the return.
			Exceptions - Reasonable cause and not willful neglect.	

Penalty Name	IRC Section	R&TC Section	Penalty Reason	Computation
Failure to Pay Tax/Late Payment Penalty	6651	19132	Taxpayer failing to pay tax by the due date. This penalty is not imposed if, for the same tax year, the sum of Sections 19131 and 19133 penalties are equal to or greater than this penalty.	5% of the total tax unpaid plus 1/2 of 1% for every month the payment of tax was late up to 40 months. Not to exceed 25% of the total unpaid tax.
			Exceptions - Reasonable cause and not willful neglect.	
Failure to Provide Information Requested/ Failure to File a Return Upon Demand	None	19133	Any taxpayer for failing to provide requested information, or failing to file a return after notice and demand.	25% of total tax liability assessed without regard to any payments or credits.
			Exceptions - Reasonable cause and not willful neglect.	
Penalty for Failure to Make a Small Business Stock Report	6652(k)	19133.5	Taxpayer for failing to make a small business report.	$50 for each report. $100 per report if the failure is due to negligence or intentional disregard.
			Exceptions - Reasonable cause and not willful neglect.	
Dishonored Payments	6657	19134	Any taxpayer who makes a payment by check that is dishonored. Includes payments made by credit card or EFT.	For payments received after January 1, 2011: • An amount equal to 2% of the amount of the dishonored payment, or • If the amount of the check is less than $1,250, $25 or the amount of the check, whichever is less.
			Exceptions - Reasonable cause and good faith.	
Unqualified or Suspended Corporation Doing Business in this State	None	19135	Any foreign corporation which fails to qualify to do business, or whose powers have been forfeited, or any domestic corporation which has been suspended, and is doing business in this state, within the meaning of Section 23101.	$2,000 per taxable year.
			Exceptions - Reasonable cause and not willful neglect.	

Penalty Name	IRC Section	R&TC Section	Penalty Reason	Computation
Underpayment of Estimated Tax (Addition to Tax)	6654	19136 et seq., 19142-19151	Any taxpayer who fails to pay estimated tax in the required installments.	An amount determined by applying the underpayment rate specified in Section 19521 to the amount of the underpayment for the period of the underpayment.
			Exceptions - (1) Safe harbors under 6654 as modified. (2) Underpayment created or increased by any provision of law that is chaptered during and operative for the taxable year of the underpayment (3) underpayment was created or increased by the disallowance of a credit under Section 17053.80(g) or 23623(g).	
Large Corporate Understatement of Tax	None	19138	When a corporation has an understatement of tax for: Tax years beginning January 1, 2003, through December 31, 2009, that exceeds $1 million. Tax years beginning January 1, 2010, that exceeds the greater of: • $1 million. • 20% of tax shown on original return or shown on amended return filed on or before original or extended due date of return for taxable year.	20% of the understatement of tax.
			Exceptions - Understatement is attributable to (1) a change in law after earlier of date return is filed or extended due date of return or (2) reasonable reliance on legal ruling by the Chief Counsel.	
Corporation Officer Statement Penalty	None	19141	Upon certification by the Secretary of State, penalty for taxpayer's failure to provide a Statement of Information.	$250 upon certification by the Secretary of State under Corporations Code Sections 2204 and 17653. $50 upon certification by the Secretary of State under
			Exceptions - None.	

Penalty Name	IRC Section	R&TC Section	Penalty Reason	Computation
Information With Respect to Certain Foreign Corporations (IRS Form 5471, *Information Return of U.S. Persons With Respect To Certain Foreign Corporations)*	6038	19141.2	Failure to file and furnish certain information about certain foreign corporations.	$1,000 for each annual accounting period. $1,000 for each 30-day period up to a maximum of $24,000 when failure continues after 90-day of notification.
			Exceptions - Reasonable cause and not willful neglect.	
Failure to File and Furnish Information About Foreign-Owned Corporations (IRS Form 5472, *Information Return of a 25% Foreign-Owned U.S. Corporation or a Foreign Corporatio n Engaged in a U.S. Trade or Business)*	6038A	19141.5	Failure to file and furnish information or to maintain required records about foreign-owned corporations, under IRC Section 6038A.	$10,000 for each taxable year for which the taxpayer fails to file required information or fails to maintain the required records. $10,000 for each 30-day period when failure continues after 90-day of notification.
			Exceptions - Reasonable cause.	

Penalty Name	IRC Section	R&TC Section	Penalty Reason	Computation
Failure to File - Notice of Certain Transfers to Foreign Corporation (IRS Form 926, *Return by a U.S. Transferor of Property to a Foreign Corporation*)	6038B	19141.5	Failure to file/furnish information records about transfers or distributions to foreign-owned corporations, under IRC Section 6038B.	10% of fair market value at time of exchange, not to exceed $100,000 unless failure due to intentional disregard. Plus recognition of gain required as if property sold based on that value.
			Exceptions - Reasonable cause and not willful neglect.	
Failure to File or Furnish Information About Foreign Corporations Engaged in U.S. Business (IRS Form 5472)	6038C	19141.5	Failure to file and furnish information or to maintain required records about a foreign corporation engaged in a trade or business within the U.S., under IRC Section 6038C.	$10,000 for each taxable year for which the taxpayer fails to provide the required information or fails to maintain the required records. $10,000 for each 30-day period, when failure continues after 90-day of notification.
			Exceptions - Reasonable cause.	
Failure to Retain Unitary Records Penalty	None	19141.6	Any taxpayer engaged in a unitary business that fails to maintain records relating to unitary combination, apportionment and allocation, and application of federal law.	$10,000 for each year that the taxpayer fails to maintain or causes another to fail to maintain the required records. If the failure continues beyond 90 days of notice from us, an additional penalty of $10,000 for each 30-day period is imposed up to a maximum of $50,000 if the taxpayer's conduct is not willful.
			Exceptions - None.	

Penalty Name	IRC Section	R&TC Section	Penalty Reason	Computation
Accuracy Related Penalty	6662	19164	Any underpayment of tax required to be shown on a return, attributable primarily to negligence or disregard of rules and regulations or a substantial understatement of income tax.	20% of the underpayment of tax. 40% unless certain exceptions apply for amnesty eligible years, which are tax years prior to January 1, 2003.
			Exceptions - The defenses to an accuracy related penalty include (1) substantial authority, (2) adequate disclosure and reasonable basis or (3) reasonable cause and good faith, depending on the grounds for imposing the penalty. In addition, see underlying regulation regarding unitary and business and nonbusiness income determinations.	
Accuracy Related Penalty – Substantial Valuation Misstatement	6662(e)(1)	19164	A substantial valuation misstatement exists when the value (or adjusted basis) of any property claimed on a return is 150% or more of the correct amount. Transactional Penalty – The price reported for any property or services claimed on a return is 200% or more (or 50% or less) of the correct figure. Net Adjustment Penalty – When the transfer price of any property or services increases the taxable income for the taxable year by the lesser of $5 million or 10% of the taxpayer's gross receipts.	20% of the portion of the underpayment of tax attributable to the misstatement. No penalty imposed unless the portion of the underpayment exceeds $5,000 ($10,000 for corporations other than S corporations or personal holding companies).
			Exceptions - Reasonable cause and good faith. (See Treasury Regulation Section 1.6664-4 and 1.6662-6 for special rules.) There is no disclosure exception to this penalty. Treasury Regulation Section 1.6662-5(a). When there is an underpayment due to overstated charitable deduction property, there are special rules for reasonable cause under IRC Section 6664(c) for returns filed after January 1, 2010.	
Accuracy Related Penalty - Increase in Penalty in Case of Gross Valuation Misstatements	6662(h)	19164	A gross valuation misstatement exists if: The value (or adjusted basis) of any property on a return is 200% or more of the correct amount, or The price for any property or service claimed on a return is 400% or more (or 25% or less) of the correct price, or The net Section 482 adjustment exceeds the lesser of $20 million or 20% of the taxpayer's gross receipts.	40% of the portion of the underpayment of tax attributable to the misstatement. No penalty imposed unless the amount of the underpayment exceeds $5,000 ($10,000 for corporations other than S corporations or personal holding companies).
			Exceptions - Reasonable cause and good faith. (See Treasury Regulation Section 1.6664-4 and 1.6662-6(d).) There is no disclosure exception to this penalty. Treasury Regulation Section 1.6662-5(a). When there is an underpayment due to overstated charitable deduction property, there are special rules for reasonable cause under IRC Section 6664(c) for returns filed after January 1, 2010.	

Penalty Name	IRC Section	R&TC Section	Penalty Reason	Computation
Fraud Penalty	6663	1916 4	When there is clear and convincing evidence to prove that some part of the underpayment of tax was due to civil fraud. Such evidence must show the taxpayer's intent to evade tax that the taxpayer believed to have owed.	75% of the underpayment attributable to civil fraud.
			Exceptions - Reasonable cause and good faith.	
Reportable Transaction Accuracy Related Penalty - Disclosed Reportable Transaction	6662A	19164.5	Any disclosed reportable transaction understatement for tax years beginning on or after January 1, 2005.	20% of the understatement attributed to the reportable or listed transaction if the transaction is adequately disclosed on the return.
			Exceptions - Chief Counsel relief for reportable transactions other than listed transactions. The standards in R&TC Section 19772 apply.	
Reportable Transaction Accuracy Related Penalty - Undisclosed Reportable Transaction	6662A(c)	19164.5	Any undisclosed reportable transaction understatement for tax years beginning on or after January 1, 2005.	30% of the understatement attributed to the reportable or listed transaction if the transaction is not adequately disclosed on the return.
			Exceptions - Chief Counsel relief for reportable transactions other than listed transactions. The standards in R&TC Section 19772 apply.	
Preparer Penalty	6694(a)(1)	19166(a)	When a preparer completes a return or claim for refund that results in the taxpayer's understatement based on an unreasonable position and the preparer knew or reasonably should have known of the unreasonable position.	Greater of: $250 or 50% of income derived (or to be derived) by the tax preparer with respect to each return or claim.
			Exceptions - The preparer can avoid the penalty (1) if the position is adequately disclosed and has a reasonable basis; (2) if the position is not disclosed and is not a tax shelter and there is substantial authority for the position; or (3) for a tax shelter position defined in IRC Section 6662(d) or a reportable transaction under IRC Section 6011, if the preparer reasonably believes that the position is more-likely-than-not correct. Also reasonable cause and good faith. If preparer pays at least 15% of the penalty within 30 days of the bill and files a claim for refund, the preparer may file an action in court within 30 days of the claim denial or deemed denial.	

Penalty Name	IRC Section	R&TC Section	Penalty Reason	Computation
Preparer Penalty - Reportable Transactions, Listed Transactions or Gross Misstatements	6694	19166(b)(2)	When a preparer completes a return or claim for refund that results in the taxpayer's understatement based on an undisclosed reportable transaction, a listed transaction, or a gross misstatement.	$1,000 or 50% of the income derived (or to be derived) with respect to each return or claim.
			Exceptions - Standard to avoid the penalty is more-likely-than-not. If preparer pays at least 15% of the penalty within 30 days of the bill and files a claim for refund, the preparer may file an action in court within 30 days of the claim denial or deemed denial.	
Understatement of a Taxpayer's Liability by Tax Preparer - Willful or Reckless Conduct	6694(b)	19166(a)	If the understatement of the taxpayer's tax is due to the preparer's willful attempt to understate the liability or any reckless or intentional disregard of rules or regulations.	The greater of $5,000 or 50% of the income derived (or to be derived) with respect to each return or claim.
			Exceptions - A preparer is not considered to have recklessly or intentionally disregarded a rule or regulation if the position has a reasonable basis and is adequately disclosed. If a regulation is at issue, there must be a good faith challenge. If the position is contrary to a revenue ruling or notice, the substantial authority standard applies. The same rules of paying 15% and filing a claim and suit in court apply.	
Additional Penalties - Failure to Furnish Copy to Taxpayer	6695(a)	19167(a)	Failure to furnish a completed copy of return or claim.	$50 per failure, not to exceed $25,000 during any calendar year.
			Exceptions - Reasonable cause and not willful neglect.	
Additional Penalties - Failure to Furnish Identifying Number	6695(c)	19167(b)	Failure to include on a return or claim the identifying number of the preparer, employer or both.	$50 per failure, not to exceed $25,000 during any calendar year.
			Exceptions - Reasonable cause and not willful neglect.	
Additional Penalties - Failure to Retain Copy or List	6695(d)	19167(c)	Failure to retain a completed copy of a return or claim for 3 years or a list with the taxpayer's name and identifying number and make the return or list available for inspection by FTB.	$50 per failure, not to exceed $25,000 during any calendar year.
			Exceptions - Reasonable cause and not willful neglect.	

Penalty Name	IRC Section	R&TC Section	Penalty Reason	Computation
Additional Penalties - Failure to Register as a Tax Preparer with California Tax Education Council (CTEC)	None	19167(d)(1) and (2)	Failure to register with the CTEC.	$2,500 for first failure to register. $5,000 for other than first failure.
			Exceptions - Reasonable cause and not willful neglect. The penalty may be waived if the preparer provides proof of registration to us within 90 days of mail date of notice. Certain persons are exempt from the requirement to register, such as licensed certified public accountants (CPA) and licensed attorneys.	
Negotiation of Taxpayer's Check by Tax Preparer	6695(f)	19169, 20645.7	If the tax preparer endorses or otherwise negotiates a check for the refund of tax that is issued to a taxpayer, if the person was the preparer of the return or claim that gave rise to the refund check.	$250 for each endorsement or negotiation of a check.
			Exceptions - The preparer will not be considered to have endorsed a check solely as a result of putting the taxpayer's name to a check for the purpose of depositing the check into the taxpayer's account, if authorized by the taxpayer.	
Failure to File Electronically	None	19170	If a preparer that is subject to R&TC Section 18621.9 fails to file returns electronically.	$50 for each failure.
			Exceptions - Reasonable cause and not willful neglect. Reasonable cause can be established by the taxpayer electing not to file electronically.	
Failure of Partnership to Comply with Filing Requirements	6698	19172	If a partnership: Fails to file a timely return (FTB 565 *Partnership Return of Income*/ FTB 568, *Limited Liability Return of Income*), including any extensions, or Files a return (FTB 565/568) that fails to include information required under R&TC Section 18633 or 18633.5.	$18 multiplied by the number of persons who were partners/members during any part of that taxable year for each month during which that failure continues, not to exceed 12 months.
			Exceptions - Reasonable cause.	

Penalty Name	IRC Section	R&TC Section	Penalty Reason	Computation
Failure of S Corporation to Comply with Filing Requirements	6699	19172.5	If an S Corporation: Fails to file a timely return, including extensions, or Files a return that fails to include information required under R&TC Section 18601.	$18 multiplied by the number of persons who were shareholders during any part of that taxable year for each month during which that failure continues, not to exceed 12 months.
			Exceptions - Reasonable cause.	
Failure to Comply With Request to Provide Lists - Reportable Transactions	6708	19173(a)	Failing to provide lists of advisees with respect to reportable transactions (other than a listed transaction) to FTB within 20 business days after FTB requests the list.	$10,000 for each day of such failure after the 20th business day.
			Exceptions - Chief Counsel relief for reportable transactions other than listed transactions.	
Failure to Comply With Request - Material Advisors With Respect to Listed Transactions	None	19173(b)	Material advisors who fail to meet the requirements of R&TC Section 18648(d)(1) with respect to a listed transaction.	$100,000 or 50% of gross income that the material advisor derived from that activity whichever is greater.
			Exceptions - The penalty does not apply if it is shown that the additional information required was not identified in our notice prior to the date the transaction/shelter was entered into. No Chief Counsel review for listed transactions.	
Failure to Report Personal Service Remuneration	None	19175	Any person or entity who fails to report amounts paid as remuneration for personal services may be liable for a penalty.	The maximum personal income tax rate multiplied by the unreported amounts paid as remuneration for personal services. In addition, at our discretion, we may disallow the deduction for amounts paid as remuneration.
			Exceptions - None.	
Statement That Results in Under-Withholding	6682	19176	Statement that results in a decrease in amounts deducted and withheld, if there was no reasonable basis for the statement.	$500 for the statement.
			Exceptions - Penalty may be waived if the tax paid by the individual for the taxable year is equal to or less than the sum of both certain credits allowed and payments of estimated tax.	

Penalty Name	IRC Section	R&TC Section	Penalty Reason	Computation
Promotion of Abusive Tax Shelter	6700	19177	Any person who engages in the organization of, or sale of any interest in, a partnership or other entity, an investment plan or arrangement, or any other plan or arrangement, if the person makes, furnishes, or causes another person to make or furnish: A false or fraudulent tax benefits statement as to a material matter; or A gross valuation overstatement as to a material matter.	$1,000 or 100% of the gross income derived (or to be derived) by the person from the activity whichever is less. If the activity on which the penalty is imposed involves a false or fraudulent statement as to any matter pertaining to the tax shelter plan or arrangement, the penalty is 50% of the gross income the promoter derived (or was to derive) from promoting the activity.
			Exceptions - If a penalty is imposed with respect to a gross valuation overstatement, the penalty may be waived on a showing that there was a reasonable basis for the valuation and the valuation was made in good faith.	
Aiding and Abetting Understatement of Tax Liability	6701	19178	Aiding and abetting understatement of tax.	$1,000. $10,000 if the tax liability relates to a corporation.
			Exceptions - None.	
Filing Frivolous Return	6702(a)	19179(a) and (b)	Filing a frivolous return.	$5,000 if the return does not contain sufficient information or is based on a frivolous position or reflects an attempt to delay or impede administration of the tax laws.
			Exceptions - Chief Counsel relief.	
Frivolous Submissions	6702(b)	19179(d)	Filing a specified frivolous submission.	$5,000 for "specified frivolous submissions."
			Exceptions - Chief Counsel relief.	
Failure to Comply With Original Issue Discount Reporting Requirements	6706	19181	Failing to comply with original issue discount reporting requirements.	$50 for each failure to show information on debt instrument. 1% of the aggregate issue price of each issue, up to a maximum of $50,000 for each issue for failure to furnish information to taxing agency.
			Exceptions - Reasonable cause and not willful neglect.	

Penalty Name	IRC Section	R&TC Section	Penalty Reason	Computation
Failure to Furnish Information Regarding Reportable Transaction	6707	19182	A material advisor who fails to file a return with respect to any reportable transaction before the date prescribed or who files false or incomplete information with respect to such transactions.	$50,000; for listed transactions, equal to the greater of: $200,000 or 50% (or 75% if failure is intentional) of the gross income derived by such a person.
			Exceptions - Penalty will not apply if it is shown that the additional required information was not identified in our notice issued prior to the date of the transaction. Chief Counsel relief for reportable transactions other than listed transactions.	
Failure to Disclose Quid Pro Quo Contributions	6714	19182.5	For each contribution where the organization fails to make the required disclosure.	$10 for each contribution, but the total penalty with respect to a particular fundraising event or mailing shall not exceed $5,000.
			Exceptions - Reasonable cause. No penalty imposed if requirements under IRC Section 6115 are met.	
Failure to File Correct Information Return	6652, 6721-6724	19183(a)	Failing to file information returns or failure to include all required information.	$50 for failure to file correct information returns, with respect to which such a failure occurs. Shall not exceed $250,000 during any calendar year; $100,000 for persons with gross receipts of not more than $5 million. Higher penalties (without reduction for correction) apply in the case of intentional disregard, depending on type of information return.
			Exceptions - De minimis failure exception. Reasonable cause and not willful neglect.	
Failure to File Correct Information Return	6721(b)(1)	19183(a)	Reduction in failure to file correct information return penalty when corrected within 30 days.	$15 for failure to file correct information returns, with respect to which such a failure occurs. Shall not exceed $75,000 during any calendar year. $25,000 for persons with gross receipts of not more than $5 million.
			Exceptions - Reasonable cause and not willful neglect.	
Failure to File Correct Information Return	6721(b)(2)	19183(a)	Reduction in failure to file correct information return penalty when corrected on or before August 1.	$30 for failure to file correct information returns, with respect to which such a failure occurs. Shall not exceed $150,000 during any calendar year. $50,000 for persons with gross receipts of not more than $5 million.
			Exceptions - Reasonable cause and not willful neglect.	

Penalty Name	IRC Section	R&TC Section	Penalty Reason	Computation
Failure to File Correct Information - Failure to Furnish Correct Payee Statements	6722(a)	19183(b)(1)	Failure to furnish correct payee statements.	$50 for each statement, up to a maximum of $100,000 for each calendar year. $100, or, if greater, 5% or 10% of the aggregate amount of the items required to be reported correctly, depending on the type of return required, with respect to each such failure for intentional disregard. The $100,000 limitation in IRC Section 6722(a) shall not apply.
			Exceptions - Reasonable cause and not willful neglect.	
Failure to File Correct Information - Failure to Comply With Other Information Reporting Requirements	6723	19183(c)	Failure to comply with other information reporting requirements.	$50 for each such failure, up to a maximum of $100,000 for each calendar year.
			Exceptions - Reasonable cause and not willful neglect.	
Failure to File Correct Information - Failure to Provide Written Explanation to Recipients of Distributions Eligible for Rollover Treatment.	None	19183(e)	Failure to provide written explanation to recipients of distributions eligible for rollover treatment pursuant to IRC Section 402(f).	$10 for each failure, up to a maximum of $5,000 for each calendar year after notice and demand.
			Exceptions - Reasonable cause and not willful neglect.	
Failure to File Report Regarding Tax Deferred Savings Accounts	6693	19184	Failure to file report regarding tax deferred savings accounts.	$50 for each failure.
			Exceptions - Reasonable cause.	

Penalty Name	IRC Section	R&TC Section	Penalty Reason	Computation
Failure to File Report Regarding Tax Deferred Savings Accounts - Overstatement as to Amount Designated Nondeductible Contributions	6693	19184(b)(1)(B)	Overstating the amount designated as nondeductible contributions for any taxable year.	$100 for each overstatement.
			Exceptions - Reasonable cause.	
Failure to File Report Regarding Tax Deferred Savings Accounts - Failure to File a Form Required for Nondeductible Contributions to Individual Retirement Accounts (IRA)	6693	19184(b)(2)	Failure to file a form required for nondeductible contributions to IRAs.	$50 for each failure.
			Exceptions - Reasonable cause.	
Substantial and Gross Valuation Misstatements on Appraisal	6695A	19185	Knowingly preparing an appraisal to be used in connection with a return or claim and the claimed value results in a substantial valuation misstatement, or gross valuation misstatement.	For returns or submissions filed on or after January 1, 2011: 125% of gross income from the preparation of the appraisal. Or, if less: 10% of the amount of underpayment attributable to misstatement, but not less than $1,000.
			Exceptions - Established value in the appraisal was more likely than not the proper value.	
Fraudulent Identification of Exempt Use Property	6720B	19186	Knowingly misidentifying applicable property (charitable deduction property) as having exempt use.	$10,000.
			Exceptions - None.	

Penalty Name	IRC Section	R&TC Section	Penalty Reason	Computation
Financial Institution Record Match (FIRM)	None	19266(g)	Any financial institution that willfully fails to comply with rules and regulations for the administration of delinquent tax collections.	$50 for each record not provided up to $100,000 per calendar year.
			Exceptions - Reasonable cause.	
Suspension or Disbarment From Practice Before FTB	None	19523.5	Failure to notify the Franchise Tax Board within 45 days of the issuance of a final order disbarring or suspending the person to practice.	$5,000.
			Exceptions - None.	
Failure to Provide Information Concerning State Licenses Penalty	None	19528	Licensees failing to provide identification numbers upon demand.	$100 after 30-day notice and demand.
			Exceptions - None.	
Frivolous Proceedings; Failure to Exhaust Administrativ e Remedies	6673	19714	Taxpayer's action at the State Board of Equalization (BOE) or in court that was instituted or maintained by the taxpayer for delay, or that the position was frivolous or groundless, or that administrative remedies were not pursued.	Not more than $5,000.
			Exceptions - None.	
Business Conducted After Suspension or Forfeiture of Corporate Rights	None	19719	Anyone who attempts or purports to exercise the powers, rights, and privileges of a corporation that has been suspended or forfeited.	Minimum $250 and not exceeding $1,000.
			Exceptions - Not applicable to any insurer or insurer's counsel.	
Failure to Include Information on Reportable Transactions	6707A	19772	Failure to include reportable transactions information with a return.	$15,000, $30,000 if listed transaction.
			Exceptions - Chief Counsel relief only for reportable transactions other than listed transactions.	

Penalty Name	IRC Section	R&TC Section	Penalty Reason	Computation
Noneconomic Substance Transaction Understatement	6662(b)(6) and (i)	19774	Understatement of a noneconomic substance transaction.	40% of understatement. Reduced to 20% if relevant facts adequately disclosed in the return.
			Exceptions - Chief Counsel relief.	
Interest-Based Penalty for Listed Transactions, et al.	None	19777	Taxpayer contacted by FTB concerning an abusive tax avoidance transaction.	100% of the interest payable for the period beginning on the due date of the return and ending on the date the NPA is mailed.
			Exceptions - None.	
Amnesty Program Interest Penalties	None	19777.5	An addition to tax for each tax year that was eligible for amnesty, but amnesty was not requested, and there was an unpaid amount due on March 31, 2005, (i.e., 50% Interest-Based penalty). The penalty is also imposed where FTB mails a notice of proposed assessment or a notice of tax due or where a taxpayer self assesses additional tax for an amnesty eligible tax year after the end of the amnesty period (i.e., Post-Amnesty Penalty).	The 50% Interest-Based Penalty is calculated as an amount equal to fifty percent of the interest that accrued on the unpaid daily balance from the original due date of the tax to March 31, 2005. The Post-Amnesty Penalty is calculated as an amount equal to fifty percent of the interest computed on the additional amount from the original due date of the tax year to March 31, 2005.
			Exceptions - No claim for refund allowed except on the grounds that the penalty was not properly calculated.	
150% Interest Penalty	None	19778	Amended return filed after April 15, 2004, but before taxpayer is contacted by FTB regarding a potentially abusive tax shelter.	Interest accrues at a rate of 150% of the adjusted annual rate.
			Exceptions - None.	
Relief From Contract Void-ability	None	23305.1	The period for which relief from voidability of the contract is granted.	$100 daily for each day of the period for which relief from voidability is granted, not to exceed a total penalty equal to the amount of the tax for the period for which relief is requested.
			Exceptions - None.	
Failure of Exempt Organizations and Trusts to Pay Filing Fee	6033, 6072(e)	23772(a)(3)	Failure to pay fee on or before due date (determined with regard to any extension of time for filing) for filing exempt organization or trust return.	Filing fee increased to $25.
			Exceptions - Reasonable cause.	

Penalty Name	IRC Section	R&TC Section	Penalty Reason	Computation
Failure of Exempt Organizations and Trusts to File Annual Information Return	6033, 6072(e)	23772(c)(1)	The period in which the exempt organization or trust fails to file a return after the due date.	On notice and demand $5 for each month or fraction thereof during which the failure to file a return continues, but the total amount imposed on any organization for the failure to file shall not exceed $40.
			Exceptions - Reasonable cause.	
Failure of Private Foundation to File on Demand	6033, 6072(e)	23772(c)(2)	The period in which a private foundation fails to file a return after receiving a demand for a return from FTB.	$5 for each month or fraction thereof during which the failure to file a return continues, but the total amount imposed on any organization for the failure to file shall not exceed $25 in addition to penalty provided in 23772(c)(1).
			Exceptions - Reasonable cause.	
Real Estate Investment Trust (REIT) Failure to Comply With Ascertainment of Ownership Rules	857(f)	24872.7	Failure to comply with federal regulations to ascertain ownership rules.	Penalty imposed only, and in same amount, if penalty is imposed for federal purposes: $25,000. Intentional disregard is $50,000. Failure to comply after notice an additional penalty of either $25,000 or $50,000.
			Exceptions – Reasonable cause and not willful neglect, as determined by	
Failure to Supply Information Penalty	None	25112	Taxpayer engaged in a unitary business that fails to supply requested information.	$1,000 for each taxable year. Additional penalty of $1,000 for each 30-day period up to $24,000 if failure continues for more than 90 days after we notify the taxpayer.

Chapter 15:

Innocent Spouse Relief

In 2013 the IRS issued Rev. Proc. 2013-34 providing guidance for a taxpayer seeking equitable relief from income tax liability under section 66(c) or section 6015(f) of the Internal Revenue Code (a "requesting spouse").

This revenue procedure supersedes Rev. Proc. 2003-61 and is effective for requests for relief filed on or after September 16, 2013. In addition, this revenue procedure is effective for requests for equitable relief pending on September 16, 2013 whether with the Service, the Office of Appeals, or in a case docketed with a Federal court.

This revenue procedure expands how the IRS will take into account abuse and financial control by the non-requesting spouse in determining whether equitable relief is warranted. It also broadens the availability of refunds in cases involving deficiencies.

IRS Form **8857,** *Request for Innocent Spouse Relief,* was revised in January 2014 to accommodate the terms of this new revenue procedure.

Generally, both the taxpayer and the taxpayer's spouse are responsible, jointly and individually, for paying any tax, interest, or penalties from their joint return. If a taxpayer believes his/her current or former spouse should be solely responsible for an erroneous item or an underpayment of tax from his/her joint tax return, he/she may be eligible for innocent spouse relief.

Innocent spouse relief may also be available if the taxpayer was a resident of a community property state (such as California) and did not file a joint federal income tax return and believes he/she should not be held responsible for the tax attributable to an item of community income.

When a taxpayer files a joint income tax return, the law makes both the taxpayer and his/her spouse responsible for the entire tax liability. This is called joint and several liability. Joint and several liability applies not only to the tax liability shown on the return but also to any additional tax liability the IRS determines to be due, even if the additional tax is due to the income, deductions, or credits of the spouse or former spouse. The taxpayer remains jointly and severally liable for taxes, and the IRS can still collect them from him/her, even if he/she later divorces and the divorce decree states that the former spouse will be solely responsible for the tax.

If a taxpayer believes, taking into account all the facts and circumstances, only his/her spouse or former spouse should be held responsible for all or part of the tax, he/she should request relief from the tax liability, including related penalties and interest by filing Form 8857. The IRS will use the information provided on the form, and any attachments submitted, to determine who is eligible for relief.

Married people who did not file joint returns, but who lived in community property states may request relief from liability for tax attributable to an item of community income. Community property states are Arizona, California, Idaho, Louisiana, Nevada, New Mexico, Texas, Washington, and Wisconsin.

A taxpayer should not file Form 8857 for any tax year to which the following situations apply:

- In a final decision a court considered whether to grant relief from the joint liability and decided not to do so;
- In a final decision a court did not consider whether to grant relief from the joint liability, but the taxpayer meaningfully participated in the proceeding and could have asked for relief;
- The taxpayer entered into an offer in compromise with the IRS; or
- The taxpayer entered into a closing agreement with the IRS that disposed of the same liability for which the taxpayer wants to seek relief.

Section 6013(d)(3) provides that married taxpayers who file a joint return under section 6013 will be jointly and severally liable for the income tax arising from that joint return.

Section 3201(a) of the Internal Revenue Service Restructuring and Reform Act of 1998, Pub. L. No. 105-206, 112 Stat. 685, 734 (RRA), enacted section 6015, which provides relief in certain circumstances from the joint and several liability imposed by section 6013(d)(3). Section 6015(b) and (c) specify two sets of circumstances under which relief from joint and several liability is available in cases involving understatements of tax. Section 6015(b) is modeled after former section 6013(e), the prior innocent spouse statute, and section 6015(c) provides for separation of liability for taxpayers who are no longer married to, are legally separated from, or not living together with the person with whom they filed a joint return. If relief is not available under section 6015(b) or (c), section 6015(f) authorizes the Secretary to grant equitable relief if, taking into account all the facts and circumstances, the Secretary determines that it is inequitable to hold a requesting spouse liable for any unpaid tax or any deficiency (or any portion of either).

Section 66(c) provides relief from income tax liability resulting from the operation of community property law to taxpayers domiciled in a community property state who do not file a joint return. Section 3201(b) of the RRA amended section 66(c) to add an equitable relief provision similar to section 6015(f).

Section 6015 provides relief only from joint and several liability arising from a joint return. If an individual signs a joint return under duress, the election to file jointly is not valid and there is no valid return with respect to the requesting spouse. The individual is not jointly and severally liable for any income tax liabilities arising from that return. In that case, section 6015 does not apply and is not necessary for obtaining relief.

Under section 6015(b) and (c), relief is available only from an understatement or a deficiency. Section 6015(b) and (c) do not authorize relief from an underpayment of income tax reported on a joint return. Section 66(c) and section 6015(f) permit equitable relief from an underpayment of income tax or from a deficiency. The legislative history of section 6015 provides that Congress intended for the Secretary to exercise discretion in granting equitable relief from an underpayment of income tax if a requesting spouse "does not know, and had no reason to know, that funds intended for the payment of tax were instead taken by the other spouse for such other spouse's benefit." H.R. Conf. Rep. No. 105-599, at 254 (1998). Congress also intended for the Secretary to exercise the equitable relief authority under section 6015(f) in other situations if, "taking into account all the facts and circumstances, it is inequitable to hold an individual liable for all or part of any unpaid tax or deficiency arising from a joint return." *Id.*

This revenue procedure gives greater deference to the presence of abuse than Rev. Proc. 2003-61. The Service recognizes that the issue of abuse can be relevant with respect to the analysis of other factors and can negate the presence of certain factors. This change is intended to give greater weight to the presence of abuse when its presence impacts the analysis of other factors.

The timeliness threshold condition in section 4.01(3) of this revenue procedure provides that a request for equitable relief under section 6015(f) or section 66(c) must be filed before the expiration of the period of limitation for collection under section 6502 to the extent the taxpayer seeks relief from an outstanding liability, or before the expiration of the period of limitation for credit or refund under section 6511 to the extent the taxpayer seeks a refund of taxes paid. This is a significant change to the requirement in Rev. Proc. 2003-61, section 4.01(3), and Treas. Reg. § 1.6015-5(b)(1) (TD 9003), that the requesting spouse's claim for equitable relief must be filed no later than two years after the date of the Service's first collection activity.

The attribution threshold condition in section 4.01(7) of this revenue procedure adds a new exception in paragraph (e) to the requirement that the income tax liability must be attributable to an item of the non-requesting spouse. Under section 4.01(7)(e) of the revenue procedure, relief would not be precluded for an item attributable to the requesting spouse if the non-requesting spouse's fraud gave rise to the understatement of tax or deficiency.

Streamlined determinations under section 4.02 of this revenue procedure now apply to understatements of income tax instead of only underpayments as under Rev. Proc. 2003-61. Section 4.02 also now applies to claims for equitable relief under section 66(c).

Section 4.03(2) of this revenue procedure clarifies that no one factor or a majority of factors necessarily controls the determination. Therefore, depending on the facts and circumstances of the case, relief may still be appropriate if the number of factors weighing against relief exceeds the number of factors weighing in favor of relief, or a denial of relief may still be appropriate if the number of factors weighing in favor of relief exceeds the number of factors weighing against relief.

The economic hardship factor in section 4.03(2)(b) of this revenue procedure now provides minimum standards based on income, expenses, and assets, for determining whether the requesting spouse would suffer economic hardship if relief is not granted. Section 4.03(2)(b) also now provides that the lack of a finding of economic hardship does not weigh against relief, as it did under Rev. Proc. 2003-61, and instead will be neutral.

The knowledge factor for understatement cases in section 4.03(2)(c)(i) of this revenue procedure clarifies how the factor works in cases involving equitable relief under section 66(c), in addition to cases involving equitable relief under section 6015(f). Section 4.03(2)(c)(i)(A) provides that actual knowledge of the item giving rise to an understatement or deficiency will no longer be weighed more heavily than other factors, as it did under Rev. Proc. 2003-61. Further, section 4.03(2)(c)(i)(A) clarifies that, for purposes of this factor, if the non-requesting spouse abused the requesting spouse or maintained control over the household finances by restricting the requesting spouse's access to financial information, and because of the abuse or financial control, the requesting spouse was not able to challenge the treatment of any items on the joint return for fear of the non-requesting spouse's retaliation, then that abuse or financial control will result in this factor weighing in favor of relief even if the requesting spouse knew or had reason to know of the items giving rise to the understatement or deficiency.

The knowledge factor for underpayment cases in section 4.03(2)(c)(ii) of this revenue procedure now provides that, in determining whether the requesting spouse knew or had reason to know that the non-requesting spouse would not pay the tax reported as due on the return, the Service will consider whether the requesting spouse reasonably expected that the non-requesting spouse would pay the tax liability at the time the return was filed or within a reasonable period of time after the filing of the return. In response to comments received with respect to Notice 2012-8, section 4.03(2)(c)(ii) provides that a requesting spouse may be presumed to have reasonably expected that the non-requesting spouse would pay the liability if a request for an installment agreement to pay the tax was filed by the later of 90 days after the due date for payment of the tax, or 90 days after the return was filed. Further, section 4.03(2)(c)(ii) clarifies that for purposes of this factor, if the non-requesting spouse abused the requesting spouse or maintained control over the household finances by restricting the requesting spouse's access to financial information, and because of the abuse or financial control, the requesting spouse was not able to question the payment of the taxes reported as due on the return or challenge the non-requesting spouse's assurance regarding payment of the taxes for fear of the non-requesting spouse's retaliation, then that abuse or financial control will result in this factor weighing in favor of relief even if the requesting spouse knew or had reason to know that the non-requesting spouse would not pay the tax liability. Finally, section 4.03(2)(c)(ii) provides that if the requesting spouse did not reasonably expect that the non-requesting spouse would pay the tax liability reported on an amended return that was based on items not properly reported on the original return, the Service will also consider whether the requesting spouse knew or had reason to know of the understatement on the original return.

The legal obligation factor in section 4.03(2)(d) of this revenue procedure clarifies that a requesting spouse's legal obligation to pay outstanding tax liabilities is a factor to consider in determining whether equitable relief should be granted, in addition to whether the non-requesting spouse has a legal obligation to pay the tax liabilities.

The significant benefit factor in section 4.03(2)(e) of this revenue procedure provides that any significant benefit a requesting spouse may have received from the unpaid tax or understatement will not weigh against relief (will be neutral) if the non-requesting spouse abused the requesting spouse or maintained financial control and made the decisions regarding living a more lavish lifestyle. Further, section 4.03(2)(e) provides that if only the non-requesting spouse significantly benefitted from the unpaid tax or understatement, and the requesting spouse had little or no benefit, or the non-requesting spouse enjoyed the benefit to the requesting spouse's detriment, this factor will weigh in favor of relief. Section 4.03(2)(e) also provides that if the amount of unpaid tax or understatement of tax was small such that neither spouse received a significant benefit, then this factor is neutral. In response to comments received with respect to Notice 2012-8, section 4.03(2)(e) provides that the determination that the tax liability was small such that neither spouse received a significant benefit will vary depending on the facts and circumstances of each case.

The compliance with the income tax laws factor in section 4.03(2)(f) of this revenue procedure now provides that a requesting spouse's subsequent compliance with all Federal income tax laws is a factor that may weigh in favor of relief, instead of always being neutral under Rev. Proc. 2003-61.

Section 4.04 of this revenue procedure broadens the availability of refunds in cases involving deficiencies by eliminating the rule in section 4.04(1) of Rev. Proc. 2003-61 that limited refunds in cases involving deficiencies to payments made by the requesting spouse pursuant to an installment agreement.

A requesting spouse must satisfy all of the following threshold conditions to be eligible to submit a request for equitable relief under section 6015(f). With the exception of conditions (1) and (2), a requesting spouse must satisfy all of the following threshold conditions to be eligible to submit a request for equitable relief under section 66(c). The Service may relieve a requesting spouse who satisfies all the applicable threshold conditions set forth below of all or part of the income tax liability under section 66(c) or section 6015(f) if, taking into account all the facts and circumstances, the Service determines that it would be inequitable to hold the requesting spouse liable for the income tax liability. The threshold conditions are as follows:

(1) The requesting spouse filed a joint return for the taxable year for which he or she seeks relief.

(2) Relief is not available to the requesting spouse under section 6015(b) or (c).

(3) The claim for relief is timely filed:

- (a) If the requesting spouse is applying for relief from a liability or a portion of a liability that remains unpaid, the request for relief must be made on or before the Collection Statute Expiration Date (CSED).
- (b) Claims for credit or refund of amounts paid must be made before the expiration of the period of limitation on credit or refund, as provided in section 6511.

(4) No assets were transferred between the spouses as part of a fraudulent scheme by the spouses.

(5) The non-requesting spouse did not transfer disqualified assets to the requesting spouse.

(6) The requesting spouse did not knowingly participate in the filing of a fraudulent joint return.

(7) The income tax liability from which the requesting spouse seeks relief is attributable (either in full or in part) to an item of the non-requesting spouse or an underpayment resulting from the non-requesting spouse's income. If the liability is partially attributable to the requesting spouse, then relief can only be considered for the portion of the liability attributable to the non-requesting spouse. Nonetheless, the Service will consider granting relief regardless of

whether the understatement, deficiency, or underpayment is attributable (in full or in part) to the requesting spouse if any of the following exceptions applies:

(a) Attribution solely due to the operation of community property law. If an item is attributable or partially attributable to the requesting spouse solely due to the operation of community property law, then for purposes of this revenue procedure, that item (or portion thereof) will be considered to be attributable to the non-requesting spouse.

(b) Nominal ownership. If the item is titled in the name of the requesting spouse, the item is presumptively attributable to the requesting spouse. This presumption is rebuttable.

(c) Misappropriation of funds. If the requesting spouse did not know, and had no reason to know, that funds intended for the payment of tax were misappropriated by the non-requesting spouse for the non-requesting spouse's benefit, the Service will consider granting equitable relief although the underpayment may be attributable in part or in full to an item of the requesting spouse. The Service will consider granting relief in this case only to the extent that the funds intended for the payment of tax were taken by the non-requesting spouse.

(d) Abuse. If the requesting spouse establishes that he or she was the victim of abuse prior to the time the return was filed, and that, as a result of the prior abuse, the requesting spouse was not able to challenge the treatment of any items on the return, or was not able to question the payment of any balance due reported on the return, for fear of the non-requesting spouse's retaliation, the Service will consider granting equitable relief even though the deficiency or underpayment may be attributable in part or in full to an item of the requesting spouse.

(e) Fraud committed by non-requesting spouse. The Service will consider granting relief notwithstanding that the item giving rise to the understatement or deficiency is attributable to the requesting spouse, if the requesting spouse establishes that the non-requesting spouse's fraud is the reason for the erroneous item.

Circumstances under which the Service will make streamlined determinations granting equitable relief.

If a requesting spouse who filed a joint return, or a requesting spouse who did not file a joint return in a community property state, satisfies the threshold conditions, the Service will consider whether the requesting spouse is entitled to a streamlined determination of equitable relief. If a requesting spouse is not entitled to a streamlined determination because the requesting spouse does not satisfy all the elements, the requesting spouse is still entitled to be considered for relief under the equitable factors. The Service will make streamlined determinations granting equitable relief in cases in which the requesting spouse establishes that the requesting spouse:

(1) Marital status. Is no longer married to the non-requesting spouse;

(2) Economic hardship. Would suffer economic hardship if relief were not granted; and

(3) Knowledge or reason to know.

(a) Section 6015(f) cases. Did not know or have reason to know that there was an understatement or deficiency on the joint income tax return, or did not know or have reason to know that the non-requesting spouse would not or could not pay the underpayment of tax reported on the joint income tax return. If the non-requesting spouse abused the requesting spouse or maintained control over the household finances by restricting the requesting spouse's access to financial information, and because of the abuse or financial control, the requesting spouse was not able to challenge the treatment of any items on the joint return, or to question the payment of the taxes reported as due on the joint return or challenge the non-requesting spouse's assurance regarding payment of the taxes, for fear of the non-requesting spouse's retaliation, then the abuse or financial control will result in this factor being satisfied even if the requesting spouse knew or had reason to know of the items giving rise to the understatement or deficiency or knew or had reason to know that the non-requesting spouse would not pay the tax liability.

(b) Section 66(c) cases. Did not know or have reason to know of an item of community income properly includible in gross income, which would be treated as the income of the non-requesting spouse.

IRS Topic 205 - Innocent Spouse Relief (Including Separation of Liability and Equitable Relief)

Many married taxpayers choose to file a joint tax return because of certain benefits this filing status allows. In filing jointly, both taxpayers are jointly and severally liable for the tax and any additions to tax, interest, or penalties that arise as a result of the joint return even if they later divorce. Joint and several liability means that each taxpayer is legally responsible for the entire liability. Thus, both spouses are generally held responsible for all the tax due even if one spouse earned all the income or claimed improper deductions or credits. This is also true even if a divorce decree states that a former spouse will be responsible for any amounts due on previously filed joint returns. In some cases, however, a spouse can get relief from joint and several liability.

There are three types of relief from joint and several liability for spouses who filed joint returns:

1. **Innocent Spouse Relief** provides you relief from additional tax you owe if your spouse or former spouse failed to report income, reported income improperly or claimed improper deductions or credits.
2. **Separation of Liability Relief** provides for the allocation of additional tax owed between you and your former spouse or your current spouse from whom you are separated because an item was not reported properly on a joint return. The tax allocated to you is the amount for which you are responsible.
3. **Equitable Relief** may apply when you do not qualify for innocent spouse relief or separation of liability relief for something not reported properly on a joint return and generally attributable to your spouse. You may also qualify for equitable relief if the correct amount of tax was reported on your joint return but the tax was not paid with the return.

Note: You must request innocent spouse relief or separation of liability relief no later than 2 years after the date the IRS first attempted to collect the tax from you. For equitable relief, you must request relief during the time the IRS has to collect the tax from you. If you are looking for a refund of tax you paid, then your request must be made within the time period for seeking a refund, which is generally three years after the date the return is filed or two years following the payment of the tax, whichever is later. For additional restrictions on refunds available under innocent spouse relief, equitable relief, and relief based on community property laws, see Publication 971, *Innocent Spouse Relief.* Refunds are not available under separation of liability relief.

You must meet **all** of the following conditions to qualify for **"innocent spouse relief"**:

- You filed a joint return that has an understatement of tax (deficiency) that is solely attributable to your spouse's erroneous item. An "erroneous item" includes income received by your spouse but which was omitted from the joint return. Deductions, credits, and property basis are also erroneous items if they are incorrectly reported on the joint return
- You establish that at the time you signed the joint return you did not know, and had no reason to know, that there was an understatement of tax and
- Taking into account all the facts and circumstances, it would be unfair to hold you liable for the understatement of tax

To qualify for **"separation of liability relief"** you must have filed a joint return and must meet **one** of the following requirements at the time you request relief:

- You are divorced or legally separated from the spouse with whom you filed the joint return
- You are widowed or

- You have not been a member of the same household as the spouse with whom you filed the joint return at any time during the 12-month period ending on the date you request relief

If, at the time you signed the joint return, you had actual knowledge of the item that gave rise to the understatement of tax, you do not qualify for separation of liability relief.

If you do not qualify for "innocent spouse relief" or "separation of liability relief" you may still qualify for **"equitable relief."** To qualify for equitable relief you must establish that, under all the facts and circumstances, it would be unfair to hold you liable for the understatement or underpayment of tax. In addition, you must meet other requirements listed in Publication 971, *Innocent Spouse Relief.*

To seek innocent spouse relief, separation of liability relief, or equitable relief, you should submit to the IRS a completed Form 8857 (PDF), *Request for Innocent Spouse Relief,* or a written statement containing the same information required on Form 8857, which is signed under penalties of perjury. You may also refer to Publication 971, *Innocent Spouse Relief,* for more information. If you request relief from joint and several liability, the IRS is required to notify the spouse with whom you filed the joint return of your request and allow him or her to provide information for consideration regarding your claim. To learn more about innocent spouse relief, go to Explore if you are an Eligible Innocent Spouse found under Tax Information for Innocent Spouses at the IRS.gov website.

If you lived in a community property state and did not file as "married filing jointly," you might qualify for relief from the operation of state community property law. Community property states are Arizona, California, Idaho, Louisiana, Nevada, New Mexico, Texas, Washington, and Wisconsin. Refer to Publication 971 for more details.

Relief from joint and several liability should not be confused with an injured spouse claim. You are an "injured spouse" if you file a joint return and all or part **of your share of the refund** was, or will be, applied against the separate past-due federal tax, state tax, child support, or federal non-tax debt (such as a student loan) of your spouse with whom you filed the joint return. If you are an injured spouse, you may be entitled to recoup your share of the refund. For more information, see Form 8379 (PDF), *Injured Spouse Allocation*, or refer to Topic 203.

A person seeking **Innocent Spouse Relief** will typically do so under one of the following conditions:

Material Changes

(1) Editorial changes made throughout this IRM.
(2) Throughout reference to Notice 2012-8 updated to Rev. Proc. 2013-34.
(3) IRM 25.15.3.1(2) added information regarding same sex marriage.
(4) IRM 25.15.3.2(1) instead of listing the versions of Form 8857, updated to state "Beginning in June 2007" .
(5) IRM 25.15.3.3(2) updated to reflect Letter 3284C for CCISO and L 3284 for the field.
(6) IRM 25.15.3.3.1(1) changed the beginning of the sentence to, For claims originating in CCISO.
(7) IRM 25.15.3.4.2.2(1) added caution regarding joint name line without joint filing status under SFR.
(8) IRM 25.15.3.4.4(2) removed sentence stating that Publication 594 has improved. No longer relevant.
(9) IRM 25.15.3.4.4(2) second Note removed regarding claims filed prior to July 18, 2002. No longer relevant.
(10) IRM 25.15.3.5.1(1) moved note into a) and added b) for criminal proceedings.
(11) IRM 25.15.3.5.6(5) word "determined" changed to "evaluated" .
(12) 25.15.3.7.2.1(2) moved the steps to allocate into a table format.
(13) 25.15.3.7.2.1(2) step 5 added the word Percentage of, to Percentage of adjustments allocated to the spouse.
(14) IRM 25.15.3.7.2.2 added step 7 for the allocation of the EITC.

(15) IRM 25.15.3.7.2.1.1 added instructions on how to calculate the allocation of the EITC.
(16) IPU 13U1619 issued 11-05-2013 IRM 25.15.3.7.2.1(9) corrected IRM reference for Special Rules and Exceptions.
(17) IRM 25.15.7.2.2(1) changed (7) to (8).
(18) IRM 25.15.7.2.2.1(4) added reference to IRM 25.15.3.5.6, Understatements Resulting From an Increase to Adjusted Gross Income.
(19) IRM 25.15.3.7.2.2.3 added information to help determine a fraudulent scheme.
(20) IRM 25.15.3.7.2.2.8 example changed "H" to "NRS" .
(21) IRM 25.15.3.7.2.2.12(1) updated title of Form 8615.
(22) IRM 25.15.3.7.3 b) with information for area office employees.
(23) IRM 25.15.3.8 updated to include the release of Rev. Proc 2013-34.
(24) IRM 25.15.3.8.2.1(6) added reference to the fraud indicators.
(25) IPU 13U1619 issued 11-05-2013 IRM 25.15.3.8.4(1) corrected title of IRM reference.
(26) IRM 25.15.3.8.4.1 added (1) stating that the factors listed are not an all inclusive list.
(27) IRM 25.15.3.8.4.1(2) note: added financial control and other family members living in the household to abuse.
(28) IRM 25.15.3.8.4.1.1 changed 12 month period to end on the date the service makes a determination.
(29) IRM 25.15.3.8.4.1.2(3)(a) added, and the RS does not have assets out of which payments towards the liability can be made.
(30) IRM 25.15.3.8.4.1.3 changed reasonably prompt time to reasonable period of time.
(31) IRM 25.15.3.8.4.1.3.2 clarified instructions for determining knowledge on an underpayment.
(32) IRM 25.15.3.8.4.1.5 additional information on if the amount of unpaid tax or understated tax was small.
(33) IPU 13U1379 issued 08-22-2013 IRM 25.15.3.9.1 made the Letter 3660C and Letter 3661C obsolete. Added letters used in the field.
(34) IPU 13U1379 issued 08-22-2013 IRM 25.15.3.9.2 added letters used in the field.
(35) IPU 13U0633 issued 03-28-2013 IRM 25.15.3.9.2(6) added the Letter 3323C. [This change was superseded by IPU 13U1379 issued 08–22–2013.]
(36) IPU 13U1379 issued 08-22-2013 IRM 25.15.3.9.3 removed the Letter 3323C and the Letter 3388C. Added letters used in the field. Letter 4581C made obsolete.
(37) IRM 25.15.3.9.3 added L 3657-A for use by area office employees.
(38) IRM 25.15.3.10(5) table, Letters added for field employees use.

Effect on Other Documents

IRM 25.15.3, Technical Provisions of IRC 6015, dated March 8, 2013 is superseded. The following IRM Procedural Updates (IPUs) issued from March 28 2013, through November 5, 2013 have been incorporated into this IRM: 13U0633, 13U1379, and 13U1619.

Audience

Employees in all business operating divisions who have contact with taxpayers addressing an innocent spouse issue

Effective Date

(07-29-2014)

Steve C. Klingel
Director, Reporting Compliance
Wage and Investment Division

25.15.3.1 (07-29-2014)
Introduction IRC 6015

1. This section discusses the innocent spouse provisions of IRC 6015 which provide three avenues for relief from joint and several liability:

- IRC 6015(b), **Innocent Spouse Relief**, provides an election for relief from a **deficiency/understatement** of tax liability.
- IRC 6015(c), **Separation of Liability**, provides an election to allocate a **deficiency/understatement.**
- IRC 6015(f), **Equitable Relief**, provides IRS with discretion to grant equitable relief from **deficiencies and underpayments** if the relief provisions under IRC 6015(b) or IRC 6015(c) do not apply.

2. Pursuant to *United States v. Windsor*, 570 U.S., 133 S. Ct. 2675 (2013), and Rev. Rul. 2013–17, same-sex spouses who are lawfully married under state law are considered to be married for federal tax purposes, and the terms "spouse," "husband and wife," "husband," and "wife" refer to such spouses. Accordingly, same-sex spouses who file joint returns are jointly and severally liable for any tax liability and may be entitled to innocent spouse relief so long as the conditions of IRC section 6015 are met.

   Note:

   Same-sex spouses who are lawfully married under state law are considered married for federal tax purposes even if they live in a state that does not recognize the validity of same-sex marriages. The term "marriage" does not include registered domestic partnerships, civil unions, or other similar formal relationships that are not recognized as marriage under state law.

25.15.3.2 (07-29-2014)
Election for Relief under IRC 6015

1. IRC 6015(e) was amended by the Tax Relief and Health Care Act of 2006 on December 20, 2006, so that most claims for relief made solely under IRC 6015(f) result in a prohibition on collection and a suspension of the collection statute just as elections under IRC 6015(b) and IRC 6015(c) always had, see IRM 25.15.1.8, *Statute of Limitations on Collection*, for a more detailed discussion of the suspension of the collection statute. Beginning with the June 2007 revision of Form 8857, *Request for Innocent Spouse Relief*, IRS no longer asks a requesting spouse (RS) to specifically request under which subsections of IRC 6015 the RS is seeking relief. Instead, the Service will consider relief under subsections (b), (c), and (f).
2. Because of the amendment to IRC 6015(e) and the revision to Form 8857, consider a RS's claim for relief under all subsections of IRC 6015 no matter which revision of Form 8857 is used by the RS, even if the RS used a prior version of Form 8857 and only checked the box indicating equitable relief under IRC 6015(f).
3. A RS may only withdraw a request for relief prior to the issuance of a preliminary determination letter.

25.15.3.3 (07-29-2014)
Notification to Non-requesting Spouse (NRS) per IRC 6015(h)(2)

1. The non-requesting spouse (NRS) must receive notice of, and an opportunity to participate in, any proceeding with respect to an election of relief from joint and several liability under IRC 6015.

   Note:

   Always protect the privacy and return information of the RS, per IRC 6103, disclosure statute.

2. Examiners shall issue an administrative proceeding notice (Letter 3284C for CCISO and L 3284 for the field) to the NRS giving a 30 day response time.
3. Notice to the NRS is not required to be sent certified mail but must be sent to the NRS's last known address.
4. Examiners shall notify the NRS of the preliminary determination made, and the right to an administrative appeal when relief is fully or partially allowed to the RS. The NRS may file a protest and request an Appeals conference, see Rev. Proc. 2003–19.

Exception:

Do not provide appeals rights to the NRS if the NRS is no longer liable for the tax liabilities at issue, e.g., tax liabilities were discharged in the NRS's bankruptcy proceedings and/or offer-in-compromise, or the NRS's collection statute expiration date (CSED) has expired.

5. If relief is denied in full, inform the NRS that he/she will be contacted if the RS protests the determination and Appeals proposes to increase the amount of relief granted in the preliminary determination. Do not provide appeal rights to the NRS when the account is full paid and the RS has been granted full relief under IRC 6015(c). This is because no refunds may be made under IRC 6015(c) and the NRS will not be held liable for additional amounts.

25.15.3.3.1 (07-29-2014)
Notification to NRS in Cases of Alleged Abuse

1. For claims originating in the Cincinnati Centralized Innocent Spouse Operation (CCISO), the RS will be sent a notification letter informing them the NRS will be notified and given an opportunity to participate. This is not necessary for claims filed on Form 8857, revised June 2007 or later because the instructions include this information. If it is necessary, CCISO will hold the claim; pending a response from the RS. The letter informs the RS of the following options:
    A. Should they want to proceed, the notification letter to the NRS will be sent from CCISO as an added precaution to conceal the RS's geographic location. The RS's new name, address, telephone number, or employer will not be used in correspondence to the NRS. CCISO will delay sending the notification letter to the NRS, pending a response from the RS. The RS will forward any response to the unit or area working the claim. The preliminary determination letter to the NRS will also be issued by CCISO.
    B. If the RS does not want CCISO to contact the NRS, the RS needs to withdraw their claim as indicated in the letter. If the RS does not withdraw, continue processing.
2. For claims originating in an area office, the examiner will contact the RS to determine if there is a need to take additional precautions to conceal the RS's location. The instructions for claims filed on Form 8857, revised June 2007 or later, include this information, making it unnecessary to send a notification letter to an RS who uses the revised form. If so, the area examiner will send a cover letter with Letter 3284 to the NRS stating the examiner has been notified of the innocent spouse claim and will be working the issue along with the other exam issues. The RS's new name, address, telephone number, or employer must not be used in correspondence to the NRS. The NRS should be given 30 days to respond.

25.15.3.4 (05-01-2005)
Terms and Definitions

1. The following are definitions of terms used throughout this IRM section.

25.15.3.4.1 (07-20-2009)
Deficiency/Understatement

1. The term **understatement** is defined as:
    A. the excess of the amount of the tax required to be shown on the return for the taxable year, over
    B. the amount of tax imposed which is shown on the return, reduced by any rebate (within the meaning of IRC 6015(b)(3) and IRC 6211(b)(2)). See IRC 6662(d)(2)(A).

For IRC 6015 purposes, a deficiency and understatement are treated the same. A RS can be considered for relief under IRC 6015(b), IRC 6015(c), and IRC 6015(f) for a deficiency/understatement.

2. If the RS signed a Form 870, *Waiver of Restrictions on Assessment and Collection of Deficiency in Tax and Acceptance of Overassessment*, Form 4549, *Income Tax Examination Changes*, or other report agreeing to additional joint liability, then the liability should be treated as an understatement/deficiency and the RS may be considered for relief under IRC 6015(b), IRC 6015(c), and IRC 6015(f).

25.15.3.4.1.1 (03-08-2013)
Item

1. An **item** is that which is required to be separately listed on an individual income tax return or any required attachments. Interest and dividends from the same source are considered separate items. Items include, but are not limited to, gross income, deductions, credits, and cost basis.
2. Penalties and interest are not erroneous items and relief from penalties and interest follows relief granted on the underlying item(s).

   Note:

   Although no relief is available separately for penalties and interest under IRC 6015, under the right circumstances, penalties (not interest) may be abated for reasonable cause or other penalty relief provisions.

IF	THEN
RS would qualify for relief of tax under any section of IRC 6015	Grant relief for the corresponding penalties and interest
RS is eligible for relief from an underpayment under IRC 6015	Grant relief of the penalties and interest corresponding to the underpayment
RS is not eligible for relief from the tax	RS remains liable for the penalties and interest
RS only requests an abatement of penalties	Follow procedures in IRM 25.15.7.5.8(4), *Account Problems*

25.15.3.4.1.1.1 (03-08-2013)
Erroneous Item

1. An **erroneous item** is any item resulting in an understatement or deficiency in tax to the extent such item is omitted from, or improperly reported (or improperly characterized) on, an individual income tax return. Some examples would be:
   - Unreported income from an investment asset resulting in an understatement or deficiency in tax
   - Ordinary income improperly reported as capital gain resulting in an understatement or deficiency in tax
   - A deduction for an expense that is personal in nature that results in an understatement or deficiency in tax
   - An improperly reported item that affects the liability on other returns

25.15.3.4.2 (03-01-2011)
Underpayment

1. An **underpayment** is an unpaid amount due from self-assessed taxes on either an original or amended joint return if a statutory notice of deficiency was not issued. A RS can only be considered for relief under IRC 6015(f) for an underpayment.

25.15.3.4.2.1 (03-08-2013)
Overstated Withholding

1. Overstated withholding is considered an underpayment of tax and qualifies for consideration only under IRC 6015(f). Consider it jointly attributable unless the RS establishes he/she did not receive or benefit from the overstated withholding.
2. It does not matter whether the overstated withholding was refunded or not.

Example:

Tax on original return $6,000
Withholding claimed $10,000 (actual withholding = $0)
Refund $4,000
Automated Underreporter (AUR) operations issued a CP 2000 notice to reverse the withholding, resulting in $10,000 owed. The $10,000 owed is an underpayment. Relief will be considered under IRC 6015(f) only. The examiner should consider who received and benefited from the $4,000 refund when making a determination as to relief.

3. IRC 6201(a)(3) allows the Service to immediately assess the liability resulting from overstated withholding. Thus, if the overstated withholding was refunded, there should be a transaction code (TC) 290 containing a TC 807 in the amount of the overstated withholding on the taxpayer's module. The existence of the TC 290 should be verified as soon as the claim is accepted for processing. If the TC 290 is not there and the assessment statute expiration date (ASED) has not expired (which is generally three years from the filing date of the return), then action should be taken to have the assessment made before the ASED expires. If the ASED has expired, then the Service's collection alternatives are limited. An erroneous refund suit can be considered if conditions for such a suit are met. Any questions should be immediately referred to Area Counsel.

25.15.3.4.2.2 (07-29-2014)
Substitute for Return (SFR)

1. A taxpayer's filing status on a Substitute For Return (SFR) will be either single or married filing separately. The Service cannot elect joint filing status for married taxpayers; thus, there will not be a joint liability, and there can be no relief under IRC 6015 from a liability due to an SFR. The taxpayer may later file a joint return with his/her spouse. It is not until this joint return is filed that relief under IRC 6015 can even be considered. The important thing to remember when determining whether relief under IRC 6015(b), IRC 6015(c), or IRC 6015(f) is available is the type of liability (underpayment versus understatement) generated by the joint return.

Caution:

Some prior processing issues have caused some SFR assessments to pick up the previous joint name line in the entity area. These accounts do not have a joint filing status only a joint name line. In this situation, SFR should be contacted to correct the account.

2. If the Service filed an SFR for a nonfiler spouse (and took no action against the other spouse) and the spouses later file a joint tax return before the issuance of a Statutory Notice of Deficiency, this joint return should be considered the spouse's original return for purposes of relief under IRC 6015. If the joint return properly reported all income but was not accompanied by full payment of the tax liability, the liability is an underpayment (self-assessed tax). Thus, if either the nonfiler spouse or the other spouse requests relief under IRC 6015 for this joint liability, only relief under IRC 6015(f) can be considered. If the joint return underreports income, and the Service determined a deficiency, then IRC 6015(b), IRC 6015(c), and IRC 6015(f) can be considered for either spouse for the portion that is a deficiency.
3. If the Service filed an SFR for a nonfiler spouse (and took no action against the other spouse) and an assessment was made following a Statutory Notice of Deficiency, the resulting amount owed by the nonfiler spouse is a liability due to a deficiency assessment. However, because no joint election was made, the taxpayer's liability is not eligible for relief under IRC 6015. If the nonfiler spouse and the other spouse later file a joint return that properly reported all income but

was not accompanied by full payment of the tax liability, the liability should be considered an underpayment. Thus, if either the nonfiler spouse or the other spouse requests relief under IRC 6015 for this joint liability, only relief under IRC 6015(f) can be considered. If the joint return underreports income, and the Service determines a deficiency, then IRC 6015(b), IRC 6015(c), and IRC 6015(f) can be considered for either spouse for the portion that is a deficiency.

4. If the Service filed an SFR for a nonfiler, the taxpayer may file a joint return in response. In some circumstances the service will process the return but keep the exam open because there are items still under review. See IRM 4.19.17.7.2.2, *Agreed – Partially Accepted.* In this circumstance the taxpayer and the taxpayer's spouse may sign an examination report or similar waiver agreeing to the tax prior to the issuance of a Statutory Notice of Deficiency. If this occurs the tax liability is considered an understatement. This is because signing a report or waiver is not the equivalent of signing and filing a joint return.

25.15.3.4.3 (03-08-2013)
Math Error

1. See IRM 25.15.7.5.15, *Math Error*, for instructions.

25.15.3.4.4 (03-08-2013)
Collection Activity

1. The RS must file a claim for relief under IRC 6015(b) and IRC 6015(c) with the Service no later than two years from the date of the first collection activity against the RS after July 22, 1998, with respect to the joint tax liability. Claims for equitable relief under IRC 6015 (f) are no longer subject to a two-year deadline. Collection activity against the RS means collection against property in which the RS has an ownership interest (other than solely through the operation of community property laws), including property owned jointly with the NRS. Because not all events that involve the Service's attempt to collect the liability will trigger the two year period, examiners should exercise caution when determining if an IRC 6015(b) or IRC 6015(c) claim is time barred. Collection activity for this purpose should not be confused with "prohibited collection actions." *IRM 25.15.3.4.5, Prohibited Collection Actions.*

   Note:

   Notice 2011–70 lifted the two-year rule deadline for claims filed under IRC 6015(f). A claim will be timely filed under IRC 6015(f) as long as it is filed within the time period the collection statute or refund statute remains open.

   Note:

   Per IRC 7502, timely mailing is treated as timely filing, so when the claim received date is past the two-year deadline for filing a claim, look at the *postmark date*. If the postmark date is prior to the two-year deadline, consider the claim timely.

2. The following actions by the Service constitute collection activity:
   - **Refund offsets:** The offset of an overpayment of the RS against the joint liability under IRC 6402 constitutes collection activity. See *Campbell v. Commissioner*, 121 T.C. 290 (2003), see also Treas. Reg. 1.6015–5(b).

     Note:

In *McGee v. Commissioner*, 123 T.C. 314 (2004), the Tax Court held that an IRC 6402 offset alone will not trigger the two year period for filing a claim unless the Service at the time of the offset notifies the RS of his or her right to file a claim for relief under IRC 6015. Prior to this court decision, the Service did not routinely notify taxpayers of their right to file an IRC 6015 claim at the time of the offset. On or about March 7, 2005, the Service began to provide this notice by including Publication 1 as a stuffer with all refund offset notices, and in August 2005, the offset notices themselves included language explaining the taxpayers' right to file an IRC 6015 claim. Thus, if the offset occurred prior to March 7, 2005, you should consider the claim to be timely unless there is evidence that the Service notified the RS, or the RS was otherwise aware, of his or her right to file an IRC 6015 claim at the time of the offset.

Note:

Now that more than two years have elapsed since Publication 1, *Your Rights as a Taxpayer* started being a stuffer with the refund offset notice and/or the refund offset notice itself started containing language explaining the taxpayers' right to file an IRC 6015, careful attention should be made to cases in which the Service offset a refund in April 2005 or later, especially those refunds offset after August 2005. If the Form 8857 was filed more than two years after such offset, the claim should be denied under IRC 6015(b) and IRC 6015(c).

- **IRC 6330 notices:** For claims filed on or after July 18, 2002, the sending of an IRC 6330 notice to the taxpayer will trigger the two year period for filing a claim under IRC 6015(b) and IRC 6015(c). An IRC 6330 notice is the notice sent pursuant to IRC 6330 which provides the taxpayer with notice of the Service's intent to levy and of their right to a Collection Due Process (CDP) hearing. A CDP notice will not start the two year period for filing a claim under IRC 6015(b) and IRC 6015(c) unless the CDP notice informs the taxpayer of the taxpayer's right to file a claim under IRC 6015. The Service has been informing taxpayers of the innocent spouse claim process through the inclusion of Publication 594, *The IRS Collection Process* as a stuffer with the CDP notice (either LT11 or Letter 1058). Based on the language discussing innocent spouse relief in versions of Publication 594, prior to May 2002 in cases where the Form 8857 was filed more than two years after a CDP Notice issued prior to May 2002, the Service should treat the claim for relief as being timely filed unless another collection activity occurred more than two years prior to the filing of the innocent spouse claim filed under IRC 6015(b) or IRC 6015(c) or if filed after the collection statute has expired under IRC 6015(f).

Example:

The claim for relief under IRC 6015(b) was filed on September 1, 2005, and the IRC 6330 notice was issued January 3, 2002. Although the claim for relief was filed more than two years after the issuance of the CDP Notice, this claim should be treated as timely filed because the notification of the taxpayer's right to file an innocent spouse claim that was included with the CDP notice was not sufficient. If, however, the CDP Notice was issued on January 3, 2003, then the discussion of the innocent spouse claim process in Publication 594 would have been sufficient to start the two year period. Thus, the election or request for relief must have been made by January 3, 2005. As the Form 8857 was not received until September 1, 2005, the claim is not timely filed.

Note:

For claims for relief filed on or after July 18, 2002, a TC 971 action code (AC) 069 on TXMOD, which represents the issuance of an IRC 6330 CDP notice, dated May 2002 or later will be considered the date from which the two year period runs. When an IRC 6330 notice starts the collection activity against the RS, there must be a TC 971 AC 069 present on the account for the RS. If the RS is the secondary taxpayer, the TC 971 AC 069 must contain a cross-reference (XREF) taxpayer identification number (TIN). If the RS's TC 971 AC 069 is followed by a TC 971 AC 068, the notice was returned as undeliverable, and the TC 971 AC 069 is not considered the start of collection activity against the RS. A TC 971 AC 469 indicates the IRS received no response from the Post Office; so, the TC 971 AC 069 does not start the collection activity against the RS.

- **The filing of a suit by the United States against the RS for the collection of a joint tax liability**: Triggers the two year period for claims filed under IRC 6015(b) and IRC 6015(c). If a collection suit was filed, the two year period will begin to run from date the suit is filed. See Treas. Reg. 1.6015-5(b)(4), example 4. The transcript will not state that a collection suit has been commenced by the Department of Justice (DOJ). When an examiner sees a general litigation code (TC 520 with closing code 70 ,75, 78-81, or 84) with a date more than two years before the claim is filed on a transcript, the examiner should investigate to determine if the DOJ commenced a collection suit against the RS (or filed a claim in a court proceeding to collect the RS's property more than two years before the claim was filed). A collection suit cannot be commenced in Tax Court. Thus, if the examiner sees a Tax Court litigation code (TC 520 with a 72 or 74 closing code), the examiner does not need to investigate any further (although that could be an indication that this matter was tried before, which could mean that the claim is barred by res judicata). *IRM 25.15.3.5.2, Collateral Estoppel.*

  Note:

  The two year period begins to run when the RS is named as a defendant in a complaint filed in a suit to reduce tax assessments to judgement or to foreclose even though the tax lien may not list specific assets the Service wishes to collect from.

- **Claims in judicial proceedings**: The filing of a claim by the Service in a court proceeding in which the RS is a party, or which involves the property of the RS, including claims in bankruptcy and claims in interpleader (a legal proceeding brought by a disinterested third party to determine the rightful claim to property of competing claimants) actions involving property of the RS also triggers the two year period.

  Example:

  Proof of claims (POC) filed in bankruptcy. The examiner should look at the transcripts to see if a bankruptcy litigation code is present more than two years before the IRC 6015(b) and IRC 6015(c) claim was filed. If this situation is present, the examiner should investigate to determine if the government filed a POC. First, the examiner should contact the bankruptcy unit that handled the bankruptcy case. This office should be able to obtain information regarding whether a POC was filed. If a POC was filed, the examiner should try and obtain from the Insolvency unit a filed stamped copy of the POC, along with any documentation that would establish who was served with a copy of the POC, and at what address.

  Example:

  Claims in other proceedings. Again, a general litigation code on the transcript indicates a possible claim in a judicial proceeding. If the general litigation code appears on the transcript, the examiner should contact the Chief Counsel attorney who handled the case to discuss whether a collection suit, discussed above, or claim in another proceeding was filed. The Chief Counsel attorney should be able to ascertain whether a claim was ever filed, and if so, the date the claim was filed. The two year period will begin on the date the claim was filed. In these situations, the examiner should request that the field attorney provide the examiner with copies of any documentation which establishes the date that the RS was served with a copy of the claim.

3. **"Collection activity" does not** include the following IRS actions:
   - Notices of deficiency
   - Demands for payment of tax
   - Notices of federal tax lien
4. There may be cases in which there has been no collection activity as described above, even though the RS may have received numerous demands for payment or other generic notices. Thus, the two year period for filing a claim for relief under IRC 6015(b) and IRC 6015(c) may not have expired on certain old and inactive balance due cases.

25.15.3.4.5 (03-08-2013)
Prohibited Collection Actions

1. IRC 6015(e)(1)(B) generally prohibits levies and judicial proceedings while an innocent spouse claim is pending. Refund offsets are not prohibited by statute. However, the Service has made a business decision not to offset refunds while a claim is pending.
2. If a prohibited collection action or a refund offset has occurred in violation of paragraph 1 above, corrective measures must be taken to refund the money to the RS.

25.15.3.5 (03-01-2011)
Special Considerations

1. Prior court decisions on a given tax year may affect whether a request for relief from joint and several liability can be considered. These are not limited to Tax Court decisions. These doctrines also apply to other court decisions. These actions are defined below:
   - Res Judicata - *IRM 25.15.3.5.1, Res Judicata*, discusses the principles of res judicata.
   - Collateral Estoppel - *IRM 25.15.3.5.2, Collateral Estoppel*, discusses collateral estoppel.
2. If the only basis for not considering or initially denying a claim under IRC 6015(c) was that the RS was still married when the original claim was made, and RS files a new claim, then res judicata does not apply to bar the new claim under IRC 6015(c) only.

25.15.3.5.1 (07-29-2014)
Res Judicata

1. **Res Judicata** - Res judicata generally precludes **any kind of claim** for a tax year previously litigated. In the case of any claim for relief under IRC 6015, if any court has rendered a final decision on the RS's tax liability for a tax year, such decision shall be conclusive if relief under IRC 6015 was at issue in the prior case or if the RS meaningfully participated in the proceeding and the RS could have raised relief under IRC 6015 in that proceeding. See IRC 6015(g)(2).
   A. A RS has not meaningfully participated in a proceeding prior to July 22, 1998 since, due to the effective date of IRC 6015, relief under IRC 6015 was not available in that proceeding.
   B. Res Judicata does not apply to criminal tax cases if the civil income tax liabilities were not, and could not have been, at issue.
2. **Final Tax Court Decision Prior to July 22, 1998** - A taxpayer who has unsuccessfully litigated his/her entitlement to innocent spouse relief under the prior law of IRC 6013(e) may elect relief under the new provision of IRC 6015 for the same year if a portion of the tax liability remains unpaid as of July 22, 1998. See Treas. Reg. 1.6015-1(e).
3. **Final Tax Court Decision on or after July 22, 1998** — If the issues creating the deficiency were the subject of a prior Tax Court decision entered on or after July 22, 1998, and the spouse seeking relief did not raise the issue of his/her eligibility for relief under IRC 6015 in that proceeding, the spouse may not raise it subsequently if the court determines the RS "participated meaningfully" (actively participated) in the prior proceeding. See Treas. Reg. 1.6015–1(e).
4. **Res Judicata and Bankruptcy** - Not all bankruptcy proceedings determine the merits of the tax liability; some bankruptcy proceedings merely determine the collectibility of the tax liability. If the merits of the tax liability were at issue in the bankruptcy proceeding, the RS meaningfully participated in the proceeding, and relief under IRC 6015 was raised or could have been raised, then res judicata applies and the RS is precluded from raising a subsequent request for relief under IRC 6015. If the merits of the tax liability were not at issue during the bankruptcy proceeding, res judicata will not apply and the RS will not be barred from making a subsequent request for relief under IRC 6015.
5. If the only basis for not considering or initially denying a claim under **IRC 6015(c)** was that the RS was still married when the original claim was made, and RS files a new claim, then res judicata does not apply to bar the new claim under IRC 6015(c) only.
6. **Criminal Tax Court**- Res Judicata does not apply to criminal tax cases if the civil income tax liabilities are not at issue.

25.15.3.5.2 (03-08-2013)
Collateral Estoppel

1. Collateral Estoppel, also known as issue preclusion, is a legal doctrine, which holds the findings of fact or law of a prior judicial decision are binding in a subsequent proceeding between the same parties. When collateral estoppel applies, the taxpayer is prohibited from litigating an issue that was identical to an issue previously litigated, which was part of a valid final judgment.

 Example:

 In tax year 1, the Tax Court determines that the requesting spouse was not entitled to relief under section IRC 6015(b) because he or she had knowledge of income from an illegal business operated by the non-requesting spouse. Under the doctrine of **res judicata** (see *IRM 25.15.3.5.1*), the requesting spouse could not subsequently request relief under section 6015(f) for tax year 1. The innocent spouse determination made by the Tax Court is **res judicata** for tax year 1 because the decision is final and the requesting spouse could have raised relief under (f) in that prior proceeding. However, for tax year 2, even if the requesting spouse was determined to have actual knowledge of the same illegal business in tax year 1, the requesting spouse would not be precluded from requesting relief under section 6015(f) as knowledge is only one factor to be determined under section 6015(f).
 Under the doctrine of **collateral estoppel**, the requesting spouse would be precluded from arguing that he or she did not have knowledge of the illegal business in a subsequent proceeding because the identical issue was litigated and determined by the Tax Court in its determination of tax year 1. But, collateral estoppel will not preclude the requesting spouse from raising the additional factors to be considered for relief under section 6015(f) as those factors had not been litigated and determined in the prior Tax Court proceeding.

25.15.3.5.3 (02-25-2010)
Issuance of a Second Final Determination Letter Under IRC 6015

1. Refer to IRM 25.15.17, *Reconsiderations*, for information on circumstances that allow for issuance of a second final determination letter.

25.15.3.5.4 (05-01-2005)
Prior Accepted Offer in Compromise (OIC)

1. Refer to IRM 25.15.1.2.7, *Offer in Compromise (OIC)*, for information on an OIC accepted prior to the filing of the Form 8857, *Request for Innocent Spouse Relief.*

25.15.3.5.4.1 (05-01-2005)
Pending Offer in Compromise

1. Refer to IRM 25.15.1.2.7, *Offer in Compromise (OIC)*, for information on a pending OIC.

25.15.3.5.5 (03-01-2011)
Closing Agreements

1. A closing agreement, Form 866, *Agreement as to Final Determination of Tax Liability*, closes with finality the tax year and the type of tax to which it relates. See Treas. Reg. 301.7121-1(c). If a taxpayer signed a Form 866, he or she is precluded from consideration for relief from joint and several liability.

2. A closing agreement, Form 906, *Closing Agreement on Final Determination Covering Specific Matters*, will generally relate to a specific matter or matters for a tax period, rather than to the entire liability. Only those matters covered in the closing agreement are conclusively closed. A taxpayer may request innocent spouse relief for adjustments not specifically covered in the closing agreement.
3. If the RS was not a party to the closing agreement, using either Form 866 or Form 906, then the RS may file an innocent spouse claim for that year if the RS is otherwise eligible.
4. Execution of a Form 870-AD, *Offer to Waive Restrictions on Assessment and Collection of Tax Deficiency and to Accept Overassessment*, by the RS is not considered a closing agreement and does not preclude consideration for relief.
5. Tax Equity and Fiscal Responsibility Act (TEFRA) Settlement Agreements are addressed in IRM 25.15.1.2.8, *Tax Equity and Fiscal Responsibility Act (TEFRA) Settlement Agreements.*

25.15.3.5.6 (07-29-2014)
Understatements Resulting From an Increase to Adjusted Gross Income

1. If an erroneous item (as defined in *IRM 25.15.3.4.1.1.1*) that is attributable to the NRS increases the adjusted gross income (AGI) and results in disallowance of another item on the return because of the increase to AGI, then any understatement caused by the disallowance of the other item will also be attributable to the NRS. This rule is applicable whether or not the RS received a refund (or a portion of a refund) due to the item.

   Example:

   A joint return shows a tax liability of $500 and an earned income tax credit (EITC) in the amount of $1500 which results in a refund of $1000. Upon examination NRS had additional unreported income that increased the tax liability on the return to $1000. In addition, the increase to the AGI from the unreported income resulted in the EITC being disallowed in full because the AGI now exceeded the maximum amount. The IRS determines a deficiency in the amount of $2000 ($500 from the unreported income and $1500 from the disallowed EITC). If RS requests relief under IRC 6015, the entire $2000 deficiency will be attributable to NRS because the EITC was disallowed solely due to the increase to adjusted gross income (AGI) of NRS's unreported income. Thus, RS will satisfy the attribution factors of IRC 6015(b) and IRC 6015(f). For purposes of IRC 6015(c) the deficiency related to the EITC will be initially allocated to NRS.

   Exception:

   This does not apply to the RS's social security benefits. The social security benefits will be attributable to the RS.

2. When credits are reduced or eliminated due to the increase in AGI, the changes are attributable to what caused the increase to AGI.

   Example:

   If the NRS's income caused the increase to AGI, the reduced or eliminated credits are attributable to the NRS.

3. When the education credits are reduced or eliminated due to lack of verification, then it will be attributable to the party actually having the education expenses. If the credit is due to a child having the expenses, then allocate by percentage. It is important to know why the education credit was reduced.
4. For purposes of determining whether a RS knew or had reason to know of the item that was disallowed due to the increase in AGI, the RS's knowledge or reason to know regarding the erroneous item that resulted in the increase in AGI will control.

   Example:

Thus, in the example (1) above, if RS knew or had reason to know of NRS's unreported income, then RS will have knowledge or reason to know of the deficiency related to the EITC. On the other hand, if RS did not know or have reason to know of NRS's unreported income, then RS will not have knowledge of reason to know of the deficiency related to the EITC.

5. If the item is attributable to the NRS and the RS is determined to not have knowledge or reason to know of the item, other factors still need to be evaluated.
6. For purposes of IRC 6015(b), the claim would still need to be timely and it would have to be inequitable to hold the RS liable (see *IRM 25.15.3.6.4*(1) *Inequitable to Hold Requesting Spouse Liable).*
7. Other examples of items that might result in an understatement due to an increase to AGI include, but are not limited to, itemized deductions, alternative minimum tax, student loan interest adjustment, and other credits.
8. These rules do not apply if there is another reason for disallowing the item, such as not having a qualifying child for the EITC or lacking substantiation for a claimed deduction. In that situation, the normal attribution and knowledge rules apply.

25.15.3.6 (09-01-2006)
IRC 6015(b) — Innocent Spouse Relief Qualifications

1. To qualify for innocent spouse relief under IRC 6015(b), the RS must establish each of the following elements:
   A. A joint return was filed for the year in which relief is requested;
   B. There is an understatement of tax, see *IRM 25.15.3.4.1*, *Deficiency/Understatement*, attributable to erroneous items of the NRS;
   C. The RS did not know and had no reason to know of the understatement at the time the return was signed;
   D. Taking into account all the facts and circumstances, it would be inequitable to hold the RS liable for the deficiency attributable to the understatement; and
   E. The request for relief is made within two years from the date of the first collection activity (with respect to the RS) after July 22, 1998.

25.15.3.6.1 (03-08-2013)
Joint Return

1. The **first** requirement is that there **must** be a joint return filed for the year for which relief is requested. If a joint return was not filed, relief under IRC 6015(b) is not available. If the RS is domiciled in a community property state, IRC 66 treatment may be available. See IRM 25.15.5*Relief from Community Property Laws/Community Property States.*

25.15.3.6.2 (03-08-2013)
Understatement Attributable to Erroneous Item of the Other Spouse

1. The **second** requirement provides there must be an understatement of tax attributable to erroneous items of the NRS. Attribution is a critical factor. Items attributable to the RS do not qualify for relief. You cannot be relieved of tax on your own items including joint items. In most cases, examiners should first consider attribution before other factors.
2. Math errors under IRC 6213(g)(2) are generally considered to be deficiencies for innocent spouse purposes of determining relief under IRC 6015. However, math error adjustments to withholding and estimated tax are not considered deficiency assessments. See IRC 6211(b)(1) and IRM 25.15.7.5.15, *Math Error.*
3. See *IRM 25.15.3.4.1*, *Deficiency/Understatement*, for a definition of an **understatement** of tax.
4. See *IRM 25.15.3.4.1.1.1*, *Erroneous Item*, for a definition of an **erroneous item**.

25.15.3.6.3 (03-08-2013)
Actual and Constructive Knowledge

1. The **third** requirement under IRC 6015(b) is that the RS did not know and had no reason to know of the understatement at the time the tax return was signed.
2. There are 2 standards that must be considered under this requirement:
   - Lack of **actual** knowledge ("did not know"); **and,**
   - Lack of **constructive** knowledge ("had no reason to know").

   Note:

   If a RS establishes he or she was the victim of domestic abuse prior to the time the return was signed, but did not sign the return under duress (which might invalidate the joint election), and as a result of the prior abuse, did not challenge any of the items on the return for fear of retaliation, the actual knowledge or reason to know, of IRC 6015(b) will not apply.

3. The examiner should consider the following factors (but, not limited to):
   - Nature of the erroneous item and the amount of the erroneous item relative to other items
   - The couple's financial situation
   - The RS's educational background and business experience
   - The extent of the RS's participation in the activity that resulted in the erroneous item
   - Whether the RS failed to inquire, at or before the time the return was filed, about items on the return or omitted from the return that a reasonable person would question
   - Whether the erroneous item represented a departure from a recurring pattern reflected in prior year's returns
4. See Treas. Reg. 1.6015-2(c).

25.15.3.6.4 (03-08-2013)
Inequitable to Hold Requesting Spouse Liable

1. The **fourth** requirement under IRC 6015(b) provides that, considering all the facts and circumstances, it is inequitable to hold the RS liable for the deficiency.
2. A determination of whether it is inequitable to hold the spouse liable is based on factors in IRC 6015(f). see *IRM 25.15.3.8, IRC 6015(f) Equitable Relief*, for a further discussion of equitable relief under IRC 6015(f).
3. These guidelines should be applied in a consistent and nondiscriminatory manner. Decisions to grant relief should not be based on the subjective personal and social beliefs of the IRS employee or any other inappropriate grounds.

25.15.3.6.5 (09-01-2006)
Time Period for Making Election

1. The **fifth** requirement under IRC 6015(b) is that the RS must make an election under IRC 6015(b) within two years from the first collection activity against the RS that occurred after July 22, 1998. See *IRM 25.15.3.4.4, Collection Activity*, for the definition of collection activity.

25.15.3.6.6 (03-01-2011)
Partial Relief Available

1. Partial relief may be granted when a spouse meets all of the other conditions for innocent spouse, except he or she had knowledge of, or reason to know of, some part of the understatement. IRC 6015(b) specifically allows partial relief from liability (including penalties, interest and other amounts) to the extent of the lack of knowledge and reason to know of the understatement. See Treas. Reg. 1.6015–2(e).

   Note:

The knowledge requirement applies to each item of adjustment and to the extent of the knowledge of each erroneous item.

Note:

= =
= =
= =
= = = = = = = = = = = = = = = = =

25.15.3.7 (03-08-2013)
IRC 6015(c) – Election to Allocate a Deficiency

1. An individual may request to allocate a deficiency under IRC 6015(c).
2. Both parties to a joint return may elect to allocate a deficiency. If only one spouse elects to allocate the deficiency, the liability of the NRS is not affected. The NRS would still be liable for the entire deficiency.
3. The election to allocate applies only to deficiencies.
4. If granted, the RS is relieved in whole or in part of the joint and several liability for the deficiency. The items giving rise to the deficiency are allocated in the same manner as they would have been if the spouses had filed separate returns. The analogy to separate returns goes to the allocation of items adjusted, not to the computation of allocable tax due to a separate return.

   Note:

   Refunds are not allowed under IRC 6015(c). Treat as a full allowance when granting relief under IRC 6015(c) for the balance due but not refunding any money.

5. The allocation is made without regard to community property law.

25.15.3.7.1 (03-08-2013)
Qualifications

1. To qualify for relief under IRC 6015(c), the RS must establish:
   A. A joint return was filed for the year in which relief was requested.
   B. There is a deficiency of tax attributable to erroneous items of the NRS. A spouse may be relieved for a portion of the tax liability arising from a joint item.
   C. He or she is either divorced, widowed, legally separated, or living apart for the 12 month period prior to the date the request was filed. Living apart for the 12 month period prior to the date the request was filed does not include a spouse who is temporarily absent from the household. A temporary absence exists if it is reasonable to assume the absent spouse will return to the household, or a substantially equivalent household is maintained in anticipation of such a return. Some examples may include absence due to incarceration, illness, business, vacation, military service, or education. Treas. Reg. section 1.6015-3 provides that the marital status of a deceased RS will be determined on the earlier of the date of election or the date of death in accordance with IRC 7703(a)(1). The regulations also clarify a husband and wife who reside in two separate dwellings are considered members of the same household if the spouses are not estranged, or one spouse is temporarily absent.
   D. The request for relief is made within two years from the date of the first collection activity (with respect to the RS) after July 22, 1998. The two year time period for making the election is the same as required under IRC 6015(b). See *IRM 25.15.3.6.5, Time Period for Making Election.*

25.15.3.7.1.1 (03-01-2011)
Actual Knowledge Invalidates Allocation

1. The **Service has the burden** of proving by a preponderance of the evidence that the RS had **actual knowledge** of the items giving rise to the deficiency **at the time the return was signed**. See IRC 6015(c)(3)(c).
2. This differs from the standard for relief under IRC 6015(b) which places the burden on the RS to establish he or she did not know and had no reason to know of the understatement. "Did not know" and "had no reason to know" are sometimes referred to as actual and constructive knowledge, respectively. A spouse who was disqualified for innocent spouse relief due to constructive knowledge under IRC 6015(b) may qualify for relief under IRC 6015(c) if he or she did not have actual knowledge.
3. In an omitted income case, actual knowledge includes knowledge of the receipt of the income. Knowledge of **only** the source of the income is not sufficient. Actual knowledge in an erroneous deduction or credit case means knowledge of the facts that made the item not allowable as a credit or a deduction. For example, in an erroneous deduction case involving disallowed deductions generated by a partnership, the Service must establish that the RS had actual knowledge of the factual circumstances which made the partnership items erroneous deductions. See Treas. Reg. 1.6015–3(c)(2).
4. **Actual knowledge of a portion** of the deficiency does not make the spouse ineligible for IRC 6015(c) relief for the entire deficiency. It **merely invalidates the allocation with respect to the specific items** for which the spouse had actual knowledge.

25.15.3.7.2 (05-01-2005)
Allocating a Deficiency Under IRC 6015(d)

1. The allocation must be made according to the procedures contained in IRC 6015(d). The allocation takes into consideration limitations in IRC 6015(c).

25.15.3.7.2.1 (07-29-2014)
Steps to Allocate

1. The following is an eight step approach to allocating understatements between the joint and several liability and each spouse individually. **In general, items for which the RS is granted relief are re-allocated from the joint liability to the NRS individually. Items for which relief is not granted remain part of the joint and several liability**.
2. The seven steps are summarized in the following table.

Step #	Action
1	**Determine the total deficiency** for the joint return with all adjustments.
2	**Identify and allocate separate treatment items** (credits and taxes other than tax imposed by IRC 1 or IRC 55). See *IRM 25.15.3.7.2.2.1, Separate Treatment Items.*
3	**Compute the total allocable deficiency.** This is done in order to allocate income tax before credits and other taxes. Therefore, disallowed credit items are subtracted from the total deficiency. Other taxes increased are also subtracted from the total deficiency. When applicable, credit `items increased and other taxes decreased are added back to the total deficiency. **Joint deficiency (Step 1) -/+ Separate treatment items (Step 2) = Total Allocable Deficiency (Step 3)**

Step #	Action
4	**Allocate all adjustment items between the spouses.** The allocation takes into account the following considerations, discussed in further detail below: • Actual knowledge bars relief for the item. • Fraudulent transfers invalidate election. • RS bears burden of proof for establishing the portion of deficiency allocable to them. • Allocate as if the spouses filed separate returns. • Ignoring separate return limitations. • Tax benefit limitation. • When an understatement is due to fraud. • There is no relief for items attributable to RS. **Note:** A RS can obtain relief from his or her own item to the extent that the RS does not receive a tax benefit from the item and the item offsets the NRS's income. See *Hopkins v. Commissioner* 121 TC 73 (2003). In these instances, the Service must establish that the RS had actual knowledge to invalidate the allocation to the NRS, or the RS will be able to obtain relief.
5	**Compute the allocable deficiency for each spouse.** This is the portion of the total allocable deficiency (Step 3) allocated to each spouse using the ratio of the adjustment items allocable to the spouse (Step 4) over the total of all allocable adjustment items. Percentage of adjustments allocated to the spouse (Step 4) x Total allocable deficiency (Step 3) = **Deficiency Allocable to a spouse (Step 6)**
6	**Compute the total deficiency** allocable to each spouse. This is a two-step process: • The allocable deficiency is adjusted for Separate Treatment Items (See *IRM 25.15.3.7.2.2.1*, *Separate Treatment Items*. Essentially they are removed from the total deficiency in Step 2 and put back in at Step 7. The result is the Tentative Total Deficiency Allocable to Spouse. Deficiency allocable to Spouse (Step 5) +/- Separate treatment tax items (Step 2) = **Tentative total deficiency allocable to spouse** **Note:** The total of the joint liability plus each spouse's allocated individual liability should equal the total deficiency before any allocation.
7	**Compute and adjust for any change to the EITC.** • Compute the allocation of the EITC per *IRM 25.15.3.7.2.1.1Allocation of Earned Income Tax Credit (EITC)*. Take the **Tentative total deficiency allocable to Spouse** + The **decrease** in EITC - The **increase** in EITC = **Total Deficiency Allocated to each spouse**
8	**Consider Exceptions and Special Rules** (see *IRM 25.15.3.7.2.2Special Rules and Exceptions*). Adjustment is

Step #	Action
	made for items that affect the deficiency such as: • Tax Benefit • Disqualified Assets • Household Employment Taxes • Child's Liability

3. The TC 240 penalty should be allocated based on how it was originally assessed and what the RS is being relieved of. To do this:

    A. Determine what the original TC 240 was assessed on. The type of TC 240 penalty can be determined by the reference number; e.g., ref. number 680 means that it is an accuracy related penalty.
    B. If the amount of tax you are relieving the RS of had the TC 240 assessed, abate the TC 240 for that portion, using the applicable reference number.

25.15.3.7.2.1.1 (07-29-2014)
Allocation of Earned Income Tax Credit (EITC)

1. Rev. Rul. 87-52 allows for allocation of the Earned Income Tax Credit (EITC) shown on the joint return. If EITC is not shown on the joint return, do not figure EITC on the allocation.
2. Use the appropriate EITC table and worksheet, or CC EICMP with definer R for the tax year for which the form is being worked.
3. Determine a new, separate EITC that would be available for each spouse if that spouse had filed a separate return and if EITC were available on a married filing separately return. This is a theoretical situation used for computation only.
4. Compute each spouse's separate EITC, based on each individual's **earned income**, using the same number of qualifying dependents used to compute the EITC on the joint return.
    A. Do not split the qualifying dependents between the spouses.
    B. Use the same column in the EITC table as used to determine the EITC on the original joint return.
5. Figure the RS percentage of EITC by dividing the RS's new separate EITC by the sum of the EITC for both spouses and multiply the percentage by the amount allowed on the joint return. See below for an example.

    Example:

    2012 Joint tax return with income from wages totalling 35,000. There are two qualifying children. NRS wages = $25,000 and the RS wages = $10,000. The EITC on this return is $2,550.

    - Calculate EITC for each spouse based on a single filing status with 2 qualifying children.
      NRS income consists of $25,000 in wages. EITC is $3,560.00.
      RS income consists of $10,000 in wages. EITC is $4,010.00.
    - Calculate percentages.
      Add the EITC amounts together 3,560 + 4,010 = 7,570
      NRS 3,560 divided by 7,570 = 47%
      RS 4,010 divided by 7,570 = 53%
    - Calculate EITC allocation of the $2,550 on the joint return.
      NRS 2,550 X .47 = $1,198.50
      RS 2,550 X .53 = $1,351.50

Note:

If the allocation using the above formula results in no EITC for both spouses due to a loss claimed on the joint return, the EITC is allocated to the spouse claiming the loss, since it is that loss that qualified the joint account for the EITC.

6. See *IRM 25.15.3.7.2.1.1.1Use of Heartland Disaster Tax Relief Act of 2008 Provisions When Allocating EITC*, if taxpayers are using their 2007 earned income to figure their EITC for 2008.

25.15.3.7.2.1.1.1 (07-29-2014)
Use of Heartland Disaster Tax Relief Act of 2008 Provisions When Allocating EITC

1. Provisions of the Heartland Disaster Tax Relief Act of 2008 allow impacted taxpayers to use their 2007 earned income for purposes of figuring any EITC for 2008 if the 2008 earned income is less than the 2007 earned income and:
   - the main home on the applicable disaster date was in a Midwestern disaster area listed in Table 1 of Publication 4492-B, Information for Affected Taxpayers in the Midwestern Disaster Areas; or
   - the main home on the applicable disaster date was in a Midwestern disaster area as shown in Table 2 and the taxpayer was displaced from that home because of the severe storms, tornadoes, or flooding.
2. If the taxpayer qualifies to use their 2007 earned income, you will determine the EITC allocation based on the 2007 income not the 2008 income.

25.15.3 Technical Provisions of IRC 6015 (Cont. 1)

25.15.3.7
IRC 6015(c) – Election to Allocate a Deficiency

25.15.3.7.2
Allocating a Deficiency Under IRC 6015(d)

25.15.3.7.2.2 (07-29-2014)
Special Rules and Exceptions

1. The following is a discussion of the special rules and exceptions indicated in allocation Steps 2, 4, 6 and 8 in *IRM 25.15.3.7.2.1*(2).

25.15.3.7.2.2.1 (03-08-2013)
Separate Treatment Items

1. Separate treatment items are **(nonrefundable) credits and taxes only.** They affect the deficiency dollar for dollar in the allocation computation. Examples include:
   A. Child and Dependent Care Credit,
   B. Child Tax Credit,
   C. Education Credits, and
   D. Self-employment (SE) Tax and the 10 percent penalty for early withdrawal of an Individual Retirement Account (IRA) Tax. This does not include income tax or alternative minimum tax under IRC 1 and IRC 55.
2. Because separate treatment items affect the deficiency dollar for dollar, they are allocated separately from the other adjustment items. The separate treatment items that were adjusted should be totaled and subtracted from the total

deficiency to arrive at a figure that represents only income tax. After the proportionate deficiency (the "only" income tax figure) is allocated between the spouse, then the separate treatment items are allocated between the spouses based on who they belong to and added to their share of the proportionate deficiency.

3. **Underpayment** - Separate treatment items creating a balance due are allocated based on who they belong to.

   Note:

   When allocating the non-refundable credits, allocate 50/50 unless the RS's tax is less than the amount of the credit. If that is the case apply that amount to the RS and the remainder on the NRS.

   Note:

   Refundable credits, other than the EITC, are allocated based on the percentage of income.

4. **Understatement** - When the credit is reduced or eliminated due to the increase in AGI, the changes are attributable based on where the increase is in the AGI See *IRM 25.15.3.5.6, Understatements Resulting From an Increase to Adjusted Gross Income.*

   Example:

   If it is the NRS's income that caused the increase to AGI, it would be attributable to the NRS, much like EITC and Additional Child Tax Credit (ACTC).

   A. If the education credit is reduced due to lack of verification, then it is attributable to the party actually claiming the education expenses.
   B. If the education credit is due to a child having the expenses, it is allocated by percentage.

      Note:

      It is important to read the CP 2000 or Exam workpapers to identify why AUR reduced the education credit.

25.15.3.7.2.2.2 (03-08-2013)
Actual Knowledge

1. No relief is available under IRC 6015(c) for any item(s) (or portion of an item) for which the Service establishes that the RS had actual knowledge. Therefore, such item(s) remain a joint and several liability and should not be allocated to either spouse individually. See *IRM 25.15.3.7.1*, *Qualifications*, for additional information.
2. If a RS establishes he or she was the victim of domestic abuse prior to the time the return was signed, but did not sign the return under duress (which might invalidate the joint election), and as a result of the prior abuse, did not challenge any of the items on the return for fear of retaliation, the actual knowledge limitation of IRC 6015(c) will not apply. This exception only applies if the Service first establishes actual knowledge of the item giving rise to the deficiency. See *IRM 25.15.3.7.1*, *Qualifications*, regarding the Service's burden to establish actual knowledge. See Treas. Reg. 1.6015–3(c)(2)(v).

25.15.3.7.2.2.3 (07-29-2014)
Fraudulent Transfers

1. Taxpayers are not eligible for relief under IRC 6015(c) or IRC 6015(f) if assets were transferred between spouses as part of a fraudulent scheme.

2. A fraudulent scheme includes a scheme to defraud the Service or another third party, including, but not limited to, creditors, ex-spouses, and business partners. See Treas. Reg. § 1.6015–1(d).
3. IRS bears the burden of showing assets were transferred as part of a fraudulent scheme. If the Service is unable to prove fraud, fraud indicators will still be taken into account when considering relief under the equitable factors under section 4.03 of Rev. Proc. 2013–34. For more information see IRM 25.1, *Fraud Handbook*.

25.15.3.7.2.2.4 (03-08-2013)
Taxpayer Burden of Proof to Establish Their Allocated Portion of the Liability

1. The RS bears the burden of proof in establishing his or her allocated portion of the liability per IRC 6015(c)(2). The spouse must prove that the items giving rise to an understatement are attributable to the NRS. If efforts to retrieve the administrative file are unsuccessful, and no other corroborating evidence is available to determine attribution of the erroneous items, examiners should base their determination on the credibility of the RS. IRC 6015(c) requires the Service prove actual knowledge of each item giving rise to a deficiency in order to invalidate an allocation to the NRS. In addition, the Service must prove the extent of actual knowledge for each item. See *IRM 25.15.3.7.1.1, Actual Knowledge Invalidates Allocation*, for additional information.

25.15.3.7.2.2.5 (05-01-2005)
Allocate as if Spouses Filed Separate Returns

1. In the allocation computation, adjustment items are allocated to each spouse in the same manner as they would have been had the spouses filed separate returns ignoring separate return limitations. See *IRM 25.15.3.7.2.2.6, Ignore Separate Return Limitations*, for additional information.

25.15.3.7.2.2.6 (03-08-2013)
Ignore Separate Return Limitations

1. Under IRC 6015(d)(4) if a deduction or credit would be disallowed because the taxpayer filed a separate return, the deduction should be computed as it would for a joint return and then allocated between spouses.
2. If a credit would not be allowed on a separate return, the credit should be computed as it would for a joint return and then allocated between spouses. Examples of credits generally not allowed on separate returns are the child and dependent care credit, the Hope and Lifetime Learning credits, and the EITC.
3. A similar rule applies to income and deductions (such as taxable social security and railroad retirement benefits and the IRA deduction) subject to special limitations on a joint return. The items should be computed based on a joint return and then allocated between spouses.

25.15.3.7.2.2.7 (09-01-2006)
Rules Regarding Relief for Items Attributable to RS

1. Generally, the RS may not be relieved of any part of the deficiency which relates to an item attributable to the RS. A RS can obtain relief from his or her own item to the extent that the RS does not receive a tax benefit from the item and the item offsets the NRS's income. In these instances, the Service must establish that the RS had actual knowledge to invalidate the allocation to the NRS, or the RS will be able to obtain relief.

25.15.3.7.2.2.8 (07-29-2014)
Tax Benefit Limitation

1. An erroneous item that would otherwise qualify for relief does not qualify to the extent the RS received a tax benefit from that item on the original return. Likewise, to the extent the RS did not receive a tax benefit from the item and the NRS does (offset of NRS's income), then the amount that the RS does not receive a benefit from is allocated to the NRS.

Examples of items that could result in such a benefit include deductions, losses, and credits attributable to the NRS (or joint items allocated 50–50) that reduce taxable income of the RS or vice-versa.

2. The RS received a tax benefit on the return to the extent the NRS's erroneous items (or joint items allocated 50–50) offset the RS's income or vice-versa.
3. For separate treatment items of nonrefundable credits and refundable credits, benefit is derived from the lesser of:
    - The total of such credits per return, or
    - The excess of such credits over the NRS's share of the original return liability including other taxes.

Example:

A joint return shows $50,000 of wages from RS. The return reflects a Schedule C attributable to NRS with gross receipts of $15,000 and one deduction of $20,000 for a net loss of $5,000. The return also reflects $1,000 of Lifetime Learning Credit attributable to NRS. Personal exemptions of $2,500 each were claimed along with the standard deduction of $7,000. Upon examination the $20,000 deduction and $1,000 credit are disallowed. In this case NRS has unused deductions that offset RS's income of $11,000 computed as follows:
Gross receipts $15,000
Personal exemptions ($2,500)
Standard Deduction ($3,500)
Taxable Income before erroneous item $9,000
Erroneous item ($20,000)
Taxable income ($11,000)
The unused deductions of NRS equals the tax benefit to RS. Since NRS only used $9,000 of the erroneous item to reduce his taxable income to $-0- the balance of $11,000 benefitted RS. RS's potential relief of the $20,000 item would be reduced by $11,000 to $9,000. In addition, because RS received the benefit of the $1,000 credit reported on the return, relief is not available for that item.

25.15.3.7.2.2.9 (05-01-2005)
Fraud

1. IRC 6015(d)(3)(C) provides an exception to the allocation method if the IRS establishes fraud by one or both spouses. The IRS may use an alternative allocation it deems appropriate based on the facts and circumstances.

25.15.3.7.2.2.10 (03-08-2013)
Disqualified Assets

1. A disqualified asset is any property or right to property transferred to the RS by the NRS, if the principal purpose of the transfer was the avoidance of tax or payment of tax (including additions to tax, penalties and interest) IRC 6015(c)(4)(B)(i).
    A. All assets transferred from the NRS to the RS during the 12 month period before, or any time after, the mailing date of the first letter of proposed deficiency (the 30 day letter), are presumed to be disqualified assets. See IRC 6015(c)(4)(B)(ii)(I) and Treas. Reg. 1.6015-3(c)(3)(iii).
    B. The presumption does not apply if the RS establishes that the transfer was pursuant to a divorce decree or separate maintenance agreement or a written instrument incident to such a decree or agreement.
    C. If the presumption does not apply because the transfer was pursuant to a decree or agreement, the Service can still treat the asset as disqualified, if the Service can establish that the purpose of the transfer was the avoidance of tax or payment of tax.
2. Under IRC 6015(c)(4)(B)(ii)(II), if the presumption that a transfer within 1 year of the first letter or proposed deficiency (30 day letter) is a disqualified asset applies, the RS may rebut the presumption by establishing that the principal purpose of the transfer was not the avoidance of tax or payment of tax.

25.15.3.7.2.2.11 (03-08-2013)
Household Employment Taxes

1. Because household employment taxes (reported on Form 1040, Schedule H) are employment taxes, not income taxes under Subtitle A, they do not qualify for relief. Only Subtitle A taxes are subject to relief.

25.15.3.7.2.2.12 (07-29-2014)
Child's Liability

1. The liability of a child, included on a joint return, is disregarded in computing the separate liability of either spouse. See IRC 6015(d)(5). The child's liability should be allocated equally between the spouses. For purposes of this paragraph, a child does not include the taxpayer's stepson or stepdaughter, unless such child was legally adopted by the taxpayer. If the child is the child of only one of the spouses, and the other spouse had not legally adopted such child, any portion of a deficiency relating to the liability of such child is allocated solely to the parent spouse. See Treas. Reg. 1.6015–3(d)(4)(iii). See Form 8615, *Tax for Certain Children Who Have Unearned Income* and Form 8814, *Parents' Election to Report Child's Interest and Dividends*.

25.15.3.7.3 (07-29-2014)
Worksheet

1. CCISO will refer to the worksheets and instructions on the http://win.web.irs.gov/innocentspouse/innocent_jobaids.htm, *Innocent Spouse Job Aids* website.
2. Area Office employees will refer to http://mysbse.web.irs.gov/exam/tip/innocentspouse/default.aspx, for more information and find an expert to assist at http://mysbse.web.irs.gov/exam/tip/innocentspouse/contacts/11883.aspx, for assistance in completing the computations.

25.15.3.8 (07-29-2014)
IRC 6015(f) Equitable Relief

1. IRC 6015(f) was enacted to provide relief from joint and several liability where, taking into consideration all the facts and circumstances, it is inequitable to hold the spouse liable for an understatement or underpayment when other relief provisions do not apply.
2. Notice 2011–70 eliminated the two-year time limit for filing a claim for equitable relief under IRC 6015(f). Notice 2012-8 proposed a new revenue procedure providing guidelines for equitable relief under IRC 6015(f), that superseded Rev. Proc. 2003-61, and gave the Service the authority to apply the provisions in the proposed revenue procedure instead of Rev. Proc. 2003-61. The final revenue procedure, Rev. Proc. 2013-34, was released in September 2013.
3. Rev. Proc. 2013-34 takes abuse and financial control into consideration more thoroughly in connection with the equitable factors rather than as a separate factor.
4. The guidelines should be applied in a consistent and nondiscriminatory manner. Decisions to grant relief should not be based on the subjective personal and social beliefs of the IRS employee or any other inappropriate grounds.

25.15.3.8.1 (03-08-2013)
Understatements and Underpayments

1. IRC 6015(f) applies to **understatements** (liabilities from deficiency assessments) and **underpayments** (unpaid self-assessed taxes on original or amended returns).
2. This is the only provision under IRC 6015 that provides relief for underpayments. See *IRM 25.15.3.4.2, Underpayment*, for a further explanation of underpayment.

3. Cases meeting the basic qualifying factors, see *IRM 25.15.3.8.2, Eligibility Threshold Requirements under Rev. Proc. 2013-34*, will first be evaluated using the factors discussed in Section 4.02 of Rev. Proc. 2013-34. See *IRM 25.15.3.8.3, Streamlined Determinations - Rev. Proc. 2013-34 Section 4.02.*
4. Cases that do not meet all the factors discussed in Section 4.02 of Rev. Proc. 2013-34 will be evaluated using the Equitable Relief factors discussed in Section 4.03 of Rev. Proc. 2013-34. See *IRM 25.15.3.8.4, Relief for Underpayment and Understatement Cases per Rev. Proc. 2013-34.*
5. This provision also applies to **penalties, additions to tax, and interest** where relief is granted for the underlying tax. The analysis of the factors should focus on the underlying tax. If relief would have been appropriate for the underlying tax, then relief is appropriate for the penalties and interest. This includes situations where there was an underpayment of tax on the return but subsequent payments have paid all the tax leaving only penalty and/or interest unpaid or partially unpaid. If the RS would be entitled to relief, then the RS may be considered for a refund (including a refund of any paid penalties and interest) and would be entitled to relief from the unpaid penalties and interest. This may also apply to situations where there was an understatement that has subsequently been satisfied leaving only penalties and interest on the account.

   Note:

   If the original return was full paid when filed, then there is no underpayment of tax, therefore, no relief is available under IRC 6015.

   Example:

   Taxpayers filed a joint return late, paid the tax with the return, but still owed penalties and interest for filing late, relief is not available under IRC 6015. Reasonable cause or other penalty relief provisions, outside of the innocent spouse process, may be considered. See IRM 25.15.7.5.8(4), *Account Problems* regarding requests for abatement of penalties and interest.

6. See *IRM 25.15.3.8.2.2, Availability of Refunds under IRC 6015(f)*, for refund provisions.

25.15.3.8.2 (03-08-2013)
Eligibility Threshold Requirements under Rev. Proc. 2013-34

1. For a list of requirements that must be met for the Service to **consider** relief under IRC 6015(f), see *IRM 25.15.3.8.2.1, Eligibility Threshold Conditions - Defined.*

   Note:

   IRM 25.15.3.8.2.1(1) and (2) are not relevant for requests for relief under IRC 66(c) relating to taxpayers who file separate returns in community property states. For more information about relief under IRC 66, see IRM 25.15.5.9, *IRC 66(c) - Innocent Spouse Relief.*

25.15.3.8.2.1 (07-29-2014)
Eligibility Threshold Conditions - Defined

1. **Joint Return Filed** — The individual filed a joint return for the year in which relief is requested.
2. **Unavailability of IRC 6015(b) and IRC 6015(c)** — Relief is not available under IRC 6015(b) or IRC 6015(c).
3. **Time Limitation** — The individual requested relief within any time period that the collection statute or refund statute remains open.
4. **No Fraudulent Transfers** — Equitable relief will not be considered if assets were transferred between spouses as part of a fraudulent scheme to avoid tax or payment of tax. Acts which would disqualify the RS from requesting allocation

under IRC 6015(c)(3)(A)(ii) also disqualify the RS from equitable relief. See *IRM 25.15.3.7.2.2.3*, *Fraudulent Transfers*, for a further explanation of fraudulent transfers.

5. **No Transfers of Disqualified Assets** — Equitable relief will not be considered to the extent of the value of disqualified assets which were transferred to the RS, similar to IRC 6015(c)(4)(B). See *IRM 25.15.3.7.2.2.10*, *Disqualified Assets*, for a further explanation of disqualified assets. This condition will not result in the RS being ineligible for relief if the NRS abused the RS or maintained control over the household finances by restricting the RS's access to financial information, or the RS did not have actual knowledge that assets were transferred.
6. **No Fraudulent Return** — The RS did not knowingly participate in the filing of a fraudulent joint return. Additional information can be found in IRM 25.1.2.3*Indicators of Fraud.*
7. **Attributable to the NRS** — Equitable relief will not be considered if the liability is solely attributable to the RS unless one of the following exceptions applies. If liability is attributable to both the RS and NRS, equitable relief will only be considered for the portion attributable to the NRS.

Note:

Generally erroneous items of income or erroneous deductions are allocable consistent with the rules under IRC 6015(c), see Treas. Reg. 1.6015–3(d). Joint items are generally allocable 50% to each spouse. Underpayments of tax are allocable based on each spouse's pro rata share of the joint taxable income determined as if the spouses had filed separate returns.

Note:

For purposes of determining how much of an underpayment is attributable to each spouse, the EITC and ACTC is allocated to each spouse in proportion to the spouse's share of the adjusted gross income.

Note:

When determining allocation, if you don't know who the income or deductions are attributable to, leave it on the joint account. The RS has the burden to establish who the income or deduction is attributable to.

A. **Attribution solely due to the operation of community property law.** If an item is attributable or partially attributable to the RS solely due to the operation of community property law, then that item (or portion thereof) will be considered to be attributable to the NRS.
B. **Nominal ownership.** If the item is titled in the name of the RS, the item is presumptively attributable to the RS. This presumption is rebuttable.

   Example:

   For example, NRS opens an Individual Retirement Account (IRA) in RS's name and forges RS's signature on the IRA in 2006. Thereafter, NRS makes contributions to the IRA and in 2008 takes a taxable distribution from the IRA. NRS and RS file a joint return for the 2008 taxable year, but do not report the taxable distribution on their joint return. The Service later proposes a deficiency relating to the taxable IRA distribution. RS requests relief from joint and several liability under IRC 6015. RS establishes that RS did not contribute to the IRA, sign paperwork relating to the IRA, or otherwise act as if RS were the owner of the IRA. RS thereby rebutted the presumption the IRA is attributable to RS.

C. **Misappropriation of funds**. If the RS did not know and had no reason to know, that funds intended for the payment of tax were misappropriated by the NRS for the NRS's benefit, the Service will consider granting equitable relief although the underpayment may be attributable in part or in full to an item of the RS. The Service will consider granting relief in this case only to the extent that the funds intended for the payment of tax were taken by the NRS.

D. **Abuse not amounting to duress**. If the RS establishes that he or she was the victim of abuse prior to the time the return was signed, and that, as a result of the prior abuse, the RS did not challenge the treatment of any items on the return, or question the payment of any balance due reported on the return, for fear of the NRS's retaliation, the Service will consider granting equitable relief although the deficiency or underpayment may be attributable in part or in full to an item of the RS.

E. **Fraud committed by NRS**. If the RS establishes that the NRS's fraud is the reason for the erroneous item, the Service will consider granting equitable relief although the deficiency or underpayment may be attributable in part or in full to an item of the RS.

Example:

NRS fraudulently accesses RS's brokerage account to sell stock that RS had separately received from an inheritance. NRS deposits the funds from the sale in a separate bank account to which RS does not have access. RS and NRS file a joint federal income tax return for the year, which does not report the income from the sale of the stock. The Service determines a deficiency based on the omission of the income from the sale of the stock. RS requests relief from the deficiency under IRC 6015(f). The income from the sale of the stock normally would be attributable to RS. Because NRS committed fraud with respect to RS, however, and because this fraud was the reason for the erroneous item, the liability is properly attributable to NRS.

25.15.3.8.2.2 (03-08-2013)
Availability of Refunds under IRC 6015(f)

1. **Deficiency and underpayment cases**— The RS is eligible for a refund of separate payments that he or she made after July 22, 1998, if the RS establishes that he or she provided the funds used to make the payment for which he or she seeks a refund.
2. RS is not eligible for refunds of payments made with the joint returns (including withholding, estimated tax payments, payments made with the return, a Form 1040-V voucher, or a request for an extension of time to file and includes payments made after the joint return was filed but on or before the due date for payment), joint payments, or payments made solely by the NRS.

Exception:

The RS may be eligible for a refund of the RS's portion of the joint overpayment from another tax year applied to the joint income tax liability; to the extent that the RS can establish that the RS provided the funds for the RS's portion of the overpayment.

3. The RS is entitled to his/her portion of the stimulus payments.

Note:

If the stimulus payment was attributable to children, the portion is 50% to each spouse unless there is a good reason to allocate the payment differently, i.e., there was a remarriage and the children were the children of only one spouse.

4. Allocate the Making Work Pay Credit equally between the RS and NRS, even if one spouse did not work.
5. The RS is entitled to his/her portion of the First Time Homebuyers Credit (FTHBC).

Note:

The maximum amount allowed is 50% of the allowed credit. This is because if they had filed a separate return the maximum allowable for married filing separate returns is $4,000 for each spouse.

6. **Other limitations**— The availability of refunds is subject to IRC 6511. Generally the Form 8857 is treated as a claim for refund.

25.15.3.8.3 (03-08-2013)
Streamlined Determinations - Rev. Proc. 2013-34 Section 4.02

1. If **all the threshold conditions** discussed in *IRM 25.15.3.8.2, Eligibility Threshold Requirements under Rev. Proc. 2013-34* are met and the RS **meets all of the following conditions, relief will be granted:**
    - The RS is no longer married to the NRS. See *IRM 25.15.3.8.4.1.1, Marital Status.*
    - Economic hardship will result if relief is not granted. See *IRM 25.15.3.8.4.1.2, Economic Hardship.*
    - The RS did not know or have reason to know of the understatement, or that the NRS would not or could not pay the underpayment of tax. See *IRM 25.15.3.8.4.1.3, Knowledge or Reason to Know* for additional information.
2. If relief is not granted due to failure to meet one of the factors above then the examiner must consider the equitable relief factors in Section 4.03 of Rev. Proc. 2013-34. See *IRM 25.15.3.8.4.1Equitable Relief Factors (Section 4.03).*

25.15.3.8.4 (07-29-2014)
Relief for Underpayment and Understatement Cases per Rev. Proc. 2013-34

1. In some instances, a RS with an underpayment liability or understatement who meets the threshold requirements, (see *IRM 25.15.3.8.2, Eligibility Threshold Requirements under Rev. Proc. 2013-34*), may not meet all of the Section 4.02 conditions (see *IRM 25.15.3.8.3, Streamlined Determinations - Rev. Proc. 2013 - 34 Section 4.02*), to qualify for relief. The RS may still qualify for equitable relief from a tax liability, if taking into account all the facts and circumstances, it is clearly inequitable to hold the RS liable for the **underpayment**, or for a liability arising from an **understatement** adjustment.
2. Various factors, listed in *IRM 25.15.3.8.4.1, Equitable Relief Factors (Section 4.03)*, below, should be taken into consideration for all cases. All the facts and circumstances of the case are to be taken into account. The degree of importance of each factor varies depending on the circumstances of the RS and the factual context surrounding the marriage. The factors are designed as guides. It is not intended that only the factors described below in *IRM 25.15.3.8.4.1, Equitable Relief Factors (Section 4.03)*, are to be taken into account in making the determination.
3. No one factor or majority of factors necessarily controls the determination. Therefore, depending on the facts and circumstances of the case, relief may be granted even if the number of factors weighing against relief exceeds the number of factors weighing in favor of relief, or a denial of relief may be appropriate even if the number of factors weighing in favor of relief exceeds the number of factors weighing against relief. The weight given to any one factor depends on the facts and circumstances of the case.

25.15.3.8.4.1 (07-29-2014)
Equitable Relief Factors (Section 4.03)

1. In determining whether it is inequitable to hold the requesting spouse liable for all or part of the unpaid tax liability or deficiency, and whether full or partial relief should be granted, all the facts and circumstances of the case are to be taken into account. The factors listed below are designed as guides and not intended to comprise an exclusive list. Other factors relevant to a specific claim for relief may also be taken into account in making a determination.
2. Factors to consider to determine if RS should be granted relief under Rev. Proc. 2013–34 are:
    - Marital Status, *IRM 25.15.3.8.4.1.1*
    - Economic Hardship, *IRM 25.15.3.8.4.1.2*
    - Knowledge or Reason to Know, *IRM 25.15.3.8.4.1.3*
    - Legal Obligation, *IRM 25.15.3.8.4.1.4*
    - Significant Benefit, *IRM 25.15.3.8.4.1.5*
    - Compliance with Income Tax Laws, *IRM 25.15.3.8.4.1.6*
    - Mental or Physical Health, *IRM 25.15.3.8.4.1.7*

Note:

Although abuse or the exercise of financial control is not a stand alone factor, the impact of abuse or financial control is considered under the applicable factors. Depending on the facts and circumstances, abuse of the RS's child or other family member living in the household can constitute abuse of the RS.

25.15.3.8.4.1.1 (07-29-2014)
Marital Status

1. **Marital Status** — Whether the RS is no longer married to the NRS as of the date the Service makes its determination.
2. This factor will **weigh in favor of relief** if the RS is no longer married to the NRS. The RS will be treated as being no longer married to the NRS only in the following situations, if the RS:
    - is divorced from the NRS,
    - is legally separated from the NRS under applicable state law,
    - is a widow or widower and is not an heir to the NRS's estate, which would have sufficient assets to pay the tax liability; or
    - has not been a member of the same household as the NRS at any time during the 12-month period ending on the date the service makes its determination. A temporary absence such as an absence due to incarceration, illness, business, military service, or education, shall not be considered separation for this purpose if it is reasonably expected that the absent spouse will return to the household.

    Reminder:

    A RS is a member of the same household as the NRS for any period in which the spouses maintain the same residence.

3. This **factor is neutral** if the RS is:
    - still married to the NRS, or
    - a widow or widower and an heir to the NRS's estate and there are sufficient assets in the estate to pay the tax liability.

25.15.3.8.4.1.2 (07-29-2014)
Economic Hardship

1. **Economic Hardship** - Whether the RS will suffer economic hardship if relief is not granted. An economic hardship exists if paying the tax liability in whole or part will cause the RS to be unable to pay reasonable basic living expenses.
    - If denying relief will cause the RS to suffer economic hardship, this factor will **weigh in favor of relief**.
    - If denying relief will not cause the RS to suffer economic hardship, this **factor will be neutral**.
    - If the RS is deceased, this **factor will be neutral**.
2. Consider the RS's current income, expenses and assets to determine if an economic hardship exists. In the event the information is missing from the Form 8857, you **must attempt to contact the RS**. It is not sufficient to rely on IRPTR data to determine current income. Instead, information should be solicited if omitted from the Form 8857. Also, consider whether the RS shares expenses or has expenses paid by another individual, such as a new spouse, a family member or significant other with whom the RS is living with and is paying for some or all of the household expenses.
3. An **economic hardship exists** if either situation below is present; unless the situation in the "CAUTION" below is present.

    A. Gross income is at 250% (for the RS's family size) or less of the poverty level and the RS does not have assets out of which payments towards the liability can be made.

Note:

No need to look at the expenses in this case.

B. Gross income is more than 250% of the poverty level but the income minus expenses is $300 or less.

Note:

The expenses must be for reasonable basic living expenses, not for the maintenance of an affluent or luxurious standard of living. To determine basic living expenses, consult the national and local collection financial standards.

C. The federal poverty level chart can be found at, http://coverageforall.org/pdf/FHCE_FedPovertyLevel.pdf.

Caution:

When the RS meets the above criteria but has assets such that the RS can make payments and still pay reasonable living expenses, consider this factor as neutral. Review the facts and circumstances. If neither (a) or (b) above applies, evaluate on a case-by-case basis; and if it would be an economic hardship, consider this factor in favor of relief. When evaluating the hardship, the size of the liability must be considered with the financial situation.

4. When the financial information is missing, incomplete, or appears questionable, **you must attempt telephone contact** with the RS for clarification. These calls must be documented. At least two attempts must be made. Those calls cannot be made within 48 hours of each other. The RS, if spoken with, should be given 30 days to provide additional documentation. If unable to reach the RS, issue Letter 3659C for CCISO and Letter L3659 for the field, requesting the specific information needed and informing the RS they have 30 days to respond. If no response, use the information available to determine if this factor will weigh in favor of relief or be neutral.

25.15.3.8.4.1.3 (07-29-2014)
Knowledge or Reason to Know

1. Actual knowledge or reason to know of the item giving rise to the understatement or deficiency **will not be weighed more heavily** than other factors.
2. This factor will **weigh in favor of relief** if the RS:
    - did not know and had no reason to know of the item giving rise to the understatement or deficiency at the time the RS filed the joint return (including a joint amended return), or
    - had a reasonable expectation at the time the joint return was filed that the NRS would pay the tax liability at the time the joint return was filed or within a reasonable period of time after the filing of the joint return.

Note:

If the **NRS abused the RS or maintained control over the household finances by restricting the RS's access to financial information**, and, therefore, because of the abuse or financial control, the RS was not able to challenge the treatment of any items on the joint return, or to question the payment of taxes reported as due on the joint return, or challenge the NRS's assurances regarding payment of the taxes, for fear of the NRS's retaliation, then the abuse or financial control will mitigate the RS's knowledge or reason to know. Under these circumstances, this factor **will weigh in favor of relief** because the abuse or financial control would mitigate the RS's knowledge or reason to know of the understatement.

3. This factor will **weigh against relief** if the RS:
   - knew or had reason to know of the item giving rise to the understatement or deficiency at the time the RS filed the joint return (including a joint amended return), or
   - could not reasonably expect that the NRS would or could pay the tax liability shown on the joint return within a reasonable period of time after filing of the return.

   Example:

   Prior to signing the return, the RS knew of the NRS's prior bankruptcies, financial difficulties, or other issues with the IRS or other creditors, or was otherwise aware of difficulties in timely paying bills.

4. When the information necessary for making a determination on the factor is missing, incomplete, or appears questionable, **you must attempt telephone contact** with the RS for clarification. These calls must be documented. At least two attempts must be made. Those calls cannot be made within 48 hours of each other. The RS, if spoken with, should be given 30 days to provide additional documentation. If unable to reach the RS, issue Letter 3659C for CCISO and Letter L3659 for the field, requesting the specific information needed and inform the RS they have 30 days to respond. If no response, use the information in the case to determine whether this factor should weigh in favor or against relief.

25.15.3.8.4.1.3.1 (03-08-2013)
Understatement or Deficiency

1. Determine whether the RS did not know and had no reason to know of the item giving rise to the understatement or deficiency at the time the RS filed the joint return (including a joint amended return).
2. For purposes of determining reason to know, consider:
   - the RS's level of education,
   - any deceit or evasiveness of the NRS,
   - the RS's degree of involvement in the activity and household financial matters,
   - the RS's business or financial expertise; and
   - any lavish or unusual expenditures compared with past spending levels.

   Reminder:

   Abuse and NRS's control of finances could mitigate knowledge. See *IRM 25.15.3.8.4.1.3*, *Knowledge or Reason to Know*.

25.15.3.8.4.1.3.2 (07-29-2014)
Underpayment

1. Determine whether the RS knew or had reason to know at the time the RS filed the joint return that the NRS would not or could not pay the tax liability at the time the joint return was filed or within a reasonable period of time after the return was filed. When making this determination, consider whether the RS reasonably expected that the NRS would pay the tax liability at the time the return was filed or within a reasonable period of time after filing of the return.

   Note:

   A reasonable expectation of payment will be presumed if the spouses submitted a request for an installment agreement within 90 days of the due date for payment of the tax or within 90 days of the return being filed, whichever is later. The request must detail the plan for paying the liability, satisfy the liability within a reasonable amount of time, and it must not be unreasonable for the RS to believe that the NRS will be able to make the payments contemplated in the request.

Reminder:

Abuse and NRS's control of finances could mitigate reasonable expectation. See *IRM 25.15.3.8.4.1.3, Knowledge or Reason to Know.*

2. If there was a reasonable expectation some of the liability would be paid, but not all of it, then relief may be available to the extent there was a reasonable expectation the liability would be paid.
3. The examiner making the determination must be satisfied the RS had a bona fide reasonable expectation the tax would be paid by the NRS.

Note:

An expectation the tax would be paid is not reasonable if the RS knew or had reason to know the NRS was not in an economic position, and was not expected to be in an economic position within the foreseeable future, to pay those taxes. A similar position is taken where the RS knew the NRS had a history of not paying the IRS or other creditors.

4. If there is an underpayment of tax on an amended return which is reporting a liability based on items not properly reported on the original return, consideration should be given to whether the RS had knowledge or reason to know of the original understatement.
5. For purposes of determining reason to know, consider:
    - the RS's level of education,
    - any deceit or evasiveness of the NRS,
    - the RS's degree of involvement in the activity and household financial matters,
    - the RS's business or financial expertise; and
    - any lavish or unusual expenditures compared with past spending levels.
6. The examiner should also look to prior years to determine payment history. A consistent history of underpayments that the RS was aware of may show that there was not a reasonable expectation the tax would be paid. On the other hand, a consistent history of returns showing tax due and the NRS timely paying those taxes could give a RS a reasonable expectation that the NRS would pay the tax due on the year(s) at issue. The examiner should also look at whether there were multiple returns filed (some of which would be late filed) with balances due that may make paying all of the taxes more difficult and might show that there was not a reasonable expectation that the tax would be paid.

25.15.3.8.4.1.4 (03-08-2013)
Legal Obligation

1. This factor **will weigh in favor of relief** if the NRS has the sole legal obligation to pay the outstanding income tax liability pursuant to a divorce decree or agreement.

Note:

It **will be neutral** if the RS knew or had reason to know, when entering into the divorce decree or agreement, that the NRS would not pay the income tax liability.

2. This factor **will weigh against relief** if the RS has the sole legal obligation.

Note:

The fact that the NRS has been relieved of liability for the taxes at issue as a result of a discharge in bankruptcy is disregarded in determining whether the RS has the sole legal obligation.

3. This factor **will be neutral** if any of the following:
    - both spouses have a legal obligation to pay the tax liability,
    - the spouses are not separated or divorced, or
    - the divorce decree or agreement is silent as to any obligation to pay the tax liability.

25.15.3.8.4.1.5 (07-29-2014)
Significant Benefit

1. Defined as, whether the RS received significant benefit (beyond normal support) from the unpaid income tax liability or item giving rise to the deficiency. See Treas. Reg. § 1.6015-2(d).
2. This factor **will weigh against relief** if the RS enjoyed significant benefits, for example, living a lavish lifestyle by owning luxury assets and taking expensive vacations.

    Note:

    If the NRS controlled the household and business finances or there was abuse such that the NRS made the decision on spending funds, then this mitigates this factor so that it **will be neutral**.

3. This factor **will weigh in favor of relief** if only the NRS significantly benefitted from the unpaid tax or item giving rise to an understatement or deficiency, and the RS had little or no benefit, or the NRS enjoyed the benefit to the RS's detriment.
4. This factor **is neutral** if the amount of unpaid tax or understated tax was small such that neither spouse received a significant benefit. Whether the amount of unpaid tax or understatement is small will vary depending on the facts and circumstances of each case.

25.15.3.8.4.1.6 (03-08-2013)
Compliance with Income Tax Laws

1. Defined as, whether the RS has made a good faith effort to comply with the income tax laws in the taxable years following the taxable year or years to which the request for relief relates.
2. This factor will **weigh in favor of relief** if the RS:
    - is compliant for taxable years after being divorced from the NRS, or
    - remains married to the NRS but files separate returns, and is compliant with the tax laws.
3. This factor will **weigh against relief** if the RS:
    - is not compliant for taxable years after being divorced from the NRS,
    - remains married to the NRS, whether or not legally separated or living apart, and continues to file joint returns with the NRS after requesting relief and the returns are not compliant,
    - remains married to the NRS and files separate returns, and is noncompliant with the tax laws.

    Exception:

    If the RS's noncompliance is due to the RS's poor financial or economic situation after the divorce, despite good faith efforts to comply, then this factor **will be neutral**.

4. This factor **will be neutral** if the RS:
    - made a good faith effort to comply with the tax laws but was unable to fully comply,
    - remains married to the NRS, whether or not legally separated or living apart, and continues to file joint returns with the NRS after requesting relief, even if they are compliant, or

- is not compliant because of the RS's poor financial or economic situation as a result of being separated or living apart from the NRS, despite good faith efforts to comply.

25.15.3.8.4.1.7 (03-08-2013)
Mental or Physical Health

1. Whether the RS was in poor physical or mental health will influence how this factor is weighed.
2. This factor will **weigh in favor of relief** if the RS was in poor mental or physical health at the time the RS filed the return or returns for which the request for relief relates or at the time the RS requested relief. The Service will consider the nature, extent, and duration of the condition.
3. This factor **will be neutral** if the RS was in neither poor physical nor poor mental health at the time the RS filed the return or returns for which the request for relief relates or at the time the RS requested relief.

25.15.3.8.4.2 (03-08-2013)
Other Factors (Section 4.03)

1. Other factors bearing (not only to justify relief, but perhaps to deny relief) on relief shall be considered.

25.15.3.9 (03-01-2011)
Commonly Used Letters

1. The following is a list of letters to be issued to the RS and NRS. Integrated Data Retrieval System (IDRS) letters are known as "C" letters and are to be used by CCISO. All other letters are to be used by field personnel.
2. Appeals letters are described in IRM 25.15.12.7, *Appeals Innocent Spouse Letters and Forms.*

25.15.3.9.1 (07-29-2014)
Preliminary Determination Letters

1. **Letter 3660C** — Obsolete 7/16/2013.
2. L 3660 - Advises the **NRS** of the determination and gives the opportunity to appeal the decision.
3. **Letter 3661C** — Obsolete 7/16/2013.
4. L 3661 - Advises the **RS** of the determination and gives them the opportunity to appeal the decision.
5. **Letter 4983C/ Letter 4983** — Advises the **NRS** of the determination made to allow full relief and allows 30 days to appeal. It will also be issued to advise the NRS of the determination to allow full relief based on additional information submitted by the RS and/or NRS and allows an additional 30 days to appeal.
6. **Letter 4984C/ Letter 4984** — Advises the **NRS** of the determination made to allow partial relief and allows 30 days to appeal. It will also be issued to advise the NRS of the determination to allow partial relief based on additional information submitted by the RS and/or NRS and allows an additional 30 days to appeal.
7. **Letter 4985C/ Letter 4985** — Advises the **NRS** of the determination made to disallow relief. The NRS does not get appeal rights. It will also be issued to advise the NRS of the determination to disallow relief based on additional information submitted by the RS and/or NRS.
8. **Letter 4986C/ Letter 4986** — Advises the **RS** of the determination made to allow full relief and allows 30 days to appeal when the refund is barred. It will also be issued to advise the RS of the determination to allow full relief based on additional information submitted by the RS and/or NRS and allows an additional 30 days to appeal, if necessary.
9. **Letter 4987C/ Letter 4987** — Advises the **RS** of the determination made to allow partial relief and allows 30 days to appeal. It will also be issued to advise the RS of our determination to allow partial relief based on additional information submitted by the RS and/or NRS and allows an additional 30 days to appeal.
10. **Letter 4988C/ Letter 4988** — Advises the **RS** of the determination made to disallow relief and allows 30 days to appeal. It will also be issued to advise the RS of the determination to disallow relief based on additional information submitted by the RS and/or NRS and allows an additional 30 days to appeal.

25.15.3.9.2 (07-29-2014)
Final Determination Letters

1. L 3279 - Advises the **RS** of our final determination. Informs RS of their Tax Court rights when applicable.
2. L 3323 - Advises the **NRS** of the final determination.
3. **Letter 5086C/ Letter 5086** — Advises the **RS** of the determination to allow relief. Informs RS of their Tax Court rights when applicable.
4. **Letter 5087C/ Letter 5087** — Advises the **RS** of the determination to allow partial relief. Informs RS of their Tax Court rights.
5. **Letter 5088C/ Letter 5088** — Advises the **RS** of the final determination to disallow relief. Informs RS of their Tax Court rights.
6. **Letter 3323C/ Letter 3323**— Advises the **NRS** of the final determination.

25.15.3.9.3 (07-29-2014)
Other Letters

1. **Letter 3284C/ Letter 3284** — Advises the **NRS** of their opportunity to participate in administrative proceedings.
2. **Letter 3657C/ Letter 3657** — Advises the **RS** that their claim is not necessary because he/she does not meet the basic eligibility requirements for requesting relief. It informs the RS that the claim is being closed.
3. **Letter 3658C/ Letter 3658** — Advises the **RS** that their claim is unprocessable.
4. **Letter 3659C / Letter 3659**— Advises the **RS** of receipt of their claim and provide information on the claim process (initial contact letter); also used to request additional information for making a determination on a factor if the necessary information is missing, incomplete, or appears questionable.
5. **Letter 4144C/ Letter 4144** — Advises the **RS** and **NRS** the case has been transferred to Appeals. It also advises the RS that Form 870–IS was received late and could not be accepted, when applicable.

   Note:

   CCISO will use Return Address (RA) 52 on all letters. This will ensure the correct return address is printed on each letter. All letters issued through Accounts Management Services (AMS) automatically select RA 52.

6. **Letter 4284C/ Letter 4284** — Advises the **NRS** of our determination on a reconsideration claim.
7. **Letter 4581C** *Proposed Determination on Untimely Request for Innocent Spouse Relief*— Obsolete 7/16/2013.
8. **Letter 5186C/Letter 5186** — Advises the **RS** of the determination on a reconsideration claim to allow relief.
9. **Letter 5187C/Letter 5187** — Advises the **RS** of the determination on a reconsideration claim to allow partial relief.
10. **Letter 5188C/Letter 5188** — Advises the **RS** of the determination on a reconsideration claim to disallow relief.
11. Letter 3657-A— Used by area office employees to inform the **RS** that their claim is not necessary because he/she does not meet the basic eligibility requirements for requesting relief. It informs the RS that the claim is being closed.

25.15.3.10 (07-29-2014)
Waivers

1. IRC 6015(e)(5) allows a RS who agrees with the Service's determination under IRC 6015(b), IRC 6015(c), or IRC 6015(f) (for claims filed after December 19, 2006) to waive, in writing, the collection restrictions imposed by IRC 6015(e)(1)(B). These waivers are only applicable in post-assessment cases, because in pre-assessment proposed deficiency cases there is no collection, and thus, no need for restrictions on collection, nor any need to waive those restrictions. When the RS signs Form 870-IS, Waiver of Collection Restrictions in Innocent Spouse Cases, it is anticipated that the RS will not petition the Tax Court. It should be noted; however, that Form 870–IS is not a final determination letter. Thus, even if the RS signs the Form 870-IS, the RS may petition the Tax Court at any time after six

months from filing the claim or within 90 days from the date the Service issues a final determination letter. Nonetheless, once the IRS receives the signed Form 870-IS, the Service may resume collection against the RS. It should also be noted that the suspension of the collection statute expiration date (CSED) stops 60 days after the IRS receives the signed Form 870-IS and it is signed on behalf of the Commissioner.

2. Form 870-IS can be found at http://publish.no.irs.gov/catlg.html, *Electronic Publishing*. The catalog number is 35518X.
3. The waiver is available for fully and partially disallowed preliminary determination letters upon request by the RS.
4. A faxed signature can be accepted.
5. When a signed Form 870-IS is received from the RS, ensure there has been no alteration of the original and then make a copy.

IF Signed Form 870-IS is received	AND	THEN
Partially Allowed Claim	NRS's time to appeal has not expired	Hold Form 870-IS until the time to appeal has expired or the NRS does appeal. At that time, follow the applicable instructions below.
Partially Allowed Claim	NRS's time to appeal has expired	A. Have manager sign the original and copy of Form 870-IS B. Mail copy to RS with Letter 4144C/Letter 4144. C. Prepare case for the Processing Team D. Send Letter 3323C/Letter 3323 to NRS E. Update ISTSR Input Record F. Process the claim per campus directions
Partially Allowed Claim	NRS appeals	G. Forward the case to Appeals H. Do not sign the Form 870-IS I. Do not send Form 870-IS back to RS. J. Send Letter 4144C/Letter 4144 to the RS.
Fully Disallowed Claim		K. Have manager sign original and copy of Form 870-IS L. Mail signed copy of Form 870–IS to RS with Letter 4144C/Letter 4144. M. Send Letter 3323C/Letter 3323 to NRS N. Update ISTSR Input Record O. Input TC 290.00 P. Input TC 972 AC 065 (use 60 days from the IRS received date of Form 870–IS) Q. Reverse TC 130 as appropriate. See IRM 25.15.9.1.5.1 (1)(c), *Denied under IRC 6015(b), (c), or (f)*. R. Process the claim per campus directions.

6. Sometimes the Form 870-IS is received after the final determination letter is issued or received prior to the issuance of the final determination letter, but not associated before the final determination letter is issued. In these situations, take the following actions:
   A. Advise the RS that because the final determination letter was issued before the Form 870-IS was received, the terms of the final determination letter apply.
   B. Upon receipt of an acceptable signed Form 870-IS, write on the Form 870–IS, "870-IS received after final determination issued." Purge and close the case. If the RS does petition the Tax Court, order the case back from Files.

Note:

Provided the terms of the Form 870-IS match the terms of the final determination letter, it is unlikely a RS who signed Form 870-IS will file a petition with Tax Court. Purge and close the case. If the RS does petition the Tax Court, order the case back from Files.

IF	THEN
Terms on the Form 870–IS match the terms of the final determination letter	C. Do not return Form 870-IS back to the RS D. Purge and close the case
Terms of the Form 870–IS do not match the terms of the final determination letter	E. Do not purge and close the case F. Hold the case in suspense until either the RS petitions the Tax Court or the final determination defaults
Form 870–IS is requested more than 30 days from the date of the preliminary determination letter or after the final determination letter was issued	Send Form 870–IS to the RS and advise them that the terms of the final determination letter apply
Form 870–IS is requested within 30 days from the date of the preliminary determination letter and there is not enough time for the RS to respond	Send Form 870–IS to the RS and update the purge date by 10 days

Note:

It is not necessary to issue a final determination letter when Form 870–IS is processed as acceptable.

Three Types of Relief at a Glance

Factors	Innocent Spouse Relief §6015(b)	Allocation of Liability §6015(c)	Equitable Relief §6015(f)	Equitable Relief Community Property States §66(c)
Type of Returns	Joint	Joint	Joint	Married filing separate
Type of Liability	Deficiency	Deficiency	Deficiency or underpayment	Deficiency or underpayment
Special Requirements			Relief under § 6015(b) and §6015(c) not available	
Refunds Subject to Internal Revenue Code 6511	Refunds available	No refunds	Refunds available for: **Underpayment** - if payments are made solely by the RS. **Deficiency** - payments made solely by the RS after claim filed and pursuant to installment agreement (not defaulted).	
Marital Status	Marital status considered as an equitable factor	Must be divorced, widowed; legally separated; OR not living together for at least 12 months prior to the election	Marital status considered as an equitable factor	
Knowledge	**TP must establish** had **no knowledge OR reason to know**	**IRS must establish TP** had ***actual*** knowledge of **deficiency items**	Knowledge considered as an equitable factor	
Equity	Inequitable to hold TP liable: consider all facts & circumstances		Inequitable to hold TP liable: consider all facts & circumstances	
Required Factors Tier I			Tier I Cases (Relief ordinarily granted if all 4 factors met) 1. **Underpayment** 2. No longer married, legally separated, OR living together for 12 months prior to request 3. No knowledge or reason to know when return signed 4. TP will suffer economic hardship if relief not granted	
List of Partial Factors Tier II			Tier II Cases - **Underpayment and Deficiency** Equitable Relief Factors 1. Marital status (same as 6015(c)) 2. Economic Hardship (defined in Regs. §301.6343-1(b)(4)) 3. Non requesting spouse's legal requirment to pay the liability 4. No knowledge or reason to know (that liability would not be paid (for underpayment) or of item (for deficiency) 5. Significant Benefit 6. Compliance with Income Tax Laws 7. Abuse (but not duress) 8. Mental or physical health	
Fraud	Fraud is a consideration in equity determination	Election invalid if IRS shows TP transferred assets as part of a fraudulent scheme	Relief not available if 1. Fraudulent return or 2. Assets transferred as part of fraudulent scheme	
Disqualified Assets Transferred for Avoidance of Tax or Payment of Tax	Transfer of disqualified assts is a consideration in equity determination	Amount of allocation is increased by value of disqualified assets	Relief not available to extent of value of any disqualified assets	
Time for Filing	2 years from 1st collection activity against the RS after 7/22/98	2 years from 1st collection activity against the RS after 7/22/98	Exception for equitable relief.	
Consideration in Courts	Tax Court; if full-paid, District court or Court of Federal Claims	Tax Court	Tax Court review of IRS's possible abuse of discretion	Tax Court review if part of deficiency proceedings or under Collection Due Process proceedings

State Related Innocent Spouse Relief

Some States have specific Innocent Spouse Relief codes. For example, The Franchise Tax Board ("FTB") in California will in many circumstances allow aid to a taxpayer that has been granted innocent spouse relief by the IRS, provided the taxpayer files the proper paperwork. You should refer to local tax codes as they exist in the state you are practicing,

Procedures for the Corresponding Spouse to the Spouse Seeking Innocent Relief

There are procedures that allow the non-relief seeking spouse to argue their case. The IRS must advise the non-seeking spouse once the seeking spouse has filed paperwork. Here the non-seeking spouse may defend him or herself against the seeking spouse's allegations and if warranted, may file an appeal under Revenue Procedure 2003-19. Another form of appeal may occur by the non-seeking spouse if the seeking spouse is denied relief and has their case moved to Tax Court, the non-seeking spouse may intervene and become a party to the case. In this circumstance both spouses might respectively argue why they are not responsible for paying the liability.

Exception for Equitable Relief[xvi]

On July 25, 2011, the IRS issued Notice 2011-70 expanding the amount of time to request equitable relief. The amount of time to request equitable relief depends on whether you are seeking relief from a balance due, seeking a credit or refund, or both:

Balance Due - Generally, you must file your request within the time period the IRS has to collect the tax. Generally, the IRS has 10 years from the date the tax liability was assessed to collect the tax. In certain cases, the 10-year period is suspended.

Credit or Refund - Generally, you must file your request within 3 years after the date the original return was filed or within 2 years after the date the tax was paid, whichever is later. But you may have more time to file if you live in a federally declared disaster area or you are physically or mentally unable to manage your financial affairs. See Pub. 556, for details.

Both a Balance Due and a Credit or Refund - If you are seeking a refund of amounts you paid and relief from a balance due over and above what you have paid, the time period for credit or refund will apply to any payments you have made, and the time period for collection of a balance due amount will apply to any unpaid liability.

Exception for relief based on community property laws.

If you are requesting relief based on community property laws, you must file Form 8857 no later than 6 months before the expiration of the period of limitations on assessment (including extensions) against your spouse or former spouse for the tax year for which you are requesting relief. However, if the IRS begins an examination of your return during the 6-month period the latest time for requesting relief is 30 days after the date of the IRS' initial contact letter to you. The period of limitations on assessment is the amount of time, generally 3 years, that the IRS has from the date you filed the return to assess taxes that you owe. If you do not qualify for the relief described above and are now liable for an unpaid or understated tax you believe you should be paid only by your spouse or former spouse, you may request equitable relief. See the Exception for equitable relief above.

Request for Innocent Spouse Relief Instructions (Form 8857)[xvii]

Instructions for Form 8857

(Rev. January 2014)

Request for Innocent Spouse Relief

Section references are to the Internal Revenue Code unless otherwise noted.

General Instructions

Note. In these instructions, the term "your spouse or former spouse" means the person who was your spouse for the year(s) you want relief. This is the person whose name you enter on line 5.

Future Developments

For the latest information about developments related to Form 8857 and its instructions, such as legislation enacted after they were published, go to *www.irs.gov/form8857*.

What's New

The Internal Revenue Service has issued Revenue Procedure 2013-34, available at *www.irs.gov/irb/2013-43_IRB/ar07.html*. This revenue procedure expands how the IRS will take into account abuse and financial control by the nonrequesting spouse in determining whether equitable relief is warranted. It also broadens the availability of refunds in cases involving deficiencies. See the instructions for *Line 31*, later.

Purpose of Form

When you file a joint income tax return, the law makes both you and your spouse responsible for the entire tax liability. This is called joint and several liability. Joint and several liability applies not only to the tax liability you show on the return but also to any additional tax liability the IRS determines to be due, even if the additional tax is due to the income, deductions, or credits of your spouse or former spouse. You remain jointly and severally liable for taxes, and the IRS can still collect them from you, even if you later divorce and the divorce decree states that your former spouse will be solely responsible for the tax.

If you believe, taking into account all the facts and circumstances, only your spouse or former spouse should be held responsible for all or part of the tax, you should request relief from the tax liability, including related penalties and interest. To request relief, you must file Form 8857. The IRS will use the information you provide on the form, and any attachments you submit, to determine if you are eligible for relief. The IRS will contact you if additional information is needed.

Married people who did not file joint returns, but who lived in community property states may request relief from liability for tax attributable to an item of community income. Community property states are Arizona, California, Idaho, Louisiana, Nevada, New Mexico, Texas, Washington, and Wisconsin. See *Community Property Laws*, later.

Note. We recognize that some of the questions on the form involve sensitive subjects. However, we need this information to evaluate the circumstances of your case and properly determine whether you qualify for relief.

Situations in Which You Should Not File Form 8857

Do not file Form 8857 for any tax year to which the following situations apply, even if you checked "Yes" on line 1. In a final decision a court considered whether to grant you relief from the joint liability and decided not to do so.

In a final decision a court did not consider whether to grant you relief from the joint liability, but you meaningfully participated in the proceeding and could have asked for relief.

You entered into an offer in compromise with the IRS.

You entered into a closing agreement with the IRS that disposed of the same liability for which you want to seek relief. However, see Pub. 971, Innocent Spouse Relief, for an exception that applies to TEFRA partnership proceedings.

You answered "No" to question 1.

When To File

You should file Form 8857 as soon as you become aware of a tax liability for which you believe only your spouse or former spouse should be held responsible. The following are some of the ways you may become aware of such a liability.

- The IRS is examining your tax return and proposing to increase your tax liability.
- The IRS sends you a notice.

However, you generally must file Form 8857 no later than 2 years after the first IRS attempt to collect the tax from you. (But see the **exceptions** below for different filing deadlines that apply.) For this reason, do not delay filing because you do not have all the required documentation.

Collection activities that may start the 2-year period are:

- The IRS offset your income tax refund against an amount you owed on a joint return for another year and the IRS informed you about your right to file Form 8857.
- The filing of a claim by the IRS in a court proceeding in which you were a party or the filing of a claim in a proceeding that involves your property. This includes the filing of a proof of claim in a bankruptcy proceeding.
- The filing of a suit by the United States against you to collect the joint liability.
- The issuance of a section 6330 notice, which notifies you of the IRS' intent to levy and your right to a collection due process (CDP) hearing. The IRS usually sends a section 6330 notice by issuing a Letter 11 or Letter 1058.

Exception for equitable relief. The amount of time to request equitable relief depends on whether you are seeking relief from a balance due, seeking a credit or refund, or both:

- Balance Due – Generally, you must file your request within the time period the IRS has to collect the tax. Generally, the IRS has 10 years from the date the tax liability was assessed to collect the tax. In certain cases, the 10-year period is suspended. The amount of time the suspension is in effect will extend the time the IRS has to collect the tax. See Pub. 594, The IRS Collection Process, for details.
- Credit or Refund – Generally, you must file your request within 3 years after the date the original return was filed or within 2 years after the date the tax was paid, whichever is later. But you may have more time to file if you live in a federally declared disaster area or you are physically or mentally unable to manage your financial affairs. See Pub. 556, Examination of Returns, Appeal Rights, and Claims for Refund, for details.
- Both a Balance Due and a Credit or Refund – If you are seeking a refund of amounts you paid and relief from a balance due over and above what you have paid, the time period for credit or refund will apply to any payments you have made, andthe time period for collection of a balance due amount will apply to any unpaid liability.

Exception for relief from liability for tax attributable to an item of community income. If you are requesting relief from liability for tax attributable to an item of community income (other than equitable relief), a different filing deadline applies. See *Relief from liability for tax attributable to an item of community income*, discussed later under Community Property Laws. The time in which to request equitable relief from liability for tax attributable to an item of community income follows the rules for equitable relief, earlier.

Where To File

Do not file Form 8857 with your tax return or the Tax Court. Instead, mail it to one of the following addresses.

If using the U.S. Postal Service: Internal Revenue Service
P.O. Box 120053 Covington, KY 41012

If using a private delivery service: Internal Revenue Service
201 W. Rivercenter Blvd., Stop 840F Covington, KY 41011

Alternatively, you can fax the form and attachments to the IRS at 855-233-8558.

For a list of private delivery services you can use to meet the "timely mailing as timely filing" rule for filing Form 8857 by the deadline, go to IRS.gov and enter "Private Delivery Services" in the search box.

Write your name and social security number on any attachments.

Send it to one of the above addresses or fax it to the above number even if you are communicating with an IRS employee because of an examination, examination appeal, or collection.

If you received an IRS notice of deficiency, you also should file a petition with the Tax Court before the end of the 90-day period, as explained in the notice. In your petition, you should raise innocent spouse relief as a defense to the deficiency. By doing so, you preserve your rights if the IRS is unable to properly consider your request before the end of the 90-day period.
Include the information that supports your position, including when and why you filed Form 8857 with the IRS, in your petition to the Tax Court. The time for filing with the Tax Court is not extended while the IRS is considering your request.

The IRS Must Contact Your Spouse or Former Spouse

By law, the IRS must contact your spouse or former spouse. There are **no** exceptions, even for victims of spousal abuse or domestic violence.

We will inform your spouse or former spouse that you filed Form 8857 and will allow him or her to participate in the process. If you are requesting relief from joint and several liability on a joint return, the IRS must also inform him or her of its preliminary and final determinations regarding your requested relief.

To protect your privacy, the IRS will not disclose your personal information (such as your current name, address, phone number(s), or information about your employer, your income, or your assets). Any other information you provide that the IRS uses to make a determination about your request for relief from liability could be disclosed to the person you list on line 5. If you have concerns about your privacy or the privacy of others, you should redact or black out personal information in the material you submit.

If you petition the Tax Court (explained later under What Happens After You File Form 8857*), your spouse or former spouse may see your personal information,*
unless you ask the Tax Court to withhold it.

Types of Relief

Four types of relief are available. They are:

1. Innocent spouse relief.
2. Separation of liability relief.
3. Equitable relief.
4. Relief from liability for tax attributable to an item of community income. (See Community Property Laws, later).

Innocent Spouse Relief

You may be allowed innocent spouse relief only if all of the following apply.
You filed a joint return for the year(s) entered on line 3.
There is an understated tax on the return(s) that is due to erroneous items (defined below) of the person with whom you filed the joint return.
You can show that when you signed the return(s) you did not know and had no reason to know that the understated tax existed (or the extent to which the understated tax existed).
Taking into account all the facts and circumstances, it would be unfair to hold you liable for the understated tax.

Understated tax. You have an understated tax if the IRS determined that your total tax should be more than the amount actually shown on the return.

Example. You and your former spouse filed a joint return showing $5,000 of tax, which was fully paid. The IRS later examines the return and finds $10,000 of income that your former spouse earned but did not report. With the additional income, the total tax becomes $6,500. The understated tax is
$1,500, for which you and your former spouse are both liable.

Erroneous items. Any income, deduction, credit, or basis is an erroneous item if it is omitted from or incorrectly reported on the joint return.

Partial innocent spouse relief. If you knew about any of the erroneous items, but not the full extent of the item(s), you may be allowed relief for the part of the understatement you did not know about.

Additional information. For additional information on innocent spouse relief, see Pub. 971.

Separation of Liability Relief

You may be allowed separation of liability relief for any understated tax (defined above) shown on the joint return(s) if the person with whom you filed the joint return is deceased or you and that person:
Are now divorced,
Are now legally separated, or
Have lived apart at all times during the 12-month period prior to the date you file Form 8857.

See Pub. 504, Divorced or Separated Individuals, for details on divorce and separation.

Exception. If, at the time you signed the joint return, you knew about any item that resulted in part or all of the understated tax, then your request will not apply to that part of the understated tax.

Additional information. For additional information on separation of liability relief, see Pub. 971.

Equitable Relief

You may be allowed equitable relief if both of the following conditions are met.
You have an understated tax (defined earlier) or unpaid tax (defined next), and
Taking into account all the facts and circumstances, the IRS determines it would be unfair to hold you liable for the understated or unpaid tax.

Equitable relief is the only type of relief available for an unpaid tax.

Unpaid tax. An unpaid tax is tax that is properly shown on your return but has not been paid.

Example. You and your former spouse filed a joint return that properly reflects your income and deductions but showed an unpaid balance due of $5,000. The unpaid tax is $5,000. You gave your former spouse $2,500 and he or she promised to pay the full $5,000, but paid nothing. There is still an unpaid tax of $5,000, for which you and your former spouse are both liable.

Additional information. For additional information on equitable relief, see Pub. 971 and Rev. Proc. 2013-34.

Community Property Laws

Generally, you must follow community property laws when filing a tax return if you are married and live in a community property state. Community property states are Arizona, California, Idaho, Louisiana, Nevada, New Mexico, Texas, Washington, and Wisconsin. Generally, community property laws provide that you and your spouse are both entitled to one-half of your total community income and expenses. If you and your spouse filed a joint return in a community property state, you are both jointly and severally liable for the total liability on the return. If you request relief from joint and several liability, state community property laws are not taken into account in determining whether an item belongs to you or your spouse or former spouse.

If you were a married resident of a community property state, but did not file a joint return and are now liable for an unpaid or understated tax, check "Yes" on line 1. You have the following two ways to get relief.

1. **Relief from liability for tax attributable to an item of com- munity income.** You are not responsible for the tax related to an item of community income if **all** of the following conditions exist.

You did not file a joint return for the tax year.
You did not include the item in gross income on your separate return.
Under section 879(a), the item was income that belonged to your spouse or former spouse. For details, see *Community Property Laws*, in Pub. 971.
You establish that you did not know of, and had no reason to know of, that item.
Under all facts and circumstances, it would not be fair to include the item in your gross income.

If you meet the above conditions, complete this form.

You must file Form 8857 no later than 6 months before the expiration of the period of limitations on assessment (including extensions) against your spouse or former spouse for the tax year for which you are requesting relief. However, if the IRS begins an examination of your return during that 6-month period, the latest time for requesting relief is 30 days after the date of the IRS' initial contact letter to you. The period of limitations on assessment is the amount of time, generally 3 years that the IRS has from the date you filed the return to assess taxes that you owe.

2. **Equitable relief.** If you do not qualify for the relief described in (1) above and are now liable for an unpaid or understated tax you believe should be paid only by your spouse or former spouse, you may request equitable relief. See *Equitable Relief*, earlier.

What Happens After You File Form 8857

We will review your form for completeness and contact your spouse or former spouse to ask if he or she wants to participate in the process. Generally, once we have all of the necessary information to make a decision, we will send a preliminary determination letter to you and your spouse or former spouse. If neither of you appeals the decision, we will issue a final determination letter to both of you. If either or both of you appeal to the IRS Office of Appeals, Appeals will issue a final determination letter to both of you after consideration of your appeal.

Note. If you did not file a joint return for the year you are requesting relief, we will send the determination letters only to you.

Tax Court review of request. You may be able to petition (ask) the Tax Court to review your request for relief (other than a request for relief from liability for tax attributable to an item of community income) if:
The IRS sends you a final determination letter regarding your request for relief, or
You do not receive a final determination letter from the IRS within 6 months from the date you filed Form 8857.

The petition must be filed **no later than the 90th day after** the date the IRS mails you a final determination letter. If you do not file a petition, or if you file it late, the Tax Court cannot review your request for relief. See Pub. 971 for details on petitioning the Tax Court.

Collection Statute of Limitations

Generally, the IRS has 10 years to collect an amount you owe. This is the collection statute of limitations. By law, the IRS is not allowed to collect from you after the 10-year period ends.

If you request relief for any tax year, the IRS cannot collect from you for that year while your request is pending. But interest and penalties continue to accrue. Your request is generally considered pending from the date the IRS receives your Form 8857 until the date your request is resolved. This includes the time the Tax Court is considering your request.

After your case is resolved, the IRS can begin or resume collecting from you any tax for which you are determined to remain responsible. The 10-year period will be increased by the amount of time your request for relief was pending plus 60 days.

How To Get Help

See Pub. 971, Innocent Spouse Relief. To get Pub. 971 and other IRS forms and publications, go to IRS.gov or call 1-800-TAX-FORM (1-800-829-3676).

The IRS can help you with your request. If you are working with an IRS employee, you can ask that employee, or you can call 1-855-851-2009.

You can use the Innocent Spouse Tax Relief Eligibility Explorer by going to IRS.gov and entering "Innocent Spouse" in the search box.

The Taxpayer Advocate Service Is Here To Help You

The Taxpayer Advocate Service (TAS) is your voice at the IRS. Our job is to ensure that every taxpayer is treated fairly and that you know and understand your rights.

What can TAS do for you? We can offer you free help with IRS problems that you can't resolve on your own. We know this process can be confusing, but the worst thing you can do is nothing at all! TAS can help if you can't resolve your problems with the IRS and:
Your problem is causing financial difficulties for you, your family, or your business.
You face (or your business is facing) an immediate threat of adverse action.
You have tried repeatedly to contact the IRS but no one has responded, or the IRS has not responded to you by the date promised.

If you qualify for our help, you'll be assigned to one advocate who'll be with you at every turn and will do everything possible to resolve your problem. Here's why we can help:
TAS is an independent organization within the IRS. Our advocates know how to work with the IRS.
Our services are free and tailored to meet your needs.
We have offices in every state, the District of Columbia, and Puerto Rico.

How can you reach us? If you think TAS can help you, call your local advocate, whose number is in your local directory and at *www.irs.gov/advocate*, or call us toll-free at 1-877-777-4778.

How else does TAS help taxpayers?

TAS also handles large-scale, systemic problems that affect many taxpayers. If you know of one of these broad issues, please report it through the Systemic Advocacy Management System at *www.irs.gov/sams*.

For additional information about TAS, visit *www.taxpayeradvocate.irs.gov* or see Pub. 1546, The Taxpayer Advocate Service of the IRS – How to Get Help With Unresolved Tax Problems.

Low Income Taxpayer Clinics

Low Income Taxpayer Clinics (LITCs) serve individuals whose income is below a certain level and need to resolve tax problems such as audits, appeals and tax collection disputes. Some clinics can provide information about taxpayer rights and responsibilities in different languages for individuals who speak English as a second language. Visit *www.irs.gov/litc* or see IRS Publication 4134, Low Income Taxpayer Clinic List.

Representation

You may either represent yourself or, with proper written authorization, have someone else represent you. Your representative must be someone who is allowed to practice before the IRS, such as an attorney, certified public accountant, or enrolled agent (a person enrolled to practice before the IRS). Use Form 2848, Power of Attorney and Declaration of Representative, to authorize someone else to represent you before the IRS.

Specific Instructions

Note. If you need more room to write your answer for any question, attach more pages. Be sure to write your name and social security number on the top of all pages you attach.

Also write your name and social security number on the top of any other documents and statements you attach.

Line 1

Complete line 1 to determine if you should file Form 8857.

Whether you check "Yes" or "No," you should go to line 2 (discussed next) to find out if you should file another form (Form 8379) to request *injured spouse relief*. Injured spouse relief is different from innocent spouse relief and you cannot request it by filing Form 8857. You must file Form 8379. For example, if
you check "Yes" on line 1 and "Yes" on line 2, you will have to file both Forms 8857 and 8379.

Line 2

Complete line 2 to determine if you should file Form 8379.

Check "Yes" for any tax year to which all of the following apply.
You filed a joint return.
At the time you filed the joint return, your spouse owed past-due federal tax, state income tax, state unemployment compensation debts, child support, spousal support, or federal nontax debt, such as a student loan.
The IRS used (offset) the refund to pay your spouse's past-due amount.
If all three of the above apply, you may be able to get back your share of the refund for that tax year if you file Form 8379, Injured Spouse Allocation.

If you checked "Yes" on line 1, and all three of the above do not apply, check "No" and go to line 3.

Example 1. You and your spouse filed your joint tax return showing a refund of $3,200. At the time you filed the return, your spouse owed $2,400 in back child support. The IRS used $2,400 of your refund to pay your spouse's back child support and refunded the remaining $800 to you and your spouse. You check "Yes" on line 2 because you meet all of the conditions listed above. If you want to get back your share of the $2,400 refund that the IRS used to pay your spouse's back child support, you must file Form 8379.

Example 2. The facts are the same as in Example 1, but the IRS audited your return and disallowed a $5,000 alimony deduction, which was actually child support paid by your spouse. Child support is not deductible. The disallowance resulted in additional tax, interest, and penalties. As explained earlier under *Innocent Spouse Relief*, this deduction is an erroneous item attributable to your spouse. You believe you meet the other requirements in that discussion for getting innocent spouse relief. You check "Yes" on line 1. In addition to Form 8379, you also should file Form 8857.

Line 4

Enter your current name, social security number, current mailing address (including county), and best or safest daytime phone number (between 6 a.m. and 5 p.m. Eastern Time) to call you if we need more information.

If your current name is different from your name as shown on your tax return for any year for which you are requesting relief, enter your former name in parentheses after your current name. For example, enter "Jane Maple (formerly Jane Oak)."

Foreign address. Enter the information in the following order: City, province, county, or state, and country. Follow the country's practice for entering the postal code. **Do not** abbreviate the country name.

Change of address. The IRS will send the initial correspondence about Form 8857 to the address you enter on line 4. However, the IRS is required to send all other correspondence to the most recent address it has for you in its records. This is usually the address shown on your most recently filed tax return or amended return. If you want us to update our records to use the address you entered on line 4 for all correspondence, you will have to file Form 8822, Change of Address. Send Form 8822 to the address shown in the instructions for that form. Do **not** send it to either of the addresses shown in these Form 8857 instructions. Generally, it takes 4 to 6 weeks to process your change of address.

If the address on line 4 matches the address in our records, you do not need to file Form 8822 unless you move. If you move after you file Form 8857, please use Form 8822 to notify the IRS of your new address.

Line 5

Enter the current name and SSN (if known) of the person to whom you were married at the end of the year(s) listed on line 3.

P.O. box. Enter the box number **only** if: You do not know the street address, or

The post office does not deliver mail to the street address.

Foreign address. See the instructions for line 4, earlier.

Line 8

If you wish to have the note removed from your account, call us at 1-855-851-2009 or write us at either of the addresses or the fax number listed earlier under *Where To File*. Please include your social security number on your written request.

Line 12

By law, if a person's name is signed to a return, it is presumed to be signed by that person, unless that person proves otherwise. If you believe your signature was forged or you signed under duress, explain in the space provided.

If you sign a joint return under duress or your signature was forged, the election to file jointly is not valid and you have no valid return. You are not jointly and severally liable for any income tax liabilities arising from that return. In that case, innocent spouse relief does not apply and is not necessary for obtaining relief. If you file Form 8857, but also maintain that there is no valid joint return due to duress or forgery, the IRS will first make a determination as to the validity of the joint return and may accordingly deny the request for innocent spouse relief based on the fact that no joint return was filed (and thus, relief is not necessary). If it is ultimately determined that a valid joint return was filed, the IRS will then consider whether you would be entitled to innocent spouse relief on the merits.

Forged signature. Your signature on the joint return is considered to be forged if it was not signed by you and you did not authorize (give tacit consent) the signing of your name to the return.

Tacit consent. Tacit consent means that, based on your actions at the time the joint return was filed, you agreed to the filing of the joint return even if you now claim the signature on the return is not yours. Whether you have tacitly consented to the filing of the joint return is based on an examination of all the facts of your case. Factors that may support a finding that you consented to the filing of the joint return include the following.

You gave tax information (such as Forms W-2 and 1099) to your spouse.

You did not object to the filing. There was an apparent advantage to you in filing a joint return.

You filed joint returns with your spouse or former spouse in prior years.

You failed to file a married filing separate return and you had a filing requirement.

Signed under duress. You are considered to have signed under duress (threat of harm or other form of coercion) if you were unable to resist demands to sign the return and you would not have signed the return except for the constraint applied by your spouse or former spouse. The duress must be directly connected with the signing of the joint return.

Line 20

You may not be entitled to relief if either of the following applies.

Your spouse (or former spouse) transferred property (or the right to property) to you for the main purpose of avoiding tax or payment of tax. A transfer will be presumed to meet this condition if the transfer is made after the date that is 1 year before the date on which the IRS sent its first letter of proposed deficiency.

The IRS proves that you and your spouse (or former spouse) transferred property to one another as part of a fraudulent scheme. A fraudulent scheme includes a scheme to defraud the IRS or another third party such as a creditor, former spouse, or business partner.

For more information about transfers of property, see Pub. 971.

Fair market value. Fair market value (FMV) is the price at which property would change hands between a willing buyer and a willing seller when both have reasonable knowledge of the relevant facts and neither has to buy or sell. FMV is not necessarily the cost of replacing the item.

Line 21

See the instructions for line 20 for the definition of fair market value.

Line 31

You must indicate that you want a refund of any payments you made in order for the IRS to consider whether you are entitled to it. Payments include refunds from another tax year applied to this tax liability. If you are granted relief, refunds are:

Permitted under innocent spouse relief and equitable relief as explained below under *Limit on Amount of Refund.*

Not permitted under separation of liability relief.

Proof Required

The IRS will only refund payments you made with your own money. However, you must provide proof that you made the payments with your own money. Examples of proof are a copy of your bank statement or a canceled check. No proof is required if your individual refund was used by the IRS to pay a tax you owed on a joint tax return for another year.

Limit on Amount of Refund

You are not eligible for refunds of payments made with the joint return, joint payments, or payments that your spouse (or former spouse) made. For example, withholding tax and estimated tax payments cannot be refunded because they are considered made with the joint return. However, you may be entitled to a refund of your portion of a joint overpayment from another year that was applied to the joint tax for a different year. You will need to show your portion of the joint overpayment.

The amount of your refund is limited. Read the chart at the top of the next page to find out the limit.

IF you file Form 8857 . . .	**THEN the refund cannot be more than . . .**
Within 3 years after filing your return	The part of the tax paid within the 3 years (plus any extension of time for filing your return) before you filed Form 8857.
After the 3-year period, but within 2 years from the time you paid the tax	The tax you paid within the 2 years immediately before you filed Form 8857.

Sign Form 8857

If you do not sign Form 8857, the IRS cannot consider your request and will return it to you. Also be sure to date it.

Keep a copy of the completed form for your records.

Paid Preparer Must Sign

Generally, anyone you pay to prepare Form 8857 must sign it and include their Preparer Tax Identification Number (PTIN) in the space provided. The preparer must give you a copy of Form 8857 for your records. Someone who prepares Form 8857 but does not charge you should not sign it.

Privacy Act and Paperwork Reduction Act Notice. We ask for the information on this form to carry out the Internal Revenue laws of the United States. We need it to determine the amount of liability, if any, of which you may be relieved. Internal Revenue Code sections 66(c) and 6015 allow relief from liability.
Requesting relief from liability is voluntary. If you request relief from liability, you must give us the information requested on this form. Code section 6109 requires you to provide your social security number. Routine uses of this information include giving it to the Department of Justice for civil and criminal litigation, and to cities, states, the District of Columbia, and U.S. commonwealths and possessions for use in administering their tax laws. We may also disclose this information to other countries under a tax treaty, to federal and state agencies to enforce federal nontax criminal laws, or to federal law enforcement and intelligence agencies to combat terrorism. If you do not provide all the information in a timely manner, we may not be able to process your request.

You are not required to provide the information requested on a form that is subject to the Paperwork Reduction Act unless the form displays a valid OMB control number. Books or records relating to a form or its instructions must be retained as long as their contents may become material in the administration of any Internal Revenue law. Generally, tax returns and return information are confidential, as required by Code section 6103.

The time needed to complete and file this form will vary depending on individual circumstances. The estimated average time is:

Learning about the law or the form . . . . 1 hr., 9 min. **Preparing the form** . . . . 2 hr., 36 min.
Copying, assembling, and sending the form to the IRS . . . . 1 hr., 3 min.

If you have comments concerning the accuracy of this time estimate or suggestions for making this form simpler, we would be happy to hear from you. You can send your comments from *www.irs.gov/formspubs*. Click on "More Information" and then on "Give us feedback." Or you can send your comments to the Internal Revenue Service, Tax Forms and Publications, 1111 Constitution Ave. NW, IR-6526, Washington, DC 20224. **Do not** send the form to this address. Instead, see *Where To File*, earlier.

Request for Innocent Spouse Relief Form[xviii]

Form **8857**
(Rev. January 2014)
Department of the Treasury
Internal Revenue Service (99)

Request for Innocent Spouse Relief

▶ Information about Form 8857 and its separate instructions is at *www.irs.gov/form8857.*

OMB No. 1545-1596

Important things you should know

- **Do not file this form with your tax return.** See *Where To File* in the instructions.
- Review and follow the instructions to complete this form. Instructions can be obtained at *www.irs.gov/form8857* or by calling 1-800-TAX-FORM (1-800-829-3676).
- While your request is being considered, the IRS generally cannot collect any tax from you for the year(s) you request relief. However, filing this form extends the amount of time the IRS has to collect the tax you owe, if any, for those years.
- The IRS is required by law to notify the person on line 5 that you requested this relief. That person will have the opportunity to participate in the process by completing a questionnaire about the tax years you enter on line 3. This will be done before the IRS issues preliminary and final determination letters.
- The IRS will not disclose the following information: your current name, address, phone numbers, or employer.

Part I Should you file this form?

Generally, both you and your spouse are responsible, jointly and individually, for paying any tax, interest, or penalties from your joint return. If you believe your current or former spouse should be solely responsible for an erroneous item or an underpayment of tax from your joint tax return, you may be eligible for innocent spouse relief.

Innocent spouse relief may also be available if you were a resident of a community property state (see list of community property states in the instructions) and did not file a joint federal income tax return and you believe you should not be held responsible for the tax attributable to an item of community income.

1 **Do either of the paragraphs above describe your situation?**

☐ Yes. You should file this Form 8857. Go to question 2.

☐ No. Do not file this Form 8857, but go to question 2 to see if you need to file a different form.

2 **Did the IRS take your share of a joint refund from any tax year to pay any of the following past-due debt(s) owed ONLY by your spouse?** • Child support • Spousal support • Student loan (or other federal nontax debt) • Federal or state taxes

☐ Yes. You may be able to get back your share of the refund. See Form 8379, Injured Spouse Allocation, and the instructions to that form. Go to question 3 if you answered "Yes" to question 1.

☐ No. Go to question 3 if you answered "Yes" to question 1. If you answered "No" to question 1, do not file this form.

3 **If you determine you should file this form, enter each tax year you want innocent spouse relief.** It is important to enter the correct year. For example, if the IRS used your 2011 income tax refund to pay a 2009 joint tax liability, enter tax year 2009, not tax year 2011.

Tax Year ________ Tax Year ________ Tax Year ________
Tax Year ________ Tax Year ________ Tax Year ________

Part II Tell us about yourself and your spouse for the tax years you want relief

4 Your current name (see instructions) | **Your social security number**

Address where you wish to be contacted. If this is a change of address, see instructions.

Number and street or P.O. box | Apt. no. | **County**

City, town or post office, state, and ZIP code. If a foreign address, see instructions. | Best or safest daytime phone number (between 6 a.m. and 5 p.m. Eastern Time)

5 **Who was your spouse for the tax years you want relief?** File a separate Form 8857 for tax years involving different spouses or former spouses.

That person's current name | **Social security number** (if known)

Current home address (number and street) (if known). If a P.O. box, see instructions. | Apt. no.

City, town or post office, state, and ZIP code. If a foreign address, see instructions. | Daytime phone number (between 6 a.m. and 5 p.m. Eastern Time)

For Privacy Act and Paperwork Reduction Act Notice, see instructions. Cat. No. 24647V Form **8857** (Rev. 1-2014)

Form 8857 (Rev. 1-2014) Page 2

Note. If you need more room to write your answer for any question, attach more pages. Be sure to write your name and social security number on the top of all pages you attach.

Part II **Tell us about yourself and your spouse for the tax years you want relief** *(Continued)*

6 **What is the current marital status between you and the person on line 5?**

☐ Married and still living together

☐ Married and living apart since ________ MM DD YYYY

☐ Widowed since ________ MM DD YYYY Attach a photocopy of the death certificate and will (if one exists).

☐ Legally separated since ________ MM DD YYYY Attach a photocopy of your entire separation agreement.

☐ Divorced since ________ MM DD YYYY Attach a photocopy of your entire divorce decree.

Note. A divorce decree stating that your former spouse must pay all taxes does not necessarily mean you qualify for relief.

7 **What was the highest level of education you had completed when the return(s) were filed?** If the answers are **not** the same for all tax years, explain.

☐ Did not complete high school

☐ High school diploma or equivalent

☐ Some college

☐ College degree or higher. List any degrees you have ▶ ________

List any college-level business or tax-related courses you completed ▶ ________

Explain ▶ ________

8 **Were you or other members of your family a victim of spousal abuse or domestic violence, or suffering the effects of such abuse during any of the tax years you want relief or when any of the returns were filed for those years?**

☐ Yes. If you want the IRS to consider this information in making its determination, complete Part V of this form in addition to other parts of the form. First read the instructions for Part V, to understand how the IRS will proceed with evaluating your claim for relief in these circumstances.

If you checked "Yes" above, we will put a note on your separate account. This will enable us to respond appropriately and be sensitive to your situation. We will remove the note from your account if you request it (as explained in the instructions).
If you do not want us to put a note on your account, check here . . . . ▶ ☐

☐ No. Complete the other parts of this form except for Part V.

9 **When any of the returns listed on line 3 were filed, did you have a mental or physical health problem or do you have a mental or physical health problem now?** If the answers are **not** the same for all tax years, explain below.

☐ Yes. **Attach a statement** to explain the problem and **when** it started. Provide photocopies of any documentation, such as medical bills or a doctor's report or letter.

☐ No.

Explain ▶ ________

10 **Is there any information you are afraid to provide on this form, but are willing to discuss?**

☐ Yes ☐ No

Part III **Tell us if and how you were involved with finances and preparing returns for those tax years**

11 **Did you agree to file a joint return?** ☐ Yes ☐ No

Explain why or why not ▶ ________

12 **Did you sign the joint return?** See instructions. ☐ Yes ☐ No

Explain why or why not ▶ ________

Note. If you need more room to write your answer for any question, attach more pages. Be sure to write your name and social security number on the top of all pages you attach.

Part III Tell us if and how you were involved with finances and preparing returns for those tax years *(Continued)*

13 **What was your involvement with preparing the returns?** Check all that apply and explain, if necessary. If the answers are **not** the same for all tax years, explain.

- ☐ You were not involved in preparing the returns.
- ☐ You filled out or helped fill out the returns.
- ☐ You gathered receipts and cancelled checks.
- ☐ You gave tax documents (such as Forms W-2, 1099, etc.) for the preparation of the returns.
- ☐ You reviewed the returns before they were filed.
- ☐ You did not review the returns before they were filed. Explain below why you did not review the returns.
- ☐ You did not know a joint return was filed.
- ☐ Other ▶ ____________

Explain how you were involved ▶ ____________

14 **When the returns were filed, what did you know about any incorrect or missing information?** Check all that apply and explain, if necessary. If the answers are **not** the same for all tax years, explain below.

- ☐ You knew something was incorrect or missing, but you said nothing. Explain below.
- ☐ You knew something was incorrect or missing and asked about it. Explain below.
- ☐ You did not know anything was incorrect or missing.
- ☐ Not applicable. There was no incorrect or missing information.

Explain ▶ ____________

15 **When any of the returns were filed, what did you know about the income of the person on line 5?** Check all that apply and explain, if necessary. If the answers are **not** the same for all tax years, explain.

- ☐ You knew that the person on line 5 had income.

  List each type of income on the lines provided below. (Examples are wages, social security, gambling winnings, or self-employment business income.) Enter each tax year and the amount of income for each type you listed. If you do not know any details, enter "I don't know."

  ____

- ☐ You knew that the person on line 5 was self-employed and you helped with the books and records.
- ☐ You knew that the person on line 5 was self-employed and you did not help with the books and records.
- ☐ You knew that the person on line 5 had no income.
- ☐ You did not know whether the person on line 5 had income.

Explain why you did not know whether the person on line 5 had income ▶ ____________

16 **When the returns were filed, did you know if the returns showed a balance due to the IRS for those tax years?** If the answers are **not** the same for all tax years, explain.

- ☐ Yes. Explain when and how you thought the amount of tax reported on the return would be paid ▶ ____________
- ☐ No. Explain why you did not know the return showed a balance due. ▶ ____________
- ☐ Not applicable. There was no balance due on the return.

17 **When any of the returns were filed, were you having financial problems** (for example, bankruptcy or bills you could not pay)? If the answers are **not** the same for all tax years, explain.

- ☐ Yes. Explain ▶ ____________
- ☐ No.
- ☐ Did not know. Explain ▶ ____________

Form 8857 (Rev. 1-2014) Page **4**

Note. If you need more room to write your answer for any question, attach more pages. Be sure to write your name and social security number on the top of all pages you attach.

Part III **Tell us if and how you were involved with finances and preparing returns for those tax years** *(Continued)*

18 **For the years you want relief, how were you involved in the household finances?** Check all that apply. If the answers are **not** the same for all tax years, explain.

☐ You were not involved in handling money for the household. Explain below.
☐ You knew the person on line 5 had separate accounts.
☐ You had joint accounts with the person on line 5, but you had limited use of them or did not use them. Explain below.
☐ You used joint accounts with the person on line 5. You made deposits, paid bills, balanced the checkbook, or reviewed the monthly bank statements.
☐ You made decisions about how money was spent. For example, you paid bills or made decisions about household purchases.
☐ Other ▶ ____________________

Explain anything else you want to tell us about your household finances ▶ ____________________

19 **Did you (or the person on line 5) incur any large expenses, such as trips, home improvements, or private schooling, or make any large purchases, such as automobiles, appliances, or jewelry, during any of the years you want relief or any later years?**

☐ Yes. Describe (a) the types and amounts of the expenses and purchases and (b) the years they were incurred or made.

☐ No.

20 **Has the person on line 5 ever transferred assets (money or property) to you?** (Property includes real estate, stocks, bonds, or other property that you own or possess now or possessed in the past.) See instructions.

☐ Yes. List the assets, the dates they were transferred, and their fair market values on the dates transferred. If the property was secured by any debt (such as a mortgage on real estate), explain who was responsible for making payments on the debt, how much was owed on the debt at the time of transfer and whether the debt has been satisfied. Explain why the assets were transferred to you. If you no longer possess or own the assets, explain what happened with the assets.

☐ No.

Part IV **Tell us about your current financial situation**

21 **Tell us about your assets.** Your assets are your money and property. Property includes real estate, motor vehicles, stocks, bonds, and other property that you own. In the table below, list the amount of cash you have on hand and in your bank accounts. Also list each item of property, the fair market value (as defined in the instructions) of each item, and the balance of any outstanding loans you used to acquire each item. Do not list any money or property you listed on line 20.

Description of Assets	Fair Market Value	Balance of Any Outstanding Loans You Used To Acquire the Asset

Form **8857** (Rev. 1-2014)

Note. If you need more room to write your answer for any question, attach more pages. Be sure to write your name and social security number on the top of all pages you attach.

Part IV Tell us about your current financial situation *(Continued)*

22 How many people are currently in your household, including yourself? Adults ________ Children ________

23 Tell us your current average monthly income and expenses for your entire household.

Monthly Income — If family or friends are helping to support you, include the amount of support as gifts below.	**Amount**
Gifts	
Wages (Gross pay)	
Pensions	
Unemployment	
Social security	
Government assistance, such as housing, food stamps, grants	
Alimony	
Child support	
Self-employment business income	
Rental income	
Interest and dividends	
Other income, such as disability payments, gambling winnings, etc. List each type below:	
Type	
Type	
Type	
Total Monthly Income	

Monthly Expenses — Enter all expenses, including expenses paid with income from gifts.	**Amount**
Food and Personal Care:	
Food	
Housekeeping supplies	
Clothing and clothing services	
Personal care products and services	
Transportation:	
Auto loan/lease payment, gas, insurance, licenses, parking, maintenance, etc.	
Public transportation	
Housing and Utilities:	
Rent or mortgage	
Real estate taxes and insurance	
Electric, oil, gas, water, trash, etc.	
Telephone and cell phone	
Cable and Internet	
Medical:	
Health insurance premiums	
Out-of-pocket expenses	
Other:	
Child and dependent care	
Caregiver expenses	
Income tax withholding (federal, state, and local)	
Estimated tax payments	
Term life insurance premiums	
Retirement contributions (employer required)	
Retirement contributions (voluntary)	
Union dues	
Unpaid state and local taxes (minimum payment)	
Student loans (minimum payment)	
Court-ordered debt payments (for example, court- or agency-ordered child support, alimony and garnishments). List each type below:	
Type	
Type	
Type	
Miscellaneous	
Total Monthly Expenses	

Form 8857 (Rev. 1-2014) Page **6**

Note. If you need more room to write your answer for any question, attach more pages. Be sure to write your name and social security number on the top of all pages you attach.

Part V **Complete this part if you were (or are now) a victim of domestic violence or spousal abuse**

As stated in line 8, providing this additional information is not mandatory but may strengthen your request. **Additionally, if you prefer to provide this information orally, check the "Yes" box on line 10.**

If you were (or are now) a victim of domestic violence or spousal abuse by the person on line 5, the IRS will consider the information you provide in this part to determine whether to grant innocent spouse relief. However, the IRS is required by law to notify the person on line 5 that you requested this relief. There are no exceptions to this rule. That person will have the opportunity to participate in the process by completing a questionnaire about the tax years you entered on line 3. This will be done before the IRS issues preliminary and final determination letters. However, the IRS is also required by law to keep all the personal identifying information (such as current names, addresses, and employment-related information) of both you and the person on line 5 confidential. This means that the IRS cannot disclose one person's information to the other person. If the IRS does not grant you relief and you choose to petition the Tax Court, your personal identifying information is available, unless you ask the Tax Court to withhold it.

The person on line 5 will receive a questionnaire about the tax years you entered on line 3. Except for your current name, address, phone numbers, and employer, this form and any attachments could be disclosed to the person on line 5. If you have any privacy concerns, see instructions.

The IRS understands and is sensitive to the effects of domestic violence and spousal abuse, and encourages victims of domestic violence to call 911 if they are in immediate danger. **If you have concerns about your safety,** please consider contacting the 24-Hour (Confidential) National Domestic Violence Hotline at 1-800-799-SAFE (7233), or 1-800-787-3224 (TTY), or 1-855-812-1001 (Video Phone Only for Deaf Callers) before you file this form.

A representative from the IRS may call you to gather more information and discuss your request. Be sure you enter your correct contact information on line 4.

24a During any of the tax years for which you are seeking relief or when any of the returns were filed for those years, did the person on line 5 do any of the following? Check all that apply. (Note. If this does not apply to you, skip lines 24a, b, and c, and complete lines 25 through 29.)

- ☐ Physically harm or threaten you, your children, or other members of your family.
- ☐ Sexually abuse you, your children, or other members of your family.
- ☐ Make you afraid to disagree with him/her.
- ☐ Criticize or insult you or frequently put you down.
- ☐ Withhold money for food, clothing, or other basic needs.
- ☐ Make most or all the decisions for you, including financial decisions.
- ☐ Restrict or control who you could see or talk to or where you could go.
- ☐ Isolate you or keep you from contacting your family members and/or friends.
- ☐ Cause you to fear for your safety in any other way.
- ☐ Stalk you, your children, or other members of your family.
- ☐ Abuse alcohol or drugs.

b Describe the abuse you experienced, including approximately when it began and how it may have affected you, your children, or other members of your family. Explain how this abuse affected your ability to question the reporting of items on your tax return or the payment of the tax due on your return.

____

____

____

c Attach photocopies of any documentation you have, such as:

- Protection and/or restraining order.
- Police reports.
- Medical records.
- Doctor's report or letter.
- Injury photographs.
- A statement from someone who was aware of or witnessed the abuse or the results of the abuse (notarized if possible).
- Any other documentation you may have.

25 Are you afraid of the person listed on line 5?

☐ Yes ☐ No

26 Does the person listed on line 5 pose a danger to you, your children, or other members of your family?

☐ Yes ☐ No

27 Were the police, sheriff, or other law enforcement ever called?

☐ Yes ☐ No

28 Was the person listed on line 5 charged or arrested for abusing you, your children, or other members of your family?

☐ Yes. Provide details below.

____

____

☐ No

29 Have you sought help from a local domestic violence program?

☐ Yes. Provide details below.

____

____

____

☐ No

Form **8857** (Rev. 1-2014)

Form 8857 (Rev. 1-2014) Page **7**

Note. If you need more room to write your answer for any question, attach more pages. Be sure to write your name and social security number on the top of all pages you attach.

Part VI Additional Information

30 **Please provide any other information you want us to consider in determining whether it would be unfair to hold you liable for the tax.**

Part VII Tell us if you would like a refund

31 **By checking this box and signing this form, you are indicating that you would like a refund if you qualify for relief and if you already paid the tax. See instructions** . . . . ☐

Caution

By signing this form, you understand that, by law, we must contact the person on line 5. See instructions for details.

Sign Here

Keep a copy for your records.

Under penalties of perjury, I declare that I have examined this form and any accompanying schedules and statements, and to the best of my knowledge and belief, they are true, correct, and complete. Declaration of preparer (other than taxpayer) is based on all information of which preparer has any knowledge.

Your signature	Date

Paid Preparer Use Only

Print/Type preparer's name	Preparer's signature	Date	Check ☐ if self-employed	PTIN
Firm's name ▶			Firm's EIN ▶	
Firm's address ▶			Phone no.	

Form **8857** (Rev. 1-2014)

Chapter 16:

Appeals[xix]

In this chapter you will learn about the different types of appeal processes as well as how to submit the various appeals. The IRS has done a good job via their instructions explaining how to submit an appeal so we defer to them in this instance.

Your Appeal Rights and How to Prepare a Protest If You Don't Agree

Publication 5 **(Rev. 01-1999)** Catalog Number **46074I**

Introduction

This Publication tells you how to appeal your tax case if you don't agree with the Internal Revenue Service (IRS) findings.

If You Don't Agree

If you don't agree with any or all of the IRS findings given you, you may request a meeting or a telephone conference with the supervisor of the person who issued the findings. If you still don't agree, you may appeal your case to the Appeals Office of IRS.

If you decide to do nothing and your case involves an examination of your income, estate, gift, and certain excise taxes or penalties, you will receive a formal Notice of Deficiency. The Notice of Deficiency allows you to go to the Tax Court and tells you the procedure to follow. If you do not go to the Tax Court, we will send you a bill for the amount due.

If you decide to do nothing and your case involves a trust fund recovery penalty, or certain employment tax liabilities, the IRS will send you a bill for the penalty. If you do not appeal a denial of an offer in compromise or a denial of a penalty abatement, the IRS will continue collection action.

If you want an Appeals conference, follow the instructions in our letter to you. Your request will be sent to the Appeals Office to arrange a conference at a convenient time and place. You or your representative should prepare to discuss all issues you don't agree with at the conference. Most differences are settled at this level.

In most instances, you may be eligible to take your case to court if you don't reach an agreement at your Appeals conference, or if you don't want to appeal your case to the IRS Office of Appeals. See the later section *Appeals to the Courts.*

Protests

When you request an appeals conference, you may also need to file a formal written protest or a small case request with the office named in our letter to you. Also, see the special appeal request procedures in Publication 1660, Collection Appeal Rights, if you disagree with lien, levy, seizure, or denial or termination of an installment agreement.

You need to file a written protest:

In all partnership and S corporation cases without regard to the dollar amount at issue.

In all other cases, unless you qualify for the small case request procedure, or other special appeal procedures such as requesting Appeals consideration of liens, levies, seizures, or installment agreements. See Publication 1660.

How to prepare a protest:

When a protest is required, **send it within the time limit specified in the letter you received.** Include in your protest:

1) Your name and address, and a daytime telephone number,
2) A statement that you want to appeal the IRS findings to the Appeals Office,
3) A copy of the letter showing the proposed changes and findings you don't agree with (or the date and symbols from the letter),
4) The tax periods or years involved,
5) A list of the changes that you don't agree with, and why you don't agree.
6) The facts supporting your position on any issue that you don't agree with,
7) The law or authority, if any, on which you are relying.
8) You must sign the written protest, stating that it is true, under the penalties of perjury as follows:

"Under the penalties of perjury, I declare that I examined the facts stated in this protest, including any accompanying documents, and, to the best of my knowledge and belief, they are true, correct, and complete." If your representative prepares and signs the protest for you, he or she must substitute a declaration stating:

1) That he or she submitted the protest and accompanying documents and
2) Whether he or she knows personally that the facts stated in the protest and accompanying documents are true and correct.

We urge you to provide as much information as you can, as this will help us speed up your appeal. This will save you both time and money.

Small Case Request:

Representation

You may represent yourself at your appeals conference, or you may have an attorney, certified public accountant, or an individual enrolled to practice before the IRS represent you. Your representative must be qualified to practice before the IRS. If you want your representative to appear without you, you must provide a properly completed power of attorney to the IRS before the representative can receive or inspect confidential information. Form 2848, Power of Attorney and Declaration of Representative, or any other properly written power of attorney or authorization may be used for this purpose.

If you don't agree, we urge you to appeal your case to the Appeals Office of IRS. The Office of Appeals can settle most differences without expensive and time-consuming court trials. [Note: Appeals cannot consider your reasons for not agreeing if they don't come within the scope of the tax laws (for example, if you disagree solely on moral, religious, political, constitutional, conscientious, or similar grounds.)]

The following general rules tell you how to appeal your case.

Appeals Within the IRS

Appeals is the administrative appeals office for the IRS. You may appeal most IRS decisions with your local Appeals Office. The Appeals Office is separate from - and independent of - the IRS Office taking the action you disagree with. The Appeals Office is the only level of administrative appeal within the IRS.

Conferences with Appeals Office personnel are held in an informal manner by correspondence, by telephone or at a personal conference. There is no need for you to have representation for an Appeals conference, but if you choose to have a representative, see the requirements under **Representation.**

In all employee plan and exempt organization cases without regard to the dollar amount at issue. If the total amount for any tax period is not more than $25,000, you may make a small case request instead of filing a formal written protest. In computing the total amount, include a proposed increase or decrease in tax (including penalties), or claimed refund. For an offer in compromise, in calculating the total amount, include total unpaid tax, penalty and interest due. For a small case request, follow the instructions in our letter to you by: sending a letter requesting Appeals consideration, indicating the changes you don't agree with, and the reasons why you don't agree.

You can get copies of Form 2848 from an IRS office, or by calling 1-800-TAX-FORM (1-800-829-3676). You may also bring another person(s) with you to support your position.

Appeals To The Courts

other matters from the Clerk of the Tax Court, 400 Second St. NW, Washington, DC 20217.

Frivolous Filing Penalty

Caution: If the Tax Court determines that your case is intended primarily to cause a delay, or that your position is frivolous or groundless, the Tax Court may award a penalty of up to $25,000 to the United States in its decision.

Reasonable amounts for court costs or any administrative fees or similar charges by the IRS.
Reasonable expenses of expert witnesses.
Reasonable costs of studies, analyses, tests, or engineering reports that are necessary to prepare your case.

You substantially prevailed on the amount in controversy, or on the most significant tax issue or issues in question.

You meet the net worth requirement. For individuals or estates, the net worth cannot exceed $2,000,000 on the date from which costs are recoverable. Charities and certain cooperatives must not have more than 500 employees on the date from which costs are recoverable. And taxpayers other than the two categories listed above must not have net worth exceeding $7,000,000 and cannot have more than 500 employees on the date from which costs are recoverable.

The United States establishes that its position was substantially justified. If the IRS does not follow applicable published guidance, the United States is presumed to not be substantially justified. This presumption is rebuttable. Applicable published guidance means regulations, revenue rulings, revenue procedures, information releases, notices, announcements, and, if they are issued to you, private letter rulings, technical advice memoranda and determination letters. The court will also take into account whether the Government has won or lost in the courts of appeals for other circuits on substantially similar issues, in determining if the United States is substantially justified.

The final judgment on your case is less than or equal to a "qualified offer" which the IRS rejected, and if you meet the net worth requirements referred to above.

If you and Appeals don't agree on some or all of the issues after your Appeals conference, or if you skipped our appeals system, you may take your case to the United States Tax Court, the United States Court of Federal Claims, or your United States District Court, after satisfying certain procedural and jurisdictional requirements as described below under each court. (However, if you are a nonresident alien, you cannot take your case to a United States District Court.) These courts are independent judicial bodies and have no connection with the IRS.

Tax Court

If your disagreement with the IRS is over whether you owe additional income tax, estate tax, gift tax, certain excise taxes or penalties related to these proposed liabilities, you can go to the United States Tax Court. (Other types of tax controversies, such as those involving some employment tax issues or manufacturers' excise taxes, cannot be heard by the Tax Court.) You can do this after the IRS issues a formal letter, stating the amounts that the IRS believes you owe. This letter is called a notice of deficiency. You have 90 days from the date this notice is mailed to you to file a petition with the Tax Court (or 150 days if the notice is addressed to you outside the United States). The last date to file your petition will be entered on the notice of deficiency issued to you by the IRS. If you don't file the petition within the 90-day period (or 150 days, as the case may be), we will assess the proposed liability and send you a bill. You may also have the right to take your case to the Tax Court in some other situations, for example, following collection action by the IRS in certain cases. See Publication 1660.

District Court and Court of Federal Claims

If your claim is for a refund of any type of tax, you may take your case to your United States District Court or to the United States Court of Federal Claims. Certain types of cases, such as those involving some employment tax issues or manufacturers' excise taxes, can be heard only by these courts.

Generally, your District Court and the Court of Federal Claims hear tax cases only after you have paid the tax and filed a claim for refund with the IRS. You can get information about procedures for filing suit in either court by contacting the Clerk of your District Court or the Clerk of the Court of Federal Claims.

If you file a formal refund claim with the IRS, and we haven't responded to you on your claim within 6 months from the date you filed it, you may file suit for a refund immediately in your District Court or the Court of Federal Claims. If we send you a letter that proposes disallowing or disallows your claim, you may request Appeals review of the disallowance. If you wish to file a refund suit, you must file your suit no later than 2 years from the date of our notice of claim disallowance letter.

Note: Appeals review of a disallowed claim doesn't extend the 2 year period for filing suit. However, it may be extended by mutual agreement.

Recovering Administrative and Litigation Costs

You may be able to recover your reasonable litigation and administrative costs if you are the prevailing party, and if you meet the other requirements. You must exhaust your administrative remedies within the IRS to receive reasonable litigation costs. You must not unreasonably delay the administrative or court proceedings

You are the prevailing party if you meet all the following requirements:

You are not the prevailing party if:

You are also the prevailing party if:

If you dispute not more than $50,000 for any one tax year, there are simplified procedures. You can get information about these procedures and Attorney fees that generally do not exceed $125 per hour. This amount will be indexed for a cost of living adjustment.

A court will generally decide who the prevailing party is, but the IRS makes a final determination of liability at the administrative level. This means you may receive administrative costs from the IRS without going to court. You must file your claim for administrative costs no later than the 90th day after the final determination of tax, penalty or interest is mailed to you. The Appeals Office makes determinations for the IRS on administrative costs. A denial of administrative costs may be appealed to the Tax Court no later than the 90th day after the denial.

Administrative costs include costs incurred on or after the date you receive the Appeals decision letter, the date of the first letter of proposed deficiency, or the date of the notice of deficiency, whichever is earliest.

Recoverable litigation or administrative costs may include:

If you discuss your case with the IRS during the 90-day period (150-day period), the discussion will not extend the period in which you may file a petition with the Tax Court.

The court will schedule your case for trial at a location convenient to you. You may represent yourself before the Tax Court, or you may be represented by anyone permitted to practice before that court.

Note: If you don't choose to go to the IRS Appeals Office before going to court, normally you will have an opportunity to attempt settlement with Appeals before your trial date.

Collection Appeal Rights (CDP vs. CAP)[xx]

Collection Appeal Rights

You may appeal many IRS collection actions to the IRS Office of Appeals (Appeals). Appeals is separate from and independent of the IRS Collection office that initiated the collection action. Appeals ensures and protects its independence by adhering to a strict policy of prohibiting certain ex parte communications with the IRS Collection office or other IRS offices, such as discussions regarding the strengths or weaknesses of your case. Revenue Procedure 2012-18 has more information about Appeals' independence and ex parte communication and is available at www.IRS.gov.

The two main procedures are **Collection Due Process** and **Collection Appeals Program**. Other procedures are described on page four of this publication and at www.IRS.gov.

Collection Due Process (CDP) is available if you receive one of the following notices:

- *Notice of Federal Tax Lien Filing and Your Right to a Hearing under IRC 6320*
- *Final Notice - Notice of Intent to Levy and Notice of Your Right to a Hearing*
- *Notice of Jeopardy Levy and Right of Appeal*
- *Notice of Levy on Your State Tax Refund – Notice of Your Right to a Hearing*
- *Post Levy Collection Due Process (CDP) Notice*

Collection Appeals Program (CAP) is available for the following actions:

- *Before or after the IRS fi les a Notice of Federal Tax Lien*
- *Before or after the IRS levies or seizes your property*
- *Termination, or proposed termination, of an installment agreement*
- *Rejection of an installment agreement*
- *Modification, or proposed modification, of an installment agreement*

CAP generally results in a quicker Appeals decision and is available for a broader range of collection actions. However, you cannot go to court if you disagree with the CAP decision. CAP procedures are described on pages three and four of this publication.

You may represent yourself at CDP, CAP and other Appeals proceedings. Or, you may be represented by an attorney, certified public accountant, or a person enrolled to practice before the IRS. Also, you may be represented by a member of your immediate family, or in the case of a business, by regular full-time employees, general partners or bona fi de officers.

A Low Income Taxpayer Clinic (LITC) may represent you if you qualify. LITCs are independent from the IRS and most provide representation before the IRS or in court on audits, tax collection disputes, and other issues for free or for a small fee. Some clinics can provide multilingual information about taxpayer rights and responsibilities. Publication 4134, *Low Income Taxpayer Clinic List*, provides information on clinics in your area and is available at your local IRS office, by calling 1-800-829-3676, or from www.IRS.gov.

If you want your representative to contact us or appear without you and to receive and inspect confidential material, you must fi le a properly completed Form 2848 (no earlier than 10/2011 revision), *Power of Attorney and Declaration of Representative*. You may also authorize an individual to receive or inspect confidential material but not represent you before the IRS, by fi ling a Form 8821, *Tax Information Authorization*. These forms are available at your local IRS office, by calling 1-800-829-3676, or from www.IRS.gov.

HEARING AVAILABLE UNDER COLLECTION DUE PROCESS (CDP)

For Lien and Levy Notices

By law, you have the right to a CDP hearing when you receive a Notice advising you of this right and you timely postmark a request for a hearing to the address indicated on the Notice. You are limited to one hearing under section 6320 (Notice and opportunity for hearing upon filing of notice of lien) and 6330 (Notice and opportunity for hearing before levy) for each tax assessment within a tax period.

You may contest the CDP determination in the United States Tax Court.

Lien Notice: The IRS is required to notify you the first time a Notice of Federal Tax Lien is filed for each tax and period. The IRS must notify you within 5 business days after the lien filing. This notice may be mailed, given to you, or left at your home or office. You then have 30 days, after that 5-day period, to request a hearing with Appeals. The lien notice you receive will indicate the date this 30-day period expires.

Levy Notice: For each tax and period, the IRS is required to notify you the first time it collects or intends to collect a tax liability by taking your property or rights to property. The IRS does this by issuing you a pre-levy or post-levy notice. The notice is mailed, given to you, or left at your home or office. During the 30-day period from the date of the notice, you may request a hearing with Appeals. There are four exceptions to issuing this notice before levy:

1. When collection of the tax is in jeopardy.
2. When the IRS levies your state tax refund.
3. When the criteria for a Disqualified Employment Tax Levy is met.
4. When the IRS serves a federal contractor levy.

You may request a hearing after the levy action in these instances.

If your request for a CDP hearing is not timely, you may request an equivalent hearing. To receive an equivalent hearing, your request must be postmarked on or before the end of the one-year period after the date of the levy notice or on or before the end of the one-year period plus 5 business days after the filing date of the Notice of Federal Tax Lien.

How do you request a CDP or equivalent hearing with the Office of Appeals?

Complete Form 12153, *Request for a Collection Due Process or Equivalent Hearing*, or other written request with the same information and send it to the address shown on your lien or levy notice. To request an equivalent hearing, you must check the Equivalent Hearing box on line 7 of Form 12153, or if you don't use Form 12153 write that you want an equivalent hearing if the CDP hearing request is late. If you received both a lien and a levy notice, you may appeal both actions by checking the boxes on line 6 of Form 12153 or if you don't use Form 12153, you may appeal both actions in one written request. You must identify your alternatives to, or your reasons for disagreeing with, the lien filing or the levy action. Alternatives or reasons for disagreeing may include:

- Collection alternatives such as installment agreement or offer in compromise.
- Subordination or discharge of lien.
- Withdrawal of Notice of Federal Tax Lien.
- Appropriate spousal defenses.
- The existence or amount of the tax, but only if you did not receive a notice of deficiency or did not otherwise have an opportunity to dispute the tax liability.
- Collection of the tax liability is causing or will cause an economic or other hardship.

Note: You may not raise an issue that was raised and considered at a prior administrative or judicial hearing, if you, or your representative, participated meaningfully in the prior hearing or proceeding. Also, you may not challenge the existence or amount of an assessment made based on court ordered restitution.

Form 12153 is available at your local IRS Office, by calling 1-800-829-3676, or from www.IRS.gov. Include a copy of your lien and/or levy notice. List all taxes and tax periods included on the notice you received for which you are requesting a hearing. You are entitled to only one hearing relating to a lien notice and one hearing relating to a levy notice, for each taxable period.

In general, the IRS will deny a hearing request that only raises issues identified by the IRS as frivolous or that are made solely to delay or impede collection. For a nonexclusive listing of issues identified by the IRS as frivolous, see "The Truth About Frivolous Tax Arguments" on www.IRS.gov.

To preserve your right to go to court, you must request a CDP hearing within the time period provided by law. Your request for a CDP hearing must be sent to the address on the lien or levy notice and postmarked on or before the date shown in the lien notice or on or before the 30th day after the date of the levy notice.

Before you formally appeal a lien or levy notice by sending us Form 12153, you may be able to work out a solution with the Collection office that sent the notice. To do so, call the telephone number on the lien or levy notice and explain to the IRS employee listed on the notice or other representative why you disagree with the action.

If a telephone number is not shown on the notice, you can call 1-800-829-1040. This contact, however, does NOT extend the 30-day period to make a written request for a CDP hearing.

What will happen when you request a CDP or equivalent hearing with the Office of Appeals?

After you request a hearing, you may still discuss your concerns with the Collection office that sent the lien or levy notice. If you are able to resolve the issues with that office, you may withdraw your request for a hearing. If you are unable to, or do not choose to, resolve the issues with the Collection office, your case will be forwarded immediately to Appeals.

Appeals will contact you to schedule a conference. Your conference may be held by telephone, correspondence, or, if you qualify, in a face-to-face conference at the Appeals office closest to your home, school or place of business. To qualify for a face-to-face conference, you must not raise any issues that are deemed as frivolous or made with a desire solely to delay or impede collection. If you are proposing a collection alternative, it may be necessary for you to submit financial information or tax returns to qualify for a face-to-face conference. The Appeals officer will notify you by letter if you need to take steps to qualify for a face-to-face conference.

Unless one of the exceptions in section 6330(f) applies, for Jeopardy situations, State Income Tax levies, Federal Contractor levies or Disqualified Employment Tax levies, levy action is not permitted for the subject tax and periods during the 30 days after the levy notice and during the timely requested CDP hearing process. Normally, there will be no levy action during the period you have to request a hearing from a lien notice and during the related CDP hearing process.

If your request for a CDP hearing is timely, the 10-year period the IRS has to collect your taxes will be suspended until the date Appeals' determination becomes final or you withdraw your request for a hearing in writing.

At the conclusion of the CDP hearing, Appeals will issue a determination letter unless you have withdrawn your hearing request. If you don't agree with Appeals' determination, you may request judicial review of the determination by petitioning the United States Tax Court within the time period provided for in the Appeals' determination letter. You may not be able to raise issues in the Tax Court if you do not raise them during the Appeals hearing, and the Tax Court may limit the evidence you can present to the evidence you submitted to Appeals during the hearing. You should, therefore, raise all issues and present all evidence during the Appeals hearing, in order to preserve your rights to raise issues and have evidence considered in subsequent court proceedings.

Appeals will retain jurisdiction over its determination. You may return to Appeals if you believe that the Collection function did not carry out Appeals' determination as it was stated or if there is a change in your circumstances that affects Appeals' determination. However, you must first try to work with Collection to resolve the problem.

If your request for a CDP hearing is not timely and you request an equivalent hearing, the law does not prohibit levy and the collection statute is not suspended. Furthermore, you cannot go to court if you disagree with Appeals' decision.

HEARING AVAILABLE UNDER COLLECTION APPEALS PROGRAM (CAP)

For Liens, Levies, Seizures and Installment Agreements

The CAP procedure is available under more circumstances than Collection Due Process (CDP). Unlike CDP, you may not challenge in CAP the existence or amount of your tax liability. You also cannot proceed to court if you don't agree with Appeals' decision in your CAP case. Collection actions you may appeal under CAP are:

Notice of Federal Tax Lien. You may appeal the proposed filing of a Notice of Federal Tax Lien (NFTL) or the actual fi ling of an NFTL at the first and each subsequent fi ling of the NFTL. You may also appeal denied requests to withdraw a NFTL, and denied discharges, subordinations, and non-attachments of a lien.

Third parties may file a CAP appeal regarding the fi ling of a notice of lien against alter ego or nominee property. There are no CDP rights available for persons determined to be nominees or alter egos. Persons assessed as transferees under Internal Revenue Code (IRC) Section 6901, however, are entitled to CDP rights.

Notice of Levy. You may appeal before or after the IRS places a levy on your wages, bank account or other property. Once the levy proceeds have been sent to the IRS, you may also appeal the denial by the IRS of your request to have levied property returned to you. Please note that a request to return levy proceeds must be made within 9 months from the date of such levy. See IRC Section 6343(d). You may also have additional CDP appeal rights. See the preceding information regarding Hearing Available under Collection Due Process.

Seizure of Property. You may appeal before or after the IRS makes a seizure but before the property is sold.

Rejection, Modification or Termination of Installment Agreement. You may appeal when the IRS rejects your request for an installment agreement. You may also appeal when the IRS proposes to terminate or terminates your installment agreement.

In addition, you may also appeal when the IRS proposes to modify or modifies your installment agreement.

Wrongful Levy. If you are not liable for tax and the IRS has levied or seized property that you believe belongs to you or in which you have an interest superior to the IRS, you may appeal the denial by the IRS of your request to release the levy or seizure, or return the property or its value. Please note that a request to the IRS to return wrongfully levied property must be in writing, fi led within 9 months of the levy or seizure and must satisfy certain specific requirements. See Publication 4528, Making an Administrative Wrongful Levy Claim Under Internal Revenue Code (IRC) Section 6343(b).

How do you appeal a lien or levy action if your only collection contact has been a notice or telephone call?

1. Call the IRS at the telephone number shown on your notice or identified by the IRS employee in a prior telephone contact. Be prepared to explain which action(s) you disagree with and why you disagree. You must also offer a solution to your tax problem.

2. If you can't reach an agreement with the employee, tell the employee that you want to appeal his or her decision. The employee must honor your request and will refer you to a manager. The manager will either speak with you then or will return your call within 24 hours.

3. Explain to the manager which action(s) you disagree with and why. The manager will make a decision on the case. If you don't agree with the manager's decision, your case will be forwarded to Appeals for review. You do not have to submit the appeal request in writing. *How do you appeal a lien, levy or seizure action if you have been contacted by a Revenue Officer?*

1. If you disagree with the decision of the Revenue Officer, you must first request a conference with the Collection manager.

2. If you do not resolve your disagreement with the Collection manager, you may submit a written request for Appeals consideration, preferably by completing Form 9423, *Collection Appeal Request*. This form is available at your local IRS office, by calling 1-800-829-3676, or from www.IRS.gov. Check the action(s) you disagree with and explain why you disagree. You must also offer a solution to resolve your tax problem.

3. Submit the Form 9423 to that Collection office.

4. If you request an appeal after the IRS makes a seizure, you must appeal to the Collection manager within 10 business days after the Notice of Seizure is given to you or left at your home or business.

5. You should let the Revenue Officer or manager know within 2 business days after your conference with the Collection manager if you want to appeal under CAP or the IRS will resume collection action. Your Form 9423 must be postmarked within 3 business days after the date of your conference with the Collection manager in order to prevent the resumption of collection action.

6. If you request a conference and are not contacted by a manager or his/her designee within two (2) business days of making the request, you can contact Collection again or submit Form 9423. If you submit Form 9423, note the date of your request for a conference in Block 15 and indicate that you were not contacted by a manager. The Form 9423 should be received or postmarked within four (4) business days of your request for a conference as collection action may resume.

How do you appeal the denial by the IRS of your request to release or return levied or seized property, if you believed the property was wrongfully levied or seized?

1. If you do not agree with the denial of the request to release or return wrongfully levied/seized property or its value, you must first request a conference with the manager of the Advisory Group denying your request.

2. Call the telephone number on the letter denying your request and explain that you want a conference with the Advisory Group manager.

3. If you do not resolve your disagreement with the Advisory Group manager, you must submit a written request for Appeals consideration, preferably on Form 9423, *Collection Appeal Request*. This form is available at your local IRS office, by calling 1-800-829-3676, or from www.IRS.gov. Check the action you disagree with and explain why you disagree.

4. Submit the completed Form 9423 to the Advisory Group office that denied your request to release or return of wrongfully levied/seized property or its value. *How do you appeal the rejection of a proposed installment agreement?*

1. Call the telephone number shown on the letter rejecting your proposed installment agreement and explain that you want to appeal the rejection. Your appeal need not be in writing unless the rejection letter was sent by a Revenue Officer, in which case your request for an appeal must be in writing, preferably using Form 9423, *Collection Appeal Request.* While a conference is recommended, you need not have a conference with a Collection manager before appealing the rejection of a proposed installment agreement.

2. Your request for an appeal of the rejection of a proposed installment agreement must be made on or before the 30th day after the date of the rejection letter (the mailing of a written request, including a Form 9423, must be postmarked on or before such day).

How do you appeal the termination of an installment agreement?

1. Call the telephone number shown on the notice that indicates that the IRS intends to terminate your installment agreement. If you are unable to resolve the matter, then explain that you want to appeal the termination. Your appeal need not be in writing unless the notice of intent to terminate your installment agreement was sent by a Revenue Officer, in which case your request for an appeal must be in writing, preferably using Form 9423, *Collection Appeal Request.* While a conference is recommended, you need not have a conference with a Collection manager before appealing the termination of an installment agreement.

2. You will have 76 days from the date of the notice of intent to terminate in which to request an appeal. Unless you appeal within 30 days after the date of the notice, or cure your default of the installment agreement, the installment agreement will terminate automatically on the 46th day after the date of the notice. After the 46th day, and the termination of your agreement, your right to appeal will continue for an additional 30 days. Accordingly, your request must be made on or before the 76th day after the date of the notice of intent to terminate (the mailing of a written request, including a Form 9423, must be postmarked on or before such 76th day).

How do you appeal a proposed modification or modification of an installment agreement?

The IRS may propose to modify the terms of your installment agreement based on your financial information. If the IRS does not hear from you after proposing to modify your installment agreement, it may proceed to modify your installment agreement. If you are informed that your agreement is being modified or has been modified, you may request an Appeals hearing under CAP procedures. If you wish to fi le an appeal concerning a proposed modification or modification of your installment agreement, please follow the directions under the section entitled, *"How do you appeal the termination of an installment agreement?"*

What will happen when you appeal your case?

Lien, Levy and Seizure: Normally, the IRS will not take any action to collect the tax for the tax periods Appeals is considering, unless the IRS believes the collection of the tax is at risk or you are a business meeting the criteria for a Disqualified Employment Tax Levy.

Installment Agreements: ***IMPORTANT*** - The IRS can't levy until 30 days after the rejection or termination of your agreement. If you appeal within the 30-day period, the IRS will be prohibited from levying until your appeal is completed unless the IRS believes the collection of the tax is in jeopardy.

Once Appeals makes a decision regarding your case, that decision is binding on both you and the IRS. You cannot obtain judicial review of Appeals' decision following a CAP hearing. However, there may be other opportunities to obtain administrative or judicial review of the issue raised in the CAP hearing. For example, a third party may contest a wrongful levy by fi ling an action in district court. See Publication 4528, *Making an Administrative Wrongful Levy Claim Under Internal Revenue Code (IRC) Section 6343(b).*

Note: Providing false information, failure to provide all pertinent information or fraud will void Appeals' decision.

APPEAL OF OTHER COLLECTION ACTIONS

You may also appeal other collection actions:

- Rejected Offer in Compromise
- Proposed Trust Fund Recovery Penalty
- Denied Trust Fund Recovery Penalty Claim
- Denied request to abate penalties (i.e., late payment, late fi ling, or deposit penalties)

To dispute a penalty in Appeals, follow the protest requirements in Publication 5, *Your Appeal Rights and How To Prepare A Protest If You Don't Agree*. Also, the correspondence you receive on these types of cases will explain where you should send your protest.

Help if you are experiencing economic harm...

The Taxpayer Advocate Service (TAS) helps taxpayers whose problems with the IRS are causing financial difficulties; who have tried but haven't been able to resolve their problems with the IRS; and those who believe an IRS system or procedure is not working as it should. If you believe you are eligible for TAS assistance, you can reach TAS by calling the TAS toll-free number at 1-877-777-4778 or TTY/TDD 1-800-829-4059. For more information, go to www.irs.gov/advocate.

TAS cannot extend the time you have to request a CDP, equivalent or CAP hearing. The timeframes for requesting these hearings are explained in this publication.

Publication 1660 (Rev. 10-2012) Catalog Number 14376Z Department of the Treasury - **Internal Revenue Service** www.irs.gov

Request for CDP Hearing or Equivalent Form[xxi]

Form **12153** (Rev. 12-2013)	**Request for a Collection Due Process or Equivalent Hearing**

Use this form to request a Collection Due Process (CDP) or equivalent hearing with the IRS Office of Appeals if you have been issued one of the following lien or levy notices:

- Notice of Federal Tax Lien Filing and Your Right to a Hearing under IRC 6320,
- Notice of Intent to Levy and Notice of Your Right to a Hearing,
- Notice of Jeopardy Levy and Right of Appeal,
- Notice of Levy on Your State Tax Refund,
- Notice of Levy and Notice of Your Right to a Hearing.

Complete this form and send it to the address shown on your lien or levy notice. Include a copy of your lien or levy notice to ensure proper handling of your request.

Call the phone number on the notice or 1-800-829-1040 if you are not sure about the correct address or if you want to fax your request.

You can find a section explaining the deadline for requesting a Collection Due Process hearing in this form's instructions. If you've missed the deadline for requesting a CDP hearing, you must check line 7 (Equivalent Hearing) to request an equivalent hearing.

1. Taxpayer Name: (Taxpayer 1) ____________________

Taxpayer Identification Number ____________

Current Address ____________________

City ____________ State ______ Zip Code ______

2. Telephone Number and Best Time to Call During Normal Business Hours	Home (___) ___ - ______ ________ ☐ am. ☐ pm. Work (___) ___ - ______ ________ ☐ am. ☐ pm. Cell ( ) - ☐ am. ☐ pm.

3. Taxpayer Name: (Taxpayer 2) ____________________

Taxpayer Identification Number ____________

Current Address ____________________

(If Different from Address Above) City ____________ State ______ Zip Code ______

4. Telephone Number and Best Time to Call During Normal Business Hours	Home (___) ___ - ______ ________ ☐ am. ☐ pm. Work (___) ___ - ______ ________ ☐ am. ☐ pm. Cell ( ) - ☐ am. ☐ pm.

5. Tax Information as Shown on the Lien or Levy Notice *(If possible, attach a copy of the notice)*

Type of Tax (Income, Employment, Excise, etc. or Civil Penalty)	Tax Form Number (1040, 941, 720, etc)	Tax Period or Periods

Form **12153** (Rev. 12-2013) Catalog Number 26685D www.irs.gov Department of the Treasury - **Internal Revenue Service**

Form **12153** (Rev. 12-2013)

Request for a Collection Due Process or Equivalent Hearing

6. Basis for Hearing Request (Both boxes can be checked if you have received both a lien and levy notice)

☐ Filed Notice of Federal Tax Lien ☐ Proposed Levy or Actual Levy

7. Equivalent Hearing (See the instructions for more information on Equivalent Hearings)

☐ I would like an Equivalent Hearing - I would like a hearing equivalent to a CDP Hearing if my request for a CDP hearing does not meet the requirements for a timely CDP Hearing.

8. Check the most appropriate box for the reason you disagree with the filing of the lien or the levy. **See page 4 of this form for examples.** You can add more pages if you don't have enough space. If, during your CDP Hearing, you think you would like to discuss a Collection Alternative to the action proposed by the Collection function it is recommended you submit a completed Form 433A (Individual) and/or Form 433B (Business), as appropriate, with this form. See www.irs.gov for copies of the forms. Generally, the Office of Appeals will ask the Collection Function to review, verify and provide their opinion on any new information you submit. We will share their comments with you and give you the opportunity to respond.

Collection Alternative ☐ Installment Agreement ☐ Offer in Compromise ☐ I Cannot Pay Balance

Lien ☐ Subordination ☐ Discharge ☐ Withdrawal

Please explain:

My Spouse Is Responsible ☐ Innocent Spouse Relief (Please attach Form 8857, *Request for Innocent Spouse Relief,* to your request.)

Other (*For examples, see page 4*) ☐

Reason (*You must provide a reason for the dispute or your request for a CDP hearing will not be honored. Use as much space as you need to explain the reason for your request. Attach extra pages if necessary.*):

9. Signatures

I understand the CDP hearing and any subsequent judicial review will suspend the statutory period of limitations for collection action. I also understand my representative or I must sign and date this request before the IRS Office of Appeals can accept it. If you are signing as an officer of a company add your title (*president, secretary, etc.*) behind your signature.

SIGN HERE

Taxpayer 1's Signature	Date
Taxpayer 2's Signature (*if a joint request, both must sign*)	Date

☐ I request my CDP hearing be held with my authorized representative (*attach a copy of Form 2848*)

Authorized Representative's Signature	Authorized Representative's Name	Telephone Number

IRS Use Only

IRS Employee (Print)	Employee Telephone Number	IRS Received Date

Information You Need To Know When Requesting A Collection Due Process Hearing

What Is the Deadline for Requesting a Timely Collection Due Process (CDP) Hearing?

- Your request for a CDP hearing about a Federal Tax Lien filing must be postmarked by the date indicated in the *Notice of Federal Tax Lien Filing and Your Right to a Hearing under IRC 6320* (lien notice).
- Your request for a CDP hearing about a levy must be postmarked within 30 days after the date of the *Notice of Intent to Levy and Notice of Your Right to a Hearing* (levy notice) or Notice of Your Right to a Hearing After an Actual Levy.

Your timely request for a CDP hearing will prohibit levy action in most cases. A timely request for CDP hearing will also suspend the 10-year period we have, by law, to collect your taxes. Both the prohibition on levy and the suspension of the 10-year period will last until the determination the IRS Office of Appeals makes about your disagreement is final. The amount of time the suspension is in effect will be added to the time remaining in the 10-year period. For example, if the 10-year period is suspended for six months, the time left in the period we have to collect taxes will be extended by six months.

You can go to court to appeal the CDP determination the IRS Office of Appeals makes about your disagreement.

What Is an Equivalent Hearing?

If you still want a hearing with the IRS Office of Appeals after the deadline for requesting a timely CDP hearing has passed, you can use this form to request an equivalent hearing. You must check the Equivalent Hearing box on line 7 of the form to request an equivalent hearing. **An equivalent hearing request does not prohibit levy or suspend the 10-year period for collecting your taxes; also, you cannot go to court to appeal the IRS Office of Appeals' decision about your disagreement.** You must request an equivalent hearing within the following timeframe:

- Lien Notice—one year plus five business days from the filing date of the Notice of Federal Tax Lien.
- Levy Notice—one year from the date of the levy notice.
- Your request for a CDP levy hearing, whether timely or Equivalent, does not prohibit the Service from filing a Notice of Federal Tax Lien.

Where Should You File Your CDP or Equivalent Hearing Request?

File your request by mail at the address on your lien notice or levy notice. You may also fax your request. Call the telephone number on the lien or levy notice to ask for the fax number. **Do not send your CDP or equivalent hearing request directly to the IRS Office of Appeals, it must be sent to the address on the lien or levy notice. If you send your request directly to Appeals it may result in your request not being considered a timely request. Depending upon your issue the originating function may contact you in an attempt to resolve the issue(s) raised in your request prior to forwarding your request to Appeals.**

Where Can You Get Help?

You can call the telephone number on the lien or levy notice with your questions about requesting a hearing. The contact person listed on the notice or other representative can access your tax information and answer your questions.

In addition, you may qualify for representation by a low-income taxpayer clinic for free or nominal charge. Our Publication 4134, Low Income Taxpayer Clinic List, provides information on clinics in your area.

If you are experiencing economic harm, the Taxpayer Advocate Service (TAS) may be able to help you resolve your problems with the IRS. TAS cannot extend the time you have to request a CDP or equivalent hearing. See Publication 594, *The IRS Collection Process*, or visit www.irs.gov/advocate/index-html. You also can call 1-877-777-4778 for TAS assistance.

Note–The IRS Office of Appeals will not consider frivolous requests. You can find examples of frivolous reasons for requesting a hearing or disagreeing with a tax assessment in Publication 2105, *Why do I have to Pay Taxes?*, or at www.irs.gov by typing "frivolous" into the search engine.

You can get copies of tax forms, schedules, instructions, publications, and notices at www.irs.gov, at your local IRS office, or by calling toll-free *1-800-TAX-FORM (829-3676).*

Information You Need To Know When Requesting A Collection Due Process Hearing

What Are Examples of Reasons for Requesting a Hearing?

You will have to explain your reason for requesting a hearing when you make your request. Below are examples of reasons for requesting a hearing.

You want a collection alternative— "I would like to propose a different way to pay the money I owe." Common collection alternatives include:

- Full payment—you pay your taxes by personal check, cashier's check, money order, or credit card.
- Installment Agreement—you pay your taxes fully or partially by making monthly payments.
- Offer in Compromise—you offer to make a payment or payments to settle your tax liability for less than the full amount you owe.

"I cannot pay my taxes." Some possible reasons why you cannot pay your taxes are: (1) you have a terminal illness or excessive medical bills; (2) your only source of income is Social Security payments, welfare payments, or unemployment benefit payments; (3) you are unemployed with little or no income; (4) you have reasonable expenses exceeding your income; or (5) you have some other hardship condition. The IRS Office of Appeals may consider freezing collection action until your circumstances improve. Penalty and interest will continue to accrue on the unpaid balance.

You want action taken about the filing of the tax lien against your property—You can get a Federal Tax Lien released if you pay your taxes in full. You also may request a lien subordination, discharge, or withdrawal. See www.irs.gov for more information.

When you request **lien subordination**, you are asking the IRS to make a Federal Tax Lien secondary to a non-IRS lien. For example, you may ask for a subordination of the Federal Tax Lien to get a refinancing mortgage on your house or other real property you own. You would ask to make the Federal Tax Lien secondary to the mortgage, even though the mortgage came after the tax lien filing. The IRS Office of Appeals would consider lien subordination, in this example, if you used the mortgage proceeds to pay your taxes.

When you request a **lien discharge**, you are asking the IRS to remove a Federal Tax Lien from a specific property. For example, you may ask for a discharge of the Federal Tax Lien in order to sell your house if you use all of the sale proceeds to pay your taxes even though the sale proceeds will not fully pay all of the tax you owe.

When you request a **lien withdrawal**, you are asking the IRS to remove the Notice of Federal Tax Lien (NFTL) information from public records because you believe the NFTL should not have been filed. For example, you may ask for a withdrawal of the filing of the NFTL if you believe the IRS filed the NFTL prematurely or did not follow procedures, or you have entered into an installment agreement and the installment agreement does not provide for the filing of the NFTL. A withdrawal does not remove the lien from your IRS records.

Your spouse is responsible—"My spouse (or former spouse) is responsible for all or part of the tax liability." You may believe that your spouse or former spouse is the only one responsible for all or a part of the tax liability. If this is the case, you are requesting a hearing so you can receive relief as an innocent spouse. You should complete and attach Form 8857, *Request for Innocent Spouse Relief*, to your hearing request.

Other Reasons—"I am not liable for (I don't owe) all or part of the taxes." You can raise a disagreement about the amount you owe only if you did not receive a deficiency notice for the liability (a notice explaining why you owe taxes—it gives you the right to challenge in court, within a specific timeframe, the additional tax the IRS says you owe), or if you have not had another prior opportunity to disagree with the amount you owe.

"I do not believe I should be responsible for penalties." The IRS Office of Appeals may remove all or part of the penalties if you have a reasonable cause for not paying or not filing on time. See Notice 746, Information About Your Notice, Penalty and Interest for what is reasonable cause for removing penalties.

"I have already paid all or part of my taxes." You disagree with the amount the IRS says you haven't paid if you think you have not received credit for payments you have already made.

See Publication 594, *The IRS Collection Process*, for more information on the following topics: Installment Agreements and Offers in Compromise; Lien Subordination, Discharge, and Withdrawal; Innocent Spouse Relief; Temporarily Delay Collection; and belief that tax bill is wrong.

Collection Appeal Request Form[xxii]

Form **9423** (August 2014)	Department of the Treasury - Internal Revenue Service **Collection Appeal Request** (Instructions are on the reverse side of this form)		
1. Taxpayer's name		2. Representative *(Attach a copy of Form 2848, Power of Attorney)*	
3. SSN/EIN	4. Taxpayer's business phone	5. Taxpayer's home phone	6. Representative's phone
7. Taxpayer's street address			

8. City	9. State	10. ZIP code
11. Type of tax *(Tax form)*	12. Tax periods being appealed	13. Tax due

Collection Action(s) Appealed

14. Check the Collection action(s) you are appealing

☐ Federal Tax Lien ☐ Levy or Proposed Levy ☐ Seizure

☐ Rejection of Installment Agreement ☐ Termination of Installment Agreement ☐ Modification of Installment Agreement

Explanation

15. Explain why you disagree with the collection action(s) you checked above and explain how you would resolve your tax problem. Attach additional pages if needed. Attach copies of any documents that you think will support your position. Generally, the Office of Appeals will ask the Collection Function to review, verify and provide their opinion on any new information you submit. We will share their comments with you and give you the opportunity to respond.

Under penalties of perjury, I declare that I have examined this request and any accompanying documents, and to the best of my knowledge and belief, they are true, correct and complete. A submission by a representative, other than the taxpayer, is based on all information of which the representative has any knowledge.

16. ☐ Taxpayer's or ☐ Authorized Representative's signature *(Only check one box)*	17. Date signed

IRS USE ONLY

18. Revenue Officer's name	19. Revenue Officer's signature	20. Date signed
21. Revenue Officer's phone	22. Revenue Officer's email address	23. Date received
24. Collection Manager's name	25. Collection Manager's signature	26. Date signed
27. Collection Manager's phone	28. Collection Manager's email address	29. Date received

Form **9423** (Rev. 8-2014) Catalog Number 14169I www.irs.gov Department of the Treasury - Internal Revenue Service

Instructions for Form 9423, Collection Appeal Request

For Liens, Levies, Seizures, and Rejection, Modification or Termination of Installment Agreements

A taxpayer, or third party whose property is subject to a collection action, may appeal the following actions under the Collection Appeals Program (CAP):

a. Levy or seizure action that has been or will be taken.
b. A Notice of Federal Tax Lien (NFTL) that has been or will be filed.
c. The filing of a notice of lien against an alter-ego or nominee's property.
d. Denials of requests to issue lien certificates, such as subordination, withdrawal, discharge or non-attachment.
e. Rejected, proposed for modification or modified, or proposed for termination or terminated installment agreements.
f. Disallowance of taxpayer's request to return levied property under IRC 6343(d).
g. Disallowance of property owner's claim for return of property under IRC 6343(b).

How to Appeal If You Disagree With a Lien, Levy, or Seizure Action

1. If you disagree with the decision of the IRS employee, and wish to appeal, you must first request a conference with the employee's manager. If you do not resolve your disagreement with the Collection manager, submit Form 9423 to request consideration by Appeals. Let the Collection office know within two (2) business days after the conference with the Collection manager that you plan to submit Form 9423. The Form 9423 must be received or postmarked within three (3) business days of the conference with the Collection manager or collection action may resume.

   NOTE: If you request an appeal after IRS makes a seizure, you must appeal to the Collection manager within 10 business days after the Notice of Seizure is provided to you or left at your home or business.

2. If you request a conference and are not contacted by a manager or his/her designee within two (2) business days of making the request, you can contact Collection again or submit Form 9423. If you submit Form 9423, note the date of your request for a conference in Block 15 and indicate that you were not contacted by a manager. The Form 9423 should be received or postmarked within four (4) business days of your request for a conference as collection action may resume.

3. On the Form 9423, check the collection action(s) you disagree with and explain why you disagree. You must also explain your solution to resolve your tax problem. Submit Form 9423 to the Collection office involved in the lien, levy or seizure action.

4. In situations where the IRS action(s) are creating an economic harm or you want help because your tax problem has not been resolved through normal channels, you can reach the Taxpayer Advocate Service at 877-777-4778.

How to Appeal An Installment Agreement Which Has Been Rejected, Proposed for Modification or Modified, or Proposed for Termination or Terminated

1. If you disagree with the decision regarding your installment agreement, you should appeal by completing a Form 9423, Collection Appeal Request.
2. You should provide it to the office or revenue officer who took the action regarding your installment agreement, within 30 calendar days.

   NOTE: A managerial conference is not required. However, it is strongly recommended a conference be held with the manager whenever possible.

   IMPORTANT: Never forward your request for an Appeals conference directly to Appeals. It must be submitted to the office which took the action on your installment agreement.

What Will Happen When You Appeal Your Case

Normally, we will stop the collection action(s) you disagree with until your appeal is settled, unless we have reason to believe that collection or the amount owed is at risk.

You May Have a Representative

You may represent yourself at your Appeals conference or you may be represented by an attorney, certified public accountant or a person enrolled to practice before the IRS. If you want your representative to appear without you, you must provide a properly completed Form 2848, Power of Attorney and Declaration of Representative. You can obtain Form 2848 from your local IRS office, by calling 1-800-829-3676, or by going to www.irs.gov.

Decision on the Appeal

Once Appeals makes a decision regarding your case, that decision is binding on both you and the IRS. You cannot obtain a judicial review of Appeals' decision following a CAP. However, there may be other opportunities to obtain administrative or judicial review of the issue raised in the CAP hearing. For example, a third party may contest a wrongful levy by filing an action in district court. See Publication 4528, *Making an Administrative Wrongful Levy Claim Under Internal Revenue Code (IRC) Section 6343(b).*

Note: Providing false information, failing to provide all pertinent information or fraud will void Appeals' decision.

Refer to Publication 594, *The IRS Collection Process*, and Publication 1660, *Collection Appeal Rights*, for more information regarding the Collection Appeals Program. Copies of these publications can be obtained online at www.irs.gov.

Privacy Act

The information requested on this Form is covered under Privacy Acts and Paperwork Reduction Notices which have already been provided to the taxpayer.

Chapter 17:

Tax Liens

Introduction

In order to protect their interest, the IRS often records a tax lien against a delinquent taxpayer within the county that they own real property. Unlike a bank levy or a wage garnishment, a tax lien is typically not a "call to action" That is, a tax lien with usually not prohibit a delinquent taxpayer from continuing with their everyday living unless of course a taxpayer is in the process of (1) selling their real property or (2) looking to borrow money or conduct some other type of transaction in which their credit will be a factor

Although the IRS may file a lien against one's real or personal property, it is unsual for the IRS to attach a lien to personal property unless the delinquent taxpayer has a valuable asset such as a classic car, art collection or a coin collection.

Once a lien has been filed by the IRS, the taxpayer will receive a notice indicating that the lien has been filed. Many delinquent taxpayers assume that the notice they receive is an indication that the IRS is about to performing active collection against them. While active collection will most likely occur in the near future, a filing of a lien is not directly related.

There are ways a delinquent taxpayer may avoid a lien from being filed. The most obvious way is of course to fully pay their liablity. This rarely occurs as most delinquent taxpayers cannot afford to full pay their liablilty. Another way to avoid a lien from being filed is to enter into an installment agreement over an extended period of time. In order to qualify, the taxpayer must (1) owe less than $25,000, (2) be able to fully pay the liability within 72 months and (3) have not defaulted on a previous agreement with the IRS.

There are four ways in which a lien may affects a delinquent taxpayer. They are as follows:

- **They affect one's assets** - a lien attaches to one's current assets as well as one's future assets acquired over the duration that the lien remains in effect.
- **They affect one's credit** - once a Notice of Federal Tax Lien has been sent, a taxpayer's credit score generally is reduced greatly affected their ability to borrow.
- **They affect businesses** – a Federal tax lien attaches to all business property and to all rights to business property, including accounts receivable over the duration of the lien. This not only prohibits businesses from seeking financing but usually ends existing borrowing relationships.
- **They may affect one's ability to discharge debt in bankruptcy** — if a taxpayer files for bankruptcy, their tax debt, lien, and Notice of Federal Tax Lien may continue to exist after the bankruptcy is complete.

If a tax lien exists, there are options allowing a delinquent taxpayer to withdrawl a Federal tax lien.

Withdrawal[xxiii]

A "withdrawal" removes the public Notice of Federal Tax Lien and assures that the IRS is not competing with other creditors for your property; however, you are still liable for the amount due. For eligibility, refer to Form 12277, Application for the Withdrawal of Filed Form 668(Y), Notice of Federal Tax Lien (Internal Revenue Code Section 6323(j)) (PDF) and the video Lien Notice Withdrawal.

Two additional Withdrawal options resulted from the Commissioner's 2011 Fresh Start initiative.

One option may allow withdrawal of your Notice of Federal Tax Lien after the lien's release. General eligibility includes:

Your tax liability has been satisfied and your lien has been released; and also:

- You are in compliance for the past three years in filing - all individual returns, business returns, and information returns;
- You are current on your estimated tax payments and federal tax deposits, as applicable.

The other option may allow withdrawal of your Notice of Federal Tax Lien if you have entered in or converted your regular installment agreement to a Direct Debit installment agreement. General eligibility includes:

- You are a qualifying taxpayer (i.e. individuals, businesses with income tax liability only, and out of business entities with any type of tax debt)
- You owe $25,000 or less (If you owe more than $25,000, you may pay down the balance to $25,000 prior to requesting withdrawal of the Notice of Federal Tax Lien)
- Your Direct Debit Installment Agreement must full pay the amount you owe within 60 months or before the Collection Statute expires, whichever is earlier
- You are in full compliance with other filing and payment requirements
- You have made three consecutive direct debit payments
- You can't have defaulted on your current, or any previous, Direct Debit Installment agreement.

Discharge of Federal Tax Lien[xxiv]

Instructions on how to apply for

Certificate of Discharge From Federal Tax Lien

IRS

A Certificate of Discharge under Internal Revenue Code Section 6325(b) removes the United States' lien from the property named in the certificate. Discharge of property under Internal Revenue Code Section 6325(c) subject to an Estate Tax Lien is not covered in this publication. For Estate Tax Lien discharges see instead the application and instructions found in Form 4422

1. Complete Form 14135, *Application for Certificate of Discharge of Federal Tax Lien* attached with this publication.
2. Mail the completed Form 14135 and the appropriate attachments to:
   IRS, Attn: Advisory Group Manager
   (Refer to **Publication 4235** *Collection Advisory Group Addresses* for the correct address. The correct address is the office assigned to the location where the property is located.)

If you have any questions, contact the applicable Advisory Office.

If you want to know how much you owe in order to pay the lien(s) in full, call 1-800-913-6050, visit the nearest Taxpayer Assistance Center, or contact the revenue officer assigned to your case.

Important!
Please submit your application at least 45 days before the transaction date that the certificate of discharge is needed. Doing so will allow sufficient time for review, determination, notification and the furnishing of any applicable documents by the transaction date.

Information Required on the Application

Section 1 - Taxpayer Information

1. Enter the name and address of the individual(s) or business as it appears on the Notice of Federal Tax Lien (NFTL). A second name line is provided if needed.
2. Enter, if known, the last 4 digits of the social security number (SSN) or full employer identification number as it appears on the NFTL.
3. Enter, if known and if applicable, the last 4 digits of any spousal SSN (secondary SSN) associated with the tax debt listed on the NFTL.
4. Provide a daytime phone number and a fax number.

Section 2 - Applicant Information

1. Check the box on the first line of Section 2 if you are both the taxpayer and the applicant. If you are not the taxpayer, attach a copy of the lien.
2. If you have checked the box indicating that you are the taxpayer **and** your information is the same as listed on the lien, enter "same as taxpayer" on the name line.
3. If you are **not** the taxpayer **or** you are the taxpayer but your information is no longer the same as the information on the Notice of Federal Tax Lien, enter your name (include any name changes), current address, daytime phone number and fax number.
4. If you are **not** the taxpayer, enter in the box next to "Name" your relationship to the taxpayer (e.g. parent, uncle, sister, no relation, etc).

Section 3 - Purchaser/Transferee/New Owner

1. Check the box on the first line of Section 3 if you are both the property owner and the applicant.
2. Enter the name of the property owner. **Or** enter "NA" if you have checked the box indicating you are both the applicant and the property owner, enter, "same as applicant".
3. Enter the property owner's relationship to the taxpayer (e.g. taxpayer, parent, no relation, etc.).

Section 4 - Attorney/Representative Information

This section is used to list the taxpayer's representative or a representative of a party other than the taxpayer, such as the lender, needing to receive information from the IRS. However, you do not need a representative to request discharge of the federal tax lien.

1. Check the box on the first line of Section 4 if you are attaching a Form 8821 (Tax Information Authority) or Form 2848 (Power of Attorney) with your application. If you are attaching one of these forms, please make sure it is completely filled out, signed, and dated. You must provide one of these forms if the representative represents an interest other than the taxpayer.
2. Enter the name, address, phone number, and fax number of your representative in this action. The IRS will work with you and your representative to process your application. **Or** enter "NA" on the name line if you are not using a representative.
3. Enter whose interest the representative represents (e.g. taxpayer, lender, title company, etc.). This allows the IRS to determine what information can be shared with the representative.

Section 5 – Lender/Finance Company Information

(Settlement/Escrow Company for Section 6325(b)(3) only)

Enter the company name, contact name, and phone number for the title or escrow company that will be used at settlement.

Section 6 – Monetary Information

1. Provide the proposed property sale amount
2. Provide the amount of proceeds the IRS can expect for application to the tax liability.
3. Enter NA for the amount of proceeds the IRS can expect, if you anticipate there will be no proceeds.

Section 7 - Basis for Discharge

Discharge of property from the federal tax lien may be granted under several Internal Revenue Code (IRC) provisions. After reviewing the discharge sections, explanations, and examples below, select the discharge section that best applies to your application. If the IRS does not agree with your selection after its review, an explanation of the decision will be provided.

1. **6325(b)(1)** – a discharge may be issued under this provision if the value of the taxpayer's remaining property encumbered by the federal tax lien is equal to at least twice the amount of the federal tax liability secured by the lien and any encumbrance entered into before the IRS filed its public notice of the lien. If there are mortgages, state and/or local taxes, mechanics liens, etc., the amount of these debts would be added to the amount of the tax liability and multiplied by 2.

   Example

Tax liability	$15,500
Other Debts +	23,334
	38,834
X	2
	$77,668

   The property remaining subject to the lien must be at least $77,668.

2. **6325(b)(2)(A)** – a discharge may be issued under this provision when the tax liability is partially satisfied with an amount paid that is not less than the value of the United States' interest in the property being discharged. **For example**, the IRS has a lien totaling $203,000 and with the ...

· Property selling for:	$215,000
· Minus encumbrances senior to IRS lien:	$135,000
· Minus proposed settlement costs:	$ 15,000
· The IRS lien interest equals:	$ 65,000

   After the IRS receives and applies the $65,000 in partial satisfaction of the tax liability, there remains an outstanding tax debt of $138,000.

   In the case of Tenancy by Entireties property, the United States is generally paid one-half of the proceeds in partial satisfaction of the liability secured by the tax lien.

3. **6325(b)(2)(B)** - a discharge may be issued under this provision when it is determined that the government's interest in the property has no value. The debts senior to the federal tax lien are greater than the fair market value of the property or greater than the sale value of the property. Submit a copy of the proposed escrow agreement as part of the application.

4. **6325(b)(3)** – a discharge may be issued under this provision if an agreement is reached with the IRS allowing the property to be sold. Per an escrow agreement the sale proceeds must be held in a fund subject to the claims of the United States in the same manner and priority the claims had prior to the property being discharged. **For example**, there are two mortgages senior to the IRS tax lien totaling $32,000 and $5,000. The government's interest in the property is $40,000 and there are liens on the property junior to the IRS lien in the amount of $3,000, $12,000 and $2,990. The proceeds from the sale would be dispensed by paying the debts in the following sequence.

   a. $32,000
   b. $5,000
   c. $40,000
   d. $3,000
   e. 12,000
   f. $2,990

   Submit a copy of the proposed escrow agreement.

5. **6325(b)(4)** – a discharge will be issued under this provision to a third party who owns the property if a deposit is made or an acceptable bond provided equal to the government's interest in the property. **In the case of Tenancy by Entireties property,** a deposit or an acceptable bond totaling one-half the government's interest in the property must be made. If you are the property owner (but not the taxpayer, i.e., you are not responsible for the tax liability) and you make a deposit or post an acceptable bond to obtain a discharge under this section, you have 120 days to file an action in federal district court, under section 7426(a)(4), challenging the IRS' determination of the government's lien interest. **This is the exclusive remedy available to the third party for the return of the deposit or accepted bond or a portion thereof.** An administrative request for refund and a refund suit in district court is not available. The *Circular 570*, available at http://fms.treas.gov/c570/index.html contains a list of companies certified by the Secretary of the Treasury as providers of acceptable securities.

6. **6325(c)** – a discharge of property subject to an Estate Tax Lien is not covered in this publication. Please refer to Form 4422.

Section 8 - Description of Property

1. Enter a detailed description of the property to be discharged from the federal tax lien.
2. When the property is real estate include the type of property, for example, 3-bedroom house; etc. When the property is personal property include serial or vehicle numbers, as appropriate, for example, 2002 Cessna twin engine airplane, serial number AT919000000000X00; etc.
3. Provide the physical address if real estate or physical location address if personal property.
4. Check the appropriate box to indicate whether you attached a copy of the title or deed to the property.
5. If you are applying under 6325(b)(1) check the "Attached" box **and** attach copies of the titles or deeds for property remaining subject to the lien. If you are not applying under 6325(b)(1) check the "NA" box.

Section 9 - Appraisal and Valuations

1. Check the "Attached" box after "Required Appraisal" indicate whether you have attached the required appraisal by a disinterested third party. This is typically a professional appraisal providing neighborhood analysis; description of the site; description of the improvements; cost approach; comparable sales; definition of market value; certification; contingent and limiting conditions; interior and exterior photos of the property; exterior photos of comparable sales used; comparable sales location map; sketch of subject property showing room layout; flood map and qualifications of the appraiser.
2. Check the appropriate box under the "**Plus** One of the Following Additional Valuations" section to indicate which other type of property value verification is attached with your application.

   Note: For applications under IRC 6325(b)(1), valuation information described above must also be provided for property remaining subject to lien.

   Note: For property being sold at public auction, provide the date and place of the sale, the proposed amount for which the property will be sold, and a statement that the United States will be paid in the proper priority from the proceeds.

Section 10 - Federal Tax Liens

This section is important when the applicant and the taxpayer are different. If the applicant and the taxpayer are the same, this section may be skipped.

1. Check the "attached" box if you have attached copies of the liens with your application.
2. If you checked the "no" box list the System Lien Identification Number (SLID) found in the top right hand box of the lien document, if available. If you do not have the number(s) enter "unknown" in the first box.

Section 11 - Sales Contract/Purchase Agreement

1. Check the box indicating whether the proposed sales contract or purchase agreement is attached.
2. If you checked the "no" box, describe how the taxpayer named on the lien will be divested of their interest in the property or why they have no interest in the property.

Section 12 - Title Report

1. Check the box indicating whether the title report is attached.
2. If you checked the "no" box, use the space provided to list any encumbrances (liens or claims) against the property that came into existence before the United States' lien interest or which have priority over the lien. Include name and address of holder; description of encumbrance, e.g., mortgage, state lien, etc.; date of agreement; original amount and interest rate; amount due at time of application; and family relationship of the holder, if applicable.
3. Attach a separate sheet with the information in item # 2 above if there is not enough space provided on the form.

Section 13 - Closing Statement

1. Check the box indicating whether the proposed closing statement is attached. This statement is often referred to as a HUD-1.
2. If you checked the "no" box, use the space provided to itemize all proposed costs, commissions, and expenses of any transfer or sale associated with property.
3. Attach a separate sheet with the information in item # 2 above if there is not enough space provided on the form.

Section 14 - Additional Information

1. Check the box indicating whether you are attaching other documents relevant to the discharge application. This could include affidavits or court documents.
2. Check the "no" box if you do not have any additional documentation.

Section 15 - Escrow Agreement

1. Check the box indicating whether you are attaching a draft escrow agreement. This is only applicable if you are applying under 6325(b)(3).
2. An escrow agreement must specify type of account, name and depositary for account, conditions under which payment will be made, cost of escrow, and the name and address of any party identified as part of the escrow agreement.

Section 16 - Waiver

This section applies only if you are:

- The property owner, but
- Not liable for the tax debt *(i.e. not named on the lien)*, and
- Applying under 6325(b)(2)(A).

By checking the "Waive" box you are waiving the option to have the payment treated as a deposit under section 6325(b)(4) which has the accompanying right to request a return of funds and to bring an action under section 7426(a)(4).

If you check the "no" box, your application will automatically be considered under 6325(b)(4) which provides for return of deposited funds and a court challenge under 7426(b)(4).

Section 17 - Declaration

The applicant or their authorized Power of Attorney signs the application form. You must sign your application under penalties of perjury attesting to having examined the application, accompanying schedules or documents, exhibits, affidavits, and statements and declaring to the best of your knowledge and belief that it is true, correct and complete.

Frequently Asked Questions

Q1: When do I make a payment?

The Internal Revenue Code section under which the certificate of discharge will be issued or granted determines the details regarding making a payment.

- Discharge under **6325(b)(1)** or **6325(b)(2)(B)** does not require a payment.
- Discharge under **6325(b)(2)(A)** requires a payment, but do not send a payment with the application. The Advisory Group Manager will notify you, after determining the amount due, when to send payment.

NOTE: If a **mortgage foreclosure** is anticipated, the application is made under section 6325(b)(2)(A) or 6325(b)(2)(B). A determination will be made that either an amount is required for discharge or the United States' interest is valueless.

In the case of foreclosure you will receive, within 30 days of the receipt of a complete and approved application, a conditional commitment letter for a certificate of discharge.

NOTE: Relocation Expenses - If a discharge under 6325(b)(2)(A) or 6325(b)(2)(B) is issued and if the sale is of the principal residence, the *taxpayer* may be eligible for a relocation expense allowance because of an inability to pay. The relocation expense allowance is subject to limitations. To apply for the allowance complete and submit Form 12451, "Request for Relocation Expense Allowance" with the application for discharge.

- Discharge under **6325(b)(3)** requires a payment, but do not send a payment with the application. First, the draft escrow agreement must be submitted.

  Second, the Advisory Group Manager approves the escrow agent selected by the applicant; any reasonable expenses submitted as incurred in connection with the sale of the property; the claim amounts and priorities, and the distribution timing of the fund.

  Third, the agreement is finalized and contains signatures of all parties involved including Advisory Group Manager prior to the discharge being issued.

Note: The escrow account must be funded before payment of any claim or lien through money paid by the applicant or from the sale proceeds.

- Discharge under **6325(b)(4)** requires a bond or deposit but do not send one with the application. The Advisory Group manager must first determine the amount of bond or deposit needed for the discharge and determine that the bond company, if applicable, is from the approved list.

Q2: What is an acceptable form of payment?

Make payments in cash or by the following types of checks: certified; cashiers; or treasurer's check. The check must be drawn on any bank or trust company incorporated under the laws of the United States, or of any state, or possession of the United States. Payment can also be made using a United States postal, bank, express or telegraph money order.

Important! If you pay by personal check, issuance of the certificate of discharge will be delayed until the bank honors the check.

Q3: Who makes the decision to issue a Certificate of Discharge?

In all cases Advisory staff will review and verify the information provided, determine whether a certificate of discharge should be issued, and contact you with any questions. Advisory may contact you, your representative, or any person relative to the transaction for additional information.

The Advisory Group Manager has the responsibility to review and approve the determination and let you know the outcome. If approved, you will receive a conditional commitment letter.

Q4: When will I receive the Certificate of Discharge?

The Internal Revenue Code under which the certificate of discharge will be issued or granted and the time at which you are divested of your interest in the property determines when you will receive the certificate.

- Under **6325(b)(1)** you will receive the certificate when it is determined the remaining property meets the criteria of the provision.
- Under **6325(b)(2)(A)** you will receive the certificate after IRS receives payment of the agreed upon amount in partial satisfaction of the tax liability, proof that the taxpayer has been divested of title, and receipt of a copy of the final settlement statement.
- Under **6325(b)(2)(B)** you will receive the certificate when it is determined that the government's interest in the property is valueless, the IRS has received proof that the taxpayer has been divested of title, and a copy of the final settlement statement.

NOTE: Under provisions **6325(b)(2)(A)** and **6325(b)(2)(B)** at the conclusion of a mortgage foreclosure the certificate will be issued in accordance with the terms of the conditional commitment letter. Also see, Publication 487, *How to Prepare an Application Requesting the United States to Release Its Right to Redeem Property Secured by a Federal Tax Lien.*

- Under **6325(b)(3)** you will receive the certificate when the amount of the government's interest in the property has been placed in the approved escrow account.
- Under **6325(b)(4)** you will receive the certificate when the amount equal to the government's interest in the property is received or an approved bond has posted.

Q5: What happens if my application is denied?

If your application is denied, you will receive Form 9423, Collection Appeal Request and Publication 1660, Collection Appeal Rights, with an explanation of why your application was denied.

Privacy and Paperwork Reduction Act Notice

The Privacy act of 1974 says that when we ask you for information about yourself, we must first tell you our legal right to ask for the information, why we are asking for it, and how it will be used. We must also tell you what could happen if you do not provide it and whether or not you must respond under the law.

We ask for the information on this form to carry out the Internal Revenue laws of the United States. This information requested on this form is needed to process your application and to determine whether the federal tax lien can be discharged. You are not required to apply for discharge; however, if you want the federal tax lien to be discharged, you are required to provide the information requested on this form. Section 6109 requires you to provide the requested identification numbers. Failure to provide this information may delay or prevent processing your application; providing any false information may subject you to penalties.

The time needed to complete and file this form will vary depending on individual circumstances. The estimated burden for individuals filing this form is approved under OMB control number 1545-2174. The estimated burden for those who file this form is shown below.

- Recordkeeping 2 hr., 45 min.
- Learning about the law or the form 2 hr.
- Preparing the form 1 hr., 30 min.
- Copying, assembling, and sending the form to the IRS 85 min.

Routine uses of this information include giving it to the Department of Justice for civil and criminal litigation, and to cities, states, the District of Columbia, and United States commonwealths and possessions for use in administering their tax laws. Advisory may contact you, your representative, or any person relative to the transaction for additional information. We may also disclose this information to other countries under a tax treaty, to federal and state agencies to enforce federal nontax criminal laws, or to federal law enforcement and intelligence agencies to combat terrorism.

Form **14135** (June 2010)

Department of the Treasury — Internal Revenue Service

Application for Certificate of Discharge of Property from Federal Tax Lien

OMB No. 1545-2174

Complete the entire application. Enter NA *(not applicable)*, when appropriate. Attachments and exhibits should be included as necessary. Additional information may be requested of you or a third party to clarify the details of the transaction(s).

1. Taxpayer Information *(Individual or Business named on the notice of lien)*:

Name *(Individual First, Middle Initial, Last)* or *(Business)* as it appears on lien		Primary Social Security Number *(last 4 digits only)*
Name Continuation *(Individual First, Middle Initial, Last)* or *(Business d/b/a)*		Secondary Social Security Number *(last 4 digits only)*
Address *(Number, Street, P.O. Box)*		Employer Identification Number
City	State	ZIP Code
Telephone Number *(with area code)*	Fax Number *(with area code)*	

2. Applicant Information: ☐ Check if also the Taxpayer *(If not the taxpayer, attach copy of lien. See Sec.10)*

Name *(First, Middle Initial, Last)*		Relationship to taxpayer
Address *(Number, Street, P.O. Box)*		
City	State	ZIP Code
Telephone Number *(with area code)*	Fax Number *(with area code)*	

3. Purchase/Transferee/New Owner ☐ Check if also the Applicant

	Relationship to taxpayer

4. Attorney/Representative Information **Attached:** Form 8821 or Power of Attorney Form 2848 ☐ Yes ☐ No

Name *(First, Middle Initial, Last)*		Interest Represented *(e.g. taxpayer, lender, etc.)*
Address *(Number, Street, P.O. Box)*		
City	State	ZIP Code
Telephone Number *(with area code)*	Fax Number *(with area code)*	

5. Lender/Finance Company Information - or *(Settlement/Escrow Company for applications under Section 6325(b)(3) only)*

Company Name	Contact Name	Contact Phone Number

6. Monetary Information

Proposed sales price	
Expected proceeds to be paid to the United States in exchange for the certificate of discharge *(Enter NA if no proceeds are anticipated)*	

7. Basis for Discharge: Check the box below that best addresses what you would like the United States to consider in your application for discharge. *(Publication 783 has additional descriptions of the Internal Revenue Code sections listed below.)*

- ☐ 6325(b)(1) Value of property remaining attached by the lien(s) is at least double the liability of the federal tax lien(s) plus other encumbrances senior to the lien(s)
- ☐ 6325(b)(2)(A) The United States receives an amount not less than the value of the United States' interest. *(Note: If you are applying under 6325(b)(2)(A) and are the property owner but not the taxpayer, see also section 16.)*
- ☐ 6325(b)(2)(B) Interest of the United States in the property to be discharged has no value.
- ☐ 6325(b)(3) Proceeds from property sale held in escrow subject to the liens and claims of the United States.
- ☐ 6325(b)(4) Deposit made or bond furnished in an amount equal to the value of the United States' interest. *(Note: This selection provides a remedy under 7426(a)(4) for return of deposit but is exclusively for a property owner not named as the taxpayer on the lien)*

8. Description of property *(for example, 3 bedroom rental house; 2002 Cessna twin engine airplane, serial number AT919000000000X00; etc.):*

Address of real property *(If this is personal property, list the address where the property is located)*:

Address *(Number, Street, P.O. Box)*		
City	State	ZIP Code

FOR REAL ESTATE: a legible copy of the deed or title showing the legal description is required	☐ Attached ☐ NA
FOR Discharge Requests under Section 6325(b)(1): copy of deed(s) or title(s) for property remaining subject to the Federal Tax Lien is required	☐ Attached ☐ NA

9. Appraisal and Valuations

REQUIRED APPRAISAL Professional appraisal completed by a disinterested third party	☐ Attached
PLUS ONE OF THE FOLLOWING ADDITIONAL VALUATIONS:	
County valuation of property *(real property)*	☐ Attached
Informal valuation of property by disinterested third party	☐ Attached
Proposed selling price *(for property being sold at auction)*	☐ Attached
Other: ______________________	☐ Attached

AND for applications under Section 6325(b)(1), valuation information (of the type described above in this section) must also be provided for property remaining subject to the lien.

10. Copy of Federal Tax Lien(s) *(Complete if applicant and taxpayer differ)* ☐ Attached ☐ No

OR list the lien number(s) found near the top right corner on the lien document(s) *(if known)*

11. Copy of the sales contract/purchase agreement *(if available)* ☐ Attached ☐ No

OR

Describe how and when the taxpayer will be divested of his/her interest in the property:

12. Copy of a current title report ☐ Attached ☐ No

OR

List encumbrances senior to the Federal Tax Lien. Include name and address of holder; description of encumbrance, e.g., mortgage, state lien, etc.; date of agreement; original loan amount and interest rate; amount due at time of application; and family relationship, if applicable *(Attach additional sheets as needed)*:

13. Copy of proposed closing statement *(aka HUD-1)* ☐ Attached ☐ No

OR

Itemize all proposed costs, commissions, and expenses of any transfer or sale associated with property *(Attach additional sheets as needed)*:

14. Additional information that may have a bearing on this request, such as pending litigation, explanations of unusual situations, etc., is attached for consideration ☐ Attached ☐ No

15. Escrow Agreement *(For applications under IRC 6325(b)(3))* ☐ Attached ☐ No

Escrow agreement must specify type of account, name and depositary for account, conditions under which payment will be made, cost of escrow, name and address of any party identified as part of escrow agreement, and signatures of all parties involved including Advisory Group Manager. Terms for agreement must be reached before discharge approved.

16. WAIVER *(For applications made by third parties under IRC 6325(b)(2))*

If you are applying as an owner of the property and you are not the taxpayer, to have this application considered under section 6325(b)(2), you must waive the rights that would be available if the application were made under section 6325(b)(4). If you choose not to waive these rights, the application will be treated as one made under 6325(b)(4) and any payment will be treated like a deposit under that section. Please check the appropriate box.

I understand that an application and payment made under section 6325(b)(2) does not provide the judicial remedy available under section 7426(a)(4). In making such an application / payment, I waive the option to have the payment treated as a deposit under section 6325(b)(4) and the right to request a return of funds and to bring an action under section 7426(a)(4). ☐ Waive ☐ No

17. Declaration

Under penalties of perjury, I declare that I have examined this application, including any accompanying schedules, exhibits, affidavits, and statements and to the best of my knowledge and belief it is true, correct and complete.

______________________ Signature/Title ______________ Date

______________________ Signature/Title ______________ Date

Catalog Number 54727S www.irs.gov Form **14135** (Rev. 06-2010)

Subordination of Federal Tax Lien[xxv]

Instructions on how to apply for a

Certificate of Subordination of Federal Tax Lien

IRS

A Certificate of Subordination under Internal Revenue Code Section 6325(d)(1) and 6325(d)(2) allows a named creditor to move their junior creditor position ahead of the United States' position for the property named in the certificate. For *How to Apply for a Certificate of Subordination of Federal Estate Tax Lien* Under Section 6325(d)(3) of the Internal Revenue Code use Publication 1153.

1. Complete Form 14134, *Application for Certificate of Subordination of Federal Tax Lien* attached with this publication.
2. Mail the completed Form 14134 and the appropriate attachments to:
   IRS, Attn: Advisory Group Manager
   (Refer to Publication 4235, *Collection Advisory Group Addresses* for the correct address. The correct address is the office assigned to the location where the property is located.)

If you have any questions, contact the applicable Advisory Office.

If you want to know how much you owe in order to pay the lien(s) in full, call 1-800-913-6050, visit the nearest Taxpayer Assistance Center, or contact the revenue officer assigned to your case.

Important!

Please submit your application at least 45 days before the transaction date that the certificate of subordination is needed. Doing so will allow sufficient time for review, determination, notification and the furnishing of any applicable documents by the transaction date.

Information Required on the Application

Section 1 - Taxpayer Information

1. Enter the name and address of the individual(s) or business as it appears on the Notice(s) of Federal Tax Lien (NFTL). A second name line is provided if needed.
2. Enter, if known, the last 4 digits of the social security number (SSN) or full employer identification number as it appears on the NFTL.
3. Enter, if known and if applicable, the last 4 digits of any spousal SSN (secondary SSN) associated with the tax debt listed on the NFTL.
4. Provide a daytime phone number and a fax number.

Section 2 - Applicant Information

1. Check the box on the first line of Section 2 if you are both the taxpayer and the applicant. If you are not the taxpayer, attach a copy of the lien.
2. If you have checked the box indicating that you are the taxpayer and your information is the same as listed on the lien, enter "same as taxpayer" on the name line.
3. If you are not the taxpayer or you are the taxpayer but your information is no longer the same as the information on the Notice of Federal Tax Lien, enter your name (include any name changes), current address, daytime phone number and fax number.
4. If you are not the taxpayer, enter in the box next to "Name" your relationship to the taxpayer (e.g. parent, uncle, sister, no relation, etc.).

Section 3 - Property Owner

1. Check the box on the first line of Section 3 if you are both the property owner and the applicant.
2. Enter the name of the property owner. Or if you have checked the box indicating you are both the applicant and the property owner, enter, "same as applicant".
3. Enter the property owner's relationship to the taxpayer (e.g. taxpayer, parent, no relation, etc.).

Section 4 - Attorney/Representative Information

This section is used to list the taxpayer's representative or a representative of a party other than the taxpayer, such as the lender, needing to receive information from the IRS. However, you do not need a representative to request subordination of the federal tax lien.

1. Check the box on the first line of Section 4 if you are attaching a Form 8821 (Tax Information Authority) or Form 2848 (Power of Attorney) with your application. If you are attaching one of these forms, please make sure it is completely filled out, signed, and dated. You must provide one of these forms if the representative represents an interest other than the taxpayer.
2. Enter the name, address, phone number, and fax number of your representative in this action. The IRS will work with you and your representative to process your application. Or enter "NA" on the name line if you are not using a representative.
3. Enter whose interest the representative represents (e.g. taxpayer, lender, title company, etc.). This allows the IRS to determine what information can be shared with the representative.

Section 5 - Lender/Finance Company Information

1. Enter the company name, contact name, phone number, and fax number for the lender you are requesting the United States subordinate its interest to.
2. Enter the type of transaction. For example, a loan consolidation or refinance often prompts a subordination request.

Section 6 - Monetary Information

1. Enter the amount of your existing or outstanding financing.
2. Enter the amount of new financing you are seeking.
3. Enter the amount anticipated being paid toward the United States' interest (For applications requested under 6325(d)(1) only).

Section 7 - Basis for Subordination

A subordination may be granted under Internal Revenue Code (IRC) 6325(d)(1) or 6325(d)(2). Review the information below and select the section which best applies to your subordination request. If the IRS does not agree with your selection after its review, an explanation of the decision will be provided.

6325(d)(1) - a subordination may be issued under this section if you pay an amount equal to the lien or interest to which the certificate subordinates the lien of the United States. The following example uses an 80% loan to value and a 3% closing cost to financing ratio.

Example:

	Current/New	Original
Fair Market Value	$200,000	N/A
Refinance	$160,000	$145,000
Closing Costs	$ 4,800	N/A
United States Interest	$ 10,200	N/A

In this example the United States' interest is the equity you obtain from your refinanced loan after paying off the existing loan of $145,000 and paying the closing costs to obtain the loan. ($200,000 property value x 80% loan to value ratio = $160,000 refinance loan amount. $160,000 - $145,000 loan payoff = $15,000 potential equity. $160,000 x 3% = $4800 closing costs to obtain the loan. $15,000 potential equity - $4,800 closing costs = $10,200) The IRS would ask for $10,200 in return for the United States subordinating its interest to the refinanced loan. The lien remains on the property but the refinanced loan has priority over the lien.

4. 6325(d)(2) – a subordination may be issued under this section if the IRS determines that the issuance of the certificate will increase the amount the government realizes and make collection of the tax liability easier. This might involve a refinance to a lower interest rate which would, if the subordination were granted, allow a larger monthly repayment rate on the tax liability. Or the situation might be more complex. For example, AAA Auto Sales currently pays the IRS $2000 per month on a $120,000 tax debt. Their inventory needs replenishing but their wholesaler is reluctant to provide added inventory because of the federal tax lien. AAA requests subordination and provides the IRS with documentation that an inventory replenishment of 500 cars could allow them to increase their monthly payment to $3000 as well as increase their pay back rate to bi-weekly. In this example the United States' interest would be second on the new inventory, if the subordination is granted.

   For applications under section 6325(d)(2), complete and attach a signed and dated statement describing how the amount the United States may ultimately realize through this subordination will increase and how collection will be facilitated by the subordination.

5. 6325(d)(3) - Questions and applications for this section refer to Publication 1153 for instructions.

Section 8 - Description of Property

1. Enter a detailed description of the collateral you will use for the loan or other financing. This is the collateral on which you want the lien interest subordinated to the loan or financing. If this is real estate, you must provide the legal description.
2. When the property is real estate include the type of property. For example, 3-bedroom house; etc. When the property is personal property include serial or vehicle numbers, as appropriate. For example, 2002 Cessna twin engine airplane, serial number AT919000000000X00; etc.
3. Provide the property's physical address if it is real estate or provide the physical address where the property is located, if it is personal property.
4. Check the appropriate box to indicate whether you attached a copy of the title or deed to the property.

Section 9 - Appraisal and Valuations

1. Check the "Attached" box after "Appraisal" to indicate whether you have attached an appraisal completed by a disinterested third party. This is typically a professional appraisal providing neighborhood analysis; description of the site; description of the improvements; cost approach; comparable sales; definition of market value; certification; contingent and limiting conditions; interior and exterior photos of the property; exterior photos of comparable sales used; comparable sales location map; sketch of subject property showing room layout; flood map and qualifications of the appraiser. **This type of appraisal is not required for a certificate of subordination.**
2. Check the appropriate box under the "Or One of the Following Valuations" section to indicate which type of property value verification is attached with your application.

Section 10 - Federal Tax Liens

This section is important when the applicant and the taxpayer are different. If the applicant and the taxpayer are the same, this section may be skipped.

1. Check the "Attached" box if you have attached copies of the lien(s) with your application.
2. If you checked the "no" box list the System Lien Identification Number (SLID) found in the top right hand box of the lien document, if available. If you do not have the numbers enter "unknown" in the first box.

Section 11 - Proposed loan agreement

1. Check the "attached" box if you have attached the proposed mortgage contract and describe how subordination is in the best interests of the United States
2. If you checked the "no" box, describe how subordination is in the best interests of the United States.

Section 12 - Current title report

1. Check the "attached" box if you attached the title report. This is required for subordination.
2. If you checked the "no" box and the title report is not attached, use the space provided to list any encumbrances (liens or claims) against the property and whether those encumbrances are senior to the United States' lien interest. Include the name and address of the holder; description of the encumbrance, e.g., mortgage, state lien, etc.; date of agreement; original loan amount and interest rate; amount due at time of application; and family relationship, if applicable.
3. If any mortgages listed on your title report are home equity lines of credit (HELOCs), the NFTL takes priority over advances made via the HELOC on the 46th day after the NFTL is filed. This means any advances made to you more than 46 days after the NFTL is filed, were made subject to the NFTL. The advances need to be included in the equity interest to which the United States attaches. To make an accurate value determination and to avoid processing delays with your application, provide documentation on any HELOC advances from the 46th day after the NFTL was filed, through the date you submit your application, and include expected advances through the date the certificate will be issued.
4. Attach a separate sheet titled "Section 12" with the information in item # 2 and # 3 above if there is not enough space provided on the form.

Section 13 - Proposed closing statement

1. Check the "attached" box if you attached the proposed closing statement. This statement is often referred to as a HUD-1.
2. If you checked the "no" box and you did not attach the proposed closing statement, use the space provided to itemize all proposed costs, commissions, and expenses to refinance the property.
3. Attach a separate sheet titled "Section 13" with the information in item # 2 above if there is not enough space provided on the form.

Section 14 - Additional Information

1. Check the "attached" box if you have attached other documents relevant to the subordination application. This could include affidavits or court documents.
2. Check the "no" box if you do not have any additional documentation.

Section 15 - Declaration

The applicant or their authorized Power of Attorney signs the application form. You must sign your application under penalties of perjury attesting to having examined the application, accompanying schedules or documents, exhibits, affidavits, and statements and declaring to the best of your knowledge and belief that the application is true, correct and complete.

Frequently Asked Questions

Q1: When do I make a payment?

The Internal Revenue Code section under which the certificate of subordination will be issued or granted determines the details regarding making a payment.

- Subordination under 6325(d)(1) requires a payment, but do not send a payment with the application. The Advisory Group Manager will notify you after determining the amount due and when to send payment.
- Subordination under 6325(d)(2) does not require a payment.

Q2: What is an acceptable form of payment?

Make payments in cash or by the following types of checks: certified; cashiers; or treasurer's check. The check must be drawn on any bank or trust company incorporated under the laws of the United States, or of any state, or possession of the United States. Payment can also be made using a United States postal, bank, express or telegraph money order.

Important! If you pay by personal check, issuance of the certificate of subordination will be delayed until the bank honors the check.

Q3: Who makes the decision to issue a Certificate of Subordination?

In all cases Advisory staff will review and verify the information provided, determine whether a certificate of subordination should be issued, and contact you with any questions. Advisory may contact you, your representative, or any person relative to the transaction for additional information.

The Advisory Group Manager has the responsibility to review and approve the determination and let you know the outcome. If approved, you will receive a conditional commitment letter.

Q4: When will I receive the Certificate of Subordination?

The Internal Revenue Code under which the certificate of subordination will be issued or granted determines when you will receive the certificate.

- Under 6325(d)(1), you will receive the certificate upon receipt of the amount determined to be the interest of the United States in the property subject to the federal tax lien.
- Under 6325(d)(2), you will receive the certificate after your application has been investigated and the information verified. The Advisory Group Manager will notify you of the decision and provide you with a projected date for mailing the certificate of subordination.

Q5: What happens if my application is denied?

If your application is denied, you will receive Form 9423, *Collection Appeal Request* and Publication 1660, *Collection Appeal Rights*, with an explanation of why your application was denied.

Privacy and Paperwork Reduction Act Notice

The Privacy act of 1974 says that when we ask you for information about yourself, we must first tell you our legal right to ask for the information, why we are asking for it, and how it will be used. We must also tell you what could happen if you do not provide it and whether or not you must respond under the law.

We ask for the information on this form to carry out the Internal Revenue laws of the United States. This information requested on this form is needed to process your application and to determine whether the federal tax lien can be discharged. You are not required to apply for discharge; however, if you want the federal tax lien to be discharged, you are required to provide the information requested on this form. Section 6109 requires you to provide the requested identification numbers. Failure to provide this information may delay or prevent processing your application; providing any false information may subject you to penalties.

The time needed to complete and file this form will vary depending on individual circumstances. The estimated burden for individuals filing this form is approved under OMB control number 1545-2174. The estimated burden for those who file this form is shown below.

- Recordkeeping 2 hr., 45 min.
- Learning about the law or the form 2 hr.
- Preparing the form 1 hr., 30 min.
- Copying, assembling, and sending the form to the IRS 85 min.

Routine uses of this information include giving it to the Department of Justice for civil and criminal litigation, and to cities, states, the District of Columbia, and United States commonwealths and possessions for use in administering their tax laws. Advisory may contact you, your representative, or any person relative to the transaction for additional information. We may also disclose this information to other countries under a tax treaty, to federal and state agencies to enforce federal nontax criminal laws, or to federal law enforcement and intelligence agencies to combat terrorism.

Form **14134** (June 2010)

Department of the Treasury — Internal Revenue Service

Application for Certificate of Subordination of Federal Tax Lien

OMB No. 1545-2174

Complete the entire application. Enter NA *(not applicable)*, when appropriate. Attachments and exhibits should be included as necessary. Additional information may be requested to clarify the details of the transaction*(s)*.

1. Taxpayer Information ***(Individual or Business named on the notice of lien)***

Name *(Individual First, Middle Initial, Last)* or *(Business)* as it appears on lien	Primary Social Security Number *(last 4 digits only)*
Name Continuation *(Individual First, Middle Initial, Last)* or *(Business d/b/a)*	Secondary Social Security Number *(last 4 digits only)*
Address *(Number, Street, P.O. Box)*	Employer Identification Number

City	State	ZIP Code
Telephone Number *(with area code)*	Fax Number *(with area code)*	

2. Applicant Information ☐ Check if also the Taxpayer *(If not the taxpayer, attach copy of lien. See Sec.10)*

Name *(First, Middle Initial, Last)*	Relationship to taxpayer
Address *(Number, Street, P.O. Box)*	

City	State	ZIP Code
Telephone Number *(with area code)*	Fax Number *(with area code)*	

3. Property Owner ☐ Check if also the Applicant

	Relationship to Taxpayer

4. Attorney/Representative Information **Attached:** Form 8821 or Power of Attorney Form 2848 ☐ Yes ☐ No

Name *(First, Middle Initial, Last)*	Interest Represented *(e.g. taxpayer, lender, etc.)*
Address *(Number, Street, P.O. Box)*	

City	State	ZIP Code
Telephone Number *(with area code)*	Fax Number *(with area code)*	

5. Lending/Finance Company

Company Name	Contact Name	Contact Phone Number

Type of transaction *(For example, loan consolidation, refinance, etc)*

6. Monetary Information

Amount of existing loan *(if refinancing)*	
Amount of new loan	
Amount to be paid to the United States *(6325(d)(1) applications only)*	

7. Basis for Subordination: Check the box below that best addresses what you would like the United States to consider in your application for subordination. *(Publication 784 has additional descriptions of the Internal Revenue Code sections listed below.)*

☐ 6325(d)(1) the United States will receive an amount equal to the lien or interest to which the certificate of subordination is issued *(provide amount in Section 6 above)*

☐ 6325(d)(2) the issuance of the certificate of subordination will increase the government's interest and make collection of the tax liability easier. ***(Complete and attach a signed and dated statement describing how the amount the United States may ultimately realize will increase and how collection will be facilitated by the subordination.)***

Statement ☐ Attached ☐ NA

8. Description of property *(For example, 3 bedroom rental house; 2002 Cessna twin engine airplane, serial number AT919000000000X00; etc.)*:

Address of real property ***(If this is personal property list the address where the property is located)*:**		
Address *(Number, Street, P.O. Box)*		
City	State	ZIP Code
Real Estate: Legible copy of deed or title showing legal description		☐ Attached ☐ NA

9. Appraisal and Valuations

<u>**Appraisal**</u>: (Professional appraisal completed by a disinterested third party but it is not required for a subordination)	☐ Attached
<u>OR</u> ONE OF THE FOLLOWING VALUATIONS:	
County valuation of property *(real property)*	☐ Attached
Informal valuation of property by disinterested third party	☐ Attached
Proposed selling price *(for property being sold at auction)*	☐ Attached
Other:________________________	☐ Attached

Catalog Number 54726H www.irs.gov Form **14134** (Rev. 06-2010)

10. Copy of Federal Tax Lien(s) *(Complete if applicant and taxpayer differ)* ☐ Attached ☐ No

OR list the lien number(s) found near the top right corner on the lien document(s) *(if known)*

11. Copy of the proposed loan agreement *(if available)* ☐ Attached ☐ No

AND

Describe how subordination is in the best interests of the United States:

12. Copy of a current title report *(required for subordination)* ☐ Attached ☐ No

OR

List encumbrances with seniority over the Federal Tax Lien. Include name and address of the holder; description of the encumbrance, e.g., mortgage, state lien, etc.; date of agreement; original loan amount and interest rate; amount due at time of application; and family relationship, if applicable. Include any home equity line of credit (HELOCs) advances beginning the 46th day after the NFTL was filed, through the date you submit your application, and include expected advances through the date the certificate will be issued. *(Attach additional sheets as needed):*

13. Copy of proposed closing statement *(aka HUD-1)* ☐ Attached ☐ No

OR

Itemize all proposed costs, commissions, and expenses of any transfer or sale associated with property *(Attach additional sheets as needed):*

14. Additional information that may have a bearing on this request, such as pending litigation, explanations of unusual situations, etc., is attached for consideration ☐ **Yes** ☐ **No**

15. Declaration

Under penalties of perjury, I declare that I have examined this application, including any accompanying schedules, exhibits, affidavits, and statements and to the best of my knowledge and belief it is true, correct and complete.

______________________________ Signature/Title ______________ Date

______________________________ Signature/Title ______________ Date

APPLICATION FOR CERTIFICATE OF SUBORDINATION OF FEDERAL TAX LIEN

Since there is no standard form available for an application for certificate of subordination of Federal Tax lien, you should consider our typewritten request as an application. All accompanying documents will be submitted in duplicate to:

Send to: District Director of Internal Revenue Service
Address to District where the property is located

Attention: Chief, Special Procedures Staff

Date of application

Please give the name and address of the person applying, under Section 6325 (d)(1) or Section 6325 (d)(2) of the Internal Revenue Code, for a certificate of subordination. See the reverse of this publication for applicable Internal Revenue Code sections. Give name and address of the taxpayer, and describe property as follows:

Give a detailed description, including the location of the property for which you are requesting the certificate of subordination. If real property is involved give the description contained in the title or deed to the property, and the complete address (street, city, state).

Attach a copy of each notice of Federal tax lien or furnish the following information as it appears on each filed notice of Federal tax lien.

The name of the Internal Revenue District;

The name and address of the taxpayer against whom the notice was filed;

The date and place the notice was filed.

Describe the encumbrance to which the Federal tax lien is to be subordinated, including:

The present amount of the encumbrance;

The nature of the encumbrance (such as mortgage, assignment, etc.)

The date the transaction if to be completed.

List the encumbrances (or attach a copy of the instrument that created each encumbrance) on the property which you believe have priority over the Federal tax lien. For each encumbrance show:

The name and address of the holder;

A description of the encumbrance;

The date of the agreement;

The original principal amount and the interest rate;

The amount due as of the date of the application for certificate of subordination, if known (show costs and accrued interest separately);

Your family relationship, if any, to the taxpayer and to the holders of any other encumbrances on the property.

Furnish an estimate of the fair market value of the property for which you would like a certificate of subordination.

If you are submitting the application under the provisions of section 6325(d)(1), show the amount to be paid to the United States.

If you are submitting the application under the provisions of section 6325(d)(2), attach a complete statement showing how the amount the United States may realize will ultimately increase and how collection of the tax liability will be made easier.

Furnish any other information that might help the district Director decide whether to issue a certificate of subordination.

The District Director may request you to furnish additional information.

Give a daytime telephone number where you may be reached.
Give the name, address and telephone number of your attorney or other representative, if any.
Make the following declaration over your signature and title:

"Under penalties of perjury, I declare that I have examined this application (including any accompanying schedules, exhibits, affidavits, and statements) and to the best of my knowledge and belief it is true, correct, and complete."

Please follow the instructions in this publication when applying for a Certificate of Discharge of Property From Federal Tax Lien.

The District Director has the authority to issue a certificate of discharge of a lien that is filed on any part of a taxpayer's property subject to the lien. The following sections and provisions of the Internal Revenue Code apply:

Section 6325(b)(1), a specific property may be discharged; if the taxpayer's property remaining subject to the lien has a Fair Market Value (FMV) which is double the sum of the balance due

All Federal Tax Liens.
All other liens (FMV=(a+b) x 2).

Section 6325(b)(2)(A), if there is paid in partial satisfaction of the liability secured by the lien an amount determined to be not less than the value of the interest of the United States in the property to be discharged.

Section 6325(b)(2)(B), if it is determined that the interest of the United States in the property to be discharged has no value.

Section 6325(b)(3), if the property subject to the lien is sold and, under an agreement with the Internal Revenue Service, the proceeds from the sale are to be held as a fund subject to the liens and claims of the United Sates in the same manner, and with the same priority, as the liens and claims on the discharged property.

Also see, Application Requesting the United States to Release its Right to redeem Property Secured by a Federal Tax Lien, Publication 487.

If application is made under the provisions of section 6325(b)(3), the District Director has the authority to approve an escrow agent selected by the applicant. Any reasonable expenses incurred in connection with the sale of the property, the holding of the fund, or the distribution of the fund shall be paid by the applicant or from the proceeds of the sale before satisfaction of any claims and liens. Submit a copy of the proposed escrow agreement as part of the application.

Sample letter used to apply for subordination:

May 25, 2008

Internal Revenue Service
Attn: Revenue Officer
6230 Van Nuys Blvd.
Van Nuys, CA 91401

Re: Client Name, Client Federal ID#
Application for Subordination Agreement

To Whom it May Concern:

Please consider the following application for subordination agreement under IRC section 6325(d)(2) for the above referenced taxpayer. [Your Clients Name] would like the Internal Revenue Service subordinate to current (and future) lenders all accounts receivable, inventory & fixed assets owned by [Your Clients Name].

AB Factors, Inc. dba AB Bancorp the company's current lender is now in 1st position with respect to the above referenced collateral, including but not limited to all accounts receivable, inventory and fixed assets owned or hereafter acquired by the company. AB Factors, Inc. dba AB Bancorp will agree to continue the 45 day rule AB Factors, Inc. dba AB Bancorp will be forced to discontinue lending resulting in the possible bankruptcy of the taxpayer.

[Lessor Name] is the current lessor of equipment to [Your Client's Name] (See payment proposal below).

We estimate the fair market value of the referenced assets at approximately $1,500,000. we propose to pay the appropriate amount owing of $560,000 as follows:

$80,000 down payment

$10,000 per month until August 2009

$25,000 per month beginning August 2009 until paid.

The payment of approximately $70,000 per month to Lessor end in July 2009 which would give the company sufficient cash flow to facilitate this large increase in payment.

Background: The Company has been in business since 1978 and has no prior history of tax delinquency. From late 2003 until early 2005 the taxpayer's contact manufacturing industry suffered from a number of significant negative factors as follows:

A stagnant economy, both domestically and abroad, which is our customer base;

The Administration's failed steel tariff policy leading to record high steel prices (50% increase in 6 months), which represents about 30% of our total operating expense;

Skyrocketing health and worker's compensation insurance costs in California;

Dramatic rises in utilities and transportation costs.

These factors lead to over $1 million of losses in 2004 and the first half of 2004, during which time the company fell behind in its payment of these taxes. Since then, however, things have turned around by controlling costs while all of the above factors have begun to improve. Since the 3rd quarter of 2005 customers have become less resistant to rising prices which has also helped offset most of these rising costs. The company is currently profitable.

We believe that this course of action is in the best interest of the United States in that the only source of repayment is the continuing operation of the business which would be impossible without continued funding by AB Factors, Inc. dba AB Bancorp and subordination by the Internal Revenue Service.

I am the Taxpayer's legal representative and I am submitting the protest and accompanying documents, which have been provided to me by the Taxpayer. Please feel free to contact me at the above referenced telephone number if you have any questions or need clarification of the foregoing.

Sincerely,

Your Name

Chapter 18:

45-Day Rule

(Requirement - 6323 n 43)

The United States Congress instituted the 45-Day Rule in 1966 to correct a problem experienced by commercial lenders who suddenly found themselves losing their loan collateral when being set against a federal tax lien. The most basic principle employed in the adjudication of the priority of liens is "first in time is the first in right." When the IRS makes an assessment for unpaid payroll taxes against a business, a statutory lien arises in favor of the federal government. The lien attaches to all property or rights to property belonging to the business. This lien is called a "silent" lien because it comes into existence without notice to the world. The lien, however, does not necessarily entitle the IRS to priority against most other secured parties unless the IRS files a notice of a federal tax lien.

Once the IRS has filed an official notice of a federal tax lien against a business, both the business and the creditors of the business are placed in financial jeopardy. If you find your company in such a situation and the 45 days are passing, your future viability is being placed in serious crisis. If such a tax lien has been placed on your business and you are in a revolving loan agreement with an asset based lender such as a bank or a factor based on your assets or accounts receivable, please contact Peter Stephan and the Tax Resolution Institute before your cash flow evaporates and your business is closed down.

The 45-day rule gives the IRS special rights against lenders that secured themselves with their customers' collateral. The rule, which appears in Section 6323(d) of the Internal Revenue Code, (26 U.S.C.) states as follows:

Even though notice of a lien imposed by section 6321 has been filed, such liens shall not be valid with respect to a security interest which came into existence after the tax lien filing by reason of disbursements made before the 46th day after the date of tax lien filing, or (if earlier) before the person making such disbursements had actual notice or knowledge of tax lien filing, but only if such security interest (1) is in property (A) subject, at the time of tax lien filing, to the lien imposed by section 6321, and (B) covered by the terms of a written agreement entered into before tax lien filing, and (2) is protected under local law against a judgment lien arising, as of the time of tax lien filing, out of an unsecured obligation.

Translated, the 45-day rule states that a lender, whose collateral can be identified only after the federal tax lien filing, receives a priority of first position subject to the following five restrictions:

The security agreement must predate the tax lien filing.

The holder of the interest may make disbursements no more than 45 days after the tax lien filing.

The collateral securing those disbursements must be acquired within those 45 days.

At the time of the disbursement, the holder cannot have "actual knowledge or notice" of the tax lien filing (this term is discussed later).

Despite the basic principle of the 45-Day Rule, a federal tax lien by the IRS has always enjoyed certain advantages when it comes to deciding first position. For instance, courts have long held that to be first in time, the nonfederal lien must first be "choate," that is, the identity of the lien and the property subject to the lien are reasonably determinable.

The first-in-time rule created a hardship for commercial lenders and factors in particular. After all, commercial lenders have loans and collateral that change daily. For this reason, in the Federal Tax Lien Act of 1966, Congress changed the law to give commercial lenders a limited priority in certain contests involving federal tax liens. However, the priority Congress granted to commercial lenders in the form of the 45-Day Rule is far from absolute.

If we take a closer look at the key provisions of the 45-Day Rule, there are a number of requirements that must be met. To prevail against the IRS, the lender must confirm beyond any question and the bar is set quite high in these cases:

The date that the notice of the federal tax lien was filed.

A written security agreement was entered into before that date.

The collateral at issue relates to the subject agreement and to loans made under the agreement.

The bank disbursed the loan no more than 45 days after the tax lien filing.

The customer has acquired the collateral and can identify the collateral inside the 45-day window.

The lender did not have actual notice or knowledge of the tax lien filing when it made the disbursements.

Under local law, the security interest would trump a hypothetical unsecured judgment lien arising as of the tax lien filing date.

Let us take a step back from the direct examination of the 45-Day Rule and the Internal revenue Code in regards to Payroll Taxes. To begin with, let us explain why a business would choose to enter into a Factoring relationship. For many companies, there are periods in the business cycle where cash flow becomes hard to manage and you look for alternatives. A workable alternative that many consider is an Accounts Receivable Financing Program or an Asset Based Financing program, commonly referred to as Asset-Based Lending or Factoring.

If your company is in financial difficulty, these types of revolving loans can sometimes accelerate the problem, but they can often help a company out of a bad situation. If you have identified the problem and have a plan in place to fix the problem within a specified period of time, accelerating cash flow can be a direct benefit that ends the crisis. It is essential to realize that such a loan agreement places your company in direct jeopardy if you fail to properly cover your payroll taxes or pay them on time.

Overall, the asset based lending industry has acquired an image that is far from ideal. Business owners assume that asset based loans are not as good as unsecured loans. In truth, asset based lending is used with all size companies and can allow an asset-rich corporation to receive financing when you have not met standard credit requirements. You do not always pay a higher rate of interest.

True asset based or "Equity based" lending is easier to obtain for borrowers who do not conform to typical lending standards. You may have no, little or terrible credit. You may have little income to support the payments, and may need to rely on the loan itself to pay back the lender until the property is either sold, refinanced, or your income resumes.

An important part of the decision to take such a loan is to compare the cost of the program to the benefit that the business will receive. It may help our business in the short-term, but if it costs more than increases profit, it is a bad solution. It is best to have a fixed, up-front cost structure that you can budget into your pricing and to know that no additional fees can be added to your cost.

In reality, with the pressure on and payroll taxes around the corner, how much time does a program like this save you and your company. If you spend large amounts of time tracking everything to manage the program and to comply with regulations, you may find yourself again losing money.

Asset based lenders typically limit the loans to a 50 or 65 loan to value ratio or "LTV". For example: If the appraisal is valued at $1,000,000.00 a lender might lend between $500,000.00 and $650,000.00. In the event of a default resulting in a foreclosure, the first lien position lender is entitled to repayment first, out of the proceeds of the sale.

You generate accounts receivable by selling goods or services to your customers on credit. If a cash squeeze develops, you may extend credit to your customers and sell your accounts receivable to a factor. A factor is a specialized financial intermediary who purchases accounts receivable at a discount. Factoring is a technique used to manage your accounts receivable and provide financing.

Under the lending (often called "factoring") agreement, you sell or assign your accounts receivable to the factor in exchange for a cash advance. The factor typically charges interest on the advance plus a commission, not mention several service fees along the way. If you are a lender in the position of the factor and your borrower has failed to pay their payroll taxes, your collateral could be in real jeopardy. When it comes to the Trust Fund Recovery Penalty and the enforcing the strictures of the 45-Day Rule, the IRS Collection Officers are orthodox and inflexible.

According to the IRS Code, IRS Collection Officers only invalidate a tax lien against the security interests of a lender that satisfy traditional choateness doctrine within 45 days after the filing of a tax lien. This 45-Day Rule is not a parity rule as it provides for "sudden death" of a security interest that is not acquired within stated period. This "sudden death" potential is essential for lenders to understand in light of a borrower failing to pay their payroll taxes and a tax lien against the company being filed by the IRS.

To avoid the "sudden death" outcome, a factor's (or lender's) security interest in the business owner's (or taxpayer's) "accounts receivable" must meet federal standards of choateness within 45 days after the filing of the tax lien to have priority over the tax lien. In other words, the security interest must have been "acquired" by the factor (or lender) within that period. In contrast, a security interest in account receivables cannot be acquired until the accounts receivable comes into existence. As a result, the IRS deems such a security interest incomplete.

Security interest arising within 45 days after a federal tax lien is filed takes priority under three specific conditions:

If your security interest stems from a written agreement entered into before the federal tax lien was filed and it qualifies as a "commercial transactions financing agreement".

If your underlying loans were made pursuant to a written agreement within 45 days of the filing of the tax lien or prior to receiving the notice of the tax lien's being filed

The agreement covers "qualified property" which was acquired by the taxpayer within 45 days of the filing of the tax lien, and local law gives the security interest holder priority over a judgment lien by an unsecured creditor as of the time the federal lien was filed.

The Internal Revenue Service considers security interest obligation, which arises from optional advance made during the 45-day period without actual notice or knowledge of existence of federal tax lien protected. However, it is essential for the lender to understand that such knowledge must be categorically proved which can be challenging to say the least.

If you are a lender and your borrower has failed to properly cover the payroll taxes of their business and the trust fund recovery penalty has come into play, the collateral your loans are based on could be in real jeopardy.

The 45-Day Requirement (Superseded)

The IRS Code only invalidates tax lien as against security interests of lenders or purchasers that satisfy traditional choateness doctrine within 45 days after filing of tax lien; rule is not parity rule as it provides for "sudden death" of security interest that is not acquired within stated period; lender's or purchaser's security interest in taxpayer's "accounts receivable" must meet federal standard of choateness within 45 days after filing of tax lien to have priority over tax lien; security interest must have been "acquired" by lender or purchaser within that period; security interest in account receivable is not acquired, and is therefore inchoate, until account receivable comes into existence. Texas Oil & Gas Corp v United States (1972, CA5 Tex) 466 F2d 1040, 11 UCCRS 575, cert den 410 US 929, 35 L Ed 2d 591, 93 S Ct 1367.

Security interest arising within 45 days after federal tax lien is filed takes priority if security interest stems from written agreement entered into before federal tax lien was filed and it qualifies as "commercial transactions financing agreement", underlying loans were made pursuant to written agreement within 45 days of filing of tax lien or prior to receiving notice of tax lien's being filed, agreement covers "qualified property" which was acquired by taxpayer within 45 days of filing of tax lien, and local law gives security interest holder priority over judgment lien by unsecured creditor as of time federal lien was filed. Donald v Madison Industries, Inc. (1973, CA10) 73-2 USTC 9623.

Absent contrary local law or specific statutory priority rules relating to judgment liens, Internal Revenue Service considers security interest obligation which arises from optional advance made during 45 day period without actual notice or knowledge of existence of federal tax lien protected; rule applies only to security interest under 26 USCS 6323 (c) (2) and (d). Rev Rul 72-290, FLAG 1972-1 p 385.

6321 n 14. Accounts receivable or payable

Taxpayer's invoice instructions to his customer to make checks payable jointly to the taxpayer and the taxpayer's creditors did not constitute an assignment of the customer's account to the creditors; hence, although the tax was not assessed until after instructions were mailed to the customer, the tax lien attached to the entire amount due from the customer. Harbert Constr. Corp. v United Iron Works, Inc. (1967, DC Ala) 67-2 USTC 9668.

Accounts receivable for "future" sales to taxpayer's customer assigned by the taxpayer to his supplier in payment for logs to be delivered to the taxpayer, was not subject to Treasury's tax lien. Harter v District Director of Internal Revenue (1968, DC Wash) 68-2 USTC 94.

Chapter 19:

IRS Criminal Investigation Division ("CI")

Overview

Headquartered in Washington DC, the IRS Criminal Investigation (CI) is comprised of approximately 3,700 employees worldwide, approximately 2,600 of whom are special agents whose investigative jurisdiction includes tax, money laundering and Bank Secrecy Act laws. While other federal agencies also have investigative jurisdiction for money laundering and some bank secrecy act violations, IRS is the only federal agency that can investigate potential criminal violations of the Internal Revenue Code.

Compliance with the tax laws in the United States relies heavily on self-assessments of what tax is owed. This is called voluntary compliance. When individuals and corporations make deliberate decisions to not comply with the law, they face the possibility of a civil audit or criminal investigation which could result in prosecution and possible jail time. Publicity of these convictions provides a deterrent effect that enhances voluntary compliance.

As financial investigators, CI special agents fill a unique niche in the federal law enforcement community. Today's sophisticated schemes to defraud the government demand the analytical ability of financial investigators to wade through complex paper and computerized financial records. Due to the increased use of automation for financial records, CI special agents are trained to recover computer evidence. Along with their financial investigative skills, special agents use specialized forensic technology to recover financial data that may have been encrypted, password protected, or hidden by other electronic means.

Criminal Investigation's conviction rate is one of the highest in federal law enforcement. Not only do the courts hand down substantial prison sentences, but those convicted must also pay fines, civil taxes and penalties.[xxvi]

History

The **Criminal Investigation Division** of the IRS **("CI")** was created on July 1, 1919. At the time, the Commissioner of the IRS created the Division which at the time was called the Intelligence Unit to probe in assertions of tax fraud. The division was originally composed of a small group of postal inspectors which is quite different from the current group of highly trained, individuals that make up the department today.[xxvii]

The CI became known nationwide when they assisted in the conviction of Al Capone for income tax evasion.

In 1978 the agency changed its name to **Criminal Investigation** which has transformed to its currently known name, the CI. Over time, in addition to investigating tax law violations, the CI expanded its duties to include investigating currency and money laundering violations. But the CI's primary objective is to ensure the integrity and fairness of the United States tax system.

Since the CI since its creation has continually been able to convict no less than 90% of the taxpayers they alleged to have violated U.S. tax law. This conviction rate is unmatched to all other branches of Federal law enforcement.[xxviii]

Background

The Criminal Investigation Division ("CI") is the "policing" arm of the IRS. When a taxpayer's actions are scrutinized as having potentially violated U.S. tax law, they may be assigned to the CI and in turn assigned an IRS Special Agent. The IRS Special Agent must adhere to strict rules set forth in the Internal Revenue Manual ("IRM") which include warning a taxpayer that he or she is under criminal investigation as well as providing credentials if requested.

A taxpayer is under no obligation to speak to a Special Agent, and in fact may and probably should remain silent when questioned by a Special Agent. If your Client is going to be or has been approached by the CI, it is in their best interest not to respond to any request of a Special Agent without having proper representation.

The IRS CI will evaluate several criteria in order to determine if a taxpayer should or should not be investigated by their Department. The main determination in deciding to proceed is based upon whether or not the CI believes their recommendation to prosecute will lead to a conviction. If the CI determines that their subject should be prosecuted, the case is then reviewed by the District Counsel ("DC") of the IRS and if passed by the DC, it is then referred to the Tax Division of the Department of Justice ("DOJ"). If the DOJ determines that the case is worthy of prosecution, it is then referred to the U.S. Attorney and prosecuted pending final approval.

In order for a taxpayer to be charged with a felony, a Federal Grand Jury must vote in favor of issuing an indictment. Here the Grand Jury has to make some subjective decisions based upon whether they believe there has been a violation in Federal tax law as well as whether they believe that the accused has broken said tax law under the same standard. A Grand Jury is composed of anywhere from16 to 23 people that are picked by the U.S. District Court. At least 12 jurors must vote to proceed with an indictment. If less than twelve agree, the case will not proceed.

How the CI works

It is the goal of an IRS Special Agent to investigate, discover and provide proof that the taxpayer had criminal intent when the performed the act/s for which they are being investigated. Keep in mind that the Special Agents best resource is the taxpayer themselves. Giving false testimony or admitting to something that is not necessary will most definitely assist the Special Agent in their case. Therefore a taxpayer under investigation should consult a qualified representative to advise them through this process.

A taxpayer with proper representation will most likely remain silent when questioned by a Special Agent. This causes the Special Agent to turn to other investigative means including third party interviews via Summons and interviewing the taxpayer's tax return preparer to establish intent via circumstantial evidence. The Special Agent may also examine the taxpayer's past and present bank account statements, financial records and tax returns. Keep in mind that if the Special Agent cannot directly establish proof, he or she may attempt to provide indirect evidence that the taxpayer intended to commit fraud.

There are 3 main concerns for which IRS CI conducts an investigation:

1. Tax evasion.
2. Filing a false return.
3. Failure to file a tax return.

Keep in mind that millions of people each year act in a way that would fall into one of the above-mentioned categories. In addition to committing the act, there is the severity of how the act was committed that must be considered as well.

Under USC § 7206 Any person who…

(1) **Declaration under penalties of perjury**

willfully makes and subscribes any return, statement, or other document, which contains or is verified by a written declaration that it is made under the penalties of perjury, and which he does not believe to be true and correct as to every material matter; or

(2) **Aid or assistance**
willfully aids or assists in, or procures, counsels, or advises the preparation or presentation under, or in connection with any matter arising under, the internal revenue laws, of a return, affidavit, claim, or other document, which is fraudulent or is false as to any material matter, whether or not such falsity or fraud is with the knowledge or consent of the person authorized or required to present such return, affidavit, claim, or document; or

(3) **Fraudulent bonds, permits, and entries**
simulates or falsely or fraudulently executes or signs any bond, permit, entry, or other document required by the provisions of the internal revenue laws, or by any regulation made in pursuance thereof, or procures the same to be falsely or fraudulently executed, or advises, aids in, or connives at such execution thereof

…shall be guilty of a felony and, upon conviction thereof, shall be fined not more than $100,000 ($500,000 in the case of a corporation), or imprisoned not more than 3 years, or both, together with the costs of prosecution.[xxix]

According to section ***25.1.1.2.4 (12-16-2011)*** of the Internal Revenue Manual ("irm") tax avoidance is not a criminal offense and tax evasion is.

Avoidance vs. Evasion

1. Avoidance of tax is not a criminal offense. Taxpayers have the right to reduce, avoid, or minimize their taxes by legitimate means. One who avoids tax does not conceal or misrepresent, but shapes and preplans events to reduce or eliminate tax liability within the perimeters of the law.

2. Evasion involves some affirmative act to evade or defeat a tax, or payment of tax. Examples of affirmative acts are deceit, subterfuge, camouflage, concealment, attempts to color or obscure events, or make things seem other than they are.

3. Common evasion schemes include:

    - Intentional understatement or omission of income,
    - Claiming fictitious or improper deductions,
    - False allocation of income, and/or
    - Improper claims, credits, or exemptions,
    - Concealment of assets.

Examples (see Appendix D for actual case studies)

Employment Tax Evasion Schemes[xxx]

Employment tax evasion schemes can take a variety of forms. Some of the more prevalent methods of evasion include pyramiding, employee leasing, paying employees in cash, filing false payroll tax returns or failing to file payroll tax returns.

Pyramiding

"Pyramiding" of employment taxes is a fraudulent practice where a business withholds taxes from its employees but intentionally fails to remit them to the IRS. Businesses involved in pyramiding frequently file for bankruptcy to discharge the liabilities accrued and then start a new business under a different name and begin a new scheme.

Employment Leasing

Employee leasing is another legal business practice, which is sometimes subject to abuse. Employee leasing is the practice of contracting with outside businesses to handle all administrative, personnel, and payroll concerns for employees. In some instances, employee-leasing companies fail to pay over to the IRS any portion of the collected employment taxes. These taxes are often spent by the owners on business or personal expenses. Often the company dissolves, leaving millions in employment taxes unpaid.

Paying Employees in Cash

Paying employees, whole or partially, in cash is a common method of evading income and employment taxes resulting in lost tax revenue to the government and the loss or reduction of future social security or Medicare benefits for the employee.

Filing False Payroll Tax Returns or Falling to File Payroll Tax Returns

Preparing false payroll tax returns understating the amount of wages on which taxes are owed, or failing to file employment tax returns are methods commonly used to evade employment taxes.

Statistical Data - Employment Tax Evasion

How to Interpret Criminal Investigation Data

Since actions on a specific investigation may cross fiscal years, the data shown in cases initiated may not always represent the same universe of cases shown in other actions within the same fiscal year.

Year-Over-Year Comparison (2010 – 2012)

	FY 2012	FY 2011	FY 2010
Investigations Initiated	148	153	166
Prosecution Recommendations	86	110	115
Indictments/Informations	92	85	83
Sentenced	79	79	62
Incarceration Rate*	**81.0%**	**81.0%**	**82.3%**
Average Months to Serve	**24**	**24**	**19**

*Incarceration includes confinement to federal prison, halfway house, home detention, or some combination thereof.

Data Source: Criminal Investigation Management Information System

Fiscal Year 2013 (Second Quarter - October 2012 - March 2013)

How to Interpret Criminal Investigation Data

Since actions on a specific investigation may cross fiscal years, the total shown under Investigations Initiated may not represent the same universe of investigations displayed under other actions within the same fiscal year. (Example: an investigation initiated in fiscal year 2012 may not be sentenced until fiscal year 2013)

Actions	Totals
Investigations Initiated	2709
Prosecution Recommendations	2213
Informations/Indictments	1902
Convictions	1515
Sentenced*	1329
Percent to Prison	82.3%
Average Months to Serve	46

'Sentence includes confinement to federal prison, halfway house, home detention, or some combination thereof.

Data Source: Criminal Investigation Management Information System. Fiscal years run from October through September.

Options

If a taxpayer suspects that he or she may be subject to a criminal investigation by the IRS, they may consider making a voluntary disclosure to the CI to avoid prosecution. The IRS has established policy surrounding voluntary disclosures that if properly complied with ensure that the majority of taxpayers who make a proper voluntary disclosure need not fear criminal prosecution. *Keep in mind that a voluntary disclosure is not the same as an admission against your interest. If you wait until the IRS has caught, it may be too late.*

Keep in mind that **the IRS's voluntary disclosure policy does not guarantee a grant of amnesty or immunity from prosecution**. The IRS states that a voluntary disclosure occurs when a taxpayer makes a truthful, timely, and complete disclosure, and the taxpayer cooperates with the IRS and makes a good faith arrangement with the IRS to pay all determined deficiencies, including interest and penalties. To qualify as a true voluntary disclosure, the disclosure must be made before the disclosing individual is aware of events that indicate the government is likely to discover the crime being disclosed. Given the technical and tactical aspects of making voluntary disclosure, experienced tax counsel should be engaged.

What is the consequence of a taxpayer lying to an IRS agent?

At some point during a civil examination or criminal investigation taxpayers may find themselves explaining their previous actions regarding their tax return to an IRS Special Agent. Because it is a crime in and of itself, to lie or mislead a federal agent, the taxpayer really only has one of two choices when faced with an interview by and IRS agent; (1) say nothing or (2) "fess up" and tell the truth. If the taxpayer knows that they substantially understated income, overstated deductions and or falsely claimed credits then it is imperative that they seek counsel from an experienced professional before continuing any further communication with the IRS. Better to say nothing than say something that can be used against you.

In 2012 IRS CI released its ***Annual Report*** highlighting strong gains in enforcement actions and penalties imposed on convicted tax criminals.

The 28-page report summarizes a wide variety of CI activity on a range of tax related issues during the fiscal year ending Sept. 30, 2012.

Richard Weber, the Chief of Criminal Investigation states "The key to our successes is perseverance and dedication to working complex financial investigations aimed at stopping tax fraud, identity theft, offshore tax evasion, public corruption, money laundering and other financial crimes…"

Highlights of the Annual Report include:

Investigations initiated and prosecution recommendations were both up nearly 9 percent in fiscal 2012 compared to the prior year. Filings of indictments and other charging documents rose 13 percent.

Meanwhile, convictions and those sentenced both gained roughly 12 percent from the prior year.

Criminal investigation initiations totaled 5,125 cases in fiscal 2012 while investigations completed were 4,937 – up 5 percent from fiscal 2011.

Convictions totaled 2,634 in fiscal 2012 while the conviction rate edged up slightly to 93 percent.

Mr. Weber also indicated "This annual report showcases some of the many significant cases that were completed by CI during fiscal year 2012 and the many program areas we cover as an organization. These cases are just a few examples of the thousands of investigations initiated by CI last year, as we continue to make our mark as the finest financial investigators in the world…"

Relative to the total number of taxpayers, an extremely small amount of individuals are criminally investigated; however, keep in mind that if an investigation is opened, one must be prepared to defend themselves because prosecutions are on the rise.

The IRS tends to be meticulous when investigating a taxpayer at this level, even more so than a typical Police Department. It is not uncommon for an investigation to span several years and may involve gathering information form the taxpayer's family, friends, neighbors, and business associates. The IRS is able to enlist the USPS to keep tabs on a taxpayer's mail correspondence. In addition a taxpayers financial advisors including banker and accountants may be required to divulge otherwise private information to the IRS.

IRS Summons from CI (*sample*)

12:22:27 04-22-2013 | 1

Summons

In the matter of [redacted]

Internal Revenue Service (Division): Criminal Investigation

Industry/Area (name or number): Houston Field Office

Periods: 2007-2012

The Commissioner of Internal Revenue

To: [redacted]

At: [redacted]

You are hereby summoned and required to appear before Special Agent [redacted] or his designee an officer of the Internal Revenue Service, to give testimony and to bring with you and to produce for examination the following books, records, papers, and other data relating to the tax liability or the collection of the tax liability or for the purpose of inquiring into any offense connected with the administration or enforcement of the internal revenue laws concerning the person identified above for the periods shown.

See Attachment:

If the production of the requested records is anticipated to cost more than $500 please contact [redacted] at [redacted] prior to production.

Attestation

I hereby certify that I have examined and compared this copy of the summons with the original and that it is a true and correct copy of the original.

[redacted] Signature of IRS officer serving the summons — Special Agent, Title

Business address and telephone number of IRS officer before whom you are to appear:

Place and time for appearance at [redacted]

on the 29 day of April 2013 (year) at 10 o'clock a m.

Issued under authority of the Internal Revenue Code this 17 **day of** April, 2013 (year).

[redacted] Signature of issuing officer — Special Agent, Title

Signature of approving officer (*if applicable*) — N/A, Title

IRS
Department of the Treasury
Internal Revenue Service
www.irs.gov
Form 2039 (Rev. 10-2010)
Catalog Number 21405J

Part A - to be given to person summoned

Chapter 20:

Request for Taxpayer Advocate Service Assistance

Request for Taxpayer Advocate Service Assistance

Seven Things to Know About the Taxpayer Advocate Service

The **Taxpayer Advocate Service** is an independent organization within the Internal Revenue Service whose employees assist taxpayers who are experiencing economic harm, who are seeking help in resolving problems with the IRS, or who believe that an IRS system or procedure is not working as it should. Here are seven things every taxpayer should know about **Taxpayer Advocate Service**.

Taxpayer Advocate Service is your voice at the IRS.

Taxpayer Advocate Service is free, confidential, and tailored to meet your needs.

You may be eligible for **Taxpayer Advocate Service** help if you've tried to resolve your tax problem through normal IRS channels and have gotten nowhere, or you think an IRS procedure just isn't working as it should.

Taxpayer Advocate Service helps taxpayers whose problems are causing financial difficulty or significant cost, including the cost of professional representation. This includes businesses as well as individuals.

Taxpayer Advocate Service employees know the IRS and how to navigate it. They will listen to your problem, help you understand what needs to be done to resolve it, and stay with you every step of the way until your problem is resolved.

Taxpayer Advocate Service has at least one local taxpayer advocate in each state, the District of Columbia, and Puerto Rico. You can call your local advocate, whose number is in your phone book, in Pub. 1546, Taxpayer Advocate Service -- Your Voice at the IRS, and at ***www.irs.gov/advocate***. You can also call our toll-free number at 1-877-777-4778 or TTY/TDD 1-800-829-4059.

You can learn about your rights and responsibilities as a taxpayer by visiting the **Taxpayer Advocate Service** online tax toolkit at ***www.taxtoolkit.irs.gov***. You can also check out the **Taxpayer Advocate Service** YouTube channel at ***www.youtube.com/tasnta***.

Request for Assistance Form[xxxi]

OMB No. 1545-1504

Department of the Treasury - Internal Revenue Service

Request for Taxpayer Advocate Service Assistance
(And Application for Taxpayer Assistance Order)

Form **911** (Rev. 6-2007)

Section I – Taxpayer Information *(See Pages 3 and 4 for Form 911 Filing Requirements and Instructions for Completing this Form.)*

1a. Your name as shown on tax return	2a. Your Social Security Number	
1b. Spouse's name as shown on tax return	2b. Spouse's Social Security Number	
3a. Your current street address *(Number, Street, & Apt. Number)*		
3b. City	3c. State *(or Foreign Country)*	3d. ZIP code
4. Fax number *(if applicable)* / 5. E-mail address		
6. Employer Identification Number *(EIN) (if applicable)*	7. Tax form(s)	8. Tax period(s)
9. Person to contact	10. Daytime phone number ☐ Check if Cell Phone	11. Best time to call

12. Indicate the special communication needs you require *(if applicable)*

☐ TTY/TDD Line ☐ Interpreter - Specify language other than English *(including sign language)* ____________

☐ Other *(please specify)*

13a. Please describe the tax problem you are experiencing *(If more space is needed, attach additional sheets.)*

13b. Please describe the relief/assistance you are requesting *(If more space is needed, attach additional sheets.)*

I understand that Taxpayer Advocate Service employees may contact third parties in order to respond to this request and I authorize such contacts to be made. Further, by authorizing the Taxpayer Advocate Service to contact third parties, I understand that I will not receive notice, pursuant to section 7602(c) of the Internal Revenue Code, of third parties contacted in connection with this request.

14a. Signature of Taxpayer or Corporate Officer, and title, if applicable	14b. Date signed
15a. Signature of spouse	15b. Date signed

Section II – Representative Information *(Attach Form 2848 if not already on file with the IRS.)*

1. Name of authorized representative	2. Centralized Authorization File (CAF) number
3. Current mailing address	4. Daytime phone number ☐ Check if Cell Phone
	5. Fax number
6. Signature of representative	7. Date signed

Catalog Number 16965S www.irs.gov Form **911** (Rev. 6-2007)

Section III is to be completed by the IRS only

Section III – Initiating Employee Information

Taxpayer name			Taxpayer Identification Number *(TIN)*	
1. Name of employee	2. Phone number	3a. Function	3b. Operating division	4. Organization code no.

5. How identified and received *(Check the appropriate box)*

6. IRS received date

IRS Function identified issue as meeting Taxpayer Advocate Service (TAS) criteria

☐ (r) Functional referral (Function identified taxpayer issue as meeting TAS criteria).
☐ (x) Congressional correspondence/inquiry not addressed to TAS but referred for TAS handling.
Name of Congressional Representative ______________________________

Taxpayer or Representative requested TAS assistance

☐ (n) Taxpayer or representative called into a National Taxpayer Advocate (NTA) Toll-Free site.
☐ (s) Functional referral (taxpayer or representative specifically requested TAS assistance).

7. TAS criteria *(Check the appropriate box.* ***NOTE: Checkbox 9 is for TAS Use Only)***

☐ (1) The taxpayer is experiencing economic harm or is about to suffer economic harm.
☐ (2) The taxpayer is facing an immediate threat of adverse action.
☐ (3) The taxpayer will incur significant costs if relief is not granted (including fees for professional representation).
☐ (4) The taxpayer will suffer irreparable injury or long-term adverse impact if relief is not granted.
☐ (5) The taxpayer has experienced a delay of more than 30 days to resolve a tax account problem.
☐ (6) The taxpayer did not receive a response or resolution to their problem or inquiry by the date promised.
☐ (7) A system or procedure has either failed to operate as intended, or failed to resolve the taxpayer's problem or dispute within the IRS.
☐ (8) The manner in which the tax laws are being administered raise considerations of equity, or have impaired or will impair the taxpayer's rights.
☐ (9) The NTA determines compelling public policy warrants assistance to an individual or group of taxpayers (**TAS Use Only**).

8. What action(s) did you take to help resolve the problem *(Must be completed by the initiating employee)*

9. State the reason(s) why the problem was not resolved *(Must be completed by the initiating employee)*

10. How did the taxpayer learn about the Taxpayer Advocate Service

Catalog Number 16965S **Page 2** www.irs.gov Form **911** (Rev. 6-2007)

Instructions for completing Form 911 (Rev. 6-2007)

Form 911 Filing Requirements

When to Use this Form: Use this form if any of the following apply to you:

1. You are experiencing economic harm or are about to suffer economic harm.
2. You are facing an immediate threat of adverse action.
3. You will incur significant costs if relief is not granted (including fees for professional representation).
4. You will suffer irreparable injury or long-term adverse impact if relief is not granted.
5. You have experienced a delay of more than 30 days to resolve a tax account problem.
6. You have not received a response or resolution to your problem or inquiry by the date promised.
7. A system or procedure has either failed to operate as intended, or failed to resolve your problem or dispute within the IRS.
8. The manner in which the tax laws are being administered raise considerations of equity, or have impaired or will impair your rights.
9. The NTA determines compelling public policy warrants assistance to an individual or group of taxpayers.

If an IRS office will not grant the assistance requested or will not grant the assistance in time, you may submit this form. The Taxpayer Advocate Service will generally request that certain activities be stopped while your request for assistance is pending (e.g., lien filings, levies, and seizures).

Where to FAX or Mail this Form: Submit this request to the Taxpayer Advocate office located in the city or state where you reside. For the address of the Taxpayer Advocate office near you or for additional information, call the National Taxpayer Advocate Toll-Free Number: 1-877-777-4778. You can also find the address, phone and fax number of your local Taxpayer Advocate office in the government listings in your local telephone directory. Information can also be found on the IRS website, **www.irs.gov**, under Taxpayer Advocate.

Third Party Contact: You should understand that in order to respond to this request you are authorizing the Taxpayer Advocate Service to contact third parties when necessary, and that you will not receive further notice regarding contacted parties. See IRC 7602(c).

Overseas Taxpayers: Taxpayers residing overseas can submit this application by mail to the Taxpayer Advocate Service, Internal Revenue Service, PO Box 193479, San Juan, Puerto Rico 00919-3479, or in person at San Patricio Office Center, #7 Tabonuco Street, Room 202, Guaynabo, PR 00966. The application can also be faxed to 1-787-622-8933.

Caution: Incomplete information or requests submitted to a Taxpayer Advocate office outside of your geographical location may result in delays. If you do not hear from us within one week of submitting Form 911, please contact the Taxpayer Advocate office where you originally submitted your request. The Taxpayer Advocate Service will not consider frivolous arguments raised on this form, such as those listed in Notice 2007-30. Frivolous arguments may include arguments that the income tax is illegal or that the IRS has no authority to assess and collect tax. You can find additional examples of frivolous arguments in *Publication 2105, Why do I have to Pay Taxes?*. If you use this form to raise frivolous arguments, you may be subject to a penalty of $5,000.

Paperwork Reduction Act Notice: We ask for the information on this form to carry out the Internal Revenue laws of the United States. Your response is voluntary. You are not required to provide the information requested on a form that is subject to the Paperwork Reduction Act unless the form displays a valid OMB control number. Books or records relating to a form or its instructions must be retained as long as their contents may become material in the administration of any Internal Revenue law. Generally, tax returns and return information are confidential, as required by Code section 6103. Although the time needed to complete this form may vary depending on individual circumstances, the estimated average time is 30 minutes.

Should you have comments concerning the accuracy of this time estimate or suggestions for making this form simpler, please write to: **Internal Revenue Service,** Tax Products Coordinating Committee, Room 6406 , 1111 Constitution Ave. NW, Washington, DC 20224.

Instructions for Section I

1a. Enter your name as shown on the tax return that relates to this request for assistance.

1b. Enter your spouse's name (if applicable) if this request relates to a jointly filed return.

2a. Enter your Social Security Number.

2b. Enter your spouse's Social Security Number if this request relates to a jointly filed return.

3a-d. Enter your current mailing address, including the street number and name, and if applicable, your apartment number, your city, town, or post office, state or possession or foreign country, and ZIP code.

4. Enter your fax number, including the area code.

5. Enter your e-mail address. We may use this to contact you if we are unable to reach you by telephone. We will not, however, use your e-mail address to discuss the specifics of your case.

6. Enter your Employer Identification Number if this request involves a business or non-individual entity (e.g., a partnership, corporation, trust, or self-employed individual).

7. Enter the number of the Federal tax return or form that relates to this request. For example, an individual taxpayer with an income tax issue would enter Form 1040.

Instructions for Section I continue on the next page ▶

Instructions for Section I - *(Continued from Page 3)*

8. Enter the quarterly, annual, or other tax period that relates to this request. For example, if this request involves an income tax issue, enter the calendar or fiscal year; if an employment tax issue, enter the calendar quarter.

9. Enter the name of the individual we should contact. For partnerships, corporations, trusts, etc., enter the name of the individual authorized to act on the entity's behalf. If the contact person is not the taxpayer or other authorized individual, please see the Instructions for Section II.

10. Enter your daytime telephone number, including the area code. If this is a cell phone number, please check the box.

11. Indicate the best time to call you. Please specify a.m. or p.m. hours.

12. Indicate any special communication needs you require (such as sign language). Specify any language other than English.

13a. Describe the problem. Specify the actions that the IRS has taken (or not taken) to resolve the problem. If the problem involves an IRS delay of more than 30 days in resolving your issue, indicate the date you first contacted the IRS for assistance in resolving your problem.

13b. Please describe the relief/assistance you are requesting. Specify the action that you want taken and that you believe necessary to resolve the problem. Furnish any documentation that you believe would assist us in resolving the problem.

14-15. If this is a joint assistance request, both spouses must sign in the appropriate blocks and enter the date the request was signed. If only one spouse is requesting assistance, only the requesting spouse must sign the request. If this request is being submitted for another individual, only a person authorized and empowered to act on that individual's behalf should sign the request. Requests for corporations must be signed by an officer and include the officer's title.

Note: The signing of this request allows the IRS by law to suspend, for the period of time it takes the Taxpayer Advocate Service to review and decide upon your request, any applicable statutory periods of limitation relating to the assessment or collection of taxes. However, it does not suspend any applicable periods for you to perform acts related to assessment or collection, such as petitioning the Tax Court for redetermination of a deficiency or requesting a Collection Due Process hearing.

Instructions for Section II

Taxpayers: If you wish to have a representative act on your behalf, you must give him/her power of attorney or tax information authorization for the tax return(s) and period(s) involved. For additional information see Form 2848, Power of Attorney and Declaration of Representative, or Form 8821, Tax Information Authorization, and the accompanying instructions. Information can also be found in Publication 1546, The Taxpayer Advocate Service of the IRS-How to Get Help With Unresolved Tax Problems.

Representatives: If you are an authorized representative submitting this request on behalf of the taxpayer identified in Section I, complete Blocks 1 through 7 of Section II. Attach a copy of Form 2848, Form 8821, or other power of attorney. Enter your Centralized Authorization File (CAF) number in Block 2 of Section II. The CAF number is the unique number that the IRS assigns to a representative after Form 2848 or Form 8821 is filed with an IRS office.

Note: Form 8821 does not authorize your appointee to advocate your position with respect to the Federal tax laws; to execute waivers, consents, or closing agreements; or to otherwise represent you before the IRS. Form 8821 does authorize anyone you designate to inspect and/or receive your confidential tax information in any office of the IRS, for the type of tax and tax periods you list on Form 8821.

Instructions for Section III *(For IRS Use Only)*

Enter the taxpayers name and taxpayer identification number from the first page of this form.

1. Enter your name.
2. Enter your phone number.
3a. Enter your Function (e.g., ACS, Collection, Examination, Customer Service, etc.).
3b. Enter your Operating Division (W&I, SB/SE, LMSB, or TE/GE).
4. Enter the Organization code number for your office (e.g., 18 for AUSC, 95 for Los Angeles).
5. Check the appropriate box that best reflects how the need for TAS assistance was identified. For example, did taxpayer or representative call or write to an IRS function or the Taxpayer Advocate Service (TAS).
6. Enter the date the taxpayer or representative called or visited an IRS office to request TAS assistance. Or enter the date when the IRS received the Congressional correspondence/inquiry or a written request for TAS assistance from the taxpayer or representative. If the IRS identified the taxpayer's issue as meeting TAS criteria, enter the date this determination was made.
7. Check the box that best describes the reason TAS assistance is requested. **Box 9 is for TAS Use Only.**
8. State the action(s) you took to help resolve the taxpayer's problem.
9. State the reason(s) that prevented you from resolving the taxpayer's problem. For example, levy proceeds cannot be returned because they were already applied to a valid liability; an overpayment cannot be refunded because the statutory period for issuing a refund expired; or current law precludes a specific interest abatement.
10. Ask the taxpayer how he or she learned about the Taxpayer Advocate Service and indicate the response here.

Chapter 21:

Bulk Transfer

Sample

May 25, 2008

<Client >
<Business, Inc.>
<Address>

MEMORANDUM OF UNDERSTANDING

Re: Business, Inc. Chapter # 11
941 liability re draw vs. loan re officers compensation
Informal cram down of unsecured creditors
Administrative procedure and Administrative remedy
Avoid successor liability, fraudulent conveyance

Dear Client:

As per our conversation, the following may represent Administrative Procedure and Administrative Remedy:

- *File amended return 941-X, Re draw / loan from officers and/or stockholders.*
- ***Organize** and **Strategize** Bulk Transfer for Corporate Industries, Inc.*
- *Including Buy-Sell agreement (Purchase Agreement)*
- *File notice of Bulk Transfer to Creditors*
- ***Pre sanctioned IRS Bulk Transfer with Revenue Officer.***
- *Provide IRS with copy of F.F.E. **(see Bulk Transfer documents).***
- *Hire auctioneers acceptable to IRS.*
- *Avoid Successor liability / fraudulent conveyance re new company.*
- *Provide list of items we need for IRS **(see documents -blue backed)***
- *Place ad with newspaper.*
- *UCC1 due diligence*
- *Establish escrow.*

Chapter 11 perils avoided:

- *Avoid chapter 11, D I P account*
- *Avoid interim & operating reports*
- *Avoid Quarterly Bankruptcy fees*
- *Avoid plan of reorganization confirmation fees*
- *Avoid bankruptcy exit fees*
- *Dismiss Chapter 11 without prejudice **(provided IRS sanctions).***

IRS "Offer in Compromise"

Defend all officers re: Trust Fund Assessment, Draw vs. Salary accounting methodology.
Strategize and complete "Offer in Compromises"

Contingent liability
(see Processing an Offer)
Abate penalty & interest

Adequate representation- Trust Fund Recovery "4180"
Provide a formal 2751 Appeals defense

Bulk Transfer Process

The following is an overview/continuum of the **Bulk Transfer** Process which we have discussed with the Revenue Officer to avoid a **"Writ to enter and seize."**

I. Statutory Foundation

A. 6101 - Short Title

This process shall be known and may be cited as Uniform Commercial Code- Bulk Transfers.

This article attempts to simplify and make uniform the bulk sales laws of the states that adopt this Act.

Many states have bulk sales laws, of varying type and coverage.

Their central purpose is to deal with two common forms of commercial fraud, namely:

- The merchant, owing debts, who sells out his stock in trade to a friend for less than it is worth, pays his creditors less than he owes them, and hopes to come back into the business through the back door sometime in the future.
- The merchant, owing debts, who sells out his stock in trade to any one for any price, pockets the proceeds, and disappears leaving his creditors unpaid.

B. 6102 - Bulk Transfer, Transfer of Equipment

A "bulk transfer" is any transfer in bulk and not in the ordinary course of the transferor's business of a substantial part of the materials, supplies, merchandise, or other inventory (Section 9109) of an enterprise subject to this division.

C. 6103 - Transfers exempt from this article

The following transfers are not subject to this division:

- Assignments for the benefit of all the creditors of the transferor, and subsequent transfers by the assignee hereunder.
- Transfers of property subject to a lien or other security interest in settlement or realization of such lien or other security interest.
- Sales by executors, administrators, receivers, trustees in bankruptcy, or any public officer under judicial process.
- Transfers of property which is exempt from enforcement of a money judgment.

D. 6105 - Notice to Creditors

- Any bulk transfer subject to this division except one made by auction sale (Section 6108) is fraudulent and void against any creditor of the transferor unless the transferee gives notice of the transfer in the manner and within the time hereafter provided.
- The term "noticed sale date" as used in this division means the date set forth in the notice provided for in subdivision (1) of Section 6107 on or after which the bulk transfer may be consummated.

E. 6106 - Transferee to apply consideration to pay debts of transferor

- This section applies only to a bulk transfer where the consideration is less than one million dollars ($1,000,000) and is substantially all cash or an obligation of the transferee to pay cash in the future to the transferor or a combination thereof.
- Upon every bulk transfer subject to this section except one made by sale at auction it is the duty of the transferee (or, if the transaction is handled through an escrow, the escrow agent) to apply the consideration in accordance with the provisions of this section so far as necessary to pay those debts of the transferor for which claims are due and payable on or before the noticed sale date and are filed in writing on or prior to the date specified as the last date to file claims with the person designated in the notice to receive claims. This duty of the transferee or escrow agent runs to each creditor timely filing such a claim.
- The notice shall state, in addition to the matters required by Section 6107, the name and address of the person with whom claims may be filed and the last date for filing claims, which shall be the business day before the noticed sale date. Claims shall be deemed timely filed only if actually received by the person designated in the notice to receive claims before the close of business on the day specified in the notice as the last date for filing claims.

F. 6106.1 - Claims against transferor handled through escrow

In any case where the notice of a bulk transfer subject to Section 6106 states that claims may be filed with a person who is an escrow agent, the intended transferee shall deposit with the escrow agent the full amount of the purchase price or consideration. If at the time the transfer is otherwise ready to be consummated the amount of cash deposited or agreed to be deposited at or prior to consummation in the escrow is insufficient to pay in full all of the claims filed with the escrow agent, the escrow agent shall:

1a. Delay the distribution of the consideration and the passing of legal title for a period of not less than 25 days nor more than 30 days from the date the notice required in paragraph (b) of this subdivision is mailed; and

1b. Within five business days after the time the transfer would otherwise have been consummated, send a written notice to each claimant who has filed a claim stating the total consideration deposited or agreed to be deposited in the escrow, the name of each claimant who filed a claim against the escrow and the amount of each claim, the amount proposed to be paid to each claimant, the new date scheduled for the passing of legal title pursuant to paragraph (a) of this subdivision and the date on or before which distribution will be made to claimants which shall not be more than five days after the new date specified for the passing of legal title.

2. Distribute the consideration in the following order of priorities:
    - All obligations owing to the United States, to the extent given priority by federal law.
    - Secured claims, including statutory and judicial liens, to the extent of the consideration fairly attributable to the value of the properties securing such claims and in accordance with the priorities provided by law; provided, however, that a secured creditor shall participate in the distribution pursuant to this subdivision only if a release of lien is deposited by such secured creditor conditioned only upon receiving an amount equal to such distribution.
        - Escrow and professional charges and broker's fees attributable directly to the sale.
        - Wage claims given priority by Section 1205 of the Code of Civil Procedure.
        - All other tax claims.
        - All other unsecured claims pro rata, including any deficiency claims of partially secured creditors.

3. To the extent that an obligation of the transferee to pay cash in the future is a part of the consideration and the cash consideration is not sufficient to pay all claims filed in full, apply all principal and interest received on such obligation to the payment of claims in accordance with subdivision (2) until they are paid in full before making any payment to the transferor. In such case, the notice pursuant to subdivision (1) shall state the amount, terms and due dates of the obligation and the portion of the claims expected to be paid thereby. No funds shall be drawn from the escrow, prior to the actual closing and completion of the escrow, for the payment, in whole or in part, of any commission, fee or other consideration as compensation for a service which is contingent upon the performance of any act, condition, or instruction set forth in an escrow.

G. 6107 - Notice

1. **The notice to creditors (Section 6105) shall state:**
    - **That a bulk transfer is about to be made;**
    - **The names and business addresses of the transferor and, except in the case of a sale at auction, the transferee, and all other business names and addresses used by the transferor within three years last past so far as known to the transferee;**
    - **The location and general description of the property to be transferred;**
    - **The place, and the date on or after which, the bulk transfer is to be consummated; and**
    - **Whether or not the bulk transfer is subject to Section 6106, and if so subject, the matters required by subdivision (3) of Section 6106.**
2. **The notice shall be:**
    - **Recorded in the office of the county recorder in the county or counties in which the property to be transferred is located at least 12 business days before the bulk transfer is to be consummated or the sale by auction is to be commenced; and**
    - **Published at least once in a newspaper of general circulation published (i) in the judicial district in which the property is located and (ii) in the judicial district, if different, in which the chief executive officer of the transferor, or, if the chief executive office is not in California, the principal business in California, is located, if in either case there is one, and if there is none, then in a newspaper of general circulation in the county embracing such judicial district, at least 12**

business days before the bulk transfer is to be consummated or the sale by auction is to be commenced; and

- **Delivered or sent by registered or certified mail at least 12 business days before the bulk transfer is to be consummated or the sale by auction is to be commenced to the county tax collector in the county or counties in which the property to be transferred is located.**

If the property to be transferred is located in more than one judicial district, the publication required by paragraph (b) of subdivision (2) shall be in a newspaper published in the judicial district where a greater portion of the property is located, on the date the notice is published, than in any other judicial district, or in the county embracing such judicial district, as the case may be. As used in this section, "business day" means any day other than a Saturday, Sunday or a day observed as a holiday by the California state government.

H. 6108 - Auction Sales

1. A bulk transfer is subject to this division even though it is by sale at auction, but only in the manner and with the results stated in this section.
2. The person or persons other than the transferor who direct, control or are responsible for the auction are collectively called the "auctioneer." The auctioneer shall be responsible for giving the notice of the transfer (Section 6107). In the cause of a sale by auction, in addition to the matters specified in Section 6107, the notice shall state that the sale is to be by auction, the name of the auctioneer, and the time and place of the auction.
3. Failure of the auctioneer to give the notice of the transfer does not affect the validity of the sale to or the title of the purchasers, but such failure renders the auctioneer liable to the creditors of the transferor as a class for the sums owing to them from the transferor up to but not exceeding the reasonable value of the assets sold. If the auctioneer consists of several persons their liability is joint and several.

I. 6109 - What creditors protected

The creditors of the transferor mentioned in this division are those holding claims based on transactions or events occurring before the bulk transfer.

J. 6110 - Subsequent Transfers

When the title of a transferee to property is subject to a defect by reason of his noncompliance with the requirements of this division, then:

- A purchaser of any such property from such transferee who pays no value or who takes with notice of such noncompliance takes subject to such defect, but
- A purchaser for value in good faith and without such notice takes free of such defect.

K. 6111 - Limitations of Actions and Levies

- No action under this division shall be brought nor levy made more than one year after the date on which the transferee took possession of the goods unless the transfer has been concealed. If the transfer has been concealed, an action may be brought or levy made within one year after its discovery by the creditor bringing such action or making such levy or after it should have been discovered by such creditor in the exercise or reasonable diligence, whichever first occurs.

If a bulk transfer is subject to and complies with Section 6106, no levy shall be made by a creditor of the transferor on the proceeds of sales in the hands of transferee or escrow agent after the transferee takes legal title to the goods, except to the extent of that creditor's share of the proceeds pursuant to Section 6106 and 6106.1.

II. Step by Step overview of the process

- Implement due diligence of all UCC-1 filings with the Secretary of State.
- Compile list of **all** creditors.
- C. Appraise all relevant Furniture, Fixtures, and Equipment (See attachment 1).
- Advertise sale of Furniture, Fixtures, and Equipment (See attachment 2).
- Mail notice of sale to all creditors 12 business days before consummation of said sales (See attachment 3).
- Establish new corporation.
- Open up escrow.
- Provide IRS and State escrow number.
- Proceeds of sale remitted to regulatories and any other secured creditors.
- Old company closes doors.
- Abatement of penalty and interest via 4180 defense also referred to as Trust Fund Recovery.

FOR DISCUSSION PURPOSES ONLY:

If you opted for Chapter 7, debtors are not liable to IRS for interest and penalties on pre-petition tax claim under 11 USCS SS. 507 where: (1) claim has been or will be paid in full; and (2) failure to make payments to IRS resulting in interest and penalty liability is fault of trustee who has failed to make timely payments. Re Irvin (1989, BC WD Mo) 95 BR 1014, 20 CBC2d 1007.

Regarding any Revenue Officer's tax examination and all its ramifications could take 30 to 60 days to complete. IRS officer and I would work on the document request list. We would isolate the issue from the other ones, this is the one that carries the most exposure, remember it is legal to avoid but illegal to evade.

SEC. 7602 - Examination of Books and Witnesses.

For the purpose of ascertaining the correctness of any return, making a return where none has been made, determining the liability of any person for any internal revenue tax or the liability at law or in equity of any transferee or fiduciary of any person in respect of any internal revenue tax, or collecting any such liability, the Secretary or his delegate is authorized:

(1) To examine any books, papers, records or other data which may be relevant or material to such inquiry;

To summon the person liable for tax or required to perform the act, or any officer or employee of such person, or any person having possession, custody, or care of books of account containing entries relating to the business of the person liable for tax or required to perform the act, or any other person the Secretary or his delegate may deem proper, to appear before the Secretary or his delegate at a time and place named in the summons and to produce such books, papers, records, or other data, and to give such testimony, under oath, as may be relevant or material to such inquiry; and

(2) To take such testimony of the person concerned, under oath, as may be relevant or material to such inquiry.

Upon further research, we should note how the conspiracy statute and fraud statues can affect you within adequate representation.

Definition of Fraud

Fraud is not defined either in Section 6653(b) or in the regulations. Some clue to the meaning of the term may be found from the version of the penalty contained in the 1939 Code, which imposed the penalty for "fraud with intent to evade tax." The change in Section 6653(b) to the imposition of the penalty for "fraud" from "fraud with intent to evade tax" was made without an apparent legislative purpose to change meaning. This means that the fraud referred to in Section 6653(b) is fraud with intent to evade tax. Also, fraud itself signifies an intent to deceive, and this intent to deceive overlaps to some extent the conduct involved in evasion. This overlap is reflected in cases holding that a taxpayer convicted of evasion is collaterally stopped from contesting the issue of fraud in a civil penalty case because the conviction necessarily carries with it the ultimate factual determination that the deficiency was due to fraud. Accordingly, a taxpayer who willfully attempts to evade tax also underpays tax with the requisite fraudulent intent for purposes of the civil penalty statute. The evasion element in fraud makes principles announced in evasion cases that willful conduct is an intentional violation of a known legal duty (Pomponio) and that "conduct, the likely effect of which would be to mislead or conceal" is evidence from which a willful attempt may be inferred (Spies), seem to apply as well to the civil fraud penalty. Thus, the long-standing definition of fraud articulated in Mitchell V. Comm's under the 1939 Code version of the penalty remains authoritative.

"Negligence", whether slight or great, is not equivalent to the fraud with intent to evade tax named in the statute. The fraud meant ***is actual****, intentional wrongdoing, and the intent required is the specific* ***purpose to evade a tax believes to owe****.*

The Conspiracy Status: 18 USC SS 371

The Offense of criminal conspiracy has two elements: (1) an agreement between two or more persons either (a) to commit an offense against or (b) to defraud the United States in any manner or for any purpose, and (2) an overt act committed by one or more of the conspirators to accomplish the object of the conspiracy. Conspiracy reaches farther into criminal activity than evasion, which is an attempt-type crime requiring affirmative conduct, by punishing mere agreement to commit a crime. In tax cases, the conspiracy charged is usually an agreement to commit a substantive tax offense (e.g., evasion) or to defraud the United States (e.g., by impeding the IRS in the determination or collection of tax). All that need be established is that two or more persons have agreed to commit a substantive tax offense or to defraud the United States in some manner. The overt act requirement of the federal conspiracy statute serves to establish the existence of the agreement, and need not be particularly significant if it is, in fact, in furtherance of the conspiracy.

Procedurally, the crime of conspiracy differs from other crimes in ways that give prosecutors the following advantages at trial:

(1) A conspiracy prosecution may be brought in a judicial district where an overt act took place. The venue rule gives prosecutors an opportunity to elect a place of trial at which conviction is more likely or which may be inconvenient to the defendants.

    There are rules of evidence peculiar to conspiracy prosecutions. A general rule, subject to many exceptions, is that hearsay is not admissible; one particular exception is that a statement by a co-conspirator during the course and in furtherance of the conspiracy does not constitute hearsay and is admissible against the defendant. Thus, if conspirator X told witness W that X along with Y and Z planned to hold back business receipts of their corporation, W could testify about the statement and it would be admissible against both Y and Z, as well as against X. The rationale of this rule is the legal fiction that a conspiracy makes the co-conspirators mutual agents. Moreover, although the statement is required to have been made during the course and in furtherance of the conspiracy, any statement relating to the conspiracy frequently is admitted. Also, the defendant's difficulties are exacerbated by the willingness of courts to admit these statements before the existence of a conspiracy has actually been established, subject only to an instruction cautioning the jury that evidence is not to be considered unless the conspiracy is proved by independent evidence.

    To establish the existence of a conspiracy, prosecutors in addition enjoy a wide latitude in offering circumstantial evidence to establish a conspiracy. This procedure is justified by the difficulties prosecutors would otherwise face in proving the existence of a conspiracy, which by its nature requires secrecy and concealment. When several defendants have been charged, they may face joint trial where evidence damaging to one may be used against all.

(2) Finally, the procedural advantages prosecutors have are coupled with the substantive vagueness and ambiguity of the crime itself. It is not certain, for example what constitutes an agreement for purposes of the conspiracy and what mental state must be shown. This uncertainty and the unfairness it may occasion have prompted the Supreme Court to discourage extensions of the conspiracy offense and the Service and Justice Department's Tax Division to utilize

the charge with restraint.

The rationale of the conspiracy statute is that collective or group activity ought to be punished separate and apart from any substantive crime because it represents a grave threat to society than individual criminal activity. A partnership in crime "both increases the likelihood that the criminal object will be fully attained and decreases the probability that the individuals involved will depart their path of criminality." For this reason, as we shall see, the conspiracy offense is separate and distinct from the crime the conspirators agree to commit, so a conspirator may be punished both for conspiracy and for the contemplated crime. For example, if A and B agree to raise the deductions of their corporation falsely and in fact file false returns for the corporation, they could receive maximum sentences for both evasion and conspiracy. Punishment under the conspiracy statute, however, has gradations, depending upon the offense that the conspirators have agreed to commit. A conspiracy to evade is punishable as a felony in the same manner as the evasion itself; but if the conspiracy is one to fail to file a tax return, the offense is punished as a misdemeanor with the same punishment Section 7203 provides.

Conspiracy to Defraud

A conspiracy to defraud combines the vagueness of a conspiracy charge with broad allegations of an attempt to impede or obstruct government functions. In United States v. Klein, the indictment charged the defendants with a conspiracy to defraud the United States "by impeding, obstructing and defeating the functions of the Department of the Treasury in the collection of the revenue, to wit, income taxes." Inter-corporate transactions of considerable complexity were alleged to have concealed the nature and source the income realized from an immense whiskey-selling business. The Second Circuit said that mere failure to disclose income would not be sufficient to establish the crime of conspiracy to defraud the United States, but that such a charge does include interference or obstruction of lawful government functions by deceit, craft, or trick, or dishonest means. In Klein, the acts of concealment were various acts of alteration of books and false statements on tax returns and to IRS agents.

The Klein-type conspiracy (i.e., a conspiracy to defraud by acts of concealment) may be charged against a tax adviser as well as a taxpayer. Just when tax planning becomes concealment is unclear, and determining where the line is to be drawn in the contest of a criminal conspiracy trial represents a prospect both difficult and dangerous.

Transferee Liability in Equity

The elements of transferee liability in equity derive in substantial part from the requirements of state fraudulent conveyance laws. A proper understanding of transferee liability in equity therefore requires some background in the law of fraudulent conveyances.

Fraudulent Conveyances

The substantive law of transferee liability varies from state to state, but in most transferee liability cases the state law involved is its fraudulent conveyances law. With some understanding of this body of law, the elements of transferee liability are made comprehensible. The modern law of fraudulent conveyances derives from a statute enacted in 1570 during the reign of Queen Elizabeth, which in substance provided that any transfer made "to delay, hinder or defraud creditors or others" was voidable by the persons hindered, delayed or defrauded. Since proof of fraudulent intent was difficult, circumstantial evidence from which an intent to defraud could be inferred, called "badges of fraud," came to be recognized. In the United States, the states recognized different badges of fraud, but intra-family transfers, transfers of property without consideration, and transfers of all or a substantial amount of property immediately before anticipated litigation are facts generally considered to be badges of fraud.

Because of the variations in the fraudulent conveyance statues and common law, a Uniform Fraudulent Conveyance Act (UFCA) has been proposed and adopted in almost half the states. Different types of fraudulent conveyances are described in Sections 4 through 8 of the UFCA, but Section 4 (conveyances by insolvents) and Section 7 (conveyances made with intent to defraud) are the ones most commonly used. Under Section 4, every conveyance made (1) "without fair consideration" (2) by a person who is or will thereby be rendered insolvent constitutes a fraudulent conveyance without regard to the actual intent of the debtor. For the purposes of the UFCA, "fair consideration" uses two comparative value standards: "Fair equivalent" if the transfer is an absolute transfer such as an exchange of property or a gift; and "not disproportionately small" if the transfer is a transfer for security, for example, under Article 9 of the Uniform Commercial code. Fair consideration also requires good faith, which has been interpreted to exist where there is (1) an honest belief in the propriety of the activities in question: (2) no attempt to made unconscionable advantage of others; and (3) no attempt to, or knowledge of the fact that the activities in question will hinder, delay or defraud others. The other element of a Section 4 fraudulent conveyance is "insolvency," which is defined by Section 2 to exist "when the present fair salable value" of the debtor's assets is less than "the amount that will be required to pay his probable liability on his existing debts as they become absolute and matured."

A conveyance is fraudulent under Section 7 of the UFCA when it is made "with actual intent, as distinguished from intent presumed in law, to hinder, delay, or defraud either present or future creditors.." for Section 7 purposes, the focus is on intent, not the adequacy of the consideration or the financial condition of the transferor as it is under Section 2. Usually, this actual intent to defraud is established by the same evidence that constitutes "badges of fraud" under prior law.

Under the UFCA, the rights of creditors depend on whether their claims have matured. Where a creditor's claim has matured, the creditor may either (1) have the conveyance set aside to the extent necessary to satisfy his claim, or (2) disregard the conveyance and levy execution on the property conveyed. In this respect the UFCA restates the remedies available to a creditor at common law. The remedy of having the conveyance set aside was an equitable remedy usually enforced by a creditor's bill. This remedy was preferable to disregarding the conveyance and attaching or levying execution on the property conveyed, because the validity of the conveyance was determined in advanced of the sale of the property, so that the amount received on the sale would probably be higher. Where the rights of creditors have not matured, under the UFCA a creditor still may proceed in court and may ask the court to (1) restrain the defendant from disposing of his property; (2) appoint a receiver to take charge of the property; (3) set aside the conveyance or annul the obligation; or (4) make any order which the circumstances of the case may require. The

UFCA somewhat expands the rights of creditors with un-matured interests in the extent of the remedies available. A prior judgment was generally necessary to maintain an action to set aside a fraudulent conveyance. It was not necessary, however, that the creditor's claim be reduced to judgment at the time of the conveyance was made, so long as the creditor has a claim at the time of the conveyance, whether that claim was liquidated or contingent.

Fraudulent transfers

Successor corporation was liable for assessed taxes, interest and fraud penalty of predecessor corporation where successor corporation was formed subsequent to claims by Treasury for income tax deficiencies, civil fraud penalties and interest; assets were transferred for inadequate consideration and with no provision for assumption of impending tax liability; after successor corporation was formed, predecessor corporation stipulated for decision against it determining deficiencies and fraud penalties; transfer was void for fraud of creditors, and at most paper transaction, since same business was conducted by same principals before and after formation of successor corporation and liability was imposed upon successor corporation without invocation of doctrine of transferee liability and all assets of successor would be considered property of predecessor for purposes of satisfying judgment. United States v. Plastic Electro-Finishing Corp. (1970, Ed NY) 313 F Supp 330.

Taxpayer made fraudulent transfer where he was informed by IRS that it was considering assessment against him for taxes arising out of his 1969 gambling activities in October 1970 and on Oct. 20, 1976, he transferred his residence to his wife, making himself insolvent; although liability was not assessed until May of 1971, transfer was fraudulent as debt existed at time of transfer. United States v. Watkins (1976, DC Ga) 77-1 USTC Par. 16242.

Transfers to controlled corporation were fraudulent where individual, who was later convicted for income tax evasion, made transfers of $186,000 in assets to controlled corporation without consideration, such transfers leaving him with assets of $45,000 and liability for taxes, penalties and interest of over $213,000, and where, in addition, extensive use of cash and concealment of assets in bank accounts were further evidence of attempt to hinder, delay and defraud Treasury. Wills corp. v. Commissioner (1969) 28 TCM 174.

Corporations

Transferee of corporate assets was bound by acts of directors of corporation, such directors also representing transferee. Warner Collieries Co. v United States (1933, CA6 Ohio) 63 F2d 34.

Corporation taking long-term lease of property of another corporation, of which it was a stockholder, and agreeing in such lease to pay rental to stockholders of lessor, was not liable as a transferee though rental distributed was in excess of taxes. Western Union Tel. Co. v. Commissioner (1933, CA2) 68 F2d 16, cert den 292 US 636, 78 L Ed 1489, 54 S Ct 715.

Liability of corporation as transferee is not obviated because transaction by which it acquires the assets of transferor is taxable transfer; agreement of transferee corporation to pay debts of transferor company can be enforced by government in proceeding for assessment of tax against transferee though amount of tax is not ascertained at time of transfer; proceedings against predecessor-transferor corporation and successor-transferee corporation at same time were distinct and not incongruous, particularly where it was manifest that transferor had disposed of all its property and that proceeding against it would be unavailing. California Iron Yards Corp. v. Commissioner (1936, CA9) 82 F2d 776, cert den 299 US 553, 81 L Ed 407, 57 S Ct 15.

New corporation organized to take over assets of old corporation, and which owned shares in old corporation, was charged with tax liabilities of old corporation. Delacroix Corp. v. Commissioner (1936, CA5) 84 F2d 442.Board's (now Tax Court's) determination of liability of corporate transferee of assets of corporation which owned entire capital stock of three other companies for which consolidated return for period in question was filed by petitioner, would be affirmed. Continental Oil Co. v. Helvering (1938) 69 App DC 236, 100 F2d 101.

Corporation organized to hold all stock of taxpayer corporation was liable for taxes assumed. Hatch v Morosco Holding Co. 91929, DC NY) 34 F2d 579, affd (CA2 NY) 50 F2d 138, cert den 284 US 668, 76 L Ed 565, 52 S Ct 42. General equitable liability of transferee for initial tax liability of transferor corporation is recognized by predecessor to 26 USCS Sect. 6901. United States v Barber (1938, DC Md) 24 F Supp. 229.

Transferees of Corporations

Mere proof of taking over assets and assumption of liabilities of dissolved corporation did not show liability as distributee. People's Industrial Life Ins. Co. v United States (1928, CA5 La) 29 F2d 650.

Petitioners were not transferees of assets of corporation under such circumstances

as to make them liable under trust fund doctrine where government did not meet its burden of proving that its claim against corporation for previous years constituted "current bill" within agreement by former stockholders for payment of current bills. Commissioner v Keller 91932, CA7) 59 F2d 499.

Our purpose in this communiqué is not to frighten you but to educate you. We feel this is not a simple matter and must be handled with diplomacy and skill. We welcome any communication with your corporate council on these pending matters.

Processing of an Offer Re: 941 liability of approximately $_________

Upon receipt of an Offer, it is processed by the Service Center where a thorough search of the taxpayer's computerized tax records is conducted to determine the exact amount and nature of all taxes owed by Officers/ Stockholders. This process takes from two weeks to two months. Subsequent to the processing by the Service Center, a proposed Offer in Compromise based upon <u>inability</u> to pay is sent to the Special Procedures Branch of the IRS District Office where it is reviewed by an advisory Revenue Officer. Most Offers based upon doubt as to liability are forwarded to the Examination Division, but Offers on 100% penalties are considered by the Collection Division. If the advisory Revenue Officer in Special Procedures determines that the Offer is totally inappropriate and insufficient, she will recommend that a summary rejection letter be issued by the Chief of the Collection Division. The Internal Revenue Manual sets forth grounds upon which an Offer might be summarily rejected as follows:

Summary rejection in SPF can be made on the grounds that the Offer is frivolous, was filed merely to delay collection, or where there is no basis for compromise. Although not all-inclusive, the following list provides guidelines on the criteria for summary rejection most often encountered:

- Taxpayer has equity in assets subject to the Federal tax lien clearly in excess of the total liability sought to be compromised.
- The total liability is extremely large and the taxpayer has offered only a minimal sum well below his equity and earnings potential, (e.g., offering $100 to compromise a $50,000 tax liability).
- The taxpayer is not current in his filing or payment requirements for periods not included in the offer.
- The taxpayer refuses to submit a complete financial statement (Form 433).
- Acceptance of the offer would adversely affect the image of the government.

- Taxpayer has submitted a subsequent offer which is not significantly different from a previously rejected offer and the taxpayer's financial condition has not changed.
- In cases involving doubt as to liability for the 100% penalty the liability is clearly established and the taxpayer has offered no new evidence to cast doubt on its validity. (IRM 57(10)7.1(2).)

Transmittal to a Revenue Officer

If the advisory Revenue Officer determines that the Offer deserves further consideration, the Offer will be transmitted to a Revenue Officer for further investigation. The Revenue Officer will investigate the taxpayer's current financial condition as disclosed on the Form 433. The taxpayer may be required to submit appraisals of property if its value is not readily determinable. The taxpayer may also be required to submit all of his financial records for review by the Revenue Officer including, but not limited to, bank statements, canceled checks and receipts.

Adequacy of Offer

The IRS is very stringent in its consideration of the adequacy of an Offer. A settlement amount which would be considered fair and adequate by an average person may not be acceptable to the Service.

An Offer in Compromise must reflect the taxpayer's maximum capacity to pay, i.e., all that can be collected from the taxpayer's equity in assets and income, present and prospective. In addition, the Service will consider amounts which may be collectible through transferee assessment or suit, 100% penalty assessments, and from assets or income that are available to the taxpayer, but beyond the reach of the government. In considering Offers based on inability to pay, the Service will investigate the priority of the federal tax claim in relation to other claims, and the liquidating value of the taxpayer's assets.

Quick Sale Value of Assets as Basis of Considering Offer

The starting point in the consideration of an Offer submitted on the basis of inability to pay is ordinarily the liquidating or quick sale value of the taxpayer's assets. The quick sale value is the amount which would be realized from the sale of an asset in a situation where financial pressures cause the taxpayer to sell in a short period of time. For Offer purposes, the taxpayer's equity in assets is defined as the quick sale value less any encumbrances against the assets which have priority over the Federal Tax Lien. Quick sale value is a valuation unique to the Offer process. It is employed because of the nature of the Offer investigation and the fact that the taxpayer and the Service are in a position to negotiate, to make mutual concessions.

Forced Sale Value vs. Fair Market Value

The two values normally considered in the collection of accounts are forced sale value and fair market value. The former represents the amount the Service can collect from a distrait sale of the taxpayer's assets; therefore, this value does not represent any concession on the taxpayer's part. The latter represents the value arrived at between a willing buyer and willing seller and normally indicates the maximum valuation for the taxpayer's assets. Between these two values there exists a wide range of possible asset valuations (i.e. quick sale value) and any asset valuation in this range can be acceptable if negotiated and agreed upon by the taxpayer and Offer examiner. If the Service is in a position to gain more revenue at less cost than can be secured through the enforced collection of all the taxpayer's assets, then the Offer might be accepted. The negotiation process involved reading agreement on asset valuations (including determination of forced sale, quick sale and fair market value). An offer should not be rejected based on a narrow criterion of asset values. We will argue your position aggressively and support valuations with appraisals by a reputable appraiser.

Calculation of Quick Sale Value

Although no specific guidelines can be formulated to compute quick sale value, certain general guidelines can be presented to indicate how quick sale values can vary depending on local conditions and the type of property involved. Local factors affecting quick sale value may conclude availability of mortgage money, appropriateness of the assets to local conditions (e.g., farm equipment in a mostly urban area), health of the local economy, etc. Also, the type of asset will in general affect the quick sale value. Unusual items are hard to sell. Quick sale value should be a reasonable reflection of the value of the property. Normally the service will not set quick sale value at less than 70% of fair market value. However, even within this range, the revenue officer will have considerable discretion in negotiating asset valuations with the taxpayer to arrive at an acceptable Offer. The basis used to calculate quick sale value will depend on the facts and circumstances of the individual case.

Although assets will normally be valued at their quick sale value, an Offer can be considered based on the forced sale value of assets if it can be shown that accepting this valuation for Offer Purposes would be in the best interest of the Government. The reasons for such a valuation must be extensively documented by the proponent and the IRS will rarely accept forced sale value.

Other Considerations

In addition to the taxpayer's equity in assets the taxpayer's earning capacity will be evaluated. Information about the taxpayer's education, profession or trade, age and experience, health, past and present income, and future prospects will be considered by the Service. We will aggressively present negative factors about any of the above listed factors (IRM 57(10)7.51).

During the course of negotiating an inability to pay the Offer, the major disputes will center on the value of Officers/ Stockholders' assets. One convention that the IRS uses is to find the average balance in a taxpayer's bank account over a period of time to determine cash on hand. The minimum time frame for averaging that we observed is six months. The IRS will not accept an Offer unless it is allowed to inspect the taxpayer's safe deposit box.

Closely Held Companies

Particularly tough valuation disputes arise when valuing securities in closely held companies. The IRS will normally require substantial disclosure of company financial data for the purposes of valuation. It also may require submission of independent appraisals. If the taxpayer's interest in such entitles is very limited, the investigating Revenue Officer is required by the IRS Manual to be more flexible in his or her disclosure demands.

Going Concern Value

The IRS takes the position that in consideration of an Offer it can reflect "going concern value" in its valuation. Therefore, it will not normally accept the liquidation value of tangible company assets to be the sole measure of quick sale value.

Pension Plan

Pension plans can also pose a problem for valuation purposes. The Internal Revenue Manual sets forth the following guidelines:

- Where under the terms of employment, a taxpayer is required to contribute a percentage of your gross earnings to a retirement plan and the amount contributed, plus any increments cannot be withdrawn until separation, retirement, demise, etc., this asset will be considered as having no realizable equity.
- If the taxpayer is within five years of retirement (including early retirement and the plan permits the taxpayer to take the pension in a lump sum, a collateral agreement must be secured whereby the taxpayer agrees to request the lump sum and to pay over to the Service the amount of the lump sum when received. This is required because if the taxpayer had access to the funds at the time of submitting the offer, the full amount would have been considered an asset and therefore payable in full as part of the offer.
- Where the taxpayer is not required, as a condition of employment, to participate in a pension plan, but voluntarily elects to do so, the realizable equity for compromise purposes shall be the gross amount in the taxpayer's plan reduced by the employer's contributions. However, in these situations each case should stand on its own merits.
- If the taxpayer is permitted to borrow up to the full amount of his/her equity in a plan, this should be taken into

consideration in the computation of realizable equity.

- The current value of property deposited in an Individual Retirement Account (IRA) or Keogh Act Plan Account should be considered in the computation of realizable equity. Cash deposits should be included at full value. If assets other than cash are invested (e.g. stock, mutual funds), the IRA should be valued at the quick sale value, less expenses. The penalty for early withdrawal should be subtracted in computing net realizable equity (IRC 57(10)8.4).

Note: Negotiations concerning the terms and requirements of pension plans will require extensive information from the employer. Start gathering the information early in the process.

Inspection of Assets

The revenue officer investigating the Offer will normally require the taxpayer to allow inspection of the household and all of the personal effects and household goods. Expensive art work, coins, stamps, silverware, china, antique furniture and glassware will all be evaluated by a Revenue Officer during such visits to a taxpayer's residence.

Note: If any officers or stockholders had substantial assets, we would make sure the amount offered is a reflection of the substantial assets' quick sale value. Remember, we don't want you to be criminally charged if materially misrepresents assets.

Joint Ownership

The Service may grant special relief for taxpayers who own property in tenancy by the entirety with an innocent spouse (irm 57(108.1(12)3(2)). The IRS may consider such interests to be less than 50% of the total value of the property as long as at least 20% is offered. Tenancy in common and joint tenancy property, however, are normally considered to be valued based upon the taxpayer's entire interest.

Approval Process

If after investigation, the Revenue Officer determines that approval is appropriate, she will submit reports to her superiors recommending approval. The Offer in Compromise will then be processed by the Special Procedures Function through the bureaucracy to the District Director for his or her final approval. Any of the various managers in the chain of review may return it to the Revenue Officer for further investigation, if it is determined that there are unresolved issues within the compromise.

Appeals

During the course of an investigation, a proponent of an Offer may request a conference before and/or after the Offer is rejected. If the proponent disagrees with the recommendation of the investigating officer, he or she may appeal the proposed rejection. The initial conference takes place at the District Director's level. The proponent may appeal the Director's decision to the appropriate District Appeals Office and request a hearing. The Appeals Office may overrule the Director's rejection and accept the Offer.

Public Policy

All accepted Offers become public record and are maintained in the local District Office for public viewing. The Service is, therefore, very reluctant to accept Offers from certain individuals because of the adverse publicity that might be generated by acceptance. The Service will reject an Offer even though it can be conclusively shown that the amounts offered are greater than can be reasonably collected in any other manner, if it believes acceptance would be detrimental to the Government's interest. The following are examples of where the IRS might invoke public policy considerations.

- Taxpayer's notoriety is such that acceptance of an Offer will hamper future Service collection and/or compliance efforts.
- There is a possibility of establishing a precedent which might lead to numerous Offers being submitted on liabilities

revealed as a result of occupational drives to enforce tax compliance.

- Taxpayer has been recently convicted of tax related crimes. Again, the notoriety of the individual will be considered when making a public policy determination. The publicity surrounding the case, taxpayer's compliance since the case was concluded, or the taxpayer's position in the community will all be considered prior to rejecting an otherwise acceptable Offer.
- Situations where the Service suspects that the financial benefits of criminal activity are concealed or the criminal activity is continuing would normally preclude acceptance of the Offer for public policy reasons. Criminal investigation function might be contacted to coordinate the government's action in such cases.

The examples are not all inclusive and we have found that mere perception of a client as a "dishonorable person" can doom an Offer. As in any negotiation with the IRS Collection division, personalities have an impact on success.

Collateral Agreements

Revenue regulations provide that as a condition of accepting an Offer in Compromise, the taxpayer may be required to enter into a collateral agreement or to post security deemed sufficient to protect the interests of the United States. If the taxpayer has future earning potential, the Service will normally require a Future Income Collateral Agreement wherein the taxpayer agrees to payment of a percentage of his excess earnings over necessary living expenses for a period of several years following acceptance of the Offer (App 6-C). Generally, we recommend that you try to keep the period of the collateral to a minimum number of years. The Service will normally request a five year collateral. The Service also has sometimes accepted other types of collateral, including waivers of certain tax benefits and the pledging of assets. Each Offer is negotiated separately and the practitioner has an opportunity to be innovative when offering a collateral agreement.

Offers which cast doubt as to liability, other than 100% penalties, will be reviewed by the Examination Division of the Service rather than the Collection Division. In reviewing such Offers, the Examination Division will use guidelines similar to those used in making audit determinations. Usually, the proponent must establish a valid question of law or fact which would render the liability in question doubtful. Generally, a more appropriate means of determining such issues would be to seek a determination by the Tax Court or via refund litigation. Most Districts seldom grant offers on this basis.

In summary, it would be our agenda to abate the penalty and interest and negotiate our ultimate dollar amount to approximately 30% of trust fund taxes owed. This will have tremendous impact on your ability to put the past behind you. Please read this material, it may be germane to your case. Thank you for your time and attention and please do not hesitate to call me if you have any questions.

Suggested Minimum Retainer Amount: **$<u>20,00</u>**

Chapter 22:

Taxes and Bankruptcy

Dischargeability of Taxes in Bankruptcy

It is a common misunderstanding that bankruptcy cannot eliminate any tax liability. Although treatment of tax liability is one of the most complicated aspects of consumer bankruptcy law, the Bankruptcy Code can offer many debtors substantial income tax relief. Whether or not your bankruptcy filing relieves your tax debt depends on several factors including the nature and the status of tax liability as well as the type of bankruptcy proceeding.

Bankruptcy Tax Dischargeability Rules:

Three-year Rule - 3 years from the Due Date of a Return including extensions.

Two-year Rule – 2 years from the date the Tax Return was filed (we say assessed) for delinquent returns.

240-day Rule - 240 days from the date of assessment (for audited and amended returns)

Type of Tax

Only individuals (not businesses) can discharge (wipe out) certain taxes through bankruptcy. The only taxes eligible for discharge are personal income taxes. Bankruptcy offers no relief from taxes for which the debtor/taxpayer was responsible for collecting from others such as FICA withheld from employees. Bankruptcy also may not relieve liability for most excise taxes such as estate and gift tax, sales tax, or fuel taxes.

Secured Tax Debts

In the course of its collection efforts, the IRS has the power to file a tax lien to "perfect" its tax claim against individuals. A tax lien, having been filed becomes a secured lien on all of the taxpayer's property. If a tax lien is in place prior to your filing bankruptcy, the IRS's secured tax lien has priority over the bankruptcy filing, and bankruptcy will not disassociate the lien from your property. Even property which would otherwise be exempt in a bankruptcy, such as a homestead cannot be sold or transferred without payment of the IRS tax lien. In this instance a bankruptcy would provide no tax relief.

Tax Relief in a Chapter 7 Bankruptcy Chapter 7 Bankruptcy will eliminate all income taxes except the following:

a. Taxes for which a tax return was due to be filed within three years (plus extensions) prior to the date of filing bankruptcy. For example, the tax return for 2003 income taxes was due to be filed on April 15, 2004 (plus any extensions), and therefore, these income taxes cannot be discharged by filing bankruptcy on or before April 15, 2007 (plus the time of extensions); OR

b. Taxes assessed by the IRS within 240 days before the filing of bankruptcy. Assessment date is the date that tax liability is entered on IRS records; OR

c. Taxes not yet assessed but still assessable; OR

d. Taxes for which a tax return was filed late and filed within two years prior to filing bankruptcy; OR

e. Taxes of a debtor who committed fraud related to a tax return or willfully attempted to evade or defeat taxes sought to be discharged.

Income taxes that do not fail any of the above five tests may be wiped out in a Chapter 7 Bankruptcy.

Tax Relief in a Chapter 13 Bankruptcy Taxes which are non-dischargeable in Chapter 13 are considered priority debts and must be paid in full during the Chapter 13 plan without interest.

Other Points to Remember

1. **Chapter 7 vs. Chapter 13**
    a. Dischargeable taxes are eliminated in Chapter 7.
    b. Dischargeable taxes are treated as general, unsecured creditors in Chapter 13.
    c. Secured tax liens cannot be discharged in Chapter 7.
2. **Tolling Events/Rules (Statutes of Limitation)**

    The Statute of Limitation for collection by the IRS tolls (is extended) under the following circumstances:

    a. For income taxes and taxes on gross receipts to be discharged, the taxing authority must have assessed (entered the liability on the taxing authority's records) the tax against the tax debtor at least the following number of days or months before the filing of the tax debtor's bankruptcy petition:
        i. 240 days; plus
        ii. The number of days each offer in compromise for the applicable tax had been pending; plus
        iii. The number of days each prior bankruptcy proceeding had been pending after the related tax return due date with valid extensions; plus
        iv. Thirty days for each applicable offer in compromise; plus
        v. Six months[xxxii] for each applicable bankruptcy proceeding. §5523 (a)(l)(A) & 507 (a)(S)(A)(ii). Prior bankruptcies and other occurrences may extend the 240-day period. Here too, the taxing authority's records are the starting point to verify the assessment date and the dates offers in compromise were pending.

    b. The period of time taxpayer spends living outside the country (It is important to verify that your client has been a U.S. resident for the entire term of the statute of limitation).

    c. The period of time between the date the IRS has created a Substitute for Return (SFR) and the time an actual Tax Return has been filed.

Sales Tax Dischargeability & "Responsible Persons"

(The State of California used as an example)

11 U.S.C. § 507 specifies the kinds of claims that are entitled to priority in distribution, and the order of the priority. The eighth priority is for certain taxes. 11 U.S.C. § 507(a)(8).

Allowed unsecured claims of governmental units are granted priority, "only to the extent that such claims are for...an excise tax on a transaction occurring before the date of the filing of the petition for which a return, if required, is last due, under applicable law or under any extension, after three years before the date of the filing of the petition." 11 U.S.C. § 507(a)(8)(E).

Sales tax under California law is an excise and privilege tax levied on a retailer for the privilege of selling tangible property. Cal. Rev. & Tax Code § 6051. See Livingston Rock & Gravel Co. v. De Salvo, 136 Cal App 2nd 156, 288 P.2d 317 (1955). Opinion followed in Xerox Corp. v. Orange County (1977) 66 CA3d 746; Bar Master Inc. v. State Board of Equalization (1976) 65 CA3d 408.

Thus, when sales tax is a tax imposed on the retailer or seller for the privilege of doing business in the state, as is the law in California, the tax is dischargeable if the transaction or event giving rise to the tax is more than three years prior to the bankruptcy filing.

In re Raiman, 172 B.R. 933 (9th Cir. BAP 1994), the Bankruptcy Appellate Panel found California's sales tax to be a tax akin to a personal income tax measured by income or gross receipts, and thus subject to a priority tax analysis under 11 U.S.C. § 507(a)(8)(A). The BAP raised but refused to rule on whether the California sales tax was also an excise tax. The ruling would make it irrelevant whether it was an excise tax or not ... it could be both an excise tax and a tax measured on gross receipts.

If California "sales tax is a tax measured by gross receipts," then under 11 U.S.C. § 507(a) (8) (A) it will not be a Priority Tax Claim if it meets the same criteria as that for a personal income tax claim, i.e. the tax year is over three years old and it has been assessed more than 240 days previous to the bankruptcy filing.

Also, since sales tax in California requires a quarterly return and payment, the excise tax is dischargeable in Chapter 7 only if the required quarterly returns were actually filed by the taxpayer at least two years prior to the bankruptcy, pursuant to 11 U.S.C. § 523(a)(1)(B)(ii).

IRS SFRs and Bankruptcy

In order for tax liability to be discharged in bankruptcy, it must stem from liability assessed based upon tax returns filed by the taxpayer that meet the aging requirements (see the 3-year rule, 2-year rule and 240-day rule). A question has come up whether liability assessed by the IRS via a Substitute for Return ("SFR") prior to the late filing of a tax return by a taxpayer can be discharged in bankruptcy.

In 2014 and 2015 the First, Fifth and Tenth circuit courts determined that liability assessed prior to a tax return being filed could not be discharged in bankruptcy. They indicated that in some cases if the return reflected a liability higher than the previously assessed amount, the additional liability may be able to be discharged. In most cases however it would not make sense to file a return if the taxpayer will increase their liability.

Recently the Bankruptcy Appellate Panel ("BAP") for the Ninth Circuit (whose region covers Alaska, Oregon, Washington, Idaho, Montana, California, Nevada and Arizona) sided with the taxpayer, concluding that regardless of whether liability had been assessed prior to the filing of a late return by the taxpayer, the liability may be discharged assuming it meets all other requirements. It is important to note that the Ninth Circuit's decision contradicts the findings of the First, Fifth and Tenth circuits. It remains a question as to whether these amounts may be discharged but it shows promise for the taxpayer. If you are contemplating the discharge of a client's liability for liability assessed prior to the filing of a return you need to consult with a bankruptcy attorney and realize you still may be rolling the dice if you are facing an SFR issue.

Chapter 23:

Benefits of Incorporating

It is possible to earn over $1,500 an hour providing this service. Make sure you know how to properly sell and deliver this service to your clients!!!

We will show you how!

Seven Basic Reasons for Incorporating:

1. **Protect yourself from personal liability**

Corporation signs lease.

Corporation borrows money.

Corporation buys goods and services on credit.

Employees or Independent Contractors of the Corporation injure someone while working.

You are not personally liable!

2. **Tax Advantages**

The ability to take what would otherwise be non-deductible personal expenses and turn them into deductible business expenses.

Personal liabilities relating to the business that might not otherwise be reimbursed by the Corporation can be reimbursed by the Corporation and become deductible business expenses of the Corporation by means of corporate indemnification.

Use of motor vehicle by Corporation

Use of part of your residence by the Corporation with the utilization of a lease not considered a home office.

Annual meeting of shareholders and directors in far away or a resort city and deduct for taxes

The goal is to convert as many non-deductible personal expenses into legitimate deductible business expenses, in this area, there is no limit to what the mind can conceive

IRS Form 1040, Schedule C (Profit or Loss from a Business) is the target of many IRS audits, however, compare this to the audit rates of similar businesses that have incorporated and the audit rate is almost NIL

3. **Privacy**

The Corporation can be established in such a way so that shareholder/owners remain anonymous; many times the same anonymity can be accomplished for officers and directors.

4. **Avoid Probate**

By owning shares jointly with your spouse you can avoid probate of the shares upon the death of either spouse.

5. ***Use of a Marketing framework***

Hold the business out to all as a corporation but yet still maintain centralized management

Gives the appearance that your company is much larger than it actually is.

Attracts investors more easily.

Appears more stable, established and permanent due to the perpetual nature and continuity of life of the corporation, unlike a sole proprietorship, a corporation can continue even after the death of an owner .

6. **Raising capital**

Because of the ease of transfer of ownership and the separate entity concept of the Corporation, it is much easier to attract investors than otherwise.

7. **Easy control and transfer of ownership and assets**

Put real estate in Corporation and transfer through private agreement, i.e. stock transfer rather than formal closing.

Re-title asset in a Corporation yet continue to maintain control.

Ease of transfer of ownership in the Corporation

Management and control of a corporation may be influenced by a stock option.

Chapter 24:

Ruling Procedures

Most practitioners do not deal with these terms on a daily basis so they are listed here as a reminder.

Regulation

A regulation is issued by the Internal Revenue Service and Treasury Department to provide guidance for new legislation or to address issues that arise with respect to existing Internal Revenue Code sections. Regulations interpret and give directions on complying with the law. Regulations are published in the Federal Register. Generally, regulations are first published in proposed form in a Notice of Proposed Rulemaking (NPRM). After public input is fully considered through written comments and even a public hearing, a final regulation or a temporary regulation is published as a Treasury Decision (TD), again, in the Federal Register.

Revenue Ruling

A revenue ruling is an official interpretation by the IRS of the Internal Revenue Code, related statutes, tax treaties and regulations. It is the conclusion of the IRS on how the law is applied to a specific set of facts. Revenue rulings are published in the Internal Revenue Bulletin for the information of and guidance to taxpayers, IRS personnel and tax professionals. For example, a revenue ruling may hold that taxpayers can deduct certain automobile expenses.

Revenue Procedure

A revenue procedure is an official statement of a procedure that affects the rights or duties of taxpayers or other members of the public under the Internal Revenue Code, related statutes, tax treaties and regulations and that should be a matter of public knowledge. It is also published in the Internal Revenue Bulletin. While a revenue ruling generally states an IRS position, a revenue procedure provides return filing or other instructions concerning an IRS position. For example, a revenue procedure might specify how those entitled to deduct certain automobile expenses should compute them by applying a certain mileage rate in lieu of calculating actual operating expenses.

Private Letter Ruling

A private letter ruling, or PLR, is a written statement issued to a taxpayer that interprets and applies tax laws to the taxpayer's specific set of facts. A PLR is issued to establish with certainty the federal tax consequences of a particular transaction before the transaction is consummated or before the taxpayer's return is filed. A PLR is issued in response to a written request submitted by a taxpayer and is binding on the IRS if the taxpayer fully and accurately described the proposed transaction in the request and carries out the transaction as described. A PLR may not be relied on as precedent by other taxpayers or IRS personnel. PLRs are generally made public after all information has been removed that could identify the taxpayer to whom it was issued.

Technical Advice Memorandum

A technical advice memorandum, or TAM, is guidance furnished by the Office of Chief Counsel upon the request of an IRS director or an area director, appeals, in response to technical or procedural questions that develop during a proceeding. A request for a TAM generally stems from an examination of a taxpayer's return, a consideration of a taxpayer's claim for a refund or credit, or any other matter involving a specific taxpayer under the jurisdiction of the territory manager or the area director, appeals. Technical Advice Memoranda are issued only on closed transactions and provide the interpretation of proper application of tax laws, tax treaties, regulations, revenue rulings or other precedents. The advice rendered represents a final determination of the position of the IRS, but only with respect to the specific issue in the specific case in which the advice is issued. Technical Advice Memoranda are generally made public after all information has been removed that could identify the taxpayer whose circumstances triggered a specific memorandum.

Notice

A notice is a public pronouncement that may contain guidance that involves substantive interpretations of the Internal Revenue Code or other provisions of the law. For example, notices can be used to relate what regulations will say in situations where the regulations may not be published in the immediate future.

Announcement

An announcement is a public pronouncement that has only immediate or short-term value. For example, announcements can be used to summarize the law or regulations without making any substantive interpretation; to state what regulations will say when they are certain to be published in the immediate future; or to notify taxpayers of the existence of an approaching deadline.

Appendices

Appendix A: IRS Circular 230

Treasury Department Circular No. 230

(Rev. 6-2014)

Catalog Number 16586R www.irs.gov

Department of the Treasury

Internal Revenue Service

Regulations Governing Practice before the Internal Revenue Service

Title 31 Code of Federal Regulations, Subtitle A, Part 10, published (June 12, 2014) Subject to section 500 of title 5, the Secretary of the Treasury may —

(1) regulate the practice of representatives of persons before the Department of the Treasury; and

(2) before admitting a representative to practice, require that the representative demonstrate —

 (A) good character;

 (B) good reputation;

  (a) necessary qualifications to enable the representative to provide to persons valuable service; and

  (b) competency to advise and assist persons in presenting their cases.

  (c) After notice and opportunity for a proceeding, the Secretary may suspend or disbar from practice before the Department, or censure, a representative who —

   (1) is incompetent;

   (2) is disreputable;

   (3) violates regulations prescribed under this section; or

   (4) with intent to defraud, willfully and knowingly misleads or threatens the person being represented or a prospective person to be represented.

   The Secretary may impose a monetary penalty on any representative described in the preceding sentence. If the representative was acting on behalf of an employer or any firm or other entity in connection with the conduct giving rise to such penalty, the Secretary may impose a monetary penalty on such employer, firm, or entity if it knew, or reasonably should have known, of such conduct. Such penalty shall not exceed the gross income derived (or to be derived) from the conduct giving rise to the penalty and may be in addition to, or in lieu of, any suspension, disbarment, or censure of the representative.

  (d) After notice and opportunity for a hearing to any appraiser, the Secretary may —

(1) provide that appraisals by such appraiser shall not have any probative effect in any administrative proceeding before the Department of the Treasury or the Internal Revenue Service, and
(2) bar such appraiser from presenting evidence or testimony in any such proceeding.

Nothing in this section or in any other provision of law shall be construed to limit the authority of the Secretary of the Treasury to impose standards applicable to the rendering of written advice with respect to any entity, transaction plan or arrangement, or other plan or arrangement, which is of a type which the Secretary determines as having a potential for tax avoidance or evasion.

(Pub. L. 97–258, Sept. 13, 1982, 96 Stat. 884; Pub. L. 98–369, div. A, title I, §156(a), July 18, 1984, 98 Stat. 695; Pub. L. 99–514, §2, Oct. 22, 1986, 100 Stat. 2095; Pub. L. 108–357, title VIII, §822(a)(1), (b), Oct. 22, 2004, 118 Stat. 1586, 1587; Pub. L. 109–280, title XII, §1219(d), Aug. 17, 2006, 120 Stat. 1085.)

IRS Circular 230 Table of Contents

Paragraph 1. The authority citation for 31 CFR, part 10 continues to read as follows:
Authority: Sec. 3, 23 Stat. 258, secs. 2-12, 60 Stat. 237 et. seq.; 5 U.S.C. 301, 500, 551-559; 31 U.S.C. 321; 31 U.S.C. 330; Reorg. Plan No. 26 of 1950, 15 FR 4935, 64 Stat. 1280, 3 CFR, 1949-1953 Comp., p. 1017.

§ 10.0 Scope of part.

(a) This part contains rules governing the recognition of attorneys, certified public accountants, enrolled agents, enrolled retirement plan agents, registered tax return preparers, and other persons representing taxpayers before the Internal Revenue Service. Subpart A of this part sets forth rules relating to the authority to practice before the Internal Revenue Service; subpart B of this part prescribes the duties and restrictions relating to such practice; subpart C of this part prescribes the sanctions for violating the regulations; subpart D of this part contains the rules applicable to disciplinary proceedings; and subpart E of this part contains general provisions relating to the availability of official records.

(b) *Effective/applicability date.* This section is applicable beginning August 2, 2011.

Subpart A — Rules Governing Authority to Practice

§ 10.1 Offices.

(a) *Establishment of office(s).* The Commissioner shall establish the Office of Professional Responsibility and any other office(s) within the Internal Revenue Service necessary to administer and enforce this part. The Commissioner shall appoint the Director of the Office of Professional Responsibility and any other Internal Revenue official(s) to manage and direct any office(s) established to administer or enforce this part. Offices established under this part include, but are not limited to:

  (1) The Office of Professional Responsibility, which shall generally have responsibility for matters related to practitioner conduct and shall have exclusive responsibility for discipline, including disciplinary proceedings and sanctions; and

  (2) An office with responsibility for matters related to authority to practice before the Internal Revenue Service, including acting on applications for enrollment to practice before the Internal Revenue Service and administering competency testing and continuing education.

(b) Officers and employees within any office established under this part may perform acts necessary or appropriate to carry out the responsibilities of their office(s) under this part or as otherwise prescribed by the Commissioner.

(c) *Acting.* The Commissioner will designate an officer or employee of the Internal Revenue Service to perform the duties of an individual appointed under paragraph (a) of this section in the absence of that officer or employee or during a vacancy in that office.

(d) *Effective/applicability date.* This section is applicable beginning August 2, 2011, except that paragraph (a)(1) is applicable beginning June 12, 2014.

§ 10.2 Definitions.

(a) As used in this part, except where the text provides otherwise—

(1) *Attorney* means any person who is a member in good standing of the bar of the highest court of any state, territory, or possession of the United States, including a Commonwealth, or the District of Columbia.

(2) *Certified public accountant* means any person who is duly qualified to practice as a certified public accountant in any state, territory, or possession of the United States, including a Commonwealth, or the District of Columbia.

(3) *Commissioner* refers to the Commissioner of Internal Revenue.

(4) *Practice before the Internal Revenue Service* comprehends all matters connected with a presentation to the Internal Revenue Service or any of its officers or employees relating to a taxpayer's rights, privileges, or liabilities under laws or regulations administered by the Internal Revenue Service. Such presentations include, but are not limited to, preparing documents; filing documents; corresponding and communicating with the Internal Revenue Service; rendering written advice with respect to any entity, transaction, plan or arrangement, or other plan or arrangement having a potential for tax avoidance or evasion; and representing a client at conferences, hearings, and meetings.

(5) *Practitioner* means any individual described in paragraphs (a), (b), (c), (d), (e), or (f) of §10.3.

(6) A *tax return* includes an amended tax return and a claim for refund.

(7) *Service* means the Internal Revenue Service.

(8) *Tax return preparer* means any individual within the meaning of section 7701(a)(36) and 26 CFR 301.7701-15.

(b) *Effective/applicability date.* This section is applicable on August 2, 2011.

§ 10.3 Who may practice.

(a) *Attorneys.* Any attorney who is not currently under suspension or disbarment from practice before the Internal Revenue Service may practice before the Internal Revenue Service by filing with the Internal Revenue Service a written declaration that the attorney is currently qualified as an attorney and is authorized to represent the party or parties. Notwithstanding the preceding sentence, attorneys who are not currently under suspension or disbarment from practice before the Internal Revenue Service are not required to file a written declaration with the IRS before rendering written advice covered under §10.37, but their rendering of this advice is practice before the Internal Revenue Service.

(b) *Certified public accountants.* Any certified public accountant who is not currently under suspension or disbarment from practice before the Internal Revenue Service may practice before the Internal Revenue Service by filing with the Internal Revenue Service a written declaration that the certified public accountant is currently qualified as a certified public accountant and is authorized to represent the party or parties. Notwithstanding the preceding sentence, certified public accountants who are not currently under suspension or disbarment from practice before the Internal Revenue Service are not required to file a written declaration with the IRS before rendering written advice covered under §10.37, but their rendering of this advice is practice before the Internal Revenue Service.

(c) *Enrolled agents.* Any individual enrolled as an agent pursuant to this part who is not currently under suspension or disbarment from practice before the Internal Revenue Service may practice before the Internal Revenue Service.

(d) *Enrolled actuaries.*

(1) Any individual who is enrolled as an actuary by the Joint Board for the Enrollment of Actuaries pursuant to 29 U.S.C. 1242 who is not currently under suspension or disbarment from practice before the Internal Revenue Service may practice before the Internal Revenue Service by filing with the Internal Revenue Service a written declaration stating that he or she is currently qualified as an enrolled actuary and is authorized to represent the party or parties on whose behalf he or she acts.

(2) Practice as an enrolled actuary is limited welfare benefits), 419A (relating to qualified asset accounts), 420 (relating to transfers of excess pension assets to retiree health accounts), 4971 (relating to excise taxes payable as a result of an accumulated funding deficiency under section 412), 4972 (relating to tax on nondeductible contributions to qualified employer plans), 4976 (relating to taxes with respect to funded welfare benefit plans), 4980 (relating to tax on reversion of qualified plan assets to employer), 6057 (relating to annual registration of plans), 6058 (relating to information required in connection with certain plans of deferred compensation), 6059 (relating to periodic report of actuary), 6652(e) (relating to the failure to file annual registration and other notifications by pension plan), 6652(f) (relating to the failure to file information required in connection with certain plans of deferred compensation), 6692 (relating to the failure to file actuarial report), 7805(b) (relating to the extent to which an Internal Revenue Service ruling or determination letter coming under the statutory provisions listed here will be applied without retroactive effect); and 29 U.S.C. § 1083 (relating to the waiver of funding for nonqualified plans).

(3) An individual who practices before the Internal Revenue Service pursuant to paragraph (d)(1) of this section is subject to the provisions of this part in the same manner as attorneys, certified public accountants, enrolled agents, enrolled retirement plan agents, and registered tax return preparers.

(e) *Enrolled retirement plan agents* —

(1) Any individual enrolled as a retirement plan agent pursuant to this part who is not currently under suspension or disbarment from practice before the Internal Revenue Service may practice before the Internal Revenue Service.

(2) Practice as an enrolled retirement plan agent is limited to representation with respect to issues involving the following programs: Employee Plans Determination Letter program; Employee Plans Compliance Resolution System; and Employee Plans Master and Prototype and Volume Submitter program. In addition, enrolled retirement plan agents are generally permitted to represent taxpayers with respect to IRS forms under the 5300 and 5500 series which are filed by retirement plans and plan sponsors, but not with respect to actuarial forms or schedules.

(3) An individual who practices before the Internal Revenue Service pursuant to paragraph (e)(1) of this section is subject to the provisions of this part in the same manner as attorneys, certified public accountants, enrolled agents, enrolled actuaries, and registered tax return preparers.

(f) *Registered tax return preparers.*

(1) Any individual who is designated as a registered tax return preparer pursuant to §10.4(c) of this part who is not currently under suspension or disbarment from practice before the Internal Revenue Service may practice before the Internal Revenue Service.

(2) Practice as a registered tax return preparer is limited to preparing and signing tax returns and claims for refund, and other documents for submission to the Internal Revenue Service. A registered tax return preparer may prepare all or substantially all of a tax return or claim for refund of tax. The Internal Revenue Service will prescribe by forms, instructions, or other appropriate guidance the tax returns and claims for refund that a registered tax return preparer may prepare and sign.

(3) A registered tax return preparer may represent taxpayers before revenue agents, customer service representatives, or similar officers and employees of the Internal Revenue Service (including the Taxpayer

Advocate Service) during an examination if the registered tax return preparer signed the tax return or claim for refund for the taxable year or period under examination. Unless otherwise prescribed by regulation or notice, this right does not permit such individual to represent the taxpayer, regardless of the circumstances requiring representation, before appeals officers, revenue officers, Counsel or similar officers or employees of the Internal Revenue Service or the Treasury Department. A registered tax return preparer's authorization to practice under this part also does not include the authority to provide tax advice to a client or another person except as necessary to prepare a tax return, claim for refund, or other document intended to be submitted to the Internal Revenue Service.

(4) An individual who practices before the Internal Revenue Service pursuant to paragraph (f)(1) of this section is subject to the provisions of this part in the same manner as attorneys, certified public accountants, enrolled agents, enrolled retirement plan agents, and enrolled actuaries.

(g) *Others.* Any individual qualifying under paragraph §10.5(e) or §10.7 is eligible to practice before the Internal Revenue Service to the extent provided in those sections.

(h) *Government officers and employees, and others.* An individual, who is an officer or employee of the executive, legislative, or judicial branch of the United States Government; an officer or employee of the District of Columbia; a Member of Congress; or a Resident Commissioner may not practice before the Internal Revenue Service if such practice violates 18 U.S.C. §§ 203 or 205.

(i) *State officers and employees.* No officer or employee of any State, or subdivision of any State, whose duties require him or her to pass upon, investigate, or deal with tax matters for such State or subdivision, may practice before the Internal Revenue Service, if such employment may disclose facts or information applicable to Federal tax matters.

(j) *Effective/applicability date.* Paragraphs (a), (b), and (g) of this section are applicable beginning June 12, 2014. Paragraphs (c) through (f), (h), and (i) of this section are applicable beginning August 2, 2011.

§ 10.4 Eligibility to become an enrolled agent, enrolled retirement plan agent, or registered tax return preparer.

(a) *Enrollment as an enrolled agent upon examination.* The Commissioner, or delegate, will grant enrollment as an enrolled agent to an applicant eighteen years of age or older who demonstrates special competence in tax matters by written examination administered by, or administered under the oversight of, the Internal Revenue Service, who possesses a current or otherwise valid preparer tax identification number or other prescribed identifying number, and who has not engaged in any conduct that would justify the suspension or disbarment of any practitioner under the provisions of this part.

(b) *Enrollment as a retirement plan agent upon examination.* The Commissioner, or delegate, will grant enrollment as an enrolled retirement plan agent to an applicant eighteen years of age or older who demonstrates special competence in qualified retirement plan matters by written examination administered by, or administered under the oversight of, the Internal Revenue Service, who possesses a current or otherwise valid preparer tax identification number or other prescribed identifying number, and who has not engaged in any conduct that would justify the suspension or disbarment of any practitioner under the provisions of this part.

(c) *Designation as a registered tax return preparer.* The Commissioner, or delegate, may designate an individual eighteen years of age or older as a registered tax return preparer provided an applicant demonstrates competence in Federal tax return preparation matters by written examination administered by, or administered under the oversight of, the Internal Revenue Service, or otherwise meets the requisite standards prescribed by the Internal Revenue Service, possesses a current or otherwise valid preparer tax identification number or other prescribed identifying number, and has not engaged in any conduct that would justify the suspension or disbarment of any practitioner under the provisions of this part.

(d) *Enrollment of former Internal Revenue Service employees.* The Commissioner, or delegate, may enrollment as an enrolled agent or enrolled retirement plan agent to an applicant who, by virtue of past service and technical experience in the Internal Revenue Service, has qualified for such enrollment and who has not engaged in any conduct that would justify the suspension or disbarment of any practitioner under the provisions of this part, under the following circumstances:

(1) The former employee applies for enrollment on an Internal Revenue Service form and supplies the information requested on the form and such other information regarding the experience and training of the applicant as may be relevant.

(2) The appropriate office of the Internal Revenue Service provides a detailed report of the nature and rating of the applicant's work while employed by the Internal Revenue Service and a recommendation whether such employment qualifies the applicant technically or otherwise for the desired authorization.

(3) Enrollment as an enrolled agent based on an applicant's former employment with the Internal Revenue Service may be of unlimited scope or it may be limited to permit the presentation of matters only of the particular specialty or only before the particular unit or division of the Internal Revenue Service for which the applicant's former employment has qualified the applicant. Enrollment as an enrolled retirement plan agent based on an applicant's former employment with the Internal Revenue Service will be limited to permit the presentation of matters only with respect to qualified retirement plan matters.

(4) Application for enrollment as an enrolled agent or enrolled retirement plan agent based on an applicant's former employment with the Internal Revenue Service must be made within three years from the date of separation from such employment.

(5) An applicant for enrollment as an enrolled agent who is requesting such enrollment based on former employment with the Internal Revenue Service must have had a minimum of five years continuous employment with the Internal Revenue Service during which the applicant must have been regularly engaged in applying and interpreting the provisions of the Internal Revenue Code and the regulations relating to income, estate, gift, employment, or excise taxes.

(6) An applicant for enrollment as an enrolled retirement plan agent who is requesting such enrollment based on former employment with the Internal Revenue Service must have had a minimum of five years continuous employment with the Internal Revenue Service during which the applicant must have been regularly engaged in applying and interpreting the provisions of the Internal Revenue Code and the regulations relating to qualified retirement plan matters.

(7) For the purposes of paragraphs (d)(5) and (6) of this section, an aggregate of 10 or more years of employment in positions involving the application and interpretation of the provisions of the Internal Revenue Code, at least three of which occurred within the five years preceding the date of application, is the equivalent of five years continuous employment.

(e) *Natural persons.* Enrollment to practice may be granted only to natural persons.

(f) *Effective/applicability date.* This section is applicable beginning August 2, 2011.

§ 10.5 Application to become an enrolled agent, enrolled retirement plan agent, or registered tax return preparer.

(a) *Form; address.* An applicant to become an enrolled agent, enrolled retirement plan agent, or registered tax return preparer must apply as required by forms or procedures established and published by the Internal Revenue Service, including proper execution of required forms under oath or affirmation. The address on the application will be the address under which a successful applicant is enrolled or registered and is the address to which all correspondence concerning enrollment or registration will be sent.

(b) *Fee.* A reasonable nonrefundable fee may be charged for each application to become an enrolled agent, enrolled retirement plan agent, or registered tax return preparer. See 26 CFR part 300.

(c) *Additional information; examination.* The Internal Revenue Service may require the applicant, as a condition to consideration of an application, to file additional information and to submit to any written or oral examination under oath or otherwise. Upon the applicant's written request, the Internal Revenue Service will afford the applicant the opportunity to be heard with respect to the application.

(d) *Compliance and suitability checks.*

(1) As a condition to consideration of an application, the Internal Revenue Service may conduct a Federal tax compliance check and suitability check. The tax compliance check will be limited to an inquiry regarding whether an applicant has filed all required individual or business tax returns and whether the applicant has failed to pay, or make proper arrangements with the Internal Revenue Service for payment of, any Federal tax debts. The suitability check will be limited to an inquiry regarding whether an applicant has engaged in any conduct that would justify suspension or disbarment of any practitioner under the provisions of this part on the date the application is submitted, including whether the applicant has engaged in disreputable conduct as defined in §10.51. The application will be denied only if the results of the compliance or suitability check are sufficient to establish that the practitioner engaged in conduct subject to sanctions under §§10.51 and 10.52.

(2) If the applicant does not pass the tax compliance or suitability check, the applicant will not be issued an enrollment or registration card or certificate pursuant to §10.6(b) of this part. An applicant who is initially denied enrollment or registration for failure to pass a tax compliance check may reapply after the initial denial if the applicant becomes current with respect to the applicant's tax liabilities.

(e) *Temporary recognition.* On receipt of a properly executed application, the Commissioner, or delegate, may grant the applicant temporary recognition to practice pending a determination as to whether status as an enrolled agent, enrolled retirement plan agent, or registered tax return preparer should be granted. Temporary recognition will be granted only in unusual circumstances and it will not be granted, in any circumstance, if the application is not regular on its face, if the information stated in the application, if true, is not sufficient to warrant granting the application to practice, or the Commissioner, or delegate, has information indicating that the statements in the application are untrue or that the applicant would not otherwise qualify to become an enrolled agent, enrolled retirement plan agent, or registered tax return preparer. Issuance of temporary recognition does not constitute either a designation or a finding of eligibility as an enrolled agent, enrolled retirement plan agent, or registered tax return preparer, and the temporary recognition may be withdrawn at any time.

(f) *Protest of application denial.* The applicant will be informed in writing as to the reason(s) for any denial of an application. The applicant may, within 30 days after receipt of the notice of denial of the application, file a written protest of the denial as prescribed by the Internal Revenue Service in forms, guidance, or other appropriate guidance. A protest under this section is not governed by subpart D of this part.

(f) *Effective/applicability date.* This section is applicable to applications received on or after August 2, 2011.

§ 10.6 Term and renewal of status as an enrolled agent, enrolled retirement plan agent, or registered tax return preparer.

(a) *Term.* Each individual authorized to practice before the Internal Revenue Service as an enrolled agent, enrolled retirement plan agent, or registered tax return preparer will be accorded active enrollment or registration status subject to renewal of enrollment or registration as provided in this part.

(b) *Enrollment or registration card or certificate.* The Internal Revenue Service will issue an enrollment or registration card or certificate to each individual whose application to practice before the Internal Revenue Service is approved. Each card or certificate will be valid for the period stated on the card or certificate. An enrolled agent, enrolled retirement plan agent, or registered tax return preparer may not practice before the Internal Revenue Service if the card or certificate is not current or otherwise valid. The card or certificate is in addition to any notification that may be provided to each individual who obtains a preparer tax identification number.

(c) *Change of address.* An enrolled agent, enrolled retirement plan agent, or registered tax return preparer must send notification of any change of address to the address specified by the Internal Revenue Service within 60 days of the change of address. This notification must include the enrolled agent's, enrolled retirement plan agent's, or registered tax return preparer's name, prior address, new address, tax identification number(s) (including preparer tax identification number), and the date the change of address is effective. Unless this notification is sent, the address for purposes of any correspondence from the appropriate Internal Revenue Service office responsible for administering this part shall be the address reflected on the practitioner's most recent application for enrollment or registration, or application for renewal of enrollment or registration. A practitioner's change of address notification under this part will not constitute a change of the practitioner's last known address for purposes of section 6212 of the Internal Revenue Code and regulations thereunder.

(d) *Renewal.*

(1) *In general.* Enrolled agents, enrolled retirement plan agents, and registered tax return preparers must renew their status with the Internal Revenue Service to maintain eligibility to practice before the Internal Revenue Service. Failure to receive notification from the Internal Revenue Service of the renewal requirement will not be justification for the individual's failure to satisfy this requirement.

(2) *Renewal period for enrolled agents.*

(i) All enrolled agents must renew their preparer tax identification number as prescribed by forms, instructions, or other appropriate guidance.

(ii) Enrolled agents who have a social security number or tax identification number that ends with the numbers 0, 1, 2, or 3, except for those individuals who received their initial enrollment after November 1, 2003, must apply for renewal between November 1, 2003, and January 31, 2004. The renewal will be effective April 1, 2004.

(iii) Enrolled agents who have a social security number or tax identification number that ends with the numbers 4, 5, or 6, except for those individuals who received their initial enrollment after November 1, 2004, must apply for renewal between November 1, 2004, and January 31, 2005. The renewal will be effective April 1, 2005.

(iv) Enrolled agents who have a social security number or tax identification number that ends with the numbers 7, 8, or 9, except for those individuals who received their initial enrollment after November 1, 2005, must apply for renewal between November 1, 2005, and January 31, 2006. The renewal will be effective April 1, 2006.

(v) Thereafter, applications for renewal as an enrolled agent will be required between November 1 and January 31 of every subsequent third year as specified in paragraph (d)(2)(i), (d)(2)(ii), or (d) (2)(iii) of this section according to the last number of the individual's social security number or tax identification number. Those individuals who receive initial enrollment as an enrolled agent after November 1 and before April 2 of the applicable renewal period will not be required to renew their enrollment before the first full renewal period following the receipt of their initial enrollment.

(3) *Renewal period for enrolled retirement plan agents.*

(i) All enrolled retirement plan agents must renew their preparer tax identification number as prescribed by the Internal Revenue Service in forms, instructions, or other appropriate guidance.

(ii) Enrolled retirement plan agents will be required to renew their status as enrolled retirement plan agents between April 1 and June 30 of every third year subsequent to their initial enrollment.

(4) *Renewal period for registered tax return preparers.* Registered tax return preparers must renew their preparer tax identification number and their status as a registered tax return preparer as prescribed by the Internal Revenue Service in forms, instructions, or other appropriate guidance.

(5) *Notification of renewal.* After review and approval, the Internal Revenue Service will notify the individual of the renewal and will issue the individual a card or certificate evidencing current status as an enrolled agent, enrolled retirement plan agent, or registered tax return preparer.

(6) *Fee.* A reasonable nonrefundable fee may be charged for each application for renewal filed. See 26 CFR part 300.

(7) *Forms.* Forms required for renewal may be obtained by sending a written request to the address specified by the Internal Revenue Service or from such other source as the Internal Revenue Service will publish in the Internal Revenue Bulletin (see 26 CFR 601.601(d)(2)(ii)(b)) and on the Internal Revenue Service webpage (www.irs.gov).

(e) *Condition for renewal*: continuing education. In order to qualify for renewal as an enrolled agent, enrolled retirement plan agent, or registered tax return preparer, an individual must certify, in the manner prescribed by the Internal Revenue Service, that the individual has satisfied the requisite number of continuing education hours.

(1) *Definitions.* For purposes of this section —

(i) *Enrollment year* means January 1 to December 31 of each year of an enrollment cycle.

(ii) *Enrollment cycle* means the three successive enrollment years preceding the effective date of renewal.

(iii) *Registration year* means each 12-month period the registered tax return preparer is authorized to practice before the Internal Revenue Service.

(iv) *The effective date of renewal* is the first day of the fourth month following the close of the period for renewal described in paragraph (d) of this section.

(2) *For renewed enrollment as an enrolled agent or enrolled retirement plan agent* —

(i) *Requirements for enrollment cycle.* A minimum of 72 hours of continuing education credit, including six hours of ethics or professional conduct, must be completed during each enrollment cycle.

(ii) *Requirements for enrollment year.* A minimum of 16 hours of continuing education credit, including two hours of ethics or professional conduct, must be completed during each enrollment year of an enrollment cycle.

(iii) Enrollment during enrollment cycle —

(A) *In general.* Subject to paragraph (e)(2)(iii)

(B) of this section, an individual who receives initial enrollment during an enrollment cycle must complete two hours of qualifying continuing education credit for each month enrolled during the enrollment cycle. Enrollment for any part of a month is considered enrollment for the entire month. (B) *Ethics.* An individual who receives initial enrollment during an enrollment cycle must complete two hours of ethics or professional conduct for each enrollment year during the enrollment cycle. Enrollment for any part of an enrollment year is considered enrollment for the entire year.

(3) *Requirements for renewal as a registered tax return preparer.* A minimum of 15 hours of continuing education credit, including two hours of ethics or professional conduct, three hours of Federal tax law updates, and 10 hours of Federal tax law topics, must be completed during each registration year.

(f) *Qualifying continuing education* —

(1) *General* —

(i) *Enrolled agents.* To qualify for continuing education credit for an enrolled agent, a course of learning must —

(A) Be a qualifying continuing education program designed to enhance professional knowledge in Federal taxation or Federal tax related matters (programs comprised of current subject matter in Federal taxation or Federal tax related matters, including accounting, tax return preparation software, taxation, or ethics); and

(B) Be a qualifying continuing education program consistent with the Internal Revenue Code and effective tax administration.

(ii) *Enrolled retirement plan agents.* To qualify for continuing education credit for an enrolled retirement plan agent, a course of learning must —

(A) Be a qualifying continuing education program designed to enhance professional knowledge in qualified retirement plan matters; and

(B) Be a qualifying continuing education program consistent with the Internal Revenue Code and effective tax administration.

(iii) *Registered tax return preparers.* To qualify for continuing education credit for a registered tax return preparer, a course of learning must —

(A) Be a qualifying continuing education program designed to enhance professional knowledge in Federal taxation or Federal tax related matters (programs comprised of current subject matter in Federal taxation or Federal tax related matters, including accounting, tax return preparation software, taxation, or ethics); and

(B) Be a qualifying continuing education program consistent with the Internal Revenue Code and effective tax administration.

(2) *Qualifying programs* —

(i) *Formal programs.* A formal program qualifies as a continuing education program if it —

(A) Requires attendance and provides each attendee with a certificate of attendance;

(B) Is conducted by a qualified instructor, discussion leader, or speaker (in other words, a person whose background, training, education, and experience is appropriate for instructing or leading a discussion on the subject matter of the particular program);

(C) Provides or requires a written outline, textbook, or suitable electronic educational materials; and

(D) Satisfies the requirements established for a qualified continuing education program pursuant to §10.9.

(ii) *Correspondence or individual study programs (including taped programs).* Qualifying continuing education programs include correspondence or individual study programs that are conducted by continuing education providers and completed on an individual basis by the enrolled individual. The allowable credit hours for such programs will be measured on a basis comparable to the measurement of a seminar or course for credit in an accredited educational institution. Such programs qualify as continuing education programs only if they —

(A) Require registration of the participants by the continuing education provider;

(B) Provide a means for measuring successful completion by the participants (for example, a written examination), including the issuance of a certificate of completion by the continuing education provider;

(C) Provide a written outline, textbook, or suitable electronic educational materials; and

(D) Satisfy the requirements established for a qualified continuing education program pursuant to §10.9.

(iii) *Serving as an instructor, discussion leader or speaker.*

(A) One hour of continuing education credit will be awarded for each contact hour completed as an instructor, discussion leader, or speaker at an educational program that meets the continuing education requirements of paragraph (f) of this section.

(B) A maximum of two hours of continuing education credit will be awarded for actual subject preparation time for each contact hour completed as an instructor, discussion leader, or speaker at such programs. It is the responsibility of the individual claiming such credit to maintain records to verify preparation time.

(C) The maximum continuing education credit for instruction and preparation may not exceed four hours annually for registered tax return preparers and six hours annually for enrolled agents and enrolled retirement plan agents.

(D) An instructor, discussion leader, or speaker who makes more than one presentation on the same subject matter during an enrollment cycle or registration year will receive continuing education credit for only one such presentation for the enrollment cycle or registration year.

(3) *Periodic examination.* Enrolled Agents and Enrolled Retirement Plan Agents may establish eligibility for renewal of enrollment for any enrollment cycle by —

(i) Achieving a passing score on each part of the Special Enrollment Examination administered under this part during the three year period prior to renewal; and

(ii) Completing a minimum of 16 hours of qualifying continuing education during the last year of an enrollment cycle.

(iii) *Measurement of continuing education coursework.*

(4) All continuing education programs will be measured in terms of contact hours. The shortest recognized program will be one contact hour.

(5) A contact hour is 50 minutes of continuous participation in a program. Credit is granted only for a full contact hour, which is 50 minutes or multiples thereof. For example, a program lasting more than 50 minutes but less than 100 minutes will count as only one contact hour.

(6) Individual segments at continuous conferences, conventions and the like will be considered one total program. For example, two 90-minute segments (180 minutes) at a continuous conference will count as three contact hours.

(7) For university or college courses, each semester hour credit will equal 15 contact hours and a quarter hour credit will equal 10 contact hours.

(g) *Recordkeeping requirements.*

(1) Each individual applying for renewal must retain for a period of four years following the date of renewal the information required with regard to qualifying continuing education credit hours. Such information includes —

(i) The name of the sponsoring organization;

(ii) The location of the program;

(iii) The title of the program, qualified program number, and description of its content;

(iv) Written outlines, course syllabi, textbook, and/or electronic materials provided or required for the course;

(v) The dates attended;

(vi) The credit hours claimed;

(vii) The name(s) of the instructor(s), discussion leader(s), or speaker(s), if appropriate; and

(viii) The certificate of completion and/or signed statement of the hours of attendance obtained from the continuing education provider.

(2) To receive continuing education credit for service completed as an instructor, discussion leader, or speaker, the following information must be maintained for a period of four years following the date of renewal —

(i) The name of the sponsoring organization;

(ii) The location of the program;

(iii) The title of the program and copy of its content;

(iv) The dates of the program; and

(v) The credit hours claimed.

(h) *Waivers.*

(1) Waiver from the continuing education requirements for a given period may be granted for the following reasons —

(i) Health, which prevented compliance with the continuing education requirements;

(ii) Extended active military duty;

(iii) Absence from the United States for an extended period of time due to employment or other reasons, provided the individual does not practice before the Internal Revenue Service during such absence; and

(iv) Other compelling reasons, which will be considered on a case-by-case basis.

(2) A request for waiver must be accompanied by appropriate documentation. The individual is required to furnish any additional documentation or explanation deemed necessary. Examples of appropriate documentation could be a medical certificate or military orders.

(3) A request for waiver must be filed no later than the last day of the renewal application period.

(4) If a request for waiver is not approved, the individual will be placed in inactive status. The individual will be notified that the waiver was not approved and that the individual has been placed on a roster of inactive enrolled agents, enrolled retirement plan agents, or registered tax return preparers.

(5) If the request for waiver is not approved, the individual may file a protest as prescribed by the Internal Revenue Service in forms, instructions, or other appropriate guidance. A protest filed under this section is not governed by subpart D of this part.

(6) If a request for waiver is approved, the individual will be notified and issued a card or certificate evidencing renewal.

(7) Those who are granted waivers are required to file timely applications for renewal of enrollment or registration.

(i) *Failure to comply.*

(1) Compliance by an individual with the requirements of this part is determined by the Internal Revenue Service. The Internal Revenue Service will provide notice to any individual who fails to meet the continuing education and fee requirements of eligibility for renewal. The notice will state the basis for the determination of noncompliance and will provide the individual an opportunity to furnish the requested information in writing relating to the matter within 60 days of the date of the notice. Such information will be considered in making a final determination as to eligibility for renewal. The individual must be informed of the reason(s) for any denial of a renewal. The individual may, within 30 days after receipt of the notice of denial of renewal, file a written protest of the denial as prescribed by the Internal Revenue Service in forms, instructions, or other appropriate guidance. A protest under this section is not governed by subpart D of this part.

(2) The continuing education records of an enrolled agent, enrolled retirement plan agent, or registered tax return preparer may be reviewed to determine compliance with the requirements and standards for renewal as provided in paragraph (f) of this section. As part of this review, the enrolled agent, enrolled retirement plan agent or registered tax return preparer may be required to provide the Internal Revenue Service with copies of any continuing education records required to be maintained under this part. If the enrolled agent, enrolled retirement plan agent or registered tax return preparer fails to comply with this requirement, any continuing education hours claimed may be disallowed.

(3) An individual who has not filed a timely application for renewal, who has not made a timely response to the notice of noncompliance with the renewal requirements, or who has not satisfied the requirements of eligibility for renewal will be placed on a roster of inactive enrolled individuals or inactive registered individuals. During this time, the individual will be ineligible to practice before the Internal Revenue Service.

(4) Individuals placed in inactive status and individuals ineligible to practice before the Internal Revenue Service may not state or imply that they are eligible to practice before the Internal Revenue Service, or use the terms enrolled agent, enrolled retirement plan agent, or registered tax return preparer, the designations "EA" or "ERPA" or other form of reference to eligibility to practice before the Internal Revenue Service.

(5) An individual placed in inactive status may be reinstated to an active status by filing an application for renewal and providing evidence of the completion of all required continuing education hours for the enrollment cycle or registration year. Continuing education credit under this paragraph (j)

(5) may not be used to satisfy the requirements of the enrollment cycle or registration year in which the individual has been placed back on the active roster.

(6) An individual placed in inactive status must file an application for renewal and satisfy the requirements for renewal as set forth in this section within three years of being placed in inactive status. Otherwise, the name of such individual will be removed from the inactive status roster and the individual's status as an enrolled agent, enrolled retirement plan agent, or registered tax return preparer will terminate. Future eligibility for active status must then be reestablished by the individual as provided in this section.

(7) Inactive status is not available to an individual who is the subject of a pending disciplinary matter before the Internal Revenue Service.

(j) *Inactive retirement status.* An individual who no longer practices before the Internal Revenue Service may request to be placed in an inactive retirement status at any time and such individual will be placed in an inactive retirement status. The individual will be ineligible to practice before the Internal Revenue Service. An individual who is placed in an inactive retirement status may be reinstated to an active status by filing an application for renewal and providing evidence of the completion of the required continuing education hours for the enrollment cycle or registration year. Inactive retirement status is not available to an individual who is ineligible to practice before the Internal Revenue Service or an individual who is the subject of a pending disciplinary matter under this part.

(k) *Renewal while under suspension or disbarment.* An individual who is ineligible to practice before the Internal Revenue Service by virtue of disciplinary action under this part is required to conform to the requirements for renewal of enrollment or registration before the individual's eligibility is restored.

(l) *Enrolled actuaries.* The enrollment and renewal of enrollment of actuaries authorized to practice under paragraph (d) of §10.3 are governed by the regulations of the Joint Board for the Enrollment of Actuaries at 20 CFR 901.1 through 901.72.

(m) *Effective/applicability date.* This section is applicable to enrollment or registration effective beginning August 2, 2011.

§ 10.7 Representing oneself; participating in rulemaking; limited practice; and special appearances.

(a) *Representing oneself.* Individuals may appear on their own behalf before the Internal Revenue Service provided they present satisfactory identification.

(b) *Participating in rulemaking.* Individuals may participate in rulemaking as provided by the Administrative Procedure Act. See 5 U.S.C. § 553.

(c) *Limited practice*—

(1) *In general.* Subject to the limitations in paragraph (c)(2) of this section, an individual who is not a practitioner may represent a taxpayer before the Internal Revenue Service in the circumstances described in this paragraph (c)(1), even if the taxpayer is not present, provided the individual presents satisfactory identification and proof of his or her authority to represent the taxpayer. The circumstances described in this paragraph (c)(1) are as follows:

(i) An individual may represent a member of his or her immediate family.

(ii) A regular full-time employee of an individual employer may represent the employer.

(iii) A general partner or a regular full-time employee of a partnership may represent the partnership.

(iv) A bona fide officer or a regular full-time employee of a corporation (including a parent, subsidiary, or other affiliated corporation), association, or organized group may represent the corporation, association, or organized group.

(v) A regular full-time employee of a trust, receivership, guardianship, or estate may represent the trust, receivership, guardianship, or estate.

(vi) An officer or a regular employee of a governmental unit, agency, or authority may represent the governmental unit, agency, or authority in the course of his or her official duties.

(vii) An individual may represent any individual or entity, who is outside the United States, before personnel of the Internal Revenue Service when such representation takes place outside the United States.

(2) *Limitations.*

(i) An individual who is under suspension or disbarment from practice before the Internal Revenue Service may not engage in limited practice before the Internal Revenue Service under paragraph (c)(1) of this section.

(ii) The Commissioner, or delegate, may, after notice and opportunity for a conference, deny eligibility to engage in limited practice before the Internal Revenue Service under paragraph (c)(1) of this section to any individual who has engaged in conduct that would justify a sanction under §10.50.

(iii) An individual who represents a taxpayer under the authority of paragraph (c)(1) of this section is subject, to the extent of his or her authority, to such rules of general applicability regarding standards of conduct and other matters as prescribed by the Internal Revenue Service.

(d) *Special appearances.* The Commissioner, or delegate, may, subject to conditions deemed appropriate, authorize an individual who is not otherwise eligible to practice before the Internal Revenue Service to represent another person in a particular matter.

(e) *Fiduciaries.* For purposes of this part, a fiduciary (for example, a trustee, receiver, guardian, personal representative, administrator, or executor) is considered to be the taxpayer and not a representative of the taxpayer.

(f) *Effective/applicability date.* This section is applicable beginning August 2, 2011.

§ 10.8 Return preparation and application of rules to other individuals.

(a) *Preparing all or substantially all of a tax return.* Any individual who for compensation prepares or assists with the preparation of all or substantially all of a tax return or claim for refund must have a preparer tax identification number. Except as otherwise prescribed in forms, instructions, or other appropriate guidance, an individual must be an attorney, certified public accountant, enrolled agent, or registered tax return preparer to obtain a preparer tax identification number. Any individual who for compensation prepares or assists with the preparation of all or substantially all of a tax return or claim for refund is subject to the duties and restrictions relating to practice in subpart B, as well as subject to the sanctions for violation of the regulations in subpart C.

(b) *Preparing a tax return and furnishing information.* Any individual may for compensation prepare or assist with the preparation of a tax return or claim for refund (provided the individual prepares less than substantially all of the tax return or claim for refund), appear as a witness for the taxpayer before the Internal Revenue Service, or furnish information at the request of the Internal Revenue Service or any of its officers or employees.

(c) *Application of rules to other individuals.* Any individual who for compensation prepares, or assists in the preparation of, all or a substantial portion of a document pertaining to any taxpayer's tax liability for submission to the Internal Revenue Service is subject to the duties and restrictions relating to practice in subpart B, as well as subject to the sanctions for violation of the regulations in subpart C. Unless otherwise a practitioner, however, an individual may not for compensation prepare, or assist in the preparation of, all or substantially all of a tax return or claim for refund, or sign tax returns and claims for refund. For purposes of this paragraph, an individual described in 26 CFR 301.7701-15(f) is not treated as having prepared all or a substantial portion of the document by reason of such assistance.

(d) *Effective/applicability date.* This section is applicable beginning August 2, 2011.

§ 10.9 Continuing education providers and continuing education programs.

(a) *Continuing education providers —*

(1) *In general.* Continuing education providers are those responsible for presenting continuing education

programs. A continuing education provider must —

(i) Be an accredited educational institution;

(ii) Be recognized for continuing education purposes by the licensing body of any State, territory, or possession of the United States, including a Commonwealth, or the District of Columbia;

(iii) Be recognized and approved by a qualifying organization as a provider of continuing education on subject matters within §10.6(f) of this part. The Internal Revenue Service may, at its discretion, identify a professional organization, society or business entity that maintains minimum education standards comparable to those set forth in this part as a qualifying organization for purposes of this part in appropriate forms, instructions, and other appropriate guidance; or

(iv) Be recognized by the Internal Revenue Service as a professional organization, society, or business whose programs include offering continuing professional education opportunities in subject matters within §10.6(f) of this part. The Internal Revenue Service, at its discretion, may require such professional organizations, societies, or businesses to file an agreement and/or obtain Internal Revenue Service approval of each program as a qualified continuing education program in appropriate forms, instructions or other appropriate guidance.

(2) *Continuing education provider numbers* —

(i) *In general.* A continuing education provider is required to obtain a continuing education provider number and pay any applicable user fee.

(ii) *Renewal.* A continuing education provider maintains its status as a continuing education provider during the continuing education provider cycle by renewing its continuing education provider number as prescribed by forms, instructions or other appropriate guidance and paying any applicable user fee. Fee requirements *for qualified continuing education programs.* A continuing education provider must ensure the qualified continuing education program complies with all the following requirements —

(iii) Programs must be developed by individual(s) qualified in the subject matter;

(iv) Program subject matter must be current;

(v) Instructors, discussion leaders, and speakers must be qualified with respect to program content;

(vi) Programs must include some means for evaluation of the technical content and presentation to be evaluated;

(v) Certificates of completion bearing a current qualified continuing education program number issued by the Internal Revenue Service must be provided to the participants who successfully complete the program; and

(vi) Records must be maintained by the continuing education provider to verify the participants who attended and completed the program for a period of four years following completion of the program. In the case of continuous conferences, conventions, and the like, records must be maintained to verify completion of the program and attendance by each participant at each segment of the program.

(3) *Program numbers* —

(i) *In general.* Every continuing education provider is required to obtain a continuing education provider program number and pay any applicable user fee for each program offered. Program numbers shall be obtained as prescribed by forms, instructions or other appropriate guidance. Although, at the discretion of the Internal Revenue Service, a continuing education provider may be required to demonstrate that the program is designed to enhance professional knowledge in Federal taxation or Federal tax related matters (programs comprised of current subject matter in Federal taxation or Federal tax related matters, including accounting, tax return preparation software, taxation, or ethics) and complies with the requirements in paragraph (a)(2)of this section before a program number is issued. *Update programs.* Update programs may use the same number as the program subject to update. An update program is a program that instructs on a change of existing law occurring within one year of the update program offering. The qualifying education program subject to update must have been offered within the two year time period prior to the change in existing law.

(ii) *Change in existing law.* A change in existing law means the effective date of the statute or regulation, or date of entry of judicial decision, that is the subject of the update.

(b) *Failure to comply.* Compliance by a continuing education provider with the requirements of this part is determined by the Internal Revenue Service. A continuing education provider who fails to meet the requirements of this part will be notified by the Internal Revenue Service. The notice will state the basis for the determination of noncompliance and will provide the continuing education provider an opportunity to furnish the requested information in writing relating to the matter within 60 days of the date of the notice. The continuing education provider may, within 30 days after receipt of the notice of denial, file a written protest as prescribed by the Internal Revenue Service in forms, instructions, or other appropriate guidance. A protest under this section is not governed by subpart D of this part.

(c) *Effective/applicability date.* This section is applicable beginning August 2, 2011.

Subpart B — Duties and Restrictions Relating to Practice Before the Internal Revenue Service

§ 10.20 Information to be furnished.

(a) *To the Internal Revenue Service.*

(1) A practitioner must, on a proper and lawful request by a duly authorized officer or employee of the Internal Revenue Service, promptly submit records or information in any matter before the Internal Revenue Service unless the practitioner believes in good faith and on reasonable grounds that the records or information are privileged.

(2) Where the requested records or information are not in the possession of, or subject to the control of, the practitioner or the practitioner's client, the practitioner must promptly notify the requesting Internal Revenue Service officer or employee and the practitioner must provide any information that the practitioner has regarding the identity of any person who the practitioner believes may have possession or control of the requested records or information. The practitioner must make reasonable inquiry of his or her client regarding the identity of any person who may have possession or control of the requested records or information, but the practitioner is not required to make inquiry of any other person or independently verify any information provided by the practitioner's client regarding the identity of such persons.

(3) When a proper and lawful request is made by a duly authorized officer or employee of the Internal Revenue Service, concerning an inquiry into an alleged violation of the regulations in this part, a practitioner must provide any information the practitioner has concerning the alleged violation and testify regarding this information in any proceeding instituted under this part, unless the practitioner believes in good faith and on reasonable grounds that the information is privileged.

(b) *Interference with a proper and lawful request for records or information.* A practitioner may not interfere, or attempt to interfere, with any proper and lawful effort by the Internal Revenue Service, its officers or employees, to obtain any record or information unless the practitioner believes in good faith and on reasonable grounds that the record or information is privileged.

(c) *Effective/applicability date.* This section is applicable beginning August 2, 2011.

§ 10.21 Knowledge of client's omission.

A practitioner who, having been retained by a client with respect to a matter administered by the Internal Revenue Service, knows that the client has not complied with the revenue laws of the United States or has made an error in or omission from any return, document, affidavit, or other paper which the client submitted or executed under the revenue laws of the United States, must advise the client promptly of the fact of such noncompliance, error, or omission. The practitioner must advise the client of the consequences as provided under the Code and regulations of such noncompliance, error, or omission.

§ 10.22 Diligence as to accuracy.

(a) *In general.* A practitioner must exercise due diligence—

(1) In preparing or assisting in the preparation of, approving, and filing tax returns, documents, affidavits, and other papers relating to Internal Revenue Service matters;

(2) In determining the correctness of oral or written representations made by the practitioner to the Department of the Treasury; and

(3) In determining the correctness of oral or written representations made by the practitioner to clients with reference to any matter administered by the Internal Revenue Service.

(b) *Reliance on others.* Except as modified by §§10.34 and 10.37, a practitioner will be presumed to have exercised due diligence for purposes of this section if the practitioner relies on the work product of another person and the practitioner used reasonable care in engaging, supervising, training, and evaluating the person, taking proper account of the nature of the relationship between the practitioner and the person.

(c) *Effective/applicability date.* Paragraph (a) of this section is applicable on September 26, 2007. Paragraph (b) of this section is applicable beginning June 12, 2014.

§ 10.23 Prompt disposition of pending matters.

A practitioner may not unreasonably delay the prompt disposition of any matter before the Internal Revenue Service.

§ 10.24 Assistance from or to disbarred or suspended persons and former Internal Revenue Service employees.

A practitioner may not, knowingly and directly or indirectly:

(a) Accept assistance from or assist any person who is under disbarment or suspension from practice before the Internal Revenue Service if the assistance relates to a matter or matters constituting practice before the Internal Revenue Service.

(b) Accept assistance from any former government employee where the provisions of § 10.25 or any Federal law would be violated.

§10.25 Practice by former government employees, their partners and their associates.

(a) *Definitions.* For purposes of this section —

(1) *Assist* means to act in such a way as to advise, furnish information to, or otherwise aid another person, directly, or indirectly.

(2) *Government employee* is an officer or employee of the United States or any agency of the United States, including a special Government employee as defined in *18 U.S.C. 202(a)*, or of the District of Columbia, or of any State, or a member of Congress or of any State legislature.

(3) *Member of a firm* is a sole practitioner or an employee or associate thereof, or a partner, stockholder, associate, affiliate or employee of a partnership, joint venture, corporation, professional association or other affiliation of two or more practitioners who represent nongovernmental parties.

(4) *Particular matter involving specific parties* is defined at 5 CFR 2637.201(c), or superseding post-employment regulations issued by the U.S. Office of Government Ethics.

(5) *Rule* includes Treasury regulations, whether issued or under preparation for issuance as notices of proposed rulemaking or as Treasury decisions, revenue rulings, and revenue procedures published in the Internal Revenue Bulletin (see *26 CFR 601.601(d)(2)(ii)(b)*).

(b) *General rules* —

(1) No former Government employee may, subsequent to Government employment, represent anyone in any matter administered by the Internal Revenue Service if the representation would violate *18 U.S.C. 207* or any other laws of the United States.

(2) No former Government employee who personally and substantially participated in a particular matter involving specific parties may, subsequent to Government employment, represent or knowingly assist, in that particular matter, any person who is or was a specific party to that particular matter.

(3) A former Government employee who within a period of one year prior to the termination of Government employment had official responsibility for a particular matter involving specific parties may not, within two years after Government employment is ended, represent in that particular matter any person who is or was a specific party to that particular matter.

(4) No former Government employee may, within one year after Government employment is ended, communicate with or appear before, with the intent to influence, any employee of the Treasury Department in connection with the publication, withdrawal, amendment, modification, or interpretation of a rule the development of which the former Government employee participated in, or for which, within a period of one year prior to the termination of Government employment, the former government employee had official responsibility. This paragraph (b)(4) does not, however, preclude any former employee from appearing on one's own behalf or from representing a taxpayer before the Internal Revenue Service in connection with a particular matter involving specific parties involving the application or interpretation of a rule with respect to that particular matter, provided that the representation is otherwise consistent with the other provisions of this section and the former employee does not utilize or disclose any confidential information acquired by the former employee in the development of the rule.

(c) *Firm representation* —

(1) No member of a firm of which a former Government employee is a member may represent or knowingly assist a person who was or is a specific party in any particular matter with respect to which the restrictions of paragraph (b)(2) of this section apply to the former Government employee, in that

particular matter, unless the firm isolates the former Government employee in such a way to ensure that the former Government employee cannot assist in the representation.

(2) When isolation of a former Government employee is required under paragraph (c)(1) of this section, a statement affirming the fact of such isolation must be executed under oath by the former Government employee and by another member of the firm acting on behalf of the firm. The statement must clearly identify the firm, the former Government employee, and the particular matter(s) requiring isolation. The statement must be retained by the firm and, upon request, provided to the office(s) of the Internal Revenue Service administering or enforcing this part.

(d) *Pending representation.* The provisions of this regulation will govern practice by former Government employees, their partners and associates with respect to representation in particular matters involving specific parties where actual representation commenced before the effective date of this regulation.

(e) *Effective/applicability date.* This section is applicable beginning August 2, 2011.

§ 10.26 Notaries.

A practitioner may not take acknowledgments, administer oaths, certify papers, or perform any official act as a notary public with respect to any matter administered by the Internal Revenue Service and for which he or she is employed as counsel, attorney, or agent, or in which he or she may be in any way interested.

§ 10.27 Fees.

(a) *In general.* A practitioner may not charge an unconscionable fee in connection with any matter before the Internal Revenue Service.

(b) *Contingent fees* —

(1) Except as provided in paragraphs (b)(2), (3), and (4) of this section, a practitioner may not charge a contingent fee for services rendered in connection with any matter before the Internal Revenue Service.

(2) A practitioner may charge a contingent fee for services rendered in connection with the Service's examination of, or challenge to —

(i) An original tax return; or

(ii) An amended return or claim for refund or credit where the amended return or claim for refund or credit was filed within 120 days of the taxpayer receiving a written notice of the examination of, or a written challenge to the original tax return.

(3) A practitioner may charge a contingent fee for services rendered in connection with a claim for credit or refund filed solely in connection with the determination of statutory interest or penalties assessed by the Internal Revenue Service.

(4) A practitioner may charge a contingent fee for services rendered in connection with any judicial proceeding arising under the Internal Revenue Code.

(c) *Definitions.* For purposes of this section —

(1) *Contingent fee* is any fee that is based, in whole or in part, on whether or not a position taken on a tax return or other filing avoids challenge by the Internal Revenue Service or is sustained either by the Internal Revenue Service or in litigation. A contingent fee includes a fee that is based on a percentage of the refund reported on a return, that is based on a percentage of the taxes saved, or that otherwise

depends on the specific result attained. A contingent fee also includes any fee arrangement in which the practitioner will reimburse the client for all or a portion of the client's fee in the event that a position taken on a tax return or other filing is challenged by the Internal Revenue Service or is not sustained, whether pursuant to an indemnity agreement, a guarantee, rescission rights, or any other arrangement with a similar effect.

(2) *Matter before the Internal Revenue Service* includes tax planning and advice, preparing or filing or assisting in preparing or filing returns or claims for refund or credit, and all matters connected with a presentation to the Internal Revenue Service or any of its officers or employees relating to a taxpayer's rights, privileges, or liabilities under laws or regulations administered by the Internal Revenue Service. Such presentations include, but are not limited to, preparing and filing documents, corresponding and communicating with the Internal Revenue Service, rendering written advice with respect to any entity, transaction, plan or arrangement, and representing a client at conferences, hearings, and meetings.

(d) *Effective/applicability date.* This section is applicable for fee arrangements entered into after March 26, 2008.

§ 10.28 Return of client's records.

(a) In general, a practitioner must, at the request of a client, promptly return any and all records of the client that are necessary for the client to comply with his or her Federal tax obligations. The practitioner may retain copies of the records returned to a client. The existence of a dispute over fees generally does not relieve the practitioner of his or her responsibility under this section. Nevertheless, if applicable state law allows or permits the retention of a client's records by a practitioner in the case of a dispute over fees for services rendered, the practitioner need only return those records that must be attached to the taxpayer's return. The practitioner, however, must provide the client with reasonable access to review and copy any additional records of the client retained by the practitioner under state law that are necessary for the client to comply with his or her Federal tax obligations.

(b) For purposes of this section — Records of the client include all documents or written or electronic materials provided to the practitioner, or obtained by the practitioner in the course of the practitioner's representation of the client, that preexisted the retention of the practitioner by the client. The term also includes materials that were prepared by the client or a third party (not including an employee or agent of the practitioner) at any time and provided to the practitioner with respect to the subject matter of the representation. The term also includes any return, claim for refund, schedule, affidavit, appraisal or any other document prepared by the practitioner, or his or her employee or agent, that was presented to the client with respect to a prior representation if such document is necessary for the taxpayer to comply with his or her current Federal tax obligations. The term does not include any return, claim for refund, schedule, affidavit, appraisal or any other document prepared by the practitioner or the practitioner's firm, employees or agents if the practitioner is withholding such document pending the client's performance of its contractual obligation to pay fees with respect to such document.

§ 10.29 Conflicting interests.

(a) Except as provided by paragraph (b) of this section, a practitioner shall not represent a client before the Internal Revenue Service if the representation involves a conflict of interest. A conflict of interest exists if—

(1) The representation of one client will be directly adverse to another client; or

(2) There is a significant risk that the representation of one or more clients will be materially limited by

the practitioner's responsibilities to another client, a former client or a third person, or by a personal interest of the practitioner.

(b) Notwithstanding the existence of a conflict of interest under paragraph (a) of this section, the practitioner may represent a client if—

(1) The practitioner reasonably believes that the practitioner will be able to provide competent and diligent representation to each affected client;

(2) The representation is not prohibited by law; and

(3) Each affected client waives the conflict of interest and gives informed consent, confirmed in writing by each affected client, at the time the existence of the conflict of interest is known by the practitioner. The confirmation may be made within a reasonable period of time after the informed consent, but in no event later than 30 days.

(c) Copies of the written consents must be retained by the practitioner for at least 36 months from the date of the conclusion of the representation of the affected clients, and the written consents must be provided to any officer or employee of the Internal Revenue Service on request.

(d) *Effective/applicability date.* This section is applicable on September 26, 2007.

§ 10.30 Solicitation.

(a) *Advertising and solicitation restrictions.*

(1) A practitioner may not, with respect to any Internal Revenue Service matter, in any way use or participate in the use of any form of public communication or private solicitation containing a false, fraudulent, or coercive statement or claim; or a misleading or deceptive statement or claim. Enrolled agents, enrolled retirement plan agents, or registered tax return preparers, in describing their professional designation, may not utilize the term "certified" or imply an employer/employee relationship with the Internal Revenue Service. Examples of acceptable descriptions for enrolled agents are "enrolled to represent taxpayers before the Internal Revenue Service," "enrolled to practice before the Internal Revenue Service," and "admitted to practice before the Internal Revenue Service." Similarly, examples of acceptable descriptions for enrolled retirement plan agents are "enrolled to represent taxpayers before the Internal Revenue Service as a retirement plan agent" and "enrolled to practice before the Internal Revenue Service as a retirement plan agent." An example of an acceptable description for registered tax return preparers is "designated as a registered tax return preparer by the Internal Revenue Service."

(2) A practitioner may not make, directly or indirectly, an uninvited written or oral solicitation of employment in matters related to the Internal Revenue Service if the solicitation violates Federal or State law or other applicable rule, e.g., attorneys are precluded from making a solicitation that is prohibited by conduct rules applicable to all attorneys in their State(s) of licensure. Any lawful solicitation made by or on behalf of a practitioner eligible to practice before the Internal Revenue Service must, nevertheless, clearly identify the solicitation as such and, if applicable, identify the source of the information used in choosing the recipient.

(b) *Fee information.*

(1)(i) A practitioner may publish the availability of a written schedule of fees and disseminate the following fee information—

(A) Fixed fees for specific routine services.

(B) Hourly rates.

(C) Range of fees for particular services.

(D) Fee charged for an initial consultation.

(ii) Any statement of fee information concerning matters in which costs may be incurred must include a statement disclosing whether clients will be responsible for such costs.

(2) A practitioner may charge no more than the rate(s) published under paragraph (b)(1) of this section for at least 30 calendar days after the last date on which the schedule of fees was published.

(c) *Communication of fee information.* Fee information may be communicated in professional lists, telephone directories, print media, mailings, and electronic mail, facsimile, hand delivered flyers, radio, television, and any other method. The method chosen, however, must not cause the communication to become untruthful, deceptive, or otherwise in violation of this part. A practitioner may not persist in attempting to contact a prospective client if the prospective client has made it known to the practitioner that he or she does not desire to be solicited. In the case of radio and television broadcasting, the broadcast must be recorded and the practitioner must retain a recording of the actual transmission. In the case of direct mail and e-commerce communications, the practitioner must retain a copy of the actual communication, along with a list or other description of persons to whom the communication was mailed or otherwise distributed. The copy must be retained by the practitioner for a period of at least 36 months from the date of the last transmission or use.

(d) *Improper associations.* A practitioner may not, in matters related to the Internal Revenue Service, assist, or accept assistance from, any person or entity who, to the knowledge of the practitioner, obtains clients or otherwise practices in a manner forbidden under this section.

(e) *Effective/applicability date.* This section is applicable beginning August 2, 2011.

(Approved by the Office of Management and Budget under Control No. 1545-1726)

§ 10.31 Negotiation of taxpayer checks.

(a) A practitioner may not endorse or otherwise negotiate any check (including directing or accepting payment by any means, electronic or otherwise, into an account owned or controlled by the practitioner or any firm or other entity with whom the practitioner is associated) issued to a client by the government in respect of a Federal tax liability.

(b) *Effective/applicability date.* This section is applicable beginning June 12, 2014.

§ 10.32 Practice of law.

Nothing in the regulations in this part may be construed as authorizing persons not members of the bar to practice law.

§ 10.33 Best practices for tax advisors.

(a) *Best practices.* Tax advisors should provide clients with the highest quality representation concerning Federal tax issues by adhering to best practices in providing advice and in preparing or assisting in the preparation of a submission to the Internal Revenue Service. In addition to compliance with the standards of practice provided elsewhere in this part, best practices include the following:

(1) Communicating clearly with the client regarding the terms of the engagement. For example, the advisor should determine the client's expected purpose for and use of the advice and should have a clear understanding with the client regarding the form and scope of the advice or assistance to be

rendered.

(2) Establishing the facts, determining which facts are relevant, evaluating the reasonableness of any assumptions or representations, relating the applicable law (including potentially applicable judicial doctrines) to the relevant facts, and arriving at a conclusion supported by the law and the facts.

(3) Advising the client regarding the import of the conclusions reached, including, for example, whether a taxpayer may avoid accuracy-related penalties under the Internal Revenue Code if a taxpayer acts in reliance on the advice.

(4) Acting fairly and with integrity in practice before the Internal Revenue Service.

(b) *Procedures to ensure best practices for tax advisors.* Tax advisors with responsibility for overseeing a firm's practice of providing advice concerning Federal tax issues or of preparing or assisting in the preparation of submissions to the Internal Revenue Service should take reasonable steps to ensure that the firm's procedures for all members, associates, and employees are consistent with the best practices set forth in paragraph (a) of this section.

(c) *Applicability date.* This section is effective after June 20, 2005.

§ 10.34 Standards with respect to tax returns and documents, affidavits and other papers.

(a) *Tax returns.*

(1) A practitioner may not willfully, recklessly, or through gross incompetence —

(i) Sign a tax return or claim for refund that the practitioner knows or reasonably should know contains a position that —

(A) Lacks a reasonable basis;

(B) Is an unreasonable position as described in section 6694(a)(2) of the Internal Revenue Code (Code) (including the related regulations and other published guidance); or

(C) Is a willful attempt by the practitioner to understate the liability for tax or a reckless or intentional disregard of rules or regulations by the practitioner as described in section 6694(b)(2) of the Code (including the related regulations and other published guidance).

(ii) Advise a client to take a position on a tax return or claim for refund, or prepare a portion of a tax return or claim for refund containing a position, that —

(A) Lacks a reasonable basis;

(B) Is an unreasonable position as described in section 6694(a)(2) of the Code (including the related regulations and other published guidance); or

(C) Is a willful attempt by the practitioner to understate the liability for tax or a reckless or intentional disregard of rules or regulations by the practitioner as described in section 6694(b)(2) of the Code (including the related regulations and other published guidance).

(2) A pattern of conduct is a factor that will be taken into account in determining whether a practitioner acted willfully, recklessly, or through gross incompetence.

(b) *Documents, affidavits and other papers* —

(1) A practitioner may not advise a client to take a position on a document, affidavit or other paper submitted to the Internal Revenue Service unless the position is not frivolous.

(2) A practitioner may not advise a client to submit a document, affidavit or other paper to the Internal Revenue Service —

(i) The purpose of which is to delay or impede the administration of the Federal tax laws;

(ii) That is frivolous; or

(iii) That contains or omits information in a manner that demonstrates an intentional disregard of a rule or regulation unless the practitioner also advises the client to submit a document that evidences a good faith challenge to the rule or regulation.

(c) *Advising clients on potential penalties* —

(1) A practitioner must inform a client of any penalties that are reasonably likely to apply to the client with respect to —

(i) A position taken on a tax return if —

(A) The practitioner advised the client with respect to the position; or

(B) The practitioner prepared or signed the tax return; and

(ii) Any document, affidavit or other paper submitted to the Internal Revenue Service.

(2) The practitioner also must inform the client of any opportunity to avoid any such penalties by disclosure, if relevant, and of the requirements for adequate disclosure.

(3) This paragraph (c) applies even if the practitioner is not subject to a penalty under the Internal Revenue Code with respect to the position or with respect to the document, affidavit or other paper submitted.

(d) *Relying on information furnished by clients.* A practitioner advising a client to take a position on a tax return, document, affidavit or other paper submitted to the Internal Revenue Service, or preparing or signing a tax return as a preparer, generally may rely in good faith without verification upon information furnished by the client. The practitioner may not, however, ignore the implications of information furnished to, or actually known by, the practitioner, and must make reasonable inquiries if the information as furnished appears to be incorrect, inconsistent with an important fact or another factual assumption, or incomplete.

(e) *Effective/applicability date.* Paragraph (a) of this section is applicable for returns or claims for refund filed, or advice provided, beginning August 2, 2011. Paragraphs (b) through (d) of this section are applicable to tax returns, documents, affidavits, and other papers filed on or after September 26, 2007.

§ 10.35 Competence.

(a) A practitioner must possess the necessary competence to engage in practice before the Internal Revenue Service. Competent practice requires the appropriate level of knowledge, skill, thoroughness, and preparation necessary for the matter for which the practitioner is engaged. A practitioner may become competent for the matter for which the practitioner has been engaged through various methods, such as consulting with experts in the relevant area or studying the relevant law.

(b) *Effective/applicability date.* This section is applicable beginning June 12, 2014.

§ 10.36 Procedures to ensure compliance.

(a) Any individual subject to the provisions of this part who has (or individuals who have or share) principal authority and responsibility for overseeing a firm's practice governed by this part, including the provision of advice concerning Federal tax matters and preparation of tax returns, claims for refund, or other documents for submission to the Internal Revenue Service, must take reasonable steps to ensure that the firm has adequate procedures in effect for all members, associates, and employees for purposes of complying with subparts A, B, and C of this part, as applicable. In the absence of a person or persons identified by the firm as having the principal authority and responsibility described in this paragraph, the Internal Revenue Service may identify one or more individuals subject to the provisions of this part responsible for compliance with the requirements of this section.

(b) Any such individual who has (or such individuals who have or share) principal authority as described in paragraph (a) of this section will be subject to discipline for failing to comply with the requirements of this section if—

(1) The individual through willfulness, recklessness, or gross incompetence does not take reasonable steps to ensure that the firm has adequate procedures to comply with this part, as applicable, and one or more individuals who are members of, associated with, or employed by, the firm are, or have, engaged in a pattern or practice, in connection with their practice with the firm, of failing to comply with this part, as applicable;

(2) The individual through willfulness, recklessness, or gross incompetence does not take reasonable steps to ensure that firm procedures in effect are properly followed, and one or more individuals who are members of, associated with, or employed by, the firm are, or have, engaged in a pattern or practice, in connection with their practice with the firm, of failing to comply with this part, as applicable; or

(3) The individual knows or should know that one or more individuals who are members of, associated with, or employed by, the firm are, or have, engaged in a pattern or practice, in connection with their practice with the firm, that does not comply with this part, as applicable, and the individual, through willfulness, recklessness, or gross incompetence fails to take prompt action to correct the noncompliance.

(c) *Effective/applicability date.* This section is applicable beginning June 12, 2014.

§ 10.37 Requirements for written advice.

(a) *Requirements.*

(1) A practitioner may give written advice (including by means of electronic communication) concerning one or more Federal tax matters subject to the requirements in paragraph (a)(2) of this section. Government submissions on matters of general policy are not considered written advice on a Federal tax matter for purposes of this section. Continuing education presentations provided to an audience solely for the purpose of enhancing practitioners' professional knowledge on Federal tax matters are not considered written advice on a Federal tax matter for purposes of this section. The preceding sentence does not apply to presentations marketing or promoting transactions.

(2) The practitioner must—

(i) Base the written advice on reasonable factual and legal assumptions (including assumptions as to future events);

(ii) Reasonably consider all relevant facts and circumstances that the practitioner knows or reasonably should know;

(iii) Use reasonable efforts to identify and ascertain the facts relevant to written advice on each Federal tax matter;

(iv) Not rely upon representations, statements, findings, or agreements (including projections, financial forecasts, or appraisals) of the taxpayer or any other person if reliance on them would be unreasonable

(v) Relate applicable law and authorities to facts; and

(vi) Not, in evaluating a Federal tax matter, take into account the possibility that a tax return will not be audited or that a matter will not be raised on audit.

(3) Reliance on representations, statements, findings, or agreements is unreasonable if the practitioner knows or reasonably should know that one or more representations or assumptions on which any representation is based are incorrect, incomplete, or inconsistent.

(b) *Reliance on advice of others.* A practitioner may only rely on the advice of another person if the advice was reasonable and the reliance is in good faith considering all the facts and circumstances. Reliance is not reasonable when—

(1) The practitioner knows or reasonably should know that the opinion of the other person should not be relied on;

(2) The practitioner knows or reasonably should know that the other person is not competent or lacks the necessary qualifications to provide the advice; or

(3) The practitioner knows or reasonably should know that the other person has a conflict of interest in violation of the rules described in this part.

(c) *Standard of review.*

(1) In evaluating whether a practitioner giving written advice concerning one or more Federal tax matters complied with the requirements of this section, the Commissioner, or delegate, will apply a reasonable practitioner standard, considering all facts and circumstances, including, but not limited to, the scope of the engagement and the type and specificity of the advice sought by the client.

(2) In the case of an opinion the practitioner knows or has reason to know will be used or referred to by a person other than the practitioner (or a person who is a member of, associated with, or employed by the practitioner's firm) in promoting, marketing, or recommending to one or more taxpayers a partnership or other entity, investment plan or arrangement a significant purpose of which is the avoidance or evasion of any tax imposed by the Internal Revenue Code, the Commissioner, or delegate, will apply a reasonable practitioner standard, considering all facts and circumstances, with emphasis given to the additional risk caused by the practitioner's lack of knowledge of the taxpayer's particular circumstances, when determining whether a practitioner has failed to comply with this section.

(d) *Federal tax matter.* A Federal tax matter, as used in this section, is any matter concerning the application or interpretation of---

(1) A revenue provision as defined in section 6110(i)(1)(B) of the Internal Revenue Code;

(2) Any provision of law impacting a person's obligations under the internal revenue laws and regulations, including but not limited to the person's liability to pay tax or obligation to file returns; or

(3) Any other law or regulation administered by the Internal Revenue Service.

(e) *Effective/applicability date.* This section is applicable to written advice rendered after June 12, 2014.

§ 10.38 Establishment of advisory committees.

(a) *Advisory committees.* To promote and maintain the public's confidence in tax advisors, the Internal Revenue Service is authorized to establish one or more advisory committees composed of at least six individuals authorized to practice before the Internal Revenue Service. Membership of an advisory committee must be balanced among those who practice as attorneys, accountants, enrolled agents, enrolled actuaries, enrolled retirement plan agents, and registered tax return preparers. Under procedures prescribed by the Internal Revenue Service, an advisory committee may review and make general recommendations regarding the practices, procedures, and policies of the offices described in §10.1.

(b) *Effective date.* This section is applicable beginning August 2, 2011.

Subpart C — Sanctions for Violation of the Regulations

§ 10.50 Sanctions.

(a) *Authority to censure, suspend, or disbar.* The Secretary of the Treasury, or delegate, after notice and an opportunity for a proceeding, may censure, suspend, or disbar any practitioner from practice before the Internal Revenue Service if the practitioner is shown to be incompetent or disreputable (within the meaning of §10.51), fails to comply with any regulation in this part (under the prohibited conduct standards of §10.52), or with intent to defraud, willfully and knowingly misleads or threatens a client or prospective client. Censure is a public reprimand.

(b) *Authority to disqualify.* The Secretary of the Treasury, or delegate, after due notice and opportunity for hearing, may disqualify any appraiser for a violation of these rules as applicable to appraisers.

(1) If any appraiser is disqualified pursuant to this subpart C, the appraiser is barred from presenting evidence or testimony in any administrative proceeding before the Department of Treasury or the Internal Revenue Service, unless and until authorized to do so by the Internal Revenue Service pursuant to §10.81, regardless of whether the evidence or testimony would pertain to an appraisal made prior to or after the effective date of disqualification.

(2) Any appraisal made by a disqualified appraiser after the effective date of disqualification will not have any probative effect in any administrative proceeding before the Department of the Treasury or the Internal Revenue Service. An appraisal otherwise barred from admission into evidence pursuant to this section may be admitted into evidence solely for the purpose of determining the taxpayer's reliance in good faith on such appraisal.

(c) *Authority to impose monetary penalty —*

(1) *In general.*

(i) The Secretary of the Treasury, or delegate, after notice and an opportunity for a proceeding, may impose a monetary penalty on any practitioner who engages in conduct subject to sanction under paragraph (a) of this section.

(ii) If the practitioner described in paragraph (c)(1)(i) of this section was acting on behalf of an employer or any firm or other entity in connection with the conduct giving rise to the penalty, the Secretary of the Treasury, or delegate, may impose a monetary penalty on the employer, firm, or entity if it knew, or reasonably should have known of such conduct.

(2) *Amount of penalty.* The amount of the penalty shall not exceed the gross income derived (or to be derived) from the conduct giving rise to the penalty.

(3) *Coordination with other sanctions.* Subject to paragraph (c)(2) of this section —

(i) Any monetary penalty imposed on a practitioner under this paragraph (c) may be in addition to or in lieu of any suspension, disbarment or censure and may be in addition to a penalty imposed on an employer, firm or other entity under paragraph (c)(1)(ii) of this section.

(ii) Any monetary penalty imposed on an employer, firm or other entity may be in addition to or in lieu of penalties imposed under paragraph (c) (1)(i) of this section.

(d) *Authority to accept a practitioner's consent to sanction.* The Internal Revenue Service may accept a practitioner's offer of consent to be sanctioned under §10.50 in lieu of instituting or continuing a proceeding under §10.60(a).

(e) *Sanctions to be imposed.* The sanctions imposed by this section shall take into account all relevant facts and circumstances.

(f) *Effective/applicability date.* This section is applicable to conduct occurring on or after August 2, 2011, except that paragraphs (a), (b)(2), and (e) apply to conduct occurring on or after September 26, 2007, and paragraph (c) applies to prohibited conduct that occurs after October 22, 2004.

§ 10.51 Incompetence and disreputable conduct.

(a) *Incompetence and disreputable conduct.* Incompetence and disreputable conduct for which a practitioner may be sanctioned under §10.50 includes, but is not limited to

(1) Conviction of any criminal offense under the Federal tax laws.

(2) Conviction of any criminal offense involving dishonesty or breach of trust.

(3) Conviction of any felony under Federal or State law for which the conduct involved renders the practitioner unfit to practice before the Internal Revenue Service.

(4) Giving false or misleading information, or participating in any way in the giving of false or misleading information to the Department of the Treasury or any officer or employee thereof, or to any tribunal authorized to pass upon Federal tax matters, in connection with any matter pending or likely to be pending before them, knowing the information to be false or misleading. Facts or other matters contained in testimony, Federal tax returns, financial statements, applications for enrollment, affidavits, declarations, and any other document or statement, written or oral, are included in the term "information."

(5) Solicitation of employment as prohibited under §10.30, the use of false or misleading representations with intent to deceive a client or prospective client in order to procure employment, or intimating that the practitioner is able improperly to obtain special consideration or action from the Internal Revenue Service or any officer or employee thereof.

(6) Willfully failing to make a Federal tax return in violation of the Federal tax laws, or willfully evading, attempting to evade, or participating in any way in evading or attempting to evade any assessment or payment of any Federal tax.

(7) Willfully assisting, counseling, encouraging a client or prospective client in violating, or suggesting to a client or prospective client to violate, any Federal tax law, or knowingly counseling or suggesting to a client or prospective client an illegal plan to evade Federal taxes or payment thereof.

(8) Misappropriation of, or failure properly or promptly to remit, funds received from a client for the purpose of payment of taxes or other obligations due the United States.

(9) Directly or indirectly attempting to influence, or offering or agreeing to attempt to influence, the official action of any officer or employee of the Internal Revenue Service by the use of threats, false accusations, duress or coercion, by the offer of any special inducement or promise of an advantage or by the bestowing of any gift, favor or thing of value.

(10) Disbarment or suspension from practice as an attorney, certified public accountant, public accountant, or actuary by any duly constituted authority of any State, territory, or possession of the United States, including a Commonwealth, or the District of Columbia, any Federal court of record or any Federal agency, body or board.

(11) Knowingly aiding and abetting another person to practice before the Internal Revenue Service during a period of suspension, disbarment or ineligibility of such other person.

(12) Contemptuous conduct in connection with practice before the Internal Revenue Service, including the use of abusive language, making false accusations or statements, knowing them to be false, or circulating or publishing malicious or libelous matter.

(13) Giving a false opinion, knowingly, recklessly, or through gross incompetence, including an opinion which is intentionally or recklessly misleading, or engaging in a pattern of providing incompetent opinions on questions arising under the Federal tax laws. False opinions described in this paragraph (a)(13) include those which reflect or result from a knowing misstatement of fact or law, from an assertion of a position known to be unwarranted under existing law, from counseling or assisting in conduct known to be illegal or fraudulent, from concealing matters required by law to be revealed, or from consciously disregarding information indicating that material facts expressed in the opinion or offering material are false or misleading. For purposes of this paragraph (a)(13), reckless conduct is a highly unreasonable omission or misrepresentation involving an extreme departure from the standards of ordinary care that a practitioner should observe under the circumstances. A pattern of conduct is a factor that will be taken into account in determining whether a practitioner acted knowingly, recklessly, or through gross incompetence. Gross incompetence includes conduct that reflects gross indifference, preparation which is grossly inadequate under the circumstances, and a consistent failure to perform obligations to the client.

(14) Willfully failing to sign a tax return prepared by the practitioner when the practitioner's signature is required by Federal tax laws unless the failure is due to reasonable cause and not due to willful neglect.

(15) Willfully disclosing or otherwise using a tax return or tax return information in a manner not authorized by the Internal Revenue Code, contrary to the order of a court of competent jurisdiction, or contrary to the order of an administrative law judge in a proceeding instituted under §10.60.

(16) Willfully failing to file on magnetic or other electronic media a tax return prepared by the practitioner when the practitioner is required to do so by the Federal tax laws unless the failure is due to reasonable cause and not due to willful neglect.

(17) Willfully preparing all or substantially all of, or signing, a tax return or claim for refund when the practitioner does not possess a current or otherwise valid preparer tax identification number or other prescribed identifying number.

(18) Willfully representing a taxpayer before an officer or employee of the Internal Revenue Service unless the practitioner is authorized to do so pursuant to this part.

(b) *Effective/applicability date.* This section is applicable beginning August 2, 2011.

§ 10.52 Violations subject to sanction.

(a) A practitioner may be sanctioned under §10.50 if the practitioner —

(1) Willfully violates any of the regulations (other than §10.33) contained in this part; or

(2) Recklessly or through gross incompetence (within the meaning of §10.51(a)(13)) violates §§ 10.34, 10.35, 10.36 or 10.37.

(b) *Effective/applicability date.* This section is applicable to conduct occurring on or after September 26, 2007.

§10.53 Receipt of information concerning practitioner.

(a) *Officer or employee of the Internal Revenue Service.* If an officer or employee of the Internal Revenue Service has reason to believe a practitioner has violated any provision of this part, the officer or employee will promptly make a written report of the suspected violation. The report will explain the facts and reasons upon which the officer's or employee's belief rests and must be submitted to the office(s) of the Internal Revenue Service responsible for administering or enforcing this part.

(b) *Other persons.* Any person other than an officer or employee of the Internal Revenue Service having information of a violation of any provision of this part may make an oral or written report of the alleged violation to the office(s) of the Internal Revenue Service responsible for administering or enforcing this part or any officer or employee of the Internal Revenue Service. If the report is made to an officer or employee of the Internal Revenue Service, the officer or employee will make a written report of the suspected violation and submit the report to the office(s) of the Internal Revenue Service responsible for administering or enforcing this part.

(c) *Destruction of report.* No report made under paragraph (a) or (b) of this section shall be maintained unless retention of the report is permissible under the applicable records control schedule as approved by the National Archives and Records Administration and designated in the Internal Revenue Manual. Reports must be destroyed as soon as permissible under the applicable records control schedule.

(d) *Effect on proceedings under subpart D.* The destruction of any report will not bar any proceeding under subpart D of this part, but will preclude the use of a copy of the report in a proceeding under subpart D of this part.

(e) *Effective/applicability date.* This section is applicable beginning August 2, 2011

Subpart D — Rules Applicable to Disciplinary Proceedings

§ 10.60 Institution of proceeding.

(a) Whenever it is determined that a practitioner (or employer, firm or other entity, if applicable) violated any provision of the laws governing practice before the Internal Revenue Service or the regulations in this part, the practitioner may be reprimanded or, in accordance with §10.62, subject to a proceeding for sanctions described in §10.50.

(b) Whenever a penalty has been assessed against an appraiser under the Internal Revenue Code and an appropriate officer or employee in an office established to enforce this part determines that the appraiser acted willfully, recklessly, or through gross incompetence with respect to the proscribed conduct, the appraiser may be reprimanded or, in accordance with §10.62, subject to a proceeding for disqualification. A proceeding for disqualification of an appraiser is instituted by the filing of a complaint, the contents of which are more fully described in §10.62.

(c) Except as provided in §10.82, a proceeding will not be instituted under this section unless the proposed respondent previously has been advised in writing of the law, facts and conduct warranting such action and has been accorded an opportunity to dispute facts, assert additional facts, and make arguments (including an explanation or description of mitigating circumstances).

(d) *Effective/applicability date.* This section is applicable beginning August 2, 2011.

§ 10.61 Conferences.

(a) *In general.* The Commissioner, or delegate, may confer with a practitioner, employer, firm or other entity, or an appraiser concerning allegations of misconduct irrespective of whether a proceeding has been instituted. If the conference results in a stipulation in connection with an ongoing proceeding in which the practitioner, employer, firm or other entity, or appraiser is the respondent, the stipulation may be entered in the record by either party to the proceeding.

(b) *Voluntary sanction* —

(1) *In general.* In lieu of a proceeding being instituted or continued under §10.60(a), a practitioner or appraiser (or employer, firm or other entity, if applicable) may offer a consent to be sanctioned under §10.50.

(2) *Discretion; acceptance or declination.* The Commissioner, or delegate, may accept or decline the offer described in paragraph (b)(1) of this section. When the decision is to decline the offer, the written notice of declination may state that the offer described in paragraph (b)(1) of this section would be accepted if it contained different terms. The Commissioner, or delegate, has the discretion to accept or reject a revised offer submitted in response to the declination or may counteroffer and act upon any accepted counteroffer.

(c) *Effective/applicability date.* This section is applicable beginning August 2, 2011.

§ 10.62 Contents of complaint.

(a) *Charges.* A complaint must name the respondent, provide a clear and concise description of the facts and law that constitute the basis for the proceeding, and be signed by an authorized representative of the Internal Revenue Service under §10.69(a)(1). A complaint is sufficient if it fairly informs the respondent of the charges brought so that the respondent is able to prepare a defense.

(b) *Specification of sanction.* The complaint must specify the sanction sought against the practitioner or appraiser. If the sanction sought is a suspension, the duration of the suspension sought must be specified.

(c) *Demand for answer.* The respondent must be notified in the complaint or in a separate paper attached to the complaint of the time for answering the complaint, which may not be less than 30 days from the date of service of the complaint, the name and address of the Administrative Law Judge with whom the answer must be filed, the name and address of the person representing the Internal Revenue Service to whom a copy of the answer must be served, and that a decision by default may be rendered against the respondent in the event an answer is not filed as required.

(d) *Effective/applicability date.* This section is applicable beginning August 2, 2011.

§ 10.63 Service of complaint; service of other papers; service of evidence in support of complaint; filing of papers.

(a) *Service of complaint.*

(1) *In general.* The complaint or a copy of the complaint must be served on the respondent by any manner described in paragraphs (a) (2) or (3) of this section.

(2) *Service by certified or first class mail.*

(i) Service of the complaint may be made on the respondent by mailing the complaint by certified mail to the last known address (as determined under section 6212 of the Internal Revenue Code and the regulations thereunder) of the respondent. Where service is by certified mail, the returned post office receipt duly signed by the respondent will be proof of service.

(ii) If the certified mail is not claimed or accepted by the respondent, or is returned undelivered, service may be made on the respondent, by mailing the complaint to the respondent by first class mail. Service by this method will be considered complete upon mailing, provided the complaint is addressed to the respondent at the respondent's last known address as determined under section 6212 of the Internal

Revenue Code and the regulations thereunder.

(3) *Service by other than certified or first class mail.*

(i) Service of the complaint may be made on the respondent by delivery by a private delivery service designated pursuant to section 7502(f) of the Internal Revenue Code to the last known address (as determined under section 6212 of the Internal Revenue Code and the regulations there under) of the respondent. Service by this method will be considered complete, provided the complaint is addressed to the respondent at the respondent's last known address as determined under section 6212 of the Internal Revenue Code and the regulations thereunder.

(ii) Service of the complaint may be made in person on, or by leaving the complaint at the office or place of business of, the respondent. Service by this method will be considered complete and proof of service will be a written statement, sworn or affirmed by the person who served the complaint, identifying the manner of service, including the recipient, relationship of recipient to respondent, place, date and time of service.

(iii) Service may be made by any other means agreed to by the respondent. Proof of service will be a written statement, sworn or affirmed by the person who served the complaint, identifying the manner of service, including the recipient, relationship of recipient to respondent, place, date and time of service.

(4) For purposes of this section, *respondent* means the practitioner, employer, firm or other entity, or appraiser named in the complaint or any other person having the authority to accept mail on behalf of the practitioner, employer, firm or other entity or appraiser.

(b) *Service of papers other than complaint.* Any paper other than the complaint may be served on the respondent, or his or her authorized representative under §10.69(a)(2) by:

(1) mailing the paper by first class mail to the last known address (as determined under section 6212 of the Internal Revenue Code and the regulations thereunder) of the respondent or the respondent's authorized representative,

(2) delivery by a private delivery service designated pursuant to section 7502(f) of the Internal Revenue Code to the last known address (as determined under section 6212 of the Internal Revenue Code and the regulations thereunder) of the respondent or the respondent's authorized representative, or

(3) as provided in paragraphs (a)(3)(ii) and (a)(3)(iii) of this section.

(c) *Service of papers on the Internal Revenue Service.* Whenever a paper is required or permitted to be served on the Internal Revenue Service in connection with a proceeding under this part, the paper will be served on the Internal Revenue Service's authorized representative under §10.69(a)

(1) at the address designated in the complaint, or at an address provided in a notice of appearance. If no address is designated in the complaint or provided in a notice of appearance, service will be made on the office(s) established to enforce this part under the authority of §10.1, Internal Revenue Service, 1111 Constitution Avenue, NW, Washington, DC 20224.

(d) *Service of evidence in support of complaint.* Within 10 days of serving the complaint, copies of the evidence in support of the complaint must be served on the respondent in any manner described in paragraphs (a)(2) and (3) of this section.

(e) *Filing of papers.* Whenever the filing of a paper is required or permitted in connection with a proceeding under this part, the original paper, plus one additional copy, must be filed with the Administrative Law Judge at the address specified in the complaint or at an address otherwise specified by the Administrative Law Judge. All papers filed in connection with a proceeding under this part must be served on the other party, unless the Administrative Law Judge directs otherwise. A certificate evidencing such must be attached to the original paper filed with the

Administrative Law Judge.

(f) *Effective/applicability date.* This section is applicable beginning August 2, 2011.

§ 10.64 Answer; default.

(a) *Filing.* The respondent's answer must be filed with the Administrative Law Judge, and served on the Internal Revenue Service, within the time specified in the complaint unless, on request or application of the respondent, the time is extended by the Administrative Law Judge.

(b) *Contents.* The answer must be written and contain a statement of facts that constitute the respondent's grounds of defense. General denials are not permitted. The respondent must specifically admit or deny each allegation set forth in the complaint, except that the respondent may state that the respondent is without sufficient information to admit or deny a specific allegation. The respondent, nevertheless, may not deny a material allegation in the complaint that the respondent knows to be true, or state that the respondent is without sufficient information to form a belief, when the respondent possesses the required information. The respondent also must state affirmatively any special matters of defense on which he or she relies.

(c) *Failure to deny or answer allegations in the complaint.* Every allegation in the complaint that is not denied in the answer is deemed admitted and will be considered proved; no further evidence in respect of such allegation need be adduced at a hearing.

(d) *Default.* Failure to file an answer within the time prescribed (or within the time for answer as extended by the Administrative Law Judge), constitutes an admission of the allegations of the complaint and a waiver of hearing, and the Administrative Law Judge may make the decision by default without a hearing or further procedure. A decision by default constitutes a decision under §10.76.

(e) *Signature.* The answer must be signed by the respondent or the respondent's authorized representative under §10.69(a)(2) and must include a statement directly above the signature acknowledging that the statements made in the answer are true and correct and that knowing and willful false statements may be punishable under 18 U.S.C. §1001.

(f) Effective/applicability date. This section is applicable beginning August 2, 2011.

§ 10.65 Supplemental charges.

(a) *In general.* Supplemental charges may be filed against the respondent by amending the complaint with the permission of the Administrative Law Judge if, for example —

 (1) It appears that the respondent, in the answer, falsely and in bad faith, denies a material allegation of fact in the complaint or states that the respondent has insufficient knowledge to form a belief, when the respondent possesses such information; or

 (2) It appears that the respondent has knowingly introduced false testimony during the proceedings against the respondent.

(b) *Hearing.* The supplemental charges may be heard with other charges in the case, provided the respondent is given due notice of the charges and is afforded a reasonable opportunity to prepare a defense to the supplemental charges.

(c) *Effective/applicability date.* This section is applicable beginning August 2, 2011.

§ 10.66 Reply to answer.

(a) The Internal Revenue Service may file a reply to the respondent's answer, but unless otherwise ordered by the Administrative Law Judge, no reply to the respondent's answer is required. If a reply is not filed, new matter in the answer is deemed denied.

(b) *Effective/applicability date.* This section is applicable beginning August 2, 2011.

§ 10.67 Proof; variance; amendment of pleadings.

In the case of a variance between the allegations in pleadings and the evidence adduced in support of the pleadings, the Administrative Law Judge, at any time before decision, may order or authorize amendment of the pleadings to conform to the evidence. The party who would otherwise be prejudiced by the amendment must be given a reasonable opportunity to address the allegations of the pleadings as amended and the Administrative Law Judge must make findings on any issue presented by the pleadings as amended.

§ 10.68 Motions and requests.

(a) *Motions* —

(1) *In general.* At any time after the filing of the complaint, any party may file a motion with the Administrative Law Judge. Unless otherwise ordered by the Administrative Law Judge, motions must be in writing and must be served on the opposing party as provided in §10.63(b). A motion must concisely specify its grounds and the relief sought, and, if appropriate, must contain a memorandum of facts and law in support.

(2) *Summary adjudication.* Either party may move for a summary adjudication upon all or any part of the legal issues in controversy. If the non- moving party opposes summary adjudication in the moving party's favor, the non-moving party must file a written response within 30 days unless ordered otherwise by the Administrative Law Judge.

(3) *Good Faith.* A party filing a motion for extension of time, a motion for postponement of a hearing, or any other non-dispositive or procedural motion must first contact the other party to determine whether there is any objection to the motion, and must state in the motion whether the other party has an objection.

(b) *Response.* Unless otherwise ordered by the Administrative Law Judge, the nonmoving party is not required to file a response to a motion. If the Administrative Law Judge does not order the nonmoving party to file a response, and the nonmoving party files no response, the nonmoving party is deemed to oppose the motion. If a nonmoving party does not respond within 30 days of the filing of a motion for decision by default for failure to file a timely answer or for failure to prosecute, the nonmoving party is deemed not to oppose the motion.

(c) *Oral motions; oral argument* —

(1) The Administrative Law Judge may, for good cause and with notice to the parties, permit oral motions and oral opposition to motions.

(2) The Administrative Law Judge may, within his or her discretion, permit oral argument on any motion.

(d) *Orders.* The Administrative Law Judge should issue written orders disposing of any motion or request and any response thereto.

(e) *Effective/applicability date.* This section is applicable on September 26, 2007.

§ 10.69 Representation; ex parte communication.

(a) *Representation.*
  (1) The Internal Revenue Service may be represented in proceedings under this part by an attorney or other employee of the Internal Revenue Service. An attorney or an employee of the Internal Revenue Service representing the Internal Revenue Service in a proceeding under this part may sign the complaint or any document required to be filed in the proceeding on behalf of the Internal Revenue Service.
  (2) A respondent may appear in person, be represented by a practitioner, or be represented by an attorney who has not filed a declaration with the Internal Revenue Service pursuant to §10.3. A practitioner or an attorney representing a respondent or proposed respondent may sign the answer or any document required to be filed in the proceeding on behalf of the respondent.

(b) *Ex parte communication.* The Internal Revenue Service, the respondent, and any representatives of either party, may not attempt to initiate or participate in ex parte discussions concerning a proceeding or potential proceeding with the Administrative Law Judge (or any person who is likely to advise the Administrative Law Judge on a ruling or decision) in the proceeding before or during the pendency of the proceeding. Any memorandum, letter or other communication concerning the merits of the proceeding, addressed to the Administrative Law Judge, by or on behalf of any party shall be regarded as an argument in the proceeding and shall be served on the othe party.

(c) *Effective/applicability date.* This section is applicable beginning August 2, 2011.

§ 10.70 Administrative Law Judge.

(a) *Appointment.* Proceedings on complaints for the sanction (as described in §10.50) of a practitioner, employer, firm or other entity, or appraiser will be conducted by an Administrative Law Judge appointed as provided by *5 U.S.C. 3105.*

(b) *Powers of the Administrative Law Judge.* The Administrative Law Judge, among other powers, has the authority, in connection with any proceeding under §10.60 assigned or referred to him or her, to do the following:
  (1) Administer oaths and affirmations;
  (2) Make rulings on motions and requests, which rulings may not be appealed prior to the close of a hearing except in extraordinary circumstances and at the discretion of the Administrative Law Judge;
  (3) Determine the time and place of hearing and regulate its course and conduct;
  (4) Adopt rules of procedure and modify the same from time to time as needed for the orderly disposition of proceedings;
  (5) Rule on offers of proof, receive relevant evidence, and examine witnesses;
  (6) Take or authorize the taking of depositions or answers to requests for admission;
  (7) Receive and consider oral or written argument on facts or law;
  (8) Hold or provide for the holding of conferences for the settlement or simplification of the issues with the consent of the parties;
  (9) Perform such acts and take such measures as are necessary or appropriate to the efficient conduct of any proceeding; and
  (10) Make decisions.

(c) *Effective/applicability date.* This section is applicable on September 26, 2007.

§ 10.71 Discovery.

(a) *In general.* Discovery may be permitted, at the discretion of the Administrative Law Judge, only upon written motion demonstrating the relevance, materiality and reasonableness of the requested discovery and subject to the requirements of §10.72(d)(2) and (3). Within 10 days of receipt of the answer, the Administrative Law Judge will notify the parties of the right to request discovery and the timeframe for filing a request. A request for discovery, and objections, must be filed in accordance with §10.68. In response to a request for discovery, the Administrative Law Judge may order —

(1) Depositions upon oral examination; or

(2) Answers to requests for admission.

(b) *Depositions upon oral examination* —

(1) A deposition must be taken before an officer duly authorized to administer an oath for general purposes or before an officer or employee of the Internal Revenue Service who is authorized to administer an oath in Federal tax law matter, and place of the deposition. The opposing party, if attending, will be provided the opportunity for full examination and cross-examination of any witness.

(2) Expenses in the reporting of depositions shall be borne by the party at whose instance the deposition is taken. Travel expenses of the deponent shall be borne by the party requesting the deposition, unless otherwise authorized by Federal law or regulation.

(c) *Requests for admission.* Any party may serve on any other party a written request for admission of the truth of any matters which are not privileged and are relevant to the subject matter of this proceeding. Requests for admission shall not exceed a total of 30 (including any subparts within a specific request) without the approval from the Administrative Law Judge.

(d) *Limitations.* Discovery shall not be authorized if—

(1) The request fails to meet any requirement set forth in paragraph (a) of this section;

(2) It will unduly delay the proceeding;

(3) It will place an undue burden on the party required to produce the discovery sought;

(4) It is frivolous or abusive;

(5) It is cumulative or duplicative;

(6) The material sought is privileged or otherwise protected from disclosure by law;

(7) The material sought relates to mental impressions, conclusions, of legal theories of any party, attorney, or other representative, or a party prepared in the anticipation of a proceeding; or

(8) The material sought is available generally to the public, equally to the parties, or to the party seeking the discovery through another source.

(e) *Failure to comply.* Where a party fails to comply with an order of the Administrative Law Judge under this section, the Administrative Law Judge may, among other things, infer that the information would be adverse to the party failing to provide it, exclude the information from evidence or issue a decision by default.

(f) *Other discovery.* No discovery other than that specifically provided for in this section is permitted.

(g) *Effective/applicability date.* This section is applicable to proceedings initiated on or after September 26, 2007.

§ 10.72 Hearings.

(a) *In general* —

(1) *Presiding officer.* An Administrative Law Judge will preside at the hearing on a complaint filed under §10.60 for the sanction of a practitioner, employer, firm or other entity, or appraiser.

(2) *Time for hearing.* Absent a determination by the Administrative Law Judge that, in the interest of justice, a hearing must be held at a later time, the Administrative Law Judge should, on notice sufficient to allow proper preparation, schedule the hearing to occur no later than 180 days after the time for filing the answer.

(3) *Procedural requirements.*

(i) Hearings will be stenographically recorded and transcribed and the testimony of witnesses will be taken under oath or affirmation.

(ii) Hearings will be conducted pursuant to *5 U.S.C. 556*.

(iii) A hearing in a proceeding requested under §10.82(g) will be conducted de novo.

(iv) An evidentiary hearing must be held in all proceedings prior to the issuance of a decision by the Administrative Law Judge unless —

(A) The Internal Revenue Service withdraws the complaint;

(B) A decision is issued by default pursuant to §10.64(d);

(C) A decision is issued under §10.82 (e);

(D) The respondent requests a decision on the written record without a hearing; or

(E) The Administrative Law Judge issues a decision under §10.68(d) or rules on another motion that disposes of the case prior to the hearing.

(b) *Cross-examination.* A party is entitled to present his or her case or defense by oral or documentary evidence, to submit rebuttal evidence, and to conduct cross-examination, in the presence of the Administrative Law Judge, as may be required for a full and true disclosure of the facts. This paragraph (b) does not limit a party from presenting evidence contained within a deposition when the Administrative Law Judge determines that the deposition has been obtained in compliance with the rules of this subpart D.

(c) *Prehearing memorandum.* Unless otherwise ordered by the Administrative Law Judge, each party shall file, and serve on the opposing party or the opposing party's representative, prior to any hearing, a prehearing memorandum containing —

(1) A list (together with a copy) of all proposed exhibits to be used in the party's case in chief;

(2) A list of proposed witnesses, including a synopsis of their expected testimony, or a statement that no witnesses will be called;

(3) Identification of any proposed expert witnesses, including a synopsis of their expected testimony and a copy of any report prepared by the expert or at his or her direction; and

(4) A list of undisputed facts.

(d) *Publicity* —

(1) *In general.* All reports and decisions of the Secretary of the Treasury, or delegate, including any reports and decisions of the Administrative Law Judge, under this subpart D are, subject to the protective measures in paragraph (d)(4) of this section, public and open to inspection within 30 days after the agency's decision becomes final.

(2) *Request for additional publicity.* The Administrative Law Judge may grant a request by a practitioner or

appraiser that all the pleadings and evidence of the disciplinary proceeding be made available for inspection where the parties stipulate in advance to adopt the protective measures in paragraph (d)(4) of this section.

(3) *Returns and return information* —

(i) *Disclosure to practitioner or appraiser.* Pursuant to *section 6103(l)(4) of the Internal Revenue Code,* the Secretary of the Treasury, or delegate, may disclose returns and return information to any practitioner or appraiser, or to the authorized representative of the practitioner or appraiser, whose rights are or may be affected by an administrative action or proceeding under this subpart D, but solely for use in the action or proceeding and only to the extent that the Secretary of the Treasury, or delegate, determines that the returns or return information are or may be relevant and material to the action or proceeding.

(ii) *Disclosure to officers and employees of the Department of the Treasury.* Pursuant to *section 6103(l)(4)(B) of the Internal Revenue Code* the Secretary of the Treasury, or delegate, may disclose returns and return information to officers and employees of the Department of the Treasury for use in any action or proceeding under this subpart D, to the extent necessary to advance or protect the interests of the United States.

(iii) *Use of returns and return information.* Recipients of returns and return information under this paragraph (d)(3) may use the returns or return information solely in the action or proceeding, or in preparation for the action or proceeding, with respect to which the disclosure was made.

(iv) *Procedures for disclosure of returns and return information.* When providing returns or return information to the practitioner or appraiser, or authorized representative, the Secretary of the Treasury, or delegate, will —

(A) Redact identifying information of any third party taxpayers and replace it with a code;

(B) Provide a key to the coded information; and

(C) Notify the practitioner or appraiser, or authorized representative, of the restrictions on the use and disclosure of the returns and return information, the applicable damages remedy under *section 7431 of the Internal Revenue Code*, and that unauthorized disclosure of information provided by the Internal Revenue Service under this paragraph (d)(3) is also a violation of this part.

(4) *Protective measures* —

(i) *Mandatory protection order.* If redaction of names, addresses, and other identifying information of third party taxpayers may still permit indirect identification of any third party taxpayer, the Administrative Law Judge will issue a protective order to ensure that the identifying information is available to the parties and the Administrative Law Judge for purposes of the proceeding, but is not disclosed to, or open to inspection by, the public.

(ii) *Authorized orders.*

(A) Upon motion by a party or any other affected person, and for good cause shown, the Administrative Law Judge may make any order which justice requires to protect any person in the event disclosure of information is prohibited by law, privileged, confidential, or sensitive in some other way, including, but not limited to, one or more of the following —

(1) That disclosure of information be made only on specified terms and

conditions, including a designation of the time or place;

(2) That a trade secret or other information not be disclosed, or be disclosed only in a designated way.

(iii) *Denials.* If a motion for a protective order is denied in whole or in part, the Administrative Law Judge may, on such terms or conditions as the Administrative Law Judge deems just, order any party or person to comply with, or respond in accordance with, the procedure involved.

(iv) *Public inspection of documents.* The Secretary of the Treasury, or delegate, shall ensure that all names, addresses or other identifying details of third party taxpayers are redacted and replaced with the code assigned to the corresponding taxpayer in all documents prior to public inspection of such documents.

(e) *Location.* The location of the hearing will be determined by the agreement of the parties with the approval of the Administrative Law Judge, but, in the absence of such agreement and approval, the hearing will be held in Washington, D.C.

(f) *Failure to appear.* If either party to the proceeding fails to appear at the hearing, after notice of the proceeding has been sent to him or her, the party will be deemed to have waived the right to a hearing and the Administrative Law Judge may make his or her decision against the absent party by default.

(g) *Effective/applicability date.* This section is applicable beginning August 2, 2011.

§ 10.73 Evidence.

(a) *In general.* The rules of evidence prevailing in courts of law and equity are not controlling in hearings or proceedings conducted under this part. The Administrative Law Judge may, however, exclude evidence that is irrelevant, immaterial, or unduly repetitious.

(b) *Depositions.* The deposition of any witness taken pursuant to §10.71 may be admitted into evidence in any proceeding instituted under §10.60.

(c) *Requests for admission.* Any matter admitted in response to a request for admission under §10.71 is conclusively established unless the Administrative Law Judge on motion permits withdrawal or modification of the admission. Any admission made by a party is for the purposes of the pending action only and is not an admission by a party for any other purpose, nor may it be used against a party in any other proceeding.

(d) *Proof of documents.* Official documents, records, and papers of the Internal Revenue Service and the Office of Professional Responsibility are admissible in evidence without the production of an officer or employee to authenticate them. Any documents, records, and papers may be evidenced by a copy attested to or identified by an officer or employee of the Internal Revenue Service or the Treasury Department, as the case may be.

(e) *Withdrawal of exhibits.* If any document, record, or other paper is introduced in evidence as an exhibit, the Administrative Law Judge may authorize the withdrawal of the exhibit subject to any conditions that he or she deems proper.

(f) *Objections.* Objections to evidence are to be made in short form, stating the grounds for the objection. Except as ordered by the Administrative Law Judge, argument on objections will not be recorded or transcribed. Rulings on objections are to be a part of the record, but no exception to a ruling is necessary to preserve the rights of the parties.

(g) *Effective/applicability date.* This section is applicable on September 26, 2007. § 10.74 Transcript.

§ 10.74 Transcript.

In cases where the hearing is stenographically reported by a Government contract reporter, copies of the transcript may be obtained from the reporter at rates not to exceed the maximum rates fixed by contract between the Government and the reporter. Where the hearing is stenographically reported by a regular employee of the Internal Revenue Service, a copy will be supplied to the respondent either without charge or upon the payment of a reasonable fee. Copies of exhibits introduced at the hearing or at the taking of depositions will be supplied to the parties upon the payment of a reasonable fee (Sec. 501, Public Law 82-137) (65 Stat. 290) (31 U.S.C. § 483a).

§ 10.75Proposed findings and conclusions.

Except in cases where the respondent has failed to answer the complaint or where a party has failed to appear at the hearing, the parties must be afforded a reasonable opportunity to submit proposed findings and conclusions and their supporting reasons to the Administrative Law Judge.

§ 10.76 Decision of Administrative Law Judge.

(a) *In general*—

  (1) *Hearings.* Within 180 days after the conclusion of a hearing and the receipt of any proposed findings and conclusions timely submitted by the parties, the Administrative Law Judge should enter a decision in the case. The decision must include a statement of findings and conclusions, as well as the reasons or basis for making such findings and conclusions, and an order of censure, suspension, disbarment, monetary penalty, disqualification, or dismissal of the complaint.

  (2) *Summary adjudication.* In the event that a motion for summary adjudication is filed, the Administrative Law Judge should rule on the motion for summary adjudication within 60 days after the party in opposition files a written response, or if no written response is filed, within 90 days after the motion for summary adjudication is filed. A decision shall thereafter be rendered if the pleadings, depositions, admissions, and any other admissible evidence show that there is no genuine issue of material fact and that a decision may be rendered as a matter of law. The decision must include a statement of conclusions, as well as the reasons or basis for making such conclusions, and an order of censure, suspension, disbarment, monetary penalty, disqualification, or dismissal of the complaint.

  (3) *Returns and return information.* In the decision, the Administrative Law Judge should use the code assigned to third party taxpayers (described in §10.72(d)).

(b) *Standard of proof.* If the sanction is censure or a suspension of less than six months' duration, the Administrative Law Judge, in rendering findings and conclusions, will consider an allegation of fact to be proven if it is established by the party who is alleging the fact by a preponderance of the evidence in the record. If the sanction is a monetary penalty, disbarment or a suspension of six months or longer duration, an allegation of fact that is necessary for a finding against the practitioner must be proven by clear and convincing evidence in the record. An allegation of fact that is necessary for a finding of disqualification against an appraiser must be proved by clear and convincing evidence in the record.

(c) *Copy of decision.* The Administrative Law Judge will provide the decision to the Internal Revenue Service's authorized representative, and a copy of the decision to the respondent or the respondent's authorized representative.

(d) *When final.* In the absence of an appeal to the Secretary of the Treasury or delegate, the decision of the Administrative Law Judge will, without further proceedings, become the decision of the agency 30 days after the date of the Administrative Law Judge's decision.

(e) *Effective/applicability date.* This section is applicable beginning August 2, 2011.

§ 10.77 Appeal of decision of Administrative Law Judge.

(a) *Appeal.* Any party to the proceeding under this subpart D may appeal the decision of the Administrative Law Judge by filing a notice of appeal with the Secretary of the Treasury, or delegate deciding appeals. The notice of appeal must include a brief that states exceptions to the decision of Administrative Law Judge and supporting reasons for such exceptions.

(b) *Time and place for filing of appeal.* The notice of appeal and brief must be filed, in duplicate, with the Secretary of the Treasury, or delegate deciding appeals, at an address for appeals that is identified to the parties with the decision of the Administrative Law Judge. The notice of appeal and brief must be filed within 30 days of the date that the decision of the Administrative Law Judge is served on the parties. The appealing party must serve a copy of the notice of appeal and the brief to any non-appealing party or, if the party is represented, the non-appealing party's representative.

(c) *Response.* Within 30 days of receiving the copy of the appellant's brief, the other party may file a response brief with the Secretary of the Treasury, or delegate deciding appeals, using the address identified for appeals. A copy of the response brief must be served at the same time on the opposing party or, if the party is represented, the opposing party's representative.

(d) *No other briefs, responses or motions as of right.* Other than the appeal brief and response brief, the parties are not permitted to file any other briefs, responses or motions, except on a grant of leave to do so after a motion demonstrating sufficient cause, or unless otherwise ordered by the Secretary of the Treasury, or delegate deciding appeals.

(e) *Additional time for briefs and responses.* Notwithstanding the time for filing briefs and responses provided in paragraphs (b) and (c) of this section, the Secretary of the Treasury, or delegate deciding appeals, may, for good cause, authorize additional time for filing briefs and responses upon a motion of a party or upon the initiative of the Secretary of the Treasury, or delegate deciding appeals.

(f) *Effective/applicability date.* This section is applicable beginning August 2, 2011.

§ 10.78 Decision on review.

(a) *Decision on review.* On appeal from or review of the decision of the Administrative Law Judge, the Secretary of the Treasury, or delegate, will make the agency decision. The Secretary of the Treasury, or delegate, should make the agency decision within 180 days after receipt of the appeal

(b) *Standard of review.* The decision of the Administrative Law Judge will not be reversed unless the appellant establishes that the decision is clearly erroneous in light of the evidence in the record and applicable law. Issues that are exclusively matters of law will be reviewed de novo. In the event that the Secretary of the Treasury, or delegate, determines that there are unresolved issues raised by the record, the case may be remanded to the Administrative Law Judge to elicit additional testimony or evidence.

(c) *Copy of decision on review.* The Secretary of the Treasury, or delegate, will provide copies of the agency decision to the authorized representative of the Internal Revenue Service and the respondent or the respondent's authorized representative.

(d) *Effective/applicability date.* This section is applicable beginning August 2, 2011.

§10.79 Effect of disbarment, suspension or censure.

(a) *Disbarment.* When the final decision in a case is against the respondent (or the respondent has offered his or her consent and such consent has been accepted by the Internal Revenue Service) and such decision is for disbarment, the respondent will not be permitted to practice before the Internal Revenue Service unless and until authorized to do so by the Internal Revenue Service pursuant to §10.81.

(b) *Suspension.* When the final decision in a case is against the respondent (or the respondent has offered his or her consent and such consent has been accepted by the Internal Revenue Service) and such decision is for suspension, the respondent will not be permitted to practice before the Internal Revenue Service during the period of suspension. For periods after the suspension, the practitioner's future representations may be subject to conditions as authorized by paragraph (d) of this section.

(c) *Censure.* When the final decision in the case is against the respondent (or the Internal Revenue Service has accepted the respondent's offer to consent, if such offer was made) and such decision is for censure, the respondent will be permitted to practice before the Internal Revenue Service, but the respondent's future representations may be subject to conditions as authorized by paragraph (d) of this section.

(d) *Conditions.* After being subject to the sanction of either suspension or censure, the future representations of a practitioner so sanctioned shall be subject to specified conditions designed to promote high standards of conduct. These conditions can be imposed for a reasonable period in light of the gravity of the practitioner's violations. For example, where a practitioner is censured because the practitioner failed to advise the practitioner's clients about a potential conflict of interest or failed to obtain the clients' written consents, the practitioner may be required to provide the Internal Revenue Service with a copy of all consents obtained by the practitioner for an appropriate period following censure, whether or not such consents are specifically requested.

(e) *Effective/applicability date.* This section is applicable beginning August 2, 2011.

§ 10.80 Notice of disbarment, suspension, censure, or disqualification.

(a) *In general.* On the issuance of a final order censuring, suspending, or disbarring a practitioner or a final order disqualifying an appraiser, notification of the censure, suspension, disbarment or disqualification will be given to appropriate officers and employees of the Internal Revenue Service and interested departments and agencies of the Federal government. The Internal Revenue Service may determine the manner of giving notice to the proper authorities of the State by which the censured, suspended, or disbarred person was licensed to practice.

(b) *Effective/applicability date.* This section is applicable beginning August 2, 2011.

§ 10.81 Petition for reinstatement.

(a) *In general*. A practitioner disbarred or suspended under §10.60, or suspended under §10.82, or a disqualified appraiser may petition for reinstatement before the Internal Revenue Service after the expiration of 5 years following such disbarment, suspension, or disqualification (or immediately following the expiration of the suspension or disqualification period, if shorter than 5 years). Reinstatement will not be granted unless the Internal Revenue Service is satisfied that the petitioner is not likely to engage thereafter in conduct contrary to the regulations in this part, and that granting such reinstatement would not be contrary to the public interest.

(b) *Effective/applicability date*. This section is applicable beginning June 12, 2014.

§ 10.82 Expedited suspension.

(a) *When applicable.* Whenever the Commissioner, or delegate, determines that a practitioner is described in paragraph (b) of this section, the expedited procedures described in this section may be used to suspend the practitioner from practice before the Internal Revenue Service.

(b) *To whom applicable.* This section applies to any practitioner who, within 5 years prior to the date that a show cause order under this section's expedited suspension procedures is served:

  (1) Has had a license to practice as an attorney, certified public accountant, or actuary suspended or revoked for cause (not including a failure to pay a professional licensing fee) by any authority or court, agency, body, or board described in §10.51(a)(10).

  (2) Has, irrespective of whether an appeal has been taken, been convicted of any crime under title 26 of the United States Code, any crime involving dishonesty or breach of trust, or any felony for which the conduct involved renders the practitioner unfit to practice before the Internal Revenue Service.

  (3) Has violated conditions imposed on the practitioner pursuant to §10.79(d).

  (4) Has been sanctioned by a court of competent jurisdiction, whether in a civil or criminal proceeding (including suits for injunctive relief), relating to any taxpayer's tax liability or relating to the practitioner's own tax liability, for —

    (i) Instituting or maintaining proceedings primarily for delay;

    (ii) Advancing frivolous or groundless arguments; or

    (iii) Failing to pursue available administrative remedies.

  (5) Has demonstrated a pattern of willful disreputable conduct by—

    (i) Failing to make an annual Federal tax return, in violation of the Federal tax laws, during 4 of the 5 tax years immediately preceding the institution of a proceeding under paragraph (c) of this section and remains noncompliant with any of the practitioner's Federal tax filing obligations at the time the notice of suspension is issued under paragraph (f) of this section; or

    (ii) Failing to make a return required more frequently than annually, in violation of the Federal tax laws, during 5 of the 7 tax periods immediately preceding the institution of a proceeding under paragraph (c) of this section and remains noncompliant with any of the practitioner's Federal tax filing obligations at the time the notice of suspension is issued under paragraph (f) of this section.

(c) *Expedited suspension procedures.* A suspension under this section will be proposed by a show cause order that names the respondent, is signed by an authorized representative of the Internal Revenue Service under §10.69(a)(1), and served according to the rules set forth in §10.63(a). The show cause order must give a plain and concise description of the allegations that constitute the basis for the proposed suspension. The show cause order must notify the respondent —Of the place and due date for filing a response;

(1) That an expedited suspension decision by default may be rendered if the respondent fails to file a response as required;

(2) That the respondent may request a conference to address the merits of the show cause order and that any such request must be made in the response; and

(3) That the respondent may be suspended either immediately following the expiration of the period within which a response must be filed or, if a conference is requested, immediately following the conference.

(d) *Response.* The response to the show cause order described in this section must be filed no later than 30 calendar days following the date the show cause order is served, unless the time for filing is extended. The response must be filed in accordance with the rules set forth for answers to a complaint in §10.64, except as otherwise provided in this section. The response must include a request for a conference, if a conference is desired. The respondent is entitled to the conference only if the request is made in a timely filed response.

(e) *Conference.* An authorized representative of the Internal Revenue Service will preside at a conference described in this section. The conference will be held at a place and time selected by the Internal Revenue Service, but no sooner than 14 calendar days after the date by which the response must be filed with the Internal Revenue Service, unless the respondent agrees to an earlier date. An authorized representative may represent the respondent at the conference.

(f) *Suspension—*

(1) *In general.* The Commissioner, or delegate, may suspend the respondent from practice before the Internal Revenue Service by a written notice of expedited suspension immediately following:

(i) The expiration of the period within which a response to a show cause order must be filed if the respondent does not file a response as required by paragraph (d) of this section;

(ii) The conference described in paragraph (e) of this section if the Internal Revenue Service finds that the respondent is described in paragraph (b) of this section; or

(iii) The respondent's failure to appear, either personally or through an authorized representative, at a conference scheduled by the Internal Revenue Service under paragraph (e) of this section.

(2) *Duration of suspension.* A suspension under this section will commence on the date that the written notice of expedited suspension is served on the practitioner, either personally or through an authorized representative. The suspension will remain effective until the earlier of:

(i) The date the Internal Revenue Service lifts the suspension after determining that the practitioner is no longer described in paragraph (b) of this section or for any other reason; or

(ii) The date the suspension is lifted or otherwise modified by an Administrative Law Judge or the Secretary of the Treasury, or delegate deciding appeals, in a proceeding referred to in paragraph (g) of this section and instituted under §10.60.

(g) *Practitioner demand for §10.60 proceeding.* If the Internal Revenue Service suspends a practitioner under the expedited suspension procedures described in this section, the practitioner may demand that the Internal Revenue Service institute a proceeding under §10.60 and issue the complaint described in §10.62. The demand must be in writing, specifically reference the suspension action under §10.82, and be made within 2 years from the date on which the practitioner's suspension commenced. The Internal Revenue Service must issue a complaint demanded under this paragraph (g) within 60 calendar days of receiving the demand. If the Internal Revenue Service does not issue such complaint within 60 days of receiving the demand, the suspension is lifted automatically. The preceding sentence does not, however, preclude the Commissioner, or delegate, from instituting a regular proceeding under §10.60 of this part.

(h) *Effective/applicability date.* This section is generally applicable beginning June 12, 2014, except that paragraphs (b)(1) through (4) of this section are applicable beginning August 2, 2011.

Subpart E — General Provisions

§ 10.90 Records.

(a) *Roster.* The Internal Revenue Service will maintain and make available for public inspection in the time and manner prescribed by the Secretary, or delegate, the following rosters —

(1) Individuals (and employers, firms, or other entities, if applicable) censured, suspended, or disbarred from practice before the Internal Revenue Service or upon whom a monetary penalty was imposed.

(2) Enrolled agents, including individuals —

(i) Granted active enrollment to practice;

(ii) Whose enrollment has been placed in inactive status for failure to meet the requirements for renewal of enrollment;

(iii) Whose enrollment has been placed in inactive retirement status; and

(iv) Whose offer of consent to resign from enrollment has been accepted by the Internal Revenue Service under §10.61.

(3) Enrolled retirement plan agents, including individuals —

(i) Granted active enrollment to practice;

(ii) Whose enrollment has been placed in inactive status for failure to meet the requirements for renewal of enrollment;

(iii) Whose enrollment has been placed in inactive retirement status; and

(iv) Whose offer of consent to resign from enrollment has been accepted under §10.61.

(4) Registered tax return preparers, including individuals —

(i) Authorized to prepare all or substantially all of a tax return or claim for refund;

(ii) Who have been placed in inactive status for failure to meet the requirements for renewal;

(iii) Who have been placed in inactive retirement status; and

(iv) Whose offer of consent to resign from their status as a registered tax return preparer has been accepted by the Internal Revenue Service under §10.61

(5) Disqualified appraisers.

(6) Qualified continuing education providers, including providers —

(i) Who have obtained a qualifying continuing education provider number; and

(ii) Whose qualifying continuing education number has been revoked for failure to comply with the requirements of this part.

(b) *Other records.* Other records of the Director of the Office of Professional Responsibility may be disclosed upon specific request, in accordance with the applicable law.

(c) *Effective/applicability date.* This section is applicable beginning August 2, 2011.

§ 10.91 Saving provision.

Any proceeding instituted under this part prior to June 12, 2014, for which a final decision has not been reached or for which judicial review is still available is not affected by these revisions. Any proceeding under this part based on conduct engaged in prior to June 12, 2014, which is instituted after that date, will apply subpart D and E of this part as revised, but the conduct engaged in prior to the effective date of these revisions will be judged by the regulations in effect at the time the conduct occurred. § 10.92 Special orders.

The Secretary of the Treasury reserves the power to issue such special orders as he or she deems proper in any cases within the purview of this part.

§ 10.93 Effective date.

Except as otherwise provided in each section and Subject to §10.91, Part 10 is applicable on July 26, 2002.

John Dalrymple,
Deputy Commissioner for Services and Enforcement

Approved: June 3, 2014 Christopher J. Meade,
General Counsel

[FR Doc. 2014-13739 Filed 06/09/2014 at 4:15 pm;
Publication Date: 06/12/2014]

Appendix B: Conference and Practice Requirements[xxxiii]

Statement of
Procedural Rules

Conference and Practice Requirements

Sections 601.501 through 601.509 of Subpart E of Part 601 of Title 26 Code of Federal Regulations

Department of the Treasury
Internal Revenue Service

Publication 216 (Rev. 3-92)

For sale by the Superintendent of Documents
U.S. Government Printing Office
Washington, D.C. 20402

Cat. No. 46290K

Title 26 - Internal Revenue

Chapter I - Internal Revenue Service, Department of Treasury

Subchapter H - Internal Revenue Practice: Part 601 - Conference and Statement of Procedural Rules; Subpart E - Conference and practice Requirements

This Publication contains the revision of Sections 601.501 through 601.509 of Subpart E, Part 601, Title 26, Code of Federal Regulations appearing in 32 F. R. 13058, dated September 14, 1967, and includes the following amendments:

Amendment appearing in 33 F. R. 6825, dated May 4, 1968, which adds a new paragraph (b) (4) to Section 601.502 and revises paragraph (b) of Section 601.503.

Amendment appearing in 33 F. R. 17241, dated November 21, 1968, which revises paragraph (b) (4) and adds a new subdivision (iv) to paragraph (c) (3) of Section 601.502. This amendment also revises paragraph (b) of Section 601.505.

Amendment appearing in 34 F. R. 643 1, dated April 12, 1969, which revises so much of paragraph (c) (1) as precedes subdivision (i) thereof, and paragraph (c) (2) (i) adds new paragraph (c) (5) to Section 601.502. This amendment also revises paragraph (b) of Section 601.505.

Amendment appearing in 34 E R. 14603, dated September 19, 1969, which revises paragraph (a) of Section 601.501.

Amendment appearing in 37 F. R. 1016, dated January 21, 1972, which revises paragraph (a) of Section 601.501.

Amendment appearing in 41 F. R. 20883, dated May 21, 1976, which revises paragraph (b)(1)(ii) of section 601.504.

Amendment in 43 F. R. 53030, dated November 15, 1978, which revises paragraph (b) of section 601.505.

Amendment appearing in 45 F. R. 7257-7259 dated February 1, 1980, which revises Sections 601.501, 601.502, 601.503, 601.504, 601.505, 601.506, 601.507 and 601.509 by eliminating discriminatory language and bringing certain provisions of the Statement of Procedural Rules up to date.

Amendment appearing in 46 F. R. 26055 dated May 11, 198 1, which revises paragraph (a) of Section 601.506.

Amendment appearing in 47 F. R. 39676 dated September 9, 1982, which adds a new subparagraph (b)(2) to Section 601.502. Existing subparagraphs (2), (3), and (4), are redesignated (3), (4), and (5) respectively.

Amendments appearing in 49 F. R. 19650-19651 dated May 9, 1984 which revises Sections 601.502, 601.503, 601.504, and 601.506.

Amendments appearing in 56 F. R. 24001-24009 dated May 28, 1991 which revises Sections 601.501 through 601.509.

TABLE OF CONTENTS
SUBPART E.-CONFERENCE AND PRACTICE REQUIREMENTS

Subpart E-Conference and Practice Requirements

§601.501 Scope of rules; definitions.

(a) *Scope of rules.* The rules prescribed in this subpart concern, among other things, the representation of taxpayers before the Internal Revenue Service under the authority of a power of attorney. These rules apply to all offices of the Internal Revenue Service in all matters under the jurisdiction of the Internal Revenue Service and apply to practice before the Internal Revenue Service (as defined in 31 CFR 10.2(a) and 10.7(a)(7)). For special provisions relating to alcohol, tobacco, and fire- arms activities, see §§601.521 through 601.527. These rules detail the means by which a recognized representative is authorized to act on behalf of a taxpayer. Such authority must be evidenced by a power of attorney and declaration of representative filed with the appropriate office of the Internal Revenue Service. In general, a power of attorney must contain certain information concerning the taxpayer, the recognized representative, and the specific tax matter(s) for which the recognized representative is authorized to act. (See §601.503(a).) A "declaration of representative" is a written statement made by a recognized representative that he/she is currently eligible to practice before the Internal Revenue Service and is au- thorized to represent the particular party on whose behalf he/she acts. (See §601.502(b).)

(b) *Definitions—(l) Attorney-in-fact.* An agent authorized by a principal under a power of attorney to perform certain specified act(s) or kinds of act(s) on behalf of the principal.

(2) Centralized Authorization File (CAF) system. An automated file containing information regarding the authority of an individual appointed under a power of attorney or a person designated under a tax information authorization.

(3) *Circular No. 230.* Treasury Department Circular No. 230 (codified at 31 CFR Part 10) which sets forth the regulations governing practice before the Internal Revenue Service.

(4) *Declaration of representative.* (See §601.502(b).)

(5) *Delegation of authority.* An act performed by a recognized representative whereby authority given under a power of attorney is delegated to another recognized representative. After a delegation is made, both the original recognized representative and the recognized representative to whom a delegation is made will be recognized to represent the taxpayer. (See §601.505(b)(2).)

(6) *Form 2848, "Power of Attorney and Declaration of Representative."* The Internal Revenue Service power of attorney form which may be used by a taxpayer who wishes to appoint an individual to represent him/her before the Internal Revenue Service. (See §601.503(b)(1).)

(7) *Matter.* The application of each tax imposed by the Internal Revenue Code and the regulations thereunder for each taxable period constitutes a (separate) matter.

(8) *Office of the Internal Revenue Service.* The office of each district director, the office of each service center, the office of each compliance center, the office of each regional commissioner, and the National Office constitute separate offices of the Internal Revenue Service.

(9) *Power of attorney.* A document signed by the taxpayer, as principal, by which an individual is appointed as attorney-in-fact to perform certain specified act(s) or kinds of act(s) on behalf of the principal. Specific types of powers of attorney include the following-

(i) *General power of attorney.* The attorney-in-fact is authorized to perform any or all acts the taxpayer can perform.

(ii) *Durable power of attorney.* A power of attorney which specifies that the appointment of the attorney-in-fact will not end due to either the passage of time (i.e., the authority conveyed will continue until the death of the taxpayer) or the incompetency of the principal (e.g., the principal becomes unable or is adjudged incompetent to perform his/her business affairs).

(iii) *Limited power of attorney.* A power of attorney which is limited in any facet (i.e., a power of attorney authorizing the attorney -in -fact to perform only certain specified acts as contrasted to a general power of attorney authorizing the representative to perform any and all acts the taxpayer can perform).

(10) *Practice before the Internal Revenue Service.* Practice before the Internal Revenue Service encompasses all matters connected with presentation to the Internal Revenue Service or any of its personnel

relating to a taxpayer's rights, privileges, or liabilities under laws or regulations administered by the Internal Revenue Service. Such presentations include the preparation and filing of necessary documents, correspondence with and communications to the Internal Revenue Service, and the representation of a taxpayer at conferences, hearings, and meetings.
(See 31 CFR 10.2(a).)

(11) *Principal.* A person (i.e., taxpayer) who appoints an attomey-in-fact under a power of attorney.

(12) *Recognized representative.* An individual who is recognized to practice before the Internal Revenue Service under the provisions of §601.502.

(13) *Representation.* Acts performed on behalf of a taxpayer by a representative in practice before the Internal Revenue Service. (See §601.501(b)(10).) However, any person may prepare a tax return, may appear as a witness for the taxpayer before the Internal Revenue Service, or furnish information at the request of the Internal Revenue Service or any of its officers or employees. (See 31 CFR 10.7(c).)

(14) *Substitution of representative.* An act performed by an attomey-in-fact whereby authority given under a power of attorney is transferred to another recognized representative. After a substitution is made, only the newly recognized representative will be considered the tax- payer's representative. (See §601.505(b)(2).)

(15) Tax *information authorization.* A document signed by the taxpayer authorizing any individual or entity (e.g., corporation, partnership, trust or organization) designated by the taxpayer to receive and/or inspect confidential tax return information in a specified matter. (See section 6103 of the Internal Revenue Code and the regulations there-under.)

(c) *Conferences--(I) Scheduling.* The Internal Revenue Service encourages the discussion of any Federal tax matter affecting a taxpayer. Conferences may be offered only to taxpayers and/or their recognized representative(s) acting under a valid power of attorney. As a general rule, such conferences will not be held without previous arrangement. However, if a compelling reason is shown by the taxpayer that an immediate conference should be held, the Internal Revenue Service official(s) responsible for the matter has the discretion to make an exception to the general rule.

(2) *Submission of information.* Every written protest, brief, or other statement the taxpayer or recognized representative Wishes to be considered at any conference should be submitted to or filed with the appropriate Internal Revenue Service official(s) at least five business days before the date of the conference. If the taxpayer or the representative is unable to meet this requirement, arrangement should be made with the appropriate Intemal Revenue Service official for a postponement of the conference to a date mutually agreeable to the parties. The taxpayer or the representative remains free to submit additional or supporting facts or evidence within a reasonable time after the conference.

§601.502 Recognized representative.

A recognized representative is an individual who is appointed as an attomey-in-fact under a power of attorney and is a member of one of the categories described in §601.502(a) and who files a declaration of representative, as described in §601.502(b).

(a) *Categories (1) Attorney.* Any individual who is a member in good standing of the bar of the highest court of any state, possession, territory, commonwealth, or the District of Columbia;

(2) *Certified public accountant.* Any individual who is duly qualified to practice as a certified public accountant in any state, possession, territory, commonwealth, or the District of Columbia;

(3) *Enrolled agent.* Any individual who is enrolled to practice before the Internal Revenue Service and is in active status pursuant to the requirements of Circular No. 230 (31 CFR Part 10);

(4) Enrolled actuary. Any individual who is enrolled as an actuary by and is in active status with the Joint Board for the Enrollment of Actuaries pursuant to 29 *U.S.C. 1242.*

(5) Other individuals. (i) Temporary recognition. Any individual who is granted temporary recognition as an enrolled agent by the Director of Practice (See 31 CFR *10.5(c).)*

(ii) *Practice based on a relationship or special status with a taxpayer.* Any individual authorized to represent a taxpayer with whom/which a special relationship exists (31 CFR 10.7(a)(1) through (6)). (For example, an individual may represent another individual who is his/her regular full-time employer or a member of his/her immediate family; an individual who is a bona fide officer or regular full-time employee of a corporation or certain other organizations may represent that entity.)

(iii) *Unenrolled return preparer.* Any individual not otherwise eligible to practice before the Internal Revenue Service who signs a return as having prepared it for a taxpayer, or who prepared a return with respect to which the instructions or regulations do not require that the return be signed by the preparer. The acts which an unenrolled return preparer may perform are limited to representation of a taxpayer before revenue agents and examining officers of the Examination Division in the offices of District Director with respect to the tax liability of the taxpayer for the taxable year or period covered by a return prepared by the unenrolled return preparer (31 CFR 10.7(a)(7)).

(iv) Special appearance. Any individual who, upon written application, is authorized by the Director of Prac tice to represent a taxpayer in a particular matter (See 31CFR 10.7(b).)

(b) *Declaration of representative.* A recognized representative must attach to the power of attorney a written declaration (e.g., Part 11 of Form 2848) stating the following—

(1) I am not currently under suspension or disbarment from practice before the Internal Revenue Service;

(2) 1 am aware of the regulations contained in Treasury Department Circular No. 230, (31 CFR Part 10), concerning the practice of attorneys, certified public accountants, enrolled agents, enrolled actuaries, and others);

(3) 1 am authorized to represent the taxpayer(s) identified in the power of attorney; and

(4) I am an individual described in 26 CFR 601.502(a).

If an individual is unable to make such declaration, he/she may not engage in representation of a taxpayer before the Internal Revenue Service or perform the acts described in §601.504(a)(2) through (6).

§601.503 Requirements of power of attorney, signatures, fiduciaries and Commissioner's authority to substitute other requirements.

(a) *Requirements. A* power of attorney must contain the following information —

(1) name and mailing address of the taxpayer;

(2) identification number of the taxpayer (i.e., social security number and/or employer identification number);

(3) employee plan number (if applicable);

(4) name and mailing address of the recognized representative(s);

(5) description of the matter(s) for which representation is authorized which, if applicable, must include —

(i) the type of tax involved;

(ii) the Federal tax form number;

(iii) the soecific year(s)/period(s) involved; and

(iv) in estate matters, decedent's date of death; and

(6) a clear expression of the taxpayer's intention concerning the scope of authority granted to the recognized representative(s).

(b) *Acceptable power of attorney documents—(I)Form* 2848. A properly completed Form 2848 satisfies the requirements for both a power of attorney (as described in §601.503(a)) and a declaration of representative (as described in §601.502(b)).

(2) *Other documents.* The Internal Revenue Service will accept a power of attorney other than Form 2848 provided such document satisfies the requirements of §601.503(a). However, for purposes of processing such documents onto the Centralized Authorization File (see §601.506(d)), a completed Form 2848 must be attached. (In such situations, Form 2848 is not the operative power of attorney and need not be signed by the taxpayer. How- ever, the Declaration of Representative must be signed by the representative.)

(3) *Special provision.* The Internal Revenue Service will not accept a power of attorney which fails to include the information required by §601.503(a)(1) through (5). If a power of attorney fails to include some or all of the information required by such section, the attorney- in-fact can cure this defect by executing a Form 2848 (on behalf of the taxpayer) which includes the missing information. Attaching a Form 2848 to a copy of the original power of attorney will validate the original power of attorney (and will be treated in all circumstances as one signed and filed by the taxpayer) provided the following conditions are satisfied —

(i) The original power of attorney contemplates authorization to handle, among other things, Federal tax matters, (e.g., the power of attorney includes language to the effect that the attorney-in-fact has the authority to perform any and all acts); and —

(ii) The attorney-in-fact attaches a statement (signed under penalty of perjury) to the Form 2848 which states that the original power of attorney is valid under the laws of the governing jurisdiction.

(4) *Other categories of powers of attorney.* Categories of powers of attorney not addressed in these rules (e.g., durable powers of attorney) will be accepted by the Internal Revenue Service provided such documents satisfy the requirements of §601.503(b)(2) or (3).

(c) *Signatures.* Internal Revenue Service officials may require a taxpayer (or such individual(s) required or authorized to sign on behalf of a taxpayer) to submit appropriate identification or evidence of authority. Except when Form 2848 (or its equivalent) is executed by an attorney-in-fact under the provisions of §601.503(b)(3), the individual who must execute a Form 2848 depends on the type of taxpayer involved—

(1) *Individual taxpayer.* In matter(s) involving an individual taxpayer, a power of. attorney must be signed by such individual.

(2) *Husband and wife.* In matters involving a joint return the following rules apply—

(i) *Joint representation.* In the case of any matter concerning a joint return in which both husband and wife are to be represented by the same representative(s), the power of attorney must be executed by both husband and wife.

(ii) *Individual representation.* In the case of any matter concerning a joint return in which both husband and wife are not to be represented by the same recognized representative(s), the power of attorney must be executed by the spouse who is to be represented. However, the recognized representative of such spouse cannot perform any act with respect to a tax matter that the spouse being represented cannot perform alone.

(3) *Corporation.* In the case of a corporation, a power of attorney must be executed by an officer of the corporation having authority to legally bind the corporation, who must certify that he/she has such authority.

(4) *Association.* In the case of an association, a power of attorney must be executed by an officer of the association having authority to legally bind the association, who must certify that he/she has such authority.

(5) *Partnership.* In the case of a partnership, a power of attorney must be executed by all partners, or if executed in the name of the partnership, by the partner or partners duly authorized to act for the partnership, who must certify that he/she has such authority.

(6) *Dissolved partnership.* In the case of a dissolved partnership, each of the former partners must execute a power of attorney. However, if one or more of the former partners is deceased, the following provisions apply

(i) The legal representative of each deceased partner(s) (or such person(s) having legal control over the disposition of partnership interest(s) and/or the share of partner- ship asset(s) of the deceased partner(s)) must execute a power of attorney in the place of such deceased partner(s). (See §601.503(c)(6)(ii).)

(ii) Notwithstanding §601.503(c)(6)(i), if the law of the governing jurisdiction provides that such partner(s) has exclusive right to control or possession of the firm's assets for the purpose of winding down its affairs, the signature(s) of the surviving partner(s) alone will be sufficient. (If the surviving partner(s) claims exclusive right to control or possession of the firm's assets for the purpose of winding down its affairs, Internal Revenue Service officials may require the submission of a copy of or a citation to the pertinent provisions of the law of the governing jurisdiction upon which the surviving partner(s) relies.)

(d) *Fiduciaries.* In general, when a fiduciary is involved in a tax matter, a power of attorney is not required. Instead Form 56, "Notice Concerning Fiduciary Relationship" should be filed. Types of taxpayers for which fiduciaries act are —

(1) *Dissolved corporation (i) Appointed trustee.* In the case of a dissolved corporation, Form 56, "Notice Concerning Fiduciary Relationship," should be filed by the liquidating trustee(s), if one or more have been appointed, or by the trustee(s) deriving authority under a law of the jurisdiction in which the corporation was organized. If there is more than one trustee, all must join unless it is established that fewer than all have authority to act in the matter under consideration. Internal Revenue Service officials may require the submission of a properly authenticated copy of the instrument and/or citation to the law under which the trustee derives his/her authority. If the authority of the trustee is derived under the law of a jurisdiction, Internal Revenue Service officials may require a statement (signed under penalty of perjury) setting forth the facts required by the law as a condition precedent to the vesting of authority in said trustee and stating that the authority of the trustee has not been terminated.

(ii) *No appointed trustee.* If there is no appointed trustee, a Form 56, "Notice Concerning Fiduciary Relationship," should be filed by the stockholder(s) holding a majority of the voting stock of the corporation as of the date of dissolution. Internal Revenue Service officials may require submission of a statement showing the total number of outstanding shares of voting stock as of the date of dissolution, the number of shares held by each signatory to a power of attorney, the date of dissolution,and a representation that no trustee has been appointed.

(2) *Insolvent taxpayer* In the case of an insolvent taxpayer, Form 56, "Notice Concerning Fiduciary Relationship," should be filed by the trustee, receiver, or attorney appointed by the court. Internal Revenue Service officials may require the submission of a certified order or document from the court having jurisdiction over the insolvent taxpayer which shows the appointment and qualification of the trustee, receiver, or attorney and that his/her authority has not been terminated. In cases pending before a court of the United States (e.g., U.S. District Court or U.S. Bankruptcy Court), an authenticated copy of the order approving the bond of the trustee, receiver, or attorney will meet this requirement.

(3) *Deceased taxpayers —(i) Executor, personal representative- or administrator.* In the case of a deceased taxpayer, a Form 56, "Notice Concerning Fiduciary Relationship," should be filed by the executor, personal rep- resentative or administrator if one has been appointed and is responsible for disposition of the matter under consideration. Internal Revenue Service officials may require the submission of a short-form certificate (or authenticated copy of letters testamentary or letters of administration) showing that such authority is in full force and effect at the time the Form 56, "Notice Concerning Fiduciary Relationship," is filed.

(ii) *Testamentary trustee(s).* In the event that a trustee is acting under the provisions of a will, a Form 56, "Notice Concerning Fiduciary Relationship," should be filed by the trustee, unless the executor, personal representative or administrator has not been discharged and is responsible for disposition of the matter. Internal Revenue Service officials may require either the submission of evidence of the discharge of the executor and appointment of the trustee or other appropriate evidence of the authority of the trustee.

(iii) *Residuary legatee(s).* If no executor, administrator, or trustee named under the will is acting or responsible for disposition of the matter and the estate has been distributed to the residuary legatee(s), a Form 56, "Notice Concerning Fiduciary Relationship," should be filed by the residuary legatee(s). Internal Revenue Service officials may require the submission of a statement from the court certifying that no executor, administrator, or trustee named under the will is acting or responsible for disposition of the matter, naming the residuary legatee(s), and indicating the proper share to which each is entitled.

(iv) *Distributee(s).* In the event that the decedent died intestate and the administrator has been discharged and is not responsible for disposition of the matter (or none was ever appointed), a Form 56, "Notice Concerning Fiduciary Relationship," should be filed by the distributee(s). Internal Revenue Service officials may require the submission of evidence of the discharge of the administrator (if one had been appointed) and evidence that the administrator is not responsible for disposition of the matter. It also may require a statement(s) signed under penalty of perjury (and such other appropriate evidence as can be produced) to show the relationship of the individual(s) who sign the Form 56, "Notice Concerning Fiduciary Relationship," to the decedent and the right of each signer to the respective shares of the assets claimed under the law of the domicile of the decedent.

(4) *Taxpayer for whom a guardian or other fiduciary has been appointed.* In the case of a taxpayer for whom a guardian or other fiduciary has been appointed by a court of record, a Form 56, "Notice Concerning Fiduciary Relationship," should be filed by the fiduciary. Internal Revenue Service officials may require the submission of a court certificate or court order showing that the individual who executes the Form 56, "Notice Concerning Fiduciary Relationship," has been appointed and that his/her appointment has not been terminated.

(5) *Taxpayer who has appointed a trustee.* In the case of a taxpayer who has appointed a trustee, a Form 56, "Notice Concerning Fiduciary Relationship," should be filed by the trustee. Internal Revenue Service officials may require the submission of documentary evidence of the authority of the trustee to act. Such evidence may be either a copy of a properly executed trust instrument or a certified copy of extracts from the trust instrument, showing—

(i) The date of the instrument;
(ii) That it is or is not of record in any court;
(iii) The names of the beneficiaries;

(iv) The appointment of the trustee, the authority granted, and other information as may be necessary to show that such authority extends to Federal tax matters; and

(v) That the trust has not been terminated and the trustee appointed therein is still legally acting as such. In the event that the trustee appointed in the original trust instrument has been replaced by another trustee, documentary evidence of the appointment of the new trustee must be submitted.

(e) *Commissioner's authority to substitute other requirements for power of attorney.* Upon application of a taxpayer or a recognized representative, the Commissioner of Internal Revenue may substitute a requirement(s) other than provided herein for a power of attorney as evidence of the authority of the representative.

§601.504 Requirements for filing power of attorney.

(a) *Situations in which a power of attorney is required.* Except as otherwise provided in §601.504(b), a power of attorney is required by the Internal Revenue Service when the taxpayer wishes to authorize a recognized representative to perform one or more of the following acts on behalf of the taxpayer

(1) *Representation.* (see §§601.501(b)(10) and 601.501 (b)(I 3).)

(2) *Waiver* Offer and/or execution of either—

(i) a waiver of restriction on assessment or collection of a deficiency in tax, or

(ii) a waiver of notice of disallowance of a claim for credit or refund.

(3) *Consent.* Execution of a consent to extend the statutory period for assessment or collection of a tax.

(4) *Closing agreement.* Execution of a closing agreement under the provisions of the Internal Revenue Code and the regulations thereunder.

(5) *Check drawn on the United States Treasury.* The authority to receive (but not endorse or collect) a check drawn on the United States Treasury must be specifically granted in a power of attorney. (The endorsement and payment of a check drawn on the United States Treasury are governed by Treasury Department Circular No. *21,* as amended, *31* Part CFR 240.) Endorsement of such check by any person other than the payee must be made under one of the special types of powers of attorney prescribed by Circular No. 21, as amended, (31 CFR Part 240). For restrictions on the assignment of claims, see Revised Statute section 3477, as amended (31 U.S.C. 3727).)

(6) *Signing tax returns.* The filing of a power of attorney does not authorize the recognized representative to sign a tax return on behalf of the taxpayer unless such act is both —

(i) permitted under the Internal Revenue Code and the regulations thereunder (e.g., the authority to sign income tax returns is governed by the provisions of section 1.6012-1 (a)(5) of the Income Tax Regulations); and

(ii) specifically authorized in the power of attorney.

(b) *Situations in which a power of attorney is not required—(l) Disclosure of confidential tax return information.* The submission of a tax information authorization to request the disclosure of confidential tax return information does not constitute practice before the Internal Revenue Service. (Such procedure is governed by the provisions of section 6103 of the Internal Revenue Code and the regulations thereunder.) Nevertheless, if a power of attorney is properly filed, the recognized representative also is authorized to receive and/or inspect confidential tax return information concerning the matter(s) specified in the power of attorney (provided the power of attorney places no limitations upon such disclosure).

(2) *Estate matter.* A power of attorney is not required at a conference concerning an estate tax matter if the individual seeking to act as a recognized representative presents satisfactory evidence to Internal Revenue Service officials that he/she is —

(i) an individual described in §601.502(a); and

(ii) the attorney of record for the executor, personal representative, or administrator before the court where the will is probated or the estate is administered

(3) *Bankruptcy matters.* A power of attorney is not required in the case of a trustee, receiver, or an attorney (designated to represent a trustee, receiver, or debtor in possession) appointed by a court having jurisdiction over a debtor. In such a case, Internal Revenue Service officials may require the submission of a certificate from the court having jurisdiction over the debtor showing the appointment and qualification of the trustee, receiver, or .attorney and that his/her authority has not been terminated. In cases pending before a court of the United States (e.g., U.S. District Court or U.S. Bankruptcy Court), an authenticated copy of the order approving the bond of the trustee, receiver, or attorney will meet this requirement.

(c) *Administrative requirements of filing— (I) General.* Except as provided in this section, a power of attorney (including the declaration of representative and any other required statement(s)) must be filed in each office of the Internal Revenue Service in which the recognized repre- sentative desires to perform one or more of the acts described in §601.504(a).

(2) *Regional offices.* If a power of attorney (including the declaration of representative and any other required statenient(s)) is filed with the office of a district director or with a service center which has the matter under consideration, it is not necessary to file a copy with the office of a regional commissioner which subsequently has the matter under consideration unless requested.

(3) *National Office.* In case of a request for a ruling or other matter to be considered in the National Office, a power of attorney, including the declaration of representative and any other required statement(s), must be submitted with each request or matter.

(4) Copv *of power of attornev.* The Internal Revenue Service will accept either the original or a copy of a power of attorney. A copy of a power of attorney received by facsimile transmission (FAX) also will be accepted.

(d) *Practice by correspondence.* If an individual desires to represent a taxpayer through correspondence with the Internal Revenue Service, such individual must submit a power of attorney, including the declaration of representative and any other required statement(s), even though no personal appearance is contemplated.

§601.505 Revocation, change in representation and substitution or delegation of representative.

(a) By *the taxpayer—(I) New power of attorney filed.* A new power of attorney revokes a prior power of attorney if it is granted by the taxpayer to another recognized representative with respect to the same matter. However, a new power of attorney does not revoke a prior power of attorney if it contains a clause stating that it does not revoke such prior power of attorney and there is attached to the new power of attorney either —

(i) a copy of the unrevoked prior power of attorney; or

(ii) a statement signed by the taxpayer listing the name and address of each recognized representative authorized under the prior unrevoked power of attorney.

(2) *Statement of revocation filed.* A taxpayer may revoke a power of attorney without authorizing a new representative by filing a statement of revocation with those offices of the Internal Revenue Service where the tax- payer has filed the power of attorney to be revoked. The statement of revocation must indicate that the authority of the first power of attorney is revoked and must be signed by the taxpayer. Also, the name and address of each recognized representative whose authority is revoked must be listed (or a copy of the power of attorney to be revoked must be attached).

(b) By *the recognized representative — (1) Revocation of power of attorney.* A recognized representative may withdraw from representation in a matter in which a power of attorney has been filed by filing a statement with those offices of the Internal Revenue Service where the power of attorney to be revoked was filed. The statement must be signed by the representative and must identify the name and address of the taxpayer(s) and the matter(s) from which the representative is withdrawing.

(2) *Substitution or delegation of recognized representative.* Any recognized representative appointed in a power of attorney may substitute or delegate authority under the power of attorney to another recognized representative if substitution or delegation is specifically permitted under the power of attorney. Unless otherwise provided in the power of attorney, a recognized representative may make a substitution or delegation without the consent of any other recognized representative appointed to represent the taxpayer in the same matter. A substitution or delegation is effected by filing the following items with offices of the Internal Revenue Service where the power of attorney has been filed —

(i) *Notice of substitution or delegation.* A Notice of Substitution or Delegation is a statement signed by the recognized representative appointed under the power of attorney. The statement must contain the name and mailing address of the new recognized representative and, if more than one individual is to represent the taxpayer in the matter, a designation of which recognized representative is to receive notices and other written communications;

(ii) Declaration of representative. A written declaration which is made by the new representative as required by §601.502(b); and

(iii) Power of attorney. A power of attorney which specifically authorizes the substitution or delegation.

An employee of a recognized representative may not be substituted for his/her employer with respect to the representation of a taxpayer before the Internal Revenue Service unless the employee is a recognized representative in his/her own capacity under the provisions of §601.502(a). However, even if such employee is not a recognized representative in his/her own capacity under the provisions of §601.502(a), that individual may be authorized by the taxpayer under a tax information authorization to receive and/or inspect confidential tax return information under the provisions of section 6103 of the Internal Revenue Code and the regulations thereunder.

§601.506 Notices to be given to recognized representative; direct contact with taxpayer; delivery of a check drawn on the United States Treasury to recognized representative.

(a) *General.* Any notice or other written communication (or a copy thereof) required or permitted to be given to a taxpayer in any matter before the Internal Revenue Service must be given to the taxpayer and, unless restricted by the taxpayer, to the representative according to the following procedures —

(1) If the taxpayer designates more than one recognized representative to receive notices and other written communications, it will be the practice of the Internal Revenue Service to give copies of such to two (but not more than two) individuals so designated.

(2) In a case in which the taxpayer does not designate which recognized representative is to receive notices, it will be the practice of the Internal Revenue Service to give notices and other communications to the first recognized representative appointed on the power of attorney.

(3) Failure to give notice or other written communication to the recognized representative of a taxpayer will not affect the validity of any notice or other written communication delivered to a taxpayer.

Unless otherwise indicated in the document, a power of attorney other than Form 2848 will be presumed to grant the authority to receive notices or other written communication (or a copy thereof) required or permitted to be given to a taxpayer in any matter(s) before the Internal Revenue Service to which the power of attorney pertains.

(b) *Cases where taxpayer may be contacted directly.* Where a recognized representative has unreasonably delayed or hindered an examination, collection or investigation by failing to furnish, after repeated requests, nonprivileged information necessary to the examination, collection or investigation, the Internal Revenue Service employee conducting the examination, collection or investigation may request the pen-nission of his/her immediate supervisor to contact the taxpayer directly for such information.

(1) *Procedure.* If such permission is granted, the case file will be documented with sufficient facts to show how the examination, collection or investigation was being delayed or hindered. Written notice of such permis-

sion, briefly stating the reason why it was granted, will be given to both the recognized representative and the taxpayer together with a request of the taxpayer to supply such nonprivileged information. (See section 752 1 (c) of the Internal Revenue Code and the regulations there-under.)

(2) *Effect of direct notification.* Permission to by-pass a recognized representative and contact a taxpayer directly does not automatically disqualify an individual to act as the recognized representative of a taxpayer in a matter. However, such information may be referred to the Director of Practice for possible disciplinary proceedings under Circular No. 230, (31 CFR Part 10).

(c) *Delivery of a check drawn on the United States Treasury-(I) General.* A check drawn on the United States Treasury (e.g., a check in payment of refund of internal revenue taxes, penalties, or interest, see §601.504(a)(5)) will be mailed to the recognized representative of a taxpayer provided that a power of attorney is filed containing specific authorization for this to be done.

(2) *Address of recognized representative.* The check will be mailed to the address of the recognized representative listed on the power of attorney unless such recognized representative notifies the Internal Revenue Service in writing that his/her mailing address has been changed.

(3) *Authorization of more than one recognized representative.* In the event a power of attorney authorizes more than one recognized representative to receive a check on the taxpayer's behalf, and such representatives have different addresses, the Internal Revenue Service will mail the check directly to the taxpayer, unless a statement (signed by all of the recognized representatives so authorized) is submitted which indicates the address to which the check is to be mailed.

(4) *Cases in litigation.* The provisions of §601.506(c) concerning the issuance of a tax refund do not apply to the issuance of a check in payment of claims which have been either reduced to judgment or settled in the course (or as a result) of litigation.

(d) *Centralized Authorization File (CAF) system-(I) Information recorded onto the CAF system.* Information from both powers of attorney and tax information authorizations is recorded onto the CAF system. Such information enables Internal Revenue Service personnel who do not have access to the actual power of attorney or tax information authorization to-

(i) deten-nine whether a recognized representative or a designee is authorized by a taxpayer to receive and/or inspect confidential tax return information;

(ii) determine, in the case of a recognized representative, whether that representative is authorized to perform the acts set forth in §601.504(a); and

(iii) send copies of computer generated notices and communications to a recognized representative or a designee so authorized by the taxpayer.

(2) *CAF number.* A Centralized Authorization File (CAF) number generally will be issued to-

(i) a recognized representative who files a power of attorney and a written declaration of representative; or

(ii) a designee authorized under a tax information authorization.

The issuance of a CAF number does not indicate that a person is either recognized or authorized to practice before the Internal Revenue Service. Such determination is made under the provisions of Circular No. 230, (31 CFR Part 10). The purpose of the CAF number is to facilitate the processing of a power of attorney or a tax information authorization submitted by a recognized representative or a designee. A recognized representative or a designee should include the same CAF number on every power of attorney or tax information authorization filed. However, because the CAF number is not a substantive requirement (i.e., as listed in §601.503(a)), a tax information authorization or power of attorney which does not include such number will not be rejected based on the absence of a CAF number.

(3) *Tax matters recorded on CAF* Although a power of attorney or tax information authorization may be filed in all matters under the jurisdiction of the Internal Revenue Service, only those documents which meet each of the following criteria will be recorded onto the CAF system-

(i) *Specific tax period.* Only documents which concern a matter(s) relating to a specific tax period will be recorded onto the CAF system. A power of attorney or tax information authorization filed in a matter unrelated to a specific period (e.g., the 100% penalty for failure to pay over withholding taxes imposed by section 6672 of the Internal Revenue Code, applications for an employer identification number, and requests for a private letter ruling pertaining to a proposed transaction) cannot be recorded onto the CAF system.

(ii) *Future three-year limitation.* Only documents which concern a tax period that ends no later than three years after the date a power of attorney is received by the Internal Revenue Service will be recorded onto the CAF system. For example, a power of attorney received by the Internal Revenue Service on August 1, *1990,* which indicates that the authorization applies to Forms *941* for the quarters ended December 31, *1990* through Decem- ber *31, 2000, will* be recorded onto the CAF system for the applicable tax periods which end no later than July *31, 1993* (i.e., three years after the date of receipt by the Internal Revenue Service).

(iii) *Documentsfor prior tax periods.* Documents which concern any tax period which has ended prior to the date on which a power of attorney is received by the Internal Revenue Service will be recorded onto the CAF system provided that matters concerning such years are under consideration by the Internal Revenue Service.

(iv) *Limitation on the number of representatives recorded onto the CAF system. No* more than three representatives appointed under a power of attorney or three persons designated under a tax information authorization will be recorded onto the CAF system. If more than three representatives are appointed under a power of attorney or more than three persons are designated under a tax information authorization, only the first three names will be recorded onto the CAF system.

The fact that a power of attorney or tax information authorization cannot be recorded onto the CAF system is not determinative of the (current or future) validity of such document. For example, a power of attorney or tax information authorization which concerns tax periods that end more than three years from the date of receipt by the Internal Revenue Service is not invalid for the period(s) not recorded onto the CAF system. Such power of attorney or tax information authorization may be resubmitted at a later date.

§601.507 Evidence required to substantiate facts alleged by a recognized representative.

The Internal Revenue Service may require a recognized representative to submit all documentary evidence required to substantiate alleged facts (except that of a supplementary or incidental character) over a declara- tion (signed under penalty of perjury) that the recog- nized representative prepared or reviewed such documentary evidence and that to the best of his/her knowledge or belief the facts contained therein are true. In any case in which a recognized representative is unable or unwilling to declare his/her own knowledge that the facts are true and correct, the Internal Revenue Service may require the taxpayer to make such a declaration under penalty of perjury.

§601.508 Dispute between recognized representatives of a taxpayer.

Where there is a dispute between two or more recognized representatives concerning who is entitled to represent a taxpayer in a matter pending before the Internal Revenue Service (or to receive a check drawn on the United States Treasury), the Internal Revenue Service will not recognize any of the disputing representatives. However, if the contesting recognized representatives designate one or more of their number under the terms of an agreement signed by all, the Internal Revenue Service will recognize such designated recognized representative(s) upon receipt of a copy of such agreement according to the terms of the power of attorney.

§601.509 Power of attorney not required in cases docketed in the Tax Court of the United States.

The petitioner and the Commissioner of Internal Revenue stand in the position of parties litigant before a judicial body in a case docketed in the Tax Court of the United States. The Tax Court has its own rules of practice and procedure and its own rules respecting admission to practice before it. Accordingly, a power of attorney is not required to be submitted by an attorney of record in a case which is docketed in the Tax Court. Correspondence in connection with cases docketed in the Tax Court will be addressed to the attorney of record before the Court. However, a power of attorney is required to be submitted by an individual other than the attorney of record in any matter before the Internal Revenue Service concerning a docketed case.

(Section 7805 of the Internal Revenue Code of 1986 (68A Stat. 917; 26 U.S.C. 7805) and 5 U.S.C. 301)

(SEAL)

FRED T. GOLDBERG, JR.
Commissioner of Internal Revenue

(As published in the issue of the Federal Register for May 28, 1991, 56 F. R. 24001-24009).

* U.S. GOVERNMENT PRINTING OFFICE: 1998 615-015/61844

Appendix C: Limited Practice without Enrollment[xxxiv]

Publication 470 (Rev. 1-82)
Cat. No. 46538V

Limited Practice Without Enrollment

26 CFR 601.502: Requirements for conference-recognition to practice and, in certain cases, power of attorney or tax information authorization. (Also 31 CFR Part 10, Section 10.7: Limited practice without enrollment.)

Rev. Proc. 81-38

Section 1. Purpose

The purpose of this revenue procedure is to prescribe the standards of conduct, the scope of authority, and the circumstances and conditions under which an individual preparer of tax returns may exercise, without enrollment, the privilege of limited practice as a taxpayer's representative before the Internal Revenue Service, pursuant to section 10.7(a)(7) of Treasury Department Circular No. 230, [1966-2 C.B. 1171] (31 CFR Part 10).

Sec. 2. Changes

This revenue procedure modifies Rev. Proc. 68-20, 1968-1 C.B. 812, to reflect changes in titles based on the Internal Revenue Service's reorganization effective July 2, 1978, and applicable revisions to Treasury Department Circular No. 230, [19671-C.B. 433; 1970-2 C.B. 644] relating to practice before the Internal Revenue Service.

Sec. 3. Applicability

.01 This revenue procedure, issued pursuant to section 10.7(a)(7) of Circular 230, applies to all unenrolled individual preparers of returns who seek to represent taxpayers, within the United States, before examining officers in the Examination Division of an Office of a District Director of Internal Revenue or in the Office of International Operations. Any reference herein to the District Director will be construed, where appropriate, to include the Office of International Operations or the Director of International Operations.

.02 This revenue procedure does not apply to attorneys, certified public accountants, or agents who are enrolled to practice before the Internal Revenue Service. The rules governing the practice of such persons before the Service are contained in the provisions of Circular 230.

Sec. 4. Scope of Authority

.01 An unenrolled individual who signs a return as its preparer may act as the taxpayer's representative if accompanied by the taxpayer, or by filing a written authorization from the taxpayer as provided herein in section 6. Such representation is limited to practice before examining officers of the Examination Division in the offices of District Directors and in the Office of International Operations, and may only encompass matters concerning the tax liability of the taxpayer for the taxable year covered by that return, subject to the limitations herein prescribed.

.02 Privilege of limited practice before the Internal Revenue Service is limited to any person who is not under disbarment or suspension from practice before the Internal Revenue Service or from practice of the person's profession by any other authority (in the case of attorneys, certified public accountants, public accountants, or actuaries).

.03 An unenrolled individual who prepared a return that provides no space on the prescribed form for signature of the preparer, or who prepared a return with respect to which the instructions or regulations do not require that it be signed by the preparer, may appear as the taxpayer's representative, if properly authorized, as set forth in section 4.01.

.04 If the unenrolled preparer appears before the examining officers without the taxpayer, written authorization from the taxpayer for such representation as provided in section 6 must be filed with the examining officer along with a declaration that he or she is not currently under suspension or disbarment from practice before the Internal Revenue Service. The unenrolled preparer may also be required to furnish satisfactory identification.

.05 The unenrolled preparer will be expected to recognize questions, issues and factual situations of such difficulty as to require additional expert assistance and to suggest to the taxpayer that the taxpayer seek such assistance.

.06 If a carryback or carryfoward, or both, are involved in a tax return, the unenrolled preparer will not be recognized as the taxpayer's representative with respect to the taxable year in which the carryback or carryforward arose unless that person prepared and signed a return for that year or years.

.07 The privilege to practice as a taxpayer's representative in accordance with this revenue's procedure shall not constitute enrollment nor a finding of eligibility for enrollment.

Sec. 5. Limitations of the Privilege of Limited Practice

.01 Privilege of limited practice without enrollment afforded an individual preparer of returns is restricted to representation before the examining officer stated in section 4.04. No unenrolled preparer shall represent or correspond as the taxpayer's representative before the Appeals offices nor before the officials in the National Office.

.02 In addition, the following acts on behalf of the taxpayer are beyond the scope of authority permitted an unenrolled preparer:

(a) Executing claims for refund;
(b) Receiving checks in payment of any refund of Internal Revenue taxes, penalties, or interest;
(c) Executing consents to extend the statutory period for assessment or collection of a tax;
(d) Executing closing agreements with respect to a tax liability or specific matter; and
(e) Executing waivers of restriction on assessment or collection of a deficiency in tax.

Sec. 6. Form of Authorization From the Taxpayer and Declaration by the Representative

.01 Internal Revenue Service Form 2848-D, Authorization and Declaration, which can be obtained from local Internal Revenue Service offices, may be used in meeting the authorization and declaration requirements in section 4.04 of this revenue procedure. Part I of Form 2848-D is the taxpayer's authorization for the representative to receive and inspect confidential tax information and act as the taxpayer's representative before the Internal Revenue Service and to make written or oral presentations of fact or argument on behalf of the taxpayer for the specified tax matter(s). Part II is the representative's declaration that the representative is not currently under suspension or disbarment from practice before the Internal Revenue Service and is authorized to represent the taxpayer as a certified public accountant, attorney, enrolled agent, unenrolled return preparer, etc.

.02 The use of technical language in the preparation of an authorization is not necessary, but the instrument must clearly indicate that the designated unenrolled preparer is authorized to represent the taxpayer before the Internal Revenue Service and specify the return prepared to which the authority relates. The authorization must also clearly set forth the taxpayer's name and address, the name and mailing address of the unenrolled preparer and must be signed by the taxpayer or taxpayers.

Sec. 7. Ethics and Conduct

.01 An unenrolled preparer shall act in such manner as not to commit any act of disreputable conduct. Disreputable conduct includes, but is not limited to, the items contained in section 10.51 of Circular 230.

.02 An unenrolled preparer shall not charge an unconscionable fee for representation of a client in any matter before the Internal Revenue Service.

.03 An unenrolled preparer shall not neglect or refuse to submit records or information in any matter before the Internal Revenue Service upon proper and lawful request by a duly authorized officer or employee of the Service; and the unenrolled preparer shall not interfere, or attempt to interfere, with any proper and lawful efforts by the officers of employees of the Service to obtain information, unless the preparer believes in good faith and on reasonable grounds that the request for, or effort to obtain, such record or information is of doubtful legality.

.04 Any unenrolled preparer who knows that the client has not complied with the revenue law, or that the client has made an error in or omission from any return, document, affidavit, or other paper that the client is required by law to execute in connection with any matter administered by the Service, shall advise the client promptly of the fact of the noncompliance, error, or omission.

.05 An unenrolled preparer shall exercise due diligence in preparing or assisting in the preparation, approving, and filing of returns, documents, affidavits, or other papers relating to Internal Revenue Service matters. The preparer shall also exercise due diligence in determining (1) the correctness of oral and written representations made by the preparer to the Service, and (2) the correctness of representations made by the preparer to the client with reference to any matter administered by the Service.

.06 An unenrolled preparer shall not unreasonably delay the prompt disposition of any matter before the Internal Revenue Service.

.07 An unenrolled preparer, as a Notary Public, shall not take acknowledgements, administer oaths, certify papers, or perform any official act in connection with matters relating to the client's tax liabilities, or in connection with any other matter in which the preparer may in any way have given assistance or been employed. In addition, the preparer may not take any acknowledgements, oaths, or certification as a Notary Public relating to any tax return, protest, or other document that the preparer has prepared or that the preparer has assisted in preparing. (26 OP. Atty. Gen. 236.)

.08 An unenrolled preparer shall not procure, or attempt to procure, directly or indirectly, from Government records or Government sources, information of any kind that is not made available by proper authority.

.09 An unenrolled preparer shall not represent conflicting interests in the preparer's limited practice before the Service, except by express consent of all directly interested parties after full disclosure has been made.

Sec. 8. Solicitation and Advertising

.01 An unenrolled preparer shall not make, directly or indirectly, an uninvited solicitation of employment, except as noted below, in matters relating to the Internal Revenue Service. Solicitation includes, but is not limited to, in-person contacts, telephone communications, and personal mailings directed to the specific circumstances unique to the recipient. This restriction does not apply to (1) seeking new business from an existing or former client in a related matter or (2) solicitation by mailings, the contents of which are designed for the general public.

.02 No unenrolled preparer shall, with respect to any Internal Revenue Service matter, in any way use or participate in the use of any form of public communication containing false, fraudulent, misleading, deceptive, unduly influencing, coercive, or unfair statement or claim. This prohibition includes, but is not limited to, statements pertaining to the quality of services rendered unless subject to factual verification, claims of specialized expertise not authorized by state or federal agencies having jurisdiction over the preparer, and the statements or suggestions that the ingenuity and/or prior record of a representative rather than the merit of the matter are principal factors likely to determine the result of the matter.

.03 An unenrolled preparer may, in a dignified manner, publish, use, or broadcast through any means of communication:

(a) The name, address, telephone number and office hours of the preparer or firm;
(b) The names of individuals associated with the firm;
(c) A factual description of the services offered;
(d) That certain credit cards and other credit arrangements will be accepted;
(e) Foreign language ability;
(f) Appropriate fee information; and
(g) Other facts relevant to the selection of an unenrolled preparer, which are not prohibited by the provisions of this revenue procedure.

Sec. 9. Persons Ineligible To Practice Under This Revenue Procedure

.01 The following persons shall be ineligible to exercise the privilege of limited practices before the Internal Revenue Service:

(a) Any individual who has been convicted of any criminal offense under the Revenue Laws of the United States or any offense involving dishonesty or breach of trust within 5 years of the date of attempt to exercise the privilege. Individuals who have been so convicted more than 5 years before the date of attempt to exercise the privilege may be permitted to practice upon showing of evidence of rehabilitation satisfactory to the Director of the Examination Division;
(b) Any individual who is under disbarment or suspension from practice as an attorney, certified public accountant, public accountant, or actuary by any duly constituted authority of any state, possession, territory, Commonwealth, the District of Columbia, any federal court of record, or any federal agency, body or board;
(c) Any individual who is disbarred or suspended from practice before the Internal Revenue Service;
(d) Any individual whose application for enrollment to practice before the Internal Revenue Service has been denied;
(e) Any individual who refuses or has refused to comply with this revenue procedure;
(f) Any individual whose conduct or practices have been or are such as to constitute a violation of SEC.7 or 8 of this revenue procedure;
(g) Any individual who is an officer or employee of the United States or of the District of Columbia; and
(h) Any individual who is an officer or employee of any state or any subdivision thereof, whose duties authorize such individual to investigate, pass upon, or act with respect to tax matters of that state or subdivision, if such employment may make or makes available to the individual facts or information applicable to federal tax matters.

.02 In addition, corporations, associations, partnerships, or other business entities are ineligible to practice before the Internal Revenue Service.

Sec. 10. Rules Governing Recognition of Unenrolled Preparers

.01 Any examining officer, or other Service officer or employee who has reason to believe that an unenrolled preparer's conduct has been or is such as would render the preparer ineligible to appear as the taxpayer's representative before the Internal Revenue Service, shall communicate this information to the District Director of the taxpayer.

.02 In administering this revenue procedure, each District Director exercises original jurisdiction in determining whether an unenrolled preparer is eligible to appear as a taxpayer's representative. When the District Director receives information, either before or after an unenrolled preparer has been recognized, indicating that the preparer's conduct , practice, or employment has been or may be such as to render the preparer ineligible to represent taxpayers, the District Director will issue a written notice to the unenrolled preparer of proposed determination of ineligibility. This notice will contain information sufficient to apprise the unenrolled preparer of the basis for the proposed determination of ineligibility and will contain a request for a written reply within 30 days, and advise as to whether a conference is desired with the District Director of the District Director's delegate. if the unenrolled preparer fails to reply, or upon review if a reply is filed, or after a conference if one is held, the District Director will notify the unenrolled preparer in writing of the District Director's final determination. When warranted, the determination will state the unenrolled preparer is ineligible to exercise the privilege of limited practice before the Service and that the District Director's determination may be appealed to the Director, Examination Division. A copy of each final determination of ineligibility issued by the District Director will be fowarded to the Director, Examination Division, National Office, Internal Revenue Service, together with copies of the notice of proposed determination of ineligibility, the unenrolled prepare's reply, if one is filed, and any other related papers or documents.

.03 An unenrolled preparer who wishes to appeal a District Director's final determination of ineligibility may, within 30 days of receipt of the final determination, submit a signed, written appeal together with the preparer's reasons in support of it, addressed to the Internal Revenue Service, Assistant Commissioner (Compliance), Director, Examination Division, Attention: CP:E:E:C,[*] 1111 Constitution Avenue, N.W., Washington, D.C. 20224. Upon filing of the written appeal, and the reasons in support of it, the unenrolled preparer, upon request, will be afforded the opportunity of a conference with the Director, Examination Division or the Director's designee. A decision will then be rendered by the Director, Examination Division or the Director's designee affirming, reversing, or modifying the decision of the District Director upon such terms and conditions as seem warranted under the facts and circumstances of the particular appeal. The decision of the Director, Examination Division or the Director's designee on this appeal will be final.

.04 Whenever an unenrolled preparer's or conduct has been or is such as would render the preparer ineligible to appear as the taxpayer's representative before the Internal Revenue Service, Service employees will continue to recognize the representative until a final determination of ineligibility has been issued by the District Director, and either the time for appeal has expired, or all appeals have been exhausted. However, recognition will not be continued where Service employees determine, or receive instructions from the District Director or the District Director's designee, that the representative should not be recognized because significant rights or interests of the taxpayer or Internal Revenue Service could be substantially harmed by continued recognition.

Sec. 11. Special Orders

.01 The Director, Examination Division may issue such special orders as the Director may deem proper in any matter within the purview of this revenue procedure,

.02 The unenrolled preparer who has been determined ineligible for limited practice before the Internal Revenue Service may request, after 1 year following the notice of final determination of ineligibility or decision on appeal, that the preparer's eligibility for limited practice be reinstated. Requests for reinstatement will be made to the District Director who may modify or revoke any previous determination. The District Director will consider the nature of the violation that resulted in ineligilbitly, the period of ineligibility, and the preparer's current adherence to the standards of ethics and conduct established by this revenue procedure in evaluating the request for reinstatement to limited practice. The consideration of a request for reinstatement will not be a reevaluation of any original determination of ineligibilty.

Sec.12. Inquiries

Inquiries from unenrolled preparers and Service personnel regarding this revenue procedure should be addressed to the Internal Revenue Service, Assistant Commissioner (Compliance), Director, Examination Division, Attention: CP:E:E:C, [*] 1111 Constitution Avenue, N.W., Washington, D.C., 20224.

Sec.13. Effect on Other Documents

Rev. Proc. 68-20 is modified and, as modified, is superseded.

---

*Now designated as CP:E:E:S

Appendix D: Criminal Case Studies

Case Studies:

Examples of Tax Fraud Investigations
Fiscal Years 2011 - 2014[xxxv]

The following examples of employment tax fraud investigations are written from public record documents on file in the court records in the judicial district in which the cases were prosecuted.

Oregon Man Sentenced on Tax Evasion Charges

On Sept. 26, 2014, in Portland, Oregon, Stephen Gregory Nagy, of Hillsboro, Oregon, was sentenced to 19 months in prison, three years of supervised release and ordered to pay $481,517 in restitution to the IRS. Nagy, who had previously pleaded guilty to tax evasion, was the president of S&S Drywall Assemblies, a company providing drywall services in the construction industry, from January 2005 through September 2011. Nagy conducted extensive business transactions in cash in order to hide funds from the IRS. He obtained the cash by illegally hiring undocumented workers to work on prevailing wage jobs, paying them a small portion of the prevailing hourly rate, and demanding that they kick back the largest portion of their wages to him in cash. Nagy failed to report this cash to the IRS. Nagy also forced some S&S Drywall employees to file for unemployment benefits through the Oregon Employment Department. After the employees filed for unemployment coverage, Nagy fraudulently insisted that they continue to work full-time for S&S Drywall. The unemployment benefits did not fully compensate the employees at a rate equal to their previous S&S Drywall salaries. To make up the deficit, Nagy gave employees cash payments amounting to the difference between the unemployment benefits and their full-time salaries. These cash wages were not reported to the IRS. Nagy also did not withhold federal income taxes, or Social Security and Medicare taxes from these cash payments. Nagy thwarted IRS collection efforts by placing business and personal assets in the names of others, by physically hiding the assets, and by eventually transferring all S&S Drywall Assemblies income, contracts, receivables, and assets to ASM Drywall, Inc., a shell company he created and placed in his sister's name.

Wisconsin Man Sentenced for Failure to Pay Over Payroll Taxes

On Sept. 23, 2014, in Madison, Wisconsin, Jeffrey Grams, of Edgerton, was sentenced to 15 months in prison and three years of supervised release. According to court documents, Jeffrey Grams was the sole owner of Rock River Concrete and managing partner of Braton Property Group. He had corporate responsibility to collect, account for, and pay over payroll taxes for these corporations. From 2007 to 2009, Grams collected over $265,000 from his employees in federal income taxes and Medicare and social security taxes, but made no payments to the IRS for the withheld taxes.

Former Defense Contractor Sentenced to Prison for Theft of Employee Payroll Taxes and Pension Plan Contributions

On Sept. 11, 2014, in Alexandria, Virginia, William P. Danielczyk Jr., formerly of Oakton, was sentenced to 18 months in prison, three years of supervised release, and ordered to pay more than $1.6 million in restitution to the IRS. Danielczyk pleaded guilty on June 10 to failing to collect and pay more than $2.2 million in employee payroll taxes and engaging in theft of more than $186,000 from an employee pension plan. Danielczyk's sentencing will be served consecutively to a 28 month prison term he is already serving for committing campaign finance violations during the 2008 presidential primary and a 2006 U.S. Senate campaign. According to court documents, from March 2009 until December 2011, Danielczyk was the executive chairman of Innolog Holdings Corporation, which acquired Innovative Logistics Technology Inc. in March 2009. From mid-2009 through the end of 2011, Danielczyk was responsible for collecting, accounting for and paying appropriate payroll tax amounts to the IRS. Although payroll taxes were withheld from the wages of Innovative's employees, Danielczyk failed to pay both the employee withholdings amounts and the employer's matching portions to the IRS. Additionally, Innovative's employees were allowed to contribute money from their bi-weekly paychecks to a qualified pension plan that was administered by an asset custodian. Danielczyk, was the person responsible for authorizing payments to the asset custodian, and failed to send these payments over the course of three years. From 2009 through 2011, this conduct led to a total loss of $186,263. Danielczyk made a variety of purchases for his personal use from company accounts.

Pennsylvania Businessman Sentenced for Tax Crimes

On Aug. 22, 2014, in Philadelphia, Pennsylvania, Harvey G. Bitler, Sr., of Shillington, was sentenced to 46 months in prison, three years of supervised release and ordered to pay restitution of $5,078,897. Bitler previously pleaded guilty to failing to pay over to the government income taxes, social security taxes and Medicare taxes withheld from his employees' paychecks. According to court documents, Bitler was the owner of Big H Farms and BH Farms in Berks County, Pennsylvania. Big H Farms provided labor for mushroom growing facilities and BH Farms employed salaried employees associated with the operation and management of Big H Farms. The companies withheld Medicare and Social Security taxes (FICA taxes) and income taxes from their employees' paychecks but, between 2007 and 2012, Big H made no payments to the Internal Revenue Service of these withheld taxes. Between 2008 and 2012, BH Farms also failed to pay over all the taxes withheld in the first quarter of 2008, and made no payments to the Internal Revenue Service for the remaining quarters of those years.

Construction Company Owner Sentenced for Fraud in Connection With Renovation of Federal Building

On Aug. 7, 2014, in Boston, Massachusetts, Wael Isreb, of Wrentham, was sentenced to four years of probation, including 18 months of home confinement, and ordered to pay $164,627 in restitution. In March 2014, Isreb and his co-defendant, Aluisio Dasilva, of Hudson, each pleaded guilty to conspiracy to commit mail fraud and false statements in connection with the renovation of the John W. McCormack Post Office and Courthouse in Boston. According to court documents, Isreb was the owner of Taunton Forms, a now-defunct concrete construction company that was retained as a subcontractor to perform work on the McCormack Building. Taunton Forms was paid in excess of $1 million for its work. Beginning in about December 2007, Isreb conspired with Dasilva and others to pay Taunton Forms workers less than the prevailing wage while certifying that they were being paid the prevailing wage. The defendants also falsely reported that workers had been laid off which permitted the workers to offset their lower wages with unemployment benefits. Isreb also avoided making fringe benefit payments as required. Finally, Isreb failed to withhold applicable payroll taxes. On July 15, 2014, Dasilva was sentenced to one year of probation and ordered to pay restitution of $10,840.

Maine Woman Sentenced on Immigration, Money Laundering and Tax Charges

On July 1, 2014, in Bangor, Maine, Mei Ya Zhang, of Waterville, was sentenced to 15 months in prison, three years of supervised release and ordered to pay more than $88,000 in restitution to the IRS. On June 5, 2013, Zhang pleaded guilty to harboring undocumented aliens for commercial advantage and private financial gain, money laundering conspiracy, and conspiracy to file false employer's quarterly federal tax returns. According to court records, between 2006 and 2011, Zhang was the manager of a Chinese buffet restaurant that brought undocumented aliens into Maine to work. Among other actions, Zhang paid the undocumented aliens under the table with cash generated illegally by their employment. Zhang filed numerous false quarterly employment tax returns in which the undocumented aliens were not disclosed and employment taxes were not properly withheld or paid.

Georgia Business Owner Sentenced for Impeding the Collection of Payroll Taxes

On June 30, 2014, in Atlanta, Georgia, Paulette Bryant, of Stockbridge, was sentenced to 36 months in prison, one year of supervised release and ordered to pay restitution of $2,914,931. Bryant previously pleaded guilty to obstructing and impeding the IRS's collection of payroll taxes. According to court documents, Bryant owned and operated a temporary employment staffing business in Georgia. Between 1998 and 2009, except for brief periods during or relating to an IRS audit, Bryant's business failed to make the required quarterly filings and to pay the IRS the payroll taxes owed by her employees and business. Bryant used the funds that should have been paid to the IRS to operate her company and fund her personal lifestyle. Additionally, Bryant formed and used new, overlapping corporate identities that had various names and that used various pseudonyms as corporate officers. Bryant's intent was to delay and hinder the IRS's efforts to collect the employment taxes that her business owed.

Business Owner Sentenced for Failure to Pay Employment Taxes

On May 29, 2014, in Springfield, Missouri, Kerry W. May, of Ozark, was sentenced to 12 months and one day in prison and ordered to pay $94,485 in restitution, in addition to the $373,200 in restitution that May has already paid. On Oct. 3, 2012, May pleaded guilty to two counts of failure to collect, or to truthfully account for and pay over employment taxes for his two corporations, Spring Creek Antiques, Inc. and Riverview Antique Center, Inc. According to court documents, from 2003 through 2009, May engaged in a deliberate scheme to avoid reporting or paying the trust fund taxes on approximately $373,200 he withheld from his employees' paychecks. May withheld taxes from his employees' pay, but simply pocketed the funds without reporting the withholding to the IRS or making the required trust fund payments.

Missouri Man Sentenced on Conspiracy Charges

On June 2, 2014, in St. Louis, Missouri, Jason Rauschelbach, of O'Fallon, was sentenced to 24 months in prison. Rauschelbach pleaded guilty to conspiring to defraud the United States and several banks. According to court documents, Rauschelbach was the CEO of The Mortgage Store, Inc. (TMS) and the president of Title America. The businesses were operating at a financial deficit in 2008. TMS incurred over $600,000 in federal employment tax liabilities in the first three quarters of 2008 that were not paid over to the United States. There were not sufficient funds available to fund the disbursements from TMS and, in addition, to meet all of the expenses incurred by TMS. In order to meet certain expenses and, at the same time, conceal the absence of adequate funds, Rauschelbach and others at TMS caused insufficient funds checks drawn on the checking accounts of both TMS and Title America to be deposited between those accounts in such a way that the "float" concealed the true balances of each account. The TMS account had a negative balance of approximately $850,000 in June, 2008, when the banks stopped accepting the floated checks. Court documents showed that Rauschelbach received substantial distributions from TMS and Title America in 2008 despite the federal employment tax delinquencies and other unpaid liabilities. In addition, he and others at TMS directed that TMS funds be paid on loans on properties at Tan Tar A Resorts in the Lake of the Ozarks, and for a ranch property in Breckenridge, Colorado. He was a partial owner of those properties. Rauschelbach submitted a false net worth statements to HUD and failed to pay over about $31,000 in employees' withholdings for a 401K plan and health insurance. Restitution payments will be first directed to reimburse those employees.

Texas Business Owners Sentenced for Failing to Pay Taxes to IRS

On May 2, 2014, in Laredo, Texas, Jorge Montemayor and Leticia Reyna were sentenced to 30 months and 15 months in prison, respectively, and three years of supervised release. In addition, Montemayor was ordered to pay $368,025 in restitution while Reyna was ordered to pay $48,562 in restitution. Montemayor and Reyna pleaded guilty on Jan. 24, 2014, and Nov. 18, 2013, respectively, to failing to pay over employment taxes to the IRS. According to court documents, Montemayor was the chief financial officer of GDM Home Health Inc. and Reyna was the president of Professional Skilled Services Inc., both home health care businesses that provided basic skilled care in Laredo. In their roles, both had authority to conduct financial transactions and exercised signatory authority on the company's bank accounts. As part of the plea, Montemayor admitted he knowingly and willfully failed to pay approximately $368,025 of federal income and FICA and Medicare taxes withheld from employee wages from the year 2008 while Reyna admitted she failed to pay over to the IRS approximately $48,562 for the fourth quarter of 2008. In his plea agreement, Montemayor admitted that corporate funds were used for lavish trips to Europe and Las Vegas, sporting events, restaurants, jewelry and real estate. In her agreement, Reyna admitted that corporate funds were used for shopping, restaurants and private school expenses.

Owner of Trucking Company Sentenced for Failure to Collect and Pay Over FICA Taxes

On April 24, 2014, in Minneapolis, Minn., Marlin Dahl, owner of Dahl Trucking in Elmore, Minn., was sentenced to 12 months and a day in prison. Dahl was convicted on Dec. 3, 2013 of failure to collect and pay over Federal Insurance Contribution Act (FICA) taxes. According to the evidence presented at trial, from 2007 to 2010, Dahl failed to deduct more than $54,000 in FICA taxes from his employees' payroll checks. Instead, Dahl recorded wage payments as "road expenses" incurred by Dahl Trucking employees, which were falsely treated them as reimbursements and not wages.

Businessmen Sentenced for Tax Fraud

On April 15, 2014 in San Antonio, Texas, Larry Kimes and Charles Pircher were sentenced to 144 months in prison and 132 months in prison, respectively, and three years of supervised release. Both men were each ordered to pay $132 million in restitution for their roles in a tax fraud conspiracy. According to court documents, Kimes was the manager of AccounTex Financial Services, LLC, and Pircher was the manager of a series of Professional Employer Organizations (PEOs) based in San Antonio, including Service Professionals. The PEOs entered into staff leasing agreements with various client companies to manage the companies' payroll and insurance programs. Between 2002 and 2008, the defendants stole more than $130 million from the clients of a series of PEOs. Kimes, Pircher and other co-conspirators diverted to their own use and benefit clients' monies that should have been paid for payroll taxes and insurance premiums.

Indiana Physician Sentenced for Failing to Pay Employment Taxes

On April 11, 2014, in Hammond, Ind., Ronald Eugene Jamerson, of Schererville, Ind., was sentenced to 12 months and one day in prison and ordered to pay $541,083 in restitution to the IRS. On Oct. 25, 2013, Jamerson pleaded guilty to one count of willfully failing to truthfully account for, collect and pay over employment taxes to the IRS. According to court documents, Jamerson is an otolaryngologist who opened his own medical practice in the late 1990s. Jamerson deducted and collected from his employees' paychecks federal income taxes and employment taxes in the amount of $63,929 over the 11 tax quarters, but failed to file the employment tax returns and pay over the related employment taxes.

Dental Center Owner Sentenced for Tax Evasion

On April 7, 2014, in Indianapolis, Ind., Sally Metzner was sentenced to 24 months in prison. Metzner previously pleaded guilty to tax evasion and failing to withhold social security and Medicare taxes for her employees. According to court documents, Metzner owned Anderson Dental Center in Anderson, Ind., for more than 10 years. Metzner, who is not a dentist, has a background in accounting and bookkeeping and personally controlled all of Anderson Dental's financial records. Metzner did not pay or file personal income taxes from 2006 to 2010. Metzner evaded income taxes through various means, including accounting for her own income from Anderson Dental as "miscellaneous expenses," and accounting for numerous personal expenses through the business as if they were business expenses. Metzner also failed to withhold and pay over taxes she was obligated to pay for social security and Medicare on behalf of her employees. The employee's pay stubs show that the appropriate amount of taxes were being withheld, however, Metzner did not pay any of this money to the IRS.

Maine Woman Sentenced on Immigration, Money Laundering and Tax Charges

On March 25, 2014, in Bangor, Maine, Mei Juan Zhang, of Fairfield, was sentenced to 14 months in prison, three years of supervised release and ordered to pay $54,288 in restitution to the IRS. Zhang pleaded guilty on April 18, 2013 to charges of harboring undocumented aliens for commercial advantage and private financial gain, money laundering and filing false employer's quarterly federal tax returns. According to court records, between 2009 and 2011, Zhang was the manager of the two restaurants in Waterville. In that capacity, she managed a Chinese buffet restaurant that brought undocumented aliens into Maine to work at the restaurants. Zhang paid them under the table with cash and filed numerous false quarterly employment tax returns in which the undocumented aliens were not disclosed and employment taxes were not properly withheld or paid. The investigation revealed that about half of the employees at the restaurant over that period were undocumented, and that the defendant's activities concealed about $250,000 in wages and thwarted the collection of about $55,000 in employment taxes.

Business Owners Sentenced on Tax Charges

On March 17, 2014 in Los Angeles, Calif., Robert and Karen Burdett were sentenced to 18 months in prison, three years of supervised release and ordered to jointly pay $1,074,223 in restitution. The Burdetts pleaded guilty in November 2013 to embezzlement from an employee benefit plan and failure to collect or pay over tax. According to the plea agreements, beginning in January 1996, the Burdetts began serving as trustees for their employee retirement benefit plan. Beginning in June 2004, they fell behind in the transmission of funds withheld by employees from their respective paychecks for contribution to the retirement plan. By June 2006, the Burdetts stopped transmitting any funds employees withheld from their respective paychecks for contribution to the retirement plan, embezzling $102,327 from the employee-participants plan. In addition, from at least September 1996 to July 2007, the Burdetts were the responsible parties regarding the collection and payment of their employees' federal income taxes and Federal Insurance Contributions Act taxes. During this time they failed to pay to the IRS approximately $971,896 in withheld trust fund taxes.

New Jersey Attorney Sentenced for Income Tax Evasion and Failing to Pay Payroll Taxes

On March 11, 2014, in Trenton, N.J., Lee Gottesman, of Toms River, N.J., was sentenced to six months in prison, six months of home confinement, three years of supervised release and ordered to pay $27,384 representing taxes owed from 2006 to the present. Gottesman, an attorney, previously pleaded guilty to an indictment charging him with one count of federal income tax evasion and one count of failing to pay payroll taxes for the employees of his law firm. According to court documents, Gottesman operated a law firm in Toms River. In 2002, the IRS filed a levy on Gottesman's assets because of unpaid taxes. Gottesman then opened a sub-account, within his attorney trust account, in the name of his wife. His wife had never been a legal client of his. Gottesman ran nearly all of his personal and business expenses through the account, closing all other business and personal accounts in his name. His payments from the account included more than $90,000 in mortgage payments for his home; more than $17,000 in household expenses, including maintenance on his pool, landscaping services and construction costs; and thousands of dollars in other personal expenses, such as life insurance premiums, auto body repair work and personal credit card payments. The scheme allowed Gottesman to avoid paying personal income taxes on the hidden income. Gottesman also withheld payroll and other taxes from his employees' pay, but never filed the required forms or turned the withheld payments over to the IRS. Gottesman specifically admitted he did not pay all his personal income taxes owed for 2006 or payroll taxes for 2009.

San Antonio Businessmen Sentenced for Money Laundering and Mail Fraud

On Feb. 21, 2014 in San Antonio, Texas, three individuals were sentenced for their roles in a $133 million tax fraud scheme. John Bean was sentenced to 72 months in prison, three years of supervised release and ordered to pay over $120 million in restitution. Bean pleaded guilty in March 2013 to money laundering and a mail fraud conspiracy. Pat Mire was sentenced to 36 months in prison, three years of supervised release and ordered to pay $10 million in restitution. Mire pleaded guilty in November 2011 to money laundering and a mail fraud conspiracy. Mike Solis was sentenced to 24 months in prison and three years of supervised release. Solis pleaded guilty in December 2012 to mail fraud conspiracy. A fourth defendant, John D. Walker II, was sentenced to five years' probation and ordered to pay $450,000 restitution. Walker pleaded guilty in May 2012 to a Klein tax fraud conspiracy charge and a false statements charge. Two other co-defendants, Larry Kimes and Charles Pircher, have both pleaded guilty and await sentencing. According to court documents, between 2002 and 2008, the defendants participated in a scheme in which they stole more than $133 million from the clients of a series of Professional Employer Organizations (PEO) operated by the defendants. The PEOs entered into staff leasing agreements with various client companies to manage the companies' payroll and insurance programs. The co-conspirators diverted to their own use and benefit clients' monies that should have been paid for payroll taxes and insurance premiums.

New York Attorney Sentenced for Tax Violations

On Feb. 19, 2014, in Buffalo, N.Y., Edmund J. Renaud, of Olean, N.Y., was sentenced to 15 months in prison. Renaud was convicted of evading the payment of taxes involving his moving companies. According to court documents, Renaud failed to pay employment taxes for businesses he ran from 2002 through 2008. Renaud ran Southern Tier Moving and Storage, Inc., in Olean until 2002, when the IRS assessed over $48,000 in unpaid federal payroll taxes. Upon shutting down that entity, Renaud opened Southern Tier Moving and Storage, LLC, where from 2002 until 2006, Renaud similarly failed to pay over $86,000 in federal payroll taxes. Renaud provided false information to the IRS about bank accounts and other assets, including a truck he had gotten as a result of accumulating "comp" credits at a casino. Renaud also provided false information to the IRS in connection with filing an Offer in Compromise, including false claims that the company was out of business, failure to identify bank accounts and failure to disclose company assets.

Massachusetts Doctor Sentenced for Multiple Tax-Related Crimes

On Feb. 12, 2014, in Boston, Mass., Richard C. McGinn was sentenced to 30 months in prison and two years of supervised release. In 2013, a jury convicted McGinn, a doctor, of tax evasion, five counts of failing to pay over employment taxes and failure to file a tax return. According to court documents, from 2007 until 2009, McGinn owned and operated a medical practice in Greenfield, Mass. During that time, he evaded the payment of a tax liability of over $1 million which he had accumulated from 1987 to 2003. Among other things, McGinn paid personal expenses with corporate funds, and he used the bank account of a family member to conceal the income from the medical practice. During this time, McGinn also withheld employment taxes from the paychecks of his employees, and he kept the money for himself, rather than paying the money to the IRS as he was required to do. Additionally, McGinn failed to file corporate income tax returns for his medical practice.

New York Business Owner Sentenced for Failing to Pay Payroll Taxes

On January 29, 2014, in Buffalo, NY, John Creighton, of Bemus Point, N.Y., was sentenced to 12 months in prison and ordered to pay $663,627 in restitution for failing to pay payroll taxes. According to court documents, Creighton is the president and owner of Classic Brass Inc. (CBI) in Lakewood, N.Y. In 2010 and 2011, Creighton withheld payroll taxes from CBI employees. However, Creighton failed to make payroll tax payments to the IRS, and failed to file Forms 941.

North Carolina Woman Sentenced for Tax and Mortgage Fraud

On January 14, 2014, in Charlotte, N.C., Tega Burns, aka Tega Foy, was sentenced to 24 months in prison, two years of supervised release and ordered to pay $201,039 in restitution to IRS, $57,450 in restitution to Bank of America, and $48,483 in restitution to CIT Group Consumer Finance. In July 2012, Burns pleaded guilty to one count of failure to account for and pay over employment tax and one count of making a false statement on a loan application. According to court records, Burns was the owner of Family Homecare Services, a Charlotte-based company that provided in-home care services in the area from 2007 through 2011. Burns failed to pay a large part of the employment taxes her company owed for the relevant tax years. Burns had an outstanding employment tax liability of more than $200,000. To hide funds from the IRS and to evade payment of the outstanding taxes, Burns utilized nominees, including her son and her step-father. In addition, in May 2007, Burns obtained mortgage loans using false information, including fake employment documentation from her company, to purchase two homes in the name of another individual. Both of these homes were eventually foreclosed on, with losses to the banks.

Michigan Resident Sentenced for Filing False Tax Return

On November 4, 2013, in Detroit, Mich., Jason Syrek, of Adrian, Mich., was sentenced to 72 months in prison and ordered to pay $17,659,561 in restitution for healthcare fraud and filing false tax returns. According to court documents, from May 2008 to December 2010, Syrek operated a human resource company, CAS Resources of Adrian, Michigan. CAS Resources provided outsourcing of human resource services, such as payroll, taxes and employee benefits administration, including health care coverage. CAS collected $1.75 million in premiums from client companies in November and December 2010, but never paid the premiums to Blue Cross Blue Shield of Michigan. Syrek, as the Director of CAS Resources, filed a form with the IRS stating that CAS Resources paid $1,862,902 in payroll taxes. Syrek knew he had diverted these funds for his own personal use and only paid $633,332 in payroll taxes. In addition to this form for the third quarter of 2010, Syrek filed seven other forms with the IRS reporting payroll taxes that he did not pay. In total, from 2010 through 2011, Syrek's tax due was $13.4 million. He admitted diverting these funds for personal use to buy beach front properties, several cars, a boat and investment properties.

Iowa Man Sentenced for Failing to Pay Withheld Taxes

On October 22, 2013, in Cedar Rapids, Iowa, Eric Holub, of Clarence, Iowa, was sentenced to 30 months in prison, three years of supervised release and ordered to pay $438,426 in restitution to the IRS. On July 12, 2013, Holub pleaded guilty to one count of failing to pay over to the IRS money he had withheld from his employees' paychecks. According to court documents, Holub was the owner of Premier Security, a private security business previously located in Cedar Rapids, and had served as the President and Treasurer of the business from 2003 through 2011. Holub admitted that from January 2008 through December 2009, he was responsible for withholding income taxes and Federal Insurance Contributions Act (FICA) taxes from the pay of Premier Security employees and was responsible for forwarding those withholdings to the IRS. However, for six calendar quarters in 2008 and 2009, Holub failed to forward the money he withheld from his employees' pay to the IRS. In the plea agreement, Holub admitted he also failed to pay to the IRS other taxes owed by Premier Security from 2008 through 2011.

Nebraska Man Sentenced for Employment Tax Fraud

On October 21, 2013, in Lincoln, Neb., John Stanley Clabaugh, Jr. was sentenced to 6 months in prison, three years of supervised release of which 6 months will be served as home confinement, and ordered to pay $135,109 in restitution. Clabaugh was the owner/operator of an insurance agency located in Crete, Nebraska. He and a secretary were the only full time employees, although there have been occasional part time employees. Clabaugh always withheld the federal income taxes and FICA taxes from his and his employees' paychecks, until 2001 when he stopped paying these withheld funds over to the IRS and stopped filing the required quarterly forms. The total 'trust fund' taxes withheld from employee paychecks for the period of time covered by the indictment was $135,330.

Delaware Man Sentenced for Failing to Pay Over Payroll Taxes

On October 4, 2013, in Wilmington, Del., Charles Smith, of Bear, Del., was sentenced to 30 months in prison, three years of supervised release and ordered to pay $300,171 in restitution to the IRS. Smith pleaded guilty to ten counts of failure to truthfully account for and pay over payroll taxes. According to court documents, Smith was the Chief Executive Officer of eShowings, a company which provides online and telephone appointment services for real estate professionals. As the founder and CEO of eShowings, Smith was responsible for ensuring that employees' payroll tax withholdings were paid over to the government. Instead, Smith took money deducted from employees' paychecks and spent it personal items for himself and his family.

President of Virginia-Based Connection Newspapers Sentenced to Six Months In Prison for Failing to Pay Employment Taxes

On September 27, 2011, in Alexandria, Va., Peter Labovitz was sentenced to six months in prison, one year of supervised release of home confinement and ordered to pay $647,510 in restitution to the IRS as a result of failing to pay employment taxes to the Internal Revenue Service (IRS). Labovitz pleaded guilty on July 19, 2011, to willfully failing to pay over to the IRS the federal income taxes and Federal Insurance Contributions Act (FICA) taxes due and owing to the United States for Connections Newspapers LLC for the quarters ending September 30, 2007, and December 31, 2007. According to court records, Labovitz was the president of Connection Newspapers, a Northern Virginia newspaper publisher that currently publishes approximately 15 community newspapers throughout Northern Virginia and Maryland. Between 2002 and 2008, Labovitz ran Connection Newspapers' day-to-day operations, directed employees, approved payments and made financial decisions on behalf of the company. Labovitz admitted that between 2002 and 2008, he caused to be deducted and collected from the total taxable wages of his employees' federal income taxes and FICA taxes. However, Labovitz failed to timely pay over to the IRS more than $940,000 in federal income taxes and FICA taxes withheld and due and owing to the United States, despite the fact that he was required to do so by law.

Oklahoma Businesswoman Jailed for Failure to Pay Employment Taxes

On September 14, 2011, in Muskogee, Okla., Janet Christine Whelan, of Eufaula, Oklahoma, was sentenced to 24 months in prison, two years of supervised release and ordered to pay $1,000,016 to the Internal Revenue Service. According to her plea agreement, between 2002 and 2006 Whelan was owner and operator of a temporary employment agency in McAlester, Oklahoma. The temporary agency would provide businesses needing employees with the employees. The temporary agency had a duty to account for, and a duty to pay, the employees' employment taxes, including their state and federal withholding taxes. Whelan collected the taxes and willfully failed to remit them to the United States Treasury. She collected taxes due from her clients. Of the total taxes due, Whelan withheld $678,563 from her employee's payroll checks and kept the employee withholdings in the agency's business bank accounts. Her duty as an employer to pay her portion of the payroll taxes was $372,547, which was not paid. Whelan pleaded guilty to the charges in December 2010.

Owner of Temporary Services Employment Agency Sentenced for Not Paying Employee Taxes

On September 13, 2011, in Minneapolis, Minn., Neng Vang, the owner of SPTS, a temporary services employment agency, was sentenced to 12 months in prison on one count of tax evasion. Vang was charged on April 20, 2011, and pleaded guilty on May 9, 2011. In his plea agreement Vang admitted that between 2004 and 2007, he paid a large group of employees "off the books" in cash without recording or reporting their wages. That action resulted in a tax loss to the Internal Revenue Service of $342,240. In addition, Vang admitted omitting significant gross receipts earned by SPTS from the company's corporate tax returns for the years 2004 through 2007. The unreported gross receipts resulted in a tax loss of more than $60,000. In entering his plea, Vang admitted the total tax loss resulting from his tax evasion was more than $400,000.

Florida Owner of Construction Business Sentenced for Employment Tax Fraud

On August 26, 2011, in Miami, Fla., Richard Rosaire Routhier, of Lake Worth, Florida, was sentenced to 60 months in prison and ordered to pay $1,243,574 in restitution to the Internal Revenue Service (IRS). On April 25, 2011, Routhier pleaded guilty to a one-count information charging him with conspiring to defraud the IRS. According to the information, Routhier and others conspired to defraud the United States and unlawfully enrich themselves by paying employees in cash and not withholding and paying over employment taxes to the U.S. Treasury. According to court documents, Routhier owned and operated Drymension Inc., a custom drywall installation and framing contracting company in Lake Worth. From 2002 through 2008, the defendant caused Drymension checks to be issued to several shell corporations. These entities, while purporting to be legitimate subcontractors, existed only on paper and did not do any work for Drymension. The checks written to shell corporations totaled approximately $9,132,516. The checks were cashed at local check cashing stores and Routhier used the cash to pay Drymension employees. Routhier neither withheld from the cash wages nor paid over to the IRS the employment and income taxes as required by law.

Ohio Man Sentenced on Tax Charges

On August 10, 2011, in Cleveland, Ohio, Scott E. Carter, owner of Advanced Health Systems, was sentenced to 25 months in prison. Carter pleaded guilty in April 2011 to charges of failure to account for and pay over to the Internal Revenue Service (IRS) withholding taxes for 2004, 2005, 2006, and 2007 for his now defunct company, Advanced Health Systems, Inc. of Hudson, Ohio. According to court documents, Carter failed to account for and pay over to the government more than $800,000 in payroll taxes. Because other payroll taxes (employer portion) were due from Advance Health, the total amount of taxes owed by Carter and his company was more than 31 million. Carter was also pleaded guilty to two counts of tax evasion regarding the payment of taxes on his personal returns for the years 2003 and 2004.

Owner of Electrical Firms Sentenced to Prison for Employment Tax Fraud

On July 15, 2011, in Seattle, Wash., Deborah Ann Guenthner, of Arlington, Washington, was sentenced to six months in prison to be followed by six months of home electronic monitoring. Guenthner will be placed on 3 years of supervised release following her release from custody and must pay $377,667 in restitution to the Internal Revenue Service (IRS). According to court documents, Guenthner owned and operated two corporations, WRG Electric, Inc. and Electrical Construction, Inc., located In Arlington, Washington. Between October 2004 and December 2006, Guenthner withheld $377,687 from employee wages for Social Security, Medicare and federal income taxes as part of her normal responsibilities. However, she failed to pay that money over to the federal government. Instead, Guenthner used the funds for either her personal benefit or for the benefit of the companies she owned.

Former Owner of Health Care Business Sentenced for Tax Evasion

On July 14, 2011, in Hartford, Conn., John Durante, of Hope Valley, Rhode Island, formerly of Old Say brook, was sentenced to 30 months of prison, followed by two years of supervised release and ordered to pay all of his outstanding tax liabilities. Durante was sentenced for engaging in a multi-year scheme to evade payment of employee withholdings and other payroll taxes to the IRS. According to court documents and statements made in court, between 1994 and 2001, Durante was involved in the operation of several small health care businesses In Connecticut which repeatedly failed to pay corporate income and payroll taxes. Durante was liable, as the responsible person, for outstanding withholding and other tax obligations and additional penalties and interest of approximately $1.121 million. After the IRS provided Durante with notice of his legal obligation, Durante set up additional companies using nominee owners who were unaware of the existence of the companies. Then, while operating the new companies, Durante took significant funds from the companies for his personal use, including funds to support a longstanding gambling habit For approximately three years. Durante sought to evade payment of the taxes he owed by continuing to hide his interest in the health care businesses, failing to disclose his ownership interest on his personal income tax return and making false representations to the IRS. Durante's illegal conduct has resulted in a tax loss to the government, Including penalties and interest, of more than $1.3 million.

Florida Contractor Sentenced for Employment Tax Fraud

On July 6.2011, in Miami, Fla., Reynaldo Orozco was sentenced to 18 months in prison and ordered to pay $504,047 In restitution to the United States. Orozco pleaded guilty to one count of filing a false employment tax return on March 22, 2011. According to court documents, from 2004 through 2007, Orozco owned and operated Rock Construction Builders Inc. (RCB), a construction business located in Miami-Dade County. Orozco admitted that he issued RCB corporate checks to various other corporations holding them out to be legitimate subcontractors. In truth, these corporations did not perform work for RCB. Orozco cashed the checks at local check cashing stores and used the bulk of the cash to pay RCB employees. Orozco failed to report the cash wages on quarterly employment tax returns and failed to withhold and pay over employment taxes on the wages. From 2004 through 2007, RCB failed to report approximately $3,294,426 in cash wages to the IRS. Based on the conduct described above, the United States Treasury suffered an employment tax loss of approximately $504,047.

North Carolina Couple Sentenced for Health Care Fraud and Tax Offenses

On June 29, 2011, in Greensboro, N.C., Ruben D. McLain and Michelle Judge McLain, both of Winston-Salem, North Carolina, were each sentenced to 24 months in prison, followed by three years of supervised release. They were also ordered to pay restitution of $1,313,671 jointly and severally to the Internal Revenue Service. The McLains did business in Winston-Salem as Universal Services, Inc., Reynolds Home Care, and Triage Behavioral Health Systems. According to their plea agreement, the McLains admitted they established a bank account for Universal Services, Inc. using a false tax identification number. They also admitted to using business bank accounts to purchase personal items for their home, to pay school tuition for their children, and to purchase jewelry. The McLains also admitted that, from 2004 through 2007, they either failed to file tax returns or filed false tax returns that did not declare their true income. The McLain companies provided personal care and mental health services to qualified recipients, paid for by the Medicaid program. The McLains admitted that they submitted a false enrollment application to the North Carolina Division of Medical Assistance that concealed their Involvement In the companies through the use of a nominee and a fictitious person. The McLains also admitted to withholding Income, social security, and Medicare taxes from their employees' wages without paying over those withholdings to the Internal Revenue Service.

Williamsville Couple Sentenced On Money Laundering and Tax Fraud Charge

On June 27, 2011, in Buffalo, N.Y., Ralph S. Guastaferro, Jr. was sentenced to 24 months in prison and fined $100,000 after being convicted of money laundering. Karen Guastaferro, his wife, was sentenced to three years probation, including six months home confinement and ordered to pay $56,670 in restitution to the IRS following her conviction of failing to collect and pay over taxes. Ralph Guastaferro operated a business called Eclipse Processing, Inc. As part of a money laundering scheme, Guastaferro opened accounts with two payment processing companies in California and Ohio. Those accounts were used by certain unscrupulous telemarketers, many of whom were located in Canada, to process alleged sales of some product or service. Many of the victims whose checking accounts were debited had never purchased any product or service. After the victims accounts were debited, the payment processing companies transferred the funds to bank accounts controlled by the defendant in Buffalo, New York. Guastaferro then wire transferred the funds, less a percentage, to the telemarketers in Canada. This was done in an attempt to conceal the nature and source of the funds. The defendant admitted that the total amount of the funds involved in his criminal conduct was $1.2 million. Karen Guastaferro owned and operated Eclipse Glass Tinting, Inc. From 2004 through 2008, Mrs. Guastaferro employed between five and seven people at the business. Although Guastaferro had a duty to collect and truthfully account for and pay over federal employment taxes for each of her employees, she was convicted of lying to the IRS about how many employees she had and how much she paid them, thus intentionally failing to account for and pay over the required federal employment taxes for those employees.

New York Man Sentenced for Failing to Pay Employment Taxes

On June 14, 2011, in Long Island, N.Y., George Dimou was sentenced to 12 months in prison, followed by three years supervised release and ordered to pay $459,119 in restitution after pleading guilty to one count of failure to collect and pay over taxes. According to the Information, Dimou owned and operated GLIG, Inc., Evia One Enterprises, Inc. and Gutters of Long Island Inc. These companies provided gutter fabrication and installation services to homeowners and building contractors on Long Island. During 2003-2007, GLIG, Evia One and Long Island Inc. did not file Forms 941 Employer's Quarterly Federal Tax Returns for the second quarter 2003 through the fourth quarter 2007. Dimou willfully failed to collect and/or truthfully account for and pay over almost $460,000 in FICA taxes, which he had a duty to pay.

Wisconsin Businessman Sentenced To Federal Prison

On June 14, 2011, in Madison, Wis., Donald Penniston, of Brodhead, Wisconsin, was sentenced to 24 months in prison for failing to pay employment taxes and stealing funds from an employee retirement plan. Penniston was also ordered to pay restitution to the retirement plan. According to court documents, Penniston was the President of Canton Promotions, LTD, a graphic design and screen printing business in Monroe, Wis. At his plea hearing in February, Penniston admitted he withheld employment taxes from his employees' payroll checks, but willfully failed to pay over those taxes to the IRS. Penniston also admitted he stole approximately $11,000 in funds belonging to Canton Promotion's employee retirement plan, which was a simple IRA fund. Penniston further admitted he withheld employee contributions for the IRA fund from his employees' payroll checks, but then willfully failed to pay that money over to the fund. The money withheld from Penniston's employees that was not paid over to the IRS or to the IRA fund remained in the company's bank accounts, where it was used by Penniston to pay for, among other things, his own personal living expenses.

North Carolina Dermatologist Sentenced on Tax Charges

On June 13, 2011, in Greensboro, N.C., Clyde Nolan was sentenced to 24 months in prison, followed by two years of supervised release and ordered to pay $585,835 in restitution to the Internal Revenue Service. Nolan operated a dermatology practice as a sole proprietorship in Greensboro, North Carolina. Nolan employed a staff in this office and withheld taxes from his employees' paychecks. According to his plea agreement, Nolan admitted that he failed to account for and pay over $42,596 he withheld in taxes from his employees' paychecks from 2003 and 2006. Nolan used that money for his own personal use. Nolan also willfully failed to file a personal income tax return for calendar year 2004, a year in which he was required to file a return.

Wisconsin Family Sentenced In Income Tax Fraud

On June 1, 2011, in Milwaukee, Wis., James Wierzbicki, of Kenosha, and two of his children, Eric Wierzbicki and Erin Morton, were sentenced for federal tax violations. James Wierzbicki was sentenced to 32 months in prison, to be followed by three years of supervised release, and ordered to pay $418,522 in restitution to the Internal Revenue Service (IRS). Eric Wierzbicki was sentenced to four months in jail, five years probation, and ordered to pay $300,922 in restitution to the IRS. Erin Morton was sentenced to 60 days in jail, five years probation, and ordered to pay $96,000 in restitution. James Wierzbicki pleaded guilty to conspiring to defraud the United States for the purpose of Impeding the IRS. Eric pleaded guilty to two counts of failing to pay payroll taxes. Erin Morton pleaded guilty to conspiring with her family to fail to pay payroll taxes. According to court documents, the Wierzbickis were involved in one or more of a series of commercial painting and dry walling businesses operated In the Kenosha area, including Southport Remodeling and Construction, SRC Painting, and PBN, LLC. The Wierzbickis failed to file quarterly payroll tax returns, filed false payroll tax returns, and paid employees in cash to avoid payroll taxes. In addition, after accumulating substantial payroll tax liabilities, the Wierzbickis would abandon one business, transfer the business operation to a successor business, and recruit someone to act as the nominee owner for the new business. The Wierzbickis also deposited business receipts from one business into their personal accounts, as well as to accounts for successor businesses. In addition, James Wierzbicki's other son, Edmund Wierzbicki, previously pleaded guilty to failing to file a federal Income tax return for the year 2003, when he was being paid by his family's painting businesses. Edmund was sentenced on April 27, 2011, to 14 days in jail, four years probation, and ordered to pay a $3,275 fine.

Former State Delegate Sentenced to Two Years in Prison on Racketeering Charge

On June 1, 2011, in Charleston, W. Va., Joseph Cleveland Ferrell, a Logan, West Virginia business owner and former state delegate, was sentenced to two years in prison after pleading guilty in October 2010 to racketeering and failure to pay employment taxes. Ferrell was also fined $250,000, ordered to forfeit $527,540 and pay the Internal Revenue Service $75,000 in unpaid employment taxes. At his plea hearing in October, Ferrell admitted his association with Southern Amusement and White Amusement, corporations which conducted legal and illegal gambling operations in Logan County and other locations in West Virginia and Kentucky. To protect his gambling operations, Ferrell admitted he gave cash bribes to an inspector with the West Virginia Lottery Commission from approximately the summer of 2004 until the summer of 2007. Ferrell admitted his motive for the payments was to insure that she continue to be immediately available to him when he needed access to the sealed areas of his video lottery machines and to insure her continuing favorable treatment during her inspections. Ferrell also admitted that from approximately the fall of 2003 until April of 2008, Ferrell conducted, financed and managed an illegal gambling business in Kentucky. This operation consisted in large part of several video poker machines owned by White Amusement. These machines paid cash jackpots to winning players and were operating in violation of Kentucky state law. White Amusement then shared the proceeds from the operation of these machines with the owner/operator of the establishment. Ferrell traveled or had others to travel to Kentucky from West Virginia to collect White Amusement's share of the proceeds, to disburse money from the operation of the machines, and to perform repairs and maintenance on the machines. The gambling operation Ferrell led involved five or more persons who conducted, managed, and supervised the gambling business.

Florida Man Sentenced on Tax Charges

On June 1, 2011, in Tampa, Fla., Stuart M. Register, of Brandon, Florida, was sentenced to 27 months in prison. In February 2011,

Register pleaded guilty to 13 counts of failure to pay over federal income tax and four counts of filing false income tax returns. According to court documents, from 2003 through 2007, Register owned and operated Criminal Research Bureau Inc., in Brandon, Florida. He employed individuals and had a duty to withhold and pay over federal employment taxes from those employees to the Internal Revenue Service (IRS). From the first quarter of 2003, through the fourth quarter of 2007, Register withheld federal employment taxes from his employees totaling $316.220, but failed to pay it over to the IRS. In addition, for the tax years 2003 to 2006, Register failed to pay personal income tax, filed false individual income tax returns with the IRS, and collected federal income tax refunds to which he was not entitled. Register's failure to pay over taxes he withheld from his employees, together with his filing of false income tax returns resulting in undue refunds, resulted in a total tax loss to the IRS of $345,612.

Illinois Contractor Sentenced to Prison on Fraud and Tax Charges

On May 9, 2011, in Rockford, Ill., John M. Volpentesta, formerly of Marengo, Illinois, was sentenced to 133 months in prison, five years of supervised release, and was ordered to pay $1,378,127 in restitution to the victims of his fraud scheme. Volpentesta was convicted in July 2010 of various charges, including failure to pay over to the IRS taxes he withheld from the wages of his employees, failure to file unemployment tax returns, and failure to file personal income tax returns. According to the indictment, Volpentesta operated a residential construction business, known as Volpentesta Construction, Inc. (VCI). He defrauded his construction company customers and investors out of more than $1 million. In addition, from the second quarter of 2003 through the fourth quarter of 2005, Volpentesta collected federal income tax, Medicare, and Social Security taxes from the wages of VCI's employees but failed to pay those monies to the IRS. He also failed to file Form 940, Federal Unemployment Tax returns, on behalf of VCI for the years 2003, 2004, and 2005; and, he failed to file personal income tax returns on behalf of himself and his wife for the same years.

California Payroll Company CEO Sentenced in $20 Million Tax Fraud Scheme

On May 6, 2011, in Sacramento, Calif., Albert Cipoletti, of Northport, N.Y., was sentenced to 78 months in prison, three years of supervised release, and ordered to pay $19,141,618 in restitution. Cipoletti was sentenced in connection with a scheme to divert more than $20 million from Sacramento County as well as two other businesses: SanDisk Corporation (SanDisk) and The Stanley Works and Stanley Solutions Inc. (Stanley). According to court documents, Cipoletti was the Chief Executive Officer (CEO) of Ingentra HR Services Inc., a payroll services corporation in Hauppauge, N.Y. As part of the payroll services, Ingentra calculated the tax payments for the clients and the clients' employees and then transmitted the payments to the state and federal tax authorities. As stated in Cipoletti's plea agreement, from 2005 until April 2010, he and co-defendant Kerry Seaman, comptroller for Ingentra, devised a scheme to defraud the County of Sacramento, SanDisk, and Stanley of the tax withholdings intended to be paid to the Internal Revenue Service (IRS) by collecting the correct amount from the clients but under-reporting to the IRS the amount owed. They diverted the difference to Ingentra's operating account for Ingentra's use. Cipoletti and Seaman sent funding letters to the clients that correctly calculated payroll and federal tax withholdings for the clients' employees, and these clients wire transferred funds to Ingentra for the purposes of paying both the payroll and taxes. Cipoletti and Seaman then filed false Forms 941, Employer's Quarterly Federal Tax Form, to the IRS, understating the true employee tax withholdings for these clients. Cipoletti and Seaman wrongfully diverted in excess of $20 million in tax withholdings from clients Stanley, SanDisk, and Sacramento County that should have been remitted to the IRS on behalf of these clients and these clients' employees. Seaman is awaiting sentencing.

Owner of Community Support Service Corporation Sentenced

On April 26, 2011, in Raleigh, N.C., Shirlene Reese Boone, of Murfreesboro, North Carolina, was sentenced to 144 months in prison, followed by three years of supervised release, and was ordered to pay restitution of $3,550,840 to the Medicaid Investigations Unit, $1,061,820 to the Internal Revenue Service, and $46,059 to the North Carolina Employment Security Commission. Boone previously pleaded guilty to multiple charges including conspiracy to commit health care fraud, aggravated identity theft, and failure to collect and pay over payroll taxes. Boone was the principal owner, manager, and registered agent for Metropolitan Counseling Services, Inc. (MCS), a registered non-profit North Carolina corporation that provided community support services and HIV case management. From 1997 to May 2010, Boone, through MCS, routinely submitted claims for reimbursement to the Medicaid program for community support services and HIV case management. Community support and HIV case management services were designed to assist the state's disabled and economically disadvantaged individuals diagnosed with certain medical conditions. Many of the claims Boone submitted to Medicaid were false in that they demanded payment for services that never happened. As the president of the corporation, Boone held back federal withholding taxes and FICA taxes from employee wages. While Boone filed quarterly payroll tax reports for all of the quarters during the period July 1, 2005, through September 30, 2006, she did not pay any of these taxes.

Final Defendant Sentenced In Illegal Worker Scheme

On April 25, 2011, in Pittsburgh, Pa, Alexander Litt, the sixth and final defendant of an illegal worker scheme was sentenced to 56 months in prison, followed by three years supervised release, on his conviction of conspiracy to harbor illegal aliens for commercial gain and money laundering conspiracy. The court also ordered the forfeiture of cash and property to the United States. According to information presented to the court, Litt, through his company, ARRA Corporation, of Cincinnati, Ohio, conspired to furnish out-of-status alien employees to various hotels in the Cincinnati, Cleveland, Columbus, and Pittsburgh areas as housekeeping personnel between 1998 and 2006. Litt, along with a co-conspirator, received a kickback of $1.50 per hour per employee for hours worked. Agents estimate that over 100 such out-of-status aliens were employed in the Pittsburgh area alone by the Pittsburgh franchise of the company, Citiwide Management Group (CMG) and that, during peak season, the aliens worked up to 20 hours per day. While working for CMG, the aliens, typically from former Soviet countries, were forced to live together in rented housing chosen by CMG, for which they were required to pay the rent. The aliens were transported to and from the hotels in a company van, for which they paid a transportation fee. Five other defendants pleaded guilty to their roles in the conspiracy and have received prison terms ranging from 33 to 56 months.

Former Illinois City Councilman Sentenced for Tax Evasion, Failure to File Income Tax Returns, and Election Fraud

On April 13, 2011, in Fairview Heights, Ill., Michael V. Collins, of Swansea, Illinois, was sentenced to 50 months in prison, followed by three years supervised release, and ordered to pay $342,375 in restitution to the Internal Revenue Service (IRS). Collins was convicted by a trial jury of tax evasion, failure to file federal income tax returns, and election fraud. According to evidence submitted at trial, Collins had not filed a federal tax return in 13 years at the time he became aware of the federal investigation. He attempted to conceal his income by commingling business and personal assets. Collins also failed to provide his correct social security number, operated a business under an Invalid Employer's Identification Number, and submitted false certified payrolls which falsely reflected that his employees' federal income tax withholdings and FICA taxes were withheld and paid. He operated through the receipt and expenditure of cash, without record keeping, and failed to maintain accurate books and records. At trial, evidence showed that Collins knowingly and willfully gave false information as to his address for the purpose of establishing his eligibility to vote in a voting district In East St. Louis and during that same period of time, he was elected to be a precinct committeeman in East St Louis when he was living in Swansea.

Owner of Superior Protection Inc., Sentenced to Prison for Conspiracy, Tax Fraud, Bankruptcy Fraud, Bribery and Other Charges

On April 8, 2011, in Houston, Texas, John Heard, Jr., was sentenced to 151 months in prison and ordered to pay more than $8.7 million in restitution. According to court documents, Heard, the owner of Superior Protection, Inc (SPI), was convicted of conspiring to defraud the United States of millions in employment taxes as well as income tax evasion in 2001 and 2003, willfully making and subscribing to a false income tax return in 2007, bribery and corrupt interference with the tax laws. Heard operated and controlled several security companies, including SPI since 1987 and failed to pay employment taxes totaling more than $5.7 million. In the scheme, Heard opened and closed numerous corporations and used fictitious names for numerous documents, including tax returns, corporate documents, bank documents and payroll checks. He also named lower-level employees as company officials in corporate documents in an effort to impede the Internal Revenue Service (IRS) by concealing the true individuals who operated and controlled the security guard companies. Heard failed to file numerous IRS Forms 941, and when he did, they were often false. He did not report funds on his personal income tax returns in 2001 and 2003 that he pulled out of SPI for his personal use. He also did not report any of the income that he earned in 2007 on his personal income tax return. He also provided airline tickets, lodging and access to two celebrity golf tournaments to a government contracting official who oversaw a federal security guard contract in exchange for a favorable reference, on behalf of SPI, to a contracting official and for pre-signed security-guard forms from the General Services Administration.

Owner of Arizona Auto Body Repair Shop Sentenced for Employment Tax Fraud

On April 4, 2011, in Tucson, Ariz., Daniel Enrique Paz, Jr., was sentenced to 27 months in prison, followed by three years of supervised release, and ordered to pay a $100 special assessment. In addition, Paz was ordered to cooperate with the Internal Revenue Service (IRS) in filing correct income tax returns for tax years 2003 through 2009 and pay all taxes, interest and penalties. Paz must also pay ail federal income and FICA taxes owed by his business and its employees for tax years 2003 through 2005. Paz pleaded guilty in February 2011 to failure to account for and pay over to the IRS federal income taxes and FICA taxes. According to court documents, Paz was the owner of Spectrum Auto Collision an auto body repair shop. Paz willfully failed to pay over approximately $340,724 in employment taxes for three tax years.

Owner of Drywall Business Sentenced for Failure to Remit More Than $1 Million in Taxes

On March 29, 2011, in Sacramento, Calif., William Roseberry was sentenced to 28 months in prison for evading and failing to remit over $1 million in taxes to the Internal Revenue Service (IRS). In addition, Roseberry was ordered to pay $1,040,500 in restitution to the IRS. Roseberry pleaded guilty in September 2009 to willfully attempting to evade or defeat taxes. According to court documents, between October 2003 and September 2006, Roseberry owned and operated a drywall business in Rocklin as a sole proprietorship under the name of Western Wallboard and/or Bustos Drywall. During this time period, Roseberry evaded or failed to remit more than $1 million in employment and income taxes owed to the IRS in connection with the 350-plus employees of the drywall business. Roseberry falsely reported to the IRS that the total wages paid to employees by the drywall business were approximately $229,972 and that the total amount of Social Security taxes and Medicare taxes due thereon were approximately $35,185 when, in fact, the total wages subject to taxation were approximately $5,638,917, and the corresponding taxes owed were $862,754. In addition, Roseberry collected income taxes from employees in the approximate amount of $236,379, but did not remit the same to the Internal Revenue Service.

California Trucking Company Owners Sentenced for Tax and Bribery Conspiracy

On March 21, 2011, in Fresno, Calif., Kulwant and Tarlochan Lasher, owners of Lasher Brothers Trucking Company Inc., based in Los Baños, were sentenced to 57 months and 12 months in prison, respectively. The brothers were each sentenced to three years of supervised release following their prison terms and ordered to pay no less than $739,787 in restitution, with the final amount to be determined by the IRS. Kulwant and Tarlochan pleaded guilty In October 2010 to conspiring to failing to account for and pay employee withholding and FICA taxes for tax years 2003 through 2007. Kulwant Lasher also admitted that he had offered to pay an undercover IRS Revenue Officer $600,000 in cash to eliminate the Lasher Brothers Trucking Company's $2.4 million tax liability. In meetings at a restaurant and gas station, Kulwant Lasher gave the Revenue Officer $56,500 in cash, handed over his 2003 BMW 745L, and gave him a quitclaim deed for his residence in Los Baños. Immediately, after delivering his BMW to the Revenue Officer, Kulwant Lasher called a BMW dealership in Fresno and asked to be picked up, because he wanted to buy a new BMW. When the dealership asked about a $747,000 tax lien on his credit record, Kulwant Lasher, knowing of his tax liability to the IRS, told the salesman that he had already paid it. Kulwant Lasher then purchased a new 745 BMW for approximately $95,000.

Brooklyn Man Sentenced to Prison for Harboring Aliens, Money Laundering and Tax Evasion

On March 3, 2011, in Pittsburgh, Pa., Yaroslav Rochniak was sentenced to 51 months in prison, followed by three years supervised release on his conviction of conspiracy to harbor aliens, money laundering, and tax evasion. According to information presented to the court, Rochniak was the President of Citiwide Management Group (Citiwide), the Pittsburgh subsidiary of a company which supplied housekeeping staff to Pittsburgh-area hotels. Over 100 of the employees provided were out -of-status aliens who had initially entered the United States legally, but had either overstayed the term limits of their visas or were not authorized to work in the United States under the terms of their visas. Thus, they had illegally remained in the United States. Most of the aliens were citizens of former Soviet bloc countries. Rochniak and his co-conspirators made kickbacks of $1.50 per hour per employee to ARRA Corporation, the parent company in Cincinnati. Citiwide housed the employees in company-leased apartments. They also transported the employees to and from the hotels, charging them both rent and transportation fees. The employees' first two weeks' wages were retained by the company as a security deposit, which the company kept as a penalty if the employees did not work at least six months. Citiwide paid no overtime or benefits and failed to pay taxes on the employees' wages, resulting in a tax loss of $1.5 million. In addition, the parent company maintained offices in Cleveland and Columbus, Ohio. Rochniak was also in charge of the Cleveland branch of the company during part of the conspiracy.

Health Services Entrepreneur Sentenced for Not Paying Taxes

On March 3, 2011, in Kansas City, Kan., Jeffrey Phillips was sentenced to 42 months in prison and ordered to pay $5.8 million in restitution. According to court documents, Phillips pleaded guilty to one count of failure to pay employment taxes. In his plea, Phillips admitted that from 2001 to 2005 his companies withheld tax payments from employee's paychecks including federal income taxes, Medicare, and Social Security taxes totaling about $4 million, but failed to make payments to the IRS.

Brothers Sentenced for Conspiring to Evade Employment Taxes

On February 17, 2011, in Minneapolis, Minn., brothers Joseph and John Riley were each sentenced to 42 months in prison and each received a $250,000 fine and were ordered to pay all taxes and penalties owed to the Internal Revenue Service (IRS) for a tax evasion scheme that involved concealing income they and many of their employees received from their road construction business. According to court documents, the brothers own Riley Bros. Companies, Inc., a holding company that owns 100 percent of Riley Bros. Construction as well as a number of other companies in whole or in part. Between 1984 and 2003, the Riley's conspired to defraud the U.S. by concealing income earned by Riley Bros. Companies, Inc. and evaded paying income taxes, social security taxes, Medicare taxes, and unemployment taxes. The Riley's also used unreported company income to pay for their personal expenses.

Colorado Man Sentenced on Charges of Tax Evasion and Harboring Illegal Aliens

On February 10, 2011, in Denver, Colo., Opas Sinprasong was sentenced to 12 months and a day in prison and ordered to pay a $4,000 fine and $754.975 in restitution. In addition, Sinprasong was ordered to forfeit $766,000 and two residential properties in Boulder. As part of his plea agreement, following his incarceration, Sinprasong, a Thai national, will be deported. According to court documents, Sinprasong, while in the United States on an E2 Non-Immigrant Principal Investor status Visa, ran Thai and Japanese restaurants in Boulder, Louisville, and Broomfield. From 2001 through 2008, Sinprasong sponsored Thai nationals' admission to the United States as specialty workers for his restaurants. He claimed these workers possessed specialized skills that were essential to the efficient operation of his businesses. Sinprasong required all Thai employees to enter into a two-year employment contract. The terms of employment per the contract included that employees pay Sinprasong a "bond" of approximately $1,500; a payment of approximately $18,000 if the employee violated a term of the contract or caused damage to Sinprasong; and a payment of $3,000 for a "visa preparation fee." Sinprasong paid employees "under-the-table" while deducting portions of the $3,000 "visa preparation fee" and other fees from their paycheck. Once these fees had been fully paid, which typically took between three and four months, the defendant helped the Thai employees obtain Social Security numbers and then started to report a portion of their wages and placed them on the official payroll of the restaurants. Court documents showed that Sinprasong used a dual payroll system whereby he concealed from his payroll records the substantial overtime hours he directed the Thai employees to work, which was typically between 26 and 32 hours of overtime each week. As a result, Sinprasong failed to report all of the wages paid to the Thai employees and failed to pay the Thai employees the overtime wages required by federal law. He filed employer's quarterly federal tax returns with the Internal Revenue Service (IRS) as required, but the returns were materially false in that they failed to report the total wages paid to the Thai employees. By failing to report all of the wages paid to the Thai employees, Sinprasong evaded paying the employer's portion of the Social Security and Medicare taxes due and owing on the unreported wages.

Florida Contractor Sentenced for Employment Tax Fraud

On January 13, 2011, in Miami, Fla., Axel Rafael Mercado, owner of Mercado Enterprises, Inc., was sentenced to 24 months in prison and ordered to pay $352,605 in restitution to the United States. According to court documents, from 2005 through 2007, Mercado attempted to evade a large part of his company's federal employment taxes. Mercado caused the company's checks to be written to shell companies, which were supposedly legitimate subcontractors, but did not work for Mercado Enterprises. Mercado would then direct those checks to be cashed at a local check-cashing store, which was aware of the scheme, and use the cash to pay his workers. Mercado never reported the existence of the employees, never reported the cash wages of the employees, never filed employment tax returns and never paid the required employment tax.

Former Owner of Illinois Payroll Processing Company Sentenced for Employment Tax Evasion

On December 22, 2010, in Urbana, Ill., Gary A. Gerberding, former owner of Premier Data Solutions, was sentenced to 60 months in prison, followed by three years of supervised release, and ordered to pay $1,585,009 in restitution. Gerberding pleaded guilty in June 2010 to defrauding former clients of his payroll processing company. According to court documents, Gerberding, of Kankakee, Illinois, admitted that from January 2007 to April 2008, he failed to pay payroll taxes due to the Internal Revenue Service (IRS) and the Illinois Department of Revenue on behalf of clients who had contracted with Premier Data Solutions to process weekly and bi-weekly payrolls. As part of their arrangement, clients provided Premier Data Solutions with the funds necessary to cover both the payroll and payroll taxes. Premier Data Solutions then provided clients with a payroll package consisting of several reports and payroll checks. Gerberding admitted that he manipulated the payment of clients' payroll tax liabilities using one client's payroll tax monies to pay another client's outstanding payroll tax liabilities. Gerberding further admitted that he provided false check reconciliation journals to clients to cover the fraud. The journals falsely indicated that Premier Data Solutions was remitting payroll taxes to the IRS and the Illinois Department of Revenue, when in fact, it was not.

Ohio Woman Sentenced on Conspiracy and Taxes Charges

On December 17, 2010, in Columbus, Ohio, Maria Terechina, a national of the Russian Federation, was sentenced to 12 months in prison, followed by three years of supervised release, and ordered to pay nearly $250,000 in restitution to her victims. During her guilty plea hearing in April 2010, Terechina admitted that she engaged in the harboring and transporting of dozens of illegal aliens from Russia, Estonia, Belarus, Ukraine, and other Eastern European nations. The illegal aliens worked for Terechina in various hotels in and around Columbus. Terechina admitted that she agreed to hold some of the workers' passports and immigration documents in order to prevent them from leaving their employment. Terechina also defrauded the United States of approximately $185,000 in employment taxes.

Texas Restaurant Owner Sentenced for Filing False Income Tax Returns

On December 13, 2010, in Houston, Texas, Maria F. Argueta, the owner of Taqueria Arandas No. 13 Inc., was sentenced to 12 months and one day in prison, one year of supervised release, and ordered to pay $237,561 in restitution to the IRS. According to court documents, Argueta owned Taqueria Arandas No. 13 Inc., through which she operated a restaurant in Houston. In a plea agreement executed on May 17, 2010, Argueta admitted she had helped file Corporate Income Tax Returns for Taqueria Arandas No. 13 Inc., for tax years 2000 through 2004 that under-reported sales by approximately $1,432,236 and taxable wages to employees by approximately $343,782. She further admitted that because of the false filings, the corporation underpaid income taxes by approximately 3184,962 and underpaid employment taxes by approximately $52,599. Argueta is one of 13 local Taqueria Arandas Restaurant owners charged with filing false federal income and employment tax returns for their restaurants. To date, these defendants have paid the IRS almost $5.5 million in delinquent taxes, penalties and interest and all remain subject to audit and further assessment of taxes, penalties and interest.

Texas Man Sentenced for Failure to Pay More Than $2 Million in Employment Taxes

On December 9, 2010, in Houston, Texas, Gary Quintinsky was sentenced to 42 months in prison and ordered to pay nearly $2.28 million in restitution for failing to pay federal income taxes, Social Security taxes, and Medicare taxes withheld from employees. According to court documents, Quintinsky admitted that he operated a group of r elated crane corporations, including United Crane and United Payroll Services. He ran the financial affairs of the corporations even though Ellynn Ogilvie appeared as the sole shareholder and president of the corporations and the sole signatory on all corporate bank accounts. Quintinsky admitted that he signed numerous letters as president of United Crane and signed title documents as president of the corporation in the related group owning the cranes. Quintinsky further admitted that he signed Ogilvie's name on numerous other important corporate documents, including signing her name on the false employer's federal quarterly tax return, IRS Form 941, for United Crane's third quarter of 2003. Quintinsky also admitted to using Ogilvie's signature stamp to disburse funds from corporate bank accounts.

Owner of Payroll and Tax Services Company Sentenced on Tax Evasion and Embezzlement Charges

On November 23, 2010, in Memphis, Tenn., Venetia Smith was sentenced to 14 months in prison, to be followed by three years of supervised release and ordered to pay $61,291.97 to the Internal Revenue Service (IRS) and $24,948 in restitution to The Regional Medical Center at Memphis (The MED). Smith pleaded guilty in June 2010 to willful failure to collect or pay over tax and embezzlement charges. According to court documents, Smith owned VS Payroll and Tax Service, which was contracted by The MED to handle payroll services for the Health Loop, including the preparation and filing of federal employment tax returns and payment of employment taxes to the IRS on a regular basis. As part of this contract, Smith was responsible for preparing employee payroll checks and withholding federal income tax, as well as Federal Insurance Contribution Act (FICA) taxes. Smith was also supposed to pay to the IRS the amount of federal income tax withheld and the total FICA taxes owed, file quarterly Forms 941 with the IRS for The Health Loop, and issue annual Forms W-2 to the employees of The Health Loop. Additionally, Smith admitted that she embezzled more than 384,000 belonging to The MED.

New York Man Sentenced on Charges of Tax Evasion, Money Laundering and Harboring Aliens

On November 18, 2010, in Pittsburgh, Pa., Gregory Kucher, a resident of Brooklyn, New York, was sentenced to 51 months in prison to be followed by two years of supervised release. Kucher pleaded guilty in February 2010 to charges of alien harboring, money laundering conspiracy, and tax evasion. According to court documents, Kucher employed and contracted out to client businesses in Western Pennsylvania more than 100 "out of status aliens" between approximately 2002 and 2006. The term "out of status aliens" refers to individuals who may have lawfully entered the United States, but have either overstayed the terms of their visas or were not permitted to be employed while in the United States under the terms of their visas. Kucher failed to declare and pay taxes on the wages earned by the out of status workers contracted to various businesses in the Greater Pittsburgh area. The total tax loss was approximately $1.5 million. He also laundered the profits generated through the wages of these out of status workers.

South Dakota Business Owner Sentenced for Failing to Pay Employment Taxes

On November 15, 2010, in Sioux Falls, S.D., Michael Hoppe was sentenced to 21 months in prison, three years of supervised release and ordered to pay more than $670,000 in restitution to the Internal Revenue Service (IRS). According to court documents, from July 2005 through January 2009, he owned and operated ABM Manufacturing and Mad Dog Haulers in Brookings, S.D. During those years, he collected federal withholding income taxes and FICA taxes from his employees' paychecks. However, he failed to report and remit the taxes withheld from employees' wages, and he failed to pay the employer's share of FICA taxes. Over a period of approximately four and a half years, Hoppe failed to remit and pay more than $670,000.

Northern Virginia Business Owner Sentenced for Failing to Pay Over $200,000 In Employment Taxes

On November 12, 2010, in Alexandria, Va., Eric Jon Eisenhower, a resident of Fairfax Station, Va. was sentenced to 19 months in prison and ordered to pay $88,826 in restitution to the Internal Revenue Service (IRS). According to court documents, Eisenhower was the president of CoManage Inc., a computer software development company. From December 2004 through June 2008, Eisenhower failed to pay over to the IRS more than $200,000 in withholding taxes from employees' paychecks. The monies included withholdings for Social Security, Medicare and federal income taxes.

Dallas Realtor Sentenced for Failing to Pay Federal Income Taxes

On November 5, 2010, in Dallas, Texas, Eleanor Sheets was sentenced to 12 months in prison which will be served in strict home confinement to include electronic monitoring. In addition, Sheets was sentenced to three years of supervised release and ordered to pay more than $1.37 million in back taxes. She pleaded guilty in July 2010 to four counts of failure to pay income taxes. According to the plea documents, Sheets admitted that she willfully failed to pay both individual income and corporate taxes during tax years 2003 through 2007. Since 1996, Eleanor and her husband, John Nicholas "Nicky" Sheets successfully worked as real estate agents and established multiple closely-held corporations, including, EMS, Inc., E-Residential, LLC and Dallas EMS, LLC. In court hearings, Eleanor Sheets stipulated that they failed to pay personal and/or employments taxes for tax years 1997 through 1999 and 2003 through 2007 which totaled approximately $1.3 million. Nicky Sheets was sentenced to 40 months for tax evasion in August 2010.

Florida Contractor Sentenced for Employment Tax Fraud

On November 3, 2010, in Miami, Fla., Victor Manuel Amaya, owner of Amaya Contracting and Stucco Inc. (ACS), was sentenced to 24 months in prison and ordered to pay $319,585 in restitution to the Internal Revenue Service (IRS). According to court documents, from 2004 through 2007, Amaya filed fraudulent employment tax returns with the IRS and caused his company to underpay its federal employment taxes. To avoid having to report all of ACS's employment tax obligations, Amaya regularly cashed checks made out to ACS at a local check cashing store instead of depositing them into the company's account. Additionally, Amaya wrote ACS checks to fictitious companies and cashed them at local check cashing stores. Amaya then used the cash to pay his workers, which allowed him to report lower wages and lower employment taxes due on ACS's employment tax returns. Amaya also used the cash for materials and personal expenses. Amaya failed to report to the IRS approximately $2,130,568 in wages, which resulted in a tax loss of approximately $319,585.

Father and Son Sentenced for Employment Tax Fraud; Ordered to Pay Over $500,000 in Restitution

On November 2, 2010, in Columbus, Ga., Edward Griffin, Sr. and Edward Griffin, Jr., were sentenced for their roles in an employment tax fraud investigation. Edward Griffin, Sr. was sentenced to 18 months in prison, three years of supervised release, and ordered to pay $367,526 in restitution to the Internal Revenue Service (IRS). Edward Griffin, Jr. was sentenced to 12 months and one day in prison, three years of supervised release, and ordered to pay $148,705 in restitution to the IRS. On July 28, 2010, both Edward Griffin, Sr. and his son, Edward Griffin, Jr., pleaded guilty to failure to pay over withholding and F.I.C.A. taxes.

Owner of Rhode Island Temporary Employment Agency Sentenced for Failing to Pay Millions of Dollars in Withholding Taxes

On October 7, 2010, in Providence, R.I., Cheang Chea, owner of S&P Temporary Help Service, Inc., was sentenced to 24 months in prison and ordered to pay the government $14 million in workers' taxes. According to court documents, since 2003, Chea operated S&P Temporary Help Service, a Providence based company which has supplied hundreds of workers to approximately 30 Rhode Island companies. Chea's workforce is made up of primarily East Asian, non-English speaking immigrants. S&P Temporary Help Service agreed to be responsible for all payroll and employment tax withholdings and carry workers compensation insurance coverage for its employees. Chea underreported substantial amounts of wages and failed to pay millions of dollars in federal withholding, social security and Medicare taxes.

South Jersey Business Owner Sentenced for Evading Employment Taxes

On September 28, 2012, in Trenton, N.J., Vanna Kem, of Sicklerville, N.J. was sentenced to 18 months in prison, three years of supervised release and ordered to pay $163,838 in restitution to the IRS for evading employment taxes. Kem plead guilty to an Information charging her with one count of tax evasion. According to court documents and statements made in court, Kem was the owner and operator of the New Jersey-based temporary employment agency Tri State Labor Services Inc. (Tri State). Despite being the true owner of Tri State, Kem incorporated the business and maintained the corporate bank account in a nominee's name. From the first quarter of 2006 through the last quarter of 2008, Kem paid Tri State employees more than $1 million in cash wages without withholding employment taxes. She also failed to file IRS 941 forms - Employer's Quarterly Federal Tax Returns - in which she was required to report the wages she paid her employees.

Former Flagstaff Tax Preparer Sentenced for Filing False Payroll Tax Returns

On September 26, 2012, in Phoenix, Ariz., Devon M. Scott was sentenced to 15 months in prison, one year of supervised release, and ordered to pay $107,775 in restitution. On February 6, 2012, Scott pleaded guilty to aiding and assisting in the preparation of false and fraudulent tax returns. According to court documents, Scott, aka Roland J. Rojas, owned and operated the now defunct Devero Premier Services Group, a payroll tax service in Flagstaff, Arizona with approximately 40 clients. Among the services Devero performed for its clients was collecting and paying its clients' payroll taxes to the IRS. From January to July 2005, in eleven specific instances, Scott filed tax returns that fraudulently and falsely stated the amount of payroll taxes that Devero had deposited with the IRS on behalf of clients.

Texas Man Sentenced for Failing to File and Pay Employment Tax

On September 20, 2012, in Oklahoma City, Okla., James Davis from Edmond, Okla., was sentenced to 20 months in prison, three years of supervised release, and ordered to pay $476,493 in restitution. Davis pleaded guilty in November 2011 to failure to collect and pay federal employment tax to the IRS. According to court documents, Davis was the owner of Hardcore Management, LLC which served other businesses owned and operated by Davis in Oklahoma City, Oklahoma, including an ice vending company and several gentlemen's clubs. From September of 2004 through January of 2008, Davis failed to collect and pay the IRS federal employment payroll taxes owed by Hardcore.

Massachusetts Tax Fraud Promoters Sentenced for Conspiracy to Obstruct and Impede the IRS

On September 27, 2012, in Boston, Mass., Charles Adams, of Norwood, Mass., was sentenced to 48 months in prison and ordered to pay $401,000 in restitution. On April 2, 2012, a federal jury convicted Adams, Catherine Floyd and William Scott Dion, both of Sanbornville, N.H., for conspiracies to defraud the United States through the promotion and use of multiple tax fraud schemes. The jury convicted all three of conspiracy to defraud the IRS by promoting an "under the table" payroll scheme. Dion and Floyd were also convicted for conspiracy to defraud the IRS through the use of an "underground warehouse banking" scheme designed to conceal customer income and assets from the IRS. Floyd and Dion were also convicted separately for corruptly endeavoring to obstruct the IRS's ability to determine their own income. Adams was separately convicted of tax evasion with respect to his own taxes. On September 21, 2012, in Worcester, Mass., Catherine June Floyd was sentenced to 60 months in prison and ordered to pay $3 million in restitution. According to the evidence presented at trial, Floyd, Dion and Adams ran a payroll tax scheme to pay employees "under the table" without properly accounting for, withholding, and paying over to the IRS the payroll taxes required by law. The three promoted the payroll scheme to employers and individuals who wanted to avoid paying employer and individual payroll taxes. They ran the payroll scheme under three different names: Contract America, Talent Management and New Way Enterprises. Approximately 150 individuals subscribed to the payroll scheme and more than S2.5 million in unreported wages and compensation were paid through the system. The evidence at trial also established that Floyd and Dion were promoting and operating an "underground warehouse banking" scheme which helped subscribers conceal income and assets from the IRS. The warehouse scheme operated under three different names: Your Virtual Office, Office Services and Calico Management. Under the warehouse banking scheme, the defendants maintained accounts at several banks and used the accounts to deposit and commingle business receipts and other funds received from subscribers to mask the true ownership of the funds. More than $28 million was deposited into the various bank accounts. Four other defendants in this case have previously pleaded guilty and await sentencing. On September 6, 2012, Dion was sentenced to 84 months in prison and ordered to pay $3 million in restitution.

Defendant Sentenced in Scheme to Defraud the IRS

On September 18, 2012, in Cincinnati, Ohio, Larry Lough, of West Chester, Ohio, was sentenced to 24 months in prison, three years of supervised release, and ordered to pay $757,751 in restitution to defrauded investors and $145,175 in restitution to the IRS. Lough pleaded guilty on February 15, 2012, to conspiracy to commit mail and wire fraud, conspiracy to commit employment tax fraud and income tax evasion. According to court documents, during 2005, Lough and another individual operated a research and development company known as Tri E Technologies (TET). As an employer, Lough was required to file Forms 941, Quarterly Employment Tax Forms, and to collect and pay over federal employment taxes on the employees. Lough issued checks to the employees and himself, and withheld the employee's share of the payroll taxes, but failed to remit the employment taxes collected along with the appropriate employer's matching contributions to the IRS. Lough filed false quarterly employment tax returns with the IRS for 2005 and 2006 under-reporting wages by over $750,000. In addition, through the false accounting records and the false partnership returns, Lough evaded the assessment, reporting, and payment of taxes, including those associated with Medicare, Social Security, and personal income taxes, which he had an obligation as employers to pay.

Landscaping Executive Sentenced for Evading Employment Taxes

On September 6, 2012, in Richmond, Va., Mark S. Holpe, of Midlothian, Va., was sentenced to 18 months in prison and fined $40,000 for evading the payment of employment taxes on unreported cash wages he paid employees of Nature's Way Landscaping, Inc. Holpe pleaded guilty to evading the assessment of $326,196 of employment taxes. Holpe worked for Nature's Way, a business that did residential and commercial landscaping in the Richmond metro area. He was originally the president, but became the treasurer in 2007 when he sold a portion of the business. In entering his plea, Holpe acknowledged that the company had two groups of employees during tax years 2006 through 2009. Holpe admitted that he paid one group of approximately 30 employees $2,132,000 in cash wages during that period, without withholding social security taxes. He did not issue them Forms W-2 or 1099, or file Employer's Quarterly Tax Returns for them. He further admitted that, when supplying expense information to the company's tax preparer for years 2006 through 2009, he did not identify the employees who were paid in cash.

Massachusetts Tax Fraud Promoter Sentenced

On September 6, 2012, in Worcester, Mass., William Scott Dion was sentenced to 84 months in prison and ordered to pay $3 million in restitution. A federal jury convicted Dion on April 2, 2012, for conspiring to defraud the United States by promoting and using multiple tax fraud schemes. According to the evidence presented at trial, Dion and others ran a payroll tax scheme to pay employees "under the table" without properly accounting for withholdings or paying the payroll taxes to the IRS. He promoted the payroll scheme to employers and individuals who wanted to avoid paying employer and individual payroll taxes. The payroll scheme operated under three different names: Contract America, Talent Management and New Way Enterprises. Approximately 150 individuals subscribed to the payroll scheme and more than $2.5 million in unreported wages and compensation were paid through the system. Dion and others also conspired to defraud the United States by promoting and operating an "underground warehouse banking" scheme, which helped subscribers conceal income and assets from the IRS. The warehouse scheme operated under three different names: Your Virtual Office, Office Services and Calico Management. As part of the warehouse banking scheme, the defendants maintained accounts at several banks and used the accounts to deposit and commingle business receipts and other funds received from subscribers to mask the true ownership of the funds. More than $28 million in deposits were made into the various bank accounts used in the scheme.

North Carolina Businessman Sentenced for Payroll Tax Fraud

On September 5, 2012, in Charlotte, N.C., Bruce Harrison, III, of Greensboro, was sentenced to 144 months in prison and ordered to pay more than $43 million in restitution for payroll tax fraud and failure to file individual income tax returns. According to court documents, Harrison owned or controlled temporary staffing companies operating in at least nine states under various corporate names. Harrison's staffing companies were headquartered in Guilford County, N.C., and contracted with client businesses to provide temporary workers. Harrison's companies promised to assume full responsibility for paying wages and withholding and transmitting taxes to the IRS for those employees. Instead, Harrison failed to account for and pay over in excess of $40 million in federal payroll taxes for the employees. Harrison created false bank statements for auditors to conceal the nonpayment of the payroll taxes. Harrison was also convicted of corruptly endeavoring to obstruct the IRS by means of false statements to IRS revenue officers. He used company funds to purchase personal residences, buy a yacht and finance commercial motion pictures. Harrison was also convicted of failing to timely file his own income tax returns for 2004, 2005 and 2006.

Florida Man Sentenced for Tax Fraud

On August 16, 2012, in Orlando, Fla., Daniel Thomas, Jr., of Ocala, Fla., was sentenced to 30 months in prison and three years of supervised release for attempting to evade federal income tax. The court also ordered him to pay $334,742 in restitution. According to court documents, Thomas operated Key Business Solutions and Payroll Advisors in Ocala, under "Dan Thomas, Inc." Between 2007 and 2009, Thomas defrauded his clients of funds they owed to the IRS as payroll taxes. Thomas embezzled these funds to pay business expenses and to pay his own personal expenses. In total, Thomas diverted $852,036 from seven different Ocala companies. He also failed to file personal income tax returns for 2007, 2008, and 2009, resulting in a tax loss of $45,533.

Former Nursing Home Operator Sentenced for Health Care Fraud and Tax Fraud

On August 13, 2012, in Rome, Ga., George D. Houser, of Sandy Springs, Ga., was sentenced to 240 months in prison and three years of supervised release on charges of conspiring with his wife to defraud the Medicare and Georgia Medicaid programs by billing them for "worthless services" in the operation of three nursing homes. Houser was also ordered to pay $6,742,807 in restitution to Medicaid and Medicare and $872,515 in restitution to the IRS. According to court documents, Medicare and Medicaid paid Houser more than $32.9

million between July 2004 and September 2007 for food, medical care, and other services for nursing home residents. Evidence presented at trial showed that instead of providing sufficient care for the nursing home residents, Houser diverted more than $8 million of Medicare and Medicaid funds to his personal use. In addition to the health care fraud count, Houser was convicted of eight counts of deducting $806,305 in federal payroll taxes from his employees' paychecks, but not paying that money over to the IRS. Houser was also convicted of failing to file personal income tax returns for 2004 and 2005.

President of Oakland Roofing Company Sentenced for Tax Evasion Scheme

On August 8, 2012, in Oakland, Calif., Tae Son Lee, aka Mike Lee, the president of Westco Roofing Inc. was sentenced to 24 months in prison, three years of supervised release, ordered to pay $367,656 in restitution, and ordered to cooperate with the IRS to pay any outstanding tax liability, including interest and penalties. Lee pleaded guilty on April 4, 2012, to conspiracy to defraud the United States of tax revenue. According to the plea agreement and evidence presented in court at sentencing, Lee was the sole shareholder and corporate officer of Oakland based Westco Roofing Company Inc. Lee established a series of shell companies to defraud the United States for tax years 2003 through 2008 by impeding the IRS in its assessment and collection of Social Security and FICA taxes. To accomplish his scheme, Lee made "subcontractor" payments to conspiracy-controlled shell companies that had no real employees and performed no real work. Cash was withdrawn from the shell companies' bank accounts and Westco employees received cash wages. Westco failed to report, withhold and pay the FICA taxes on these cash wages.

Connecticut Man Sentenced for Operating Decade-Long Tax Evasion Scheme

On July 30, 2012, in New Haven, Conn., Sherwood Schaub, aka Andy Sherwood, was sentenced to 30 months in prison and two years of supervised release for operating a decade-long tax evasion scheme. He also agreed to cooperate with the IRS and to pay all back taxes, penalties and interest. On February 28, 2012, Schaub waived his right to indictment and pleaded guilty to two counts of tax evasion. According to court documents and statements made in court, Schaub has owned and operated an executive search business and other businesses that have used a variety of names, including Goodrich & Sherwood Company, Goodrich & Sherwood Associates, Inc., Whittenwood Associates, Inc., Whittenwood International, Inc., GSA International, Inc., Stanton Chase of New York and G&S Holding Limited Partnership. From approximately 1994 through 2006, Schaub's business entities repeatedly failed to pay federal taxes that had been withheld from employees' paychecks. During these years, the IRS assessed Schaub penalties for not paying the withholding taxes, but he did not pay these penalties. As part of the scheme, Schaub willfully attempted to avoid paying taxes by causing his business entities to operate under various names and his income to be paid in his wife's name, rather than his own, in the form of checks and wire transfers to her bank account. Through this scheme, Schaub evaded paying $1,314,146 in taxes, interest and penalties. In addition, in 2005, Schaub received taxable income of $164,100 in the form of checks deposited into his wife's bank account. He did not pay taxes on this income and did not file an income tax return for tax year 2005.

Minnesota Woman Sentenced for Failing to Pay Employment Taxes Withheld from Employee Paychecks

On July 19, 2012, in Minneapolis, Minn., Doris Ruiz was sentenced to 12 months and one day in prison on one count of failure to pay over federal employment taxes. Ruiz was indicted on October 4, 2011, and pleaded guilty on January 17, 2012. According to court records, between 2005 and 2007, Ruiz, the owner of Olen Staff Company, a temporary work agency in Minneapolis, deducted and collected federal employment taxes, including certain federal income taxes, such as Federal Insurance Contribution Act (FICA) taxes, from her employees' wages. Under the law, she was required to pay those withholdings to the IRS. However, Ruiz failed to do so and, instead, used more than $150,292.00 in employee withholdings for her own personal benefit,

Kansas Business Man Sentenced for Tax Evasion and Bank Fraud

On July 16, 2012, in Kansas City, Kan., James Clark, Overland Park, Kan., a former owner of the Kansas City Knights basketball team, was sentenced to 51 months in prison and ordered to pay more than $1.3 million in restitution. Clark pleaded guilty to one count of tax fraud and one count of bank fraud. According to court documents, Clark withheld payroll taxes from employees of his company, SWISH Holding Corp., while failing to pay more than $502,000 to the IRS. He diverted the funds and used them for his own purposes, including the operation of the basketball franchise. Clark also admitted submitting false information to a bank when he applied for a line of credit. He overstated the income, profits and assets of SWISH. He gave the bank purported copies of federal income tax returns for SWISH for 2002 and 2003. The returns had not actually been filed with the IRS and falsely overstated SWISH's income. Additionally, as a personal guarantor of the loan, Clark gave the bank statements that over-stated the value of the Kansas City Knights and misrepresented that he had an ownership interest in the American Basketball Association.

President of Florida Employer Solutions, Inc. Sentenced on Tax Charges

On July 12, 2012, in Orlando, Fla., Luis Armando Ferrer, of Pembroke Pines, was sentenced to 24 months in prison and ordered to pay $640,707 in restitution. According to court documents, Ferrer was the President of Florida Employer Solutions, Inc. (FES). FES's business included performing payroll services for client companies and collecting, accounting for, and paying over social security, Medicare taxes, and federal incomes taxes to the IRS on behalf of those companies. Instead of paying this money over to IRS, Ferrer diverted it to his own personal bank account. He used it, in part, to start a landscaping business, Florida Outdoor Impressions, Inc.

Employee Sentenced on Tax Charges

On July 11, 2012, in Memphis, Tenn., Christopher Jones was sentenced to 24 months in prison, three years of supervised release and ordered to pay $287,000 in restitution to the IRS. According to court documents, Jones pleaded guilty on February 1, 2012, to obstructing or impeding the administration of Internal Revenue laws and making false statements to federal agents. Jones admitted that he collected $146,458 in employee withholding taxes from Rippee Rehab, Inc.; Rippee Rehab; Rippee Rehab, LLC; and Dental Connection East, PC, and then converted the funds for his personal use rather than sending the funds to the IRS.

Owner of Virginia Business Sentenced for $1.1 Million Tax Fraud

On June 29, 2012, in Alexandria, Va., Willard Douglas Kerr, of Phoenix, Ariz., was sentenced to 24 months in prison, three years of supervised release, and ordered to pay $1,111,352 in restitution. According to court records, from 2003 through 2009, Kerr operated DK Coatings LLC, a painting and wall covering company in Manassas, Va. He was responsible for collecting, accounting for, and paying over employment taxes on behalf of DK Coatings employees to the Internal Revenue Service. From at least September 30, 2004, through December 31, 2009, Kerr withheld trust fund taxes from his employees' paychecks but did not pay over those taxes to the IRS. From 2003 through 2009, Kerr also failed to pay the employer matching portion of FICA taxes. Kerr failed to pay over more than 31.1 million in taxes. Kerr admitted that he spent the money he withheld from his employees' paychecks on other aspects of the business and on personal expenses, including purchasing multiple vehicles and repairing his swimming pool.

Former Operators of Texas Medical Center are Sentenced Following Tax Convictions

On June 15, 2012, in Lubbock, Texas, Herschel A. Breig and James Cheek, both of Springfield, Mo., were each sentenced to 60 months in prison and ordered to pay a $10,000 fine and $5,049,875 in restitution. In addition, Breig and Cheek have paid a total of $120,000 in restitution to the individual victims identified by the U.S. Department of Labor. Breig and Cheek each pleaded guilty in February 2012 to one count of failure to pay over payroll taxes and aiding and abetting. According to court documents, in March 2006, Breig and Cheek acquired control of the Highland Medical Center (HMC), located in Lubbock, Texas, after Shiloh Health Services purchased the clinic. From March 2006 to May 2008, Cheek controlled every aspect of HMC's business affairs and Breig controlled HMC's financial business affairs, including paying HMC's payroll taxes, federal income taxes, Federal Insurance Contributions Act (FICA) taxes and Medicare taxes. During 2006, 2007 and 2008, HMC withheld payroll taxes from employees' paychecks, but from December 2006 through May 2008, HMC made no payments to the Internal Revenue Service.

New York Certified Public Accountant (CPA) Sentenced for Failing to Pay Employment Taxes

On June 12, 2012, in New York, NY, Silford Warren, of Queens, N.Y., was sentenced to 24 months in prison and ordered to pay S184.263 in restitution to the IRS. Warren pleaded guilty on December 9, 2011, to willful failure to pay over employment taxes on behalf of his accounting business, Silford Warren, CPA PC. According to court documents, from 2006 through 2008, Warren under-reported his employees' salaries on tax filings with the IRS. The court ordered restitution includes the employment taxes he failed to pay over from his employees and his obligation, as an employer, to pay over a matching portion of those employment taxes, as well as the tax loss resulting from his filing false corporate income tax returns for 2005 through 2008.

Ohio Man Sentenced on Tax Conviction

On June 7, 2012, in Cleveland, Ohio, Michael R. Tucker, of Canton, Ohio, was sentenced to 15 months in prison and three years of supervised release. Tucker pleaded guilty on March 27, 2012, to charges of willful failure to pay withheld federal income and FICA taxes to the Internal Revenue Service and filing a false individual income tax return. According to the Indictment, from 2004 through 2008, Tucker operated and was the majority partner and general manager of Computology, LLC. In that capacity, Tucker was required to pay over federal income taxes and Federal Insurance Contributions Act (FICA) taxes that the business withheld from the wages of its employees. From December 2005 through March 2008, Tucker willfully failed to pay over taxes totaling $263,188 that had been withheld from the employees. The indictment also charged Tucker with filing false individual income tax returns for 2005, 2006, and 2007. The indictment alleged that on those returns, Tucker claimed federal income tax withholding totaling $34,775, which he knew had not been paid over to the Internal Revenue Service and, as a result, he received tax refunds to which he was not entitled.

Maryland Business Owner Sentenced for Failing to Pay Employment Taxes

On June 1, 2012, in Greenbelt, Md., Richard Stewart, of Mitchellville, Md., was sentenced to 24 months in prison and ordered to pay $5,414,647 in restitution to the Internal Revenue Service (IRS). According to the plea agreement and criminal information, from at least 2003 through 2008, Stewart owned and operated Montgomery Mechanical Services, a company that installed plumbing, heating, and air conditioning in commercial buildings. From 2003 through at least 2008, Stewart did not collect, truthfully account for and pay over approximately $3,969,337 in employment taxes from his employees' wages.

California Restaurant Owners Sentenced on Tax Fraud and Other Federal Charges

On April 24, 2012, in Oakland, Calif., Marino Sandoval and his wife, Nicole Sandoval, were sentenced on various immigration, Social Security and tax charges related to the operation of their San Francisco Bay area restaurant chain, El Balazo. Marino Sandoval was sentenced to 41 months in prison. Nicole Sandoval was sentenced to five years probation and 12 months of community confinement. They were ordered to pay $2,216,010 in restitution to the Internal Revenue Service (IRS). According to court documents, the Sandovals owned and operated the El Balazo Restaurants with Marino Sandoval's brother, Francisco Sandoval. Marino and Nicole Sandoval acknowledged that they were responsible for withholding federal taxes, including employment and unemployment taxes, from their employees' pay. Nicole Sandoval admitted that she under-reported the employees correct wages to the payroll company that the defendants used to prepare the tax returns. Marino and Nicole Sandoval admitted that, based upon their actions, the amount of employment taxes paid to the Internal Revenue Service was understated. In addition, Marino Sandoval also admitted to hiring employees he knew were not legally authorized to work in this country. Nicole Sandoval also pleaded guilty to misusing El Balazo employees' social security numbers that were provided to the Social Security Administration and the IRS. Between 2002 and 2007, Nicole Sandoval submitted, on behalf of El Balazo, the employer's quarterly contribution and wage reports to the Social Security Administration. The reports included the names of undocumented alien employees receiving wages from their employment. In court, Nicole Sandoval admitted that she was aware that the social security numbers she submitted were false and were not the social security numbers assigned to the employees as reported. Francisco Sandoval, of Alameda, Calif., was sentenced on December 8, 2010, to three years probation for failure to account and pay over payroll taxes and for harboring illegal aliens for financial gain. He was also ordered to pay $50,000 in restitution to the IRS.

Missouri Business Owner Sentenced for Failing to Pay $1.1 Million in Payroll Taxes

On April 18, 2012, in Springfield, Mo., Gregory Crocker was sentenced to 30 months in prison and ordered to pay $1,586,024 in restitution. According to court documents, Crocker pleaded guilty to failing to account for and pay over to the Internal Revenue Service (IRS) the federal income taxes and Social Security and Medicare taxes deducted from employee paychecks. Crocker was an owner and the executive officer of a cemetery and marketer of pre-need funeral services in Joplin, Mo. Crocker admitted that for the quarters ending March 31, 2002, through March 31, 2010, he failed to pay over payroll taxes to the IRS, and to file employers' federal quarterly income tax returns. The total tax harm Crocker caused was $1,152,550.

Extradited Defendant Sentenced for Tax Fraud in Employee Leasing Scheme

On April 18, 2012, in Miami, Fla., Lucia Kanis was sentenced to 27 months in prison and ordered to pay $1,973,266 in restitution. On the same day, Kanis pleaded guilty to one count of conspiring to impede and obstruct the Internal Revenue Service in the collection of payroll taxes as a part of an alien employee leasing scheme. Kanis, who previously lived in Coral Springs, Florida, fled the United States to avoid prosecution. She was extradited from Italy to the United States to face the federal charges filed against her in 2005 for her role in a nationwide employee leasing conspiracy. According to the indictment, Kanis and her co-defendants conspired to provide unauthorized workers, mostly Eastern Europeans who had entered the United States on tourist visas, to American companies with whom the defendants had contracted to provide legally authorized foreign workers. The co-defendants brought more than 550 illegal aliens into the United States. The alien workers obtained tourist visas to enter the United States and were employed illegally in the Midwest and Southeastern United States on farms, dairies and factories. The defendants contracted with American employers to provide workers, for whom the defendants were to pay payroll taxes and workers' compensation deductions. The defendants did not pay the taxes or workers' compensation deductions. During her plea hearing, Kanis admitted that from 2000 to 2002, she participated in a scheme through which she failed to pay more than $1,973,266 in payroll taxes.

Two Former Executives of Payroll Services Company Sentenced for Conspiracy on Wire and Tax Fraud Charges

On April 11, 2012, in Newark, N.J., the former vice president of operations and the former director of sales for a payroll services company based in Hoboken, N.J., were both sentenced to prison for defrauding clients of almost $1 million and failing to pay $400,000 in taxes. Jose Figueroa, of Northampton County, Pa., was sentenced to 41 months in prison and Carlos Chorro, also of Northampton, was sentenced to 12 months in prison. Both men previously pleaded guilty to Informations charging them with one count each of conspiracy to commit wire fraud and one count each of subscribing to false tax returns. According to court documents and statements made in court, from January 2008 through November 2009, Figueroa and Chorro conspired to enrich themselves by manipulating the company computer system to divert clients' payroll tax funds to bank accounts and monetary devices controlled by Figueroa and Chorro. Specifically, Figueroa, who was responsible for setting up the computer files that allowed money to be transferred from clients' bank accounts to the company's tax accounts and thereafter to the IRS, manipulated the company computer files to divert clients' tax funds onto prepaid debit cards controlled by Figueroa and Chorro. Both Figueroa and Chorro then used the diverted funds for personal expenditures. About 128 cash transactions totaling $306,140 were deposited into bank accounts controlled by Figueroa, and 200 transactions totaling $278,125 were deposited into bank accounts controlled by Chorro. From July 2009 through November 2009, Figueroa caused 24 wire transfers totaling $588,366 to be transferred from clients' bank accounts to a bank account controlled by Figueroa. Around September 25, 2009, Figueroa transferred $95,000 by bank check from a bank account controlled by Figueroa to Chorro. For the tax years 2008 and 2009, Figueroa and Chorro did not disclose to the IRS the income they received in connection with their conspiracy. Figueroa failed to disclose $894,477, resulting in a tax loss to the United States of $278,477. Chorro failed to disclose $373,125, resulting in a tax loss of $107,184. In addition to their prison terms, Figueroa and Chorro were ordered to serve three years each of supervised release, Figueroa has agreed to pay $469,737 in restitution to victims, $278,133 to the IRS and forfeit S438.000. Chorro was ordered to pay $373,125 in restitution and forfeit $184,000.

Colorado Man Sentenced for Failure to Pay Over $1.3 Million to the IRS and Theft from 401(k) Plan

On April 4, 2012, in Denver, Colo., John C. Walshe was sentenced to 46 months in prison, three years of supervised release, and ordered to pay $1,330,333 in restitution to the Internal Revenue Service (IRS). Walshe was convicted by trial jury on November 14, 2011, for failure to pay taxes and theft from an employee benefit plan. According to court records, as well as evidence presented at trial, Walshe was the owner and principal officer of Finzer Business Systems of Colorado, Inc., dba Finzer Imaging Systems, located in Denver. Walshe was required to withhold from payroll checks issued to his employee's federal income taxes on their taxable wages and salaries, Social Security taxes and Medicare taxes. Walshe and his company, Finzer, were required to pay the employer's matching portion of Social Security and Medicare taxes which he failed to pay to the IRS. During the period of quarters ending June 30, 2005, through December 31, 2007, Walshe deducted and collected from Finzer employees, federal income taxes, Social Security taxes, and Medicare taxes totaling over $900,000. However, Walshe willfully failed to pay the IRS the money due to the federal government. Furthermore, Walshe did unlawfully and willfully abstract and convert to his own use money in the approximate amount of $18,853 of Finzer Business Systems of Colorado, Inc. 401(k) Plan and a fund connected with such plan. Specifically, from June 15, 2006 through December 31, 2006, Walshe withheld money from employees' pay checks that the employees elected to be paid to their 401 (k) plan; however, Walshe failed to pay this money over to the plan.

Wisconsin Woman Sentenced for Tax Fraud

On March 16, 2012, in Milwaukee, Wis., Connie Sax was sentenced to six months in prison and six months home confinement and ordered to pay $168,091 in restitution to the IRS for tax fraud. According to court documents, Sax was the owner and former operator of Connie's Day Care, a child care center that she had operated in Kenosha. From the third quarter of 2005 through the first quarter of 2009, Sax withheld more than $168,000 from her employees but failed to pay the money to the Internal Revenue Service. She used these funds for her own benefit.

Florida Man Sentenced for Tax Fraud

On February 22, 2012, in Miami, Fla., Osvaldo Martinez, of Hollywood, Fla., was sentenced to 24 months in prison. According to the plea agreement, Martinez operated Clinicas Finlay, Inc., a medical services company in Miami-Dade County until 2007. Although Martinez withheld employee payroll taxes from his employees' salaries, he failed to pay $1,781,294 to the IRS, as required by law. In November 2011, Martinez pleaded guilty to one count of willfully failing to pay to the Internal Revenue Service federal income taxes.

New York Man Sentenced on Tax Fraud Charges

On February 21, 2012, in Rochester, N.Y., Jeffrey Sykes, of Canandaigua, N.Y., was sentenced to 96 months in prison, three years of supervised release, and ordered to pay $3,714,649 in restitution. According to the plea agreement, Sykes owned and operated Paybooks, Inc., a payroll servicing company that serviced approximately 1,100 clients in Western New York area. Between January 1,2008, and June 30, 2009, Sykes received from Paybooks' clients proceeds that were to be used to pay employment taxes on behalf of the clients. However, Sykes failed to remit the funds to the appropriate taxing agencies. In addition to not paying over employment tax liabilities, Sykes failed to file Forms 941 on behalf of the clients. In an effort to conceal his fraudulent conduct, Sykes falsely represented to his clients that Paybooks had filed the Forms 941, and paid the employment taxes by mailing to the client's letters, stating that the returns and all tax payments had been filed.

Business Owner and Employee Sentenced for Conspiring to Defraud the IRS

On February 3, 2012, in Pittsburgh, Pa., Richard Swartz and Richard J. Connell were sentenced in federal court on their convictions of conspiracy to defraud the Internal Revenue Service. Swartz, of Coraopolis, Pa., was sentenced to 15 months in prison, three years of supervised release and pay a $30,000 fine. Connell, of Pittsburgh, Pa., was sentenced to 12 months and one day in prison and three years of supervised release. According to information presented to the court, Swartz owned and controlled Ace Tire and Parts, Inc., a retail auto parts and repair business, and Mariclare of Pa., doing business as Installer's Supply, a wholesale automobile supply and parts business. Connell was an employee and the controller of Ace Tire and Parts, Inc., and also performed financial services for Mariclare of Pa. From January 2000 through January 2006, Swartz and Connell conspired to defraud the Internal Revenue Service (IRS), by defeating and obstructing the IRS in the collection of income and employment taxes, as well as filing false tax returns.

Arkansas Man Sentenced on Bank Fraud and Failure to Pay Payroll Tax

On February 1, 2012, in Little Rock, Ark., Scott Keith Voss, of Jonesboro, Ark., was sentenced to 33 months in prison, five years of supervised release and ordered to pay restitution of $450,000 to a bank and $148,564 to the Internal Revenue Service (IRS). Voss, who served as pastor and president of a church in Jonesboro, pleaded guilty to one count of bank fraud and one count of willful failure to pay over tax in November 2011. Voss admitted during his plea hearing that from September 2007 until June 26, 2010, he devised a scheme to defraud a bank. As part of the scheme, Voss applied for a loan from the bank, pledging as collateral the Jonesboro worship center real estate where he served as pastor. Voss then failed to obtain appropriate board of directors' authorization to so encumber the church real estate. Additionally, Voss admitted that from 2006 through 2010, the church withheld tax payments from its employees' paychecks. However, through this same period, the church failed to make any payments to IRS of these withholdings.

Former Owner of Temporary Labor Firm Sentenced for Bribery and Tax Scheme

On January 26, 2012. in Camden, N. J., Channavel "Danny" Kong, of Philadelphia, Pa., was sentenced to 24 months in prison, three years of supervised release and ordered to cooperate fully with the IRS in paying his outstanding federal tax obligations and pay the state of New Jersey S15.000 in restitution. According to court documents and statements made in court, from 2006 to 2009, Kong owned and operated Sunrise Labor, which was in the business of providing temporary employees to client businesses, including businesses located in New Jersey. During this time period, Kong admitted that he made illegal cash payments to Joseph Rivera, a senior investigator with the New Jersey Department of Labor & Workforce Development's Division of Wage and Hour Compliance. Kong admitted he paid Rivera bribes totaling approximately S55.281 with the intent to influence Rivera not to conduct audits and inspections, including inspections and audits examining Sunrise's compliance with state payroll tax obligations. Kong also admitted that he was responsible, as the operator of Sunrise, for withholding, collecting, and accounting for and paying to the U.S. all employment taxes imposed by the Internal Revenue Code and that he willfully failed to collect and truthfully account for these taxes, which caused a tax loss to the IRS of between $80,000 and $200,000.

Missouri Business Owner Sentenced for Failing to Pay Employment Taxes

On January 24, 2012, in Springfield, Mo., Robert Landis was sentenced to 37 months in prison and ordered to pay $6.26 million in restitution for failing to pay employment taxes. According to court documents, from December 2003 until June 2007, Landis was the owner of Priority Personnel of Missouri and Priority Personnel of Kansas, temporary employment agencies. Landis was also the owner of Loma Landis LLC, which managed residential structures known as villas and operated nearby golf courses. Landis operated Loma Landis from 2005 to 2009. Each of those firms deducted payroll taxes from employees' pay, however, he failed to truthfully account for or pay to the IRS payroll taxes that were deducted and withheld from the paychecks of Priority Personnel of Missouri employees.

Virginia Businessman Sentenced for Tax Evasion Scheme

On January 20, 2012, in Alexandria, Va., Russell Foumier, of Stafford, Va., was sentenced to 25 months in prison and three years of supervised release for failing to pay more than $700,000 in employment taxes from 2000 to 2008. According to court documents, Foumier was a co-owner of Virginia Mobile Homes, Inc. (VMH), a Virginia corporation that sold mobile home trailers. In that capacity, Foumier was responsible for VMH's tax and financial affairs, including the filing of VMH's quarterly employment tax returns and paying over to the IRS the Federal Insurance Contributions Act and federal income taxes that were withheld from VMH employees. For nearly a decade, Fournier failed to file his company's tax returns and pay to the IRS his company's taxes. As a result, Fournier deprived the federal government of $722,485 between 2000 and 2008. In that time, Fournier used company funds to purchase for himself and his family luxury cars and trips abroad.

Virginia Woman Sentenced for Tax Evasion

On December 22, 2011, in Richmond, Va., Kim Jenkins Brandveen, of Petersburg, Va., was sentenced to 60 months in prison and three years of supervised release on her conviction for tax evasion. According to court documents, Brandveen admitted being the owner of Healthcare Solutions Medical Supply, LLC, a business that sold durable medical equipment and provided home health services. Brandveen directed the withholding of federal employment taxes from the paychecks of that business's employees, but regularly and systematically failed to pay those taxes over to the Internal Revenue Service (IRS), instead using those funds for other business ventures and personal expenses. When the IRS undertook collection efforts, Brandveen shut down that business and abandoned its bank accounts. She then operated as Healthcare Solutions Service Corporation, a virtually identical business performing largely the same functions from the same location with the same employees. Healthcare Solutions Service Corporation also failed to pay over employees' withheld employment taxes to the IRS, again using them for Brandveen's other business ventures and personal expenses.

Connecticut Accountant Sentenced for Stealing from Clients and Failing to Pay Employment Taxes

On December 20, 2011, in Hartford, Conn., Felix Robert LaSaracina, of Norwich, was sentenced to 63 months in prison and three years of supervised release for defrauding clients of approximately $4.1 million and for failing to pay more than $700,000 in employment taxes. According to court documents and statements made in court, LaSaracina, the owner and operator of F. Robert

LaSaracina CPA, LLC, provided accounting and tax preparation services to clients in the New London and Norwich areas and served as the trustee for a series of trusts set up by a family for the benefit of their three children. As part of a scheme to defraud, LaSaracina falsely represented to numerous individuals and clients that he had investment opportunities in which their money would be invested in real estate, that the investment would pay 8 percent interest and other false promises. There were no actual investment opportunities and LaSaracina used the invested funds for his own benefit. To create the appearance of legitimacy to prospective investors, he prepared official-looking documents or investment contracts termed "Promissory Note(s)". As a trustee, LaSaracina controlled and was responsible for managing the assets of the trusts, including the real estate holdings owned by the trusts, LaSaracina took out a series of mortgages using the real estate that was owned by the trusts as collateral. Through this scheme, LaSaracina diverted more than $1.2 million in mortgage funds for his own personal use. In addition, between 2005 and 2010, LaSaracina failed to remit to the Internal Revenue Service approximately $734,359 in federal income taxes and Federal Insurance Contributions Act (FICA) taxes that he had collected from the wages of employees of his business.

Ohio Man Sentenced for Failing to Pay Employment Taxes

On December 14, 2011, in Cleveland, Ohio, Charles J. Matthews, of Shaker Heights, Ohio, was sentenced to 15 months in prison after pleading guilty to six counts of willful failure to collect or pay over taxes. According to court documents, Matthews was the senior pastor at Mt. Sinai Baptist Church, located in Cleveland, as well as chief executive officer of the council overseeing the financial affairs. Matthews failed to pay Federal Insurance Contributions Act (FICA) taxes that were withheld from employees at Mount Sinai Baptist Church and Ministries over six quarters between October 2005 and January 2007. The taxes were collected and withheld from Mt. Sinai employees, but Matthews willfully failed to report and pay over the monies to the IRS. Instead, Matthews caused those funds to be used for other purposes, including transfers to the Pastor's account for his own personal use. He also failed to report and pay over the employer's share of the FICA taxes.

Owner of Maryland-Based Dental Corporation Sentenced for Failing to Pay Employment Taxes

On December 7, 2011, in Baltimore, Md., Jay Wayne Hustead, of Annapolis, Md., was sentenced to 24 months in prison, three years of supervised release and ordered to perform 200 hours of community service for failure to pay employment taxes related to his corporation, Hustead Dental and Orthodontics, PA. Hustead was also ordered to pay $65,913 in restitution and enter into a closing agreement with the IRS to pay the full amount of taxes due. According to his plea agreement, Jay Hustead and his wife, Susan K. Hustead, operated Hustead Dental and Orthodontics, PA, which employed several dentists, technicians and office employees and, from 2001 to 2006, had annual payrolls exceeding $1 million. From 2001 to 2006, Hustead Dental paid $25,000 in employment taxes and owed an additional $1.9 million. For the tax quarter that ended on December 31, 2003, the period charged in the criminal information, the tax loss associated with the Husteads' failure to pay to the IRS the employment taxes was $65,913. Susan K. Hustead also pleaded guilty to her role in the scheme and awaits sentencing.

Kansas Lawyer Sentenced on Employment Tax Evasion Charges

On November 18, 2011, in Kansas City, Kan., Rosie Quinn, a lawyer, was sentenced to 36 months in prison for failing to pay employment and personal taxes. According to court documents, Quinn was the sole proprietor of Rosie M, Quinn Attorney At Law, where she usually employed three to five people to assist with her practice. For calendar years 1995 through 2008, Quinn withheld more than $235,600 in payroll taxes from employees while submitting only $10,232 in payroll taxes to the IRS. In addition, Quinn failed to pay $8,435 in personal income taxes in 2002 and $19,905 in personal income taxes in 2003. Altogether, Quinn failed to pay more than $1 million including interest and penalties, for payroll and personal income taxes since 1995.

Virginia Man Sentenced for Failing to Pay Over $1.7 Million In Taxes

On November 18, 2011, in Alexandria, Va., James Miller, of Lorton, Va., was sentenced to 18 months in prison, three years of supervised release and ordered to pay $965,006 in restitution for willful failure to collect, account for, and pay over withholdings from employees' paychecks to the Internal Revenue Service. Miller pleaded guilty in August 2011. According to court documents, Miller served as the President and CEO of Team, Inc., a janitorial company located in Virginia from 1997 through 2008. Team provided janitorial services for organizations and businesses located throughout the Washington, D.C., area. Due to the positions he held at

Team, Miller had a duty to collect, account for, and pay over federal taxes withheld from his employees' paychecks. According to court documents, beginning with the first quarter of 2003 and continuing through the fourth quarter of 2008, Team withheld federal taxes from employees' paychecks, including Federal Insurance Contribution Act taxes, but Miller willfully and knowingly failed to pay over any of the withheld taxes to the government. As a result of Miller's conduct, the total federal tax loss was approximately $1.7 million.

New York Contractor Sentenced in Payroll Tax Evasion Scheme

On November 15, 2011, in Manhattan, N.Y., Michael Mahoney was sentenced to 24 months home confinement, two years of supervised release and ordered to pay $306,765 in restitution. According to the information, from 2004 through 2006, Mahoney, owner and operator of a construction company known as EMC of New York, took checks that represented receipts of EMC and, rather than depositing them in the corporate bank accounts, cashed them at a check-cashing establishment in New York City. The cash that Mahoney received was used, in part, to pay employees all or a portion of their wages avoiding federal tax reporting and withholding requirements and defrauding the IRS of taxes owed under FICA.

Internet Communications Firm Owners Sentenced

On November 9, 2011, in Washington, D.C., Frank G. Bivings and Isabelle Blanco, of Washington, D.C., husband and wife, and co-owners of The Bivings Group, Inc, were sentenced on charges stemming from the failure to pay more than $2 million in employment taxes to the Internal Revenue Service (IRS). Bivings was sentenced to 30 months in prison, three years of supervised release and required to perform 100 hours of community service. Blanco was sentenced to 10 months in prison, one year of supervised release and required to perform 100 hours of community service. Under terms of their plea agreements, both agreed to pay $2,420,927 in restitution. The Bivings Group, Inc. was a full service Internet communications business. In their plea agreements, Bivings and Blanco both admitted that between January 1, 2002, and June 30, 2008, The Bivings Group, Inc., failed to pay over to the IRS a total of $2,420,927 in employment taxes, which includes withholding and FICA taxes. Of this amount, $1,813,488 represented the money that was withheld from employees for taxes but was not paid over to the IRS.

Kentucky Man Placed On House Arrest for Tax Crimes

On November 8, 2011, in Cincinnati, Ohio, Andrew E. Williams, of Villa Hills, Kentucky, was sentenced to 15 months of home confinement and ordered to pay $49,991 in restitution to the Internal Revenue Service (IRS). Williams pleaded guilty on August 11, 2011, to one count of failure to collect and pay over employment taxes to the IRS. According to court records, Williams was the owner of Club Aqua, Inc., which at the time was doing business under the name Club Ritz, withheld federal income tax, social security tax and Medicare tax from club employees' paychecks but failed to pay the taxes to the IRS or file quarterly federal income tax returns as required. Williams also admitted that he did not pay his employer's portion of these taxes. The total loss to the IRS from Williams' conduct was $81,712, with the unpaid portion of this loss being the restitution ordered at sentencing. Williams' plea agreement also obligates him to file complete and accurate tax returns with the IRS for all tax years and periods up to and including the date of sentencing, which were required to be filed under U.S. tax laws but have not yet been filed. He also agreed to file with the IRS complete and accurate amended returns for all previously filed incomplete or inaccurate tax returns, and pay all taxes, penalties, and interest due and owing to the IRS.

Florida Owner of Construction Business Sentenced

On November 3, 2011, in Miami, Fla., Braynert Marquez, of Miami, Fla., was sentenced to 30 months in prison, one year of supervised release and ordered to pay restitution of $280,362 to the IRS. Marquez pleaded guilty on July 21, 2011, to a one-count information charging him with aiding or assisting in the preparation of a false employment tax return. Specifically, the information charged that on or about January 31, 2008, Braynert Marquez willfully aided and assisted in and caused the preparation and presentation of a fraudulent Employer's Quarterly Federal Tax Return, IRS Form 941, for Bema Group for the calendar quarter ending December 31, 2007. The return was fraudulent in that it underreported wages, tips, and other compensation paid to employees. According to court documents, Marquez operated and at least partly owned two construction companies known as Bema Block Corp. and Bern a Group Corp. From 2004 through 2007, Marquez paid employees of Bema Block and Bema Group "off-the-books" wages. Marquez failed to report these wages on quarterly employment tax returns and failed to withhold and pay over employment taxes on the wages.

Oregon Woman Sentenced for Evading Employment Taxes

On October 28, 2011, in Oklahoma City, Okla., Skoshi Farr, of Grants Pass, Oregon, was sentenced to 33 months in prison, three years of supervised release and ordered to pay $72,076 in restitution for tax evasion. According to court documents, Farr's deceased husband owned and operated an alternative medicine practice, Genesis Medical Center, in southwest Oklahoma City from 1984 until his death in December 1998. In 1999, Farr owned and operated the clinic with the assistance of other medical personnel. The clinic had collected, but failed to pay to the IRS, the quarterly employment taxes at the clinic for three quarters in 1999. As the Administrator of the clinic, Farr was personally obligated to pay those taxes through the trust fund recovery penalty. Farr evaded her obligation to pay these taxes by hiding assets from the IRS and using a nominee bank account in the name of a corporation controlled by her adult children.

Former Owner of Massachusetts Temporary Employment Agency Sentenced for Under-the-Table Scheme

On October 26, 2011, in Boston, Mass., Michael Powers, the former owner of a Stoughton temporary employment agency, was sentenced to 84 months in prison, two years of supervised release, and ordered to pay more than $9 million in restitution to the Internal Revenue Service (IRS), the Massachusetts Department of Unemployment Assistance, and two insurers. Powers and John Mahan, of Stoughton, were convicted in July 2011 of one count of conspiracy to defraud the IRS and various workers' compensation insurers, one count of mail fraud and two counts of filing false tax returns. According to court documents, between 2000 and 2004, Powers and Mahan owned and operated Commonwealth Temporary Services, Inc., which supplied hundreds of temporary laborers to businesses throughout Eastern Massachusetts. To avoid paying employment taxes, such as social security and Medicare, and to fraudulently reduce the businesses' insurance premiums, Powers and Mahan under-reported their payrolls. To hide their fraud, they arranged to pay more than $30 million of their payroll in cash, under the table. The scheme avoided more than $9 million in federal and state payroll taxes and workers' compensation insurance premiums.

Glossary

Collection

The IRS charges a late-payment penalty of 0.5% per month as well as interest as the federal rate on past-due tax payments. In addition, if a return is not filed by the due date, a late-filing penalty of 5% per month, up to 25% of the tax due, is charged. Extensions of time of file are obtained using form 4868; see Tab 1. An extension of time to pay tax may be obtained using form 1127, Application for Extension of Time for Payment of Tax. The taxpayer must show that timely payment would result in undue hardship.

Liens

A lien is a claim against property for the satisfaction of a debt. The IRS has an automatic lien on a taxpayer's property if the taxpayer owes tax that is not currently being disputed. The IRS may file a Notice of Federal Tax Lien to protect its right to the taxpayer's property if the not paid.

The IRS must notify any person subject to a lien of the existence of the lien within five days of the lien being filed, with a notice given in person, left at the taxpayer's home or place of business, or sent by certified or registered mail to the person's last known address. The notice must explain (1) the amount of the unpaid tax, (2) the person's right to request a hearing during the 30-days beginning on the fifth day after the lien is filed, (3) the available administrative appeals and their procedures, and (4) the procedures relating to the release of liens.

Any tax lien against an individual's property will be released within 30 days after tax (along with applicable penalties and interest) is paid. In some circumstance the IRS will release a tax lien while the tax is still owed. See IRS Publication 1660, collection Appeals Rights, for information.

Levies

A levy is a seizure of property to satisfy a debt. The IRS must give 30 days notice of its intent to seize a taxpayer's property. The IRS may generally levy any property the taxpayer owns at the time of the levy. Certain property is exempt from levy.

- Clothing and school books needed by the taxpayer and family member
- Furniture and personal effects in the taxpayer's household up to $8,230 in value (for 2009)
- Books and tools of the taxpayer's trade, business, or profession up to $4,120 in value (for 2009)
- Unemployment benefits, including any portion payable with respect to dependents
- Undelivered mail
- Annuity or person payments under the Railroad Retirement Act; benefits under the Railroad Unemployment Insurance Acts; special pension payment received by a person whose name has been entered on the Army, Navy, Air force, and Coast Guard Medal of Honor roll: and annuities based on retired or retainer pay under chapter 73 of title 10 USC
- Worker's compensation, including any portion payable with respect to dependents
- Salary, wages, or other income necessary to comply with any child support judgment
- Wages or salary received by an individual for personal services, or income from other sources, up to the "exempt amount" stated in the statute. This amount consists of the sum of the individual's standard deduction and personal exemption for the tax year, divided by the number of payments during the year (for example, 52 in the case of weekly wage or salary payments).
- Certain amounts payable to an individual as a service-connected disability benefit
- Any amount payable to an individual as a recipient of public assistance under supplemental security income for the aged, blind, and disabled of the social Security Act, or state or local government public assistance or public welfare programs for which eligibility is determined by a needs or income test
- Any amount payable to a participant under the Job Training Partnership Act (29 U.S.C 1501 et seq.) from funds appropriated to the act

- If the amount of the levy does not exceed $5,000, the residence of the taxpayer; or any real property of the taxpayer (other than which is rented) used by another individual as a residence
- The principle residence of the taxpayer (unless the levy is approved by a judge or magistrate of a federal district court), as well as tangible personal or real property (other than that which is rented) used in the trade or business of an individual taxpayer (unless the levy is approved by an appropriate IRS official, or it is determined that the collection of the tax is in jeopardy) Personal property that is exempt from levy is not exempt from attachment by a federal tax lien.

Relief from Collection Activity and Delays of collection activity

If a taxpayer's income is below an amount based on the HHS poverty guidelines, the IRS may delay collection activities. Low-income taxpayers may file Form 433-A, Collection Information Statement for Wage Earners and Self-Employed Individuals, or form 433-B, Collection Information Statement for Business to prove that their income in insufficient to pay the tax owed and also meet basic living expense and that the taxpayer has no assets the IRS might levy to secure payment of the tax.

Taxpayer Advocate Service

Collection activity may be suspended if the taxpayer faces significant hardship. The Taxpayer Advocate Service assists taxpayers who have an issue that has not been resolved through normal channels. The taxpayer advocate independently represents taxpayer interests and concerns within the IRS. Taxpayer advocates are independent of other divisions of the IRS and report directly to the National Taxpayer Advocate. This service is provided for the following situation:

- The taxpayer is suffering, or is about to suffer, a significant hardship as a result of administration of the tax laws.
- The taxpayer is facing an immediate threat of adverse action.
- The taxpayer will incur significant costs in resolving the tax problem through normal channels (including fees for professional representation).
- The taxpayer will suffer irreparable injury or long-term adverse impact as a result of IRS action.
- There had been a delay of more than 30 days beyond normal processing times to resolve a tax account problem.
- A response had not been received by the date promised.

Situations are reviewed on a case-by-case basis. An Issue is submitted for consideration by the taxpayer advocate service in one of three ways

- By phone at 877-777-4778 (TTY/TTD, call 800-829-4059).
- By filing form 911, Request for Taxpayer Advocate Service Assistance (and application for taxpayer Assistance Order), with the Taxpayer Advocate Service.
- By written request for assistance or in person at the local Taxpayer Advocate office.

Injured Spouse Claim

The IRS may offset overpayments of taxes for past-due federal debts, child support payments, and some other debts. If the debt is attributable to one spouse, and a joint return was filed, the other spouse may be entitled to receive a refund of his or her share of the overpayment by filing Form 8379, Injured Spouse Claim and Allocation.

Innocent Spouse Relief

If a joint return is filed, each spouse is responsible for the accuracy of the return and for the payment of the tax. Under certain circumstances, one spouse may claim relief by filing form 8857, Request for Innocent Spouse Relief, no later than two years after the tax. Married taxpayers who live in community property states may qualify for relief even if a join return is not failed.

The following conditions must be met to qualify for innocent spouse relief:

1. The joint return had an understatement of tax due to erroneous items of the spouse or former spouse.
2. At the time the spouse requesting relief signed the joint return, he or she did not know or have reason to know that there was an understatement of tax.
3. Taking into account all the facts and circumstances, it would be unfair to hold the spouse requesting relief for the understatements of tax.

Relief by Separation of Liability

Under separation of liability, income, deduction, credits, and other items are allocated to each spouse in a method similar to that which would have been used if the spouses had filed separate returns, and each spouse is liable only for his or her portion of the tax. Only unpaid liabilities may be treated in this way. If the tax has been paid, relief by separation of liability is not available.

This type of relief applies only if the spouse are divorced or legally separated (or the other spouse has died), or if the spouse were not members of the same household at any time during the last 12 months. Also the spouse applying for relief must not have had actual knowledge of the disputed items.

Equitable relief

Spouses who do not qualify for innocent spouse relief by separation for innocent spouse relief or relief by separation of liability may qualify for equitable relief. The IRS automatically considers whether equitable relief is appropriate if an application for another form of relief is received and declined. This type of relief may apply to both understatement of tax and to underpayment of tax. For example, if the taxpayer believed that his or her spouse paid the tax but the tax has in fact not been paid.

See IRS Publication 971, Innocent Spouse Relief (and Separation of Liability and Equitable Relief), for more details.

Appeals of Collections

There are various collection appeal procedures available to taxpayers who have received a bill or notice of deficiency from the IRS. The two main procedures are the Collection Due Process (CDP) hearing and the Collection Appeals Program (CPA).

Installment Agreements

Installment agreements are used when a taxpayer cannot fully and immediately pay the amount due. The IRS will generally grant an installment agreement in cases where the liability can be paid within three years and in "small dollar" cases, defined now as "streamlined agreements." A $105 fee is charged by the IRS for setting up an installment agreement ($52 for those with a direct agreement; $43 for those below a certain income level). If a taxpayer has an installment restructured or reinstated, the user fee is $45. An installment agreement reduces the late-payment penalty to 0.25% per month.

The IRS is authorized to enter into installment agreements with taxpayers that provide for partial payment of the tax liability (in contrast to prior law, which required an installment agreement to provide for payment in full of the tax liability). The IRS is required to review partial payment agreements every two years. If payment in full can be made within three years, however, and the taxpayer's liability is less than $10,000 (and if certain other conditions are met), the IRS can only accept an agreement providing full payment, and the partial payment option is not available.

Offers in Compromise

Sometimes the IRS settles tax collection matters for less than the full amount of tax due. There are three potential grounds for an offer in compromise: doubt as to collectability, doubt as to liability, and effective tax administration or special circumstances.

A Taxpayer makes an offer using form 656, Offer in Compromise, or, if the offer in Compromise (Doubt as to Liability). A $150 application fee is required, but the fee may be waived for low-income taxpayers who file form 656-A, Income Certification for Offer in Compromise Application fee. If form 656-L is filed, the fee may be waived. See form 656-B, Offer in Compromise booklet.

If an offer is accepted based on doubt as to collectability, the IRS will determine the reasonable the reasonable collection potential of case (an amount less than the total debt owed), Taking into account the taxpayer's basic living expenses. In addition, the agency may accept less than that amount if there are special circumstances. However, if a taxpayer's tax liability can be paid in full in a lump sum or through an installment agreement. The taxpayer will not be considered for an offer in compromise. The only exception is if the taxpayer can demonstrate special circumstances that would show full payment of the liability would result in economic hardship or be detrimental to voluntary compliance.

In a case where the IRS accepts an offer based on the promotion of effective tax administration (that is, the IRS had decided that collection the full amount owed would be possible, but would create economic hardship for the taxpayer or would be unfair or inequitable), the decision will be based on the taxpayer's individual circumstances. The structure of these agreements is based on the IRS's goal of collecting as much of the tax as possible in situations in which the taxpayer lacks the resources to meet the tax liability.

A taxpayer is required to make partial payments while an offer in compromise is being considered. If the offer is of a lump sum payment, then the taxpayers must make a nonrefundable down payment of 20 percent of the amount of the offer. The relevant fee must also be submitted with the appropriate partial payment; that amount will be applied to the taxpayer's tax liability.

Bankruptcy and taxes

A separate estate, for tax purposes, is created for an individual who files a petition under chapter 7 or 11 of Bankruptcy Code. A separate estate is not created under chapter 12 or 13 of the Bankruptcy Code.

The individual taxpayer should continue to file the same federal income tax return, reporting all income received and deducting all allowable expenses. Debt canceled because of bankruptcy is not included in income, but may reduce losses and credits (the extent that the taxpayer has them).

The estate is represented by a trustee appointed by the bankruptcy court to administer the estate and liquidate nonexempt assets. In Chapter 11, the debtor usually remains in control of the assets as a "debtor-in-possession.''

A bankruptcy estate may produce its own income as well as incur its own expenses, and the trustee must file a tax return on form 1041, US Income Tax Return for Estates and Trusts, for the estates if its income is greater than sum of personal exemption amount and the basic standard deduction for a married individual filing separately. If a return is required, the trustee (or debtor-in-possession) completes the identification area at the top of the form 1041 and lines 23-29 (total tax amount on line 23 is taken from form 1040). And signs and dates it. For bankruptcy estates, Form 1041 is used as a transmittal for form 1040, U.S. Individual Income Tax Return. Complete form 1040 and figure the tax using the tax rate schedule for a married person filing separately. In the top margin of form 1040, written "Attachment to Form 1041. DO NOT DETACH.'' Attach form 1040 to the form 1041.

Index

1

4

A

B

C

D

E

F

H

I

L

N

O

P

R

S

T

V

End Notes

---

i IR-2007-04, Jan. 9, 2007

ii IRS Form 2848 (Rev. 3-2012)

iii IRS Form 8821 (Rev. 4-2004)

iv http://www.irs.gov/uac/Form-9465,-Installment-Agreement-Request-2

v https://www.google.com/search?q=irs+4506&ie=utf-8&oe=utf-8

vi IRS Form 2848 (Rev. 3-2012)

vii http://www.irs.gov/uac/Form-4506,-Request-for-Copy-of-Tax-Return

viii http://www.irs.gov/Individuals/Understanding-Your-IRS-Notice-or-Letter

ix IRC section 6672

x IRS Form 433-A (Rev. 12-2012)

xi IRS Form 433-B (Rev. 12-2012)

xii IRS Form 433-F (Rev. 1-2013)

xiii www.irs.gov

xiv See www.irs.gov/taxtopics/tc757.html

xv Courtesy of the Franchise Tax Board (FTB") Use this chart for reference purposes only. We list penalty codes by Revenue and Taxation Code (R&TC) sections and reference comparable Internal Revenue Code (IRC) sections. These penalties reflect the law as enacted on September 21, 2011, for taxable years beginning on or after January 1, 2011.

xvi See www.irs.gov

xvii http://www.irs.gov/uac/Form-8857,-Request-for-Innocent-Spouse-Relief

xviii IRS Form 8857 (Rev. 6-2007) for more info. see IRS *"Publication 971"*

xix IRS Publication 5 (Rev. 1-1999)

xx IRS Publication 1660 (Rev. 3-2007)

xxi http://www.irs.gov/Individuals/Collection-Due-Process-%28CDP%29

xxii http://www.irs.gov/Individuals/Collection-Appeals-Program

xxiii http://www.irs.gov/Businesses/Small-Businesses-&-Self-Employed/Understanding-a-Federal-Tax-Lien

xxiv http://www.irs.gov/Businesses/Small-Businesses-&-Self-Employed/Understanding-a-Federal-Tax-Lien

xxv http://www.irs.gov/Businesses/Small-Businesses-&-Self-Employed/Understanding-a-Federal-Tax-Lien

xxvi Criminal Investigation (CI) At-a-Glance *US Department of Treasury*

xxvii History of IRS Criminal Investigation (CI) *US Department of Treasury*

xxviii Criminal Investigation (CI) At-a-Glance *US Department of Treasury*

xxix Cornell University Law School *www.law.cornell.edu/uscode/text/26/7206*

xxx www.irs.gov

xxxi IRS Form 911 (Rev. 6-2007)

xxxii IRM 5.1.19.3.1 (03-01-2006) The collection statute of limitations, in a case under the Bankruptcy Code, is suspended while the Service is prohibited by reason of the case from collecting, and for 6 months thereafter. For more information see IRC 6503(h)(2). Thus, the collection statute of limitations is generally suspended while the automatic stay imposed by the bankruptcy is in effect. Even if the suspension of the collection statute under IRC 6503(h) no longer applies, the collection statute still may be suspended when substantially all the debtor's assets remain in the custody or control of the bankruptcy court under IRC 6503(b). For more information see IRM 5.9.4.2

xxxiii IRS Publication 216 (Rev. 3-92)

xxxiv IRS Publication 470 (Rev. 1-82)

xxxv www.irs.gov